Intermediate
Macroeconomics

Robert J. Barro
Angus C. Chu
Guido Cozzi

FIRST EDITION

**Intermediate Macroeconomics,
1st Edition**
Robert J. Barro, Angus C. Chu and
    Guido Cozzi

Publisher: Annabel Ainscow

Commissioning Editor: Abigail Coppin

Content Project Manager: Sue Povey

Manufacturing Manager: Eyvett Davis

Marketing Manager: Vicky Pavlicic

Typesetter: DiacriTech

Cover design: Cyan Design

Text design: Design Deluxe Ltd

While the publisher has taken all reasonable care in the preparation of this book, the publisher makes no representation, express or implied, with regard to the accuracy of the information contained in this book and cannot accept any legal responsibility or liability for any errors or omissions from the book or the consequences thereof.

Products and services that are referred to in this book may be either trademarks and/or registered trademarks of their respective owners. The publishers and authors make no claim to these trademarks. The publisher does not endorse, and accepts no responsibility or liability for, incorrect or defamatory content contained in hyperlinked material.

All the URLs in this book are correct at the time of going to press; however, the Publisher accepts no responsibility for the content and continued availability of third party websites.

For product information and technology assistance,
contact **emea.info@cengage.com**

For permission to use material from this text or product,
and for permission queries,
email **clsuk.permissions@cengage.com**

British Library Cataloguing-in-Publication Data

A catalogue record for this book is available from the British Library.

ISBN: 978-1-4737-2509-6

Cengage Learning EMEA
Cheriton House, North Way, Andover, Hampshire SP10 5BE
United Kingdom

Cengage Learning products are represented in Canada by Nelson Education Ltd.

For your lifelong learning solutions, visit
www.cengage.co.uk

Purchase your next print book or e-book at
www.cengagebrain.com

Printed in the United Kingdom by Ashford Colour Press Ltd
Print Number: 04   Print Year: 2019

Robert J. Barro: To Rachel, Zac and Wiggles.
Angus C. Chu: To Amanda, Alvin and Alice.
Guido Cozzi: To Silvia, Diana and Aurelio.

Brief contents

Contents

Preface

Sound theory and a unified approach

Macroeconomics and microeconomics are the two pillars of economics. Yet, there is a wide gulf between the two pillars in the undergraduate curriculum. Micro courses teach material that is easier but basically consistent with the content taught to graduate students and used by economists in their research. In contrast, macro courses often bear little resemblance to graduate courses or academic research. Undergraduate macro textbooks and courses seem frequently to compromise good economics for presentations that are breezy, closely linked to arguments found in the popular press and not very intellectually challenging. But sacrificing solid economics to capture student interest is not necessary – sound theory can be clearly written with vivid examples to reinforce it.

This dissatisfaction with the textbook environment motivated Barro to write his first intermediate macro textbook in 1984. That book appeared in five editions, and he likes to think it had a positive impact – directly and also indirectly – in terms of influencing the subject matter and approaches of competitor works. Yet, there have been tremendous advances in macroeconomic theory and evidence over the last 30 years, and much of this research was left out of his earlier books. Hence, we decided to put our energies into this new book, *Intermediate Macroeconomics*, which is an adaptation of Barro's earlier book, *Macroeconomics: A Modern Approach*, with new materials and new data.

In addition to providing a more accurate presentation of the current state of macroeconomic thought, this text provides a unified approach that most macro textbooks lack. Rather than presenting a completely new model when shifting from a discussion of long-run theory to short-run theory, this book develops short-run and long-run models that build on one another in a natural, comprehensible and elegant way. And all this is done *without* ignoring the important differences between the economy in the long run and the short run. Similarly, we bring in the Keynesian idea of sticky prices as a new idea, but one that builds coherently on the structure of the basic equilibrium model.

Organizational structure

LONG-TERM GROWTH

Part I begins with long-run macroeconomics; that is, with the determinants of long-term economic growth. Great advances in theory and empirical analysis have taken place in this area since the late 1980s. Fortunately, it is possible to convey these important findings to undergraduates in a manageable and interesting way. In fact, as can be seen from Part II, students can understand the exciting results (in Chapters 3–5) without having, first, to master the details of the underlying microeconomic foundations (which come in Chapters 7 and 8). This early consideration of results with important policy implications helps to drive home the impact and relevance of macroeconomics.

THE EQUILIBRIUM BUSINESS-CYCLE MODEL

In Chapter 6, we begin Part III by reviewing some traditional Keynesian models that often appear in many macroeconomic textbooks. However, a complete microeconomic framework is more important for satisfactory analyses of economic fluctuations. Therefore, we apply the micro foundations from Chapters 7 and 8 to the development of an equilibrium business-cycle model in Chapters 9 and 10. This model generalizes the real business-cycle model, which has become a centrepiece of macroeconomic research since the mid-1980s. In Parts IV and V, Chapters 11–15 extend the equilibrium model to allow for money and inflation, and for the government sector (expenditure, taxes, transfers and public debt). In these Parts, we highlight some differences between the traditional Keynesian approach and the equilibrium business-cycle approach to macroeconomics.

INCOMPLETE INFORMATION AND STICKY PRICES

Part VI focuses on interactions between money and the real economy. Chapter 16 extends the equilibrium business-cycle model to allow for incomplete information about prices in a setting of rational expectations. Chapter 17 introduces the Keynesian idea of sticky prices and wages, with a focus on the new Keynesian model, another major development since the mid-1980s. This model recognizes that, rather than being perfect competitors, producers typically set prices that represent mark-ups on costs of production. Most importantly, these prices adjust only infrequently to changed circumstances. Together, Chapters 16 and 17 usefully supplement the equilibrium business-cycle model to allow for significant real effects from monetary policy.

THE OPEN ECONOMY

In Part VII, Chapters 18 and 19 extend the equilibrium model to an open economy. In Chapter 18, we deal, first, with a purely real setting in which the home and foreign countries share a common currency. One significant topic is the current-account deficit, a great concern for many countries in recent years. Chapter 19 introduces different moneys and allows for the determination of exchange rates. An important issue here – relevant today to debates about China's currency – concerns the relative merits of fixed versus flexible exchange rates.

Acknowledgements

Throughout the writing and development of this book, many dedicated professors have generously contributed their time and comments to help improve its presentation. We are grateful for their consideration and assistance. Angus Chu and Guido Cozzi would like especially to thank Margaret Davenport and Michael Ellington for their excellent research assistance.

The publisher would like to thank the following reviewers for their helpful feedback on this edition:

John Gathergood, University of Nottingham, UK

Katerina Raoukka, University of Bristol, UK

Tommaso Trani, Universidad de Navarra, Spain

Fang Xu, University of Reading, UK

About the authors

ROBERT J. BARRO

I was born in New York City, then moved to Los Angeles, where I attended high school. After studying physics at Caltech, including classes from Richard Feynman, I switched to economics for graduate school at Harvard. The change to economics was a great move for me! After jobs at Brown, Chicago and Rochester, I returned to Harvard as a professor in 1987. I am presently a senior fellow of Stanford's Hoover Institution and a research associate of the National Bureau of Economic Research. I co-edit Harvard's *Quarterly Journal of Economics* and was president of the Western Economic Association and vice president of the American Economic Association. I have been visiting China a great deal recently and am now honorary dean of the China Economics & Management Academy of the Central University of Beijing. My research has focused on macroeconomics and economic growth but includes recent work with my wife, Rachel, on the economics of religion. I am also studying the economic effects of rare disasters, such as depressions, world wars, epidemics and natural disasters. Aside from academic research, I enjoy more popular writing, including work as a viewpoint columnist for *Business Week* from 1998 to 2006 and as a contributing editor of *The Wall Street Journal* from 1991 to 1998. My recent books include *Economic Growth* (2nd edn, with Xavier Sala-i-Martin, who astoundingly served for a time as acting president of the famous soccer team F.C. Barcelona), *Nothing Is Sacred: Economic Ideas for the New Millennium, Determinants of Economic Growth* and *Getting It Right: Markets and Choices in a Free Society*, all from MIT Press.

ANGUS C. CHU

I was born in Hong Kong and moved to Vancouver, Canada, to attend high school, and to complete undergraduate studies at Simon Fraser University and graduate studies at the University of British Columbia. I then went to study at the University of Michigan in the United States and obtained my doctoral degree in Economics there in 2008. Recently, I have joined Fudan University in China as Professor of Economics. Before that, I served as Chair in Economics at the University of Liverpool, UK, where I still hold an honorary appointment. My research focuses on macroeconomics, monetary economics, economic growth, innovation and intellectual property rights. I have published my research in journals such as the *European Economic Review, International Economic Review, Journal of Development Economics, Journal of Economic Dynamics and Control, Journal of Economic Growth, Journal of International Economics, Journal of Money, Credit and Banking, Journal of Urban Economics, Macroeconomic Dynamics* and the *Review of Economic Dynamics*. Currently, I serve as an associate editor for the *Bulletin of Economic Research, Economic Modelling* and the *Singapore Economic Review*.

GUIDO COZZI

I was born in Rome and graduated in Economics at the University of Rome 'La Sapienza'. I continued my post-graduate studies at New York University, gaining my PhD in Economics in 2000. I have spent the past few years in Switzerland as Professor of Macroeconomics at the University of St Gallen. Before that, I served as Chair in Economics at the University of Durham, UK. My research focuses on macroeconomics, economic growth, innovation and intellectual property rights. I have published my research articles in journals such as the *Journal of Political Economy, American Economic Review, Review of Economics and Statistics, Journal of Economic Theory, Journal of* the *European Economic Association, European Economic Review, International Economic Review, Journal of Economic Growth, Journal of International Economics, Review of Economic Dynamic, Journal of Development Economics* and the *Journal of Economic Dynamics and Control*. I have collaborated with several private and public institutions, including the European Commission.

CENGAGE
Learning®

Digital
Support
Resources

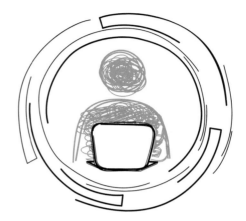

All of our Higher Education textbooks are accompanied by a range of digital support resources. Each title's resources are carefully tailored to the specific needs of the particular book's readers. Examples of the kind of resources provided include:

- A password protected area for instructors with, for example, a testbank, PowerPoint slides and an instructor's manual;

- An open-access area for students including, for example, useful weblinks and glossary terms.

Lecturers: to discover the dedicated lecturer digital support resources accompanying this textbook, please register here for access: login.cengage.com

Students: to discover the dedicated student digital support resources accompanying this textbook, please search for **INTERMEDIATE MACROECONOMICS** on: cengagebrain.co.uk

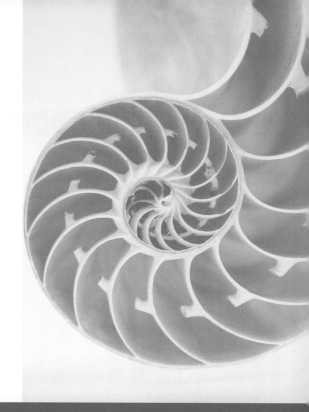

Introduction

PART I

1 Thinking about macroeconomics

Macroeconomics deals with the overall, or aggregate, performance of an economy. We study the determination of the economy's total production of goods and services, as measured by the real **gross domestic product (GDP)**. We analyze the breakdown of GDP into its major components: consumption, gross investment (purchases of new capital goods – equipment and structures – by the private sector), government purchases of goods and services, and net exports of goods and services. We also examine the aggregates of **employment** (persons with jobs) and **unemployment** (persons without jobs who are seeking work).

These terms refer to quantities of goods or labour. We are also interested in the prices that correspond to these quantities. For example, we consider the prices of the goods and services produced in an economy. When we look at the price of the typical or average item, we refer to the **general price level**. We also study the **wage rate**, which is the price of labour; the **rental price**, which is the price paid to use capital goods; and the **interest rate**, which determines the cost of borrowing and the return to lending. When we consider more than one economy, we can study the **exchange rate**, which is the rate at which one form of money (e.g., the euro) is exchanged for another form of money (e.g., the British pound).

We will set up an economic model, which will allow us to study how the various quantities and prices are determined. We can use the model to see how the quantities and prices respond to technological advances, government policies and other variables. For example, we will consider monetary policy, which involves the determination of the quantity of money and the setting of interest rates. We will also study fiscal policy, which describes the government's expenditures, taxes and fiscal deficits.

The performance of the overall economy matters for everyone because it influences incomes, job prospects and prices. Thus, it is important for us – and even more important for government policymakers – to understand how the macroeconomy operates. Unfortunately, as is obvious from reading the newspapers, macroeconomics is not a settled scientific field. Although there is consensus on many issues – such as some of the determinants of long-run economic growth – there is also controversy about many topics, such as the sources of economic fluctuations and the short-run effects of monetary policy. The main objective of this book is to convey the macroeconomic knowledge that has been attained, as well as to point out areas in which a full understanding has yet to be achieved.

Output, unemployment and prices

To get an overview of the subject, we can look at the historical record of some of the major macroeconomic variables. Figure 1.1 shows the total output or production of goods and services in the world from 1950 to 2014. (The starting date is determined by the available data.)[1] Our measure of aggregate output is known as the **real gross world product**, which is computed as the combined **real gross domestic product** (GDP) of all countries in the world. Therefore, **gross world product** (GWP) is also known as the world GDP. Real GDP expresses quantities in

[1] DeLong (1998) provides estimates of the gross world product for some years between one million years BCE and the present time.

Figure 1.1 Real GWP, 1950–2014

The graph shows the real gross world product (GWP) on a proportionate (logarithmic) scale, and the numbers are in billions of 1990 international dollars.[2]

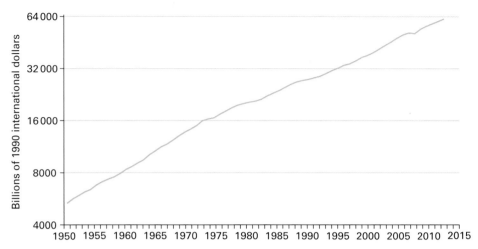

Sources: Data until 2010 on real GWP per capita are from the Maddison Project Database. Data on world population are from the United Nations Population Database. Data from 2011 on real GWP are from the World Bank, International Comparison Program database.

terms of a base year – in our case, 1990. Chapter 2 considers **national-income accounting** and thereby provides the conceptual details for measuring **real gross domestic product**.

The general upward trend of real GWP in Figure 1.1 reflects the long-term growth of the world economy. Figure 1.2 plots the growth rate of real GWP for each year from 1951 to 2014. A simple way to compute the growth rate for year t is to take the difference between the levels of real GWP in years t and $t-1$, $Y_t - Y_{t-1}$, and then divide by year $t-1$'s level of real GWP, Y_{t-1}:

$$growth\,rate\,of\,real\,GWP\,for\,year\;t=\left(Y_t-Y_{t-1}\right)/Y_{t-1}$$

If we then multiply by 100, we get the growth rate of real GWP in percent per year.

The mean growth rate of real GWP from 1951 to 2014 was 3.9% per year. This growth rate meant that the level of real GWP, shown in Figure 1.1, expanded more than ten-fold from 1950 to 2014. If we divide through by population to determine real per capita GWP, it turns out that the mean per capita growth rate was 2.2% per year. This rate equals the 3.9% per-year growth rate of real GWP less the 1.7% per-year growth rate of population. The growth rate of real per capita GWP of 2.2% per year meant that real GWP per capita increased four-fold from 1950 to 2014.

Figure 1.2 shows that the year-to-year growth rates of real GWP varied substantially around their mean of 3.9%. These variations are called **economic fluctuations** or, sometimes, the **business cycle**.[3] When real GWP expands towards a high point or peak, the world economy is in a **boom**, or an economic expansion. When real GWP falls towards a low point or trough, the world economy is potentially in a **recession**, or an economic contraction. One condition that the International Monetary Fund uses to define a global recession is a decline in annual per capita real GWP. There are many other ways to classify periods of recession. In Chapter 9, we use a more sophisticated method to classify recessions at the national level.

Note in Figure 1.3 the global **Great Recession** in 2008, during which per capita real GWP declined by 2%. The other sharp reductions in the growth rates of real GWP in Figure 1.3 capture the effects of the oil crisis in 1973, the energy crisis in 1979, the oil price shock in 1990, the Asian financial crisis in 1997 and the burst of the dot-com bubble in 2000. Each of these shocks caused major recessions in different parts of the world.

---

[2]The graph uses a proportionate scale, so that each unit on the vertical axis corresponds to the same percentage change in real GDP. The international dollar, also known as the Geary-Khamis dollar, is constructed in such a way that this hypothetical unit of currency has the same purchasing power as the US dollar in the United States at a given point in time.

[3]The term 'business cycle' can be misleading because it suggests a more regular pattern of ups and downs in economic activity than actually appears in the data.

Figure 1.2 **Growth rate of real GWP, 1951–2014**

The graph shows the annual growth rate of real GWP. The growth rates are calculated from the values of real GWP shown in Figure 1.1.

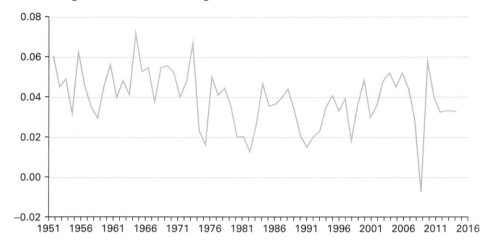

Figure 1.3 **Growth rate of per capita real GWP, 1951–2014**

The graph shows the annual growth rate of per capita real GWP.

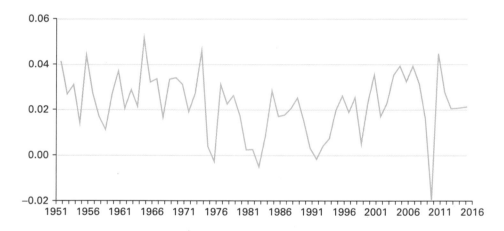

Economics in Practice
The Great Recession

The global Great Recession was partly triggered by the subprime mortgage crisis in the United States. In 2006–07, the US housing bubble burst led to many homeowners defaulting on their mortgage payments. These mortgage defaulters were often subprime borrowers, defined as people who have higher-than-normal credit risks and a below-average credit history. These US mortgages were marketed as mortgage-backed securities around the world and held by major financial institutions due to their higher yields than US government bonds. When homeowners started to default on these mortgages, the value of the mortgage-backed securities collapsed causing substantial losses to major financial institutions. The most notable example was Lehman Brothers, which declared bankruptcy in 2008. The resulting panic on the inter-bank loan market led to severe financial losses by many large and well-established banks in the United States and Europe. This financial crisis also led to sharp reductions in household spending and business investment, partly triggering the global recession.

Another way to gauge recessions and booms is to consider the **unemployment rate** – the fraction of persons seeking work who have no job. Figure 1.4 shows the unemployment rates of the world and a number of countries for each year from 1991 to 2013. The mean unemployment rate of the world was 6.1% and fluctuated moderately from 5.4% to 6.5%. However, mean unemployment rates are quite different across countries and also more volatile within each country. For example, the mean unemployment rate of France was 10.0% whereas it was only 4.4% in China. The mean unemployment rates of other countries were somewhere in between: Saudi Arabia (5.6%), United Kingdom (7.0%) and United States (6.2%). From 1991 to 2013, the unemployment rates were more volatile in France, the United Kingdom and the United States than in China and Saudi Arabia. During recessions, the unemployment rate typically rises sharply. An example is the Great Recession in 2008, during which the unemployment rates rose from 7.4% to 9.1% in France, from 5.4% to 7.8% in the United Kingdom and from 5.9% to 9.4% in the United States within a year.

Figure 1.5 shows the evolution of the price levels of the world and a number of countries from 1991 to 2013. This graph measures the price level as the deflator for the GDP (we discuss the details of this price index in Chapter 2). For present purposes, the important point is that the GDP deflator is a broad index, corresponding to the prices of all the items that enter into the gross domestic product. One striking observation is the persistent rise in price levels across most countries. The only notable exception is Saudi Arabia, where there were clear up and down movements in the price level. For example, during the Asian financial crisis in 1997 and the Great Recession in 2008, the price level fell significantly in Saudi Arabia.

Figure 1.6 shows the annual **inflation rates** of the world and a number of countries from 1991 to 2013. Each year's inflation rate is calculated as the growth rate in percent per year of the price level of a country shown in Figure 1.5. A simple way to compute the inflation rate for year t is to take the difference between the price levels in years t and $t - 1$, $P_t - P_{t-1}$, and then divide by year $t -1$'s price level, P_{t-1}:

$$inflation\ rate\ for\ year\ t = (P_t - P_{t-1})/P_{t-1}$$

If we then multiply by 100, we get the inflation rate in percent per year.

Notice from Figure 1.6 that the inflation rates in France, the United Kingdom and the United States were all greater than zero with mean inflation rates of 1.5% in France, 2.5% in the United Kingdom and 2.1% in the United States. In contrast, mean inflation rates were much higher in China (5.5%) and Saudi Arabia (4.5%), and inflation fell below zero in two major crises: the Asian financial crisis and the Great Recession. In subsequent chapters, we will relate the behaviour of inflation to the character of monetary institutions and monetary policy. Notably, central banks in developed countries, such as France, the United Kingdom and the United States, have successfully pursued a policy of low and stable inflation.

Figure 1.4 World unemployment rates, 1991–2013

The graph shows the unemployment rates of the world and a number of countries.

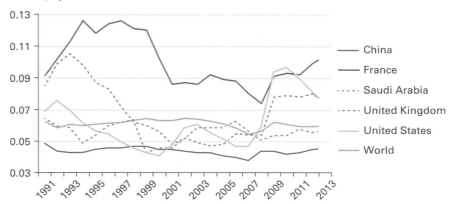

Source: Data on unemployment rates estimated by the International Labour Organization (ILO) are from the World Development Indicators. The ILO establishes international standards for labour statistics so that the ILO's data on unemployment rates can be compared between countries.

Figure 1.5 World price levels, 1991–2013

The graph shows the GDP price deflators of the world and a number of countries. The numbers are on a proportionate (logarithmic) scale, with the value for the year 1991 set at 100. Data are from the World Development Indicators.

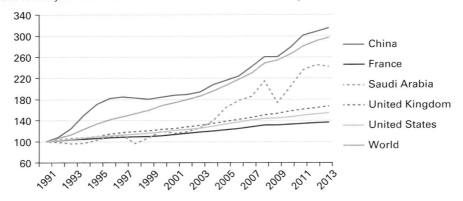

Figure 1.6 World inflation rates, 1991–2013

The graph shows the annual inflation rate based on the GDP deflator. The inflation rate is the annual growth rate of the price level shown in Figure 1.5.

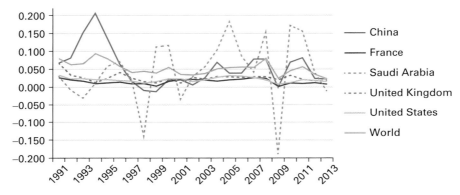

Economic models

As mentioned, we want to understand the determinants of major macroeconomic variables, such as real GDP and the general price level. To carry out this mission, we will construct a macroeconomic model. A model can be a group of equations or graphs, or a set of conceptual ideas. We will use all of these tools in this book – some equations but, more often, graphs and ideas.

An economic model deals with two kinds of variables: endogenous variables and exogenous variables. The **endogenous variables** are the ones that we want the model to explain. For example, the endogenous variables in our macroeconomic model include real GDP, investment, employment, the general price level, the wage rate and the interest rate.

The **exogenous variables** are the ones that a model takes as given and does not attempt to explain. A simple example of an exogenous variable is the weather (at least in models that do not allow the climate to affect the economy). In many cases, the available technologies will be exogenous. For a single country's economy, the exogenous variables include the world prices of commodities such as oil and wheat, as well as levels of income in the rest of the world. In many cases, we will treat government policies as exogenous – for example, choices about monetary policy, and government spending and taxes. We also treat as exogenous war and peace, which have important macroeconomic consequences.

The central idea of a model is that it tells us how to go from the exogenous variables to the endogenous variables; Figure 1.7 illustrates this process. We take as given the group of exogenous variables shown in the left-hand box in the diagram. The model tells us how to go from these exogenous variables to the group of endogenous variables shown in the right-hand box of the diagram. Therefore, we can use the model to predict how changes in the exogenous variables affect the endogenous variables.

Figure 1.7 The workings of an economic model

A model is a theory that tells us how to go from a group of exogenous variables to a group of endogenous variables. The model may be a list of equations or graphs or a set of conceptual ideas. The exogenous variables come from outside the model and are therefore not explained by the model. The endogenous variables are the ones that the model seeks to explain. With the help of the model, we can predict how changes in the exogenous variables affect the endogenous variables.

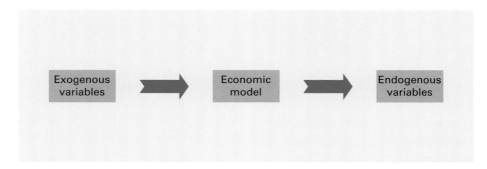

In macroeconomics, we are interested in the determination of macroeconomic – that is, economy-wide aggregate – variables, such as real GDP. However, to construct a useful macroeconomic model, we will find it helpful to build on a microeconomic approach to the actions of individual households and businesses. This microeconomic approach investigates individual decisions about how much to consume and save, how much to work, and so on. Then we can add up, or aggregate, the choices of individuals to construct a macroeconomic model. This underlying microeconomic analysis is called **microeconomic foundations**.

A SIMPLE EXAMPLE: THE COFFEE MARKET

To illustrate general ideas about models and markets, we can examine the market for a single product, such as coffee. Our analysis will focus on three key tools used by economists: demand curves, supply curves, and market-clearing conditions (quantity demanded equals quantity supplied).

Individuals decide how much coffee to buy; that is, the quantity of coffee to demand. Influences on this demand include the individual's income, the price of coffee, P_c, and the price of a substitute good, say, P_T, the price of tea. Since each individual is a negligible part of the coffee and tea markets, it makes sense that each individual would neglect the effect of his or her coffee and tea consumption on P_c and P_T. That is, each individual is a **price taker**; he or she simply decides how much coffee and tea to buy at given prices, P_c and P_T. Economists use the term **perfect competition** to describe a market in which there are so many buyers and sellers that no individual can noticeably affect the price.

Reasonable behaviour for an individual household dictates that each household's quantity of coffee demanded would rise with income, fall with the coffee price, P_c, and rise with the price of the substitute good, P_T. These results for individual households are examples of microeconomic analysis. When we add up across all households, we determine the aggregate quantity of coffee demanded as a function of aggregate income, denoted by Y, and the prices P_c and P_T. We can isolate the effect of the coffee price, P_c, on the total quantity of coffee demanded by drawing a market **demand curve**. This curve shows the total quantity of coffee demanded, Q_c^d, as a function of P_c.

Figure 1.8 shows the market demand curve for coffee. As already noted, a decrease in P_c increases Q_c^d. Recall, however, that the demand curve applies for given values of aggregate income, Y, and the price of tea, P_T. If Y rises, the quantity of coffee demanded, Q_c^d, increases for a given price, P_c. Therefore, the demand curve shown in Figure 1.8 shifts to the right. If P_T falls, the quantity of coffee demanded, Q_c^d, decreases for a given price, P_c. Therefore, the demand curve shifts to the left.

Figure 1.8 Demand curve for coffee

The market demand curve shows the total quantity of coffee demanded, Q_c^d, as a function of the price of coffee, P_c. A decrease in P_c raises Q_c^d. The demand curve applies for given aggregate income, Y, and the price of tea, P_T. If Y rises, the quantity of coffee demanded, Q_c^d, increases for a given P_c. Therefore, the demand curve in the diagram shifts to the right. If P_T falls, the quantity of coffee demanded, Q_c^d, decreases for a given P_c. Therefore, the demand curve shifts to the left.

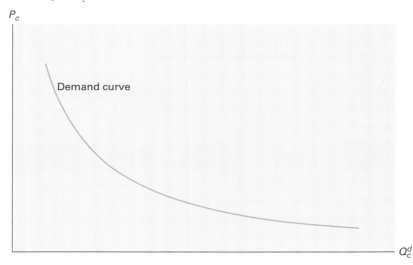

We also have to consider how individual producers of coffee decide how much to offer for sale on the market; that is, how much coffee to supply. Influences on this supply include the price of coffee, P_c, and the cost of producing additional coffee. We assume, as in our analysis of demand, that the suppliers of coffee are price takers with respect to P_c. This assumption could be questioned because some producers of coffee are large and might consider the effects of their actions on P_c. However, an extension to allow for this effect would not change our basic analysis of the market for coffee.

Reasonable behaviour by an individual producer dictates that the quantity of coffee supplied would rise with the price of coffee, P_c, and fall with an increase in the cost of producing additional coffee. For example, bad weather that destroys part of the coffee crop in Brazil would raise the cost of producing coffee and, thereby, reduce the coffee supplied by Brazilians. These results for individual producers are examples of microeconomic analysis.

When we add up across all producers, we determine the aggregate quantity of coffee supplied. One result is that a rise in P_c increases the aggregate quantity of coffee supplied, Q_c^s. The total quantity supplied also depends on weather conditions in coffee-producing areas, such as Brazil and Colombia.

Extending the Model
Demand and supply curves are functions

The market demand for coffee can be written as a function:

$$Q_c^d = D(P_c, Y, P_T)$$

The function $D(\cdot)$ determines the quantity of coffee demanded, Q_c^d, for any specified values of the three demand determinants, P_c, Y, and P_T. We assume that the function $D(\cdot)$ has the properties that Q_c^d decreases with the price of coffee, P_c, rises with income, Y, and rises with the price of tea, P_T. Figure 1.8 graphs Q_c^d against P_c for given values of the other demand determinants, Y and P_T. It is important to distinguish the demand curve, $D(\cdot)$, shown in Figure 1.8, from the quantity demanded, Q_c^d, at a given price, P_c (and for given Y and P_T). The demand curve refers to the whole functional relationship between quantity demanded and price, $D(\cdot)$, whereas the quantity demanded, Q_c^d, refers to one of the points along the curve.

The market supply of coffee is also a function, which can be written as:

$$Q_c^s = S(P_c, weather)$$

We assume that the function $S(\cdot)$ has the properties that the quantity supplied, Q_c^s, rises with P_c and with better weather in coffee-producing areas. Figure 1.9 graphs the quantity supplied, Q_c^s, against P_c, for given weather conditions. It is important to remember that the supply curve, $S(\cdot)$, refers to the whole functional relationship between quantity supplied and price, whereas the quantity supplied, Q_c^s, refers to one of the points along the curve.

As in our analysis of demand, we can isolate the effect of the coffee price, P_c, on the total quantity of coffee supplied by drawing a market **supply curve**. This curve, shown in Figure 1.9, gives the total quantity of coffee supplied, Q_c^s, as a function of P_c. As already noted, an increase in P_c raises Q_c^s. This supply curve applies for given cost conditions for producing coffee and, in particular, for given weather in coffee-producing areas. If bad weather destroys part of Brazil's coffee crop, the market quantity of coffee supplied, Q_c^s, decreases for a given price, P_c. Therefore, the supply curve shown in Figure 1.9 shifts to the left.

Figure 1.10 shows the clearing of the market for coffee. The price of coffee, Q_c^s, is assumed to adjust to equate the quantity supplied, P_c, to the quantity demanded, Q_c^d. This market-clearing price is the value $(P_c)^*$ shown in the figure. The corresponding market-clearing quantity of coffee is $(Q_c)^*$.

Why do we assume that the coffee price, P_c, adjusts to the market-clearing value, $(P_c)^*$? For any other price, the quantities supplied and demanded would be unequal. For example, at point 1 in Figure 1.10, where P_c is less than $(P_c)^*$, the quantity demanded, Q_c^d, would be greater than the quantity supplied, Q_c^s. In that case, some coffee drinkers must be unsatisfied; they would not be able to buy the quantity of coffee that they want at the price P_c. That is, suppliers would be unwilling to provide enough coffee to satisfy all of the desired purchases at this low price. In this circumstance, we would think that competition among the eager demanders of coffee would raise the market price, P_c, towards $(P_c)^*$.

Figure 1.9 Supply curve for coffee

The market supply curve shows the total quantity of coffee supplied, Q_c^s, as a function of the price of coffee, P_c. An increase in P_c raises Q_c^s. The supply curve applies for given conditions that affect the cost of producing coffee. For example, a harvest failure in Brazil would decrease the total quantity of coffee supplied, Q_c^s, for a given price, P_c. Therefore, the supply curve shifts to the left.

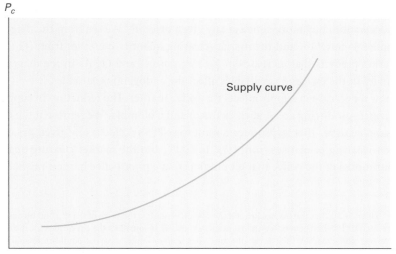

Figure 1.10 Clearing of the market for coffee

The coffee market clears at the price $(P_c)^*$ and quantity $(Q_c)^*$ At this point, the quantity of coffee supplied equals the quantity demanded.

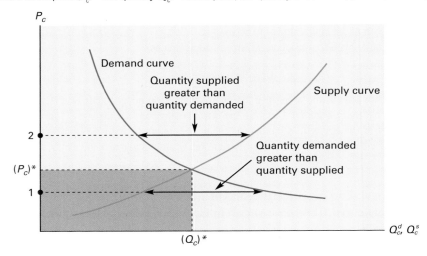

Conversely, at point 2 in Figure 1.10, where P_c is higher than $(P_c)^*$, the quantity demanded, Q_c^d, would be less than the quantity supplied, Q_c^s. In this case, some coffee producers must be unsatisfied; they would not be able to sell the full quantity of coffee that they want to sell at the price P_c. That is, coffee drinkers would be unwilling to buy all the coffee that the producers offer at this high price. In this situation, we would expect that competition among the eager suppliers of coffee would reduce the market price, P_c, towards $(P_c)^*$.

The market-clearing price, $P_c = (P_c)^*$, is special because only at this price is there no pressure for the coffee price to rise or fall. In this sense, the market-clearing price is an **equilibrium** price. This price tends to remain the same unless there are shifts to the demand curve or the supply curve.

We can think of our market-clearing analysis of the coffee market as a model of how the coffee market operates. The two endogenous variables in the model are the price, P_c, and quantity, Q_c, of coffee. We can use the market-clearing analysis from Figure 1.10 to see how changes in exogenous variables affect the endogenous variables in the model. The exogenous variables are the outside forces that shift the demand and supply curves for coffee. For demand, we referred to two exogenous variables: income, Y, and the price of tea, P_T.[4] For supply, we mentioned as exogenous variables the weather conditions in coffee-producing areas, such as Brazil.

Figure 1.11 shows how an increase in demand affects the coffee market. The rise in demand could reflect an increase in income, Y, or the price of tea, P_T. We represent the increase in demand by a rightward shift of the demand curve. That is, consumers want to buy more coffee at any given price, P_c. We see from the diagram that the market-clearing price rises from $(P_c)^*$ to $(P_c)^{*\prime}$, and the market-clearing quantity increases from $(Q_c)^*$ to $(Q_c)^{*\prime}$. Thus, our model of the coffee market predicts that increases in Y or P_T raise P_c and Q_c. As in the diagram in Figure 1.7, the model tells us how changes in the exogenous variables affect the endogenous variables.

Figure 1.12 shows how a decrease in supply affects the coffee market. The reduction in supply could reflect poor weather conditions in coffee-producing areas, such as Brazil and Colombia. We represent the decrease in supply by a leftward shift of the supply curve. That is, producers want to sell less coffee at any given price, P_c. We see from the diagram that the market-clearing price rises from $(P_c)^*$ to $(P_c)^{*\prime}$, and the market-clearing quantity decreases from $(Q_c)^*$ to $(Q_c)^{*\prime}$. Thus, our model of the coffee market predicts that a poor coffee harvest raises P_c and lowers Q_c.

---

[4]From a broader perspective that encompasses the tea market and the overall economy, the price of tea, P_T, and incomes would also be endogenous variables. This broader analysis is called general-equilibrium theory; that is, it considers the conditions for the clearing of all markets simultaneously. The limitation to a single market, such as the one for coffee, is an example of partial-equilibrium analysis. In this case, we assess the clearing of the coffee market while taking as given the outcomes in the other markets.

Figure 1.11 Effect of an increase in demand on the coffee market

In Figure 1.10, the coffee market cleared at the price $(P_c)^*$ and quantity $(Q_c)^*$. An increase in income, Y, or in the price of tea, P_T, raises the demand for coffee. Therefore, the demand curve shifts rightward from the solid blue curve to the dashed blue curve. The market-clearing price of coffee rises to $(P_c)^{*\prime}$, and the market-clearing quantity of coffee rises to $(Q_c)^{*\prime}$.

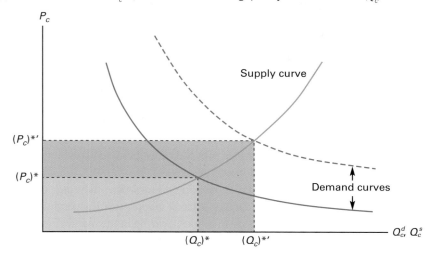

Figure 1.12 Effect of a decrease in supply on the coffee market

In Figure 1.10, the coffee market cleared at the price $(P_c)^*$ and quantity $(Q_c)^*$. A harvest failure in Brazil reduces the supply of coffee. Therefore, the supply curve shifts leftward from the solid blue curve to the dashed blue curve. The market-clearing price of coffee rises to $(P_c)^{*\prime}$, and the market-clearing quantity of coffee falls to $(Q_c)^{*\prime}$.

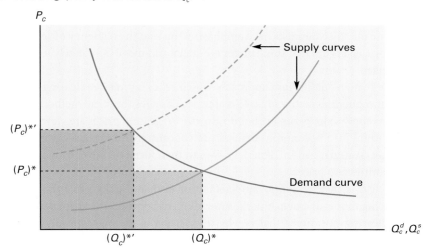

Table 1.1 summarizes the results from the market-clearing model of the coffee market. As in Figure 1.7, the model tells us how changes in the exogenous variables affect the endogenous variables.

Our macroeconomic model will use this kind of market-clearing analysis to predict how changes in exogenous variables affect the endogenous macroeconomic variables. However, we will not study an array of goods, such as coffee, tea, and so on. Rather, we will consider the aggregate demand for and supply of a composite good that corresponds to the economy's overall output, the real GDP. We will also analyze the demand for and supply of factors of production – labour and capital services.

Table 1.1 Effects of changes in exogenous variables on the endogenous variables in the coffee market

Change in exogenous variable	Effect on P_c	Effect on Q_c
Increase in income Y	rises	rises
Increase in price of tea P_T	rises	rises
Poor coffee harvest	rises	falls

FLEXIBLE VERSUS STICKY PRICES

When we studied the market for coffee, we focused on market-clearing conditions. Therefore, when an exogenous variable changed, we based our predictions on how this change altered the market-clearing price and quantity. The assumption that underlies this analysis is that the price of coffee adjusts rapidly to clear the market for coffee; that is, to equate the quantity demanded to the quantity supplied. We observed that, if the price differed from its market-clearing value, either demanders or suppliers of coffee could not be satisfied in their offers to buy or sell at the established price. Consequently, there was always pressure for the coffee price to adjust towards its market-clearing value – the market-clearing price was the only equilibrium price.

Although most economists accept the focus on market-clearing prices when analyzing coffee or similar products, there is less agreement on whether macroeconomics should focus on market-clearing conditions. In particular, not all economists agree that we should consider only situations of market clearing in the market for the composite good that represents real GDP or in the market for labour. For long-run analysis, there is a consensus that the market-clearing framework provides the best guide to how an economy operates. Therefore, in our study of long-run economic growth in Chapters 3–5, we use a market-clearing, equilibrium approach. However, for analyses of short-run macroeconomic fluctuations, there is a sharp divide among economists as to whether a market-clearing model provides useful insights.

The famous economist John Maynard Keynes, writing in the wake of the **Great Depression** in the 1930s, argued that the labour market typically did not clear – he thought that the labour market was usually in a state of **disequilibrium**, by which he meant a discrepancy between the quantities of labour demanded and supplied. In particular, he argued that wage rates were sticky and adjusted only slowly to generate equality between the quantities of labour demanded and supplied. In Chapter 6, we will examine the **Keynesian IS-LM model** that was developed based on the insights of Keynes. Some macroeconomists have emphasized instead the tendency of some goods markets to be in disequilibrium. This approach argues that some prices are sticky and move only slowly to equate the quantities of goods demanded and supplied.

Other economists argue that an equilibrium approach, which relies on market-clearing conditions, gives us the best insights into short-run economic fluctuations. This approach applies the same methodology to short-run fluctuations as most economists apply to long-run economic growth. Wages and prices are viewed as sufficiently flexible in the short run so that a useful macroeconomic analysis can concentrate on market-clearing situations. As in our analysis of the coffee market (summarized in Table 1.1), we can then focus on how changes in exogenous variables affect market-clearing quantities and prices.

One point that seems clear is that we cannot understand or evaluate sticky-price models unless we have the flexible-price, market-clearing model as a benchmark. After all, macroeconomists agree that the economy is always approaching the market-clearing position – that is why this setting is the one typically used to study long-run economic growth. A reasonable inference is that, whatever the ultimate verdict on the significance of sticky prices in the short run, it is best to begin macroeconomic analysis with a market-clearing model.

We set out the basic market-clearing model of economic fluctuations in Chapters 7–11. We call this model an equilibrium business-cycle model (a broader term than 'real business-cycle model', which often appears in the economics literature). We extend the model to allow for inflation in Chapter 12 and for government spending, taxes, and fiscal deficits in Chapters 13–15. Chapter 16 allows for misperceptions about prices and wages but continues to assume a market-clearing framework. In Chapter 17, we extend the equilibrium business-cycle model to allow for the sticky wages and sticky prices that are the hallmarks of the Keynesian IS-LM model, and the resulting model is known as the **new Keynesian model**.

Key Terms and Concepts

boom
business cycle
demand curve
disequilibrium
economic fluctuations
employment
endogenous variables
equilibrium
exchange rate

exogenous variables
general price level
Great Depression
Great Recession
gross domestic product
  (GDP)
gross world product (GWP)
inflation rate
interest rate

Keynesian IS-LM model
microeconomic foundations
national-income accounting
new Keynesian model
perfect competition
price taker
real GDP
real gross domestic
  product

real gross world product
recession
rental price
supply curve
unemployment
unemployment rate
wage rate

2 National-income accounting: Gross domestic product and the price level

In Chapter 1, we used terms such as *gross domestic product (GDP)* and the *price level* without defining them precisely. Now, by looking at national-income accounting, we develop the meanings of these terms. Many challenging issues arise in the construction of the national-income accounts. However, for our purposes, we will deal only with the basic concepts.

Nominal and real GDP

We begin with the gross domestic product, or GDP. **Nominal GDP** measures the euro (or British pound, etc.) value of all the goods and services that an economy produces during a specified period, such as a year. For example, in 2014, the euro area's nominal GDP was €10.1 trillion. The nominal GDP is a **flow variable**: it measures the euro value of goods and services produced per unit of time, such as a year.

Consider the definition of nominal GDP one step at a time. The word 'nominal' means that the goods produced during a year are measured as values in euros (or in units of another currency, such as British pounds). For most goods and services – pencils, cars, haircuts, and so on – the euro value is determined by the price at which these items sell in the marketplace.

Some goods and services, including many produced by governments, are not exchanged on markets. For example, the government does not sell its services for national defence, the justice system and the police. These items enter into nominal GDP at their nominal (euro) cost of production. This treatment is problematic because it amounts to assuming that government employees experience no changes over time in their productivity. However, in the absence of market prices, it is unclear what alternative approach would be more accurate.

Another item, owner-occupied housing, enters into GDP as an estimate of what this housing would fetch on the market if the owner rented the property to another person. This amount is called the **imputed rental income** on owner-occupied housing. Conceptually, the same approach ought to apply to consumer durables, such as households' automobiles, furniture and appliances. However, this treatment has not been followed; that is, the GDP does not include the estimated rental income on consumer durables.[1] For government-owned property, the assumption in the national accounts is that the imputed rental income equals the estimated depreciation. This assumption is troublesome but, again, a preferred alternative method is not obvious.

It is important to understand that the nominal GDP includes the value of the goods and services produced during a specified time interval, such as a year. That is, GDP measures current production. For example, if a carmaker manufactures and sells a new car in 2017, the full value of the car counts in the GDP for 2017. However, if someone sells in 2017 a used car that was built in 2016, this sale does not count in the GDP for 2017.

The nominal GDP can be misleading because it depends on the overall level of prices, as well as on the physical quantity of goods produced. Table 2.1 illustrates this problem. Think about a simple economy that produces only

---

[1] The capital owned by businesses (such as factories and machinery) contributes to the goods and services produced by the businesses. Therefore, the market value of output already includes the rental income on business capital. For this reason, it is unnecessary for measures of GDP to include an imputed rental income on business capital.

Table 2.1 The calculation of nominal and real GDP: A simple example

	2016a	2016b	2017a	2017b
Prices				
Butter	€2.00 per pound	€2.00 per pound	€3.00 per pound	€1.50 per pound
Golf balls	€1.00 per ball	€1.00 per ball	€1.10 per ball	€0.89 per ball
Quantities				
Butter	50 pounds	50 pounds	40 pounds	70 pounds
Golf balls	400 balls	400 balls	391 balls	500 balls
Nominal market values				
Butter	100.0	100.0	120.0	105.0
Golf balls	400.0	400.0	430.1	445.0
Nominal GDP	500.0	500.0	550.1	550.0
2016–17 average price				
Butter	€2.50 per pound	€1.75 per pound	€2.50 per pound	€1.75 per pound
Golf balls	€1.05 per ball	€0.945 per ball	€1.05 per ball	€0.945 per ball
Market values at 2016–17 average prices				
Butter	125.0	87.5	100.0	122.5
Golf balls	420.0	378.0	410.6	472.5
Total	545.0	465.5	510.6	595.0
Ratio to 2016	1.0	1.0	0.937	1.278
Chained real GDP, 2016 base	500.0	500.0	468.5	639.0
Implicit GDP deflator, 2016 base	100	100	117	86

butter and golf balls. The table shows the hypothetical quantities and prices of these goods in 2016 and 2017. In 2016, the economy produces 50 pounds of butter, which sell at €2.00 per pound. Thus, the euro value of 2016's butter output is €100. In 2016, the economy also produces 400 golf balls, priced at €1.00 per ball, for a golf-ball output of €400. The nominal GDP for 2016 is the sum of the euro values of butter and golf-ball output: €100 + €400 = €500.

The columns labelled 2017a and 2017b show two possibilities for prices and quantities in 2017. In case *a*, the prices of both goods rise – to €3.00 per pound of butter and €1.10 per golf ball. In case *b*, the prices of both goods decline – to €1.50 per pound of butter and €0.89 per golf ball. In case *a*, the quantities of both goods decline – to 40 pounds of butter and 391 golf balls. In case *b*, the quantities of both goods rise – to 70 pounds of butter and 500 golf balls.

We have assumed numbers so that the nominal GDP in 2017 is about the same in both cases. In case *a*, the nominal GDP is €120 for butter plus €430 for golf balls, a total of €550. In case *b*, the nominal GDP is €105 for butter plus €445 for golf balls, again a total €550. However, the quantities of both goods are higher in case *b* than case *a*. Thus, any sensible measure of real GDP in 2017 would show a higher value in case *b* than case *a*. Thus, the equality of the nominal GDPs is misleading. Identical figures on nominal GDP can conceal very different underlying differences in levels of production.

CALCULATING REAL GDP

Economists solve the problem of changing price levels by constructing measures of real GDP. Until recently, the most common way to compute real GDP was to multiply each year's quantity of output of each good by the price of the good in a base year, such as 2010. Then all of these multiples were added to get the economy's aggregate real GDP.

The resulting aggregate is called 'GDP in 2010 euro values' (if 2010 is the base year). Sometimes, the result is called **GDP in constant prices**, because we use prices (for the base year, 2010) that do not vary over time. In contrast, the nominal GDP is sometimes called **GDP in current prices**, because this calculation of GDP uses each good's price in the current year.

Since the prices from the base year (say, 2010) do not vary over time, the method just described provides a reasonable measure of changes over time in the overall level of production. That is, it provides a sensible measure of real GDP. However, a shortcoming of this approach is that it weighs the outputs of the various goods by their prices in the base year, which happened to be 2010. For example, suppose that a personal computer costs more than a sofa in 2010. In this case, each computer produced in 2017 (of the same quality as ones produced in 2010) would count more than each sofa for 2017's real GDP, even though computers were then cheaper than couches. More generally, the base-year weights become less relevant over time as relative prices of goods change. The response had been to make frequent shifts in the base year. However, a more accurate solution, called the chain-weighted method, has been adopted by most countries to get a better measure of real GDP. The resulting variable is called **chain-weighted real GDP**. This chain-weighted measure is the one publicized in the media, and it is the one we shall use in this book to measure real GDP.[2]

To illustrate how chain-weighting works, we can again use our hypothetical data for a simple economy from Table 2.1. The method starts by computing the average price of each good for two adjacent years – 2016 and 2017 in the table. For example, in scenario *a*, the average price of butter for 2016 and 2017 is €2.50 per pound. In scenario *b*, it is €1.75 per pound.

In each year – 2016 and 2017 in the table – the quantities produced of each good are multiplied by the average prices for the two adjacent years. For example, in case *a*, the value of the butter produced in 2016 is €125 when calculated at the average price for 2016 and 2017, compared to €100 when the (lower) price for 2016 is used. For 2017, in case *a*, the value of the butter is €100 when computed at the average price, compared to €120 when the (higher) price for 2017 is used.

Using these average-price numbers, we sum the values of the goods produced in each year to get the totals shown in Table 2.1. For example, for 2016, in case *a*, the total value is €545, compared to €500 when we used prices for 2016. For 2017, in case *a*, the total value is €510.6, compared to €550.1 when we used prices for 2017.

Next we compute the ratios of each of these totals to the totals for 2016. Thus, the ratios are 1.0 for the two cases (*a* and *b*) that apply to 2016. For 2017, the ratio is 0.937 in case *a* and 1.278 in case *b*.

To get chained real GDP on a 2016 base, we multiply the ratios just calculated by the nominal GDP (€500) for 2016. Thus, chained real GDP for 2016 on a 2016 base is the same as nominal GDP – €500 (for cases *a* and *b*). For 2017, chained real GDP on a 2016 base is €468.5 in case *a* and €639.0 in case *b*. Thus, although the nominal GDPs for 2017 are the same, the chained real GDP is substantially higher in case *b*. This result makes sense because the quantities of butter and golf balls are both higher in case *b* than in case *a*.

We can proceed the same way for other years. For example, when we get data for 2018, we can calculate the ratio of the value of output in 2018 to that for 2017. These ratios are analogous to those calculated for 2017 compared to 2016 in Table 2.1. We then want to express the results for 2018 on a 2016 base, so that all the chained values apply to the same base year. To do this, we multiply the ratio for 2018 compared to 2017 by the ratio for 2017 compared to 2016. This gives us the ratio of 2018 values to 2016 values. Finally, we multiply the last ratio by nominal GDP for 2016 to get the chain-weighted GDP for 2018 on a 2016 base. This procedure is called *chain-linking*. If we carry out this procedure from one year to the next, we end up with a time series for chain-weighted real GDP expressed in terms of a single base year.

In Table 2.1, the base year for chain-weighted real GDP is 2016. However, the actual base year used by Eurostat in the early 2010s was 2010. With the chain method, the choice of which year to use for the base is not important. We use a single base year only to ensure that the real GDPs for each year are comparable. (The ratio of chain-weighted real GDPs for two years, such as 2016 and 2017, is the same for any choice of base year.)

---

[2]At the end of the chapter, there is a question that involves calculating real GDP using constant prices and comparing this *constant-price* real GDP with chain-weighted real GDP.

We can use the results on real GDP to construct an index for the overall level of prices. In Table 2.1, where 2016 is the base year, we can think of the overall price level for 2016 as '100'. This number is arbitrary; it just serves as a comparative position that can be related to price levels in other years.

For case *a* in 2017, the nominal GDP is €550, and the chain-weighted real GDP on a 2016 base is €468.5. We can think of an implicit price level used to convert a euro value – the nominal GDP of €550 – into a real value – the real GDP of €468.5:

$$(nominal\ GDP)/(implicit\ price\ level) = real\ GDP$$

If we rearrange the terms in the equation, we have:

$$implicit\ price\ level = (nominal\ GDP)/(real\ GDP)$$

For example, for 2017 in case *a*, in Table 2.1, we have:

$$implicit\ price\ level = (550/468.5) = 1.17$$

In contrast, for 2017 in case *b*, we have:

$$implicit\ price\ level = (550/639.0) = 0.86$$

The numbers 1.17 and 0.86 do not mean anything as absolute magnitudes. However, they have meaning when compared with similarly calculated price levels for other years. As mentioned, the usual convention is to think of a price index that takes on the value 100 for the base year, which is 2016 in our example. When compared to this base, the price level for 2017 in case *a* is 1.17*100 = 117, whereas in case *b* it is 0.86*100 = 86. These values are shown in Table 2.1. The usual name for these price indexes is the **implicit GDP deflator** (on a 2016 base). That is, these values are the ones implicitly used to convert from nominal GDP to real GDP (on a 2016 base).

REAL GDP AS A MEASURE OF WELFARE

Although real GDP reveals a great deal about an economy's overall performance, it is not a perfect measure of welfare. Some of the shortcomings of real GDP from a welfare standpoint include:

- The aggregate real GDP does not consider changes in the distribution of income.
- The calculated real GDP excludes most non-market goods. The exclusions include legal and illegal transactions in the 'underground economy', as well as services that people perform in their homes. For example, if a person cares for his or her child at home, the real GDP excludes this service. But if the person hires someone to care for the child at home or at a day-care centre, the real GDP includes the service.
- Real GDP assigns no value to leisure time.
- Measured real GDP does not consider environmental damage, such as air and water quality, except to the extent that this pollution affects the market value of output.

Despite these shortcomings, the real GDP tells us a great deal about how an economy's standard of living changes over time. It also allows us to compare standards of living across countries. Measured real GDP helps us to understand short-run economic fluctuations as well as long-term economic development.

Alternative views of GDP: Expenditure, income and production

We can think about the gross domestic product, or GDP, in three different ways. First, we can consider expenditure on goods and services produced domestically by households, businesses, government and foreigners. Second, we can calculate the incomes earned domestically in the production of goods and services – compensation of employees, rental income, corporate profits, and so on. Finally, we can measure the domestic production of goods and services by industry – agriculture, manufacturing, wholesale and retail trade, and so on. An important point is that all three approaches will end up with the same totals for nominal and real GDP. To see this, we take up each approach in turn, beginning with the breakdown by type of expenditure.

MEASURING GDP BY EXPENDITURE

The national accounts divide GDP into four parts, depending on who or what buys the goods or services. The four sectors are households, businesses, all levels of government and foreigners. In this section, we use mainly the United Kingdom (UK) as an illustrative example but also discuss data from a number of countries. Table 2.2 shows the details of this breakdown for the UK in 2012. The first column lists values in current (2012) British pounds, and the second column expresses each amount as a percentage of nominal GDP. The nominal GDP for 2012 of £1655.4 billion corresponds to £1628.3 billion in 2011 (base year) British pound value. If we make these calculations for other years, we can compare across years to see how real GDP has changed over time.

1 **Household consumption expenditure.** The purchases of goods and services by households for consumption purposes are called **household consumption expenditure**. This variable, like GDP, is a flow concept. Thus, nominal household consumption expenditure has units of British pounds per year. This spending typically, but not always, accounts for more than half of GDP in developed countries. For example, Table 2.2 shows that, in 2012, the nominal household consumption expenditure of £1072.5 billion was 64.8% of the nominal UK GDP of £1655.4 billion. In 2012, the percentages of household consumption expenditure in GDP were 36.7% in China, 55.5% in France, 56.0% in Germany, 28.5% in Saudi Arabia, 60.5% in South Africa and 68.6% in the United States.

Table 2.2 Expenditure components of UK gross domestic product in 2012

Category of expenditure	Billions of British pounds	% of nominal GDP
Gross domestic product	1655.4	100.0
Household consumption expenditure	1072.5	64.8
Durable goods	96.5	5.8
Semi-durable goods	106.6	6.4
Non-durable goods	248.9	15.0
Services	562.7	34.0
Non-profit institutions serving households plus adjustments*	57.8	3.5
Gross domestic investment	273.4	16.5
Corporations	147.4	8.9
Households	72.4	4.4
Government	49.0	3.0
Change in inventories**	4.6	0.3
Government consumption expenditure	343.9	20.8
Collective goods	127.8	7.7
Individual goods	216.1	13.1
Net exports of goods and services	−34.5	−2.1
Exports	500.7	30.2
Imports	535.2	32.3

Source: United Kingdom National Accounts, The Blue Book, 2014 edition.

* We have added to this item adjustments due to UK resident households' consumption outside the UK and foreign resident households' consumption in the UK.

** We have added to this item the value of acquisitions less disposals of valuables, such as jewellery, precious metals, works of art and antiques.

The national accounts distinguish purchases of consumer goods that are used up quickly, such as toothpaste and various services, from those that last for an extended period of time. The first group is called **consumer non-durables and services**, and the second is called **consumer semi-durables and durables**. Semi-durable goods, such as clothes, tend to have shorter lifespans and lower prices than durable goods, such as cars and furniture. An important point is that consumer durables yield a flow of services for an extended period. A car, for instance, can be used by the owner for many years, or can be sold or rented to another driver. Therefore, purchases of consumer durables can be viewed as a type of investment. Table 2.2 shows the division of households' consumption expenditure among durable goods, semi-durable goods, non-durable goods and services. In 2012, nominal spending on durables and semi-durables of £203.1 billion constituted about one-fifth of household consumption expenditure. Non-durable goods and services are the most important component (75%) of household consumption expenditure, whereas non-profit institutions, such as churches, trade unions and political parties, serving households are responsible for the remaining 5% of household consumption expenditure.

We can also look at each individual component of GDP in chained 2011 British pound value. For example, the nominal household consumption expenditure, of £1072.5 billion in 2012 corresponds to £1050.8 billion in 2011 British pound value. If we apply this calculation to other years, we can compute the changes over time in real household consumption expenditure, or in the other real components of GDP. However, there are difficulties in comparing the level of real household consumption expenditure in a given year with the level of real GDP in the same year. As already mentioned, the nominal household consumption expenditure for 2012 was 64.8% of nominal GDP. However, a comparison of real household consumption expenditure with real GDP depends on which base year one happens to use. The reason is that the comparison of real consumer expenditure with real GDP depends on the changes in relative prices that occurred between the base year (say, 2011) and the comparison year (say, 2012). In particular, the results depend on how prices of items contained in household consumption expenditure changed compared to the prices of the other items that entered into GDP.

2 **Gross domestic investment.** The second major category of GDP is **gross domestic investment**, also known as gross fixed capital formation. Investment, like consumption expenditure, is a flow variable, measured in British pounds per year. Corporate investment comprises purchases by domestic businesses of new capital goods, such as factories and machinery. These capital goods are durables, which serve as inputs to production for many years. Thus, these goods are analogous to the consumer durables that we have already mentioned. In fact, in the national accounts, an individual's purchase of a new home – which might be considered the ultimate consumer durable – is counted as household investment, rather than consumption expenditure. Finally, there is also government investment, which includes public spending on infrastructure.

Gross domestic investment also includes the net change in businesses' **inventories** of goods. In 2012, this net inventory change was a comparatively small amount, £4.6 billion. The total nominal gross domestic investment in the UK was £273.4 billion, which constituted 16.5% of nominal GDP. In 2012, the percentages of gross domestic investment in GDP were 48.7% in China, 22.7% in France, 19.2% in Germany, 26.3% in Saudi Arabia, 20.1% in South Africa and 19.2% in the United States. Therefore, investment tends to be a smaller component of GDP than consumption, except in China where investment was almost half the size of the economy in 2012.

One common error about national-income accounting arises because the spending on new physical capital is called 'investment'. This terminology differs from the concept of investment used in normal conversation, where investment refers to the allocation of financial assets among stocks, bonds, real estate, and so on. When economists refer to a business's investment, they mean the business's purchases of newly produced goods, such as a factory or machine.

Another point about investment concerns **depreciation**. The stock of capital goods is the outstanding quantity of goods in the form of factories, machinery, and so on. Thus, the capital stock is a **stock variable**, measured as a quantity of goods. Since capital goods wear out or depreciate over time, a part of gross investment merely replaces the old capital that has depreciated. Depreciation is a flow variable – the nominal value of the goods that wear out per year. Depreciation is comparable in units to GDP and gross domestic investment.

The difference between gross domestic investment and depreciation – called **net domestic investment** – is the net change in the value of the stock of physical capital goods. The GDP includes gross domestic investment. If we replace this gross investment by net investment (by subtracting depreciation), we also subtract depreciation from GDP. The difference between GDP and depreciation is called **net domestic product (NDP)**. The NDP is a useful concept because it measures GDP net of the spending needed to replace worn-out or depreciated capital goods.

3 **Government purchases of goods and services**. The third component of GDP is government consumption expenditure. This category includes consumption outlays (such as salaries of military personnel and public-school teachers). Table 2.2 shows the division of government consumption expenditure among collective goods and individual goods. Collective goods, such as national defence and public safety, benefit society as a whole. Individual goods, such as social services, healthcare and education, primarily benefit individual citizens. One important point is that the government sector includes all levels of government, whether central or local. Another point is that government purchases of goods and services exclude transfers, such as payments to retirees and welfare recipients. These transfers do not represent payments for currently produced goods and services. Therefore, these outlays do not appear in GDP. In 2012, nominal government consumption expenditure totalled £343.9 billion, or 20.8% of nominal GDP. The percentages of government consumption expenditure in GDP were 13.7% in China, 23.8% in France, 19.0% in Germany, 20.0% in Saudi Arabia, 19.9% in South Africa and 15.8% in the United States.

4 **Exports and imports.** Some of the goods and services produced domestically are exported to foreign users. These **exports** of goods and services must be added to domestic purchases to compute the economy's total domestic production (GDP). Foreigners also produce goods and services that are imported into the home country – for use by households, businesses and government. These **imports** of goods and services must be subtracted from domestic purchases to calculate the economy's total production (GDP). The foreign component therefore appears in GDP as **net exports**: the difference between spending of foreigners on domestic production (exports) and spending by domestic residents on foreign production (imports). Net exports may be greater than zero or less than zero. Table 2.2 shows that, in 2012, net nominal exports were −£34.5 billion, or −2.1% of nominal GDP. The net export component breaks down into £500.7 billion of exports (30.2% of GDP) less £535.2 billion of imports (32.3% of GDP). In 2012, the percentages of exports of goods and services in GDP were 26.8% in China, 28.1% in France, 45.9% in Germany, 54.5% in Saudi Arabia, 29.7% in South Africa and 13.6% in the United States. The percentages of imports of goods and services in GDP were 24.0% in China, 30.1% in France, 40.0% in Germany, 29.3% in Saudi Arabia, 31.0% in South Africa and 17.1% in the United States.

Economists often use a theoretical model that omits net exports. This model applies to a **closed economy**, which has no trade linkages to the rest of the world. In contrast, an economy that is linked through trade to the rest of the world is called an **open economy**. Reasons for using a closed-economy model include the following:

● It simplifies the analysis.
● The world as a whole really is a closed economy, so we have to carry out a closed-economy analysis to assess the world economy.

We follow the closed-economy tradition of macroeconomics until Chapter 18, which allows for international trade.

MEASURING GDP BY INCOME

Another way to look at GDP is in terms of the income earned by various factors of production. This concept is called **gross domestic income (GDI)**. To make clear the relation between production and income, we can think of a simple closed economy that has only two businesses. One, a mill, uses only labour to produce flour. The second, a bakery, uses flour and labour to produce bread. Bread is the only final product. Flour is the only intermediate product – it is used up entirely in the production of the final good, bread. Notice that, to simplify matters, we are ignoring capital inputs, such as factories and machines.

Income statements for the two businesses appear in Table 2.3. The nominal GDP for this economy is the value of the final product, bread, of £600. This amount is also the revenue of the bakery. The income statement shows that the costs and profit for the bakery break down into £350 for flour, £200 for labour (for workers in the bakery) and £50 for profit (of the bakery). For the mill, the £350 of revenue divides into £250 for labour (for workers at the mill) and £100 of profit (of the mill). The GDI equals the total labour income of £450 plus the total profit of £150, or £600. Thus, in this simple economy, GDI equals GDP, which is also true in general.

Table 2.3 Hypothetical data for calculation of national income

Type of revenue	Amount £	Type of cost or profit	Amount £
Bakery (produces final good)			
Sale of bread	£600	Labour	200
		Flour	350
		Profit	50
		Total cost and profit	600
Mill (produces intermediate good)			
Sale of flour	£350	Labour	250
		Profit	100
		Total cost and profit	350

Notice that the GDP counts the value of the final product, bread, as £600, but does not count separately the value of the flour, £350. The flour is used up in the production of bread; that is, the £600 in bread sales already takes into account the £350 cost of the intermediate good, flour. If we added the £350 in sales of flour to the £600 in sales of bread, we would *double-count* the contribution of the intermediate good, flour. To put it another way, the **value added** by the bakery is only £250 – sales of £600 less payments for flour of £350. The value added by the mill is the full £350, because we assumed that the mill uses no intermediate goods. Therefore, if we combine the value added of £350 for the mill with the value added of £250 for the bakery, we get the GDP of £600. Hence, GDP equals the sum of value added from all sectors. The GDI equals the GDP and, therefore, also equals the sum of value added from all sectors.

Table 2.4 shows the breakdown of UK GDI by sources of income in 2012. The total nominal GDI was £1655.4 billion, which is also the nominal GDP. Although the method for computing GDI is conceptually the same as that in Table 2.3, the UK economy includes additional forms of income. The largest part of the UK economy was compensation of employees: £849.4 billion, or 51.3% of GDP. This component is analogous to the labour income shown in Table 2.3.

Table 2.4 UK gross domestic income by type in 2012

Type of income	Billions of British pounds	% of GDI
Gross domestic income (GDI)	**1655.4**	**100.0**
Compensation of employees	849.4	51.3
Operating surplus:		
Private corporations	347.5	21.0
Households	125.8	7.6
Central government and public corporations	34.7	2.1
Mixed income	96.6	5.8
Taxes on production and imports	213.9	12.9
Less: subsidies	(12.6)	(0.8)

Source: United Kingdom National Accounts, The Blue Book, 2014 edition.

Several parts of the UK GDI in Table 2.4 represent income that accrues to capital. These amounts did not appear in Table 2.3 because we did not consider that the bakery and mill each have capital equipment, such as machinery, that contributes to the production of goods. In the UK national accounts, the categories of income from capital comprise operating surplus by private corporations, households, central government and public corporations. The total operating surplus of £508.0 billion represented 30.7% of GDI.

The UK national income for 2012 also includes mixed income of £96.6 billion (5.8% of the total). This income represents payments to self-employed persons, including unincorporated businesses. This income represents a mix of payments to labour and capital. The breakdown into labour and capital is unknown, although economists have made estimates.

Taxes on production – sales, excise and value added (or VAT)[3] – are included in market prices of goods. Therefore, these taxes on production appear in GDP, which is calculated from market values of output. The tax revenues are also part of government revenue – therefore, these revenues enter into GDI as income of the government sector. Subsidies paid to producers by government amount to negative production taxes. Therefore, subsidies enter with a negative sign in GDI. In 2012, the total of taxes on production less subsidies was £201.3 billion, or 12% of GDI.

Differences between GDI and national income

In the simplified economy of Table 2.3, GDI and national income were equal. In practice, divergences between GDI and national income reflect two main items: income receipts and payments involving the rest of the world, and depreciation of capital stocks. We take up these two items in turn.

The GDP is the value of goods and services produced within the UK, which is also equal to GDI. The UK national income is the income received by all sectors residing in the UK. One source of divergence between GDI and national income is that residents of the UK receive income from the rest of the world. The main item is the income on capital (assets) owned by UK residents but located abroad. A secondary part is labour income of UK residents working abroad. The counterpart to the UK factor income from abroad is the UK payments to factors abroad. These payments are to capital (assets) located in the UK but owned by foreigners and to foreigners working in the UK. The net factor income from abroad is the difference between UK income receipts from the rest of the world and UK income payments to the rest of the world: –£5.3 billion as shown in Table 2.5. The addition of this amount to the GDI of £1655.4 billion yields the gross national income (GNI) of £1650.1 billion, as shown in Table 2.5. The GNI gives the total gross income to UK factors of production, whether located in the UK or abroad.

One part of UK GDI covers the depreciation of the fixed capital stock located in the UK. This depreciation does not show up as income for factors of production. In particular, depreciation is subtracted from gross business revenue to calculate corporate profits or proprietors' income. If we subtract from GNI the estimated depreciation of £218.7 billion, we get the net national income (NNI) for 2012 of £1431.4 billion.

Table 2.5 **Relations between UK GDI and national income in 2012**

Category of product or income	Billions of British pounds
Gross domestic income (GDI)	**1655.4**
Plus: Net income receipts from rest of world	(5.3)
Equals: Gross national income (GNI)	**1650.1**
Less: Depreciation of capital stock	(218.7)
Equals: Net national income (NNI)	**1431.4**

Source: United Kingdom National Accounts, The Blue Book, 2014 edition.

MEASURING GDP BY PRODUCTION

We can also break down GDP according to the sectors of production that generate the income. Table 2.6 shows this breakdown for the UK in 2012. The nominal GDP of £1655.4 billion breaks down into the gross value added (GVA)

---

[3]The value-added tax is important in many countries but does not exist in some countries; e.g., the United States.

Table 2.6 UK GDP by sector of production in 2012

Sector of production	Billion of British pounds	% of GVA
Agriculture	10.0	0.7
Construction	88.7	6.0
Production		
Manufacturing	146.9	10.0
Mining	29.3	2.0
Utilities	37.0	2.5
Services		
Accommodation and food services	43.3	2.9
Finance and insurance	119.8	8.1
Government, healthcare and education	281.9	19.1
Information	92.2	6.2
Professional and business services	175.8	11.9
Transportation and storage	62.1	4.2
Real estate	167.3	11.3
Wholesale and retail trade	162.0	11.0
Other services	59.7	4.0
Gross value added (GVA)	1475.9	100.0
Plus: Value-added taxes on products	113.9	
Plus: Other taxes on products	72.7	
Less: Subsidies on products	(7.2)	
Gross domestic product (GDP)	1655.4	

Source: United Kingdom National Accounts, The Blue Book, 2014 edition.

of £1475.9 billion and net taxes on products of £179.5 billion. Table 2.6 shows how the nominal GVA of £1475.9 billion divides into different sectors: 0.7% in agriculture, 6.0% in construction, 14.5% in production and 78.8% in services. The largest shares of GVA in services are 19.1% in government, healthcare and education; 11.9% in professional and business services; 11.3% in real estate; 11.0% in retail and wholesale trade; and 8.1% in finance and insurance.

In developed countries, services tend to be the largest sector in the economy, and this is also true in some developing countries. For example, the shares of GVA in China are 10.4% in agriculture, 7.1% in construction, 39.8% in production and 42.7% in services. The shares of GVA in France are 1.9% in agriculture, 6.1% in construction, 13.8% in production and 78.2% in services. The shares of GVA in Germany are 0.9% in agriculture, 4.5% in construction, 26.1% in production and 68.4% in services. The shares of GVA in South Africa are 2.4% in agriculture, 3.8% in construction, 26.0% in production and 67.9% in services. The shares of GVA in the United States are 1.2% in agriculture, 3.6% in construction, 16.5% in production and 78.7% in services. However, Saudi Arabia is an exception to this pattern because production is the largest sector in the economy. The shares of GVA in Saudi Arabia are 1.8% in agriculture, 4.3% in construction, 58.6% in production and 35.3% in services.

SEASONAL ADJUSTMENT

Data on GDP and its components are available for the UK and most other countries on a quarterly basis. These data allow us to study economic fluctuations at a quarterly frequency. However, one problem with the raw data is that they include sizeable systematic variations due to seasonal factors. The typical pattern is that UK real GDP rises during a calendar year and reaches a peak in the fourth quarter (October–December). Then, real GDP usually falls sharply in the first quarter of the next year (January–March) before rebounding from the second to the fourth quarters.

The seasonal fluctuations in real GDP and other macroeconomic variables reflect the influences of weather and holidays (notably the Christmas period and summer vacations). For most purposes, we want to use the national-accounts data to study economic fluctuations that reflect factors other than normal seasonal patterns. For this reason, real GDP and its components are adjusted to filter out the typical seasonal variation. Variables adjusted this way are called **seasonally adjusted data**. The national-accounts information reported in the news media and used for most macroeconomic analyses comes in this seasonally adjusted form. We use seasonally adjusted quarterly data in this book to analyze economic fluctuations.

Seasonal adjustments apply also to many of the monthly variables reported in the news media and used for macroeconomic analyses. These variables include employment and unemployment, labour earnings, industrial production, retail sales and the consumer price index. When we discuss these monthly variables in this book, we refer to seasonally adjusted data.

Prices

We have already discussed how the computation of chained real GDP generates an implicit price deflator for the GDP. The resulting series gives us a good measure of an overall price index. That is, we get a price index that matches the overall market basket of goods and services produced domestically. We can also use this approach to get implicit price deflators for the components of GDP. For example, we have a deflator for household consumption expenditure, one for gross private domestic investment, and so on.[4] In addition to these implicit price deflators, there are also measures of consumer price inflation.

Economics in Practice
Problems with the consumer price index

The **consumer price index (CPI)** receives considerable attention because it provides monthly information on the prices of a broad market basket of goods and services bought by households. Part of the attention arises because some public and private contracts index nominal payments to the CPI. Many economists think that the reported increases in the CPI overstate inflation and, hence, that the automatic adjustments of CPI-indexed payments may have been too large to keep the outlays fixed in real terms. Naturally, this assessment is controversial, because any repairs would have significant consequences for real transfer payments, real tax collections, and so on. One reason for the overstatement of inflation is called substitution bias. The idea is that changes in supply conditions shift the relative prices of various goods and services, and households respond by shifting expenditure towards the goods and services that have become relatively cheaper. However, because the weights in the CPI are fixed for long intervals, the formula for computing the CPI responds only with a substantial lag to changes in the pattern of purchases. In particular, the CPI fails to give increasing weight to the cheaper items that tend to become more important in the typical household's expenditure. This problem is conceptually easy to fix by shifting to the chain-weighting approach already described for the calculation of the implicit GDP deflator. This deflator is free of substitution bias because the weights change almost continuously over time. Another, more challenging problem – which applies to the implicit GDP deflator as well as the CPI – involves quality change. Despite attempts to measure improvements in quality, these changes tend to be underestimated. Therefore, some of the price increases that are recorded as inflation should actually be viewed as increases in money spent to get better quality products. A full accounting for quality improvements would therefore lower

---

[4]However, the deflator for government purchases of goods and services is not very useful. Since most of the government's output is not sold on markets, this price deflator reflects arbitrary assumptions about costs of providing public services. The main assumption is that the productivity of government employees does not vary over time.

the inflation rate. Some improved measurement has been made for goods such as cars, computers, houses and television sets. Interesting proposals for measuring quality change have also been offered in the medical area, where technical advances that save lives or improve the quality of life tend to be labelled as inflation. Another problem is that the various price indices do not consider the effective reductions in the price level due to the introduction of new products. For example, when personal computers or DVD players became available, households were made better off for a given income – even if the new goods were initially 'expensive'. The same idea applies to the invention of new prescription drugs, even if the prices of these drugs are 'high' at the outset. The creation of useful new products tends to raise households' real income or, equivalently, lower the effective price level. Thus, a proper accounting for new products would lower the average inflation rate. The economy's real economic growth would also look stronger if the effects of new products were properly considered.

In the UK, the Office for National Statistics (ONS) computes the CPI and the **retail price index (RPI)**. Both price indices are produced by tracking the prices of goods and services based on monthly information on approximately 180 000 price quotes for over 650 representative items. However, the RPI inflation rate has historically been higher than the CPI inflation rate for the following reasons. First, the two indices are based on different baskets of goods and services. The RPI includes items such as owner-occupiers' housing costs, council tax, building insurance and house depreciation, whereas the CPI does not. The CPI includes items such as university accommodation fees, foreign student university tuition fees, unit trust and stockbroker charges, whereas the RPI does not. Second, the two price indices have different target populations. The CPI covers domestic expenditure by all households and foreign visitors in the UK. In contrast, the RPI excludes expenditure by very high-income households and some pensioners. Finally, the most important reason for the two indices to produce different inflation rates is that they use different formulae to compute the price indices, and this is known as the formula effect; see the Economics in Practice box for details. In 2013, the ONS announced that because the RPI does not meet international standards, it is no longer considered an official national statistic, but the ONS continues to compute its value.

Economics in Practice
Problems with the retail price index

The RPI was introduced in 1947 and was the official measure of consumer price inflation from 1956 until it was replaced by the CPI. The CPI was introduced in 1996 as the Harmonized Index of Consumer Prices, which is produced by all countries in the European Union. In 2003, the inflation target of the Bank of England was changed from 2.5% of RPI to 2% of CPI. This change in the value of the target inflation is due to the fact that the RPI inflation rate has generally overestimated inflation and been higher than the CPI inflation rate by an average of about 0.9 percentage points. This difference is mostly due to the different formulae used in the construction of the CPI and the RPI, which can be explained as follows. The CPI is predominantly based on the so-called Jevons index, which takes the geometric mean of prices, whereas the RPI is mainly based on the so-called Carli index, which takes the arithmetic mean of prices. Mathematically, the Carli index always yields a higher price level and a higher inflation rate than the Jevons index. Because the Carli index does not meet international standards for price indices, in 2013 the ONS announced that the RPI is no longer considered an official national statistic.

Key Terms and Concepts

chain-weighted real GDP
closed economy
consumer semi-durables
 and durables
consumer non-durables and
 services
consumer price index (CPI)
depreciation
exports
flow variable

GDP in constant prices
GDP in current prices
gross domestic income
 (GDI)
gross domestic investment
gross national income (GNI)
gross value added (GVA)
household consumption
 expenditure
implicit GDP deflator

imports
imputed rental income
inventories
national income
net domestic investment
net domestic product (NDP)
net exports
net factor income from
 abroad
net national income (NNI)

nominal GDP
open economy
retail price index (RPI)
seasonally adjusted data
stock variable
value added

Questions and Problems

A   Review questions

1   Define nominal and real GDP. Are these flow
 or stock concepts? Explain why the differences
 between nominal and real GDP are important.

2   From Table 2.1, compute the value of *constant-
 price* real GDP in 2017 using the prices in 2016
 and compare it to the chain-weighted real GDP in
 Table 2.1.

3   Define the implicit price deflator. Where does this
 concept come from? How does it relate to nominal
 and real GDP?

4   We discussed alternative views of GDP from
 the perspectives of expenditure, income and
 production. What are the basic differences in
 these approaches? Why do they add to the same
 total for GDP?

5   We discussed the concepts of GDI and GNI. What
 are the basic differences in these concepts?

B   Problems for discussion

6   Table 2.5 shows the relation between GDP and
 income for the UK in 2012. Replicate this table for
 any country.

7   Download data for the CPI and the GDP deflator
 of any country. Compare the inflation rates calculated from these two price indices.

8   What are some of the shortcomings of real GDP
 from a welfare perspective? Do you have any practical suggestions for revising the computation of
 GDP to achieve a better measure of welfare?

Economic growth

PART II

3 Introduction to economic growth

In 2014, the gross domestic product, or GDP, per person in the European Union was $36 699 (valued in international dollars for the year 2014). This high output per person meant that the typical EU resident had a high **standard of living**, which refers to the quantity and quality of the goods and services consumed. Most families had their own home, at least one car, several television sets, education at least through high school and often college, and a level of health that translated into a life expectancy at birth of nearly 80 years. Such high standards of living also applied to other advanced countries, such as Australia, Canada, Japan, New Zealand, Singapore, South Korea and the United States.

The residents of most other countries were not nearly as well off. For example, in 2014, the GDP per person (valued in international dollars for the year 2014) was $17 950 in Mexico, $5808 in India, and $6054 in Nigeria, the most populous country in Africa. Lower real GDPs per person meant lower standards of living. The typical resident of Mexico could afford food, shelter and basic health care but could not attain the range and quality of consumer goods available to most residents in rich countries. Even more seriously, the typical Nigerian had concerns about nutrition and housing, and faced a life expectancy at birth of less than 52 years.

How can countries with low real GDP per person catch up to the high levels enjoyed by rich countries? The only answer is to have a high **rate of economic growth** – the rate at which real GDP per person increases – over long periods, such as 20 or 40 years. To illustrate, Table 3.1 shows the level of real GDP per person that China would attain in 2036, based on its growth rate of real GDP per person from 2011 to 2036. It would take a growth rate of about 6.3% per year – a considerable accomplishment for 25 years – for China's real GDP per person in 2036 to approach the level of the USA and other rich countries in 2011. Thus, differences in rates of economic growth, when sustained for 20 years or more, make an enormous difference to standards of living, measured by levels of real GDP per person.

The benefits of sustained economic growth apply to all nations. Thus, the universal question is, what can we – or our governments – do to increase the rate of economic growth? The importance of this question inspired economist Robert Lucas (1988) to ask: 'Is there some action a government of India could take that would lead the Indian economy to grow like Indonesia's or Egypt's? If so, what, exactly? If not, what is it about the "nature of India" that makes it so? The consequences for human welfare involved in questions like these are simply staggering: once one

Table 3.1 Economic growth and China's real GDP per person in 2036*

Growth rate of real GDP per person from 2011 to 2036	Real GDP per person in 2036 (in 2005 dollars)
2% per year	14 670
5% per year	31 060
10% per year	108 420

*China starts with real per capita GDP of $8900 in 2011. We calculate the level of real GDP per person in 2036 as follows: start with the natural logarithm of real GDP per person in 2011: ln (8900) = 9.094. Then multiply the number of years, 25, by the growth rate – for example, 0.02 if the growth rate is 2% per year: 25 × 0.02 = 0.50. Add this to 9.094 to get 9.594. Then take the exponential of 9.594 to get the answer, 14 670.

starts to think about them, it is hard to think about anything else.' (p. 5)[1] Questions like these underline the challenge of developing policies that promote economic growth. This challenge motivates the study that we begin in this chapter and continue in the following two chapters.

We start by presenting key facts about economic growth; first, for a large number of countries since 1960 and, second, for a number of rich countries for over a century. These observations bring out patterns that we need to understand to design policies to promote economic growth. As a way to gain this understanding, we construct a model of economic growth, called the Solow model. In Chapters 4 and 5, we extend this model and see how these extensions relate to patterns of economic growth and to Lucas's policy challenge.

Facts about economic growth

ECONOMIC GROWTH AROUND THE WORLD, 1960 TO 2011

We start our study of economic growth by comparing living standards – gauged by real GDP per person – for a large number of countries. This comparison will allow us to see at a glance which countries are rich and which are poor. In Figure 3.1, the horizontal axis plots real GDP per person (in international dollars for the year 2005), and the vertical axis shows the number of countries with each real GDP per person in 2011. The graph applies to 160 countries with data, and representative countries (or economies) are labelled for each bar.

The highest-income country in the sample was Luxembourg with a real GDP per person of $79 300, almost two times that of the United States with $42 700, which was ranked 7th. More generally, the top positions were dominated by the long-term members of the rich countries' club, which is known as the Organisation for Economic Cooperation and Development (OECD). This elite group includes most of Western Europe, Estonia, Slovenia, the Slovak Republic, the United States, Canada, Australia, New Zealand, Chile, Israel, South Korea and Japan. Overall, 21 of the richest 25 economies in 2011 were OECD members. The other four economies were Macao (ranked 2nd), Singapore (3rd), Hong Kong (5th) and Taiwan (19th).

The poorest country in Figure 3.1 is Congo (Kinshasa), a sub-Saharan African country, with a real GDP per person of $406, again in 2005 international dollars. Therefore, in 2011, the richest country (Luxembourg) had a real GDP per person that was 195 times that of the poorest country. If we exclude Luxembourg because of its small size and compare instead with the United States, we find that the United States had a real GDP per person that was 105 times as large as Congo's.

Economists use the term **poverty** to describe low standards of living. A person or family living in poverty has difficulty affording the basic necessities of life – food, clothing, shelter and health – and can only dream about cars and television sets. Poverty reflects low real incomes of individuals and families. According to one definition used by international organizations such as the United Nations and the World Bank, an individual was living in poverty in 2011 if their annual income was less than $460 per year in 2005 prices. The value of $460 per year is a modification of a well-known standard established in the 1980s that viewed the poverty line as an income of $1 per person per day. Therefore, we can refer to $460 per year as the $1-per-day poverty standard.

The number of persons living in poverty in a country depends on two things. One is the way that the country's income is distributed among persons; for example, the total income might be distributed nearly evenly, or a small proportion of the population might have most of the income. The second is the country's average real income, which

---

[1]When Lucas wrote these words in the mid-1980s, India had been growing more slowly than Egypt and Indonesia for some time. The growth rates of real GDP per person from 1960 to 1980 were 2.5% per year in Egypt, 3.5% in Indonesia and 1.6% in India. However, India did manage to surpass Indonesia in terms of growth rates from 1980 to 2011: the growth rates of real GDP per person were 5.5% per year for Egypt, 3.0% for Indonesia and 4.1% for India. Thus, the Indian government may have met Lucas's challenge.

Figure 3.1 World distribution of real GDP per person in 2011

The graph shows the distribution of real gross domestic product (GDP) per person for 160 countries (or economies) in 2011. The horizontal axis is in 2005 US dollars and uses a proportionate scale. Representative countries (or economies) are indicated for the ranges of real GDP per person.

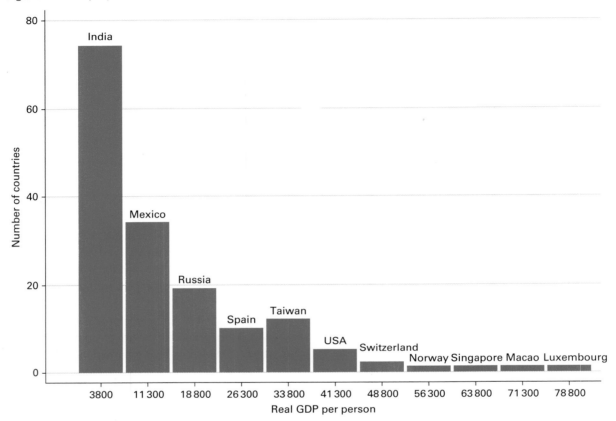

can be approximated by real GDP per person. If this average is very low, the typical resident will be living in poverty even if income is distributed evenly.

In practice, the second factor – a country's real GDP per person – is the most important determinant of the number of people living in poverty. Countries with very low real GDP per person are the ones in which a large proportion of the population lives in poverty. Therefore, the data plotted in Figure 3.1 tell us that world poverty in 2011 was dominated by sub-Saharan Africa – an amazing 23 of the lowest 25 real GDPs per person were in this region. The two other countries in this poorest group were El Salvador (11th from the bottom) and Nepal (19th). (A list of the data used to plot this graph is not given here.)

Real GDP per person in 2011 gives us a snapshot of the standard of living at a point in time. The rich countries, such as the OECD members, were rich in 2011 because their levels of real GDP per person rose over a long period. Similarly, the levels of real GDP per person in poor countries in 2011 – especially in sub-Saharan Africa – had not been growing. In fact, as we shall see, many of these growth rates were negative, so that real GDP per person fell over time.

To measure economic growth, we have to compare the levels of real GDP per person in 2011 with those from earlier years. Figure 3.2 begins this comparison by showing a graph of real GDP per person over 50 years earlier, in 1960. This graph is similar to the one in Figure 3.1. The horizontal axis again shows real GDP per person, still using international dollars in the year 2005. The vertical axis shows the number of countries with each real GDP per person in 1960. The total number of countries is only 107, given the availability of data for 1960.

In 1960, Switzerland was at the top with a real GDP per person of $17 200, and Norway was second, at $16 700. The top 25 was dominated by the long-term members of the OECD – 22 of the richest 25 countries were OECD members.

Figure 3.2 World distribution of real GDP per person in 1960

The graph shows the distribution of real gross domestic product (GDP) per person for 107 countries in 1960. The horizontal axis is in 2005 international dollars and uses a proportionate scale. Representative countries are indicated for the ranges of real GDP per person.

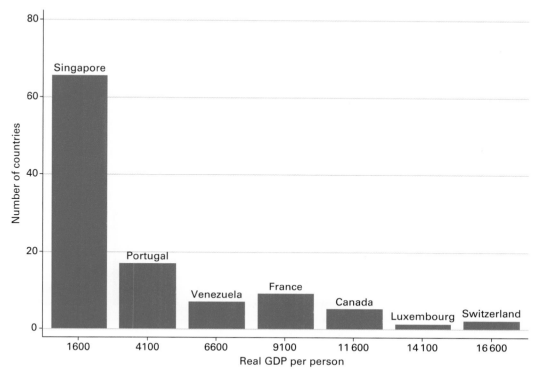

One difference from 2011was that no Asian countries were in the top 25 in 1960. A couple of Latin American countries (Uruguay and Venezuela) were in the top group, but none remained in 2011. Trinidad and Tobago, and Barbados, were also in this group in 1960 but not in 2011 (at which point Trinidad and Tobago ranked 31st and Barbados 33rd).

The low end for real GDP per person was dominated somewhat less by sub-Saharan Africa in 1960 than in 2011. The poorest country in 1960 was Botswana, at $390, but 'only' 18 of the 25 countries with the lowest real GDPs per person were in sub-Saharan Africa. Five of the poorest 25 in 1960 were in Asia – Pakistan, Thailand, Nepal, India and Indonesia. The other members of the lowest 25 were Egypt (6th from the bottom) and El Salvador (11th from the bottom). Most of the seven non-African countries grew rapidly enough over the next 40 years to escape the lowest category. In fact, the high growth in Asia and the low growth in many sub-Saharan African countries from 1960 to 2011 were major parts of the story about world standards of living in 2011. In the next section, we discuss how these developments affected world poverty.

In 1960, the richest country (Switzerland) had a real GDP per person that was 44 times that of the poorest country (Botswana). This spread was lower than was the case in 2011, where the US real GDP per person was 105 times that of Congo (Kinshasa).

If we compare the levels of real GDP per person in 2011 and 1960 for each country, we can compute the country's growth rate of real GDP per person over the 51 years.[2] Figure 3.3 shows the distribution of these growth rates for the 107 countries with the necessary data. The construction of this graph is similar to those of Figures 3.1 and 3.2. The horizontal axis now shows the growth rate of real GDP per person from 1960 to 2011, and the vertical axis shows the number of countries with each growth rate.

The average growth rate of real GDP per person from 1960 to 2011 for 107 countries was 2.2% per year. The fastest-growing country was Botswana, with a rate of 7.1%. More generally, many of the fast growers from 1960

[2]The easiest way to compute the growth rate of real GDP per person from 1960 to 2011 is to calculate $(1/(2011-1960)) * \log$ (real GDP per person in 2011/real GDP per person in 1960), where log is the natural logarithm.

Figure 3.3 World distribution of growth rates of real GDP per person, 1960–2011

The graph shows the distribution of the growth rate of real GDP per person for 107 countries from 1960 to 2011. Representative countries are indicated for the ranges of growth rates. The unweighted average growth rate was 2.2% per year.

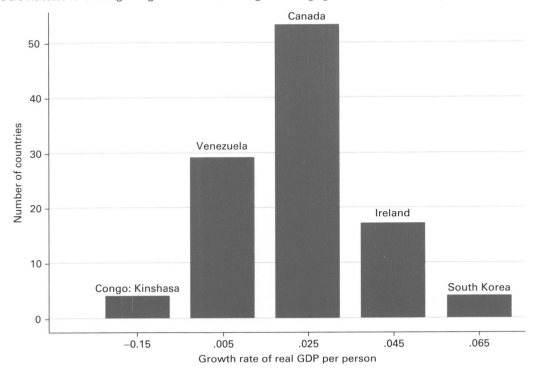

to 2011 – seven of the top 12 – came from East Asia. The East Asian economies in the top 20 were China, Hong Kong, Japan (which grew rapidly mainly up until the early 1970s), Malaysia, Singapore, South Korea, Taiwan and Thailand. Some long-term OECD countries were among the top 20 for economic growth: Ireland and Portugal. The other members of the top 20 were Botswana, Gabon and Equatorial Guinea (the star performers of sub-Saharan Africa), Cyprus, Romania, Egypt, Tunisia, Iran, Malta and Argentina.

At the bottom end, 17 of the 20 worst performers for economic growth from 1960 to 2011 were in sub-Saharan Africa. The three non-African slow growers were Jamaica (0.3% per year), Bangladesh (0.6%) and Honduras (0.8%). Among the 17 African countries, seven experienced negative growth of real GDP per person, with Congo (Kinshasa) the worst at –2.1% per year. Thus, the reason for low levels of real GDP per person in 2011 is partly that countries in this region started off badly in 1960 (around the time of independence for most of the countries) and, even more so, that they performed so poorly in terms of the growth of real GDP per person from 1960 to 2011. The poorest countries in 2011 – especially in sub-Saharan Africa – were poor mainly because they had grown at low or negative rates since 1960. Thus, to go further, we have to understand why these countries failed to grow at higher rates, particularly when growth in other countries in the region began to accelerate.[3]

We have also learned that a group of economies in East Asia grew at high rates from 1960 to 2011. This strong growth enabled these countries to move from low levels of real GDP per person in 1960 to much higher levels in 2011. To understand this change, we have to understand why these countries grew at high rates.

To appreciate the high levels of real GDP per person in the OECD countries in 2011, we have to look at data before 1960. That is, these countries were rich in 2011 partly because they grew from 1960 to 2011 but, even more so,

---

[3]One important recent development has been the accelerated growth rates in many countries in sub-Saharan Africa. Not only Botswana and Equatorial Guinea, who ranked 1st and 2nd within the sample of 107 countries, but also Gabon and Cape Verde experienced average growth rates in excess of 3.0%.

because they were already rich in 1960. To get a feel for these longer-term developments in currently rich countries, we will look at historical data for a number of rich countries later in this chapter.

WORLD POVERTY AND INCOME INEQUALITY

We noted that poverty refers to a minimally acceptable level of real income, such as the World Bank's $1-per-day standard (which actually corresponds to $460 per year in 2005 prices). The term **inequality** is often used interchangeably with poverty but is actually different in meaning. Inequality describes an unequal distribution of income across individuals at a point in time within a country or around the world. One common measure of inequality is the proportion of a nation's income received by persons in the lowest fifth of the distribution. If income were equally distributed, this number would be 20%. The greater the shortfall of this share from 20%, the higher the income inequality. Similarly, we can look at the proportion of income received by persons in the upper fifth of the distribution. The greater the excess of this share above 20%, the higher the income inequality.

In practice, the distribution of income is far from equal – for 100 countries with data around 2010, the average amount of the income received by the lowest fifth was 6.7%, whereas the average for the highest fifth was 45%. These income shares were 5.0% and 46% for the United States (higher than average inequality based on the lowest fifth, and about average inequality based on the highest fifth), 7.1% and 42% for the United Kingdom (less unequal than the USA at the bottom and the top), 8.0% and 39.3% for Germany (a country with relatively little inequality), and 3.2% and 58.3% for Brazil (a country with considerable inequality).

For a given average income per person, the degree of inequality determines the proportion of the population that falls below the $1-per-day poverty line. Unless average real income is extremely low, more inequality means that a higher proportion of the population falls below the poverty line. However, when average real income changes – for example, when real GDP per person rises – inequality and poverty behave differently.

To understand why, suppose that everyone's real income were to double. In this case, inequality would not change – for example, if the lowest fifth of the distribution started with 6% of total income, the lowest fifth would still have 6% after everyone's income doubled. In contrast, poverty would fall sharply if everyone's real income doubled – because more people's real incomes would exceed the $1-per-day standard. If we think that a person's welfare depends on his or her real income, rather than income measured relative to that of other persons, then poverty is more meaningful than inequality as a measure of welfare.

Pinkovskiy and Sala-i-Martin (2009) showed that economic growth led to a dramatic fall in world poverty from 1970 to 2006. The estimated number of people below the $1-per-day poverty line fell from 967 million, or 27% of the world's population in 1970, to 350 million, or 5% of the population in 2006.[4] Figure 3.4 shows how these changes occurred. Figure 3.4(a) describes the distribution of income for the world's people in 1970. The horizontal axis plots real income on a proportionate scale, and the vertical axis shows the number of people with each level of income. The vertical lines marked $1 show the income levels that correspond to the $1-per-day poverty line.[5] Consider the area below the upper curve and to the left of the $1 line. To find the proportion of the world's population with incomes below $1 per day, we take the ratio of this area to the total area under the upper curve. The result is 27%.

World economic growth from 1970 to 2006 led to a shift from Figure 3.4(a) to Figure 3.4(b). Notice that the whole distribution of income shifted to the right, because larger proportions of the world's people had higher real incomes. Hence, the proportion of the world's population with incomes below the $1-per-day poverty line was much smaller in 2006 than in 1970. The percentage for 2006 was 5%, compared with 27% in 1970. This sharp decline in poverty rates shows the dramatic progress over three decades as a result of economic growth.

---

[4]The proportion of the population living in poverty is called the *poverty rate,* whereas the number of people living in poverty is called the *poverty headcount.* The decrease in the poverty rate from 1970 to 2006 was so sharp that the world poverty headcount decreased, despite the substantial rise in world population.

[5]The two vertical lines at $312 and $554 represent real incomes corresponding to the $1 dollar per day lines in 2006 dollars according to estimates from Pinkovskiy and Sala-i-Martin ($312) and estimates from the World Bank ($554).

Figure 3.4 (a) At the head of the figure for 1970; (b) At the head of the figure for 2006

Figure 3.4(a) is for 1970 and Figure 3.4(b) is for 2006. In each case, the horizontal axis plots real income in 2006 international dollars on a proportionate scale. For the upper curves in the two figures, the vertical axis shows the number of people in the world with each level of income. The vertical lines marked $1 show the annual real incomes that correspond to the standard poverty line of $1 per day ($312 per year in 2006 prices). The income distributions for countries are grouped into regions: East Asia (labelled EA), Eastern Europe (EEU), Former Soviet Union (FSU), High Income Non-OECD countries (HNOECD), Latin America (Latam), Middle East and North Africa (MENA), South Asia (SA) and sub-Saharan Africa (SSA). The values shown on the upper curves for numbers of people in the world are the vertical sums of the numbers of people in all of the individual countries.

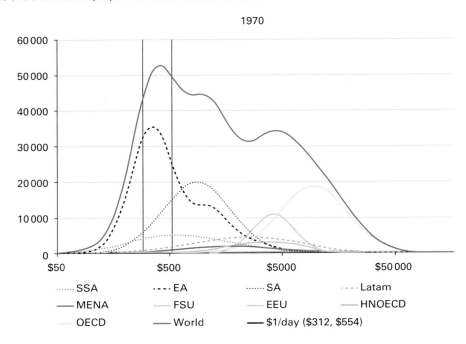

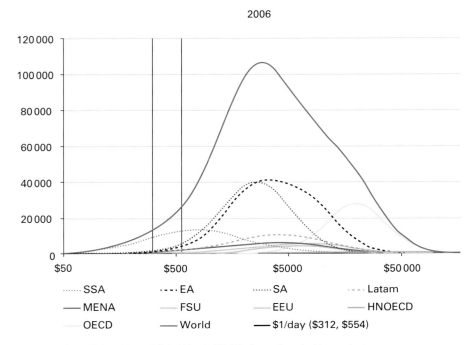

Source: These graphs come from Pinkovskiy and Sala-i-Martin (2009). Reproduced with permission.

The graphs also show how some of the world's regions fared from 1970 to 2006. For poverty, the biggest changes occurred in China and India, which accounted for nearly 40% of world population in 2006. In 1970, many residents of China and India and other Asian countries were below the $1-per-day poverty line – East Asia accounted for 53% and South Asia for 15% overall of persons living in poverty. However, Figures 3.4(a) and 3.4(b) show that the income distribution curves for East and South Asia shifted dramatically to the right from 1970 to 2006. This change reflected the strong economic growth in Asia, particularly since the late 1970s for China and the mid-1980s for India. Consequently, by 2006, East Asia accounted for only 7% and South Asia for 11% of persons living in poverty.

We also know that recent decades saw very low economic growth in sub-Saharan Africa. Consequently, the poverty numbers soared. In 1970, sub-Saharan Africa accounted for only 12% of persons living in poverty. However, in 2006, this region accounted for 68% of persons in poverty. Thus, poverty shifted from primarily an Asian problem to mainly an African problem. If recent strong growth in several African economies continues, it may help to mitigate this problem.

The results are more complicated for world inequality. We can think of the changes in two parts: the first is within countries and the second is across countries. Inequality rose from 1970 to 2006 within several large countries, including the United States, the United Kingdom and China. However, Pinkovskiy and Sala-i-Martin showed that these changes within countries had only minor effects on inequality across persons in the entire world.

The second factor is the dispersion of average incomes across countries. We know from Figures 3.1 and 3.2 that the ratio of the highest real GDPs per person (concentrated in the OECD countries) to the lowest (primarily in sub-Saharan Africa) rose from 1960 to 2011. However, since world inequality involves numbers of people, rather than numbers of countries, we have to give more weight to the larger countries. The income changes in the larger countries, especially China and India, matter much more than the changes in the smaller countries. Since China and India had very low average real incomes in 1970, their strong economic growth from 1970 to 2011 contributed heavily to a reduction of world income inequality. It turns out that this force dominated the others and led to a decrease in standard measures of world income inequality over a similar time period.

LONG-TERM GROWTH IN RICH COUNTRIES

We mentioned that for the rich countries, the main reason for high real GDP per person in recent years is that these countries already had high real GDP per person in 1960. Therefore, to understand the prosperity of these countries, we have to take a long-term view that starts well before 1960.

We begin our discussion with the United States due to the availability of reliable historical data. If we go back more than a century, we find that US real GDP per person in 1850 (the first year for which reliable, cross-country annual data are available) was $1850, measured in 1990 prices. Therefore, the real GDP per person of $42 700 in 2011 was 23 times that of 1850. An increase in real GDP per person and, hence, in the typical person's real income by a factor of 23, makes an enormous difference to the standard of living. In 2011, unlike in 1850, the typical US family not only owned a comfortable home and had ample food and clothing, but also possessed many things not even imagined in 1850: cars, television sets, telephones, personal computers and a connection to the Internet. Also, compared with 161 years earlier, education levels were much higher, life expectancy was substantially longer and a much larger proportion of the population lived in cities.

The average growth rate of real GDP per person in the United States from 1850 to 2011 was 1.9% per year. This growth rate does not seem all that impressive – it is lower than the average rate of 2.2% per year from 1960 to 2011 for the 107 countries shown in Figure 3.3. Moreover, the long-term US growth rate is much lower than the growth rates in excess of 6% per year achieved by some East Asian and African countries from 1960 to 2011. Nevertheless, the US growth rate of 1.9% per year – when sustained for such a long time – was enough to make the United States one of the world's ten richest countries in 2011.

Living standards in the United States in 2011 would have been very different if the average growth rate of real GDP per person since 1850 had been much lower or higher than 1.9%. If the growth rate had been 1.0% per year, real GDP per person in 2011 would have been $9255, only five times the value in 1850. In this case, the typical American family would possess reasonable food and healthcare but would lack a comfortable home and a fine car, would be missing an array of pleasant consumer products and would have lower levels of education. Alternatively, if the growth rate had been 3.0%, the level of real GDP per person in 2005 would have been \$231 600, 125 times the level in 1850. A real GDP per person of \$231 600 means that the typical family would have a grand home, a couple of nice cars, no problems with expensive private schooling and healthcare, and so on.

Similar calculations apply to other OECD countries, many of which are now nearly as rich as or richer than the United States. These countries also came to be rich because their real GDP per person grew for a long time at the unspectacular rate of around 2% per year.

Although average growth rates of real GDP per person over a century or more were around 2% per year, the growth rates were not constant over time. To see this, consider Table 3.2, which shows growth rates for 21 OECD countries, including the United States. The table shows unweighted averages for the 21 countries of the growth rates of real GDP per person over 30-year periods from 1800 to 2010. The average growth rate over the full 210 years was 1.4% per year, with no clear trend. However, the average growth rates since 1920 were somewhat higher: 2.2% per year.

The decline in the growth rate of real GDP per person from 3.4% per year for 1950–1980 to 1.7% per year for 1980–2010 is sometimes called the **productivity slowdown**. Measures of productivity – such as output per person and per worker – did not grow as rapidly from 1980 to 2010 as in the previous 30 years. However, the growth rate of 1.7% per year for 1980–2010 exceeded the average growth rate since 1800. Thus, the high growth rate for 1950–1980 (and, it turns out, for 1950–1970) may have been the outlier. In addition, the lower growth rates from 1980–2010 are heavily influenced by the impact of the economic crises hitting the United States and Europe beginning in 2008. A reasonable guess from the numbers in Table 3.2 is that future growth rates of real GDP per person will average something close to 2% per year.

Table 3.2 Long-term economic growth in OECD countries

Period	Growth rate of real GDP per person (per cent per year)	Number of countries
1800–1830	0.1	5
1820–1850	1.0	13
1850–1880	1.2	20
1860–1890	1.2	18
1890–1920	1.0	20
1920–1950	1.5	20
1950–1980	3.4	21
1980–2010	1.7	21

Note: The data are from the Angus Maddison Project described in Bolt and van Zanden (2014). The 21 countries included are Australia, Austria, Belgium, Canada, Denmark, Finland, France, Germany, Greece, Italy, Ireland, Japan, Netherlands, New Zealand, Norway, Portugal, Spain, Sweden, Switzerland, the United Kingdom and the United States. The growth rates are unweighted averages for the countries with available data. Fewer countries have data for the earlier periods.

PATTERNS OF WORLD ECONOMIC GROWTH

In looking at the data, we observed some important patterns in economic growth. First, some economies, such as those in East Asia, grew rapidly from 1960 to 2011 and thereby raised their levels of real GDP per person substantially over 51 years. Second, over the same period, other countries – especially many in sub-Saharan Africa – grew at low or negative rates and therefore ended up with low levels of real GDP per person in 2011. Third, the United States and other OECD countries had high levels of real GDP per person in 2011 mostly because they grew at moderate rates – around 2% per year – for a century or more.

These observations suggest questions that we would like to answer about economic growth:

- What factors caused some countries to grow rapidly and others to grow slowly over periods such as 1960 to 2011? In particular, why did the East Asian countries do so much better than the sub-Saharan African countries?
- How did countries such as the OECD members sustain growth rates of real GDP per person of around 2% per year for a century or more?
- What can policymakers do to increase growth rates of real GDP per person?

The answers to these questions could contribute a great deal to the living standards of future generations. The theories about economic growth that we turn to next bring us closer to finding these answers.

Theory of economic growth

Now we will build a model of economic growth to help understand the patterns found in the international data. We start by considering the *production function*, which tells us how goods and services are produced.

THE PRODUCTION FUNCTION

We begin our theoretical study of economic growth by considering how a country's technology and factors of production – or factor inputs – determine its output of goods and services, measured by real GDP. The relation of output to technology and the quantities of factor inputs is called a **production function.**

We will build a simplified model that has two factor inputs: **capital stock**, K, and labour, L. In this model, capital takes a physical form, such as machines and buildings used by businesses. A more complete model would include **human capital**, which embodies the effects of education and training on workers' skills, and the effects of medical care, nutrition and sanitation on workers' health. In our simplified model, the amount of labour input, L, is the quantity of working hours per year for labour of a standard quality and effort. That is, we imagine that, at a point in time, each worker has the same skill. For convenience, we often refer to L as the **labour force** or the number of workers – these interpretations are satisfactory if we think of each labourer as working a fixed number of hours per year.

We use the symbol A to represent the **technology level**. For given quantities of the factor inputs, K and L, an increase in A raises output. That is, a more technologically advanced economy has a higher level of overall **productivity**. Higher productivity means that output is higher for given quantities of the factor inputs.

Mathematically, we write the production function as:

Key equation (production function):

$$Y = A \bullet F(K, L) \tag{3.1}$$

One way to see how output, Y, responds to the variables in the production function – the technology level, A, and the quantities of capital and labour, K and L – is to change one of the three variables while holding the other two fixed. Looking at the equation, we see that Y is proportional to A. Hence, if A doubles, while K and L do not change, Y doubles.

For a given technology level, A, the function $F(K, L)$ determines how additional units of capital and labour, K and L, affect output, Y. We assume that each factor is productive at the margin. Hence, for given A and L, an increase in K – that is, a rise in K at the margin – raises Y. Similarly, for given A and K, an increase in L raises Y.

The change in Y from a small increase in K is called the **marginal product of capital**, which we abbreviate as **MPK**. The MPK tells us how much Y rises when K increases by one unit, while A and L do not change. The corresponding change in Y from a small increase in L is called the **marginal product of labour (MPL)**. The MPL tells us how much Y rises when L increases by one unit, while A and K do not change. We assume that the two marginal products, MPK and MPL, are greater than zero.

Figure 3.5 shows how output, Y, responds to an increase in capital input, K. This figure is a graph of the production function, $A \bullet F(K, L)$, from equation (3.1). The special feature of this graph is that we are holding constant the values of A and L. Therefore, the graph shows how increases in K affect Y when A and L do not change.

The curve in Figure 3.5 goes through the origin, because we assume that output, Y, is zero if the amount of capital stock, K, is zero. The slope of the curve at any point is the marginal product of capital; that is, the change in Y from a small increase in K. Since we have assumed that this marginal product, MPK, is always greater than zero, the slope of the curve is positive throughout. We also assume that the slope flattens as K rises. The curve has this shape because we assume that the MPK declines as K rises, for given A and L. This property is known as **diminishing marginal product of capital**. As an example, at a low K, such as point a in the graph, an increase in K by one unit might raise

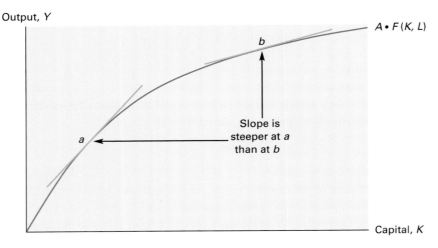

Output, Y

A • F (K, L)

b

Slope is
steeper at a
than at b

a

Capital, K

Figure 3.5 The production function in terms of capital input

The curve shows the effect of capital input, K, on output, Y. We hold fixed the technology level, A, and the quantity of labour input, L. Therefore, the slope of the curve at any point is the marginal product of capital, MPK. This slope gets less steep as K rises because of diminishing marginal product of capital. Therefore, the slope at point a is greater than that at point b.

Y by 0.1 units per year. However, at a high K, such as point b, an increase in K by one unit might raise Y by only 0.05 units per year.

Figure 3.6 shows the corresponding graph for output, Y, as a function of labour input, L. This figure is again a graph of the production function, $A • F (K, L)$, from equation (3.1). The special feature now is that we are holding constant the values of A and K. This graph shows how increases in L affect Y when A and K do not change. Again, the curve goes through the origin, because we assume that Y is zero if L is zero. The positive slope of the curve at any point is the marginal product of labour, MPL. The flattening of the curve as L rises indicates that the MPL falls as L increases, for given A and K. Hence, we are assuming **diminishing marginal product of labour**. As an example, at a low L, such as point a in the graph, an increase in L by one unit might raise Y by 0.1 units per year. However, at a high K, such as point b, an increase in L by one unit might raise Y by only 0.05 units per year.

Another assumption is that the production function in equation (3.1) exhibits **constant returns to scale** in the two factor inputs, K and L. The idea is that if we double the scale of inputs – double K and L – the output, Y, doubles. As an example, assume that a business starts with 5 machines, $K = 5$, and 5 workers, $L = 5$. The business has a given technology level, A, and is able to produce an output, Y, of, say, 100 widgets per year. Now, suppose that K and L double, so that the business has $K = 10$ machines and $L = 10$ workers. The technology level, A, is the same as before. Our assumption is that, with twice as many machines and workers and the same technology level, the business can produce twice as much output. That is, Y is now 200 widgets per year.

More generally, if the production function exhibits constant returns to scale, a multiplication of the two factor inputs, K and L, by any positive number leads to a multiplication of output, Y, by the same number. Therefore, if we multiply K and L by the quantity $1/L$ in equation (3.1), we also multiply Y by $1/L$ to get:

$$Y/L = A • F(K/L, L/L)$$

The value L/L on the right-hand side equals 1.0 (a constant) and can therefore be ignored. By writing the production function this way, we see that output per worker, Y/L, depends only on the technology level, A, and the quantity of capital per worker, K/L. We can show this property more clearly by defining $y \equiv Y/L$ to be output per worker and $k \equiv K/L$ to be capital per worker, and then defining a new function, f that relates y to k:

$$y = A • f(k) \qquad (3.2)$$

Figure 3.7 shows the graph of output per worker, y, versus capital per worker, k, for a given technology level, A. This graph looks the same as the one in Figure 3.5. The slope of the curve in Figure 3.7 again tells us the effect of more capital on output; that is, it measures the marginal product of capital, MPK. Note that the marginal product of capital diminishes as capital per worker, k, rises.

Output, Y

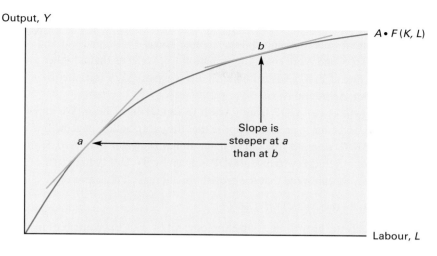

Figure 3.6 The production function in terms of labour input

The curve shows the effect of labour input, L, on output, Y. We hold fixed the technology level, A, and the quantity of capital input, K. Therefore, the slope of the curve at any point is the marginal product of labour, MPL. This slope gets less steep as L rises because of diminishing marginal product of labour. Therefore, the slope at point a is greater than that at point b.

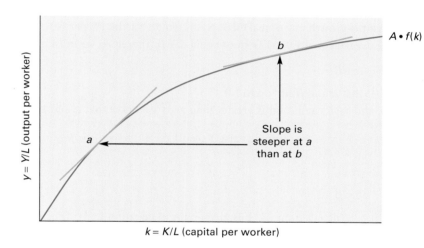

Figure 3.7 Output per worker versus capital per worker

This method for showing the production function plots output per worker, $y = Y/L$, against capital per worker, $k = K/L$. We hold fixed the technology level, A. The slope of the curve at any point is the marginal product of capital, MPK. This slope gets less steep as k rises because of diminishing marginal product of capital. Therefore, the slope at point a is greater than that at point b.

GROWTH ACCOUNTING

The production function in equation (3.1) determines the level of output or real GDP, Y, at a point in time for given values of its three determinants: the technology level, A, and the quantities of capital and labour, K and L. However, the production function is also the starting point for our investigation of economic growth. To use the production function to study growth, we use a method called **growth accounting** to consider how growth in Y depends on growth in A, K and L. Whereas *the production function is a relation between the level of Y and the levels of A, K and L, growth accounting is a relation between the growth rate of Y and the growth rates of A, K and L.*

To begin the analysis of growth accounting, let ΔY represent the change in Y over an interval of time – say, one year. (The symbol Δ, the Greek letter capital delta, represents the change in a variable.) The growth rate of Y over the year is given by $\Delta Y/Y$. For example, if $Y = 100$ and $\Delta Y = 1$ over one year, the growth rate is $\Delta Y/Y = 1\%$ per year. Similarly, if we use ΔA, ΔK and ΔL to represent the changes in technology, capital and labour, the growth rates of each are $\Delta A/A$, $\Delta K/K$ and $\Delta L/L$, respectively.

Our next task is to explain precisely how $\Delta A/A$, $\Delta K/K$ and $\Delta L/L$ contribute to the growth rate of real GDP, $\Delta Y/Y$. Start with the contribution of technology. We see from the production function expressed in equation (3.1):

$$Y = A \cdot F(K, L) \tag{3.1}$$

that Y would grow at the same rate as A if K and L were unchanged. For example, if $\Delta A/A = 1\%$ per year and K and L are constant, then $\Delta Y/Y = 1\%$ per year. Even if K and L are changing, equation (3.1) tells us that a higher growth rate of A would contribute to a higher growth rate of Y. If $\Delta A/A$ is higher by 1% per year, $\Delta Y/Y$ is higher by 1% per year, for given growth rates of capital and labour, $\Delta K/K$ and $\Delta L/L$.

Now consider the contributions to the growth of real GDP from growth in capital and labour. We know that $\Delta Y/Y$ increases when $\Delta K/K$ and $\Delta L/L$ increase. To be more precise, suppose that the contribution of growth in capital to the growth of real GDP is given by $\alpha \cdot \Delta K/K$, where α (the Greek letter alpha) is greater than zero. Similarly, suppose that the contribution of growth in labour to the growth of real GDP is given by $\beta \cdot \Delta L/L$, where β (the Greek letter beta) is also greater than zero. In this case, we can write that the growth rate of real GDP is given by:

$$\Delta Y/Y = \Delta A/A + \alpha \cdot (\Delta K/K) + \beta \cdot (\Delta L/L) \tag{3.3}$$

That is, the growth rate of real GDP, $\Delta Y/Y$, equals the growth rate of technology, $\Delta A/A$, plus the contributions from the growth of capital, $\alpha \cdot (\Delta K/K)$, and labour, $\beta \cdot (\Delta L/L)$. Notice that, since Y is proportional to A in the production function, equation (3.1), the coefficient on $\Delta A/A$ in equation (3.3) is 1.0.

To think about the effects from the growth rates of capital, $\Delta K/K$, and labour, $\Delta L/L$, let's simplify matters for the moment by neglecting growth of technology, so that $\Delta A/A = 0$. If $\Delta K/K$ and $\Delta L/L$ were the same, say, 1% per year, the condition of constant returns to scale tells us that the growth rate of real GDP, $\Delta Y/Y$, would also be 1% per year. But we see from equation (3.3) that, if $\Delta K/K$ and $\Delta L/L$ each equal 1.0, $\Delta Y/Y$ must equal $\alpha + \beta$. Therefore, we must have:

$$\alpha + \beta = 1$$

The condition of constant returns to scale implies that α and β add up to 1.0.

Since the coefficients α and β add up to 1.0, and each coefficient is greater than zero, we know that α and β are each less than 1.0. That is, the coefficients satisfy:

$$0 < \alpha < 1$$

and

$$0 < \beta < 1$$

Notice that, if $\Delta K/K = 1\%$ per year and $\Delta L/L = 0$, the effect on $\Delta Y/Y$ is given by α in equation (3.3). Thus, if K grows while L stays fixed, Y grows at α rate slower than the growth rate of K (because $\alpha < 1$). Similarly, if $\Delta L/L = 1\%$ per year and $\Delta K/K = 0$, the effect on $\Delta Y/Y$ is given by β in equation (3.3). Thus, if L grows while K stays fixed, Y grows at a rate slower than the growth rate of L (because $\beta < 1$).

We know from Chapter 2 that – if we neglect net flows of income from the rest of the world – the economy's total real income equals real GDP, Y, less depreciation of capital stocks. If the depreciation of capital is small, Appendix A to this chapter shows that the coefficient α approximates the share of capital income in the economy's total real income. For example, if $\alpha = \frac{1}{3}$ – a commonly assumed value for the share of capital income – then α growth rate of capital, $\Delta K/K$, of 1% a year would contribute $\frac{1}{3}\%$ per year to the growth rate of real GDP, $\Delta Y/Y$.

Similarly, under the conditions explored in Appendix A to this chapter, β approximates the share of labour income in the economy's total real income. For example, if $\beta = \frac{2}{3}$ – a commonly assumed value for the share of labour income – a growth rate of labour, $\Delta L/L$, of 1% a year would contribute $\frac{2}{3}\%$ per year to $\Delta Y/Y$.

The interpretations of α and β as shares of capital and labour in total real income fit with our result that $\alpha + \beta = 1$. That is, we have:

$$\textit{share of capital income} + \textit{share of labour income} = 1$$
$$\alpha + \beta = 1$$

Thus, payments to capital and labour exhaust all of the real income in the economy.

We can rearrange the condition $\alpha + \beta = 1$ to substitute $1 - \alpha$ for β on the right-hand side of equation (3.3) to get equation (3.4), which says that we can break down the growth rate of real GDP, $\Delta Y/Y$, into the growth rate of technology, $\Delta A/A$, and a weighted average of the growth rates of capital and labour, $\alpha \cdot \Delta K/K$ and $(1 - \alpha) \cdot \Delta L/L$.

Key equation (growth-accounting formula):

$$\Delta Y/Y = \Delta A/A + \alpha \cdot (\Delta K/K) + (1-\alpha) \cdot (\Delta L/L) \qquad (3.4)$$

The growth rate of capital gets the weight α (corresponding to capital's share of income), and the growth rate of labour gets the weight $1 - \alpha$ (corresponding to labour's share of income).

We now simplify by assuming that the coefficient α, which we interpret as capital's share of income, is fixed. That is, we assume that this coefficient does not change as the economy grows. The constancy of income shares does not always apply in the real world, but it does work as a reasonable approximation for the United States and many other countries. In Appendix C to this chapter, we show that the constancy of α holds for a commonly assumed form of the production function, $A \cdot F(K, L)$.

THE SOLOW GROWTH MODEL

We learned from growth accounting in equation (3.4) that the growth rate of real GDP, $\Delta Y/Y$, depends on the growth rate of technology, $\Delta A/A$, and a weighted average of the growth rates of capital and labour, $\Delta K/K$ and $\Delta L/L$. To go from growth accounting to a theory of economic growth, we have to explain the growth rates of technology, capital and labour. We begin this explanation by constructing the **Solow growth model**.

The Solow model makes several simplifying assumptions. First, labour input, L, equals the labour force, which is the number of persons seeking work. That is, the model does not allow for unemployment – labour input equals the labour force, all of which is employed. However, the important assumption is that the unemployment rate is constant, not necessarily zero. For example, if 96% of the labour force is always employed, labour input would always be a fixed multiple of the labour force and would grow at the same rate as the labour force.

The relation between the labour force, L, and population is given by:

labour force, $L = $ (labour force/population) $\bullet$ population

The ratio of labour force to population is the **labour-force participation rate**. In OECD countries, in recent years, the labour-force participation rate has been close to one-half. For example, in Germany in 2013, the civilian labour force (42.6 million) and armed forces (165 000) was 52% of the total population.[6] The second assumption in the Solow model is that this participation rate does not change over time. In this case, the equation tells us that the growth rate of labour input, L, equals the growth rate of population.

Third, the model ignores a role for government, so that there are no taxes, public expenditures, government debt or money. Fourth, the model assumes a closed economy; that is, there is no international trade in goods and services or in financial assets.

To begin our analysis of the Solow model, consider again the growth-accounting equation:

$$\Delta Y/Y = \Delta A/A + \alpha \cdot (\Delta K/K) + (1-\alpha) \cdot (\Delta L/L) \qquad (3.4)$$

We focus initially on growth of the two inputs, K and L, and ignore changes in the technology level, A. That is, we assume $\Delta A/A = 0$. In this case, the growth-accounting equation simplifies to:

$$\Delta Y/Y = \alpha \cdot (\Delta K/K) + (1-\alpha) \cdot (\Delta L/L) \qquad (3.5)$$

Hence, in this version of the Solow model, the growth rate of real GDP, $\Delta Y/Y$, is a weighted average of the growth rates of capital, $\Delta K/K$, and labour, $\Delta L/L$.

---

[6]The Bureau of Labor Statistics in the United States computes a different measure of the labour-force participation rate – the ratio of the civilian labour force to the civilian non-institutional population, which is the population (aged 16 and over) not on active military duty and not in institutions such as prisons.

Economics in Practice
Intellectual origin of the Solow growth model

The Solow model was created during the 1950s by the MIT economist Robert Solow. This research led eventually to a Nobel Prize in 1987 for 'contributions to the theory of economic growth'. The Solow model was extended during the 1960s, especially by David Cass (1965) and Tjalling Koopmans (1965), and became known as the **neoclassical growth model**. The Solow model and the 1960s extensions were actually anticipated in theoretical work done by the mathematician Frank Ramsey in the 1920s. Hence, this growth model is often called the **Ramsey model**. Unfortunately, Ramsey's brilliant career was cut short by his death in 1930 at the age of 26.

We will find it useful to focus on real GDP per worker, $y = Y/L$, rather than the level of real GDP, Y. If Y were fixed, growth in L means that y would decline over time. For example, with a fixed Y, growth in workers at 1% per year implies that y falls by 1% per year. More generally, we have the formula:

$$\Delta y/y = \Delta Y/Y - \Delta L/L \tag{3.6}$$

growth rate of real GDP per worker = growth rate of real GDP − growth rate of labour

Using the same reasoning, the growth rate of capital per worker, $\Delta k/k$, falls short of the growth rate of capital, $\Delta K/K$, by the growth rate of the number of workers:

$$\Delta k/k = \Delta K/K - \Delta L/L \tag{3.7}$$

growth rate of capital per worker = growth rate of capital − growth rate of labour

Hence, for a given $\Delta K/K$, a higher $\Delta L/L$ means that, over time, each worker has less capital to work with.

If we rearrange the terms on the right-hand side of equation (3.5), we get:

$$\Delta Y/Y = \alpha \bullet (\Delta K/K) - \alpha \bullet (\Delta L/L) + \Delta L/L$$

Then, if we move $\Delta L/L$ from the right-hand side to the left-hand side and combine the two terms on the right-hand side that involve α, we get;

$$\Delta Y/Y - \Delta L/L = \alpha \bullet (\Delta K/K - \Delta L/L)$$

We see from equation (3.6) that the left-hand side is the growth rate of real GDP per worker, $\Delta y/y$, and from equation (3.7) that the term in parentheses on the right-hand side is the growth rate of capital per worker, $\Delta k/k$. Therefore, the key result is that the growth rate of real GDP per worker depends only on the growth rate of capital per worker:

$$\Delta y/y = \alpha \bullet (\Delta k/k) \tag{3.8}$$

We see from equation (3.8) that, to analyze the growth rate of real GDP per worker, $\Delta y/y$, we need only to determine the growth rate of capital per worker, $\Delta k/k$. Moreover, we know from equation (3.7) that $\Delta k/k$ is the difference between the growth rate of capital, $\Delta K/K$, and the growth rate of labour, $\Delta L/L$. We first assess $\Delta K/K$ and then turn to $\Delta L/L$.

The growth rate of the capital stock

The change in the stock of capital, ΔK, will depend on the economy's **saving**, which is the income that is not consumed. In our analysis in Chapter 8, we analyze saving behaviour by considering the optimal choices of individual households. However, we simplify matters here by using Solow's assumption that each household divides up its real income in a fixed proportion s to saving and $1 - s$ to consumption, C.

For the economy as a whole, we know from our study of national-income accounting in Chapter 2 that national income equals net domestic product (NDP), which equals GDP less depreciation of capital stocks. In our model, some of the national income is labour income, which goes to workers, and some is capital income, which goes to owners of capital. However, all income must flow eventually to households, partly in their role as workers and partly in their role as owners of capital (or owners of businesses). We assume that saving depends only on households' total income, not on how this income divides up between labour income and capital income.

Depreciation arises because capital stocks wear out over time. Buildings need repairs, machines deteriorate and vehicles require new parts. We capture depreciation in a simple way by assuming that all forms of capital depreciate at the same constant rate, δ (the Greek letter delta). Therefore, the flow quantity ΔK is the amount of capital that depreciates or disappears each year. In practice, the value of δ depends on the type of building or machine, but a reasonable average number is 5% per year. For example, if the stock of capital, K, is 100 machines, and δ is 5% per year, depreciation equals 5 machines per year.

The economy's real national income equals real NDP, which equals real GDP, Y, less depreciation, δK. From now on, we shorten the term national income to income. If households save the proportion s of all income, the economy's total real saving is:

$$real\ saving = s \bullet (Y - \delta K)$$

$$real\ saving = (saving\ rate) \bullet (real\ income)$$

Since household real income, $Y - \delta K$, goes either to consumption, C, or real saving, $s \bullet (Y - \delta K)$, we can also write:

$$Y - \delta K = C + s \bullet (Y - \delta K)$$

$$real\ income = consumption + real\ saving$$

(3.9)

In a closed economy with no government sector, real GDP, Y, must be either consumed or invested. That is, the goods and services produced are used for only two purposes: consumption and outlays on capital goods or **gross investment**, I. Therefore, we have:

$$Y = C + I$$

$$real\ GDP = consumption + gross\ investment$$

If we subtract depreciation, δK, from both sides, we get:

$$Y - \delta K = C + (I - \delta K)$$

$$real\ NDP = consumption + net\ investment$$

(3.10)

Notice on the right-hand side that we have defined **net investment** as gross investment, I, less the part of that investment, δK, needed to make up for the depreciation of existing capital.

Equations (3.9) and (3.10) have the same variable on the left-hand side (because real national income equals real NDP). Consequently, the right-hand sides must be equal:

$$C + s \bullet (Y - \delta K) = C + I - \delta K$$

If we cancel out the variable C on the two sides of the equation, we get a key equality between real saving and net investment:

$$s \bullet (Y - \delta K) = I - \delta K$$

$$real\ saving = net\ investment$$

(3.11)

The change in the capital stock equals gross investment, I – the purchases of new capital goods – less the depreciation of existing capital:

$$\Delta K = I - \delta K$$

change in capital stock = gross investment − depreciation

change in capital stock = net investment

Since net investment equals real saving from equation (3.11), we also have:

$$\Delta K = s \bullet (Y - \delta K) \tag{3.12}$$

change in capital stock = real saving

If we divide through each side of equation (3.12) by K, we get the formula we are seeking for the growth rate of the capital stock:

$$\Delta K/K = s \bullet Y/K - s\delta \tag{3.13}$$

This result for $\Delta K/K$ is one of the two pieces needed to determine the growth rate of capital per worker:

$$\Delta k/k = \Delta K/K - \Delta L/L \tag{3.7}$$

We now turn to the second piece – the growth rate of labour, $\Delta L/L$.

The growth rate of labour

Given our previous assumptions (a constant labour-force participation rate and a constant unemployment rate), the growth rate of labour, $\Delta L/L$, equals the growth rate of population. Thus, we now consider **population growth**.

Population growth rates vary across countries and over time. The world population growth rate was around 2% from 1960 to 1975, but has been falling since, reaching 1.2% from 2010 onwards. In many Western European countries, population growth rates fell from around 1% per year in the 1960s to less than 0.5% starting in the mid-1990s. In China and India, population growth rates have declined from over 2% per year in the 1960s to recent values between 0.5% and 1.3% per year, respectively. Many low-income countries still have population growth rates above 2% per year. However, there has been a worldwide tendency for population growth rates to decline over time.

In the model, we assume that population grows at a constant rate, denoted by n, where n is a positive number ($n > 0$). At this point, we do not attempt to explain the population growth rate within the model; that is, we take n to be exogenous. We assume that labour, L, begins at an initial year, denoted by year 0, at the quantity $L(0)$, as shown in Figure 3.7. Thereafter, the growth rate of L, $\Delta L/L$, equals the exogenous population growth rate, n:

$$\Delta L/L = n \tag{3.14}$$

Since n is constant, Figure 3.8 shows the time path of L as a straight line (using a proportionate scale on the vertical axis).

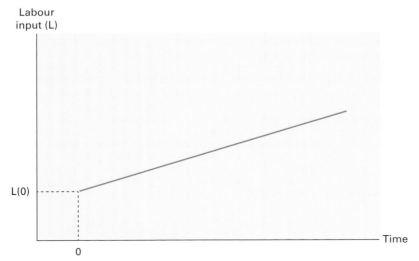

Figure 3.8 Time path of labour input

Labour input, L, starts at time 0 at $L(0)$. Labour input then grows with population at the constant rate n. On a proportionate scale, L follows a straight line, as shown in the figure.

The growth rate of capital and real GDP per worker

We can substitute our result for the growth rate of capital, $\Delta K/K$, from equation (3.13) and for the growth rate of labour, $\Delta L/L$, from equation (3.14) into equation (3.7) to determine the growth rate of capital per worker, $\Delta k/k$. We get:

$$\Delta k/k = \Delta K/K - \Delta L/L$$
$$\Delta k/k = s \bullet (Y/K) - s\delta - n \tag{3.15}$$

Equation (3.15) is a key result in the Solow growth model. Because of the importance of this equation, we will examine the various terms. On the left-hand side, the growth rate of capital per worker has units of per year. For example, a value for $\Delta k/k$ of 0.02 per year means that capital per worker is growing at 2% per year.

The terms on the right-hand side of equation (3.15) are determinants of the growth rate of capital per worker. Hence, each of these terms must also have units of per year. Consider the term $s \bullet (Y/K)$, which is the product of the saving rate, s, and Y/K. The saving rate, s, is a pure number; that is, a number without units of time or goods. For example, if $s = 0.2$, households save 20% of their income. The term Y/K – output per unit of capital – is called the **average product of capital**. The units for Y – a flow variable – are goods per year and those for K – a stock variable – are goods. Therefore, the average product of capital has units of:

$$(goods\ per\ year)/goods = per\ year$$

Since s is a pure number, the units of $s \bullet (Y/K)$ are the same as the units of Y/K, which are per year, just like $\Delta k/k$.

The other terms on the right-hand side of equation (3.15) also have units of per year. The term $s\Delta$ is the product of a pure number, s, and Δ, which has units of per year. The population growth rate, n, also has units of per year.

We will find it useful to express the average product of capital, Y/K, in terms of real GDP per worker, y, and capital per worker, k. The relation is:

$$Y/K = \frac{Y/L}{K/L}\ or$$

$$Y/K = \frac{y}{k}$$

If we substitute this result for Y/K into equation (3.15), we get the central relation of the Solow model:

Key equation (Solow growth model):

$$\Delta k/k = s \bullet (y/k) - s\delta - n \tag{3.16}$$

Finally, once we know the growth rate of capital per worker from equation (3.16), we can use equation (3.8) to determine the growth rate of real GDP per worker:

$$\Delta y/y = \alpha \bullet (\Delta k/k)$$
$$\Delta y/y = \alpha \bullet [s \bullet (y/k) - s\delta - n] \tag{3.17}$$

If the capital-share coefficient, α, is fixed, we can go readily from the growth rate of capital per worker, $\Delta k/k$, in equation (3.16) to the growth rate of real GDP per worker, $\Delta y/y$, in equation (3.17). Since the number of workers grows at the same rate, n, as population, $\Delta y/y$ also equals the growth rate of real GDP per person.

The transition and the steady state

The key to the Solow growth model is equation (3.16), which determines the growth rate of capital per worker, $\Delta k/k$. The equation shows that $\Delta k/k$ depends on the saving rate, s, the depreciation rate, δ, the population growth rate, n, and the average product of capital, y/k. We have assumed that s, δ and n are constants. Therefore, the only reason that $\Delta k/k$ varies over time is that the average product of capital, y/k, varies. We will now consider how this average product depends on capital per worker, k. In this way, we will find that changes over time in k lead to changes in y/k and, thereby, to changes in $\Delta k/k$.

We have already considered the marginal product of capital, MPK, which is the ratio of a change in real GDP, ΔY, to a change in capital, ΔK. Geometrically, the marginal product was given by the slope of the production function shown in Figure 3.7. We reproduce this construction in Figure 3.9. In this new graph, we compute the average product of capital, y/k, as the ratio of y (the variable on the vertical axis) to k (the variable on the horizontal axis). This ratio equals the slope of a straight line from the origin to the production function. The graph shows two such lines, one from the origin to point a and another from the origin to point b. The first line corresponds to capital per worker k_a and the second to the larger capital per worker k_b. The graph shows that the average product of capital, y/k, declines as capital per worker, k, rises; for example, from k_a to k_b. This **diminishing average product of capital** is analogous to the diminishing marginal product of capital, which we discussed before.

We can show diagrammatically how equation (3.16) determines the growth rate of capital per worker, $\Delta k/k$, by graphing the terms on the right-hand side of the equation versus capital per worker, k. In the first term, $s \cdot (y/k)$, the crucial property is the one just derived: the average product of capital, y/k, diminishes as k rises. Hence, the curve for $s \cdot (y/k)$ slopes downward versus k, as shown in Figure 3.10.

The remaining terms on the right-hand side of equation (3.16) can be written as $-(s\Delta + n)$. The term $s\Delta + n$ is described by the horizontal line in Figure 3.10. Since $s\Delta + n$ enters with a minus sign in equation (3.16), we have to subtract the position along the horizontal line from that of the curve (which gives $s \cdot [y/k]$) to determine $\Delta k/k$.

To study how the growth rate of capital per worker, $\Delta k/k$, changes over time, we have to know the capital per worker that the economy has initially; that is, at year 0. The economy begins with an accumulated stock of capital in the forms of machines and buildings. We represent this starting stock by $K(0)$. Since the initial labour is $L(0)$, the initial capital per worker is:

$$k(0) = K(0)/L(0)$$

Recall that the production function in per-worker form is:

$$y = A \cdot f(k) \tag{3.2}$$

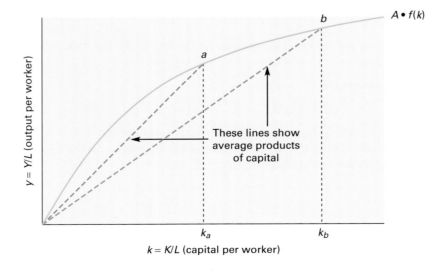

Figure 3.9 The average product of capital

The graph shows the production function for output per worker, $y = Y/L$, versus capital per worker, $k = K/L$, as in Figure 3.7. The slope of a straight line from the origin to the production function gives the average product of capital, y/k, at the associated value of k. As k rises, for a given technology level, A, the average product of capital falls. For example, the slope of the dashed blue line, from the origin to point a, is greater than that of the dashed blue line, from the origin to point b. Therefore, the production function exhibits diminishing average product of capital.

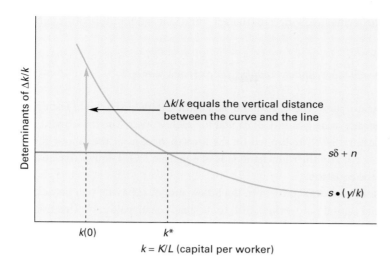

Figure 3.10 Determination of the growth rate of capital per worker in the Solow model

The technology level, A, is fixed. The vertical axis plots the two determinants of the growth rate of capital per worker, $\Delta k/k$, from the right-hand side of equation (3.16). $\Delta k/k$ equals the vertical distance between the negatively sloped $s \cdot (y/k)$ curve and the horizontal line at $s\delta + n$. At the steady state, where $k = k^*$, the curve and line intersect, and $\Delta k/k = 0$. The initial capital per worker, $k(0)$, is assumed to be less than k^*. Therefore, when $k = k(0)$, $\Delta k/k$ is greater than zero and equal to the vertical distance shown by the blue arrows.

Therefore, the initial level of real GDP per worker is given by:

$$y(0) = Y(0)/L(0)$$
$$y(0) = A \cdot f[k(0)]$$

In Figure 3.10, the growth rate of capital per worker, $\Delta k/k$, is the vertical distance between the $s \cdot (y/k)$ curve and the horizontal line, $s\delta + n$; see equation (3.16). We assume that, when $k = k(0)$, the curve lies above the line. In this case, capital per worker grows initially. That is, $\Delta k/k$ is greater than zero and is given by the distance marked by the blue arrows. This positive growth rate means that capital per worker, k, increases over time; that is, k moves to the right in Figure 3.10. Notice that the distance between the curve and the horizontal line diminishes over time. Since this distance equals $\Delta k/k$, we have shown that the growth rate of capital per worker slows down over time. This result is an important property of the Solow model.

Eventually, the increase in capital per worker, k, eliminates the gap between the $s \cdot (y/k)$ curve and the $s\Delta + n$ line in Figure 3.10. The gap gets close to zero when k approaches the value k^* on the horizontal axis. When $k = k^*$, $\Delta k/k$ equals zero. Therefore, k no longer moves to the right – with $\Delta k/k = 0$, k stays fixed at the value k^*. For this reason, we call k^* the capital per worker in the **steady state**. The corresponding real GDP per worker in the steady state is given from the production function in per-worker form in equation (3.2) by:

$$y^* = f(k^*)$$

The results tell us that capital per worker, k, follows a **transition path** from its initial value, $k(0)$, to its steady-state value, k^*. Figure 3.11 shows this transition path as the blue curve. Note that k starts at $k(0)$, rises over time, and eventually gets close to k^*, shown as the dashed blue line.

Recall that the formula for the growth rate of capital per worker is:

$$\Delta k/k = s \cdot (y/k) - s\delta - n \tag{3.16}$$

In the steady state, $\Delta k/k$ equals zero. Therefore, the right-hand side of equation (3.16) must also be zero in the steady state:

$$s \cdot (y^*/k^*) - s\delta - n = 0$$

If we move n to the right-hand side, combine the terms involving s on the left-hand side, and multiply through by k^*, we get:

$$s \bullet (y^* - \delta k^*) = nk^* \tag{3.17}$$

steady-state saving per worker = steady-state capital provided for each new worker

The left-hand side is saving per worker in the steady state. The right-hand side is the capital provided to each new worker in the steady state. Recall that k^* is the steady-state quantity of capital for each worker. The investment per worker needed to generate the necessary new capital is k^* multiplied by the growth rate, n, of the labour force. Therefore, the steady-state investment per worker, nk^*, on the right-hand side of equation (3.17) equals the steady-state saving per worker on the left-hand side of the equation.

Our analysis allows us to think of the process of economic growth in the Solow model as having two phases. In the first phase, there is a transition from an initial capital per worker, $k(0)$, to its steady-state value, k^*. This transition is shown by the blue curve in Figure 3.11. During this transition, the growth rate of capital per worker, $\Delta k/k$, is

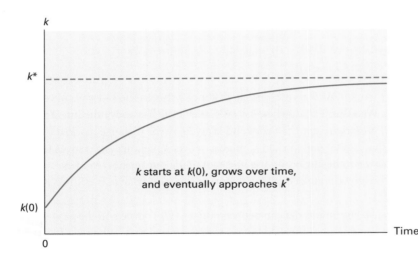

k starts at k(0), grows over time, and eventually approaches k*

Figure 3.11 The transition path for capital per worker

In the Solow model, described by Figure 3.10, capital per worker, k, starts at $k(0)$ and then rises over time. The growth rate of k slows down over time, and k gradually approaches its steady-state value, k^*. The transition path from $k(0)$ to k^* is shown by the solid blue curve. The dashed blue line shows the steady-state value, k^*.

Do the Maths

We have seen how Figure 3.10 determines the steady-state capital per worker, k^*. We can also determine k^* algebraically. If we set $\Delta k/k = 0$ in equation (3.16), the right-hand side of the equation must be zero, so that:

$$s \bullet (y^*/K^*) - s\delta - n = 0$$

If we rearrange the terms in this equation and divide by s, we find that the average product of capital in the steady state is:

$$y^*/k^* = \delta + n/s \tag{3.18}$$

If we use equation (3.2) to substitute $A \bullet f(k^*)$ for y^*, we find that the steady-state capital per worker, k^*, must satisfy:

$$A \bullet f(k^*)/k^* = \delta + n/s \tag{3.19}$$

This algebraic result for k^* will be helpful in Chapter 4, when we work further with the Solow model.

greater than zero but declining gradually towards zero. In the second phase, the economy is in (or near) the steady state, represented by the dashed blue line in Figure 3.11. In this phase, $\Delta k/k = 0$.

Our goal was to determine how the growth rate of real GDP per worker (and per person), $\Delta y/y$, varies over time. We can now reach this goal, because $\Delta y/y$ equals the growth rate of capital per worker, $\Delta k/k$, multiplied by α, which we assume to be constant (with $0 < \alpha < 1$):

$$\Delta y/y = \alpha \cdot (\Delta k/k) \tag{3.8}$$

Therefore, everything that we said about $\Delta k/k$ applies also to $\Delta y/y$, once we multiply by α. In particular, starting at the initial capital per worker $k(0)$ shown in Figure 3.10, we have that $\Delta y/y$ starts out positive, then declines as capital per worker, k, and real GDP per worker, y, rise. Eventually, when k reaches its steady-state value, k^*, $\Delta y/y$ falls to zero; this is because equation (3.8) implies $\Delta y/y = 0$ when $\Delta k/k = 0$. In the steady state, real GDP per worker, y, equals its steady-state value, y^*.

In Figure 3.11, we can view the transition as applying to real GDP per worker, y, as well as to capital per worker, k. That is, the blue curve also describes the transition from the initial real GDP per worker, $y(0)$, to its steady-state value, y^*.

Summing Up

We began our study of economic growth with observations about the importance of growth for standards of living. Now we have constructed the Solow growth model and are ready to work with it to understand how economic variables influence growth. We will begin to put the model to use in Chapter 4.

Key Terms and Concepts

average product of capital	gross investment	marginal product of labour (MPL)	Ramsey model
capital stock	growth accounting	neoclassical growth model	rate of economic growth
constant returns to scale	human capital	net investment	saving
diminishing average product of capital	inequality	population growth	Solow growth model
diminishing marginal product of capital	labour force	poverty	standard of living
diminishing marginal product of capital	labour-force participation rate	production function	steady state
diminishing marginal product of labour	marginal product of capital (MPK)	productivity	technology level
		productivity slowdown	transition path

Questions and Problems

A Review questions

1 Explain why an increase in capital per worker, k, reduces the growth rate of capital per worker, $\Delta k/k$. How does this result depend on diminishing productivity of capital?

2 Does a positive saving rate, $s > 0$, mean that output per worker, y, grows in the long run? Explain.

3 What is a production function? In what way does it represent a relation between factor inputs and the level of output?

4 Does a positive saving rate, $s > 0$, mean that capital per worker, k, rises over time? Explain by referring to equation (3.16).

5 Explain the concepts of marginal and average products of capital. What is the difference between the two? Is the average product always greater than the marginal product?

B Problems for discussion

6 Growth without diminishing productivity of capital

Suppose that the production function is $Y = AK$ (the so-called AK model).

a What is the condition for the growth rate of capital per worker, $\Delta k/k$, in equation (3.16)? What does the $s \cdot (y/k)$ curve look like in Figure 3.10?

b What are the growth rates of capital and output per worker, $\Delta k/k$ and $\Delta y/y$? Are these growth rates greater than zero? Do these growth rates decline during a transition?

c Discuss how your results relate to diminishing productivity of capital. Is it plausible that diminishing productivity would not apply?

7 Growth with a Cobb-Douglas production function

Suppose that the production function takes the Cobb-Douglas form, discussed in Problem 7: $Y = A \cdot F(K, L) = AK^a L^{1-a}$, where $0 < \alpha < 1$.

a In the steady state, $\Delta k/k$, given by equation (3.16), equals zero. Use this condition, along with the form of the production function, to get a formula for the steady-state capital and output per worker, k^* and y^*.

b Let $c = C/L$ be consumption per worker. What is steady-state consumption per worker, c^*?

c Use equation (3.16) to work out a formula for the growth rate of capital per worker, $\Delta k/k$. Can you show that $\Delta k/k$ falls during the transition as k rises? What happens during the transition to the growth rate of output per worker, $\Delta y/y$?

8 Constant returns to scale

We have assumed that the production function, $A \cdot F(K, L)$, exhibits constant returns to scale. That is, if we multiply the inputs, K and L, by any positive number, we multiply output, Y, by the same number. Show that this condition implies that we can write the production function as in equation (3.2):

$$y = A \cdot f(k)$$

where $y = Y/L$ and $k = K/L$.

9 Determination of steady-state capital per worker

Consider the steady-state capital per worker, k^*, determined in Figure 3.10. How is k^* affected by the following?

a An increase in the saving rate, s.

b An increase in the technology level, A.

c An increase in the depreciation rate, δ.

d An increase in the population growth rate, n.

10 Cobb-Douglas production function

The Cobb-Douglas production function, discussed in the Appendix to this chapter, is given by:

$$Y = AK^\alpha L^{1-\alpha}$$

where $0 < \alpha < 1$.

a Define A, K and L.

b What does it mean that Y is proportional to A?

c What does it mean that the marginal product of capital (or labour), MPK (or MPL), is greater than zero? Show that the marginal products are positive in the Cobb-Douglas case.

d What does it mean that the marginal product of capital (or labour), MPK (or MPL), is decreasing? Show that the marginal products are diminishing in the Cobb-Douglas case.

e Does the Cobb-Douglas production function satisfy the property of constant returns to scale, discussed in Problem 6? Explain your answer.

Appendix

This appendix comprises three parts. Part A provides a formal derivation of the growth-accounting equation, given in equation (3.4). Part B shows how to use the growth-accounting equation to analyze productivity growth. Part C discusses a common form of the production function, known as the Cobb-Douglas production function.

Part A: The Growth-Accounting Equation

The growth-accounting equation is:

$$\Delta Y/Y = \Delta A/A + \alpha \cdot (\Delta K/K) + (1-\alpha) \cdot (\Delta L/L) \tag{3.4}$$

We derive this equation more formally here and work out a formula for the coefficient α.

The production function is:

$$Y = A \cdot F(K, L) \tag{3.1}$$

The form of this equation tells us that, for given K and L, an increase in the growth rate of technology, $\Delta A/A$, by 1% per year raises the growth rate of real GDP, $\Delta Y/Y$, by 1% per year. This reasoning explains why the term $\Delta A/A$ appears as it does in equation (3.4).

Consider now the effect from changes in K, when A and L are held fixed. If K increases by the amount ΔK, while A and L do not change, the increase in real GDP equals ΔK multiplied by the marginal product of capital, MPK:

$$\Delta Y = MPK \cdot \Delta K$$

To get the growth rate of Y divide each side by Y:

$$\Delta Y/Y = (MPK/Y) \cdot \Delta K$$

Then, if we multiply and divide by K on the right-hand side, we get:

$$\Delta Y/Y = \left(\frac{MPK \cdot K}{Y} \right) \cdot (\Delta K/K)$$

This result determines $\Delta Y/Y$ when K is growing but A and L are held fixed. More generally, it tells us the contribution of $\Delta K/K$ to $\Delta Y/Y$, even when A and L are changing. That is, to get the contribution of $\Delta K/K$ to $\Delta Y/Y$, multiply $\Delta K/K$ by the term $(MPK \cdot K)/Y$. Therefore, in equation (3.4), we must have that the coefficient α is given by:

$$\alpha = (MPK \cdot K)/Y \tag{3.20}$$

In a competitive economy, capital's marginal product, MPK, equals the real rental price paid per unit of capital. (We work out this result in Chapter 7.) In that case, the term $MPK \cdot K$ equals the amount paid per unit of capital, MPK, multiplied by the quantity of capital, K, and therefore equals the total real rental payments to capital. Therefore, α is given by:

$$\alpha = (MPK \cdot K)/Y$$

$$\alpha = (real\ rental\ payments\ to\ capital)/(real\ GDP)$$

If depreciation of capital stocks were zero, the real rental payments would equal the real income on capital and real GDP would equal the economy's total real income (that is, real national income). In this case, equation (3.20) implies that α equals the *capital share of income*. More generally, depreciation of capital stocks has to be subtracted from real rental payments and real GDP to compute real incomes. In this case, the capital share of income will be less than α. In any event, since the real rental payments to capital have to be smaller than real GDP, we have $0 < \alpha < 1$.

Now we consider the contribution to the growth of real GDP from growth in labour input. If L increases by the amount ΔL, while A and K are held fixed, the increase in real GDP equals ΔL multiplied by the marginal product of labour:

$$\Delta Y = MPL \cdot \Delta L$$

If we divide through by Y, we get:

$$\Delta Y/Y = (MPL/Y) \cdot \Delta L$$

Then, if we multiply and divide by L on the right-hand side, we get:

$$\Delta Y/Y = \left(\frac{MPL \cdot L}{Y} \right) \cdot (\Delta L/L)$$

Therefore, to get the contribution of $\Delta L/L$ to $\Delta Y/Y$, we have to multiply $\Delta L/L$ by the term $(MPL \cdot L)/Y$. Hence, in equation (3.4), we must have:

$$1 - \alpha = (MPL \cdot L)/Y \qquad (3.21)$$

In a competitive economy, labour's marginal product, MPL, equals the real wage rate. (We work out this result in Chapter 7.) Therefore, the term $MPL \cdot L$ equals the amount paid per unit of labour, MPL, multiplied by the quantity of labour, L, and therefore equals the total real wage payments to labour. If depreciation of capital stocks were zero, real GDP, Y, would equal total real income. In this case, equation (3.21) implies that $1 - \alpha$ equals the *labour share of income*. More generally, since total real income is less than Y, the labour share of income will be greater than $1 - \alpha$.

Part B: The Solow Residual

We know that the growth rate of technology, $\Delta A/A$, contributes to the growth rate of real GDP, $\Delta Y/Y$. Since the technology level, A, is not directly observable, we need some way to measure it from national-accounts data. A common approach is to rearrange the growth-accounting formula, equation (3.4), to get:

$$\Delta A/A = \Delta Y/Y - \alpha \cdot (\Delta K/K) - (1 - \alpha) \cdot (\Delta L/L) \qquad (3.22)$$
growth rate of A = growth rate of real GDP − contribution of capital and labour

The terms on the right-hand side can be measured from national-accounts data. Therefore, we can use this equation to measure the left-hand side, which equals the growth rate of technology, $\Delta A/A$.

The term $\Delta A/A$ in equations (3.4) and (3.22) is often called **total factor productivity growth**, or **TFP growth**. This concept comes from Robert Solow (1957) and is also often called the **Solow residual**. This terminology arises because equation (3.22) shows that we can compute $\Delta A/A$ as the *residual* after we take the growth rate of real GDP, $\Delta Y/Y$, and subtract out the contributions to growth from the changing factor inputs, $\alpha \cdot (\Delta K/K)$ for capital and $(1 - \alpha) \cdot (\Delta L/L)$ for labour. Economists have calculated these Solow residuals for various countries and time periods.

Part C: The Cobb-Douglas Production Function

We assumed in our analysis of the Solow model that α (which equals the capital share of income if depreciation can be neglected) was constant. That is, α did not change as capital per worker, k, varied. We can show that this assumption is valid for a particular form of the production function:

$$Y = A \cdot F(K, L)$$
$$Y = AK^{\alpha}L^{1-\alpha} \qquad (3.23)$$

In this form, the constant α appears as the exponent on capital, K, whereas $1 - \alpha$ appears as the exponent on labour, L. We assume that α is a fraction, so that $0 < \alpha < 1$. This form of the production function has been used by economists in many theoretical and empirical studies.

The function in equation (3.23) is called the **Cobb-Douglas production function**, named after the economist and US Senator Paul Douglas, who apparently teamed up with a mathematician named Cobb. It is easy to show that the Cobb-Douglas production function satisfies constant returns to scale. (Multiply K and L each by 2 and see what happens to Y.) In terms of real GDP and capital per worker, y and k, the Cobb-Douglas production function is:

$$
\begin{aligned}
y &= Y/L \\
&= AK^{\alpha}L^{1-\alpha} \cdot (1/L) \\
&= AK^{\alpha}L^{1-\alpha} \cdot L^{-1} \\
&= AK^{\alpha}L^{-\alpha} \\
&= A \cdot (K/L)^{\alpha} \\
y &= Ak^{\alpha}
\end{aligned}
\tag{3.24}
$$

We can show using calculus that the exponent α that appears in the Cobb-Douglas production function in equation (3.23) satisfies equation (3.20):

$$
\alpha = (MPK \cdot K)/Y
\tag{3.20}
$$

To verify this result, recall that MPK is the effect on Y from a change in K, while holding fixed A and L. If we take the derivative of $Y = AK^{\alpha}L^{1-\alpha}$ with respect to K, for given A and L, we get:

$$
\begin{aligned}
MPK &= dY/dK \\
&= \alpha AK^{\alpha-1}L^{1-\alpha} \\
&= \alpha AK^{\alpha}K^{-1}L^{1-\alpha} \\
&= \alpha AK^{\alpha}L^{1-\alpha} \cdot (1/K) \\
&= \alpha \cdot (Y/K)
\end{aligned}
$$

Therefore, we have:

$$
\begin{aligned}
(MPK \cdot K)/Y &= [\alpha \cdot (Y/K) \cdot K]/Y \\
&= \alpha
\end{aligned}
$$

as in equation (3.20).

4 Working with the Solow growth model

Now that we have constructed the Solow growth model, we can put it into action by seeing how various economic changes affect growth in the short and long run. We begin by studying variations in the saving rate, the technology level, the level of labour input and the population growth rate. Then we explore convergence, or a tendency for poor countries to catch up to rich ones.

We found in the Solow model that the growth rate of capital per worker, $\Delta k/k$, was given from equation (3.16). We repeat this key equation here:

$$\Delta k/k = s \bullet (y/k) - s\delta - n \tag{4.1}$$

where k is capital per worker, y is real gross domestic product (real GDP) per worker, y/k is the average product of capital, s is the saving rate, δ is the depreciation rate and n is the population growth rate. We assumed that everything on the right-hand side was constant except for y/k. We found that, in the transition to the steady state, the rise in k led to a fall in y/k and, hence, to a fall in $\Delta k/k$. In the steady state, k was constant and, therefore, y/k was constant. Hence, $\Delta k/k$ was constant and equal to zero.

The production function in per-worker form was given in equation (3.2). We repeat this equation here:

$$y = A \bullet f(k) \tag{4.2}$$

If we substitute for y from equation (4.2) into equation (4.1), we get a revised version of the basic Solow equation:

$$\Delta k/k = sA \bullet f(k)/k - s\delta - n \tag{4.3}$$

Up to now, we assumed that the saving rate, s, the technology level, A, and the population growth rate, n, were fixed. Now we allow for changes in s, A and n. We also consider changes in the level of labour input, L. We analyze the effects of these changes on the two phases of the Solow model. What are the effects on the transition to the steady state, and what are the effects on the steady state? We can think of the first part as representing the short-run effects and the second part as representing the long-run effects.

A change in the saving rate

How do differences in the saving rate, s, affect economic growth? As an example of differences in saving rates, we can compare nations in which the residents regularly save at a high rate – such as Singapore and South Korea, or certain other East Asian countries – with places in which the residents typically save at a low rate – such as most countries in sub-Saharan Africa or Latin America. Some of the differences in saving rates result from government policies and some may stem from cultural differences. The important point is that saving rates differ across societies and over time.

Figure 4.1 extends the Solow model from Figure 3.9 to consider two saving rates, s_1 and s_2, where s_2 is greater than s_1. Each saving rate determines a different curve for $s \bullet (y/k)$ – the one with s_2 lies above that for s_1. Recall that the growth rate of capital per worker, $\Delta k/k$, equals the vertical distance between the $s \bullet (y/k)$ curve and the horizontal line, $s\delta + n$. There are also two positions for this horizontal line, one for s_1 and the other for s_2. However, this shift in the horizontal line turns out to be minor. Therefore, we can see from Figure 4.1 that $\Delta k/k$ is higher at any capital per worker, k, when the saving rate is s_2 rather than s_1.[1] Specifically, at $k(0)$, $\Delta k/k$ is higher when the saving rate is s_2, rather than s_1. (We have assumed that $\Delta k/k$ is greater than zero for both saving rates.)

For either saving rate, the growth rate of capital per worker, $\Delta k/k$, declines as capital per worker, k, rises above $k(0)$. When the saving rate is s_1, $\Delta k/k$ reaches zero when k attains the steady-state value k_1^* in Figure 4.1. However, at k_1^*, $\Delta k/k$ would still be greater than zero if the saving rate were higher – for example, if it equalled s_2. If the saving rate is s_2, capital per worker, k, rises beyond k_1^* until it reaches the higher steady-state value, k_2^*. Since capital per worker is higher, we also know that real GDP per worker is greater when the saving rate is s_2; that is, $y_2^* > y_1^*$.

Figure 4.1 Effect of an increase in the saving rate in the Solow model

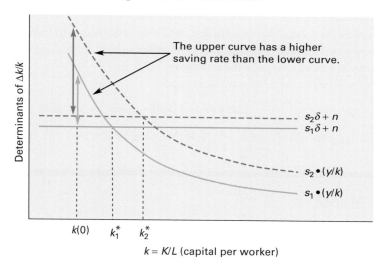

This graph comes from Figure 3.9. The curves for $s \bullet (y/k)$ are for the saving rates s_1 and s_2, where s_2 is greater than s_1. Similarly, the horizontal lines for $s\delta + n$ are for the saving rates s_1 and s_2. The growth rate of capital per worker, $\Delta k/k$, is higher at any k when the saving rate is higher. For example, at $k(0)$, when the saving rate is s_1, $\Delta k/k$ equals the vertical distance shown by the light blue arrows. When the saving rate is s_2, $\Delta k/k$ equals the vertical distance shown by the dark blue arrows. In the steady state, $\Delta k/k$ is zero, regardless of the saving rate. The higher saving rate yields a higher steady-state capital per worker; that is, k_2^* is greater than k_1^*.

Do the Maths

We can determine the steady-state capital per worker, k^*, algebraically from the steady-state condition given in equation (3.19). We repeat this result here:

$$A \bullet f(k^*)/k^* = \delta + n/s \qquad (4.4)$$

An increase in s lowers the right-hand side. Hence, the left-hand side must be lower, and this reduction can occur only through a decrease in the average product of capital, $A \bullet f(k^*)/k^*$. We know from Figure 3.8 that, if A is fixed, a decrease in the average product of capital requires an increase in capital per worker, k. Therefore, an increase in s raises k^*.

[1] The rise in the $s \bullet (y/k)$ curve is greater than the increase in the $s\delta + n$ line as long as $y/k > \delta$; that is, as long as real GDP per worker, y, is greater than depreciation per worker, δk. Thus, we need only to be sure that the net domestic product is greater than zero, as is surely the case.

To summarize, in the short run, an increase in the saving rate raises the growth rate of capital per worker. This growth rate remains higher during the transition to the steady state. In the long run, the growth rate of capital per worker is the same – zero – for any saving rate. In this long-run or steady-state situation, a higher saving rate leads to higher steady-state capital per worker, k^*, not to a change in the growth rate (which remains at zero).

One important extension of the Solow model – carried out in the mid-1960s by David Cass (1965) and Tjalling Koopmans (1965) – allowed households to choose the saving rate, s. To study this choice, we need the microeconomic analysis of how households determine consumption at different points in time. We defer this analysis to Chapter 8.

A change in the technology level

We have assumed, thus far, that the technology level, A, was fixed. In reality, technology varies over time and across locations. For examples of improvements in technology over time, we can think of the introductions of electric power, cars, computers and the Internet. For differences across locations, we can think of businesses in advanced economies, such as the United States and Western Europe, as having better access to leading technologies than their counterparts in poor countries. To assess the influences from differences in technologies, we begin by considering the effects in the Solow model from a change in the technology level, A.

The formula for the growth rate of capital per worker is again:

$$\Delta k/k = sA \bullet f(k)/k - s\delta - n \tag{4.3}$$

where $A \bullet f(k)/k$ is the average product of capital, y/k. Note that a higher A means that y/k is higher at a given k.

Extending the Model
Consumption in the Solow model

Recall that real income equals real net domestic product, $Y - \delta K$, which equals consumption, C, plus saving, $s \bullet (Y - \delta K)$. Therefore, in terms of quantities per worker, we have:

$$y - \delta k = c + s \bullet (y - \delta k)$$

where c is consumption per worker. An increase in the saving rate, s, means that c must fall for given $y - \delta k$. However, since higher saving leads in the long run to higher real GDP, consumption may increase in the long run. Here, we consider what the Solow model says about the effect of saving on consumption in the long run.

We found that an increase in the saving rate, s, raises the steady-state capital and real GDP per worker, k^* and y^*. The rise in real GDP per worker leads to an increase in the typical person's real income. However, people care about their consumption, not their income *per se*. Thus, we want to know how a rise in the saving rate affects steady-state consumption per person.

Consumption per person is given by:

consumption per person = (consumption per worker) × (workers/population)

The ratio of workers to population is the labour-force participation rate, which we have assumed to be constant. Therefore, consumption per person always moves along with consumption per worker, c. This result means that we can focus on c to see what happens to consumption per person.

Since consumption equals the real income not saved, and saving per worker in the steady state is $s \bullet (y^* - \delta k^*)$, we have:

$$c^* = y^* - \delta k^* - s \bullet (y^* - \delta k^*) \tag{4.5}$$

where c^* is the steady-state value of c. We also know from Chapter 3 that steady-state saving per worker is just enough to provide new workers with capital to work with:

$$s \bullet (y^* - \delta k^*) = nk^* \tag{3.17}$$

Therefore, we can substitute nk^* for $s \bullet (y^* - \delta k^*)$ on the right-hand side of equation (4.5) to get:

$$c^* = y^* - \delta k^* - nk^* \tag{4.6}$$

We know that a rise in the saving rate, s, raises k^*, say, by the amount δk^*. The change in c^* follows from equation (4.6) as:

$$\Delta c^* = \Delta y^* - (\delta + n) \bullet \Delta k^*$$

We can compute Δy^* by noting that it must equal Δk^* multiplied by the marginal product of capital, MPK:

$$\Delta y^* = MPK \bullet \Delta k^*$$

Therefore, if we substitute $MPK \bullet \Delta k^*$ for Δy^*, we get that the change in c^* is given by:

$$\Delta c^* = MPK \bullet \Delta k^* - (\delta + n) \bullet \Delta k^*$$
$$\Delta c^* = (MPK - \delta - n) \bullet \Delta k^* \tag{4.7}$$

We see from equation (4.7) that Δc^* is greater than zero if MPK is greater than $\delta + n$. The part $MPK - \delta$ is the net marginal product of capital; that is, the MPK net of depreciation. This term gives the rate of return on additional capital. Hence, equation (4.7) says that an increase in steady-state capital per worker, k^*, raises steady-state consumption per worker, c^*, as long as the rate of return on capital, $MPK - \delta$, is greater than the population growth rate, n. Typical estimates of rates of return on capital are around 10%, whereas population growth rates are around 0–2%. Therefore, in normal circumstances, Δc^* is greater than zero.[2]

The positive effect of the saving rate, s, on steady-state consumption per worker, c^*, and, therefore, on steady-state consumption per person, does not necessarily mean that the typical person is better off by saving more. In order to achieve the higher steady-state capital per worker, k^*, households have to save more during the transition to the steady state. Hence, levels of consumption per person during part of the transition have to be reduced. Thus, there is a trade-off – less consumption per person in the short run and more consumption per person in the long run. Whether the typical person is better or worse off depends on, first, how much consumption is gained in the long run in comparison with how much is lost in the short run and, second, on how patient people are about deferring consumption.

Figure 4.2 compares two levels of technology, A_1 and A_2, where A_2 is greater than A_1. Each technology level corresponds to a different curve for $s \bullet (y/k) = s A \bullet f(k)/k$. The curve with the higher technology level, A_2, lies above the other one. Notice that the positions of the two curves are similar to those in Figure 4.1, which considered two values of the saving rate, s. Hence, our analysis of effects from a change in A is similar to that for a change in s.

At the initial capital per worker, $k(0)$, in Figure 4.2, the growth rate of capital per worker, $\Delta k/k$, is higher with the higher technology level, A_2, than with the lower one, A_1. In both cases, $\Delta k/k$ declines over time. For the lower technology level, $\Delta k/k$ falls to zero when capital per worker, k, attains the steady-state value k_1^*. For the higher technology level, k rises beyond k_1^* to reach the higher steady-state value k_2^*. Thus, an increase in A results in a higher $\Delta k/k$ over the transition period. In the long run, $\Delta k/k$ still falls to zero, but the steady-state capital per worker, k^*, is higher. That is, k_2^* is greater than k_1^*.

[2]Caselli and Feyrer (2007) provide estimates of the marginal product of capital from around 7% for poor countries and 8% for rich countries. Their estimates adjust the marginal product of capital across countries for differences in the relative price of goods.

Figure 4.2 Effect of an increase in the technology level in the Solow model

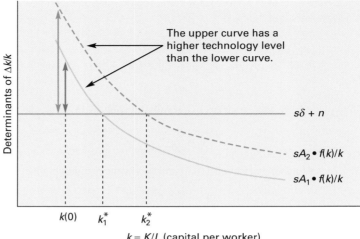

This graph comes from Figure 3.9. The two curves for $s \cdot (y/k) = sA \cdot f(k)/k$ are for the technology levels A_1 and A_2, where A_2 is greater than A_1. The growth rate of capital per worker, $\Delta k/k$, is higher at any k when the technology level is higher. For example, at $k(0)$, when the technology level is A_1, $\Delta k/k$ equals the vertical distance shown by the shorter arrows. When the technology level is A_2, $\Delta k/k$ equals the vertical distance shown by the longer arrows. In the steady state, $\Delta k/k$ is zero, regardless of the technology level. The higher technology level yields a higher steady-state capital per worker; that is k_2^*, is greater than k_1^*.

Do the Maths

We can derive the effect of A on k^* algebraically from the condition we used before:

$$A \cdot (k^*)/k^* = \delta + n/s \tag{4.4}$$

An increase in A does not affect the right-hand side. Therefore, the steady-state capital per worker, k^*, must adjust on the left-hand side to keep the steady-state average product of capital, $A \cdot f(k^*)/k^*$, the same. Since the increase in A raises this average product, k^* must change in a way that reduces the average product. As we know from Figure 3.8, a reduction in the average product of capital requires a rise in k^*. Therefore, an increase in A raises k^*.

An increase in the technology level, A, raises the steady-state real GDP per worker, $y^* = A \cdot f(k^*)$, for two reasons. First, an increase in A raises real GDP per worker, y, for given capital per worker, k. Second, the steady-state capital per worker, k^*, is higher when A is higher. On both counts, an increase in A raises y^*.

To summarize, in the short run, an increase in the technology level, A, raises the growth rates of capital and real GDP per worker. These growth rates remain higher during the transition to the steady state. In the long run, the growth rates of capital and real GDP per worker are the same – zero – for any technology level. In this long-run or steady-state situation, a higher technology level leads to higher steady-state capital and real GDP per worker, k^* and y^*, not to changes in the growth rates (which remain at zero).

Changes in labour input and the population growth rate

We can consider two types of changes in labour input, L. First, L could change at a point in time because of a sudden shift in the size of the labour force. Second, a change in the population growth rate could affect the long-term time path of labour input. We begin with a one-time change in L.

A CHANGE IN LABOUR INPUT

Changes in labour input, L, can result from shifts in the labour force. For example, the labour force could decline precipitously due to an epidemic of disease. An extreme case from the mid-1300s is the bubonic plague, or Black Death, which is estimated to have killed about 20% of the European population. The potential loss of life due to the AIDS epidemic in Africa may be analogous and, more recently, the outbreak of the Ebola virus. In these examples, physical capital does not change initially, and the starting capital per worker, $k(0) = K(0)/L(0)$, rises because of the drop in $L(0)$.

Wartime casualties are another source of decrease in the labour force. However, since wartime tends also to destroy physical capital, the effect on capital per worker depends on the circumstances. Migration can also change the labour force. One recent example is the massive influx of refugees from Syria, Iraq, Afghanistan and other war-torn countries into Europe starting in 2015. Another case is the large in-migration to Portugal in the mid-1970s by its citizens who had been residing in African colonies. When these colonies became independent, many residents returned to Portugal, and this inflow raised the domestic Portuguese population by about 10%. Finally, in Israel in the 1990s, the roughly 1 000 000 Russian Jewish immigrants constituted about 20% of Israel's 1990 population.

Figure 3.8 showed the path of labour input, L, starting at $L(0)$ and then growing at the constant rate n. In Figure 4.3, we assume that the initial level of labour input rises from $L(0)$ to $L(0)$, while n does not change. Thus, we are considering a proportionate increase in the level of labour input, L, in each year. Since the initial stock of capital, $K(0)$, does not change, the increase in $L(0)$ decreases the initial capital per worker, $k(0) = K(0)/L(0)$.

Figure 4.4 considers the effects of an increase in the level of labour input. The rise in initial labour from $L(0)$ to $L(0)'$ reduces the initial capital per worker from $k(0)$ to $k(0)'$. However, a key point is that the curve for $s \cdot (y/k)$ and the horizontal line at $s\delta + n$ do not change. The reduction in $k(0)$ raises the initial average product

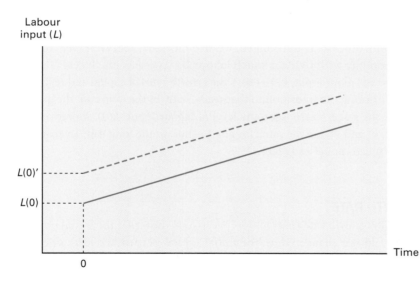

Labour input (L)

$L(0)'$

$L(0)$

0 ——— Time

Figure 4.3 An increase in the level of labour input

In year 0, labour input jumps upward from $L(0)$ to $L(0)'$. The population growth rate, n, does not change.

Do the Maths

We can again work out the steady-state results algebraically from the condition:

$$A \cdot f(k^*)/k^* = \delta + n/s \qquad (4.4)$$

Note that A, s, n and δ are constant, and the level of labour input, L, does not enter into the equation. Therefore, the steady-state capital per worker, k^*, does not change when L changes.

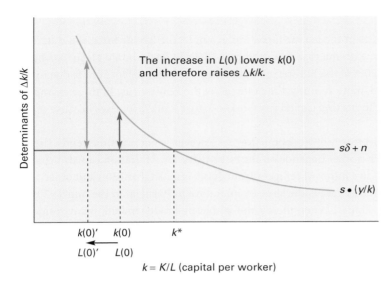

The increase in $L(0)$ lowers $k(0)$ and therefore raises $\Delta k/k$.

$s\delta + n$

$s \bullet (y/k)$

$k(0)'$ $k(0)$ k^*

$L(0)'$ $L(0)$

$k = K/L$ (capital per worker)

Figure 4.4 Effect of an increase in labour input in the Solow model

This graph comes from Figure 3.10. If the initial level of labour input rises from $L(0)$ to $L(0)'$, the initial capital per worker declines from $k(0) = K(0)/L(0)$ to $k(0)' = K(0)/L(0)'$. Therefore, the growth rate of capital per worker, $\Delta k/k$, rises initially. Note that the vertical distance shown by the arrows at $k(0)'$ is larger than that shown by the arrows at $k(0)$. The steady-state capital per worker, k^*, is the same for the two values of $L(0)$.

of capital, y/k (see Figure 3.9) and leads, thereby, to a higher $s \bullet (y/k)$ along the unchanged curve. Consequently, the growth rate of capital per worker, $\Delta k/k$, rises initially. We can see this result in Figure 4.3 because the vertical distance between the $s \bullet (y/k)$ curve and the $s\delta + n$ line is greater at $k(0)'$ than at $k(0)$. The growth rate $\Delta k/k$ remains higher during the transition to the steady state. However, $\Delta k/k$ still declines towards its long-run value of zero. Moreover, the steady-state capital per worker, k^*, is the same whether labour input starts at $L(0)'$ or $L(0)$. Thus, if $L(0)'$ is twice as large as $L(0)$, the long-run level of capital, K, is also twice as large (so that capital per worker remains the same). Since k^* is unchanged, we also have that real GDP per worker, y^*, does not change. In the long run, an economy with twice as much labour has twice as much real GDP, Y.

To summarize, in the short run, an increase in labour input, $L(0)$, raises the growth rates of capital and real GDP per worker. These growth rates remain higher during the transition to the steady state. In the long run, the growth rates of capital and real GDP per worker are the same – zero – for any level of labour input, $L(0)$. Moreover, the steady-state capital and real GDP per worker, k^* and y^*, are the same for any L. Thus, in the long run, an economy with twice as much labour input has twice as much capital and real GDP.

A CHANGE IN THE POPULATION GROWTH RATE

Figure 4.5 shows an increase in the population growth rate from n to n'. We assume now that the initial population and, hence, level of labour input, $L(0)$, do not change. Thus, the initial capital per worker, $k(0)$, does not change.

In Figure 4.6, the higher population growth rate corresponds to a higher horizontal line for $s\delta + n$. Recall that the growth rate of capital per worker, $\Delta k/k$, equals the vertical distance between the $s \bullet (y/k)$ curve and the $s\delta + n$ line. Therefore, $\Delta k/k$ is lower at any capital per worker, k, when the population growth rate is n' rather than n. We can also see this result from the formula for the growth rate of capital per worker:

$$\Delta k/k = sA \bullet f(k)/k - s\delta - n \tag{4.3}$$

A higher n lowers $\Delta k/k$ for given k. The reason that $\Delta k/k$ is lower when n is higher is that a larger portion of saving goes to providing the growing labour force, L, with capital to work with.

For either population growth rate in Figure 4.6, the growth rate of capital per worker, $\Delta k/k$, declines as capital per worker rises above $k(0)$. When the population growth rate is n', $\Delta k/k$ reaches zero when k attains the steady-state value $(k^*)'$. However, at $(k^*)'$, $\Delta k/k$ would still be greater than zero if the population growth rate were lower – in

Labour
input (*L*)

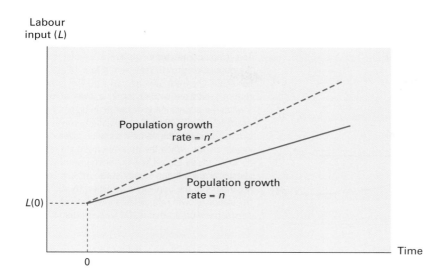

**Figure 4.5 An Increase in the
population growth rate**

The population growth rate rises in year
0 from *n* to *n'*. The initial level of labour
input, *L*(0), does not change.

particular, if it equalled *n*. Thus, if the population growth rate is *n*, capital per worker rises beyond $(k^*)'$; i.e., *k* increases until it reaches the steady-state value k^*, which is greater than $(k^*)'$.

Figure 4.6 shows that, at the initial capital per worker, $k(0)$, an increase in the population growth rate from *n* to *n'* lowers the growth rate of capital per worker, $\Delta k/k$. The growth rate of real GDP per worker, $\Delta y/y$, falls correspondingly. Thus, in the short run, a higher *n* lowers $\Delta k/k$ and $\Delta y/y$. These growth rates remain lower during the transition to the steady state. However, in the steady state, $\Delta k/k$ and $\Delta y/y$ are zero for any *n*. That is, a higher *n* leads to lower steady-state capital and real GDP per worker, k^* and y^*, not to changes in the growth rates, $\Delta k/k$ and $\Delta y/y$ (which remain at zero). A change in *n* does affect the steady-state growth rates of the levels of capital and real GDP, $\Delta K/K$ and $\Delta Y/Y$. An increase in *n* by 1% per year raises the steady-state values of $\Delta K/K$ and $\Delta Y/Y$ by 1% per year.

Do the Maths

A s usual, we can find the effect of *n* on k^* algebraically from the condition:

$$A \bullet f(k^*)/k^* = \delta + n/s \tag{4.4}$$

An increase in *n* raises the right-hand side of the equation. Hence, the steady-state average product of capital, $A \bullet f(k^*)/k^* = y^*/k^*$, has to rise on the left-hand side. Because of diminishing average product of capital (Figure 3.9), this change requires a decrease in k^*. Therefore, as we already found, an increase in *n* reduces k^*.

We can see from Figure 4.6 that an increase in the depreciation rate, δ, affects the steady-state capital per worker in the same way as an increase in the population growth rate, *n*. This result follows because equation (4.3) involves the term $s\delta + n$, which can rise either from an increase in *n* or an increase in δ. The kind of analysis that we carried out for an increase in *n* tells us that an increase in δ lowers the growth rates of capital and real GDP per worker, $\Delta k/k$ and $\Delta y/y$, in the short run. In the steady state, an increase in δ leads to lower capital and real GDP per worker, k^* and y^*, not to changes in $\Delta k/k$ and $\Delta y/y$, which remain at zero.[3]

[3]One difference is that an increase in *n* raises the steady-state growth rates of the levels of capital and real GDP, $(\Delta K/K)^*$ and $(\Delta Y/Y)^*$, whereas an increase in δ does not affect these steady-state growth rates.

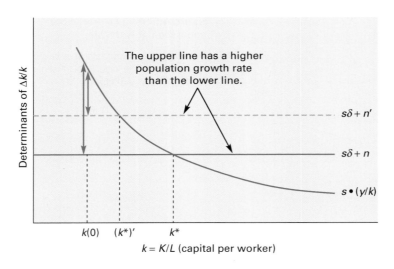

The upper line has a higher population growth rate than the lower line.

$s\delta + n'$

$s\delta + n$

$s \cdot (y/k)$

$k(0)$ $(k^*)'$ k^*

$k = K/L$ (capital per worker)

Figure 4.6 Effect of an increase in the population growth rate in the Solow model

This graph comes from Figure 3.10. An increase in the population growth rate from n to n' raises the horizontal line from $s\delta + n$ to $s\delta + n'$. The growth rate of capital per worker, $\Delta k/k$, is lower at any k when the population growth rate is higher. For example, at $k(0)$, when the population growth rate is n, $\Delta k/k$ equals the vertical distance given by the longer arrows. When the population growth rate is n', $\Delta k/k$ equals the vertical distance given by the shorter arrows. In the steady state, $\Delta k/k$ is zero, regardless of the population growth rate. A higher population growth rate yields a lower steady-state capital per worker; that is, $(k^*)'$ is less than k^*.

Convergence

One of the most important questions about economic growth is whether poor countries tend to converge or catch up to rich countries. Is there a systematic tendency for low-income countries like those in Africa to catch up to the rich OECD countries? We will start our answer to this question by seeing what the Solow model says about convergence. Then we will look at how the facts on convergence match up with the Solow model.

CONVERGENCE IN THE SOLOW MODEL

To study convergence, we focus on the transition for capital per worker, k, as it rises from its initial value, $k(0)$, to its steady-state value, k^*. In Figure 3.11, we see that k^* works like a target or magnet for k during the transition. Therefore, an important part of our analysis of convergence concerns the determination of k^*. We have studied how k^* depends on the saving rate, s, the technology level, A, the population growth rate, n, the depreciation rate, δ, and the initial level of labour input, $L(0)$. We can summarize these results in the form of a function for k^*:

$$k^* = k^*[s, A, n, \delta, L(0)]$$
$$(+)(+)(-)(-)(0)$$

(4.7)

The sign below each variable indicates its effect on k^*. Thus, equation (4.7) shows that k^* rises with s and A, falls with n and δ, and does not depend on the level of labour input, represented by $L(0)$. Table 4.1 summarizes these results.

To apply the Solow model to convergence, we have to allow for more than one economy. In making this extension, we assume that the economies are independent of each other. Specifically, they do not engage in international trade in goods and services or in financial assets. In other words, we still think of each economy as closed.

Think now of two economies, 1 and 2, and suppose that they start with capital per worker of $k(0)_1$ and $k(0)_2$, respectively, where $k(0)_1$ is less than $k(0)_2$. Each economy is assumed to have the same production function, $y = A \cdot f(k)$. Thus, economy 2 is initially more advanced in the sense of having higher capital and real GDP per worker, $k(0)$ and $y(0)$. Imagine that each economy has the same values for the determinants of k^* listed in Table 4.1, so that they have the same steady-state capital per worker, k^*.

Table 4.1 Effects on steady-state capital per worker, k^*

Increase in this variable	Effect on k^*
Saving rate, s	Increase
Technology level, A	Increase
Depreciation rate, δ	Decrease
Population growth rate, n	Decrease
Level of labour force, $L(0)$	No effect

Note: The right-hand column shows the effect of an increase in the variable in the left-hand column on the steady-state ratio of capital to labour, k^*. These results come from equation (4.7).

Extending the Model
Endogenous population growth

Our analysis treated the population growth rate, n, as exogenous – determined outside the model. However, since the writings of Thomas Malthus (1798), economists have argued that population growth responds to economic variables. Malthus was a British economist and minister who wrote his *Essay on Population* in 1798. He argued that an increase in real income per person raised population growth by improving life expectancy, mainly through better nutrition but also through improved sanitation and medical care. Another influence, Malthus believed, was that higher income encouraged greater fertility. He thought that birth rates would rise as long as real income per person exceeded a **subsistence level**, which is the amount needed to pay for the basic necessities of life.

We can incorporate Malthus's ideas about population growth into the Solow model. In Figure 3.10, for a given population growth rate, n, the economy approaches a steady-state capital per worker, k^*, and a corresponding real NDP per worker, $y^* = A \bullet f(k^*) - \delta k^*$, which equals real national income per worker. The real income per person is then:

$$real\ income\ per\ person = (real\ NDP\ per\ worker) \times (workers/population)$$

The last term on the right-hand side is the labour-force participation rate, which we assume to be fixed.

When household real income per person rose above the subsistence level, Malthus believed that the population growth rate would rise. Figure 4.6 showed the effect of a rise in the population growth rate; this change lowered the steady-state capital and real GDP per worker. According to Malthus, this process would continue until the steady-state real income per person fell to the subsistence level.

Malthus's view on the relation between real income per person and life expectancy is reasonable. Data across countries show that higher real GDP per person matches up closely with higher life expectancy at birth.[4] However, Malthus's idea about fertility seems unreasonable. At least in the cross-country data since 1960, higher real GDP per person matches up with lower fertility.[5] In fact, this relation is so strong that higher real GDP per person matches up with a lower population growth rate, even though countries with higher real GDP per person have higher life expectancy.

We can modify the Solow model to include Malthus's idea that population growth is endogenous. However, contrary to Malthus, we should assume a negative effect of real GDP per person – and, hence, of capital per worker, k – on the population growth rate, n.

[4]Although this relation is suggestive, it does not prove that the causation is from higher real income per person to greater life expectancy, rather than the reverse. In fact, both directions of causation seem to be important.
[5]This relation does not prove that the causation is from higher real income per person to lower fertility, rather than the reverse. In fact, the reverse effect is predicted by the Solow model. If a society chooses, perhaps for cultural reasons, to have higher fertility and population growth, the model predicts lower steady-state real GDP per worker. In practice, both directions of causation seem to be important.

The condition for the growth rate of capital per worker is again:

$$\Delta k/k = sA \bullet f(k)/k - s\delta - n \tag{4.3}$$

During the transition to the steady state, a rise in k reduced the average product of capital, y/k, and thereby decreased the growth rate of capital per worker, $\Delta k/k$. Now we have that a rise in k also lowers n. This change raises $\Delta k/k$ and, thus, offsets the effect from a reduced average product of capital. Hence, a declining population growth rate is one reason why rich societies can sustain growing capital and real GDP per worker for a long time.

We show this situation in Figure 4.7, which has been adapted from Figure 3.10. The only difference between the two economies is that one starts at $k(0)_1$ and the other at $k(0)_2$. Therefore, the differences in the transition paths of k depend only on the differences in these starting values. The graph in Figure 4.7 shows that the vertical distance between the $s \bullet (y/k)$ curve and the $s\delta + n$ line is greater at $k(0)_1$ than at $k(0)_2$. That is, the distance marked with arrows at $k(0)_1$ is greater than that marked with arrows at $k(0)_2$. Therefore, the growth rate of capital per worker, $\Delta k/k$, is higher initially for economy 1 than economy 2. Because k grows at a faster rate in economy 1, its level of k converges over time towards economy 2's level.

Figure 4.8 shows the transition paths of capital per worker, k, for economies 1 and 2. Note that $k(0)_1$ is less than $k(0)_2$, but k_1 gradually approaches k_2. (At the same time, k_1 and k_2 both gradually approach k^*.) Thus, economy 1 converges towards economy 2 in terms of the levels of k.

We can express the results in terms of real GDP per worker, y. The capital per worker, k, determines y from the production function:

$$y = A \bullet f(k) \tag{4.2}$$

Since economy 1 starts with lower capital per worker, $k(0)$, it must also start with lower real GDP per worker – $y(0)_1$ is less than $y(0)_2$. The growth rate of real GDP per worker relates to the growth rate of capital per worker from equation (3.8), which we repeat:

$$\Delta y/y = \alpha \bullet (\Delta k/k) \tag{4.8}$$

where α is the capital-share coefficient. (We assume that α is the same in the two economies.) We showed in Figure 4.7 that $\Delta k/k$ was higher initially in economy 1 than in economy 2. Therefore, $\Delta y/y$ is also higher initially in economy 1. Hence, economy 1's real GDP per worker, y, converges over time towards economy 2's real GDP per worker. The transition paths for y in the two economies look like those shown for k in Figure 4.8.

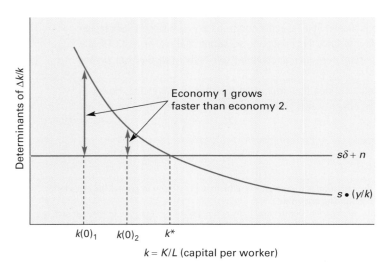

Figure 4.7 Convergence in the Solow model

This graph comes from Figure 3.10. Economy 1 starts with lower capital per worker than economy 2 – $k(0)_1$ is less than $k(0)_2$. Economy 1 grows faster initially because the vertical distance between the $s \bullet (y/k)$ curve and the $s\delta + n$ line is greater at $k(0)_1$ than at $k(0)_2$. That is, the distance marked by the arrows at $k(0)_1$ is greater than that marked by the arrows at $k(0)_2$. Therefore, capital per worker in economy 1, k_1, converges over time towards that in economy 2, k_2.

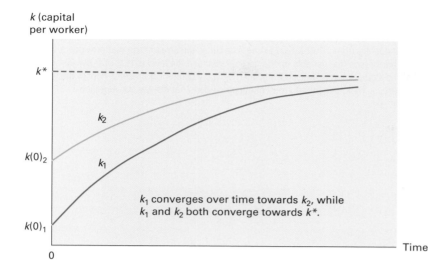

k (capital per worker)

Figure 4.8 Convergence and transition paths for two economies

Economy 1 starts at capital per worker $k(0)_1$ and economy 2 starts at $k(0)_2$, where $k(0)_1$ is less than $k(0)_2$. The two economies have the same steady-state capital per worker, k^*, shown by the dashed line. In each economy, k rises over time towards k^*. However, k grows faster in economy 1 because $k(0)_1$ is less than $k(0)_2$ (see Figure 4.7). Therefore, k converges over time towards k_2.

k_1 converges over time towards k_2, while k_1 and k_2 both converge towards k^*.

To summarize, the Solow model says that a poor economy – with low capital and real GDP per worker – grows faster than a rich one. The reason is the diminishing average product of capital, y/k. A poor economy, such as economy 1 in Figure 4.7, has the advantage of having a high average product of capital, y/k. This high average product explains why the growth rates of capital and real GDP per worker are higher than in the initially more advanced economy, economy 2. Thus, the Solow model predicts that poorer economies tend to converge over time towards richer ones in terms of the levels of capital and real GDP per worker.

FACTS ABOUT CONVERGENCE

The main problem with these predictions about convergence is that they conflict with the evidence for a broad group of countries. We have already seen, in Figure 3.3, growth rates of real GDP per person from 1960 to 2011. To apply the Solow model to these data, we have to translate from amounts per worker to amounts per person. The formula for real GDP per person is again:

$$real\ GDP\ per\ person = (real\ GDP\ per\ worker) \bullet (workers/population)$$

The ratio of workers to population is the labour-force participation rate, which we have assumed to be constant. For example, if the ratio is around one-half, as in recent OECD country experience, real GDP per person is about one-half of real GDP per worker.

With this translation, we find that the Solow model predicts convergence for real GDP per person. Specifically, the model predicts that a lower level of real GDP per person would match up with a higher subsequent growth rate of real GDP per person.

Figure 4.9 uses the data for countries from Figure 3.3 to plot growth rates of real GDP per person from 1960 to 2011 against levels of real GDP per person in 1960. If the convergence predictions from the Solow model were correct, we should find low levels of real GDP per person matched with high growth rates, and high levels of real GDP per person matched with low growth rates. Instead, it is difficult to discern any pattern in the data – if anything, there is a slight tendency for the growth rate to rise with the level of real GDP per person.

The sample of countries included in Figure 4.9 is very broad; it includes the richest and poorest economies in the world. The convergence prediction of the Solow model accords better with the data if we limit the observations to economies that have more similar economic and social characteristics. Figure 4.10 is the same as Figure 4.9, except that the sample is limited to 28 of the 34 OECD countries with available data for 1960. For this limited sample, lower levels of real GDP per person in 1960 do match up, on average, with higher growth rates from 1960 to 2011. This pattern reflects especially the catching up of some of the initially poorer OECD countries – Greece, Ireland, Portugal and Spain – to the richer ones.

Figure 4.9 Growth rate versus level of real GDP per person for a broad group of countries

The horizontal axis shows real GDP per person in 1960 in 2005 US dollars on a proportionate scale for 107 countries. The vertical axis shows the growth rate of real GDP per person for each country from 1960 to 2011. The blue line is the straight line that provides a best fit to the relation between the growth rate of real GDP per person (the variable on the vertical axis) and the level of real GDP per person (on the horizontal axis). Although this line slopes upward, the slope is – in a statistical sense – negligibly different from zero. Hence, the growth rate is virtually unrelated to the level of real GDP per person. Thus, this broad group of countries does not display convergence.

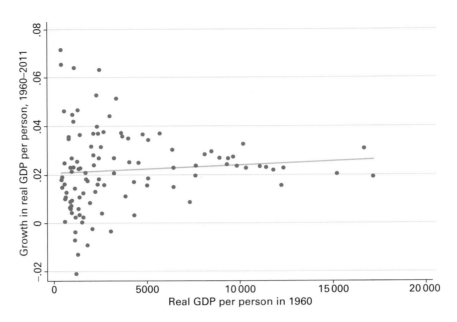

Figure 4.10 Growth rate versus level of real GDP per person for OECD countries

The horizontal axis shows real GDP per person in 1960 in 2005 US dollars on a proportionate scale for 28 of the current 34 members of OECD. The abbreviation identifies each country. The vertical axis shows the growth rate of real GDP per person for each country from 1960 to 2011. The blue line is the straight line that provides a best fit to the relation between the growth rate of real GDP per person (the variable on the vertical axis) and the level of real GDP per person (on the horizontal axis). The line has a clear negative slope – therefore, a lower level of real GDP per person in 1960 matches up with a higher growth rate of real GDP per person from 1960 to 2011. Thus, the group of OECD countries exhibit convergence.

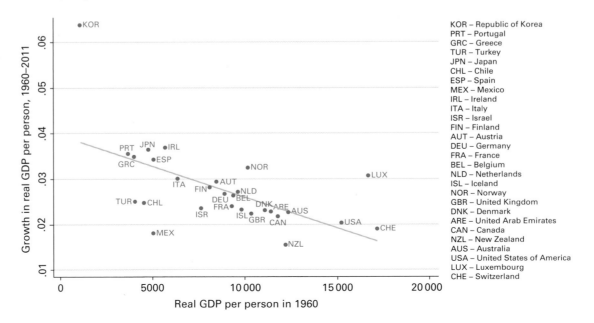

Figure 4.11 shows an even clearer pattern of convergence for a still more homogeneous group of economies – 19 members of the European Union as of 2015 with data going back to 1960. The figure again plots growth rates of real GDP per person against real GDP per person in 1960. This graph shows a dramatic tendency for the initially poorer countries in the European Union (and its predecessors) to grow faster than the initially richer ones.

Figures 4.9 to 4.11 tell us that similar economies tend to converge, whereas dissimilar economies display no relationship between the level of real GDP per person and the growth rate. Thus, the convergence pattern is strongest for advanced economies within a common region (Figure 4.11), next strongest among a group of rich countries (Figure 4.10), and weakest – in fact, absent – for the full worldwide sample of countries (Figure 4.9).

Figure 4.11 Growth rate versus level of real GDP per person for countries of europe

The horizontal axis shows real GDP per person in 1960 for 19 of the current 28 members of the European Union. The vertical axis shows the growth rate of real personal income per person for each country from 1960 to 2011. The solid line is the straight line that provides a best fit to the relation between the growth rate of real GDP per person (the variable on the vertical axis) and the level of real GDP per person (on the horizontal axis). The line has a clear negative slope – therefore, a lower level of real GDP per person in 1960 matches up with a higher growth rate of income per person from 1960 to 2011. Thus, the members of the European Union exhibit convergence.

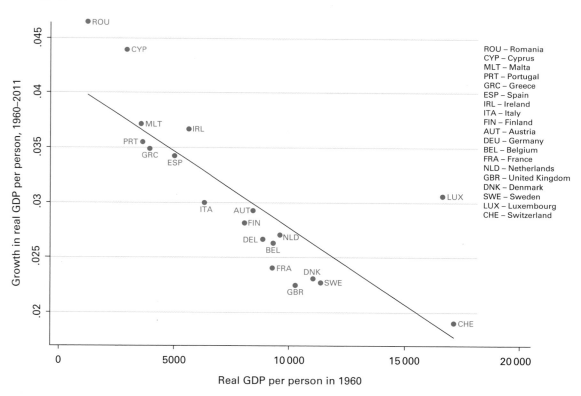

CONDITIONAL CONVERGENCE IN THE SOLOW MODEL

The Solow model's prediction of convergence seems to explain growth patterns in similar economies, and it seems to fail when we examine a dissimilar array of economies. Do these findings mean that the model is flawed? Are there changes we can make to improve its predictions?

To find the flaw and try to correct it, let's re-examine the Solow model. One key assumption was that the determinants of the steady-state capital per worker, k^*, were the same for all economies. This assumption is reasonable for similar economies but is less plausible for a broad sample of countries with sharply different economic, political and social characteristics. In particular, the assumption is unreasonable for the worldwide sample of countries considered in Figure 4.9. To explain the lack of convergence for this group, we have to allow for differences in the steady-state positions, k^*.

Suppose that countries differ with respect to some of the determinants of k^* in equation (4.7) and Table 4.1. For example, k^* could vary because of differences in saving rates, s, levels of technology, A, and population growth rates, n.[6] Figure 4.12 modifies Figure 4.7 to show how differences in saving rates affect convergence. Economy 1 has the saving rate s_1, and economy 2 has the higher saving rate s_2. We assume, as in Figure 4.7, that economy 1 has lower initial capital per worker; that is, $k(0)_1$ is less than $k(0)_2$. Remember that the growth rate of capital per worker, $\Delta k/k$, equals the vertical distance between the $s \cdot (y/k)$ curve and the $s\delta + n$ line. We see from Figure 4.12 that it is uncertain whether the distance between the $s \cdot (y/k)$ curve and the $s\delta + n$ line is greater initially for economy 1 or economy 2. The lower capital per worker, $k(0)$, tends to make the distance greater for economy 1, but the lower saving rate, s, tends to make the distance smaller for economy 1. In the graph, these two forces roughly balance, so that $\Delta k/k$ is about the same for the two economies. That is, the distance marked with the arrows at $k(0)_1$ is similar to the one marked with the arrows at $k(0)_2$. Therefore, the poorer economy, economy 1, does not necessarily converge towards the richer economy, economy 2.

To get the result in Figure 4.12, we had to assume that the economy with lower $k(0)$ – economy 1 – had a lower saving rate, s. This assumption is reasonable because an economy with a lower s has a lower steady-state capital per worker, k^*. In the long run, an economy's capital per worker, k, would be close to its steady-state value, k^*. Therefore, it is likely when we examine countries at an arbitrary date, such as date 0, that $k(0)$ will be lower in the economy with the lower s; i.e., $k(0)$ tends to be lower in economy 1 than in economy 2. Thus, the pattern that we assumed – a low saving rate matched with a low $k(0)$ – is likely to apply in practice.

We get a similar result if we consider other reasons for differences in the steady-state capital per worker, k^*. Suppose that the two economies have the same saving rates but that economy 1 has a lower technology level, A, than economy 2. In this case, the two curves for $s \cdot (y/k)$ again look as shown in Figure 4.12.[7] Therefore, it is again uncertain whether the vertical distance between the $s \cdot (y/k)$ curve and the $s \delta + n$ line is greater for economy 1 or economy 2. The lower capital per worker, $k(0)$, tends to make the distance greater for economy 1, but the lower A tends to make the distance smaller for economy 1. As before, it is possible that the two forces roughly balance, so that $\Delta k/k$ is about the same for the two economies. Thus, the poorer economy, economy 1, need not converge towards the richer economy, economy 2.

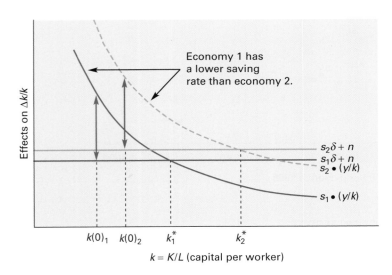

Figure 4.12 Failure of convergence in the Solow model: differences in saving rates

As in Figure 4.7, economy 1 starts with lower capital per worker than economy 2; i.e., $k(0)_1$ is less than $k(0)_2$. However, we now assume that economy 1 also has a lower saving rate; that is, s_1 is less than s_2. The two economies have the same technology levels, A, and population growth rates, n. Therefore, k_1^* is less than k_2^*. In this case, it is uncertain which economy grows faster initially. The vertical distance marked with the arrows at $k(0)_1$ may be larger or smaller than the one marked with the arrows at $k(0)_2$.

[6] Levels of population and the labour force vary greatly across countries, but the level of labour input, represented by $L(0)$, does not affect k^* in the model. The depreciation rate, δ, probably does not vary systematically across countries.
[7] In this case, unlike in Figure 4.12, the $s\delta + n$ lines are the same for the two countries.

To get this result, we had to assume that the economy with the lower starting capital per worker, $k(0)$ – economy 1 – had the lower technology level, A. This assumption is reasonable because an economy with a lower A has a lower steady-state capital per worker, k^*. Therefore, it is again likely when we look at the two economies at date 0 that $k(0)$ will be lower in economy 1 than economy 2.

The same conclusions apply if we consider differences in population growth rates. In Figure 4.13, the two economies have the same saving rates and technology levels, but economy 1 has a higher population growth rate, n. Hence, the $s\delta + n$ line is higher for economy 1. It is again uncertain whether the vertical distance between the $s \cdot (y/k)$ curve and the $s\delta + n$ line is greater for economy 1 or economy 2. The lower capital per worker, $k(0)$, for economy 1 tends to make the distance greater for economy 1, but the higher n tends to make the distance smaller for economy 1. As in our other cases, it is possible that the two forces roughly balance, so that $\Delta k/k$ would be about the same in the two economies – the distance marked with the arrows at $k(0)_1$ is similar to the one marked with the arrows at $k(0)_2$. Thus, economy 1 again need not converge towards economy 2.

To get this result, we had to assume that the economy with the lower starting capital per worker, $k(0)$ – economy 1 – had the higher population growth rate, n. This assumption makes sense because an economy with a higher n has a lower steady-state capital per worker, k^*. Therefore, it is again likely when we look at the two economies at date 0 that $k(0)$ will be lower in economy 1 than economy 2.

Now let's generalize the conclusions from our three cases. In each case, economy 1 had a characteristic – lower saving rate, s, lower technology level, A, higher population growth rate, n – that led to a lower steady-state capital per worker, k^*. For a given starting capital per worker, $k(0)$, each of the three characteristics tended to make economy 1's initial growth rate less than economy 2's initial growth rate. We see these effects in Figures 4.12 and 4.13. At a given $k(0)$, the vertical distance between the $s \cdot (y/k)$ curve and the $s\delta + n$ line is smaller if s or A is lower or if n is higher.

Since economy 1 has lower k^*, it is also likely to have lower initial capital per worker, $k(0)$. The lower $k(0)$ tends to make economy 1 grow faster than economy 2 – the convergence force shown in Figure 4.7. Whether economy 1 grows faster or slower overall than economy 2 depends on the offset of two forces. The lower $k(0)$ generates faster growth in economy 1, but the lower k^* generates slower growth in economy 1. It is possible that the two forces roughly balance, so that the two economies grow at about the same rate. That is, we need not find convergence.

Figure 4.14 shows the transition paths of capital per worker, k, for the two economies. We assume that economy 1 starts with a lower capital per worker – $k(0)_1$ is less than $k(0)_2$ – and also has a lower steady-state capital per worker – k_1^* is less than k_2^*. The graph shows that capital per worker in each economy converges towards its own steady-state level – k_1 towards k_1^*, and k_2 towards k_2^*. However, since k_1^* is less than k_2^*, k_1 does not converge towards k_2.

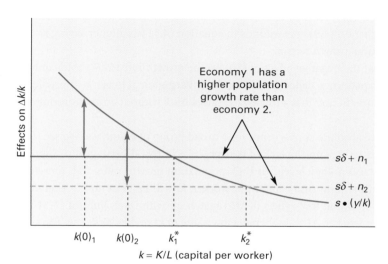

Figure 4.13 Failure of convergence in the Solow model: Differences in population growth rates

As in Figure 4.12, economy 1 starts with lower capital per worker than economy 2; i.e., $k(0)_1$ is less than $k(0)_2$. The two economies now have the same saving rates, s, and technology levels, A, but economy 1 has a higher population growth rate, n; that is, n_1 is greater than n_2. Therefore, as in Figure 4.12, k_1^* is less than k_2^*. It is again uncertain which economy grows faster initially. The vertical distance marked with the arrows at $k(0)_1$ may be larger or smaller than the one marked with the arrows at $k(0)_2$.

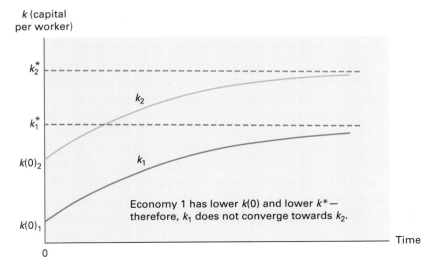

k (capital per worker)

Economy 1 has lower k(0) and lower k*— therefore, k_1 does not converge towards k_2.

Figure 4.14 Failure of convergence and transition paths for two economies

As in Figures 4.12 and 4.13, economy 1 has a lower starting capital per worker (i.e., $k(0)_1$ is less than $k(0)_2$) and also has a lower steady-state capital per worker; i.e., k_1^* is less than k_2^*. Each capital per worker converges over time towards its own steady-state value: k_1 towards k_1^*, and k_2 towards k_2^*. However, since k_1^* is less than k_2^*, k_1 does not converge towards k_2.

We can summarize our findings for the growth rate of capital per worker in an equation:

Key equation (conditional convergence in the Solow model):

$$\Delta k/k = \varphi[k(0), k^*]$$
$$(-) \ (+)$$

(4.9)

growth rate of capital per worker = function of initial and steady-state capital per worker

The function φ indicates how $\Delta k/k$ depends on the initial capital per worker, $k(0)$, and the steady-state capital per worker, k^*. The minus sign under $k(0)$ signifies that, for given k^*, a decrease in $k(0)$ raises $\Delta k/k$. The plus sign under k^* means that, for given $k(0)$, a rise in k^* increases $\Delta k/k$.

We can interpret the effects in equation (4.9) from the perspective of our equation for the growth rate of capital per worker:

$$\Delta k/k = sA \bullet f(k)/k - s\delta - n$$

(4.3)

The negative effect of $k(0)$ in equation (4.9) corresponds in equation (4.3) to a lower initial average product of capital, $A \bullet f(k)/k$. The positive effect of k^* in equation (4.9) corresponds in equation (4.3) to a higher saving rate, s, a higher technology level, A, or a lower population growth rate, n.

One important result in equation (4.9) is that the negative effect of $k(0)$ on the growth rate, $\Delta k/k$, holds only in a conditional sense; that is, for a given k^*. This pattern is called **conditional convergence**: a lower $k(0)$ predicts a higher $\Delta k/k$, conditional on k^*. In contrast, the prediction that a lower $k(0)$ raises $\Delta k/k$ without any conditioning is called **absolute convergence**.

Recall from Figure 4.9 that we do not observe absolute convergence for a broad group of countries. We see from equation (4.9) that we can use the Solow model to explain the lack of convergence in this diverse group. Suppose that some countries have low saving rates, low technology levels, or high population growth rates and, therefore, have low steady-state capital per worker, k^*. In the long run, capital per worker, k, will be close to k^*. Therefore, when we look at date 0 (say, 1960), we tend to find that low values of $k(0)$ match up with low values of k^*. A low value of $k(0)$ makes the growth rate of capital per worker, $\Delta k/k$, high, but a low value of k^* makes $\Delta k/k$ low. Thus, the data may show little relation between $k(0)$ and $\Delta k/k$. This pattern is consistent with the one found in Figure 4.9 for growth rates and levels of real GDP per person.

Where do we stand with the Solow model?

When we first considered convergence, we observed that the lack of absolute convergence for a broad group of countries, as in Figure 4.9, was a failing of the Solow model. Then we found that an extension of the model to consider conditional convergence explained this apparent failure. We show in Chapter 5 that conditional convergence allows us to understand many other features of economic growth in the world.

Although the Solow model has many strengths, we should be clear about what the model does not explain. Most important is the failure to explain how real GDP per person grows in the long run – for example, at a rate of about 2% per year for well over a century in many developed countries. In the model, capital per worker – and, hence, real GDP per worker and per person – are constant in the long run. Thus, a key objective of Chapter 5 is to extend the model to explain long-run economic growth.

Key Terms and Concepts

absolute convergence	conditional convergence	convergence	subsistence level

Questions and Problems

A   Review questions

1   For 107 countries, Figure 4.9 shows that the growth rate of real per capita GDP from 1960 to 2011 bears little relation to the level of real GDP in 1960. Does this finding conflict with the Solow model of economic growth? How does this question relate to the concept of conditional convergence?

2   What is the meaning of the term *convergence*? How does absolute convergence differ from conditional convergence?

3   If the initial level of labour input, $L(0)$, doubles, why does the steady-state capital stock, K^*, double? That is, Figure 4.4 implies that steady-state capital per worker, k^*, does not change. How does this result depend on constant returns to scale in the production function?

4   Does population growth, $n > 0$, lead to growth of output in the long run? Does it lead to growth of output per worker in the long run?

B   Problems for discussion

5   Variations in the population growth rate
Suppose that the population growth rate, n, can vary as an economy develops.

a   The equation for the growth rate of capital per worker, k, is again given from:
$$\Delta k/k = s \bullet (y/k) - s\delta - n \qquad (4.1)$$
Is this equation still valid when n is not constant?

b   Suppose that n falls as an economy develops; that is, rich countries have lower population

growth rates than poor countries. How does this behaviour affect the results about convergence?

c   Suppose, instead, that n rises as an economy develops; that is, rich countries have higher population growth rates than poor countries. How does this behaviour affect the results about convergence?

d   Which case seems more plausible – b or c above? Explain, giving particular attention to the views of Malthus about endogenous population growth.

6   Variations in the saving rate
Suppose that the saving rate, s, can vary as an economy develops.

a   The equation for the growth rate of capital per worker, k, is given by:
$$\Delta k/k = s \bullet (y/k) - s\delta - n \qquad (4.1)$$
Is this equation still valid when s is not constant?

b   Suppose that s rises as an economy develops; that is, rich countries save at a higher rate than poor countries. How does this behaviour affect the results about convergence?

c   Suppose, instead, that s falls as an economy develops; that is, rich countries save at a lower rate than poor countries. How does this behaviour affect the results about convergence?

d   Which case seems more plausible – b or c above? Explain.

Appendix

The rate of convergence

We assess here how fast convergence takes place in the Solow model. Figure 4.15 starts by reproducing the construction from Figure 3.10. The horizontal line is again at $s\delta + n$, and the capital per worker starts at $k(0)$. The saving curve is shown in the solid curve as $s \cdot (y/k)^{\text{I}}$. The growth rate of capital per worker, $\Delta k/k$, equals the vertical distance between the $s \cdot (y/k)^{\text{I}}$ curve and the $s\delta + n$ line.

As stressed before, the source of convergence in the Solow model is the diminishing average product of capital, y/k. Recall that this average product is given by:

$$y/k = A \cdot f(k)/k$$

The tendency for the average product to fall as k increases is the reason that the $s \cdot (y/k)^{\text{I}}$ curve slopes downward. The slope of the curve determines how fast convergence occurs, and this slope will depend on the form of the function $f(k)/k$.

To understand the role of the slope of the $s \cdot (y/k)$ curve, Figure 4.15 includes a second saving curve, $s \cdot (y/k)^{\text{II}}$, shown in the dashed curve. In comparison with the first curve, the second one has the same saving rate, s, and technology level, A, but a different form of the function $f(k)/k$. This different form means that the relation between k and y/k is different for curve II than for curve I. Specifically, at any value of k, the second curve does not slope downward as much as the first one. That is, the average product of capital, y/k, diminishes less rapidly with k in the second case than in the first one.

To ease the comparison, we set up the graph so that the two saving curves intersect the $s\delta + n$ line at the same point. Hence, the steady-state capital per worker, $k^\star$, is the same in the two cases. However, at the initial capital per worker, $k(0)$, the vertical distance between the saving curve and the $s\delta + n$ line is larger in the first case than in the second. In the graph, the first distance is shown by the longer arrows, and the second distance by the shorter arrows. Therefore, at $k(0)$, $\Delta k/k$ is higher in the first case. The higher growth rate means that k converges more rapidly towards its steady-state level, $k^\star$. Hence, we have shown that the rate of convergence is higher when the average product of capital diminishes more rapidly with k.

For a given technology level, A, the relation between the average product of capital, y/k, and k depends on the form of the function $f(k)/k$. To take a concrete example, consider the Cobb-Douglas production function, introduced in the Appendix, Part C, to Chapter 3, where $f(k) = k^\alpha$. In this case, the average product of capital is:

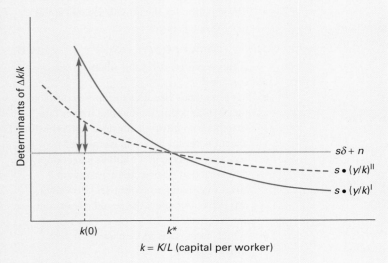

Figure 4.15 Determining the speed of convergence

This graph modifies Figure 4.4. The first saving curve, $s \cdot (y/k)^{\text{I}}$, is the same as before. The second saving curve, $s \cdot (y/k)$, does not slope downward as much as the first one. The reason is that the average product of capital, y/k, diminishes less rapidly with k in the second case. At $k(0)$, the distance between the $s \cdot (y/k)$ curve and the $s\delta + n$ line is greater in the first case (the longer arrows) than in the second (the shorter arrows). Therefore, the initial $\Delta k/k$ is higher in the first case, and the convergence to the steady state is faster. The conclusion is that convergence is faster when the average product of capital diminishes more rapidly with k.

$$y/k = A \cdot f(k)/k$$
$$= Ak^\alpha/k$$
$$= Ak^\alpha \cdot k^{-1}$$
$$= Ak^{(\alpha-1)}$$
$$y/k = Ak^{-(1-\alpha)} \tag{4.10}$$

Since $0 < \alpha < 1$, the average product of capital, y/k, falls as k rises. The value of α determines how fast y/k falls as k rises. If α is close to 1, equation (4.10) says that y/k falls slowly as k rises (curve II in Figure 4.15 is like this). If α is close to zero, y/k falls quickly as k rises (curve I is like this). Generally, the lower α is, the more quickly y/k falls as k rises.

To get a quantitative idea about the rate of convergence, consider an intermediate case in which $\alpha = 0.5$. In this case, the average product of capital is:

$$y/k = Ak^{-(1/2)}$$
$$y/k = A/\sqrt{k}$$

That is, the average product of capital declines with the square root of k.

Recall that the growth rate of k is given by:

$$\Delta k/k = s \cdot (y/k) - s\delta - n \tag{4.1}$$

If we substitute $y/k = A/\sqrt{k}$, we get:

$$\Delta k/k = sA/\sqrt{k} - s\delta - n \tag{4.11}$$

If we specify values for the saving rate, s, the technology level, A, the depreciation rate, δ, the rate of population growth, n, and the initial capital per worker, $k(0)$, we can use equation (4.11) to calculate the time path of k. Since we know $k(0)$, equation (4.11) determines k at the next point in time, $k(1)$. Then, given $k(1)$, we can use the equation to calculate $k(2)$. Proceeding in this way, we can calculate $k(t)$ at any time t.

Table 4.2 shows the solution for the path of $k(t)$. The calculations assume that the initial capital per worker, $k(0)$, is one-half of its steady-state value, k^*. The table reports the values of k/k^* and y/y^* that prevail after 5 years, 10 years, and so on. Note that it takes about 25 years – roughly a generation – to eliminate half of the initial gap between k

Table 4.2 The transition path in the Solow model

Year	k/k^*	y/y^*
0	0.50	0.71
5	0.56	0.75
10	0.61	0.78
15	0.66	0.81
20	0.71	0.84
25	0.74	0.86
30	0.78	0.88
35	0.81	0.90
40	0.83	0.91
45	0.86	0.93
50	0.88	0.94

Note: The table shows the solution of the Solow model for capital per worker, k, and real GDP per worker, y. The results are expressed as ratios to the steady-state values, k/k^* and y/y^*. The transitional behaviour of k and y comes from equation (4.11), which assumes $y = A \cdot \sqrt{k}$. The calculations assume that k/k^* starts at 0.5 and uses the values $n = 0.01$ per year and $\delta = 0.05$ per year. The values of s, A and $L(0)$ turn out not to affect the results. The initial value for k/k^* also does not matter for the speed of convergence.

and k^*. By analogy to radioactive decay in physics, we can define the time for half of the convergence to the steady state to occur as the *half-life*. Since the ratio k/k^* starts at 0.5 and the half-life of the convergence process is 25 years, the ratio reaches 0.75 in 25 years and 0.875 in 50 years. Hence, although capital per worker, k, converges towards k^*, the Solow model predicts that this process takes a long time. The same numerical results on half-lives turn out to apply to the adjustment of real GDP per worker, y, to its steady-state level, y^*.

If α is greater than 0.5, the average product of capital, y/k, declines more slowly as k rises, and the convergence to the steady state is less rapid. Therefore, the half-life is more than 25 years. Conversely, if α is less than 0.5, y/k declines more quickly as k rises, and the convergence to the steady state is more rapid. In this case, the half-life is less than 25 years.

Many interesting applications have been made for speeds of convergence and half-lives calculated from the Solow model. One implication involves the unification of Germany in 1990. The model predicts that the poor eastern parts from the formerly Communist East Germany would converge, but only slowly, to the richer western regions. (In 1990, the GDP per person of the eastern regions was about one-third that of the Western level.) This prediction for gradual convergence of real GDP per person accords with the German data for the 1990s.

5 Conditional convergence and long-run economic growth

In Chapters 3 and 4, we developed and extended the Solow model of economic growth. The most important results for short-run analysis concerned convergence during the transition to the steady state. We show in the first part of this chapter how to use these results to understand patterns of economic growth in the world.

We observed at the end of Chapter 4 that the major deficiency of the Solow model was its failure to explain long-run economic growth. In the steady state, the growth rate of real GDP per worker was zero. In the second part of this chapter, we extend the model to analyze long-run growth.

Conditional convergence in practice

We found that the Solow model predicted convergence across economies in capital per worker, k. We summarized this conclusion in an equation for the growth rate of capital per worker, $\Delta k/k$:

$$\Delta k/k = \varphi[k(0), k^*]$$
$$(-)(+)$$

(4.9)

where k^* is the steady-state value of k. For a given k^*, a lower $k(0)$ matches up with a higher $\Delta k/k$. Thus, the model has a convergence property for k. The convergence is conditional in the sense of depending on variables that affect k^*. For given $k(0)$, an increase in k^* raises $\Delta k/k$.

The production function relates real GDP per worker, y, to capital per worker, k:

$$y = A \bullet f(k)$$

(4.2)

We can use equation (4.2) in equation (4.9) to replace $\Delta k/k$ by $\Delta y/y$, $k(0)$ by $y(0)$, and k^* by y^* to get:

> Key equation (conditional convergence for real GDP per worker):
>
> $$\Delta y/y = \varphi[y(0), y^*]$$
> $$(-) (+)$$
>
> growth rate of real GDP per worker = function of initial and steady-state real GDP per worker (5.1)

Equation (5.1) shows that the Solow model determines the growth rate of real GDP per worker, $\Delta y/y$, as a function of initial real GDP per worker, $y(0)$, and steady-state real GDP per worker, y^*. For given y^*, an increase in $y(0)$ lowers $\Delta y/y$. For given $y(0)$, an increase in y^* raises $\Delta y/y$. This relation exhibits the convergence property because a poorer economy – with lower $y(0)$ – has a higher growth rate, $\Delta y/y$. However, the convergence is conditional in the sense of depending on variables that influence the steady-state position, y^*.

In our discussion in Chapter 4, we focused on three variables that influenced the steady-state capital and real GDP per worker, k^* and y^*: the saving rate, s, the technology level, A, and the population growth rate, n. Economists have extended the Solow model to allow for additional variables that affect k^* and y^*. We can understand these effects, without working through the details, by taking a broader view of the technology level, A. The important feature of a higher A is that it raises productivity; that is, it allows real GDP to rise for given inputs of capital and labour. Many variables that are not strictly technological also influence an economy's productivity. These other influences affect economic growth in ways analogous to changes in A.

As an example, productivity depends on the degree of market efficiency. Economies can enhance efficiency by removing restrictions due to government regulations, by lowering tax rates and by promoting competition, possibly through anti-trust enforcement. Another way for markets to work better, discussed in Chapter 18, is for governments to allow free trade in goods and services across international borders. This kind of international openness allows countries to specialize in the production of the goods and services in which they have natural advantages. Hence, greater international openness tends to raise world productivity. A country's legal and political system also influences its productivity; see the Economics in Practice box for a discussion of recent empirical studies. Productivity tends to rise if governments do better at enforcing property rights, if the judicial system runs more smoothly and if official corruption declines.

RECENT RESEARCH ON THE DETERMINANTS OF ECONOMIC GROWTH

Recent research has used the equation for conditional convergence, given in equation (5.1), as a framework to analyze the determinants of economic growth across countries. The idea is to measure an array of variables that influence a country's steady-state real GDP per worker, y^*. Equation (5.1) then tells us two things. First, if we hold fixed y^* (by holding fixed the variables that influence y^*), the growth rate of real GDP per worker, $\Delta y/y$, should exhibit convergence. That is, for given y^*, a lower $y(0)$ should match up with a higher $\Delta y/y$. Second, any variable that raises or lowers y^* should correspondingly raise or lower $\Delta y/y$ for given $y(0)$. In practice, because of difficulties in precisely measuring numbers of workers, most studies have measured y by real GDP per person, rather than real GDP per worker.

Figure 5.1 shows empirical results for the relation between the growth rate and level of real GDP per person. The cross-country data are for a broad group of countries and are similar to Figure 4.9.[1] However, because we are holding fixed variables that determine the steady-state real GDP per worker, y^*, the graph looks very different from before. With the other variables held constant, the convergence pattern becomes clear – low levels of real GDP per person match up with high growth rates of real GDP per person, and high levels of real GDP per person match up with low growth rates. Thus, there is evidence for conditional convergence across a broad group of countries.

The relation shown in Figure 5.1 applies when we hold constant a list of variables that influence y^*. The particular list used to construct the graph is:

- a measure of the saving rate
- the fertility rate for the typical woman (which influences population growth)
- subjective measures of maintenance of the rule of law and democracy
- the size of government, gauged by the share of government consumption purchases in GDP
- the extent of international openness, measured by the volume of exports and imports
- changes in the terms of trade (the ratio of prices of exported goods to prices of imported goods)
- measures of investment in education and health
- the average rate of inflation, which is an indicator of macroeconomic policy.

[1] One new feature is that the data are for multiple periods from 1965 to 2010. A country's real GDP per person in 1965 is matched with its growth rate of real GDP per person from 1965 to 1975; the real GDP per person in 1975 is matched with the growth rate of real GDP per person from 1975 to 1985, and so on. In Figure 4.9, a country's real GDP per person in 1960 is matched with its growth rate of real GDP per person from 1960 to 2011. Therefore, each country appears only once in this graph.

Figure 5.1 Growth rate versus level of real GDP per person: conditional convergence for a broad group of countries

The horizontal axis shows real GDP per person in 2005 US dollars. The data are for 57 countries in 1965, 62 countries in 1975, 65 countries in 1985, 69 countries in 1995 and 70 countries in 2005. (The sample was based on the availability of data.) The vertical axis shows the corresponding growth rates of GDP per capita for 1965–75, 1975–85, 1985–95, 1995–05 and 2005–10. Each of the growth rates filters out (and, therefore, holds constant) the estimated effects of the variables discussed in the text. The blue line is the straight line that provides a best fit to the relation between the growth rate of real GDP per person (the variable on the vertical axis) and the level of real GDP per person (on the horizontal axis). The line has a clear negative slope. Therefore, once we hold constant the other variables, a lower level of real GDP per person matches up with a higher growth rate of real GDP per person. This relation is called 'conditional convergence'.

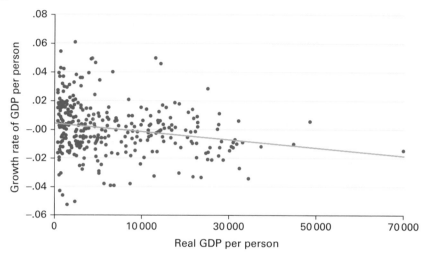

One reason that we considered these variables is to isolate conditional convergence, as shown in Figure 5.1. Equally important, however, is that we learn how the variables in the list affect economic growth. The research shows that the growth rate of real GDP per person rises in response to a higher saving rate, lower fertility, better maintenance of the rule of law, smaller government consumption purchases, greater international openness, improvement in the terms of trade, greater quantity and quality of education, better health and lower inflation.

Research on the determinants of economic growth has been lively since the early 1990s. This research has suggested numerous additional variables that influence growth. The variables considered include the scope of banking and financial markets, the degree of income inequality, the extent of official corruption, the role of colonial and legal origins, and the intensity of religious participation and beliefs. The effect of democracy on growth is also much debated in the literature. A recent empirical study by Acemoglu, Naidu, Restrepo and Robinson (2015) shows that democracy has an unambiguously positive effect on GDP per capita. In the Economics in Practice box, we discuss two other important variables: institutions and human capital.

These kinds of empirical results have raised our understanding of the determinants of economic growth, but our knowledge remains incomplete. For one thing, economists have isolated only some of the variables that influence growth. The problems relate partly to data – for example, it is difficult to quantify government distortions from regulations and taxation, or to measure various aspects of legal and political systems. Another problem is that many variables influence economic growth, making it impossible to isolate all of these effects with the limited data available. Moreover, it is often difficult to be sure whether a variable – for example, maintenance of the rule of law, or the levels of investment in education and health – affects economic growth or whether it is affected by growth. In practice, both directions of causation are often important.

Economics in Practice
Institutions versus human capital

A recent study by Acemoglu, Gallego and Robinson (2014) examines the relative importance of human capital and institutions on long-run economic growth. They look at how the quality of institutions, measured by a rule-of-law index constructed by the World Bank, affects income level across countries. To avoid reverse causality (i.e., higher-income countries can afford to have better institutions), they use the mortality rate of early settlers as an exogenous determinant (i.e., an instrumental variable) of past and current institutions, and find a large positive effect of institutions on long-run economic growth.[2] When institutions are not controlled for, human capital also has a large positive effect on long-run growth. However, when the historical determinants of institutions and human capital are properly controlled for, the effect of human capital declines drastically and even becomes insignificantly different from zero. These results suggest that institutions are a fundamental cause of long-run growth, and their effects work through many channels, including human capital accumulation.

[2]According to Acemoglu, Johnson and Robinson (2001), the mortality rate of early settlers is a useful determinant of the quality of past and current institutions in former colonies. They argue that areas with a favourable disease environment induced the early European settlers to set up institutions conducive to economic development, whereas areas with an unfavourable disease environment induced the settlers to set up institutions designed for resource extraction. Furthermore, these institutions could persist to the present day.

EXAMPLES OF CONDITIONAL CONVERGENCE

If we look at history, we find examples of conditional convergence. At the end of World War II, the economies of many nations were destroyed. Cities were levelled, factories bombed and farmland used as battlefields. By 1946, Japan, Germany, France and other countries in Europe had suffered sharp reductions in physical capital. Human capital also fell sharply, but the reductions in physical capital were larger. In our model, these events generated low starting values of capital and real GDP per worker, $k(0)$ and $y(0)$. But these countries also had characteristics that were favourable to rapid economic recovery – including strong human capital in the forms of education and health, and good legal and political traditions that encouraged markets and trade. We can represent these favourable characteristics as high values of steady-state capital and real GDP per worker, k^{*} and y^{*}. Hence, conditional convergence – summarized in equation (5.1) – predicts that these countries would have high growth rates of real GDP per person in the aftermath of World War II. This prediction fits the facts.

As another example of conditional convergence, in the 1960s, many East Asian countries, such as Singapore and South Korea, were poor and, therefore, had low values of capital and real GDP per worker, $k(0)$ and $y(0)$. However, these countries also had reasonably good legal systems, satisfactory education and health programmes, and relatively high openness to international trade. Therefore, the steady-state values, k^{*} and y^{*} were high. Hence, we predict the high growth rates of real GDP per person from 1960 to 2000.

The typical sub-Saharan African country was also poor in the 1960s; that is, capital and real GDP per worker, $k(0)$ and $y(0)$, were low. Hence, from the perspective of absolute convergence, we would predict high growth rates of real GDP per person in Africa – whereas, in fact, the growth rates were the lowest in the world from 1960 to 2000. Conditional convergence can explain this outcome, because the African countries had poorly functioning legal and political systems, weak education and health programmes, high rates of population growth and large corrupt governments. Thus, the steady-state values, k^{*} and y^{*} were low, and the sub-Saharan African countries failed to grow.

We see from these examples that the idea of conditional convergence allows us to understand many apparently dissimilar experiences of economic growth. This idea helps us to understand growth rates of real GDP per person in rich countries after World War II, as well as in East Asian and sub-Saharan African countries from 1960 to 2000. More generally, the idea of conditional convergence helps to explain the range of growth rates experienced by a broad group of countries since 1960.

Long-run economic growth

Thus far, the Solow model does not explain how capital and real GDP per worker, k and y, grow in the long run. In the model, these variables are fixed in the long run at their steady-state values, k^* and y^*. Thus, the model does not explain how real GDP per person grew at around 2% per year for well over a century in Western Europe, the United States and other currently rich countries, but only at 0.8% in Africa.

We will now consider extensions of the Solow model that explain long-run growth of capital and real GDP per worker, k and y. We begin with a model in which the average product of capital, y/k, does not diminish as k rises. Then we allow for technological progress in the sense of continuing growth of the technology level, A. We will consider first a model in which this technological progress is just assumed; that is, A grows in an exogenous manner. Then we will consider theories in which technological progress is explained within the model; that is, endogenous growth models. We will also consider models of technological diffusion, in which a country's technology level, A, rises through imitation of advanced technologies from other countries.

MODELS WITH CONSTANT AVERAGE PRODUCT OF CAPITAL

The diminishing average product of capital, y/k, plays a major role in the Solow model's transition to the steady state. As capital per worker, k, increases, the decline in y/k reduces the growth rate of capital per worker, $\Delta k/k$. Eventually, the economy approaches a steady state, in which k reaches a fixed value, k^*, and $\Delta k/k$ is zero. This sketch of the transition suggests that the conclusions would differ if y/k did not decline as k rose. Thus, we now consider a modified model in which y/k does not change as k rises. We are particularly interested in whether this modification can explain long-run growth of capital and real GDP per worker.

Recall that, in the Solow model, the growth rate of capital per worker, k, is given by:

$$\Delta k/k = s \bullet (y/k) - s\delta - n \tag{4.1}$$

Now, we want to reconsider our assumption that the average product of capital, y/k, falls as k rises. This diminishing average product makes sense if we interpret capital narrowly; for example, as machines and buildings. If a business keeps expanding its machines and buildings, without adding any workers, we would expect the marginal and average products of capital to fall. In fact, if labour input does not increase, we would expect the marginal product of capital eventually to get close to zero. If no one is available to operate an extra machine, the marginal product of that machine would be nil.

Another view is that we should interpret capital more broadly to include human capital in the forms of formal education, on-the-job training and health. Human capital is productive, and the quantity of this capital can be increased by investment. Hence, human capital is analogous to machines and buildings. We might go further to include **infrastructure capital**, which is the capital, often owned by government, to provide services such as transport, electric power and water.

The tendency for capital's marginal and average products to fall as capital per worker, k, rises is less pronounced and may be absent if we view capital in this broad sense. That is, if we double not only machines and buildings, but also human and infrastructure capital, real GDP may roughly double. All we are holding constant here, aside from the technology level, A, is the quantity of raw labour, L. If raw labour is not a critical input to production, capital's marginal and average products may not decline as capital accumulates.

To see the consequences of this modification, consider a case in which capital – broadly defined to include human and infrastructure capital – is the only factor input to production. Then, instead of the usual production function:

$$y = A \bullet f(k) \tag{4.2}$$

we might have:

$$y = Ak \tag{5.2}$$

Equation (5.2) is the special case of equation (4.2) in which $f(k) = k$. For obvious reasons, the new model is called the **Ak model**.

In the *Ak* model, the average product of capital is constant. If we divide both sides of equation (5.2) by capital per worker, *k*, we get:

$$y/k = A \tag{5.3}$$

Hence, the average product of capital equals the technology level, *A*. (The marginal product of capital also equals *A*.) If we substitute $y/k = A$ into equation (4.1), we get that the growth rate of *k* is:

$$\Delta k/k = sA - s\delta - n \tag{5.4}$$

We can use a graph analogous to Figure 3.9 to study the determination of the growth rate of capital per worker, $\Delta k/k$, in the *Ak* model. The new feature in Figure 5.2 is that the term $s \bullet (y/k) = sA$ is not downward sloping versus *k*; instead, it is a horizontal line at *sA*. The other horizontal line, at $s\delta + n$, is the same as before. Also as before, $\Delta k/k$ equals the vertical distance between the two lines. However, now this distance is constant, rather than diminishing as *k* rises.

Two important conclusions follow from Figure 5.2. First, instead of being zero, the long-run growth rate of capital per worker, $\Delta k/k$, is greater than zero and equal to $sA - s\delta - n$, as shown in the graph and in equation (5.4). This growth rate is greater than zero because we assumed that *sA* was greater than $s\delta + n$. This condition is more likely to hold the higher the saving rate, *s*,[3] and the technology level, *A*, and the lower the population growth rate, *n*, and the depreciation rate, δ.

If *sA* is greater than $s\delta + n$, as assumed in Figure 5.2, growth of capital per worker, *k*, continues forever at the rate $sA - s\delta - n$. Moreover, since $y = Ak$, real GDP per worker, *y*, grows forever at the same rate. In this case, a higher saving rate, *s*, or a higher technology level, *A*, raises the long-run growth rates of capital and real GDP per worker, $\Delta k/k$ and $\Delta y/y$. Conversely, a higher population growth rate, *n*, or a higher depreciation rate, δ, lowers the long-run values of $\Delta k/k$ and $\Delta y/y$. In contrast, in the standard Solow model, $\Delta k/k$ and $\Delta y/y$ were zero in the steady state and, therefore, did not depend on *s*, *A*, δ and *n*. The reason for the different result is that the standard model assumed diminishing average product of capital, *y/k*.

The second important result from Figure 5.2 and equation (5.4) is the absence of convergence. The growth rates of capital and real GDP per worker, $\Delta k/k$ and $\Delta y/y$, do not change as capital and real GDP per worker, *k* and *y*, rise. Consequently, poor economies – with low *k* and *y* – do not tend to grow faster than rich economies.

Economists have developed more sophisticated models in which the average product of capital does not change as capital accumulates. Some models distinguish human from non-human capital and allow for an education sector that produces human capital. However, two basic shortcomings apply to most of these models. First, the loss of

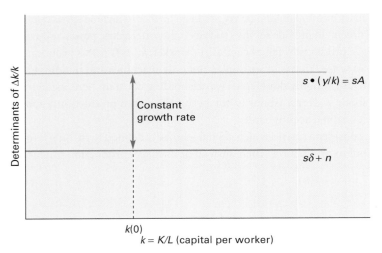

Figure 5.2 Economic growth with constant average product of capital

This graph modifies Figure 3.9 to allow for an unchanging average product of capital, *y/k*. In this *Ak* model, *y/k* equals the technology level, *A*. Therefore, the $s \bullet (y/k)$ curve becomes the horizontal line *sA*. If *sA* is greater than $s\delta + n$, as shown, the growth rate of capital per worker, $\Delta k/k$, is a positive constant equal to the vertical distance between the two horizontal lines. This distance is shown by the blue arrows.

[3]We are assuming $A > \delta$; otherwise, real net domestic product is less than zero.

the convergence prediction is a problem, because we do observe conditional convergence in cross-country data. Therefore, we cannot be satisfied with a growth model that fails to predict conditional convergence. Second, a common view among economists is that diminishing marginal and average products of capital apply eventually to the accumulation of capital even when interpreted in a broad sense to include human and infrastructure capital. If we reintroduced diminishing average product of capital, growth of capital and real GDP per worker could not continue in the long run just by accumulating capital. Therefore, we now turn to another explanation for long-run economic growth: technological progress.

EXOGENOUS TECHNOLOGICAL PROGRESS

In Chapter 4, we studied the effects of a one-time increase in the technology level, A. This change raised the growth rates of capital and real GDP per worker, $\Delta k/k$ and $\Delta y/y$, during the transition to the steady state. However, the economy still approached a steady state in which $\Delta k/k$ and $\Delta y/y$ were zero. Thus, we cannot explain long-run growth in k and y from a single increase in A. Rather, we have to allow for continuing increases in A. This regular process of improvement in technology is called **technological progress**.

Solow did extend his growth model to allow for technological progress, but he did not try to explain the sources of this progress. He just assumed that technological progress occurred and then examined the consequences for economic growth. In other words, he assumed **exogenous technological progress** – the improvements in technology were not explained within the model. This approach would be reasonable if most improvements in technology came by luck – in particular, if they did not depend much on purposeful effort by businesses (including non-profit enterprises, such as universities), workers and the government. In this section, we follow Solow's practice by assuming that the technology level, A, grows exogenously at a constant rate g:

$$\Delta A/A = g$$

In a later section, we discuss **endogenous growth theory**, which tries to explain the rate of technological progress within the model.

The steady-state growth rate

The growth-accounting equation worked out in Chapter 3 is again:

$$\Delta Y/Y = \Delta A/A + \alpha \bullet (\Delta K/K) + (1-\alpha) \bullet (\Delta L/L) \tag{3.3}$$

where Y is real GDP, K is the capital stock, and L is labour input. If we substitute $\Delta A/A = g$ and $\Delta L/L = n$, the population growth rate, we get:

$$\Delta Y/Y = g + \alpha \bullet (\Delta K/K) + (1-\alpha) \bullet n \tag{5.5}$$

Recall that the growth rate of real GDP per worker, $\Delta y/y$, is given by:

$$\Delta y/y = \Delta Y/Y - \Delta L/L \tag{3.6}$$

so that, with $\Delta L/L = n$:

$$\Delta y/y = \Delta Y/Y - n \tag{5.6}$$

If we substitute for $\Delta Y/Y$ from equation (5.5), we get:

$$\Delta y/y = g + \alpha \bullet (\Delta K/K) + (1-\alpha) \bullet n - n$$
$$= g + \alpha \bullet (\Delta K/K) + \cancel{n} - \alpha n - \cancel{n}$$
$$= g + \alpha \bullet (\Delta K/K - n)$$

The growth rate of capital per worker, $\Delta k/k$, is given by:

$$\Delta k/k = \Delta K/K - \Delta L/L \tag{3.7}$$

so that, with $\Delta L/L = n$:

$$\Delta k/k = \Delta K/K - n \tag{5.7}$$

If we substitute $\Delta k/k$ for $\Delta K/K - n$ in the formula for $\Delta y/y$, we get:

$$\Delta y/y = g + \alpha \bullet (\Delta k/k) \tag{5.8}$$

Therefore, real GDP per worker grows because of technological progress, g, and growth of capital per worker, $\Delta k/k$. The growth rate of capital per worker, $\Delta k/k$, is still determined in the Solow model by:

$$\Delta k/k = sA \bullet f(k)/k - s\delta - n \tag{4.3}$$

If we substitute this expression for $\Delta k/k$ into equation (5.8), we get:

> **Key equation (growth rate of real GDP per worker with technical progress):**
> $$\Delta y/y = g + \alpha \bullet [sA \bullet f(k)/k - s\delta - n] \tag{5.9}$$

In our previous analysis, where A was fixed, increases in k led to reductions in the average product of capital, $y/k = A \bullet f(k)/k$. Consequently, in the long run, the economy approached a steady state in which the average product of capital was low enough so that $\Delta k/k$ equalled zero in equation (4.3). Then, with $g = 0$, $\Delta y/y$ also equals zero in equations (5.8) and (5.9).

The difference now is that each increase in A raises the average product of capital, $y/k = A \bullet f(k)/k$, for given k. Hence, the negative effect of rising k on y/k is offset by a positive effect from rising A. The economy will tend towards a situation in which these two forces balance. That is, k will increase in the long run at a constant rate, and y/k will be unchanging. We call this situation **steady-state growth**.

Since the average product of capital, y/k, does not change during steady-state growth, the numerator of the ratio, y, must grow at the same rate as the denominator, k. Therefore, we have:

$$(\Delta y/y)^* = (\Delta k/k)^* \tag{5.10}$$

where the asterisks designate values in steady-state growth.

We know from equation (5.10) that capital and real GDP per worker, k and y, grow at the same rate in steady-state growth. Now, we want to determine the steady-state growth rate. Equation (5.8) implies that, in steady-state growth:

$$(\Delta y/y)^* = g + \alpha \bullet (\Delta k/k)^* \tag{5.11}$$

Using equation (5.10), we can replace $(\Delta k/k)^*$ on the right-hand side by $(\Delta y/y)^*$ to get:

$$(\Delta y/y)^* = g + \alpha \bullet (\Delta y/y)^*$$

If we move the term $\alpha \bullet (\Delta y/y)^*$ from the right-hand side to the left side, we get:

$$(\Delta y/y)^* - \alpha \bullet (\Delta y/y)^* = g$$

which implies, after we combine the terms on the left-hand side:

$$(1 - \alpha) \bullet (\Delta y/y)^* = g$$

If we divide both sides by $1 - \alpha$, we get the steady-state growth rate of real GDP per worker:

> **Key equation (steady-state growth rate with technological progress):**
> $$(\Delta y/y)^* = g/(1 - \alpha) \tag{5.12}$$

Since $0 < \alpha < 1$, equation (5.12) tells us that the steady-state growth rate of real GDP per worker, $(\Delta y/y)^*$, is greater than the rate of technological progress, g. As an example, if $\alpha = 1/2$, we have:

$$(\Delta y/y)^* = 2g$$

Thus, when $\alpha = 1/2$, $(\Delta y/y)^*$ is twice the rate of technological progress, g.

The reason that the growth rate of real GDP per worker, $(\Delta y/y)^*$, is greater than g is that the steady-state growth rate of capital per worker, $(\Delta k/k)^*$, is greater than zero, and this growth rate adds to g to determine $(\Delta y/y)^*$ – see equation (5.11). In fact, we know from equation (5.10) that the growth rates of k and y are the same in steady-state growth:

$$(\Delta k/k)^* = (\Delta y/y)^*$$

Therefore, equation (5.12) implies:

$$(\Delta k/k)^* = g/(1-\alpha) \qquad (5.13)$$

The important finding from equations (5.12) and (5.13) is that exogenous technological progress at the rate $\Delta A/A = g$ leads to long-term growth in real GDP and capital per worker, k and y, at the rate $g/(1 - \alpha)$. The technological progress offsets the tendency for the average product of capital, y/k, to fall when k rises and, thereby, allows for long-term growth of k and y.

Recall from our earlier discussion that the growth rate of real GDP per person in Western Europe, the United States and other advanced countries averaged 2% per year for well over a century. To explain this long-term growth within the Solow model, we have to look at the model's predictions for steady-state growth.

Since the labour-force participation rate is constant in the model, the growth rate of real GDP per person equals the growth rate of real GDP per worker. Therefore, to get long-term growth of real GDP per person at around 2% per year, we need the steady-state growth rate of real GDP per worker, which equals $g/(1 - \alpha)$ from equation (5.12), to be around 2% per year. If we think of α as the share of capital income and use values for α of between $\frac{1}{3}$ and $\frac{1}{2}$, the required value for g is a little over 1% per year. In other words, if the technology improves exogenously at a rate around 1% per year, the Solow model's prediction for the long-term growth rate of real GDP per person matches the long-term growth rates observed in advanced countries.

Steady-state saving

Now, we consider how technological progress affects steady-state saving. The growth rate of capital per worker, $\Delta k/k$, is again:

$$\Delta k/k = s \bullet (y/k) - s\delta - n \qquad (4.1)$$

In steady-state growth, we can replace $\Delta k/k$ from equation (5.13) with $g/(1 - \alpha)$ to get:

$$g/(1-\alpha) = s \bullet (y/k) - s\delta - n$$

We can then rearrange the terms to get:

$$s \bullet [(y/k) - \delta] = n + g/(1-\alpha)$$

If we multiply through by k, we determine saving per worker, $s \bullet (y - \delta k)$, in steady-state growth:

$$\textit{In steady-state growth: } s \bullet (y - \delta k) = nk + [g/(1-\alpha)] \bullet k \qquad (5.14)$$

When $g = 0$, steady-state saving per worker equals nk, the amount required to provide the growing labour force with capital to work with. When g is greater than zero, steady-state saving also includes the term $[g/(1 - \alpha)] \bullet k$. Since $g/(1 - \alpha)$ equals the steady-state growth rate of capital per worker, $\Delta k/k$ (equation [5.13]), this term is:

$$[g/(1-\alpha)] \bullet k = (\Delta k/k) \bullet k$$
$$= \Delta k$$

Therefore, this term is the saving per worker needed in the steady state to provide for increasing capital per worker.

The transition path and convergence

In Figure 3.11, we analyzed the transition path for capital per worker, k, in the Solow model without technological progress. We found that k gradually approached its steady-state value, k*. Thus, k* was the target that k was approaching. The model with exogenous technological progress still has a transition path for k. However, we have to think of k* as a moving target, rather than a fixed point. That is, k* moves over time along a steady-state path.

In steady-state growth, equation (5.13) says that capital per worker rises at the rate $(\Delta k/k)^* = g/(1 - \alpha)$. Hence, capital per worker, k, varies over time in the steady state – it grows at the rate $g/(1 - \alpha)$. We now define k* to be the value that k takes at each point in time along the steady-state path. We just have to remember that k* rises over time when g is greater than zero.

Capital per worker, k, again starts at some initial value, k(0). The model still has a transition in which k moves from k(0) to its steady-state path. However, we have to represent the steady-state path not by a fixed point but, rather, by the dashed line labelled k* in Figure 5.3. This line has a positive slope because capital per worker grows in the steady state. The graph shows that k begins at k(0), rises over time along the solid curve, and gradually approaches its moving target, k*.

Along the steady-state path, k = k* grows at the rate $g/(1 - \alpha)$– see equation (5.13). Therefore, in order for k to approach k*, as shown in Figure 5.3, the growth rate of k, $\Delta k/k$, must be greater than $g/(1 - \alpha)$, the growth rate of k*. Otherwise, k could not catch up during the transition to its moving target, k*.

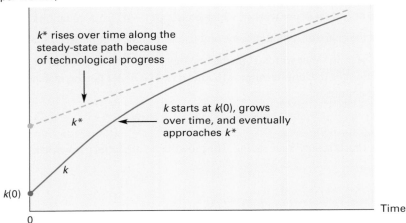

k (capital per worker)

k* rises over time along the steady-state path because of technological progress

k*

k starts at k(0), grows over time, and eventually approaches k*

k

k(0)

0

Time

Figure 5.3 The transition path for capital per worker in the Solow model with technological progress

In the Solow model with technological progress at the rate g, the steady-state level of capital per worker, k*, is not fixed; k* rises over time along the steady-state path shown by the dashed line. (Since we use a proportionate scale on the vertical axis, the straight line means that k* grows along the steady-state path at a constant rate, given by $g/[1 - \alpha]$.) In the transition, capital per worker, k, starts at k(0), rises over time along the solid curve, and gradually approaches the k* line. (We assume that k(0) lies below the k* line.)

The results for the transitional behaviour of k again tell us about convergence across economies. As before, convergence depends on whether different economies have the same or different steady states. Figure 5.4 shows a case in which two economies have the same steady-state paths, k*. Economy 1 begins at the capital per worker $k(0)_1$, and economy 2 at the higher capital per worker $k(0)_2$. The graph shows that k_1 and k_2 converge towards the steady-state path, k*, and that k_1 also converges towards k_2. Therefore, economy 1 has a higher growth rate of capital per worker, $\Delta k/k$, than economy 2 during the transition to the steady-state path. In other words, if the two economies have the same steady-state paths, absolute convergence holds, and the poorer economy (with lower k[0]) has a higher $\Delta k/k$. These results are similar to those found in Figure 4.8 for the model without technological progress, where g = 0.

Figure 5.5 considers a case in which the two economies have different steady-state paths, k*. We assume that economy 1 – with lower k(0) – also has a lower k*. We discussed in Chapter 4 why an economy with low k* tends also to have low k when observed at an arbitrary time, such as date 0. The graph shows that each economy converges over time towards its own steady-state path – k_1 towards k_1^*, and k_2 towards k_2^*. Since $k_1(0)$ is less than $k_2(0)$, and k_1^* is less than k_2^*, we cannot be sure which economy has the higher growth rate of capital per worker, $\Delta k/k$, during the transition. The lower $k(0)$ tends to make $\Delta k/k$ higher in economy 1, but the lower k^* tends to make $\Delta k/k$ lower in economy 1. Thus, convergence need not hold in an absolute sense. However, conditional convergence still applies; if we hold fixed the steady-state path, k^*, a lower $k(0)$ leads to higher growth rates of capital per worker, $\Delta k/k$, during the transition.

We expressed all the results about convergence in terms of capital per worker, k. However, the results also hold for real GDP per worker, y, once we make use of the production function, $y = A \cdot f(k)$. Therefore, we can also use Figures 5.4 and 5.5 to assess convergence of real GDP per worker across economies.

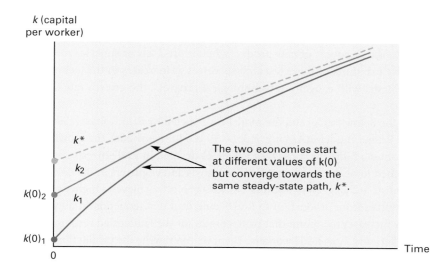

Figure 5.4 Convergence and transition paths for two economies in the Solow model with technological progress

As in Figure 5.3, the steady-state capital per worker, k^*, rises over time along the steady-state path shown by the dashed line. The first economy starts at $k(0)_1$, and the second economy starts at the higher value $k(0)_2$. During the transitions, capital per worker in each economy, k_1 or k_2, gradually approaches the common steady-state path, k^*. The first economy (the curve at $k(0)_1$) has a higher growth rate of capital per worker, $\Delta k/k$, than the second economy (the curve at $k(0)_2$), so that k_1 converges towards k_2. Therefore, absolute convergence applies.

Figure 5.5 Failure of convergence and transition paths for two economies in the Solow model with technological progress

As in Figure 5.4, the first economy starts at $k(0)_1$, and the second economy starts at the higher value $k(0)_2$. However, economy 1 now has a lower steady-state path of capital per worker; that is, the dashed line at k_1^* for lies below the dashed line at k_2^*. During the transitions, k_1 and k_2 gradually approach their respective steady-state paths, k_1^* and k_2^*. However, the growth rate of capital per worker, $\Delta k/k$, need not be higher in economy 1 than economy 2. Therefore, k_1 (the solid curve at k_1) does not necessarily converge towards k_2 (the solid curve at k_2). Hence, absolute convergence need not hold.

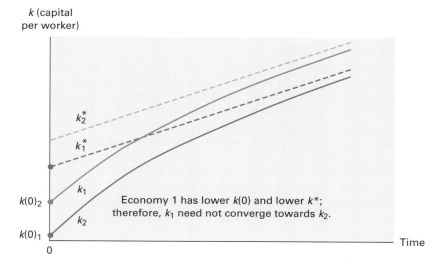

ENDOGENOUS GROWTH THEORY

The inclusion of exogenous technological progress allows the Solow model to match the long-term growth rates of real GDP per person observed in the data. However, many economists have criticized this fix of the model because the technological progress comes from nowhere – it is not explained by the model. For that reason, economists led by Paul Romer in the late 1980s and early 1990s tried to extend the model to explain why technological progress occurs. The models that Romer and others developed are called endogenous growth theory because, first, the models explain the rate of technological progress and, second, as in the Solow model, the technological progress leads to long-run growth of real GDP and capital per worker.

Most endogenous growth models focus on investments in **research and development**, or **R&D**. Data show that many countries spend a non-negligible share of their output on R&D. According to the OECD database, R&D expenditures as a percentage of GDP in 2012 are 4.2% in Israel, 2.8% in the United States, 1.9% in the European Union, 0.9% in Turkey and 0.8% in South Africa. Among the OECD countries, R&D expenditure is, on average, 2.4% of GDP. Successful R&D projects lead to the discovery of new products, better products or superior methods of production. In the Solow growth model, we can think of these research successes as increases in the technology level, A. However, in contrast to the Solow model with exogenous technological progress, the growth rate of A is explained within the model.

To illustrate this main difference between the Solow model and the model constructed by Paul Romer (1990), we write down the following key equation of the Romer model: $\Delta A/A = g(R \& D)$. In the Romer model, the growth rate of A is no longer a parameter. Instead, it becomes a function $g(R\&D)$ of resources devoted to R&D investment. The variable $R\&D$ is usually (but not always) assumed to be the number of R&D scientists and engineers in the economy. In other words, a country that has more scientists and engineers working on R&D projects achieves a higher growth rate of technology. However, reallocating resources from production to R&D could lead to a reduction in output, at least temporarily until the level of technology increases to a point that compensates for the reallocated resources. To illustrate this, we define L_Y as production workers and L_R as R&D workers. Then, we can rewrite the production function in equation (3.1) as $Y = A \bullet F(K, L_Y)$. The resource constraint on labour becomes $L = L_Y + L_R$, which shows that, for a given L, an increase in L_R leads to a decrease in L_Y. Although the increase in L_R leads to a higher growth rate $g(L_R)$, the decrease in L_Y leads to a lower level of output Y. Therefore, a natural question to ask is how the level of R&D is determined in the economy. Another important question is why R&D investment can sustain long-run economic growth but capital investment cannot. Furthermore, we can use endogenous growth models to understand how government policies and other variables influence R&D investment and, thereby, the rate of technological progress and the long-run growth rate of real GDP per person. We discuss all these points in the rest of this section.

Extending the Model
Scale effect in the Romer model

The Romer model features what is known in the literature as the scale effect. The scale effect implies that when an economy has more R&D scientists and engineers over time, its growth rate of technology also increases over time. However, Charles Jones (1995) provides empirical evidence against this theoretical prediction of an increasing growth rate in the Romer model and modifies $\Delta A/A = g(L_R)$ in such a way that it is the growth rate (rather than the level) of R&D that affects $\Delta A/A$ in the long run. For example, suppose $\Delta A = \theta L_R$, where the parameter $\theta > 0$ captures the productivity of R&D engineers and scientists. In this case, the growth rate of technology is $\Delta A/A = \theta L_R/A$. Therefore, a constant technology growth rate $\Delta A/A$ in the long run requires a constant R&D–technology ratio $\theta L_R/A$, which, in turn, implies $\Delta A/A = \Delta L_R/L_R$, in the long run. In other words, the long-run growth rate of technology is determined by the growth rate (rather than the number) of R&D engineers and scientists in the Jones model.

The Romer model specifies a connection between R&D investment and the amount of technological advance, represented by increases in A. Because research entails discovery, the outcomes are uncertain. For example, when working on new medicines, computer designs, or other original products or processes, a researcher does not know the degree of success in advance. This uncertainty is greater for basic research than for refinements of existing products or methods of production. However, we can say generally that a greater amount of R&D investment leads to a larger expected increase in the technology level, A. Therefore, to have more technological progress on average, innovators must be motivated to raise R&D outlays. For private businesses, the motivation comes from greater prospective profit. The government may affect the profit motive by subsidizing research, some of which is carried out by non-profit organizations, such as universities. The government may also contract directly for research projects, such as in defence industries and the space programme.

Economics in Practice
R&D tax incentives

Recent studies by the OECD on R&D tax incentives show that the number of countries providing R&D tax incentives has been increasing over time. In 1995, there were only 12 OECD countries that provided R&D tax incentives, and there are now more than 20. Other countries, such as Brazil, China, India, Singapore and South Africa, also provide generous tax incentives for R&D. These tax incentives usually take the form of tax credits or allowances, which reduce the amount of corporate tax payable to the government. These tax credits can take the form of volume-based credits or incremental credits. Volume-based tax credits apply to all qualified R&D expenses, whereas incremental tax credits apply only to the extra amount of R&D expenses beyond a base amount. According to the OECD, most countries are moving to volume-based R&D tax credits, which are easier to implement than incremental tax credits.

In many respects, R&D investment resembles the familiar investment in physical capital. The R&D outlays correspond to investment expenditure, and the technology level, A, corresponds to the stock of capital, K. However, there are two important differences between technological progress and increases in the stock of capital. One has to do with diminishing returns and the other with ownership rights.

A key question is whether diminishing returns apply to R&D investment. Specifically, as the technology level, A, grows, does it become increasingly expensive in terms of R&D outlays to generate expected further increases in A? If so, the R&D process exhibits diminishing returns, and it may be impossible for R&D investments to sustain technological progress and long-run growth of real GDP per worker. If not, it may be possible for R&D investments to maintain technological progress and long-run growth of real GDP per worker.

To understand how ownership rights differ between technology and the stock of capital, think of the technology level, A, as representing an idea about how to use factor inputs, K and L, to produce output, Y. In contrast, think of the stock of capital, K, as a machine or a building. If A represents an idea, all producers can use the idea simultaneously. If producer 1 uses the idea to create goods and services, producer 2 can use the same idea at the same time to create other goods and services. In a physical sense, an idea is a **non-rival good** – any number of producers can use the idea simultaneously without reducing the amount of the idea available to others. Examples of non-rival ideas are mathematical formulae in calculus, chemical formulae for drugs, codes for computer software and the notes in a song. An important point about a non-rival idea is that, once discovered, efficiency dictates sharing with all potential users.

The stock of capital differs from the stock of ideas. If one business uses a machine to produce goods, it is physically impossible for other businesses to use the same machine at the same time. This property holds also for labour input and most other goods and services. Economists say that each of these is a **rival good**.

Suppose, however, that all ideas were freely available once discovered. In this case, profit-seeking businesses would devote few resources to making inventions. The learning of an idea typically requires R&D investment, but there is no individual pay-off – no profit motive – for making the discovery. As an example, the invention of a chemical formula for a new drug typically entails substantial R&D outlays. If the formulae for successful drugs were distributed widely and all firms were allowed to use these formulae without charge, there would be no way for the innovating company to recoup its research expenses. Then – if we are relying on profit-seeking private enterprises, rather than governments – little R&D would take place, and little technological progress would occur.

Profit-seeking companies invest in R&D only if they can maintain some rights in the (good) ideas that they discover. These rights are called **intellectual property rights**. In some areas, the enforcement of intellectual property rights involves a **patent** (typically for 17 or 20 years) or a **copyright** (usually for the lifetime of the author plus 50 years). These legal protections are especially important for pharmaceuticals, software, books, music and movies.

Many basic discoveries have no patent protection, partly because of legal limitations and partly because of practical considerations in defining the scope of an idea. For example, Isaac Newton did not have patent protection for his mathematical innovations in calculus, Solow did not have property rights in his growth model and Henry Ford did not have exclusive use of the assembly line. For a more recent example, Toyota Motors did not have property rights over the idea of just-in-time inventory management, the practice of having suppliers deliver product components just before they are needed in a production process, instead of storing raw materials in physical inventory. Other car manufacturers, computer manufacturer Dell and many other companies copied this idea to reduce their inventory costs.

In many cases, businesses that make patentable inventions do not seek patents, sometimes because the approval process is costly and, more often, because businesses do not want to reveal the information needed to gain approval. Such information tends to aid competitors even when patents are granted. In the absence of formal patent protection, the main methods of maintaining intellectual property rights are secrecy and the advantages gained from moving first into a new area.

In the Romer model, an inventor retained perpetual monopoly rights over their invention. However, this extreme form of intellectual property rights is not necessary for Romer's main results. The basic idea is that some form of intellectual property rights ensured that successful innovators were rewarded for their discoveries.

The Romer model distinguishes the return to society from an invention from the private return, which is the reward to the inventor. The private return is greater than zero because of the intellectual property rights, but the social return tends to exceed the private one. For example, the social benefits from the invention of the transistor or the microchip were much greater than the pay-offs to the individuals and businesses that made the discoveries.[4] For this reason, the resources devoted to R&D and the resulting rate of technological progress tend to be too low from a social perspective. This reasoning is often used to justify government subsidy of innovative activity, especially basic research. However, government subsidies also create problems, including the politics of choosing what to subsidize and the necessity to raise revenues to pay for the subsidies.

Romer equated technology with ideas, and he assumed that the returns from generating new ideas did not diminish as the technology level advanced. His reasoning was that the number of potentially good ideas was unlimited, so the stock of remaining ideas would not be depleted as more things were discovered. Thus, at least as a working hypothesis, we might assume that the returns to the creation of ideas are constant. This assumption turns out to be consistent with a constant, steady-state growth rate of real GDP per worker, driven by technological progress at a constant rate. That is, the results look like those in the Solow model when the technology level, A, grows exogenously at the constant rate g.

In the Romer model, where R&D investment is carried out by profit-seeking businesses, the rate of technological progress depends on the private rewards from making discoveries. These rewards depend on a number of factors:

- The private return to R&D investment is higher if the costs of R&D are lower. Some of these costs depend on government policies. Costs are lower if the government subsidizes R&D. Costs are higher if there are large expenses for gaining government approval (e.g., of new drugs), or satisfying government regulations.

---

[4]Theoretically, the private returns could exceed the social ones. This situation can apply if resources are wasted when competing researchers strive to be the first to make a discovery, or if the main consequence from an improved product is the transfer of monopoly profits from the old industry leader to the new one. However, it is hard to present convincing empirical examples of this theoretical possibility.

- The reward from successful innovations depends on how much they raise sales revenue or reduce production costs. One consideration is the size of the market over which the benefits from a discovery can be spread. A bigger market, which includes domestic and foreign sales, encourages more R&D.
- The private return is higher if intellectual property rights over the use of an invention are more secure and long lasting. In many cases, these rights will be better protected domestically than internationally. Another consideration is the ease with which competitors, domestic or foreign, can imitate successful innovations. The easier the imitation, the lower the intellectual property rights over an innovation and, hence, the smaller the incentive for R&D investment.

Changes in any of these factors influence the rate of technological progress and, therefore, the economy's steady-state growth rate of real GDP per worker. These effects are analogous to those from changes in the rate of exogenous technological progress, g, in the Solow model.

Advanced countries spend the most on R&D. They have the most scientists and engineers, and are granted most of the patents. (India is an exception to the usual pattern, as a poor country with many innovations in computer software.) One reason for the concentration of R&D in rich countries is the complementary resources that support research, including a large supply of skilled workers and strong educational institutions. The large domestic market available to wealthy countries is also significant. However, a small country can successfully innovate if it is well-connected to other markets through international trade, and if intellectual property rights are respected in foreign countries. As examples, Sweden and Finland have been leaders in pharmaceuticals and telecommunications.

At the start of this chapter, we discussed cross-country empirical research on convergence and other aspects of economic growth. These empirical findings match up well with the version of the Solow growth model that includes exogenous technological progress. Thus far, less cross-country empirical work has been done on the endogenous growth models. One finding, however, is that countries that spend more on R&D investment tend to have higher growth rates of real GDP per person.[5]

Economics in Practice
The importance of innovation in the thirteenth five-year plan of China

China has adopted Five-Year Plans (FYPs) for developing social and economic blueprints since 1953. These plans are drafted and implemented by governments at all levels. The FYP for the central government is drafted by the National Development and Reform Commission and lays out specific economic targets on, for example, growth rates of GDP, and social development goals in healthcare and education. These targets guide the policymaking of government officials throughout the five-year period of each FYP. The latest FYP is for the years from 2016 to 2020. One of the main targets for this thirteenth FYP is to shift the engine of economic growth towards technological progress by boosting innovation and R&D. This policy is consistent with the theories of economic growth described in this chapter: in the long run, economic growth comes from technological progress which, in turn, is endogenously determined by the level of R&D and innovation in the economy.

THE DIFFUSION OF TECHNOLOGY

For the world as a whole, the only way to raise the technology level, A, is for someone to discover something new. However, for an individual country or producer, it is possible to raise A – the technology level available to that country or producer – by imitating or adapting someone else's innovation. For example, the first commercial steam engine was invented in Britain before the technology spread to Europe and elsewhere. Similarly, the first

---

[5]See David Coe and Elhanan Helpman (1995). For evidence on the relation between R&D and productivity at the level of industries and firms, see Zvi Griliches (1998).

handheld mobile phone was invented in the USA before the use of this technology spread to the rest of the world. In Africa, mobile phones are so widespread relative to landline phones that it is often referred to as the 'mobile-only' continent.

The term **diffusion of technology** describes the imitation and adaptation of one country's technology by another country. For low-income countries, imitation and adaptation tend to be less expensive than invention as ways to improve methods of production and introduce new and better products. Therefore, low-income countries tend to focus on diffusion of technology as the way to raise technology levels.

Businesses have used many methods to imitate leading technologies. A multinational firm from an advanced country can use an advanced technology in a foreign subsidiary. Domestic entrepreneurs then learn from the foreign-owned operations about products and production processes. These channels of technological diffusion were important in the textile industries in Hong Kong and Mauritius (an economically successful island off the east coast of Africa).

Sometimes, the transfer of technology occurs through observation and analysis of products exchanged in international trade. For example, an importer of a good may be able to deduce how the good was produced by taking it apart (through a process of 'reverse engineering'). In other cases, a foreign company licenses or sells its processes to domestically owned businesses. For example, Apple Inc. licenses the manufacturing of iPhones mainly to Foxconn, an electronics contract manufacturing company in China. In still other cases, domestic residents work or study at a business or university in an advanced country and bring back the technology to their home countries.

The diffusion of technology is another mechanism for poor countries to converge towards rich ones. Low-income countries are poor partly because they lack access to leading technologies. Therefore, these countries can grow rapidly by imitating better technologies from advanced countries. However, as imitation proceeds, the supply of useful uncopied technologies decreases, and the cost of further imitation tends to rise. This rising cost of imitation is similar to the decreasing average product of capital, y/k, in the Solow model. Therefore, growth rates of follower countries tend to decline and their levels of real GDP per worker tend to converge towards those in the advanced countries.

Studies show that the rate of technological diffusion to a developing country is high when the country has considerable trade with rich countries, has high education levels and has well-functioning legal and political systems, as in some East Asian countries.[6] Therefore, these characteristics help to explain the high rates of economic growth in East Asia since the 1960s.

Economics in Practice
Steam engine: a case of technological diffusion

A recent study by Nuvolari, Verspagen and von Tunzelmann (2011) investigates the spread of steam technology across British counties in the eighteenth century. According to their data, the first steam engine invented by Thomas Newcomen was possibly installed in Cornwall in 1710, whereas the first Newcomen engines in Fife, Lanark and Stirling were not installed until 1760–64. Other counties installed their first Newcomen engines at various points in the early to mid-eighteenth century. The delay in the spread of steam engines across counties depended on demand-and-supply factors in the local area, such as coal prices, the availability of water sites, the number of textile mills, and so on. Interestingly, the diffusion of Newcomen engines also depended on the depth of steam engineering skills in the local area because Newcomen engines were mainly installed by local manufacturers. In contrast, the diffusion of steam engines invented by James Watt did not seem to depend on local steam engineering skills because they were mainly 'installed by only one company owning a proprietary technology'.

[6]See, for example, Florence Jaumotte (2000) and Francesco Caselli and Wilbur Coleman (2001).

What do we know about economic growth?

We began our study of economic growth in Chapter 3 with the Solow growth model. In the first phase of this model, capital and real GDP per worker rise from their initial levels to their steady-state levels. The second phase is the steady state. In Chapters 3 and 4, capital and real GDP per worker did not grow in the steady state. However, in the present chapter, the inclusion of technological progress led to growth of capital and real GDP per worker in the steady state.

In Chapter 4, we used the Solow model to predict short- and long-run effects from changes in the saving rate, the technology level, the size of the labour force and the population growth rate. The transition phase of the model predicted convergence – poor economies tend to grow faster than rich ones and, therefore, tend to catch up over time to rich ones. Although this prediction conflicted with observations for a broad group of countries, a modified concept – conditional convergence – fits well with the data. Conditional convergence allows for differences in steady-state positions, due to variations in saving rates, technology levels and population growth rates. In extended models, the differences can reflect other variables, including legal and political systems, openness to international trade, and the efficiency of education and health programmes.

In the present chapter, we showed that the concept of conditional convergence explains many historical patterns of economic growth. We can understand why some war-ravaged OECD countries grew rapidly after World War II. We can also explain why, from 1960 to 2000, most East Asian countries grew rapidly but most sub-Saharan African countries grew slowly or not at all.

The basic Solow model does not explain long-run growth of real GDP per person, a pattern that applied for well over a century to Western Europe, the United States and other advanced countries. The model does explain long-term per-capita growth at around 2% per year, if we assume exogenous technological progress at about 1% per year. Endogenous growth models rely on R&D investment as the source of improvements in technology. These models predict how intellectual property rights, research subsidies and other variables affect the rate of technological progress and, hence, the long-run growth rate of real GDP per person.

Technological diffusion is the main method by which low-income countries raise their technology levels. This diffusion helps to explain convergence of poor countries towards rich countries but does not explain technological progress for the whole world.

Although we understand a great deal about economic growth, there is much that remains unexplained. For example, economists have isolated only some of the variables that underlie differences across countries in steady-state positions. In the long-run context, we are still uncertain about the sources of technological progress. In particular, we cannot say with confidence how government policies that affect incentives for R&D investment influence long-run economic growth in a single country, or in the world. Thus, although we have learned a great deal, there is still much to do.

Key Terms and Concepts

Ak model	exogenous technological progress	non-rival good	rival good
copyright	patent	steady-state growth
diffusion of technology	infrastructure capital	research and development (R&D)	technological progress
endogenous growth theory	intellectual property rights		

Questions and Problems

A Review questions

1 Most countries in sub-Saharan Africa grew at a low rate from 1960 to 2000, while many countries in East Asia grew at a high rate. How can the concept of conditional convergence help to explain these observations?

2 Suppose that the technology level, A, grows exogenously at a positive rate, $g > 0$. Does the level of output, Y, grow in the long run? Does output per worker, Y/L, grow in the long run?

B Problems for discussion

3 Convergence and the dispersion of income (difficult)

Consider a group of economies that satisfies absolute convergence; that is, poor economies tend to grow faster than rich ones.

a Does this convergence property imply that a measure of the dispersion of income per person – or income inequality – across the economies will narrow over time? (This question relates to Galton's fallacy, an idea applied by Galton to the distribution of heights and other characteristics in a population. If a parent is taller than average, the child tends to be taller than average but shorter than the parent. That is, there is reversion to the mean, an effect that parallels the idea of absolute convergence. Does the presence of reversion to the mean imply that the distribution of heights across the population will narrow over time? The answer is no, but you are supposed to explain why.)

b We found in Figure 4.9 that absolute convergence did not hold for a broad group of countries from 1960 to 2011. We did find in Figure 5.1 that conditional convergence held for these countries. A measure of the dispersion of per capita real GDP across these countries shows a mild, but persistent, increase from 1960 to 2011. How would you account for this pattern?

Appendix

The steady-state path in the Solow model with exogenous technological progress

We now derive the steady-state path, k^* in the model with exogenous technological progress. The path is shown graphically in Figure 5.3. This appendix provides an algebraic derivation.

The growth rate of capital per worker is given by:

$$\Delta k/k = s \bullet (y/k) - s\delta - n \tag{4.1}$$

Hence, along a steady-state path, the growth rate is:

$$(\Delta k/k)^* = s \bullet (y/k)^* - s\delta - n \tag{5.15}$$

where $(y/k)^*$ is the unchanging average product of capital in a position of steady-state growth. We also know that, in a situation of steady-state growth, k grows at the rate:

$$(\Delta k/k)^* = g/(1-\alpha) \tag{5.13}$$

Therefore, if we substitute $g/(1-\alpha)$ for $(\Delta k/k)^*$ on the left-hand side of equation (5.15), we get:

$$g/(1-\alpha) = s \bullet (y/k)^* - s\delta - n$$

We can rearrange the terms to get:

$$s \bullet (y/k)^* = s\delta + n + g/(1-\alpha)$$

Then, if we divide by s, we get a formula for the steady-state average product of capital:

$$(y/k)^* = \delta + (1/s) \bullet [n + g/(1-\alpha)] \tag{5.16}$$

Note that the right-hand side of the equation is constant. Therefore, this result verifies that the average product of capital, $(y/k)^*$, does not change in steady-state growth.

Since the production function is:

$$y = A \cdot f(k)$$

we can write the average product of capital, y/k, as:

$$y/k = A \cdot f(k)/k$$

Therefore, if we define k^* to be the time-varying value for k during steady-state growth, the steady-state average product of capital is:

$$(y/k)^* = A \cdot f(k^*)/k^* \tag{5.17}$$

Equations (5.16) and (5.17) give us two expressions for $(y/k)^*$. Therefore, the two right-hand sides must be equal:

$$A \cdot f(k^*)/k^* = \delta + (1/s) \cdot [n + g/(1-\alpha)] \tag{5.18}$$

The right-hand side is constant, and the technology level, A, on the left-hand side grows over time at the rate g. Therefore, if we specify the form of the production function, f, we can use equation (5.18) to determine the steady-state path, k^*.

Suppose that the production function, $f(k)$, takes the Cobb-Douglas form:

$$y = Ak^\alpha \tag{3.24}$$

which we discussed in Part C to the Appendix to Chapter 3. In this case:

$$A \cdot f(k)/k = Ak^\alpha /k$$
$$= Ak^\alpha k^{-1}$$
$$= Ak^{\alpha-1}$$
$$A \cdot f(k)/k = Ak^{-(1-\alpha)}$$

Therefore, we can substitute $A \cdot f(k^*)^{-(1-\alpha)}$ in equation (5.18) to get:

$$A \cdot (k^*)^{-(1-\alpha)} = \delta + (1/s) \cdot [n + g/(1-\alpha)]$$

If we multiply through by $(k^*)^{1-\alpha}$ and s, divide through by $[s\delta + n + g/(1 - \alpha)]$, and rearrange terms, we get:

$$(k^*)^{1-\alpha} = \frac{sA}{[s\delta + n + g/(1-\alpha)]} \tag{5.19}$$

On the right-hand side, everything except A does not vary over time. If A were constant, k^* would be constant, as in the Solow model without technological progress ($g = 0$). If A grows at the rate g, equation (5.19) implies that k^* grows at the rate $g/(1 - \alpha)$, consistent with the result in equation (5.13).

Economic
fluctuations

PART III

6 Macroeconomics without microeconomic foundations

In Chapters 7 to 10, we will develop a complete microeconomic framework and apply these microeconomic foundations to the development of an equilibrium business-cycle model, which we then use to explore the origin of economic fluctuations. This approach to understanding the macroeconomy has been a centrepiece of macroeconomic research since the mid-1980s. Before we study this modern approach to macroeconomics, we first devote this chapter to reviewing an alternative approach that appears in many undergraduate macroeconomic textbooks. This approach is known as **Keynesian economics**.

Keynesian economics originates from the work of John Maynard Keynes. In 1936, he published his famous book, *The General Theory of Employment, Interest and Money*. Prior to Keynes's research, mainstream macroeconomics was based on **classical economics** that focused on the **aggregate supply** of an economy, according to which recessions are caused by reduced capacity of producers. However, Keynes argued that the Great Depression was, instead, driven by a lack of **aggregate demand** and that the government could stimulate the economy through fiscal and monetary policies.

Some of Keynes's ideas were summarized in a mathematical model, known as the **IS-LM model**.[1] In this chapter, we first present a simple version of the IS-LM model. Then, we consider two extensions of the model and use these models to explore the effects of fiscal and monetary policies.

It is worthwhile remarking that modern New Keynesian economics has recently found ways to provide micro foundations for the IS-LM model, based on consumer intertemporal optimization and firm profit maximization in the presence of nominal rigidity. Such derivations are beyond the scope of our book, but are the subject of post-graduate studies; therefore, we proceed with the IS-LM analysis without showing their possible micro foundations. This is also in the spirit of Keynes's (1936) and Hicks's (1937) sketch of Keynes's theory based on his IS-LM diagrams, which preceded modern microeconomic foundations of macroeconomics.

Economics in Practice
The Great Depression

During the Great Depression of the 1930s, many countries suffered from a very severe decline in economic activity. From the end of the 1920s to the early 1930s, the world experienced a 15% decline in GDP. The Great Depression had damaging effects on economies across the world, with some countries experiencing an unemployment rate of as high as over 30%. In most countries, the depression started in 1929 and did not end until the late 1930s. The depression first started in the United States, where the stock market crashed in October 1929. On 28 and 29 October, the Dow Jones Industrial Index fell by over 20%. There are several plausible explanations for the Great Depression. Some have argued that the sharp reduction in consumption and investment was due to a large-scale loss of confidence, which led to a severe drop in aggregate demand. Others argue that the Great Depression was the result of contractionary monetary policy (i.e., a decrease in money supply) that exacerbated the

[1]A number of economists, such as Roy Harrod, John Hicks and James Meade, contributed to the development of this model.

impacts of an ordinary recession and turned it into an economic depression. One of the solutions to the Great Depression proposed by Keynes was to stimulate the economy by increasing government spending. Indeed, massive increases in government expenditure undertaken by F. D. Roosevelt's administration, especially towards the beginning of World War II in 1939, helped the US economy to recover.

The IS-LM model

The IS-LM model consists of two components: the IS curve and the LM curve. The IS curve stands for the **investment-saving curve**. It represents an equilibrium condition of the goods market. The IS curve is given by the following national income accounting identity of a closed economy:

$$Y = C + I + G \tag{6.1}$$

The variables in equation (6.1) denote the different components of the national income account. Y stands for the output of goods and services in the economy. C stands for household consumption. I stands for investment by firms. G stands for government expenditure. We assume that consumption, C, is increasing in disposable income given by $Y - T$, where T denotes tax payment (net of any income transfers from the government to households). In other words, when households have more disposable income, they consume more goods and services. We also assume that investment, I, is decreasing in the **real interest rate**, r, which determines the cost of borrowing for investment. In other words, when firms face a lower cost of borrowing for investment, they increase their spending on investment. Finally, we assume that government spending, G, and tax payment, T, are exogenously chosen by the government. In this case, the IS curve becomes:

$$Y = \underset{(+)}{C(Y-T)} + \underset{(-)}{I(r)} + G \tag{6.2}$$

While the relationship between consumption and disposable income and between investment and the real interest rate are here based on *ad hoc* assumptions, they could be derived from optimizing behaviours of consumers and firms.

We simplify the analysis by assuming that the consumption function is linear; i.e., $C(Y-T) = c \bullet (Y-T)$. The parameter $c < 1$ is the **marginal propensity to consume**, which measures the increase in consumption when disposable income increases by one unit. Using the linear consumption function, we can simplify the IS curve to:

$$Y = [\underset{(-)}{I(r)} + G - cT]/(1-c) \tag{6.3}$$

which describes a locus of points, showing alternative combinations of the output level, Y, and the real interest rate, r, on which the goods market is in equilibrium. Given that the investment function, $I(r)$, is decreasing in the real interest rate, r, the IS curve has a negative slope as shown in Figure 6.1. The intuition behind the IS curve is that a higher real interest rate reduces investment which, in turn, leads to a decrease in output.

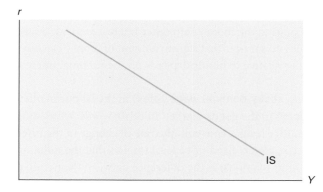

r

IS

Y

Figure 6.1 The IS curve

The IS curve shows the different combinations of Y and r under which the goods market is in equilibrium; i.e., the following condition holds: $Y = C(Y - T) + I(r) + G$.

One of the main reasons why the IS-LM model is considered a macroeconomic model without microeconomic foundations is that the aggregate supply of goods is assumed to follow aggregate demand passively. Imagine, for example, an exogenous increase in consumer confidence about their future incomes inducing families to spend a larger part of their current incomes, or else a diffused waved of optimistic 'animal spirits' (Keynes, *The General Theory*) spurring firms to buy new equipment and structures, or exogenous increases in government expenditure. The IS curve in equation (6.2) would then imply that Y would just increase as a consequence: firms would produce more goods and eventually meet all extra demand. Conversely, if demand suddenly dropped, so would Y: firms would just produce less and an economic contraction would follow.

This theory, is not telling us why increases in aggregate demand are not met by increases in the general price level, and vice versa – demand, drops generating deflationary pressures. Therefore, this theory's underlying assumption is that firms always have enough spare capacity to increase production on demand, or that there are always enough unemployed resources (in particular, labour and capital) to be utilized when demand increases. This is probably true during recessions, which is perhaps the only economic environment in which the IS curve can work at its best.

The LM curve stands for the **liquidity-money curve**. It represents an equilibrium condition of the money market and describes a theory of liquidity preference. It is meant to explain why households wish to keep part of their wealth in non-interest-earning form such as money (currency, current accounts, etc.), rather than in higher-earning assets such as bonds (treasury bills, etc.). Money is the most liquid part of household wealth, as opposed to less liquid but more lucrative interest-earning assets. The LM curve attempts to explain a potentially complex household portfolio choice in a simple and stylized manner. Therefore, we can say that, in the Keynesian theory, the LM curve is also the equilibrium condition in the broadly intended financial market, most notably the bond market. In Chapter 7, we will describe the bond market in more detail. As of now, the reader can simply think of bonds as legal obligations to pay money by entities such as the government or important firms. If, for 100 euros, I can buy a government bond promising to pay 10 euros every year forever (this bond is called an 'annuity'), then we can say that the interest rate earned on the government bond is 10/100 = 10%. If, following an increase in government bond demand, the price of that bond increases to 200 euros – while always promising to pay 10 euros each year – then we say that the interest rate of that bond has declined to 10/200 = 5%. Vice versa, if the market demand for that type of bond declines and their price drops to 50 euros, this implies that the interest rate on the bond has increased to 10/50 = 20%. Therefore, there exists an inverse relationship between bond prices and interest rates. This inverse relationship is very important for understanding Keynes's theory of financial markets, which underlies the LM curve.

The LM curve can be expressed as follows:

$$M^s/P = D(Y,i) \quad\quad\quad (6.4)$$
$$\underset{(+)(-)}{}$$

M^s denotes the level of money supply, which is exogenously chosen by the monetary authority. P denotes the price level. Therefore, M^s/P is the **real money supply**, which determines the amount of goods and services that the amount of money, M^s, can buy given the price level. $D(Y,i)$ is the **real money demand**, which determines the real amount of money demanded by households' given income, Y, and the **nominal interest rate**, i. When income rises, households want to consume more goods and services, so their demand for money increases. A higher nominal interest rate, i, increases the opportunity cost of holding money and depresses money demand. The reason is that when households hold money, they forgo the opportunity of putting the money into other interest-bearing assets. Furthermore, the real value of money (i.e., the amount of goods and services that a given amount of money can buy) is diminished by inflation; therefore, the cost of money holding relative to bonds depends on the nominal interest rate, i, instead of the real interest rate, r.

In *The General Theory*, Keynes considered wage rigidity (i.e., **sticky nominal wage rates**) in the labour market. For simplicity, here we consider price rigidity (i.e., **sticky prices**) in the goods market. In other words, we assume that the price level, P, is fixed in the short run. Given that the price level is constant, the rate of change in the price level is zero in the short run. Therefore, our assumption of a completely fixed price level implies that the inflation rate is zero. The real interest rate, r, (i.e., the rate of return in units of goods) is the difference between the nominal interest rate, i (i.e., the rate of return in units of money), and the inflation rate (i.e., the rate of change in the price of goods), which is denoted by π. The Fisher equation, named after Irvin Fisher, is then given by $r = i - \pi$, which will be discussed in more detail in Chapter 12. The assumption of zero inflation implies that $r = i$ in the short run. Therefore, we can now rewrite the LM curve, by replacing the nominal interest rate, i, with the real interest rate, r, in the money demand function, as follows:

$$M^s / P = D(Y, r) \atop (+)(-)$$ (6.5)

which describes a locus of points, showing alternative combinations of the output level, Y, and the real interest rate, r, on which the money market is in equilibrium given the real money supply, M^s / P. The LM curve has a positive slope as shown in Figure 6.2. The intuition behind the LM curve is that, when income rises, the excess demand for money must be offset by a higher interest rate.

When the money market is not in equilibrium, the bond prices change, and so will the interest rate, i, and therefore r. For example, below the LM curve are all points in which, given the level of income, Y, the interest rates i and r are too low, and therefore the right-hand sides of equations (6.4) and (6.5) are larger than their left-hand sides. This means that there is excess demand for money and, consequently, excess supply of bonds: being in excess supply, the bond prices will decline and the interest rate (which is inversely related to the price of a bond) will increase. This will continue until the economy is driven back to the LM curve. Vice versa above the LM curve: too high an interest rate, hence excess supply of money and excess demand for bonds. Consequently, the bond price will increase and the interest rate will decline.

According to this theory, since financial markets operate much faster than the goods market, the interest rate will quickly adjust to guarantee that the economy is always on the LM curve. In fact, while firms faced with excess demand or supply of goods may take weeks or months to adjust their production plans, employment decisions, and so on, in the case of excess demand/supply of money/bonds, financial markets take minutes (if not seconds) to react and reach the money/bond market equilibrium.

Figure 6.3 shows the equilibrium in the IS-LM model given by the intersection of the IS and LM curves, which represents the simultaneous equilibrium in the goods market and in the money market. The equilibrium level of

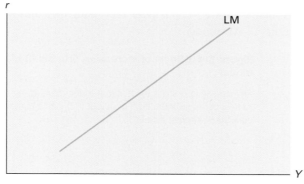

Figure 6.2 The LM curve

The LM curve shows the different combinations of y and r under which the money market is in equilibrium; i.e., the following condition holds: $M^s / P = D(Y, r)$.

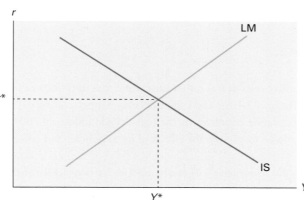

Figure 6.3 The IS-LM model

The intersection of the IS and LM curves shows the equilibrium level of output, Y^*, and the equilibrium interest rate, r^*, in the economy.

output is given by Y^*, and the equilibrium interest rate is given by r^*. In the next section, we will use the IS-LM model to explore the effects of fiscal and monetary policies on the macroeconomy.

According to this theory, the economy tends always to be at its equilibrium point (Y^*, r^*). This is guaranteed by the adjustment process that would take place if, by chance, the economy found itself at an off-equilibrium point: any excess demand for goods would be covered by increases in production by firms, with resulting increase in employment and capacity utilization. Any excess supply of goods would lead firms to produce less, lay off workers, and/or reduce capacity utilization. This process ceases only once the economy is back in equilibrium.

Similarly, excess demand for money would induce households to try to sell the bonds in their possession and replace them with more money. However, the total money supply is given, and households cannot all sell bonds without anyone buying them; therefore, the aggregate effect will just be a reduction in bond prices and an increase in the interest rate. Vice versa, any excess supply of money will be used to buy bonds, thereby increasing their prices and reducing the interest rate.

To sum up, according to this theory, the aggregate level of production adjusts to guarantee that equation (6.3) – which defines the IS curve – is satisfied, while the interest rate will guarantee that equation (6.5) – which defines the LM curve – is satisfied as well. For this reason, in order to make a successful prediction as to what the economy will do, we will only need to focus our attention on the point of intersection between the IS curve and the LM curve.

FISCAL POLICY IN THE IS-LM MODEL

We begin by exploring the short-run effects of an increase in government spending, G. From equation 6.3, we see that an increase in G shifts the IS curve to the right. Consequently, the equilibrium interest rate increases from r^* to $(r^*)'$ and the equilibrium level of output increases from Y^* to $(Y^*)'$ as shown in Figure 6.4. The increase in the interest rate depresses investment, I, whereas the increase in income, Y, stimulates consumption.[2] The increase in income and the increase in the interest rate have offsetting effects on money demand such that the overall effect on money demand, $D(Y, r)$, is neutral, which we know because the real money supply, M^s/P, is unchanged and, hence, the real money demand, $D(Y, r)$, must also remain constant in order to satisfy the money market equilibrium condition $M^s/P = D(Y, r)$. In the long run, there will be further adjustments, but we will postpone discussing the adjustment from the short run to the long run until we have presented the AS-AD model.

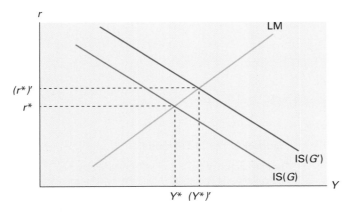

Figure 6.4 Effects of increasing G in the IS-LM model

An increase in G shifts the IS curve to the right, giving rise to a higher equilibrium level of output $(Y^*)'$ and a higher equilibrium interest rate $(r^*)'$.

Although the above analysis is transparent and yields intuitive results, it is rather unrealistic that the effects of fiscal policies are so simple unless the economy has enough underutilized labour and capital, as may happen during depressions, such as that of the USA in 1929–1938, or of some Eurozone countries in the half-decade following 2009. In Chapters 13–15, we will use the equilibrium business-cycle model to explore the effects of fiscal policies and compare

[2]Durable consumption may also depend on the interest rate. If we assume that consumption is decreasing in the interest rate, then the overall effect on consumption would be ambiguous.

its implications with those of the IS-LM model. We will find that the effects of fiscal policies can be more general in the equilibrium business-cycle model, which encompasses periods of nearly full employment.

INVESTOR SENTIMENT IN THE IS-LM MODEL

In addition to fiscal policy, one can also use the IS-LM model to explore the macroeconomic implications of a change in **investor sentiment**. Suppose we specify the investment function as $I(r,\varepsilon)$, where ε is a parameter that captures investor sentiment such that an increase in ε leads to an increase in investment, $I(r,\varepsilon)$, for a given interest rate, r. In this case, an improvement in investor sentiment (i.e., an increase in ε) shifts the IS curve to the right and gives rise to a higher equilibrium level of output and a higher equilibrium interest rate. Graphically, the effects are the same as in Figure 6.4. Conversely, a deterioration in investor sentiment, ε, shifts the IS curve to the left and leads to a lower equilibrium level of output and a lower equilibrium interest rate.

MONETARY POLICY IN THE IS-LM MODEL

We now explore the effects of an increase in money supply, M^s. From equation (6.5), we see that, for a given price level, P, an increase in money supply, M^s, leads to an increase in money demand, $D(Y,r)$, which must be accompanied by an increase in income, Y, and/or a decrease in the interest rate, r. Therefore, an increase in money supply, M^s, shifts the LM curve to the right, as shown in Figure 6.5. As a result, the equilibrium interest rate decreases

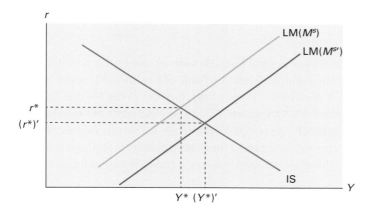

Figure 6.5 Effects of increasing M^s in the IS-LM model

An increase in M^s shifts the LM curve to the right, giving rise to a higher equilibrium level of output $(Y^*)'$ and a lower equilibrium interest rate $(r^*)'$.

Economics in Practice
Liquidity trap

On the LM curve, the nominal interest rate cannot go to zero because this would imply too high a bond price. When the interest rate is close to zero, nobody wants to invest in bonds because households would be scared that their price may drop at any moment. For this 'speculative' motive, when the interest rate is too close to zero, the households would rather hold any quantity of money: this situation is called a '**liquidity trap**' and implies that conventional monetary policy has no effect on the economy, as shown in Figure 6.6. In a liquidity trap, the LM curve becomes horizontal at an interest rate that is close to zero because the interest rate is so low that the individuals will accept any extra liquidity in their portfolios. In this case, changes in the money supply will have no effect on output. Some commentators say that the recent Eurozone experience with extremely low market interest rates is a case in point of liquidity trap, and explains why the European Central Bank is not able to make the Eurozone economy recover despite pouring huge amounts of new money into it. According to the Keynesian view, in a liquidity trap, only expansionary fiscal policy can help, as the positive effects of the US 'fiscal stimulus' and of the problematic European lack of it (with its 2011–12 'double-dip recession') seem to confirm.

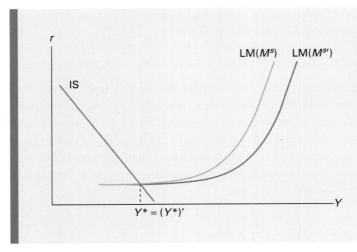

Figure 6.6 Effects of increasing *M*ˢ under a liquidity trap

An increase in M^s shifts the LM curve to the right but leaves the output level unchanged because the intersection of the two curves is at the horizontal part of the LM curve.

from r^* to $(r^*)'$, whereas the equilibrium level of output increases from Y^* to $(Y^*)'$. The decrease in the interest rate stimulates investment, I, whereas the increase in income, Y, stimulates consumption. The increase in income and the decrease in the interest rate both have positive effects on money demand, and the increase in money demand matches the increase in money supply.

The IS-MP model

A common critique of the IS-LM model is that the central bank normally sets the interest rate (rather than the level of money supply) when conducting monetary policy. For example, when the Bank of England's Monetary Policy Committee meets to conduct monetary policy, which it does twelve times a year, the committee sets the Bank of England Base Rate, which is the official interest rate in the United Kingdom. We can accommodate this by replacing the LM curve with a monetary-policy (MP) rule. A simple MP rule is that the monetary authority exogenously sets the nominal interest rate, i. Then, our assumption of a zero inflation rate in the short run implies that the monetary authority is also able to influence the real interest rate. Therefore, we specify a very simple MP rule as follows:

$$r = \bar{r} \tag{6.6}$$

In equation (6.6), $\bar{r}$ is the interest rate target chosen by the monetary authority. The IS curve is the same as in equation (6.3).

Figure 6.7 plots the equilibrium of the IS-MP model and the effects of a decrease in the interest rate, $\bar{r}$. The decrease in $\bar{r}$ shifts down the MP curve causing an increase in the level of output from Y^* to $(Y^*)'$. The decrease in the interest rate stimulates investment, I, which raises output, and then the increase in income, Y, stimulates consumption. These effects are the same as an increase in the level of money supply in the IS-LM model.

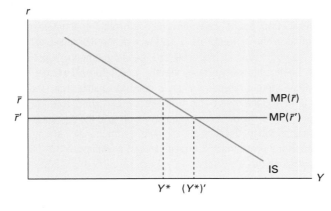

Figure 6.7 Effects of decreasing *r̄* in the IS-MP model

A decrease in $\bar{r}$ shifts down the MP curve, giving rise to a higher equilibrium level of output $(Y^*)'$.

The IS-MP-PC model

So far we have assumed a completely fixed price level that implies a zero inflation rate in the short run. This is a very extreme assumption. Some degree of price rigidity does not necessarily imply a completely fixed aggregate price level. Therefore, sticky prices do not necessarily imply a zero inflation rate. In this section, we explore the behaviour of inflation by introducing to the IS-MP model an additional component; namely, the Phillips curve. The resulting IS-MP-PC model is often referred to as the **three-equation Keynesian model**.

The Phillips curve, named after William Phillips, specifies a positive relationship between inflation, π, and the level of output, Y.[3] This relationship is based on the observation that inflation tends to be high in a booming economy, whereas it tends to be low in a recession. The version of the Phillips curve that we consider is:

$$\pi = \pi^e + \theta \bullet (Y - \bar{Y}) \tag{6.7}$$

The parameter $\theta > 0$ determines how sensitive inflation, π, is to changes in output, Y. $\bar{Y}$ is the long-run level of output determined by economic growth. Given that this is a short-run model, we take $\bar{Y}$ as given. The variable π^e denotes the expected inflation rate. There are many ways to model expectations. Here, we consider a simple formulation: extrapolative expectations. Under extrapolative expectations, firms and households expect inflation this year to equal inflation in the previous year; i.e., $\pi^e = \pi_{t-1}$, where π_{t-1} is the inflation rate in the previous period.

In order to allow inflation to affect output, we need a more general monetary policy rule. The more general version of the MP curve that we consider here is given by:

$$r = \bar{r} + \rho \bullet (\pi - \bar{\pi}) \tag{6.8}$$

The parameter $\rho > 0$ determines how sensitive the interest rate is to changes in inflation. When ρ equals zero, equation (6.8) is identical to the simple MP rule in equation (6.6). In the more general case that ρ is greater than zero, a decrease in the inflation rate, π, causes the central bank to lower the interest rate. The intuition behind this policy response is that lower inflation may be caused by a weakening economy, so the central bank should cut the interest rate to stimulate the economy. The parameter $\bar{\pi}$ denotes the inflation target of the central bank.[4] Notice that we are here assuming quite an aggressive central bank policy, which raises the nominal interest rate more than one-to-one to inflation.[5]

We now substitute the MP curve into the IS curve in equation (6.3) to obtain the following negative relationship between output, Y, and inflation, π:

$$Y = \{I[\bar{r} + \rho \bullet (\pi - \bar{\pi})] + G - cT\}/(1 - c) \tag{6.9}$$
$$\scriptstyle(-)$$

Intuitively, a higher inflation, π, leads to an increase in the interest rate, r, from the monetary policy rule which, in turn, depresses investment, I, and output, Y. Equation (6.9) is essentially an aggregate demand (AD) curve that describes a negative relationship between inflation and output. The Phillips curve can also be interpreted as an aggregate supply (AS) curve that describes a positive relationship between inflation and output as follows:

$$\pi = \pi_{t-1} + \theta \bullet (Y - \bar{Y}) \tag{6.10}$$

Figure 6.8 plots the equilibrium of the IS-MP-PC model in the AS-AD diagram.

Suppose we consider the effects of disinflation by the central bank (i.e., a decrease in the inflation target, $\bar{\pi}$). Figure 6.9 shows that a decrease in $\bar{\pi}$ shifts down the AD curve. Intuitively, the decrease in $\bar{\pi}$ causes the central bank to respond by raising the interest rate (i.e., disinflation requires an increase in the interest rate) which, in turn, depresses investment and output in the short run.

---

[3]In Phillips's original article in 1958, he identified a negative relationship between unemployment and the rate of change of nominal wages (i.e., wage inflation) in the UK economy. Given that unemployment and output are inversely related, the negative relationship between unemployment and inflation implies a positive relationship between output and inflation.

[4]Specifically, $\bar{\pi}$ is the inflation target when the equilibrium interest rate, r, is equal to $\bar{r}$.

[5]If, instead, the central bank were not increasing the nominal interest rate following an increase in the inflation rate, then, according to the previously mentioned Fisher's equation $r = i - \pi$, the increase in inflation would automatically lead to a decline of the real interest rate.

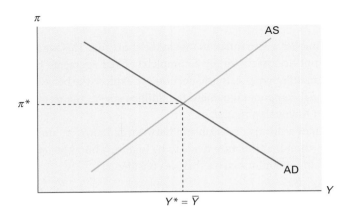

Figure 6.8 The AS-AD diagram

The intersection of the AS and AD curves shows the equilibrium level of output and the equilibrium inflation rate in the economy.

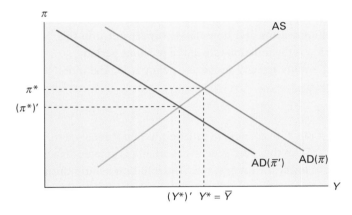

Figure 6.9 Short-run effects of disinflation

A decrease in $\bar{\pi}$ shifts down the AD curve, which gives rise to a decrease in the equilibrium level of output and inflation rate in the short run.

After one period, the decrease in the equilibrium inflation rate causes inflation expectation, $\pi^e = \pi_{t-1}$, to fall which, in turn, shifts down the AS curve. This shift in the AS curve causes a further decrease in inflation but also an increase in output. After two periods, the decrease in inflation causes inflation expectation to adjust downwards again which, in turn, shifts down the AS curve again. This process continues until the level of output returns to the long-run level, $\bar{Y}$, which is depicted in Figure 6.10. In the long run, the equilibrium rate of inflation decreases whereas the level of output returns to the initial level, $\bar{Y}$. At $Y = \bar{Y}$, the inflation rate becomes stationary. Although its long-run effect on output is neutral, disinflation causes a temporary fall in output in the short run.

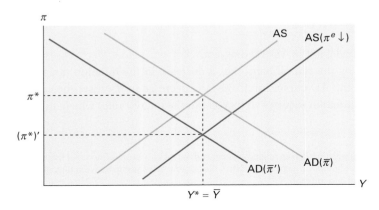

Figure 6.10 Long-run effects of disinflation

The decrease in $\pi^e = \pi_{t-1}$ shifts down the AS curve until the level of output reaches the long-run level.

Macroeconomics with microeconomic foundations

We have devoted this chapter to reviewing some popular models in Keynesian economics. These models often involve *ad hoc* assumptions, such as the relationship between consumption and income and the relationship between investment and the interest rate, that are assumed rather than being derived from optimizing rational behaviours of households and firms. In the next chapter, we will begin to develop a macroeconomic model that is derived from optimizing behaviours based on microeconomic foundations. We will then use this equilibrium business-cycle model to examine the effects of fiscal and monetary policies on the macroeconomy and compare these effects with those in this chapter. Finally, we will also introduce sticky prices into the equilibrium business-cycle model to develop a New Keynesian model in order to have a more realistic analysis of monetary policy. The resulting New Keynesian model is often viewed as an integration of the Keynesian IS-LM model and the equilibrium business-cycle model.

Key Terms and Concepts

aggregate demand	IS-LM model	marginal propensity to	real money supply
aggregate supply	Keynesian economics	consume	sticky nominal wage rates
classical economics	liquidity-money curve	nominal interest rate	sticky prices
investment-saving curve	liquidity trap	real interest rate	three-equation Keynesian
investor sentiment		real money demand	model

Questions and Problems

A   Review questions

1   Show the effects of increasing taxation, T, on the interest rate, output, consumption and investment in the IS-LM model

2   Suppose the inflation rate π is positive and exogenous in the IS-LM model. In this case, the LM curve becomes $M^s/P = D(Y, r + \pi)$. Show the effects of an exogenous increase in inflation, π, on the real interest rate, output, consumption and investment in the IS-LM model

3   Show the effects of increasing government spending, G, on the interest rate, output, consumption and investment in the IS-MP model

4   Show the short-run and long-run effects of increasing the interest rate target, $\bar{r}$, on the inflation rate and output in the IS-MP-PC model

5   Show the short-run and long-run effects of increasing the long-run level of output, $\bar{Y}$, on the inflation rate and output in the IS-MP-PC model

7 Markets, prices, supply and demand

People care a great deal about whether the economy is expanding or contracting. During a boom, when real GDP rises, consumption and investment tend to be strong, employment tends to rise and unemployment tends to fall. Conversely, during a recession, when real GDP falls, consumption, investment and employment tend to be weak, and unemployment tends to increase. During recessions, people find it hard to locate good jobs, and more workers lose jobs than find them. The inability to keep or find a good job causes hardship for job seekers and their families.

In this part of the book, our main goal is to understand these economic fluctuations; that is, the increases of real GDP during booms and the decreases during recessions. These fluctuations typically apply to relatively short periods, such as one or two years. In contrast, our study of economic growth in Chapters 3 to 5 focused on the long term: 5–10 years, or even 20–30 years or longer.

To build a model of economic fluctuations, we start by working out the model's microeconomic foundations. These foundations describe how individual consumers and producers make choices. In the present chapter, we will focus on the markets for labour and capital services. In Chapter 8, we extend the analysis to consumption and saving.

An example of a microeconomic choice is a worker's decision about how much to work. Another example is a producer's decision about how many workers to hire. In these decisions, an individual worker or producer takes as given the prices that they face. One of these prices is the *real wage rate*, which specifies the quantity of goods that a worker can buy with an hour of labour.

A key assumption in our model is that individual workers, consumers and producers are too small to have a significant impact on the prices that influence their decisions. To take a concrete example, which we detail later, consider a simple analysis of the labour market. Suppose that, in choosing how much labour to supply, each worker takes as given the real wage rate. Similarly, in deciding how much labour to demand, each producer takes as given the real wage rate. Thus, the individual choices of quantities supplied and demanded are made at given market prices. Economists say that this assumption applies under perfect competition. With perfect competition, each market participant assumes that he or she can sell or buy any quantity desired at the going price. In particular, each participant is small enough that changes in their quantity supplied and demanded have a negligible impact on the market price.

When we add up the individual choices, we determine aggregate or market supply and demand functions. For example, we determine the market supply of and demand for labour as a function of the real wage rate, w/P; Figure 7.1 shows this case. The aggregate quantity of labour supplied, L^s, is assumed to rise as w/P increases (along the light blue curve). Therefore, the L^s curve slopes upward. The aggregate quantity of labour demanded, L^d, is assumed to decline as w/P rises (along the dark blue curve). Therefore, the L^d curve slopes downward.

Once we know the market supply and demand functions, we have to consider how these functions determine the quantities and prices in the economy. Our main approach relies on market-clearing conditions. As an example, in Figure 7.1, the market supply of and demand for labour each depends on the real wage rate, w/P.

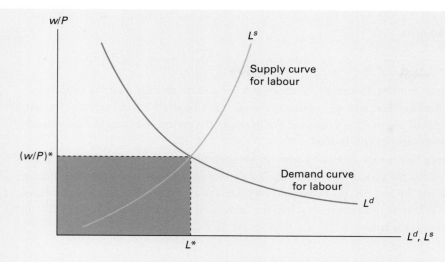

Figure 7.1 An example of market clearing: the labour market

This figure gives a simple example of how a market – in this case, the labour market – clears. The labour-demand curve, L^d, slopes downward versus the real wage rate, w/P. The labour-supply curve, L^s, slopes upward versus w/P. Market clearing corresponds to the intersection of the two curves. The market-clearing real wage rate is $(w/P)^*$, and the market-clearing quantity of labour is L^*.

Our assumption is that w/P adjusts to clear the labour market; that is, to equate the quantity of labour supplied to the quantity demanded. Thus, the market-clearing real wage rate is the value $(w/P)^*$ on the vertical axis, and the market-clearing quantity of labour is the value L^* on the horizontal axis.

With this background about markets in mind, we will now start the construction of the microeconomic foundations for our macroeconomic model. We begin by specifying the structure of the markets in the model.

Markets in the macroeconomy

Our macroeconomic model contains several markets on which exchanges occur. In this section, we describe the participants in each market and identify the goods and services exchanged on each market.

We simplify by assuming that households perform all of the functions in the economy. Each household runs a family business and uses labour, L, and capital, K, to produce goods, Y, through the production function, which we introduced in Chapter 3:

$$Y = A \cdot F(K, L) \tag{3.1}$$

More realistically, the production of goods might take place in a large corporation or a small business. However, if we included these private businesses in our model, we would have to take into account that they must ultimately be owned by households, possibly through shares traded on a **stock market**. When we think of businesses as parts of households, we avoid the complexities of ownership structure. Since we end up with the same macroeconomic results, this simplification is worth making.

THE GOODS MARKET

In the real world, the typical household uses little of the goods that it helps to produce in the marketplace. Usually, a person works on one or a few products and receives income from the sale of these products, or from the sale of the labour services that help to produce the products. The person then spends this income on an array of goods. The model would become too complex if we tried to capture this variety of goods.

We simplify by imagining that households sell all the goods they produce on a **goods market**. Then households buy back from this market the goods that they want. One reason that a household buys goods is for *consumption*.

Another reason is to increase the stock of goods in the form of capital – machines and buildings – used for production. This use of goods is called *investment*.

THE LABOUR MARKET

Households supply labour on a **labour market**. To simplify at the outset, we assume that the quantity supplied, L^s, is a constant, L. This assumption is not harmless, and we eventually change it in Chapter 9. As in previous chapters, we measure labour as the flow quantity of person-hours per year. For example, if a person works 40 hours per week, 52 weeks per year, the flow of person-hours per year is 2080.

Households, as managers of family businesses, demand labour in the quantity L from the labour market. The labour demanded is used as an input to the production of goods. Notice that each household wears two hats in our simplified economy. When wearing the first hat, the household supplies labour, looking like an employee hired by the person who buys the labour. When wearing the second hat, the household demands labour, looking like an employer who hires the person who sells the labour.

THE RENTAL MARKET

Next, we consider the capital input to production. Households own the capital stock, K. An individual household can add to its stock by buying goods from the goods market and can lower its stock by selling goods on the goods market. We can think of these trades as resales of used capital goods. For example, a household might sell a used car or a house, which are forms of capital goods. In our model, where households run businesses, we also imagine that households might sell a used machine or a whole used factory.

The stock of capital, K, is measured in units of goods; for example, numbers of cars or numbers of machines. Conceptually, we should distinguish this stock of goods from the flow of capital services. For example, suppose that a household owns a single machine. If the machine operates 8 hours per day, 5 days per week, 52 weeks per year, the machine is used for 2080 hours per year. We think of these 2080 machine-hours per year – a flow variable – as the quantity of capital services. This flow is analogous to the flow of labour services, measured in person-hours per year.

We simplify at the outset by assuming that each unit of capital – say, each machine – is used for a fixed number of hours per year, perhaps 2080. In this case, the flow of capital services is a constant multiple of the capital stock – each machine represents 2080 machine-hours per year. Therefore, in this case, we will not get into any trouble if we enter the capital stock, K, as an input to the production function, as we did in equation (3.1). This stock really represents the flow of capital services, but this flow is a fixed multiple of the stock. Since the multiple is a constant – say, 2080 – we do not have to show it explicitly in the production function, $F(K, L)$.

Although a household owns a particular unit of capital – say, a machine – it does not necessarily use that capital for its own production of goods. Rather, the household can rent the capital to another household, which then uses it as an input to production. For example, a household might rent its house or car to another household. In our model, we extend this idea of rentals to all types of capital, including machines and factories.

We shall find it convenient to assume that each household rents out all of the capital that it owns on a **rental market**. Thus, if a household owns a machine, it offers for rent all of the capital services – say, 2080 machine-hours per year – that this machine provides. In the real world, we can think of Hertz as owning cars and renting them to users. Other real-world examples are rentals of furniture from companies such as Cort Furniture and Instant Home, rentals of tools from stores such as Home Depot and Hire Station, and rentals of taxis and truck cabs from their owners. The important assumption in our model is that households do not allow any of their capital to sit idle and, rather, provide all of it for use on the rental market.

The amount of capital offered on the rental market is analogous to the amount of labour offered or supplied to the labour market, L^s. Therefore, we think of the capital offered on the rental market as the supply of capital services, K^s. Since we have assumed that each household rents out all of its capital, we have $K^s = K$. (More precisely, we should multiply by 2080 to convert from capital stock – numbers of machines – to capital services – machine-hours per year. But, since 2080 is a constant, we can ignore it.) Our assumption that the supply of capital services is constant is analogous to our assumption that the supply of labour is constant. Again, the assumption is not harmless, and we change our assumption about capital services in Chapter 10.

So far, we have assumed that each household rents out all the capital that it owns. However, households, as managers of family businesses, also use capital services to produce goods. To get this capital input, households rent it from the rental market. The amount of capital rented on the rental market is analogous to the amount of labour purchased or demanded from the labour market, L^d. Therefore, we think of the capital rented on the rental market as the demand for capital services, K^d.

Notice that we are assuming that each household rents out all of its capital, $K^s = K$, and then rents back the quantity K^d. If K^s is greater than K^d, we could think instead of the household as retaining the quantity K^d of its own capital for use in production of goods and then renting out only the remainder, $K^s - K^d$. Analogously, if K^s is less than K^d, we can think of the household as using the entire quantity K^s of its own capital for use in production of goods, and then renting the additional amount, $K^d - K^s$. The results would be the same under these alternative assumptions. Therefore, we shall find it convenient to stick with the assumption that the household rents out all of its capital, $K^s = K$, and then rents back the quantity, K^d, that it uses as an input to production.

THE BOND MARKET

The last market that we introduce is one in which households borrow or lend. A borrowing household receives a loan from another household, whereas a lending household provides a loan to another household. In the real world, this lending and borrowing would typically occur through financial institutions, such as banks. However, as in our neglect of private businesses, we simplify by assuming that households carry out all lending and borrowing directly.

We assume that a household that makes a loan receives a piece of paper – a form of contract – that specifies the terms of the loan. We call this piece of paper a *bond*, and we call the market on which households borrow or lend the **bond market**. The holder of a bond – the lender – has a claim to the amount owed by the borrower.

Money as a medium of exchange

Households buy and sell goods on the goods market, labour on the labour market, capital services on the rental market and bonds on the bond market. We assume that the exchanges on each of these markets use a single form of **medium of exchange**. In general, a medium of exchange is an object held, not for its own sake but, rather, to trade fairly soon for something else, such as goods and services. We call the medium of exchange in our model **money**. Historically, money has taken many forms, including precious commodities such as gold and silver, or sometimes beads and shells. However, in our model, we assume that money is just a piece of paper, analogous to a paper **currency** issued by a government.

Money is denominated in an arbitrary unit, such as 'the euro'. For example, a household may have €100. Euro amounts are in **nominal** terms. Thus, €100 is the value of the household's currency in nominal units. One important property of paper money is that it bears no interest. That is, if a household has €100 of money and just leaves it under the mattress, the amount of money held is still €100 the following week and the following year (assuming that it is not lost). In contrast, bonds will earn interest. We use the symbol M for the nominal quantity of money that a household holds. The sum of the individual holdings of money equals the aggregate quantity of money in the economy. We assume, for now, that this aggregate quantity of money is a given constant. Therefore, the total money held by all households must end up equalling this constant.

Economics in Practice
Common currency

Historically, most governments have issued their own currency. However, there is now a trend towards the formation of groups of countries that share a **common currency**, which is a single form of money used by several countries. This kind of group is called a **currency union.** The most important example of a currency union since 1999–2001 is the euro, which is issued by the European Central Bank and is the official currency of the Eurozone that consists of 19 of the 28 member states of the European Union. These countries are Austria, Belgium, Cyprus, Estonia, Finland, France, Germany, Greece, Ireland, Italy, Latvia, Lithuania, Luxembourg, Malta, the Netherlands, Portugal, Slovakia, Slovenia and Spain. Some other European countries are considering the adoption of the euro, although the United Kingdom, Denmark and Sweden have rejected the idea.

A number of small countries have been joined together in currency unions for some time. Examples are the 14 African countries that use the CFA franc (linked in the past to the French franc and now the euro) and the seven Caribbean countries in the Eastern Caribbean Currency Area (ECCA) that use the Caribbean dollar (linked to the US dollar). Proposals exist (or existed in the past) for the creation of new currency unions in northeast Asia (China, Japan and South Korea), southern and western Africa, the Persian Gulf, Central America, and between Australia and New Zealand. In addition, a number of small countries use (or used in the past) the currency of a large country – examples are Panama, Ecuador, Bermuda, Liechtenstein, Luxembourg and San Marino.

Markets and prices

The key macroeconomic variables in our model will be determined by the interactions of households who trade on the various markets. We will now describe the details of each market.

THE GOODS MARKET

We assume that there is a single type of good that can be used for consumption or investment. The goods market is the place in which households exchange goods for money. The price in this market, denoted by P, expresses the amount of euros that are exchanged for one unit of goods. We call P the **price level.** The consumer price index, or CPI, which we discussed in Chapter 2, is a real-world counterpart of the price level. The CPI measures the nominal cost of a representative market basket of goods and services.[1] Alternatively, we can think of the deflator for the gross domestic product (the GDP deflator), which is a price index related to the economy's overall production of goods and services (the real GDP). In the model, which has just one type of good, the price level, P, corresponds to the CPI or the GDP deflator. We assume, for now, that there is no inflation, which is the change over time in the price level. That is, we assume that P does not change over time.

Recall that households produce goods in the flow quantity Y per year, where Y is given from the production function as:

$$Y = A \bullet F(K, L) \tag{3.1}$$

Since all of these goods are sold on the goods market, the variable Y will also represent the quantity of goods per year sold and bought on the goods market. The quantity PY is the nominal value per year of the goods bought and sold on the goods market.

For a seller of goods, the price level, P, is the amount of euros obtained for each unit of goods sold. In contrast, for a buyer, P is the amount of euros paid per unit of goods. Since P euros buy 1 unit of goods, €1 buys $1/P$ units

---

[1]More precisely, the CPI measures the nominal cost of a market basket of goods in a particular year – say, 2016 – expressed relative to the nominal cost of the market basket of goods in a base year – say, 2015.

of goods. The expression $1/P$ is, therefore, the value of €1 in terms of the goods that it buys. Similarly, M euros exchange for:

$$(M) \bullet (1/P) = M/P$$

units of goods. The quantity M is the value of money in euros, and the quantity M/P is the value of this money in terms of the goods that it buys. An expression such as M/P is in **real terms** – in units of goods – whereas a quantity such as M is in nominal terms. As an example, if a household has €100 of money and the price level is 5, the real value of the household's money is:

$$100/5 = 20$$

That is, the household could buy 20 units of goods with its €100 of money. Hence, 100 is the nominal value of the household's money, and 20 is the real value of this money, measured in terms of the quantity of goods that it buys. To put it another way, each €1 of money can buy 1/5th of a unit of goods. Hence, 1/5th is the real value of each euro.

THE LABOUR MARKET

Households buy and sell labour in the labour market at the **nominal wage rate**, w. Since we measure labour, L, in units of hours worked per year, the wage rate, w, is the units of euros per hour worked. A household that buys the amount of labour L pays the nominal amount wL^d per year, and then gets to use the labour as an input to production. A household that sells the quantity of labour L^s receives the nominal wage income of wL^s per year.

The **real wage rate** is w/P. This real wage rate is the value in goods per hour received by a supplier of labour and paid by a demander of labour. For example, if the nominal wage rate is $w = $ €10 per hour and the price level is $P = 5$, the real wage rate is:

$$w/P = 10/5 = 2$$

This real wage rate – 2 goods per hour worked – determines the quantity of goods that can be bought with the nominal wage (€10) paid for an hour of work. Since people care about the goods that they get, we shall find that household decisions depend on the real wage rate, w/P, rather than the nominal wage rate, w.

THE RENTAL MARKET

In the rental market, households rent out capital, K, for euros at the **nominal rental price**, R. The price R is expressed in euros per unit of capital per year. For example, if $R = $ €100 per year, a household receives €100 per year for each unit of capital (say, a machine or a car) that the household rents out on the rental market.

A household that rents the amount of capital K^d pays the nominal amount RK^d per year and then gets to use the capital as an input to production. A household that rents out the quantity of capital K^s receives the nominal rental income of RK^s per year.

The **real rental price** is R/P. This real rental price is the value in goods per unit of capital per year received by the supplier and paid by the demander. For example, if the nominal rental price is $R = $ €100 and the price level is $P = 5$, the real rental price is:

$$R/P = 100/5 = 20$$

This real rental price – 20 goods per unit of capital per year – gives the quantity of goods that can be bought with the rental payments (€100) for each unit of capital over a year. Again, since people care about the goods that they get, we shall find that household decisions depend on the real rental price, R/P, rather than the nominal rental price, R.

THE BOND MARKET

Our model has a simple form of bond market in which households borrow and lend from each other. For example, a household might make a loan to another household that wants to buy a car, a house, a machine, or a factory. A **bond** is the piece of paper that lays out the terms of the loan contract.

A bond could be an IOU that says that household *a* owes a certain number of euros to the holder of the bond. Initially, the borrower owes the money to household *b*, which is the household that advanced the money. However, we assume that bonds can be sold on the bond market to another household, perhaps household *c*, which becomes the holder of the bond. Household *a* then owes the money to household *c*.

We define units so that each unit of bonds commits the borrower to repay €1 to the holder of the bond. This €1 is the **principal** of each bond. The principal is the initial amount advanced on a loan.

We simplify by thinking of all bonds as having very short **maturity**, by which we mean the time at which the principal must be paid back. At any point in time, the issuer of a bond – the borrower – is entitled to buy back the bond for the fixed €1 of principal. That is, the borrower can retire the loan by giving back the €1 to the holder of the bond. Similarly, the holder of the bond is entitled to return the bond to the borrower at any time in exchange for €1. That is, the holder can cancel the loan by demanding the €1 of principal.

These assumptions are not so realistic. For example, with a student loan, the lender (which might be a bank) cannot demand repayment until many years in the future; that is, the maturity is long. Similarly, home mortgages often have long maturities, although borrowers can usually pay back the principal at any time. Despite these real-world complications, our assumption that maturities are very short will capture the most important aspects of interest rates in a tractable way.

We assume that, as long as a bond is neither retired nor cancelled, each unit of bonds commits the borrower to pay the holder a flow of interest payments of €i per year. The variable i is the interest rate, which is the ratio of the interest payment, €i, to the principal, €1. The interest rate, i, can vary over time.

As an example, suppose that a household borrows €1000, so that the principal amount outstanding is €1000. Assume that the interest rate, i, is 5% per year. In this case, the annual interest payment is:

$$interest\ payment = interest\ rate \bullet principal$$
$$€50 = 5\% \bullet €1000$$

For the holder of a bond, the interest rate, i, determines the return per year to lending. For the issuer of a bond, i determines the cost per year of borrowing.

One complication is that a borrower receives euros today – say, €1000 – and pays interest over time – say, €50 per year – with euros in the future. If the price level, P, were changing – that is, if the inflation rate were not zero – today's euros and future euros would differ in their real values. Thus, when we allow for inflation in Chapter 12, we have to distinguish two concepts of interest rates – the *nominal interest rate* and the *real interest rate*. However, for now, we do not have to worry about this complication because the inflation rate is zero.

We simplify by assuming that all bonds are alike, regardless of the household that issued the bond. Most importantly, we neglect differences among issuers in the risk that payments of interest and principal will not be made. One type of risk is that a borrower will default on a loan by refusing to pay or by disappearing. Since we ignore these risks, the interest rate, i, will have to be the same on all bonds. Otherwise, borrowers would want to do all their borrowing at the lowest interest rate, whereas lenders would want to do all their lending at the highest interest rate. Since all bonds are identical, borrowers and lenders can be matched only if the interest rates on all bonds are the same.

Let B represent the number of bonds in nominal units that a household holds. This amount may be greater than zero or less than zero for an individual household. Notice, however, that for any euro borrowed by one household, there must be a corresponding euro lent by another household. Hence, the total of positive bond holdings for lenders must exactly match the total of negative bond holdings for borrowers. Therefore, when we sum up over all households, the total of the Bs must always be zero.

Finally, we consider the price of bonds. One unit of bonds was defined to have a principal of €1 – that is, each unit can always be exchanged for €1 by cancelling the loan. Therefore, the nominal price of these bonds must always be €1 per unit.[2] However, the important variable for our analysis is the interest rate, i. We can think of i as the cost

---

[2]The price is fixed at €1 per unit because we are considering bonds with very short maturity. Longer-term bonds commit the borrower to pay the bondholder a stream of nominal payments (in interim payments called *coupons* and in a final payment called the *principal*) over a period, up to the maturity date. We can define the units so that each unit of bonds commits the borrower to pay the holder €1 at the maturity date. The nominal price of these bonds will vary when the interest rate, i, changes.

or price of credit. A higher i means that obtaining credit – borrowing – is more expensive in terms of the interest that has to be paid. At the same time, a higher i means that extending credit – lending – is more rewarding, in that it yields a higher flow of interest income.

Constructing the budget constraint

The quantities and prices determined on the four markets will determine household income. Households will receive income from managing the family business, wages, rentals of capital services and interest received. These flows of income are **sources of funds** for households. Households use their sources of funds to buy goods or increase their assets; that is, to *save*. The purchases of goods and assets are **uses of funds** for households. The important point is that the total sources of funds must equal the total uses of funds. This equality is called the household **budget constraint**, which we derive in this chapter. In Chapter 8, we use the budget constraint to understand how households choose consumption and saving.

INCOME

We begin by considering household income. Households receive income in four forms: profit from the family business, wage income, rental income and interest income. We consider each of these in turn.

Profit

Households may earn **profit** – an excess of revenue over costs – from their business activities. If a household uses the quantity of labour L and the quantity of capital K^d as inputs to production, the amount of goods produced, Y, is given by the production function:

$$Y = A \cdot F(K^d, L^d) \tag{7.1}$$

Since all goods sell at the price level, P, the nominal income from sales is PY per year.

Households pay the nominal amounts wL^d per year for labour input and RK^d per year for capital input. The difference between the income from sales and the payments to labour and capital is the nominal profit per year from running the family business. This nominal profit, which we represent by Π, is given by:

$$profit = income\ from\ sales - wage\ and\ rental\ payments$$
$$\Pi = PY - (wL^d + RK^d)$$

If we substitute $A \cdot F(K^d, L^d)$ for Y, we get:

$$\Pi = PA \cdot F(k^d, L^d) - (wL^d + RK^d) \tag{7.2}$$

This expression is useful because it shows how profit, Π, depends on households' business decisions, which are the quantities demanded of capital and labour input, K^d and L^d.

Wage income

If households supply the quantity of labour L^s to the labour market, they receive the nominal wage income of wL^s per year. As already mentioned, we assume for now that the quantity of labour supplied is the fixed amount L. Therefore, the nominal wage income is wL.

Rental income

If households supply the quantity of capital K^s to the rental market, they receive the nominal rental income of RK^s per year. Since households supply all of their available capital, K, to the rental market, so that $K^s = K$, the nominal rental income is RK.

We assume, as in Chapter 3, that capital depreciates at the rate δ. Therefore, the quantity δK of capital disappears each year. The nominal value of this lost capital is $P \cdot \delta K$ per year. Hence, the net nominal rental income from ownership of capital is:

$$net\ nominal\ rental\ income = nominal\ rental\ income - value\ of\ depreciation$$
$$= RK - \delta PK$$

We want to calculate the rate of return that households get by owning capital. To compute this rate of return, we have to manipulate the expression for net nominal rental income. Start by dividing and multiplying the first term by P to get:

$$net\ nominal\ rental\ income = (R/P) \bullet PK - \delta PK$$

Next, combine the terms on the right-hand side to get:

$$net\ nominal\ rental\ income = (R/P - \delta) \bullet PK \tag{7.3}$$

The right-hand side expresses the net nominal rental income as the product of two terms: $R/P - \delta$ and PK. The second term, PK, is the nominal value of the capital owned by households. The first term, $R/P - \delta$, is the rate of return on each euro held in the form of capital. The important result is the formula for the rate of return on capital:

$$rate\ of\ return\ on\ owning\ capital = R/P - \delta \tag{7.4}$$

The rate of return on owning capital is the real rental price, R/P, less the rate of depreciation, δ.

Interest income

If a household's nominal bond holdings are B, the flow of nominal interest income received is iB per year. Notice that interest income is greater than zero for a holder of bonds (when B is greater than zero) and less than zero for an issuer of bonds (when B is less than zero). That is, an issuer of bonds – someone who owes money to another person – has to pay out interest rather than receive it. Since B equals zero for the whole economy, we have that the total of interest income equals zero. The amount paid to holders of bonds (lenders) exactly balances the amount paid by issuers of bonds (borrowers).

Total income

We can put the four types of income together to calculate households' total nominal income per year. The result is:

$$household\ nominal\ income = nominal\ profit + nominal\ wage\ income$$
$$+ nominal\ net\ rental\ income + nominal\ interest\ income$$

If, from equation (7.2), we substitute Π for nominal profit and wL for nominal wage income, and, from equation (7.3), we substitute $(R/P - \delta) \cdot PK$ for nominal net rental income, and insert iB for nominal interest income, we get:

$$household\ nominal\ income = \Pi + wL + (R/P - \delta) \bullet PK + iB \tag{7.5}$$

CONSUMPTION

So far, we have discussed household income. Now, we will consider household expenditures on goods. Households consume goods in the quantity C per year. Since the price level is P, the nominal amount spent on consumption per year is:

$$household\ nominal\ consumption = PC$$

ASSETS

Now, we will work out how households' incomes and expenditures relate to households' assets. Households hold assets in three forms: money, M; bonds, B; and ownership of capital, K. Money pays no interest. Bonds pay interest at the rate i per year. Ownership of capital yields the rate of return $R/P - \delta$ per year, as seen in equation (7.4). We assume that households can divide their assets any way they wish among the three forms. That is, at any point in time, households can exchange euros of money for euros of bonds and can exchange euros of money for units of capital at the price level, P. So, when would households choose to hold all three forms of assets?

Bonds seem to be more attractive than money if the interest rate, i, is greater than zero. Households would, however, hold some money for convenience, because they use money as a medium of exchange; for example, to buy or sell goods and labour. In contrast, our assumption is that bonds are not readily accepted in exchange for goods or labour; usually, the holder of a bond has to sell the bond for money before buying goods or labour. The special role of money in making exchanges motivates households to have a positive *demand for money*. We will postpone our study of this demand for money until Chapter 11. For now, we assume that households hold a fixed amount of money in nominal terms; that is, we assume that the change over time of a household's nominal money holdings is zero. If we use the symbol Δ to represent a change over time, we have:

$$\Delta M = 0$$

As an example, a family might want to hold €200, on average, to cover expenses for groceries, petrol and other goods. The amount of money held by an individual household would vary over time, sometimes rising above €200 and sometimes falling below €200. However, if the average money held by each household is always €200, then the total money held at every point in time by all households would tend not to vary much. Our assumption is that the change in the total amount of money held by all households, ΔM, is zero.

In considering whether to hold assets as bonds or capital, households would compare the rate of return on bonds (i.e., the interest rate, i) with the rate of return on ownership of capital (i.e., $R/P - \delta$). Would households be willing to hold both forms of assets if the rates of return differed? They might be willing to hold both types if the assets differed by characteristics other than the rate of return. In the real world, the most important difference is the *riskiness* of the returns. Some types of bonds, such as short-term bonds issued by financially solvent governments, are nearly risk-free.[3] Forms of owning capital, such as stock in Airbus Group, provide uncertain returns. In these situations, the risky asset (stock in Airbus Group) typically has to pay an expected rate of return greater than the interest rate on, say, German Treasury discount paper to induce people to hold the risky asset.

To keep things manageable in our model, we do not consider risk in the returns paid on bonds or capital. That is, we assume that, aside from rates of return, bonds and capital look the same to households as ways to hold assets. In this case, if bonds offered a higher rate of return, households would hold no capital. In contrast, if capital offered a higher rate of return, households would want to borrow a great deal to hold considerable capital (actually, an infinite amount). Since the economy's stock of capital is greater than zero but less than infinity, the two rates of return must be equal. This condition is:

Key equation:
rate of return on bonds = rate of return on ownership of capital
$i = R/P - \delta$ (7.6)

If we use this result to substitute i for $R/P - \delta$ in the expression for household nominal income in equation (7.5), we get:

$$household\ nominal\ income = \pi + wL + i \cdot (B + PK) \qquad (7.7)$$

The last term shows that assets held as bonds or ownership of capital yield the same rate of return per year, given by the interest rate, i.

HOUSEHOLD BUDGET CONSTRAINT

Now, we will use the results on household income to construct the household budget constraint. This constraint relates changes in households' assets to the flows of income.

---

[3] The holder of these bonds has virtual certainty of receiving the promised nominal amount in the future. However, the real value of this payment is uncertain because the future price level is unknown; that is, the inflation rate is uncertain. Thus, even these bonds have risk in their real returns unless their payments are indexed by inflation.

At a point in time, a household has assets in the form of money, bonds and ownership of capital:

$$nominal\ value\ of\ assets = M + B + PK$$

We define **nominal saving** to be the change over time in the nominal value of assets. Therefore, if we again use the symbol Δ to represent a change over time, we have:

$$nominal\ saving = \Delta(nominal\ assets)$$
$$= \Delta M + \Delta B + P \bullet \Delta K$$

If we use our assumption that $\Delta M = 0$, we get:

$$nominal\ saving = \Delta B + P \bullet \Delta K \tag{7.8}$$

That is, a household's saving corresponds to changes in its holdings of bonds and capital.

A household's nominal saving depends on its income and consumption. If income is greater than consumption, the difference will be saved and, therefore, added to assets. If income is less than consumption, nominal saving is less than zero, and the difference will subtract from nominal assets. Therefore, we have:

$$nominal\ saving = nominal\ income - nominal\ consumption$$

Extending the Model
Allowing for a risk premium on ownership of capital

We can make our model more realistic by allowing for a difference between the rate of return on ownership of capital, $R/P - \delta$, and the interest rate on bonds, i. We can write the relationship between the two rates of return as:

$$R/P - \delta = i + risk\ premium$$
$$rate\ of\ return\ on\ capital = interest\ rate + risk\ premium$$

Thus, the **risk premium** is the excess of the anticipated rate of return on capital – for example, the expected rate of return on holding corporate stock – over the expected rate of return on a nearly risk-free asset, such as German Treasury discount paper. The risk premium normally has to be greater than zero to induce households to hold the riskier asset. If the risk premium is constant, our analysis would not change by allowing for this premium. More interesting (and more difficult) would be to allow the risk premia to vary over time. Some reasons that risk premia change are: first, the perceived riskiness of capital changes; second, households become more or less willing to absorb risk; and, third, innovations in the financial markets or the legal system make it easier for households to reduce the overall risk in their assets and incomes.

If we substitute for nominal income from equation (7.7) and replace nominal consumption by PC, we get:

$$nominal\ saving = \Pi + wL + i \bullet (B + PK) - PC \tag{7.9}$$

Equations (7.8) and (7.9) are two ways of representing nominal saving. Therefore, the right-hand sides of the equations must be equal:

$$\Delta B + P \bullet \Delta K = \Pi + wL + i \bullet (B + PK) - PC \tag{7.10}$$

This equation says that nominal saving, $\Delta B + P \bullet \Delta K$ on the left-hand side, equals the difference between nominal income, $\Pi + wL + i \bullet (B + PK)$, and nominal consumption, PC, on the right-hand side.

If we rearrange equation (7.10) to put nominal consumption, *PC*, on the left-hand side, we get:

> **Key equation (household budget constraint in nominal terms):**
>
> $$PC + \Delta B + P \bullet \Delta K = \Pi + wL + i \bullet (B + PK)$$
>
> *nominal consumption + nominal saving = nominal income*
>
> (7.11)

The right-hand side has total nominal income, $\Pi + wL + i \bullet (B + PK)$. Equation (7.11) says that households are constrained to divide this total nominal income between the two terms on the left-hand side: nominal consumption, *PC*, and nominal saving, $\Delta B + P \bullet \Delta K$. Thus, equation (7.11) is the **household budget constraint in nominal terms**.

We shall find it useful to express the household budget constraint in real terms by dividing all the terms in equation (7.11) by the price level, *P*. After we do this division, we get:

> **Key equation (household budget constraint in real terms):**
>
> $$C + (1/P) \bullet \Delta B + \Delta K = \Pi/P + (w/P) \bullet L + i \bullet (B/P + K)$$
>
> *consumption + real saving = real income*
>
> (7.12)

This equation is the **household budget constraint in real terms**. The right-hand side has total real income, $\Pi/P + (w/P) \bullet L + i \bullet (B/P + K)$. The left-hand side has consumption, *C*, and the change in the real value of assets, $(1/P) \bullet \Delta B + \Delta K$. We refer to the change in the real value of assets as **real saving**. Notice that nominal saving, $\Delta B + P \bullet \Delta K$, which appears on the left-hand side of equation (7.11), gives the change in the nominal value of assets. In contrast, real saving, $(1/P) \bullet \Delta B + \Delta K$, which appears on the left-hand side of equation (7.12), gives the change in the real value of assets.

Figure 7.2 shows graphically the household budget constraint from equation (7.12). Suppose that a household has a given total real income, $\Pi/P + (w/P) \bullet L + i \bullet (B/P + K)$, on the right-hand side of the equation. The budget constraint says that this real income must be divided between consumption, *C*, and real saving, $(1/P) \bullet \Delta B + \Delta K$. One possibility is that the household sets real saving to zero, so that *C* equals the total real income. This choice corresponds to point 1, shown on the horizontal axis where *C* equals total real income. Another possibility is that the household sets *C* to zero, so that real saving equals total real income. This choice corresponds to point 2, shown on the vertical axis where real saving equals total real income. More commonly, the household would choose an intermediate point, such as point 3, where *C* and real saving are both greater than zero. The full range of possibilities is shown by the downward-sloping line in the figure. This line is called a **budget line**. The budget constraint in equation (7.12) tells us that, along a budget line, each increase in *C* by one unit corresponds to a decrease in real saving by one unit. Hence, the slope of a budget line is –1.

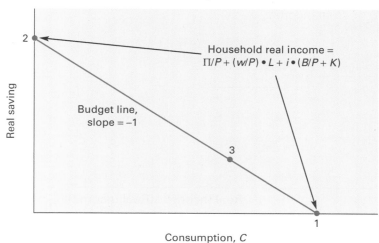

Figure 7.2 The household budget constraint

Households have a given total of real income, $\Pi/P + (w/P) \bullet L + i \bullet (B/P + K)$. This total must be divided between consumption, *C*, and real saving, $(1/P) \bullet \Delta B + \Delta K$. Thus, if real saving is zero, *C* equals the total of real income along the horizontal axis at point 1. If *C* is zero, real saving equals the total of real income along the vertical axis at point 2. The budget constraint in equation (7.12) allows the household to select any combination of consumption and real saving along the budget line such as point 3. The budget line has a slope of –1. Therefore, along this line, one unit less of consumption corresponds to one unit more of real saving.

Clearing of the markets for labour and capital services

Now that we have worked out the household budget constraint, we can consider the choices that households make. We begin by considering decisions about the family business. These decisions determine the demands for labour and capital services. Once we know these demands, we can study the clearing of the markets for labour and capital services.

PROFIT MAXIMIZATION

The two business decisions that households make are the quantities of labour and capital services to demand, L^d and K^d. These decisions determine the amount of goods produced and sold on the goods market, $A \bullet F(K^d, L^d)$, and, therefore, the amount of nominal profit from:

$$\Pi = PA \bullet F(k^d, L^d) - wL^d - RK^d \qquad (7.2)$$

To calculate real profit, we can divide through equation (7.2) by the price level, P, to get:

$$\Pi/P = A \bullet F(k^d, L^d) - (w/P) \bullet L^d - (R/P) \bullet k^d$$

$$real\ profit = output - real\ wage\ payments - real\ rental\ payments \qquad (7.13)$$

We can see from the right-hand side of the household budget constraint in equation (7.12) that an increase in real profit, Π/P, raises household real income. Figure 7.3 shows how an increase in real income affects households. An increase in real income moves the budget line outward from the solid line to the dashed line. In comparison with the solid budget line, the dashed budget line allows households to choose higher consumption, C, for any given value of real saving, $(1/P) \bullet \Delta B + \Delta K$. Therefore, as long as households like more consumption, they prefer more real income to less. This result tells us that households, as managers of family businesses, will seek to make real profit,

Figure 7.3 Effect of an increase in real income on the household budget constraint

If household real income, $\Pi/P + (w/P) \bullet L + i \bullet (B/P + K)$, rises, the budget line moves outward from the solid line to the dashed line. That is, in the graph, (real income)′ is larger than (real income). In comparison with the solid line, the dashed line allows the household to have more consumption, C, for any given value of real saving, $(1/P) \bullet \Delta B + \Delta K$. Since households like more consumption, they prefer more real income to less.

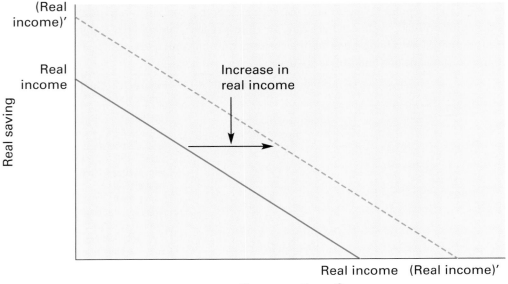

Π/P, as high as possible. That is, households will choose their demands for labour and capital services, L^d and K^d, to maximize Π/P, as given in equation (7.13).

We assume that an individual household takes as given the real wage rate for labour, w/P, and the real rental price for capital, R/P. As mentioned before, these assumptions are standard for competitive markets; an individual household is too small to have a noticeable effect on market prices. In this situation, each household can buy or sell whatever quantity of labour it wants at the going real wage rate, w/P, and can rent or rent out whatever amount of capital it wants at the going real rental price, R/P. Therefore, the household will demand quantities of labour and capital services, L^d and K^d, that maximize real profit, Π/P, for given values of w/P and R/P.

THE LABOUR MARKET

We will now consider the demand for labour and the supply of labour. Then, we will determine the real wage rate, w/P, from the market-clearing condition for the labour market: the quantity of labour demanded equals the quantity supplied.

Demand for labour

The demand for labour, L^d, comes from the objective of profit maximization. Consider the effect of an increase in labour input, L^d, by one unit on real profit, Π/P, as given in equation (7.13). The increase in L raises output, $A \cdot F(K^d, L^d)$, on the right-hand side by increasing production and, hence, sales of goods on the goods market. We know from Chapter 3 that an increase in L by one unit raises production by the marginal product of labour (MPL). An increase in L also raises the second term on the right-hand side, the real wage payments, $(w/P) \cdot L$. For a given real wage rate, w/P, an increase in L by one unit raises these payments by the amount w/P. Therefore, the overall effect from an increase in L by one unit is to change real profit by:

$$\Delta(\Pi/P) = \Delta[A \cdot F(k^d, L^d)] - w/P$$
$$= MPL - w/P$$

change in real profit = marginal product of labour − real wage rate

We know from Chapter 3 that the MPL depends on the quantity of labour input, L^d. As L^d rises, the MPL falls. This relation is shown by the downward-sloping curve in Figure 7.4. This curve applies for a given technology level, A, and capital input, K^d.

Suppose that the household selects a low labour input, such as L_1 in Figure 7.4, where the marginal product of labour, MPL_1, is greater than w/P. In this case, an increase in L by an additional unit would raise real profit, Π/P. The reason is that the addition to output – by MPL_1 units – is larger than the addition to wage payments – by w/P units.

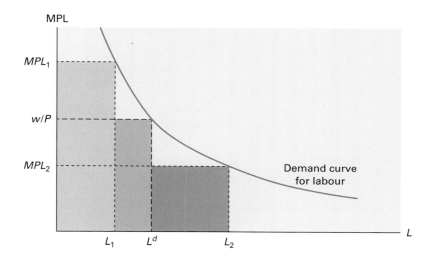

Figure 7.4 Labour demand

For a given technology level, A, and capital input, K^d, the marginal product of labour, MPL, decreases as labour input, L, increases. Therefore, the MPL, given by the downward-sloping curve, declines on the vertical axis as L rises on the horizontal axis. The household chooses labour input, L^d, where the MPL equals the real wage rate, w/P. At a lower labour input, such as L_1, MPL_1 is greater than w/P, and at a higher labour input, such as L_2, MPL_2 is less than w/P. If w/P decreases, L^d increases.

However, as L rises, the MPL falls and eventually gets as low as w/P. If the household continues to raise L^d, the MPL falls below w/P, such as at L_2 in Figure 7.4. In that situation, further increases in L^d lower Π/P. Thus, to maximize real profit, the household should stop at the point where the MPL equals w/P. The graph shows that this equality occurs where the value along the curve for the MPL equals w/P.

For a given real wage rate, w/P, on the vertical axis, the graph in Figure 7.4 shows on the horizontal axis the quantity of labour demanded, L^d. We can see that a decrease in w/P raises L^d. Hence, if we graph L^d versus w/P, we map out a downward-sloping demand curve. That is, the labour-demand curve looks as shown in Figure 7.1.

Each household determines its labour demand, L^d, as shown in Figure 7.4. Therefore, when we add up across all the households, we end up with an aggregate or market demand for labour that also looks like the curve shown in the figure. In particular, a decrease in the real wage rate, w/P, raises the market quantity of labour demanded, L^d.

Supply of labour

We are assuming that each household supplies a fixed quantity of labour to the labour market. Therefore, the aggregate or market supply of labour, L^s, is the given amount L. More realistically, the quantity of labour supplied would depend on the real wage rate, w/P. For example, we might have the upward-sloping labour-supply curve shown in Figure 7.1. However, we neglect until Chapter 9 this dependence of L^s on w/P.

Clearing of the labour market

The market labour demand, L^d, is determined from Figure 7.4 as a downward-sloping function of the real wage rate, w/P. We reproduce this curve in Figure 7.5. The market labour supply, L^s, is assumed to be the constant L. We show this fixed labour supply as the vertical line at L. Now we can determine the equilibrium value of w/P from the market-clearing condition for the labour market. Specifically, we assume that w/P is determined to equate the aggregate quantity of labour demanded, L^d, to the aggregate quantity supplied, L. This market-clearing value of w/P corresponds in Figure 7.5 to the intersection of the L curve with the vertical line at L. The market-clearing value for w/P is denoted by $(w/P)^*$ on the vertical axis. The corresponding market-clearing quantity of labour input, L^*, equals L^d on the horizontal axis.

The equality between L and L^d means that the market-clearing real wage rate, $(w/P)^*$, equals the marginal product of labour, MPL:

$$(w/P)^* = MPL \ (evaluated \ at \ L) \tag{7.14}$$

By MPL (evaluated at L), we are referring in Figure 7.4 to the value for the marginal product of labour that corresponds to the quantity of labour L.[4]

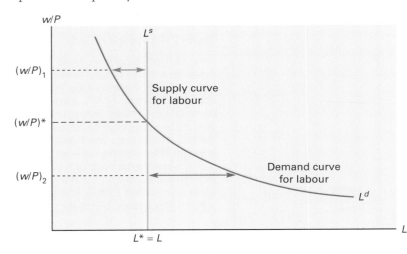

Figure 7.5 Clearing of the labour market

The downward-sloping labour-demand curve, L^d, comes from Figure 7.4. We assume that labour supply, L^s, is fixed at L. The market-clearing real wage rate is $(w/P)^*$. The market-clearing quantity of labour input is $L^* = L$. At a higher real wage rate, such as $(w/P)_1$, the quantity of labour supplied, L^s, exceeds the quantity demanded, L^d, in the amount shown by the upper arrows. At a lower real wage rate, such as $(w/P)_2$, the quantity of labour supplied, L^s, falls short of the quantity demanded, L^d, in the amount shown by the lower arrows.

[4]Note that the curve for MPL in Figure 7.4 applies for a given capital stock, K. A change in K would shift the MPL associated with a given value of L^d and would therefore change $(w/P)^*$ in Figure 7.5.

Why do we assume that the labour market clears? The idea is that only at this market-clearing position would the real wage rate, w/P, tend neither to rise nor to fall. If w/P were below $(w/P)^*$, for example, at $(w/P)_2$ in Figure 7.5, the aggregate quantity of labour demanded would exceed the quantity supplied in the amount shown by the lower arrows. In this case, demanders of labour would compete to hire scarce workers by raising w/P.[5] Conversely, if w/P were above $(w/P)^*$, for example, at $(w/P)_1$ in Figure 7.5, the aggregate quantity of labour demanded would fall short of the quantity supplied in the amount shown by the upper arrows. In this case, the eager suppliers of labour would bid down w/P. In equilibrium, w/P will be determined to clear the labour market; that is, so that the aggregate quantity of labour supplied, L, equals the quantity demanded, L^d.

THE MARKET FOR CAPITAL SERVICES

We will now consider the demand for capital services and the supply of capital services. Then, we will determine the real rental price, R/P, from the market-clearing condition for the market for capital services: the quantity of capital services demanded equals the quantity supplied.

Demand for capital services

As with the demand for labour, the demand for capital services, K^d, comes from the objective of profit maximization. Consider the effect of an increase in K^d by one unit on a household's real profit, as given again by:

$$\Pi/P = A \bullet F(k^d, L^d) - (w/P) \bullet L^d - (R/P) \bullet k^d$$

real profit = output − real wage payments − real rental payments (7.13)

We know from Chapter 3 that an increase in capital input, K^d, by one unit raises output, $A \cdot F(K^d, L^d)$, the first term on the right-hand side, by the marginal product of capital (MPK). An increase in K^d also raises the real rental payments, $(R/P) \bullet K^d$, the last term on the right-hand side. For a given real rental price, R/P, an increase in K^d by one unit raises real rental payments by the amount R/P. Therefore, the overall effect from an increase in K^d by one unit is to change real profit by:

$$\Delta(\Pi/P) = \Delta[A \bullet F(k^d, L^d)] - R/P$$
$$= MPK - R/P$$

change in real profit = marginal product of capital − real rental price

We know from Chapter 3 that the MPK depends on the amount of capital input, K^d. As K^d rises, MPK falls. This relation is shown by the downward-sloping curve in Figure 7.6. This curve applies for a given technology level, A, and labour input, L^d.

Suppose that the household selects a low value of capital input, K^d, such as K_1 in Figure 7.6, at which the marginal product of capital, MPK_1, is greater than R/P. In this case, an increase in K^d by an additional unit would raise real profit, Π/P. The reason is that the addition to output (by MPK_1 units) is greater than the increase in real rental payments (by R/P units). However, as K^d rises, the MPK falls and eventually gets as low as R/P. If the household continues to raise K^d, the MPK falls below R/P, such as at K_2 in the figure. In that case, further increases in K^d lower Π/P. Thus, to maximize real profit, the household should stop at the point where the MPK equals R/P. The graph shows that this equality occurs where the value along the curve for the MPK equals R/P.

For a given real rental price, R/P, on the vertical axis, the graph in Figure 7.6 shows on the horizontal axis the quantity of capital services demanded, K^d. We can see that a decrease in R/P increases K^d. Hence, if we graph K^d versus R/P, we determine a downward-sloping demand curve.

Each household sets its demand for capital services, K^d, as shown in Figure 7.6. Therefore, when we add up across all the households, we end up with an aggregate or market demand for capital services that also looks like the curve shown in the figure. In particular, a decrease in the real rental price, R/P, raises the market quantity of capital services demanded, K^d.

---

[5]This description views the participants in the labour market as directly setting the real wage rate, (w/P). However, our story would be the same if instead, the price level, P, were given, and the participants in the labour market adjusted the nominal wage rate, w.

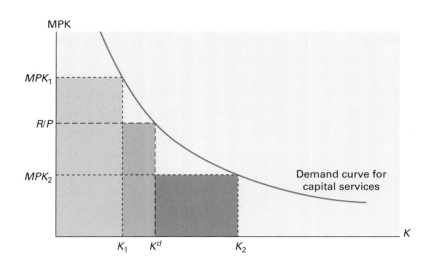

Figure 7.6 Demand for capital services

For a given technology level, A, and labour input, L^d, the marginal product of capital, MPK, decreases as capital input, K, increases. Therefore, the MPK, given by the downward-sloping curve, declines on the vertical axis as K rises on the horizontal axis. The household chooses capital input, K^d, where the MPK equals the real rental price, R/P. In contrast, at a lower capital input, such as K_1, MPK_1 is greater than R/P, and at a higher capital input, such as K_2, MPK_2 is less than R/P. If R/P decreases, K^d increases.

Supply of capital services

For the economy as a whole, the aggregate quantity of capital, K, is given from past flows of investment. That is, in the short run, the economy has a given stock of houses, cars, machines and factories. This capital stock is owned by households, and all of the services from this stock are supplied to the rental market. Therefore, in the short run, the aggregate or market quantity of capital services supplied, K^s, equals K.

Clearing of the market for capital services

The market demand for capital services, K^d, is determined from Figure 7.6 as a downward-sloping function of the real rental price, R/P. We reproduce this curve in Figure 7.7. The market supply of capital services, K^s, is the constant K. We show this fixed supply of capital services as the vertical line at K. As with the labour market, we assume that the equilibrium value of R/P is determined to clear the market – that is, so that the aggregate quantity of capital services supplied, K, equals the aggregate quantity demanded, K^d. This market-clearing value of R/P corresponds in Figure 7.7 to the intersection of the K^d curve with the vertical line at K. The market-clearing value for R/P is denoted by $(R/P)^*$ on the vertical axis. The corresponding market-clearing quantity of capital services, K^*, equals K on the horizontal axis.

The equality between K and K^d means that the market-clearing real rental price, $(R/P)^*$, equals the marginal product of capital, MPK:

$$(R/P)^* = MPK(evaluated\ at\ K) \tag{7.15}$$

By MPK (evaluated at K), we are referring in Figure 7.6 to the value for the marginal product of capital that corresponds to the capital input K.[6]

We can ask again why we assume that the market clears. The idea is that only at this market-clearing position would the real rental price, R/P, tend neither to rise nor to fall. If R/P were below $(R/P)^*$, for example, at $(R/P)_2$ on the vertical axis in Figure 7.7, the aggregate quantity of capital services demanded would exceed the quantity supplied in the amount shown by the lower arrows. In this case, demanders of capital services would compete to hire scarce capital by bidding up R/P. Conversely, if R/P were above $(R/P)^*$, for example, at $(R/P)_1$ on the vertical axis in Figure 7.7, the aggregate quantity of capital services demanded would fall short of the quantity supplied in the amount shown by the upper arrows. In this case, the suppliers of capital services would compete by lowering R/P. In equilibrium, R/P will be determined to clear the market – that is, so that the aggregate quantity of capital services supplied, K, equals the aggregate quantity demanded, K^d.

---

[6]Note that the curve for MPK in Figure 7.6 applies for a given labour input, L. A change in L would shift the MPK associated with a given value of K and would therefore change $(R/P)^*$ in Figure 7.7.

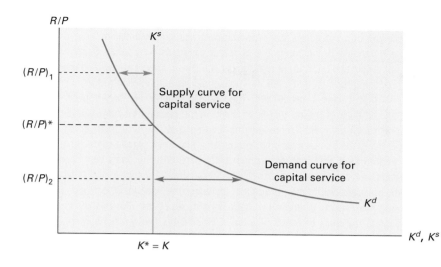

Figure 7.7 Clearing of the market for capital services

The downward-sloping demand curve for capital services, K^d, comes from Figure 7.6. The supply of capital services, K^s, is fixed at K. The market-clearing real rental price is $(R/P)^*$. The market-clearing quantity of capital services is $K^* = K$. At a higher real rental price, such as $(R/P)_1$, the quantity of capital services supplied, $K^s = K$, exceeds the quantity demanded, K^d, in the amount shown by the upper arrows. At a lower real rental price, such as $(R/P)_2$, the quantity of capital services supplied, $K^s = K$, falls short of the quantity demanded, K^d, in the amount shown by the lower arrows.

The interest rate

The market-clearing solution for the real rental price will allow us to determine the interest rate, i. We found before that i equals the rate of return to owning capital:

$$i = R/P - \delta$$

rate of return on bonds = rate of return on ownership of capital

(7.6)

Therefore, if we substitute for R/P from the formula for $(R/P)^*$ in equation (7.15), we get:

> **Key equation (equilibrium interest rate):**
>
> $$i = MPK(evaluated\ at\ K) - \delta$$
>
> (7.16)

Thus, once we determine R/P, we also determine the interest rate, i.

This last result is important. It says that the interest rate, i, cannot change unless something changes the MPK. For a given technology level, A, the MPK depends on the inputs of capital services, K, and labour, L. In our present setting, K and L are given. Therefore, i will also be given. In the real world, the interest rate, i, tends to fluctuate a good deal. Thus, to capture this aspect of reality, we have to extend our model to allow for variations in the MPK. We introduce in Chapters 9 and 10 some sources of changes in the MPK and, therefore, in the interest rate, i.

PROFIT IN EQUILIBRIUM

We determined households' demands for labour and capital services, L^d and K^d, from the objective of profit maximization. Households as business managers chose L^d and K^d to make real profit, Π/P, as high as possible. Now, we will consider the level of Π/P that households receive when the labour and rental markets clear.

When the labour and rental markets clear, so that $L^d = L$ and $K^d = K$, real profit is given from equation (7.13) by:

$$\Pi/P = A \bullet F(K, L) - (w/P) \bullet L - (R/P) \bullet K$$

(7.17)

Since the labour and rental markets clear, we also have, from equations (7.14) and (7.15):

$$w/P = MPL$$
$$R/P = MPK$$

where MPL and MPK are evaluated at the given values of L and K. If we substitute these formulas for w/P and R/P into equation (7.17), we get:

$$\Pi/P = A \bullet F(K, L) - MPL \bullet L - MPK \bullet K$$

(7.18)

Economics in Practice
Economic profit versus accounting profit

Our definition of profit differs from the standard accounting definition. The reason for the difference is the treatment of rental payments on capital. Suppose, for example, that a household (or, more realistically, a business) owns capital and uses the capital to produce goods. In that case, the household pays no explicit rental payments on the capital that it uses in production. The rental payments are only implicit – the household should think of paying rentals to itself on the capital that it owns and uses. These implicit rental payments represent the income that the household could have received by renting the capital to another producer. Thus, the foregone rental payments should be treated as a cost (called an *opportunity cost*) of using one's own capital to produce goods.

However, standard accounting practices, including the national-income accounts, do not include most forms of implicit rental payments as costs.[7] For this reason, the usual accounting measure of rental payments understates the rental payments that are appropriate from an economic perspective. Since rental payments are a negative item for real profit, Π/P, in equation (7.17), we also get that the accounting measure overstates real profit from an economic standpoint. Since the economic profit is zero in equilibrium, the accounting measure of profit must be greater than zero in equilibrium. The accounting measure of profit really measures the uncounted part of the rental income on capital.

We show in the Appendix that the expression on the right-hand side of equation (7.18) equals zero. That is, when the values for w/P and R/P satisfy the market-clearing conditions for labour and capital services, the real profit, Π/P, ends up being zero. Another way to say this is that real GDP, which equals $A \bullet F(K, L)$, just covers the payments to the two factor inputs, $(w/P) \bullet L$ for labour and $(R/P) \bullet K$ for capital services. Output equals the total of these real factor incomes and all of this income goes to either labour or capital. Nothing is left over for profit.

We therefore have something of a paradox. Households as business managers select their demands for labour and capital services, L^d and K^d, to maximize profit. However, when w/P and R/P satisfy market-clearing conditions, the resulting real profit, Π/P, is zero. That is, the highest real profit that households can attain is zero. The Economics in Practice box on this page notes that accounting measures of profit include part of rental payments to capital and tend, therefore, to be greater than zero.

From an economic perspective, the reason that profit ends up being zero in our model is that profit represents the return to a household from managing a business. We have assumed that all households are equally good at business management and that the process of managing takes no effort. Therefore, in equilibrium, business management receives zero compensation (profit is nil).

Another point is that households as business owners are the *residual claimants* on business earnings. That is, profit income is the residual after subtracting from sales the costs of factor inputs, labour and capital. In our model, profit is not risky; it equals zero in equilibrium with complete certainty. More realistically, profit involves uncertainties about sales and costs. In most circumstances, the average profit has to be greater than zero to compensate business owners for assuming the risks of being a residual claimant.

---

[7]If a business borrows money to finance purchases of capital goods, the usual accounting practice treats the interest payments on the business's debt as costs. Therefore, interest expenses, which represent the rental payments on debt-financed capital, enter as a negative item into the accounting definition of profit. Thus, standard accounting procedures include rental payments on capital as costs when the capital is debt financed but not when the capital is owned outright by a business. In the case of corporations, this ownership corresponds to finance of capital by issue of equity shares (corporate stock) or retained earnings (after-tax profit not paid out as dividends to shareholders).

Summing Up

We set up the market structure and microeconomic foundations for our macroeconomic model. We began by describing the economy's four markets – for goods, labour, rental of capital and bonds. The nominal prices on the first three markets are the price level, P, the wage rate, w, and the rental price, R. The price of short-term bonds is fixed at €1, but the interest rate, i, can vary. We can think of i as the price of credit. We have shown how the sales and purchases on the various markets determined household income from wages, returns on assets and profit.

We have examined in detail the markets for labour and capital services. As managers of family businesses, households determine their demands for labour, L^d, and capital services, K^d. We derived these demands from the objective of profit maximization, assuming that each household took as given the real wage rate, w/P, and the real rental price, R/P. We assumed that the supply of labour, L^s, was fixed at L and that the supply of capital services, K^s, was fixed at K.

We found from the labour market that the market-clearing real wage rate, $(w/P)^*$, equalled the marginal product of labour, MPL. We found from the market for capital services that the market-clearing real rental price, $(R/P)^*$, equalled the marginal product of capital, MPK. The two marginal products, MPL and MPK, were evaluated at the given values of L and K. We also showed that the market-clearing real rental price, $(R/P)^*$, determined the interest rate, i.

The results from this chapter provide essential building blocks for our model of economic fluctuations. In the next chapter, we extend the analysis to consumption, saving and investment. Then, in Chapters 9 and 10, we show how to use the model to explain real-world features of economic fluctuations.

Key Terms and Concepts

bond	household budget	nominal wage rate	sources of funds
bond market	constraint in real terms	price level	stock market
budget constraint	labour market	principal (of bond)	uses of funds
budget line	market-clearing conditions	profit	
common currency	maturity	real rental price	
currency	medium of exchange	real saving	
currency union	money	real terms	
goods market	nominal	real wage rate	
household budget constraint	nominal rental price	rental market	
in nominal terms	nominal saving	risk premium	

Questions and Problems

A   Review questions

1   How does an increase in the real rental price, R/P, affect the quantity of capital services demanded, K^d? Where does the assumption of diminishing marginal product of capital (MPK) come in?

2   How does an increase in the real wage rate, w/P, affect the quantity of labour demanded, L^d? Where does the assumption of diminishing marginal product of labour (MPL) come in?

3   Why would households be interested only in the real values of consumption, income and assets such as bonds? Think about how households would feel if the nominal values of consumption, income and assets all doubled, and the price level, P, also doubled

4   Derive the budget line shown in Figure 7.2. What does this line show?

5   Distinguish clearly between a household's initial asset position and the change in that position. If a household has negative saving, is that household necessarily a borrower in the sense of having a negative position in bonds?

B   Problems for discussion

6   Term structure of interest rates

Suppose that the economy has discount bonds (discussed in question 8) with one- and two-year maturities. Let i_t^1 be the interest rate on a one-year bond issued at the start of year t, and i^1_{t+1} the interest rate on a one-year bond issued at the start of year $t + 1$. Let i^2_t be the interest rate (per year) on a two-year bond issued at the start of year t. We can think of i^1_t as the current short-term interest rate and i^2_t as the current long-term interest rate.

a   Assume that, at the start of year t, everyone knows not only i^1_t and i^2_t, but also the next year's one-year rate, i^1_{t+1}. What must be the relation of i^2_t to i^1_t and i^1_{t+1}? Explain the answer by considering the incentives of lenders and borrowers.

b   If $i^1_{t+1} > i^1_t$, what is the relation between i^2_t, the long-term interest rate, and i^1_t, the short-term interest rate? The answer is an important result about the term structure of interest rates.

c   How would the results change if we assumed, more realistically, that there was uncertainty in year t about the future one-year interest rate, i^1_{t+1}?

7   Financial intermediaries

Consider a financial intermediary, such as a bank, that participates in the credit market. This intermediary borrows from some households and lends to others. (The loan from a customer to a bank often takes the form of a deposit account.)

a   Does the existence of intermediaries affect the result that the aggregate amount of loans is zero?

b   What interest rates would the intermediary charge to its borrowers and pay to its lenders? Why must there be some spread between these two rates?

c   Can you provide some reasons to explain why intermediaries might be useful?

8   Discount bonds

The bonds in our model have a maturity close to zero; they just pay interest in accordance with the current interest rate, i, as a flow over time. We could consider, instead, a discount bond. This type of asset has no explicit interest payments (called *coupons*) but pays a principal of, say, €1000 at a fixed date in the future. A bill with one-year maturity pays off one year from the issue date, and similarly for three-month or six-month bills. Let P be the price of a discount bond with one-year maturity and principal of €1000.

a   Is P greater than or less than €1000?

b   What is the one-year interest rate on these discount bonds?

c   If P rises, what happens to the interest rate on these bonds?

d   Suppose that, instead of paying €1000 in one year, the bond pays €1000 in two years. What is the interest rate per year on this two-year discount bond?

Appendix

Output equals real factor incomes and profit equals zero

We show here that, when capital and labour are each paid their marginal products, the total of real income payments to capital and labour equals the output or real GDP. Hence, profit is zero. These results are shown most easily using calculus.

Start with the production function for real GDP, Y:

$$Y = A \cdot F(K, L) \tag{3.1}$$

In Chapter 3, we assumed that the production function satisfied constant returns to scale in capital and labour, K and L. Therefore, if we multiply K and L each by $1/L$, we also multiply Y by $1/L$:

$$Y/L = A \cdot F(K/L, 1)$$

Thus, output per unit of labour, Y/L, depends only on capital per unit of labour, K/L. If we multiply through each side of the equation by L, we get another way to write the production function:

$$Y = AL \cdot F(K/L, 1) \tag{7.19}$$

We can use calculus to calculate the MPK from equation (7.19). The MPK is the derivative of Y with respect to K, while holding fixed A and L:

$$MPK = AL \cdot F_1 \cdot (1/L)$$

where F_1 is the derivative of the function F with respect to its first argument, K/L. We get the last term, $1/L$, from the chain rule for differentiation. That is, $1/L$ is the derivative of K/L with respect to K, while holding fixed L. If we cancel out L and $(1/L)$, we get:

$$MPK = AF_1 \qquad (7.20)$$

The MPL is the derivative of Y with respect to L, while holding fixed A and K. Since L appears in two places on the right-hand side of equation (7.19), we have to calculate the derivative with respect to L of the product of two terms, AL and $F(K/L, 1)$. The first part of the answer is the derivative of the first term, A, multiplied by the second term, $F(K/L, 1)$. The second part is the first term, AL, multiplied by the derivative of the second term. This derivative is $F_1 \bullet (-K/L)$, where F_1 is, again, the derivative of the function F with respect to its first argument, K/L. The term $-K/L$ comes from the chain rule for differentiation. That is, $-K/L$ is the derivative of K/L with respect to L, while holding fixed K. Putting the results together, we get:

$$MPL = A \bullet F(K/L, 1) + A\!\!\!L \bullet F_1 \bullet (-K/L^2)$$
$$MPL = A \bullet F(K/L, 1) - A \bullet (K/L) \bullet F_1 \qquad (7.21)$$

If the factor inputs are each paid their marginal products, so that $w/P = MPL$ and $R/P = MPK$, we can use equations (7.20) and (7.21) to calculate the total payments to labour and capital:

$$(w/P) \bullet L + (R/P) \bullet K = MPL \bullet L + MPK \bullet K$$
$$= [A \bullet F(K/L, 1) - A \bullet (K/L) \bullet F_1] \bullet L + (AF_1) \bullet K$$
$$= AL \bullet F(K/L, 1) - A\!K \bullet F_1 + A\!K \bullet F_1$$
$$= AL \bullet F(K/L, 1)$$

Equation (7.19) tells us that the last term equals real GDP Y, which equals $A \bullet F(K, L)$. Therefore, we have shown:

$$(w/P) \bullet L + (R/P) \bullet K = A \bullet F(K, L) \qquad (7.22)$$

Thus, the total real payments to labour and capital, $(w/P) \bullet L + (R/P) \bullet K$, equal real GDP, $A \cdot F(K, L)$.[8]

Recall that real profit is given by:

$$\Pi/P = A \bullet F(K, L) - (w/P) \bullet L - (R/P) \bullet K \qquad (7.17)$$

Therefore, the result in equation (7.22) proves that Π/P is zero in equilibrium, as claimed in the text.

---

[8]This result is called Euler's Theorem.

8 Consumption, saving and investment

Chapter 7 introduced the four markets in our model of the macroeconomy – goods, labour, capital services and bonds. We related household income to the prices and quantities in the four markets. We began the construction of the model's microeconomic foundations by considering how households, as managers of family businesses, determined their demands for labour and capital services. Then, we investigated the clearing of the markets for labour and capital services. For given values of labour, L, and capital, K, these market-clearing conditions determined the real wage rate, w/P, the real rental price of capital, R/P, and the interest rate, i.

In this chapter, we extend our microeconomic analysis of households to the choices of consumption and saving. Then, we will use these results to determine economy-wide levels of consumption, saving and investment. These results will form the basis for an equilibrium business-cycle model, which we will use in Chapters 9 and 10 to analyze macroeconomic fluctuations.

Consumption and saving

In this section, we study an individual household's choice of consumption, C. In making this decision, the household also determines how much to save.

Start with the household budget constraint from equation (7.12) of Chapter 7:

$$C+(1/P)\bullet\Delta B+\Delta K = \Pi/P+(w/P)\bullet L+i\bullet(B/P+K) \tag{7.12}$$

We showed in Chapter 7 that real profit, Π/P, equalled zero when the markets for labour and capital services cleared. Therefore, we can set $\Pi/P = 0$ to get a simplified form of the household budget constraint:

$$C+(1/P)\bullet\Delta B+\Delta K = (w/P)\bullet L+i\bullet(B/P+K)$$

$$consumption+real\ saving = real\ income \tag{8.1}$$

Recall that the expression $(1/P) \bullet \Delta B + \Delta K$ represents real saving – the change in the real value of assets held as bonds, B, and ownership of capital, K. Real income consists of real wage income, $(w/P) \bullet L$, plus real asset income, $i \bullet (B/P + K)$.

We want to explore how the household chooses consumption and real saving. In making these choices, we assume, as in Chapter 7, that an individual household takes as given the real wage rate, w/P. This assumption is standard for a competitive market – the individual household is too small to have a noticeable effect on w/P. Now, we go further by assuming that an individual household takes the interest rate, i, as given. This assumption is also standard for a competitive market – the individual household is too small to have a noticeable effect on i. Notice that, in this set-up, each household can lend or borrow as much as it wants at the going interest rate. A household would borrow by issuing a bond that pays the interest rate, i. A household would lend by buying a bond that pays the interest rate, i.

Suppose that a household has given labour, L, and real assets, $(B/P + K)$. Then, since the real wage rate, w/P, and the interest rate, i, are given by the market to an individual household, the total of household real income, $(w/P) \bullet L+ i \bullet (B/P + K)$, is determined on the right-hand side of equation (8.1).

With a given real income, the household's only choice is how to divide this income between consumption, C, and real saving, $(1/P) \cdot \Delta B + \Delta K$. That is, the household budget constraint in equation (8.1) constrains the total of consumption and real saving on the left-hand side. A household would like to have more of both, but this desire cannot be met for a given real income.

Figure 8.1 (similar to Figure 7.2 in Chapter 7) shows how the budget constraint from equation (8.1) allows the household to choose between consumption, C, and real saving, $(1/P) \cdot \Delta B + \Delta K$. One option is to set real saving to zero, so that C equals the total real income. This choice corresponds to point 1, shown on the horizontal axis where C equals total real income. Another option is to set C to zero, so that real saving equals total real income. This choice corresponds to point 2, shown on the vertical axis where real saving equals total real income. More typically, the household would opt for an intermediate position, where C and real saving are both greater than zero. For example, the household could pick point 3 in the graph.

The full range of possibilities is shown by the downward-sloping budget line in Figure 8.1. The budget constraint in equation (8.1) tells us that, along a budget line, each increase in C by one unit of goods corresponds to a decrease in real saving by one unit. Hence, the slope of a budget line is −1. The important point is that, if the household wants one unit more of consumption, it must give up one unit of real saving.

So far, we have considered only the choice between consumption and saving at a point in time. But the reason for saving is to raise future assets, which will allow for higher consumption in the future. Thus, the essence of the household's choice between today's consumption and today's saving is the choice between today's consumption and tomorrow's consumption. By today and tomorrow, we mean that today's consumption has to be considered as part of a long-term plan – perhaps a lifetime plan, or even a longer one that considers the well-being of one's children. The key idea is that, to understand the choice between consumption and saving, we have to study the household's choices of consumption at different points in time.

The household budget constraint, equation (8.1), applies at every point in time. The link between today's budget constraint and tomorrow's budget constraint comes from the effect of today's real saving, $(1/P) \cdot \Delta B + \Delta K$, on tomorrow's real assets, $B/P + K$. We can go a long way in exploring this linkage by considering just two periods. To be concrete, think of the first period as the current year and the second period as the following year. Once we understand this two-period framework, we can readily extend the model to determine consumption and saving over many periods.

CONSUMPTION OVER TWO YEARS

For the current year, year 1, we can write the budget constraint from equation (8.1) as:

$$C_1 + (B_1/P + K_1) - (B_0/P + K_0) = (w/P)_1 \cdot L + i_0 \cdot (B_0/P + K_0)$$

consumption in year 1 + real saving in year 1 = real income in year 1   (8.2)

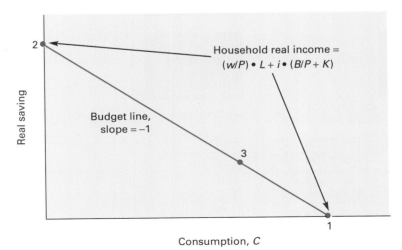

Figure 8.1 The household budget constraint

Households have a given total of real income, $(w/P) \cdot L + i \cdot (B/P + K)$. This total must be divided between consumption, C, and real saving, $(1/P) \cdot \Delta B + \Delta K$. Thus, if real saving is zero, C equals the total of real income along the horizontal axis at point 1. If C is zero, real saving equals the total of real income along the vertical axis at point 2. The budget constraint in equation (8.1) allows the household to select any combination of consumption and real saving along the budget line such as point 3. The budget line has a slope of −1. Along this line, one unit less of consumption corresponds to one unit more of real saving.

On the left-hand side, C_1 is year 1's consumption. The real assets B_1/P and K_1 are the amounts held at the end of year 1. The real assets B_0/P and K_0 are the amounts held at the end of the previous year, year 0, and therefore also the amounts held at the *beginning* of year 1. Thus, $(B_1/P + K_1) - (B_0/P + K_0)$ is the change in real assets – or real saving – in year 1.

On the right-hand side of equation (8.2), the real wage rate for year 1 is $(w/P)_1$, and the real wage income for the year is $(w/P)_1 \bullet L$. Since we assume that labour, L, is fixed over time, we do not include a year subscript. The interest rate for assets held at the end of year 0 is i_0. Thus, the real asset income for year 1 is $i_0 \bullet (B_0/P + K_0)$. When we add real wage income to real asset income, we get total real income for year 1 on the right-hand side.

The budget constraint in equation (8.2) is for year 1. The same form of budget constraint applies to year 2:

$$C_2 + (B_2/P + K_2) - (B_1/P + K_1) = (w/P)_2 \bullet L + i_1 \bullet (B_1/P + K_1)$$
consumption in year 2 + real saving in year 2 = real income in year 2 (8.3)

Our next task is to combine the budget constraints in equations (8.2) and (8.3) to describe a household's choice between consuming this year, C_1, and next year, C_2. Notice that both budget constraints include the assets held at the end of year 1, $B_1/P + K_1$. We can use equation (8.2) to solve out for this term by moving C_1 and $B_0/P + K_0$ from the left-hand side to the right-hand side and rearranging terms to get:

$$B_1/P + K_1 = B_0/P + K_0 + i_0 \bullet (B_0/P + K_0) + (w/P)_1 \bullet L - C_1$$
real assets end year 1 = real assets end year 0 + real income year 1 – consumption year 1 (8.4)

Figure 8.2 shows this relation visually. The top bin has the real assets at the end of year 0, $B_0/P + K_0$, which is the first term on the right-hand side of equation (8.4). Add to this amount the left-hand bin, which contains the real

Figure 8.2 Change in real assets in year 1

The top bin has the real assets at the end of year 0, $B_0/P + K_0$, the first term on the right-hand side of equation (8.4). The real income for year 1, $i_0 \bullet (B_0/P + K_0) + (w/P)_1 \bullet L$ in the left-hand bin, corresponds to the second term on the right-hand side of equation (8.4) and adds to the top bin. The consumption for year 1, C_1 in the right-hand bin, corresponds to the third term on the right-hand side of equation (8.4) and subtracts from the top bin. The final result is the real assets at the end of year 1, $B_1/P + K_1$ in the bottom bin. This amount is the left-hand side of equation (8.4).

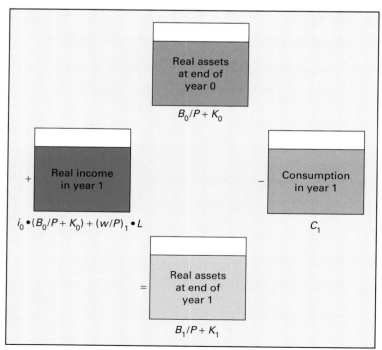

income in year 1, $i_0 \cdot (B_0/P + K_0) + (w/P)_1 \cdot L$. This income is the second term on the right-hand side of equation (8.4). Then, subtract the right-hand bin, which contains consumption in year 1, C_1, the final term on the right-hand side. We end up with the bottom bin, which contains the real assets at the end of year 1, $B_1/P + K_1$, the term on the left-hand side of equation (8.4).

The same analysis applies to year 2. The analogue to equation (8.4) is:

$$B_2/P + K_2 = B_1/P + K_1 + i_1 \cdot (B_1/P + K_1) + (w/P)_2 \cdot L - C_2$$

$$real\ assets\ end\ year\ 2 = real\ assets\ end\ year\ 1 + real\ income\ year\ 2 - consumption\ year\ 2 \tag{8.5}$$

Figure 8.3, similar to Figure 8.2, shows this relationship visually.

Going back to equation (8.4), we can combine the two terms involving $B_0/P + K_0$ on the right-hand side to get:

$$B_1/P + K_1 = (1 + i_0) \cdot (B_0/P + K_0) + (w/P)_1 \cdot L - C_1 \tag{8.6}$$

Notice, on the right-hand side, that we multiply $B_0/P + K_0$ by the term $1 + i_0$. The '1' represents the principal of year 0's assets, and the 'i_0' represents the interest paid on these assets.

We see on the right-hand side of equation (8.6) that, if the household lowers year 1's consumption, C_1, by one unit, the real assets held at the end of year 1, $B_1/P + K_1$, rise by one unit on the left-hand side. Visually, in Figure 8.2, suppose that we take one unit of goods out of the right-hand C_1 bin and do not change the top and left-hand bins.

Figure 8.3 Change in real assets in year 2

The top bin has the real assets at the end of year 1, $B_1/P + K_1$, the first term on the right-hand side of equation (8.5). The real income for year 2, $i_1 \cdot (B_1/P + K_1) + (w/P)_2 \cdot L$ in the left-hand bin, corresponds to the second term on the right-hand side of equation (8.5) and adds to the top bin. The consumption for year 2, C_2 in the right-hand bin, corresponds to the third term on the right-hand side of equation (8.5) and subtracts from the top bin. The final result is the real assets at the end of year 2, $B_2/P + K_2$ in the bottom bin. This amount is the left-hand side of equation (8.5).

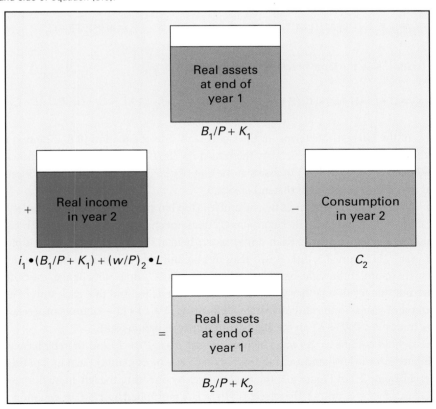

Since the right-hand bin enters with a minus sign, taking one unit out of it means that there will be one unit more left in the bottom bin, which has $B_1/P + K_1$.

If we combine the two terms involving $B_1/P + K_1$ on the right-hand side of the second year's budget constraint in equation (8.5), we get:

$$B_2/P + K_2 = (1+i_1) \bullet (B_1/P + K_1) + (w/P)_2 \bullet L - C_2 \tag{8.7}$$

This expression takes the same form as equation (8.6), except that everything is updated by one year. Notice, on the right-hand side, that a higher value of $B_1/P + K_1$, the assets held at the end of year 1, allows the household to raise year 2's consumption, C_2, also on the right-hand side. Visually, in Figure 8.3, an increase in $B_1/P + K_1$ by one unit means that we add one unit to the top bin (which has the assets at the end of year 1) and i_1 units to the left-hand bin (which includes the interest income on the assets from the end of year 1). Suppose that we do not change the bottom bin, which has the assets held at the end of year 2, $B_2/P + K_2$. In this case, we must have $1 + i_1$ units more in the right-hand bin, which contains C_2. Note that C_2 can be increased by $1 + i_1$ units without having to change the assets held at the end of year 2, $B_2/P + K_2$.

We now have the building blocks to establish the link between consuming this year, C_1, and next year, C_2. Recall from equation (8.6) and Figure 8.2 that a reduction in C_1 by one unit allows the household to increase assets at the end of year 1, $B_1/P + K_1$, by one unit. We also have from equation (8.7) and Figure 8.3 that an increase in $B_1/P + K_1$ by one unit can be used to raise C_2 by $1 + i_1$ units. Thus, if C_1 decreases by one unit, the household can increase C_2 by $1 + i_1$ units. Moreover, the household can make this switch between C_1 and C_2 without changing $B_2/P + K_2$, the real assets carried over to year 3 (and shown as the bottom bin in Figure 8.3). Thus, the household can change the timing of consumption between this year and next year, C_1 and C_2, without shortchanging or enriching the future; that is, without altering the assets available for year 3 and beyond.

To construct the full two-year budget constraint algebraically, first replace $B_1/P + K_1$ on the right-hand side of equation (8.7) by the right-hand side of equation (8.6) to get:

$$B_2/P + K_2 = (1+i_1) \bullet [(1+i_0) \bullet (B_0/P + K_0) + (w/P)_1 \bullet L - C_1] + (w/P)_2 \bullet L - C_2$$

If we multiply the terms inside the large brackets by $1 + i_1$, we get:

$$B_2/P + K_2 = (1+i_1) \bullet (1+i_0) \bullet (B_0/P + K_0) + (1+i_1) \bullet (w/P)_1 \bullet L - (1+i_1) \bullet C_1 + (w/P)_2 \bullet L - C_2 \tag{8.8}$$

Notice the effects of the interest-rate terms on the right-hand side of equation (8.8). The first term includes the assets from the end of year 0, $B_0/P + K_0$, which pay the return $i_0 \bullet (B_0/P + K_0)$ in year 1. If the household holds these assets, it ends up with $(1 + i_0) \bullet (B_0/P + K_0)$ in assets at the end of year 1. Hence, each unit of assets from the end of year 0 is multiplied by $1 + i_0$ to get assets at the end of year 1.

Equivalently, in Figure 8.2, if $B_0/P + K_0$ rises by one unit, the top bin rises by one unit and the left-hand bin rises by i_0 units. Therefore, if the right-hand bin, which contains C_1, does not change, the bottom bin increases by $1 + i_0$ units.

The same calculation applies for year 2. Each unit of assets held at the end of year 1 is multiplied by $1 + i_1$ to get assets at the end of year 2. In Figure 8.3, if $B_1/P + K_1$ rises by one unit, the top bin rises by one unit and the left-hand bin rises by i_1 units. Therefore, if the right-hand bin, which contains C_2, does not change, the bottom bin increases by $1 + i_1$ units. If we put this result together with the result for year 1, we find that each unit of assets held for two periods – from the end of year 0 to the end of year 2 – ends up as $(1 + i_1) \bullet (1 + i_0)$ units of assets. This interest-rate term is the one that multiplies $B_0/P + K_0$ on the right-hand side of equation (8.8).

Similarly, the household could save its wage income in year 1, $(w/P)_1 \bullet L$, and thereby have more assets at the end of year 1. (In Figure 8.2, the left-hand and bottom bins each rise by one unit.) Each unit of these assets becomes $1 + i_1$ units at the end of year 2. (In Figure 8.3, the top bin rises by one unit, the left-hand bin rises by i_1 units, and the bottom bin increases by $1 + i_1$ units.) Therefore, $(w/P)_1 \bullet L$ is multiplied by $1 + i_1$ in equation (8.8). In contrast, the wage income $(w/P)_2 \bullet L$ appears by itself because the household receives this income too late to get any asset returns in year 2.

To think about the consumption terms, notice in equation (8.6) that year 1's consumption, C_1, enters in the same way as year 1's real wage income, $(w/P)_1 \bullet L$, but with a minus sign.[1] The reason is that real saving is the difference between real income and consumption. We therefore find in equation (8.8) that C_1, like $(w/P)_1 \bullet L$, is multiplied by $1 + i_1$. Similarly, year 2's consumption, C_2, enters into equation (8.7) in the same way as year 2's real wage income, $(w/P)_2 \bullet L$, except for the sign.[2] Therefore, C_2, like $(w/P)_2 \bullet L$, appears in equation (8.8) without any interest-rate terms.

If we divide through everything in equation (8.8) by $1 + i_1$ and rearrange the terms to put those involving consumption on the left-hand side, we get:

Key equation (two-year household budget constraint):

$$C_1 + C_2/(1+i_1) = (1+i_0) \bullet (B_0/P + K_0) + (w/P)_1 \bullet L$$
$$+ (w/P)_2 \bullet L/(1+i_1) - (B_2/P + K_2)/(1+i_1) \qquad (8.9)$$

We get this result by using the budget constraints for years 1 and 2, as given in equations (8.2) and (8.3). Therefore, we call equation (8.9) the **two-year budget constraint**.

Observe how the wage incomes, $(w/P)_1 \bullet L$ and $(w/P)_2 \bullet L$, enter on the right-hand side of equation (8.9). We do not add the two together but, rather, divide $(w/P)_2 \bullet L$ by $1 + i_1$ before combining it with $(w/P)_1 \bullet L$. Similarly, on the left-hand side, we make the same adjustment to C_2 before combining it with C_1. To understand these adjustments, we have to explore the concept of **present value**.

Present value

If the interest rate, i_1, is greater than zero, €1 held as assets in year 1 becomes more than €1 in year 2. Therefore, €1 received or spent in year 1 is equivalent to more than €1 in year 2. Or, viewed in reverse, euros received or spent in year 2 must be **discounted** to make them comparable to euros in year 1. The general idea of discounting is that euros received later are not worth as much as euros received earlier. Here, we apply the general notion of discounting to a comparison of year 1 with year 2.

To be concrete, suppose that the interest rate is $i_1 = 5\%$ per year. Assume that a household has €100 of income in year 1 but plans to spend this income a year later, in year 2. Then, the household can buy €100 of bonds at the start of year 1 and have €105 at the start of year 2. Hence, €100 received in year 1 is worth as much as €105 received in year 2. Equivalently, the €105 from year 2 has to be discounted to get the income needed in year 1 to generate €105 in year 2. We find this amount by solving the equation:

$$\text{income needed in year } 1 \times (1+5\%) = €105$$

The required amount of income in year 1 is €105/1.05 = €100.

More generally, if we substitute i_1 for 5%, the income for year 2 has to be divided by $1 + i_1$ to find the equivalent amount for year 1. Hence, if the wage income received in year 2 is $(w/P)_2 \bullet L$, the present value (or year 1 value) of this income is $(w/P)_2 \bullet L/(1 + i_1)$. The term $1 + i_1$ is an example of what economists call a **discount factor**. When we discount by this factor – that is, divide by $1 + i_1$ – we determine the present value of year 2's income. If we went beyond year 2, we would have a different discount factor for each year.

---

[1] Equivalently, in Figure 8.2, an increase by one unit in the bin, which contains $(w/P)_1 \cdot L$, has the same effect as a decrease by one unit in the bin, which contains C_1.

[2] Equivalently, in Figure 8.3, an increase by one unit in the bin, which contains $(w/P)_2 \cdot L$, has the same effect as a decrease by one unit in the bin, which contains C_2.

The two-year budget constraint in equation (8.9) shows that we express year 2's wage income as a present value, $(w/P)_2 \bullet L/(1 + i_1)$, before combining it with year 1's income, $(w/P)_1 \bullet L$. The sum, $(w/P)_1 \bullet L + (w/P)_2 \bullet L/(1 + i_1)$, is the total present value of wage income for years 1 and 2. Similarly, we express year 2's consumption as the present value $C_2/(1 + i_1)$ before combining it with year 1's consumption, C_1. The sum, $C_1 + C_2/(1 + i_1)$, is the total present value of consumption for years 1 and 2.

Our next task is to analyze a household's choices of how much to consume in year 1 and year 2. We know that these choices have to respect the two-year budget constraint given in equation (8.9). But the household still has considerable leeway in deciding among the feasible combinations of C_1 and C_2. We have to figure out which combination the household will prefer among those that satisfy the two-year budget constraint.

Choosing consumption: income effects

To understand choices of consumption, we have to bring in *household preferences* about consuming at different points in time. By preferences, we mean a ranking of time paths of consumption in terms of the satisfaction that the household gets. Economists use the term **utility** as a synonym for satisfaction or happiness.[3] Our assumption is that the household chooses the time path of consumption – in this case, C_1 and C_2 – to maximize utility, subject to the budget constraint in equation (8.9).

We assume that, all other things remaining the same, utility increases if C_1 or C_2 (or consumption in any other year) rises. We assume further that a household likes to consume at similar levels at different points in time, rather than consuming at high levels some of the time and at low levels at other times. For example, a household prefers having C_1 and C_2 both equal to 100, rather than having C_1 equal to 0 and C_2 equal to 200. These preferences motivate a household to *smooth consumption* even when income is irregular. By 'smooth', we mean that the planned levels of consumption chosen for different years, such as C_1 and C_2, tend to be close to each other, rather than varying greatly from one year to the next.

Consider some intuitive examples of consumption smoothing. Suppose that a person gets an unexpected windfall of income, perhaps from winning the lottery or receiving a surprise cheque in the mail. The usual response is to spread the extra money over consumption at various dates, rather than spending it all at once. Similarly, because people anticipate that their incomes will go down when they retire, they tend to save in advance to avoid sharply lower consumption during retirement.

To see how the household chooses C_1 and C_2, return to the two-year budget constraint:

$$C_1 + C_2/(1+i_1) = (1+i_0) \bullet (B_0/P + K_0) + (w/P)_1 \bullet L + (w/P)_2 \bullet L/(1+i_1) - (B_2/P + K_2)/(1+i_1)$$

p.v. of consumption = value of initial assets + p.v. of wage incomes − p.v. of assets end year 2   (8.9)

where we use *p.v.* as an abbreviation for present value. The first term on the right-hand side, $(1 + i_0) \bullet (B_0/P + K_0)$, is the value in year 1 of initial assets. This term adds to the present value of wage incomes received in years 1 and 2, $(w/P)_1 \bullet L + (w/P)_2 \bullet L/(1 + i_1)$. We shall find it convenient to combine these two terms into a single measure, V, of the present value of the household's sources of funds received through year 2. Thus, we define V by:

$$V = (1+i_0) \bullet (B_0/P + K_0) + (w/P)_1 \bullet L + (w/P)_2 \bullet L/(1+i_1)$$

p.v. of sources of funds = value of initial assets + p.v. of wage incomes   (8.10)

If we substitute this definition of V into equation (8.9), we get:

$$C_1 + C_2/(1+i_1) = V - (B_2/P + K_2)/(1+i_1)$$

p.v. of consumption = p.v. of sources of funds − p.v. of assets end year 2   (8.11)

---

[3] The term **utility function** is used to express the relation between the utility obtained and the time path of consumption; in this case, the values of C_1 and C_2.

The last term on the right-hand side of equation (8.11), $(B_2/P + K_2)/(1 + i_1)$, is the present value of the real assets held at the end of year 2. These assets will help to pay for consumption in years 3 and later. We assume, for now, that this term is fixed. That is, we analyze the choices of C_1 and C_2 while holding constant the assets that a household provides for year 3 and beyond. This simplifying device allows us to carry out a two-period analysis, where we study just the choices of C_1 and C_2.

Suppose that V, the present value of the sources of funds, increases due to a rise in initial assets, $(B_0/P + K_0)$, or wage incomes, $(w/P)_1 \bullet L$ and $(w/P)_2 \bullet L$. Since we are holding fixed the term $(B_2/P + K_2)/(1 + i_1)$, equation (8.11) tells us that the total present value of consumption, $C_1 + C_2/(1 + i_1)$, must rise by the same amount as V. Since households like to consume at similar levels in the two years, we predict that C_1 and C_2 will rise by similar amounts. These responses of consumption to increases in initial assets or wage incomes are called **income effects**. An increase in V, the present value of the sources of funds, leads to higher consumption in each year, C_1 and C_2.

Choosing consumption: the intertemporal-substitution effect

The income effects that we just studied tell us about the overall level of consumption; for example, the responses of C_1 and C_2 to a change in initial assets and wage incomes. The other major decision is how much to consume in one year compared to the other year. We have already assumed that households like to have similar levels of C_1 and C_2. However, this preference is not absolute. Households would be willing to deviate from equal consumption levels if there were an economic incentive to deviate. The interest rate, i_1, provides this incentive.

Consider again the two-year budget constraint:

$$C_1 + C_2/(1 + i_1) = V - (B_2/P + K_2)/(1 + i_1)$$
$$p.v.\, of\ consumption = p.v.\, of\ sources\ of\ funds - p.v.\, of\ assets\ end\ year\ 2 \qquad (8.11)$$

The left-hand side has the present value of consumption, $C_1 + C_2/(1 + i_1)$. This expression shows that C_2 is discounted by $1 + i_1$ before adding it to C_1. This discounting means that a unit of C_2 is effectively cheaper than a unit of C_1. The reason is that, if a household defers consumption from year 1 to year 2, it can hold more assets (or borrow less) at the end of year 1. Since, in accordance with equation (8.7), each unit of assets becomes $1 + i_1$ units in year 2, one unit less of C_1 can be replaced by $1 + i_1$ units more of C_2.

As an example, suppose that you are considering taking a vacation this summer. If the interest rate is $i_1 = 5\%$, you might prefer to postpone the vacation until next summer. The reward is that you could spend 5% more and have a better vacation.

We can also use this example to see how the household responds to an increase in the interest rate. If the interest rate rises to $i_1 = 10\%$, the reward for waiting increases – now you could spend 10% more on the delayed vacation. Thus, our prediction is that the vacation is more likely to be postponed when the interest rate, i_1, rises. Hence, C_1, consumption of vacations in year 1, falls and C_2, consumption of vacations in year 2, rises.

The general point is that an increase in the interest rate, i_1, lowers the cost of C_2 compared to C_1. That is, a higher i_1 provides a greater reward for deferring consumption. Therefore, the household responds to an increase in i_1 by lowering C_1 and raising C_2. Economists call this response an **intertemporal-substitution effect**. By intertemporal, we mean that the effect refers to substitution *over time*. The household shifts consumption away from one point in time, such as year 1, and towards another point, such as year 2.[4] The By the Numbers box 'Empirical evidence on intertemporal substitution of consumption' describes empirical estimates of the strength of the intertemporal-substitution effect.

---

[4]Economists usually assume that households prefer to consume earlier rather than later. In this case, the interest rate, i_1, has to be greater than zero – perhaps 2% per year – to motivate households to choose equal values of C_1 and C_2. If i_1 is greater than 2%, the household sets C_1 below C_2, whereas if i_1 is less than 2%, the household sets C_1 above C_2. The main point is still that an increase in i_1 reduces C_1 and raises C_2.

Although we analyzed the intertemporal-substitution effect in terms of consumption in different years, we can view the results through a different lens to determine the responses of saving. That is, we can figure out the effects of the interest rate on the household's saving.

Return to the household budget constraint for year 1:

$$C_1 + (B_1/P + K_1) - (B_0/P + K_0) = (w/P)_1 \cdot L + i_0 \cdot (B_0/P + K_0)$$
$$consumption\ in\ year\ 1 + real\ saving\ in\ year\ 1 = real\ income\ in\ year\ 1 \qquad (8.2)$$

We know from the intertemporal-substitution effect that an increase in the interest rate, i_1, motivates the household to postpone consumption, so that this year's consumption, C_1, falls on the left-hand side. Since year 1's real income, $(w/P)_1 \cdot L + i_0 \cdot (B_0/P + K_0)$ on the right-hand side of equation (8.2), is given, the decline in C_1 must be matched by a rise in year 1's real saving, $(B_1/P + K_1) - (B_0/P + K_0)$. That is, the intertemporal-substitution effect motivates the household to save more when the interest rate rises.

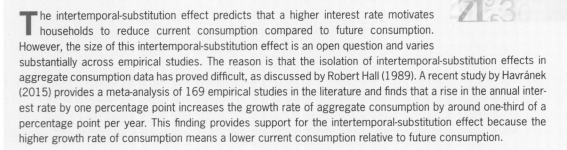

By the Numbers
Empirical evidence on intertemporal substitution of consumption

The intertemporal-substitution effect predicts that a higher interest rate motivates households to reduce current consumption compared to future consumption. However, the size of this intertemporal-substitution effect is an open question and varies substantially across empirical studies. The reason is that the isolation of intertemporal-substitution effects in aggregate consumption data has proved difficult, as discussed by Robert Hall (1989). A recent study by Havránek (2015) provides a meta-analysis of 169 empirical studies in the literature and finds that a rise in the annual interest rate by one percentage point increases the growth rate of aggregate consumption by around one-third of a percentage point per year. This finding provides support for the intertemporal-substitution effect because the higher growth rate of consumption means a lower current consumption relative to future consumption.

Our analysis of interest rates is incomplete because we have considered only the intertemporal-substitution effect. We have not yet considered whether a change in the interest rate also has an income effect.

The income effect from a change in the interest rate
We can understand the income effect from a change in the interest rate, i_1, by examining the household budget constraint for year 2:

$$C_2 + (B_2/P + K_2) - (B_1/P + K_1) = (w/P)_2 \cdot L + i_1 \cdot (B_1/P + K_1)$$
$$consumption\ in\ year\ 2 + real\ saving\ in\ year\ 2 = real\ income\ in\ year\ 2 \qquad (8.3)$$

We can see the income effect from i_1 in, $i_1 \cdot (B_1/P + K_1)$, which gives the income on assets in year 2. We can break this term down into its two parts, $i_1 \cdot (B_1/P)$ and $i_1 K_1$.

Consider first the part $i_1 \cdot (B_1/P)$, which is the interest income on bonds. This interest income is greater than zero for a holder of bonds (the lender), for whom B_1/P is greater than zero. However, this term is less than zero for an issuer of bonds (the borrower), for whom B_1/P is less than zero. For a holder of bonds, the income effect from an increase in i_1 is positive, because the interest income received on a given amount of bonds, B_1/P, is larger. For an issuer of bonds, the income effect from an increase in i_1 is negative, because the interest paid on a given amount of bonds, B_1/P, is larger. For the economy as a whole, lending and borrowing must balance – any outstanding bond has both a holder and an issuer. Therefore, for the average household, B_1/P has to be zero. Hence, for the average household, the income effect from the term $i_1 \cdot (B_1/P)$ is zero.

Households also hold assets in the form of ownership of capital, and the $i_1 K_1$ part of the shaded term in equation (8.3) represents the income received on these assets in year 2. For the economy as a whole, the capital stock, K_1, is, of course, greater than zero. Thus, in contrast to bonds, the average household's holding of claims on capital, K_1, is greater than zero. Therefore, when we consider the term $i_1 K_1$, the income effect from an increase in i_1 is positive.

To put the results together, in the aggregate, the income effect from an increase in i_1 consists of a zero effect from the term $i_1 \cdot (B_1/P)$ and a positive effect from the term $i_1 K_1$. Therefore, the full income effect from an increase in i_1 is positive.

Combining income and substitution effects

In many circumstances, an economic change will involve both income and substitution effects. Consider, for example, the effect of an increase in the interest rate, i_1, on year 1's consumption, C_1. The intertemporal-substitution effect motivates the household to reduce C_1. However, an increase in i_1 also has a positive income effect, which motivates the household to raise C_1. Therefore, the overall effect from an increase in i_1 on C_1 is ambiguous. Year 1's consumption, C_1, falls if the intertemporal-substitution effect dominates but rises if the income effect dominates. In the next section, we will use the *multiyear budget constraint* to assess the strength of the income effect. In some cases, this analysis allows us to determine whether the income effect is likely to be stronger or weaker than the substitution effect.

Figure 8.4 provides a visual summary of the intertemporal-substitution and income effects from a change in the interest rate, i_1. The upper part shows that the intertemporal-substitution effect predicts that an increase in i_1 will lower year 1's consumption, C_1, and, therefore, raise year 1's real saving, $(B_1/P + K_1) - (B_0/P + K_0)$. If i_1 falls, these intertemporal-substitution effects are in the opposite direction. The lower part shows that the income effects always offset the intertemporal-substitution effects. For example, if i_1 rises, the income effects predict that C_1 will rise and, hence, real saving, $(B_1/P + K_1) - (B_0/P + K_0)$, will fall.

CONSUMPTION OVER MANY YEARS

We now extend the household budget constraint to include consumption over many years. We start with the two-year budget constraint:

$$C_1 + C_2/(1+i_1) = (1+i_0) \cdot (B_0/P + K_0) + (w/P)_1 \cdot L$$
$$+ (w/P)_2 \cdot L/(1+i_1) - (B_2/P + K_2)/(1+i_1)$$

p.v. of consumption = value of initial assets + p.v. of wage incomes
− p.v. of assets end year 2   (8.9)

We now relax our simplifying assumption that the household could not change the present value of assets held at the end of year 2 – that is, the shaded term, $(B_2/P + K_2)/(1 + i_1)$, in equation (8.9). These assets are, in fact, not fixed. A change in $(B_2/P + K_2)$ means that the household provides more or less assets for consumption in years 3 and beyond. To understand the choice of $(B_2/P + K_2)$, we have to consider consumption and income in future years. The Appendix describes in detail how to make this extension. Here, we provide an intuitive analysis.

The left-hand side of equation (8.9) is the present value of consumption for years 1 and 2. When we consider many years, the left-hand side becomes the present value of consumption over these many years. The first term added is the present value of year 3's consumption, which is $C_3/[(1 + i_1) \cdot (1 + i_2)]$. We divide C_3 by $(1 + i_1) \cdot (1 + i_2)$, because this term measures the accumulation of interest earnings over two years, from year 1 to year 3. That is, one unit of assets in year 1 becomes $1 + i_1$ units in year 2, and each of these units becomes $1 + i_2$ units in year 3.

Figure 8.4 Effects of the interest rate on consumption and saving

If year 1's interest rate, i_1, goes up, the intertemporal-substitution effect predicts that year 1's consumption, C_1, will fall, and year 1's real saving, $(B_1/P + K_1) - (B_0/P + K_0)$, will rise. The income effects always go in the opposite direction from the intertemporal-substitution effects. For example, if i_1 goes up, the income effect predicts that consumption, C_1, will rise, and real saving, $(B_1/P + K_1) - (B_0/P + K_0)$, will fall.

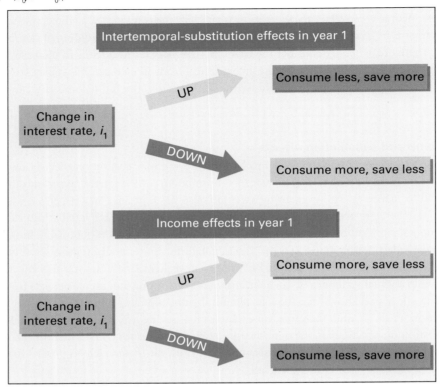

If we continue to include years further into the future, we end up with the overall present value of consumption:

$$overall\ present\ value\ of\ consumption = C_1 + C_2/(1+i_1) + C_3/[(1+i_1)\bullet(1+i_2)] + \cdots$$

The ellipses ($\cdots$) indicate that we include the present values of C_4, C_5, and so on. The multiyear budget constraint has this overall present value of consumption on the left-hand side.[5] In contrast, equation (8.9) included this present value only for years 1 and 2.

The right-hand side of equation (8.9) includes the year-1 value of initial assets, $(1 + i_0) \bullet (B_0/P + K_0)$. This term still appears in the multiyear setting. However, equation (8.9) includes the present value of wage incomes only for years 1 and 2. When we consider many years, we end up with the present value of wage incomes over these many years. By analogy with the results for consumption, we end up with:

$$overall\ present\ value\ of\ wage\ incomes$$
$$= (w/P)_1 \bullet L + (w/P)_2 \bullet L/(1+i_1) + (w/P)_2 \bullet L/[(1+i_1)\bullet(1+i_2)] + \cdots$$

Again, the ellipses indicate that we include the present values of $(w/P)_3 \bullet L$, $(w/P)_4 \bullet L$, and so on. Notice that the interest-rate terms – needed to calculate present values – are the same as those for consumption.

The final point is that the right-hand side of equation (8.9) includes the present value of assets held at the end of year 2, $(B_2/P + K_2)/(1 + i_1)$. When we consider many years, this term becomes the present value of assets held in the

---

[5]Year 4's consumption, C_4, is divided by $(1 + i_1) \bullet (1 + i_2) \bullet (1 + i_3)$ and so on.

distant future. Because of the discounting used to calculate present values, we can safely neglect this term. (See the Appendix for a discussion.) Therefore, we end up with the **multiyear budget constraint**:

Key equation (multiyear budget constraint):

$$C_1 + C_2/(1+i_1) + C_3/[(1+i_1) \bullet (1+i_2)] + \cdots = (1+i_0) \bullet (B_0/P + K_0)$$
$$+ (w/P)_1 \bullet L + (w/P)_2 \bullet L/(1+i_1) + (w/P)_3 \bullet L/[(1+i_1) \bullet (1+i_2)] + \cdots$$

Overall present value of consumption = value of initial assets
+ overall present value of wage incomes

(8.12)

The multiyear budget constraint is useful because it allows us to compare the effects of temporary and permanent changes in income. For a temporary change, we can consider an increase in year 1's wage income, $(w/P)_1 \bullet L$, by one unit while leaving unchanged the initial assets, $(B_0/P + K_0)$, and the wage incomes for the other years, $(w/P)_2 \bullet L$, $(w/P)_3 \bullet L$, and so on. An example would be a bonus that an employee does not expect to be repeated. One possibility, which satisfies the multiyear budget constraint in equation (8.12), is that the household would spend all of its extra income on year 1's consumption, C_1. However, households tend not to react this way, because they like to have similar levels of consumption in each year. Thus, we predict that the household would respond to a rise in $(w/P)_1 \bullet L$ by raising consumption by similar amounts in each year: C_1, C_2, C_3, and so on. This response means, however, that consumption in any particular year, such as year 1, cannot increase very much. Therefore, if $(w/P)_1 \bullet L$ rises by one unit, we predict that C_1 increases by much less than one unit. To put it another way, the **propensity to consume** in year 1 out of an extra unit of year 1's income tends to be small when the extra income is temporary.

We can interpret the results in terms of saving by looking again at the household's budget constraint for year 1:

$$C_1 + (B_1/P + K_1) - (B_0/P + K_0) = (w/P)_1 \bullet L + i_0 \bullet (B_0/P + K_0)$$

consumption in year 1 + real saving in year 1 = real income in year 1

(8.2)

If $(w/P)_1 \bullet L$ rises by one unit on the right-hand side, C_1 rises by much less than one unit on the left-hand side. Therefore, year 1's real saving, $(B_1/P + K_1) - (B_0/P + K_0)$, must rise by nearly one unit on the left-hand side. That is, the **propensity to save** in year 1 out of an extra unit of year 1's income is nearly 1.0 when the extra income is temporary. Saving goes up so much because additional assets are needed to provide for the planned increases in consumption in future years.

Consider, as a contrast, a permanent increase in wage income, where $(w/P)_1 \bullet L$, $(w/P)_2 \bullet L$, $(w/P)_3 \bullet L$, and so on each rise by one unit. An example would be a wage increase that an employee expects to be permanent. The multiyear budget constraint in equation (8.12) shows that it would be possible for the household to respond by increasing consumption by one unit in each year – in that case, for any $t = 1, 2, 3$, and so on, each rise in C_t would match each rise in $(w/P)_t \bullet L$. Moreover, we predict that the household would respond roughly this way because this behaviour is consistent with the desire to have similar levels of consumption each year. Thus, the prediction is that the propensity to consume out of an extra unit of year 1's income would be high – close to 1.0 – when the extra income is permanent.

For the response of saving, we can again look at year 1's budget constraint in equation (8.2). If $(w/P)_1 \bullet L$ rises by one unit on the right-hand side, and C_1 rises by roughly one unit on the left-hand side, year 1's real saving, $(B_1/P + K_1) - (B_0/P + K_0)$, must change by little or not at all. In other words, the propensity to save in year 1 out of an extra unit of year 1's income is small when the extra income is permanent. Saving does not change much because, in this case, the household does not need additional assets to provide for the planned increases in future consumption. These increases can be paid for by the higher future wage incomes: $(w/P)_2 \bullet L$, $(w/P)_3 \bullet L$, and so on.

Our findings about temporary and permanent changes of income correspond to Milton Friedman's famous concept of **permanent income**.[6] His idea was that consumption depends on a long-term average of incomes – which he called permanent income – rather than current income. If a change in income is temporary, permanent income and, hence, consumption change relatively little. Therefore, as in our analysis, the propensity to consume out of temporary income is small. The next By the Numbers box discusses empirical evidence on the propensity to consume.

We can also assess the effects from changes in anticipated future incomes. The multiyear budget constraint is again:

$$C_1 + C_2/(1+i_1) + C_3/[(1+i_1) \bullet (1+i_2)] + \cdots = (1+i_0) \bullet (B_0/P + K_0)$$
$$+ (w/P)_1 \bullet L + (w/P)_2 \bullet L/(1+i_1) + (w/P)_3 \bullet L/[(1+i_1) \bullet (1+i_2)] + \cdots$$

overall present value of consumption = value of initial assets
+ overall present value of wage incomes (8.12)

Suppose, to begin, that real wage incomes, $(w/P)_t \bullet L$, for $t = 1, 2$, and so on, are all the same. Then, assume in year 1 that the household learns that it will be getting a permanent rise the following year. Hence, expected future wage incomes, $(w/P)_2 \bullet L$, $(w/P)_3 \bullet L$, and so on, all rise. Alternatively, the household might learn in year 1 that it would be receiving in the future an inheritance payment or an insurance settlement.

The household would react to higher expected future incomes by raising consumption by similar amounts in each year: C_1, C_2, and so on. In particular, year 1's consumption, C_1, increases even though no higher income has yet shown up.

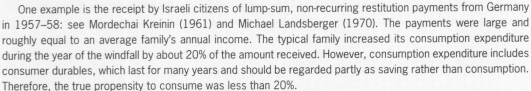

By the Numbers
Empirical evidence on the propensity to consume

Economists have found strong evidence that the propensity to consume out of permanent changes in income is much larger than that for temporary changes. Some of the clearest evidence comes from special circumstances in which people have received windfalls of income, which were clearly temporary and at least partly unanticipated.

One example is the receipt by Israeli citizens of lump-sum, non-recurring restitution payments from Germany in 1957–58: see Mordechai Kreinin (1961) and Michael Landsberger (1970). The payments were large and roughly equal to an average family's annual income. The typical family increased its consumption expenditure during the year of the windfall by about 20% of the amount received. However, consumption expenditure includes consumer durables, which last for many years and should be regarded partly as saving rather than consumption. Therefore, the true propensity to consume was less than 20%.

Another example is the payment in 1950 to US World War II veterans of an unanticipated, one-time life insurance dividend of about $175, roughly 4% of an average family's annual income at the time. In this case, consumption expenditure rose by about 35% of the windfall: see Roger Bird and Ronald Bodkin (1965). However, since consumption expenditure includes consumer durables, the true propensity to consume was less than 35%.

Broader studies of consumer behaviour show that the propensity to consume out of permanent changes in income is large and not much different from unity. In contrast, the propensity to consume out of temporary income is about 20 – 30%: see Robert Hall (1989). Although this response to temporary changes is greater than that predicted by our theory, the important point is that the response of consumption to permanent changes in income is much larger than that to temporary changes.

[6]See Friedman (1957), Chs 2 and 3.

Consider a case where wage incomes starting in year 2 (i.e., $(w/P)_2 \cdot L$, $(w/P)_3 \cdot L$, and so on) increase by one unit. Because these increases in wage incomes were anticipated in year 1, we predicted that C_1, C_2, C_3, and so on would rise by similar amounts. Therefore, although year 2 has higher wage income than year 1 (i.e., $(w/P)_2 \cdot L$ is greater than $(w/P)_1 \cdot L$) we do not predict that the rise in wage income in year 2 will be matched by a higher consumption in year 2 relative to consumption in year 1. That is, we predict that C_1 and C_2 will be similar. We get this result because the anticipated increase in income from year 1 to year 2 was already reflected in a higher C_1. The important prediction is that the household's consumption will not respond to an increase in income when that increase was already expected. The next By the Numbers box discusses empirical evidence on this proposition.

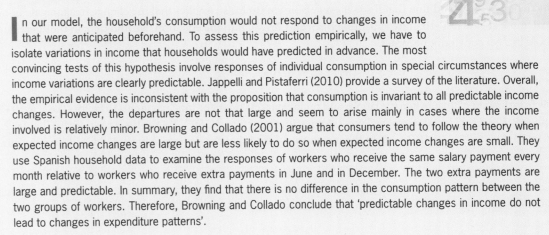

By the Numbers
The response of consumption to anticipated income changes

In our model, the household's consumption would not respond to changes in income that were anticipated beforehand. To assess this prediction empirically, we have to isolate variations in income that households would have predicted in advance. The most convincing tests of this hypothesis involve responses of individual consumption in special circumstances where income variations are clearly predictable. Jappelli and Pistaferri (2010) provide a survey of the literature. Overall, the empirical evidence is inconsistent with the proposition that consumption is invariant to all predictable income changes. However, the departures are not that large and seem to arise mainly in cases where the income involved is relatively minor. Browning and Collado (2001) argue that consumers tend to follow the theory when expected income changes are large but are less likely to do so when expected income changes are small. They use Spanish household data to examine the responses of workers who receive the same salary payment every month relative to workers who receive extra payments in June and in December. The two extra payments are large and predictable. In summary, they find that there is no difference in the consumption pattern between the two groups of workers. Therefore, Browning and Collado conclude that 'predictable changes in income do not lead to changes in expenditure patterns'.

Consumption, saving and investment in equilibrium

We will now use our analysis of a single household's choices of consumption and saving to determine the aggregate quantities of consumption and saving. This analysis will allow us to determine the aggregate quantity of investment. Once we finish this section, we will have all the building blocks in place to study economic fluctuations. Our analysis of that topic begins in Chapter 9.

We have discussed how a household divides its real income between consumption and real saving. Now, we will determine the aggregates of consumption and real saving. These quantities are the amounts that arise when the various markets clear. That is, as in Chapter 7, we go from microeconomic foundations – the behaviour of individual households – to aggregate variables by using market-clearing conditions.

Consider again the household budget constraint at a point in time:

$$C+(1/P)\cdot \Delta B+\Delta K =(w/P)\cdot L+i\cdot (B/P+K)$$

consumption + real saving = real income

(8.1)

If we separate real income on assets, $i \bullet (B/P + K)$, into its two parts, $i \bullet (B/P)$ and $i\,K$, we get the revised budget constraint:

$$C+(1/P) \bullet \Delta B + \Delta K = (w/P) \bullet L + i \bullet (B/P) + iK$$

We know from Chapter 7 that the interest rate, i, is determined from:

$$i = (R/P - \delta)$$
$$\textit{rate of return on bonds} = \textit{rate of return on ownership of capital} \qquad (7.6)$$

If we substitute $(R/P - \delta)$ for i in the iK term of the budget constraint, we get:

$$C+(1/P) \bullet \Delta B + \Delta K = (w/P) \bullet L + i \bullet (B/P) + (R/P) \bullet K - \delta K$$

Since this equation applies for each household, it also applies when we add up across all households. That is, the equation can be applied to the aggregate variables. However, we know for the aggregate of households that the total quantity of bonds, B, must be zero. That is, when the bond market clears, households in the aggregate hold a zero net quantity of bonds. The condition that $B = 0$ at every point in time also implies that the change in aggregate bond holdings, ΔB, must always be zero. If we substitute $B = 0$ and $\Delta B = 0$ into the equation, we find that, in the aggregate, the household budget constraint becomes:

$$C + \Delta K = (w/P) \bullet L + (R/P) \bullet K - \delta K$$

We know from Chapter 7 that, when the labour and rental markets clear, the total payments to factors (i.e., $(w/P) \bullet L$ for labour plus $(R/P) \bullet K$ for capital) equal real gross domestic product (real GDP), Y. (See the Appendix to Chapter 7.) If we substitute Y for $(w/P) \bullet L + (R/P) \bullet K$ in the equation, we find that the aggregate household budget constraint becomes:

Key equation (aggregate form of household budget constraint):

$$C + \Delta K = Y - \delta K$$
$$\textit{consumption} + \textit{net investment} = \textit{real GDP} - \textit{depreciation}$$
$$= \textit{real net domestic product} \qquad (8.13)$$

Recall that the real gross domestic product is determined from the production function by $Y = A \bullet F(K, L)$. Therefore, on the right-hand side of equation (8.13), the real net domestic product, $Y - \delta K$, is determined, for a given technology level, A, by the given values of K and L. Therefore, the left-hand side of the equation implies that the economy's net investment, ΔK, is determined by households' choices of consumption, C. Given the real net domestic product, one unit more of consumption, C, means one unit less of net investment, ΔK. In Chapter 9, we investigate how much households choose to consume, C, given that the interest rate, i, is determined from equation (7.6) to equal the rate of return on capital, $R/P - \delta$. This choice of C determines ΔK from equation (8.13).

Notice that, when the bond market clears, net investment, ΔK, equals economy-wide real saving. For an individual household, real saving equals $(1/P) \bullet \Delta B + \Delta K$ – the change in the real value of assets held as bonds or capital. However, for the economy as a whole, ΔB equals zero, and real saving equals ΔK.

Summing Up

We have now extended the microeconomic foundations of our model from Chapter 7 to consider a household's choices of consumption and saving. The whole point of saving is to increase assets, which will allow for more consumption in the future. Therefore, the essence of the household's choice between today's consumption and today's saving is the choice between today's consumption and tomorrow's consumption.

Using this perspective, we analyzed consumption choices in terms of income effects and intertemporal-substitution effects. Higher initial assets, or higher current or future real wage incomes, raise consumption in all years through income effects. A higher interest rate today motivates the household to lower today's consumption compared to future consumption. Through this channel, a higher interest rate raises current saving. However, a higher interest rate also has a positive income effect, which leads to more consumption and less saving today. Therefore, the overall effect of the interest rate on today's saving is ambiguous.

We have distinguished a permanent change in wage income from a temporary change. For a permanent change, the propensity to consume is high, and the propensity to save is low. In contrast, for a temporary change, the propensity to consume is low, and the propensity to save is high.

By aggregating the household budget constraint and using market-clearing conditions, we were able to determine economy-wide levels of consumption, saving and investment. As we show in Chapter 9, aggregate consumption can be derived by considering income and intertemporal-substitution effects. Net investment is, then, the difference between real net domestic product and consumption. If the quantities of capital, K, and labour, L, are given, the real net domestic product is determined. Hence, the model will determine the aggregates of consumption and net investment.

Key Terms and Concepts

discount factor	infinite-horizon budget	multiyear budget constraint	propensity to save
discounted	constraint	permanent income	two-year budget constraint
finite horizon	intertemporal-substitution	planning horizon	utility
income effects	effect	present value	utility function
infinite horizon	life-cycle models	propensity to consume	

Questions and Problems

A Review questions

1 Discuss the effects on this year's consumption, C_1, from the following changes:
   a An increase in the interest rate, i_1;
   b A permanent increase in real wage income, $(w/P) \cdot L$;
   c An increase in current real wage income, $(w/P)_1 \cdot L$, but no change in future real wage incomes;
   d An increase in future real wage income, $(w/P)_t \cdot L$, for $t = 2, 3$, and so on;
   e A one-time windfall, which raises initial real assets, $(B_0/P + K_0)$.

2 What factors determine whether the propensity to consume out of an additional unit of income is less than or equal to 1.0? Can the propensity be greater than 1.0?

3 Derive the two-year household budget constraint shown in equation (8.9). According to this constraint, if a household reduces this year's consumption, C_1, by one unit, how much would next year's consumption, C_2, rise (if nothing else changes in the equation)?

4 Show how taking a present value gives different weights to income and consumption in different years. Why is a unit of real income in the present more valuable than a unit of real income next year? Why is a unit of consumption next year cheaper than a unit this year?

B Problems for discussion

5 Income effects

Consider again the household's multiyear budget constraint in equation (8.12). What are the income effects from the following:

a An increase in the price level, P, for a household that has a positive value of initial nominal bonds, B_0. What if B_0 is zero or negative?

b An increase by 1% per year in every year's interest rate, i_t. Assume here that $B_0 = 0$.

6 Permanent income

The idea of permanent income is that consumption depends on a long-run average of income, rather than current income. Operationally, we can define permanent income as the hypothetical, constant income that has the same present value as a household's sources of funds on the right-hand side of the multiyear budget constraint:

$$C_1 + C_2/(1+i_1) + C_3/[(1+i_1) \bullet (1+i_2)] + \cdots$$
$$= (1+i_0) \bullet (B_0/P + K_0)$$
$$+ (w/P)_1 \bullet L + (w/P)_2 \bullet L/(1+i_1)$$
$$+ (w/P)_3 \bullet L/[(1+i_1) \bullet (1+i_2)] + \cdots \quad (8.12)$$

a Use equation (8.12) to get a formula for permanent income, when evaluated in year 1.

b What is the propensity to consume out of permanent income?

c If consumption, C_t, for $t = 1, 2$, and so on is constant over time, what is the value of permanent income?

Appendix

The Multiyear Budget Constraint and the Planning Horizon

We show here how to calculate the household budget constraint over many years. When we considered two years, we got the budget constraint:

$$C_1 + C_2/(1+i_1) = (1+i_0) \bullet (B_0/P + K_0) + (w/P)_1 \bullet L + (w/P)_2 \bullet L/(1+i_1)$$
$$- (B_2/P + K_2)/(1+i_1) \quad (8.9)$$

To extend to many years, we will begin with year 3.

The real assets held at the end of year 2 are given by:

$$(B_2/P + K_2) = (1+i_1) \bullet (B_1/P + K_1) + (w/P)_2 \bullet L - C_2 \quad (8.5)$$

The real assets held at the end of year 3 are given by an analogous formula, with everything updated by one year:

$$(B_3/P + K_3) = (1+i_2) \bullet (B_2/P + K_2) + (w/P)_3 \bullet L - C_3 \quad (8.14)$$

We found before that we could express the real assets held at the end of year 2 by:

$$(B_2/P + K_2) = (1+i_1) \bullet (1+i_0) \bullet (B_0/P + K_0) + (1+i_1) \bullet (w/P)_1 \bullet L$$
$$- (1+i_1) \bullet C_1 + (w/P)_2 \bullet L - C_2 \quad (8.8)$$

If we replace $(B_2/P + K_2)$ on the right-hand side of equation (8.14) by the right-hand side of equation (8.8), we get:

$$(B_3/P + K_3) = (1+i_2) \bullet [(1+i_1) \bullet (1+i_0) \bullet (B_0/P + K_0) + (1+i_1) \bullet (w/P)_1 \bullet L$$
$$- (1+i_1) \bullet C_1 + (w/P)_2 \bullet L - C_2] + (w/P) \bullet L - C_3$$

If we multiply the terms inside the brackets by the term $1 + i_2$, we get:

$$(B_3/P + K_3) = (1+i_2) \bullet (1+i_1) \bullet (1+i_0) \bullet (B_0/P + K_0)$$
$$+ (1+i_2) \bullet (1+i_1) \bullet (w/P)_1 \bullet L - (1+i_2) \bullet (1+i_1) \bullet C_1$$
$$+ (1+i_2) \bullet (w/P)_2 \bullet L - (1+i_2) \bullet C_2 + (w/P)_3 \bullet L - C_3 \quad (8.15)$$

The important result involves interest rates. The initial real assets, $(B_0/P + K_0)$, now accumulate interest over three years, up to the end of year 3. Thus, these assets are multiplied on the right-hand side of equation (8.15) by

$(1 + i_2) \bullet (1 + i_1) \bullet (1 + i_0)$. Year 1's real wage income, $(w/P)_1 \bullet L$, accumulates interest over two years and is therefore multiplied by $(1 + i_2) \bullet (1 + i_1)$. The other real income and consumption terms enter in an analogous way.

If we divide through everything in equation (8.15) by $(1 + i_2) \bullet (1 + i_1)$ and rearrange the terms to put only those involving consumption on the left-hand side, we get the three-year budget constraint:

$$C_1 + C_2/(1+i_1) + C_3/[(1+i_1) \bullet (1+i_2)] = (1+i_0) \bullet (B_0/P + K_0) + (w/P)_1 \bullet L$$

$$+ (w/P)_2 \cdot L/(1+i_1) + (w/P)_3 \bullet L/[(1+i_1) \bullet (1+i_2)] - (B_3/P + K_3)/[(1+i_1) \bullet (1+i_2)] \qquad (8.16)$$

This result extends the two-year budget constraint from equation (8.9) to three years. Everything in equation (8.16) appears as a present value (or year 1 value). But now the budget constraint includes the real wage income and consumption from year 3, $(w/P)_3 \bullet L$ and C_3, and these amounts are discounted for the accumulation of interest over two years; that is, by $(1 + i_1) \bullet (1 + i_2)$. The real assets held at the end of year 3, $(B_3/P + K_3)$, now appear on the right-hand side and are also discounted by $(1 + i_1) \bullet (1 + i_2)$.

By now, we see how to extend the budget constraint to any number of years. Each time we push forward one more year, we bring in the real income and consumption from that year. We also bring in the real assets held at the end of the new year and drop the real assets held at the end of the previous year. All of the new terms are discounted to reflect the accumulation of interest from year 1 up to the future year. For example, if we consider j years, where j is greater than 3, we get the j-year budget constraint:

$$C_1 + C_2/(1+i_1) + C_3/[(1+i_1) \bullet (1+i_2)] + \cdots$$
$$+ Cj/[(1+i_1) \bullet (1+i_2) \bullet \cdots \bullet (1+i_{j-1})] = (1+i_0) \bullet (B_0/P + K_0)$$
$$+ (w/P)_1 \bullet L + (w/P)_2 \bullet L/(1+i_1) + (w/P)_3 \bullet L/[(1+i_1) \bullet (1+i_2)]$$
$$+ \cdots + (w/P)_j \bullet L/[(1+i_1) \bullet (1+i_2) \bullet \cdots \bullet (1+i_{j-1})]$$
$$- (B_j/P + K_j)/[(1+i_1) \bullet (1+i_2) \bullet \cdots \bullet (1+i_{j-1})] \qquad (8.17)$$

We want to use equation (8.17) to understand how the household chooses year 1's consumption, C_1. That is, the household now makes this choice as part of a long-term plan that considers future consumptions and real incomes out to year j. These future values relate to the current choice through the j-year budget constraint. We can think of the number j as the **planning horizon**; that is, the number of years over which the household plans its choices of consumption and saving.

How long is the horizon that the typical household considers when making decisions? Because we are dealing with households that have access to borrowing and lending, a long horizon is appropriate. By borrowing or lending, households can effectively use future income to pay for current consumption, or current income to pay for future consumption. When expressed as a present value, future incomes are as pertinent for current decisions as today's income.

Economists often assume that the typical household's planning horizon is long but finite. For example, in theories called **life-cycle models**, the horizon, j, represents an individual's expected remaining lifetime.[7] If people do not care about things that occur after their death, they have no reason to carry assets beyond year j. Accordingly, they plan so as to set to zero the final stock of assets, $(B_j/P + K_j)$, in equation (8.17).[8] That is, each person plans to end up with no assets when he or she dies.

It is straightforward to define the anticipated lifetime and, thereby, the planning horizon for an isolated individual. The appropriate horizon is, however, not so obvious for a family in which individuals have spouses and children.

---

[7] Life-cycle models are associated particularly with the economist Franco Modigliani. See Franco Modigliani and Richard Brumberg (1954), and Albert Ando and Franco Modigliani (1963).

[8] We have to rule out the possibility of dying with negative assets. Otherwise, each person would like to set $(B^j/P + K^j)$ to be a large negative number.

Since a person cares about their spouse and children, the applicable horizon extends beyond a person's expected life-time, and households give weight to the expected future real incomes and consumptions of children. Further, since children care about their prospective children, should they have any, there is no clear point at which to draw the line.

Instead of imposing a **finite horizon** (where j is a finite number), we can think of each household's plan as having an **infinite horizon**. That is, the planning period, j, extends arbitrarily far out into the future and can be thought of as being infinite. There are two good reasons to make this assumption:

- First, if we think of the typical person as part of a family that cares about members of future generations – children, grandchildren, and so on – into the indefinite future, this set-up is appropriate;
- Second, although it is not obvious at this point, an infinite horizon is the simplest assumption.

If we use an infinite horizon, we allow the number j to become arbitrarily large in equation (8.17). In that case, there is no final year, j, and we do not have to worry about the last term on the right-hand side, which involves $(B_j/P + K_j)$.[9] Thus, the **infinite-horizon budget constraint** – the constraint that applies to an infinite planning period – is the one we used before:

$$C_1 + C_2/(1+i_1) + C_3/[(1+i_1) \bullet (1+i_2)] + \cdots = (1+i_0) \bullet (B_0/P + K_0)$$
$$+ (w/P)_1 \bullet L + (w/P)_2 \bullet L/(1+i_1) + (w/P)_3 \bullet L/[(1+i_1) \bullet (1+i_2)] + \cdots \tag{8.12}$$

The ellipses signify that we are including terms involving C_t and $(w/P)_t \bullet L$ for $t = 1, 2$, and so on; that is, extending out to arbitrarily large values of t.

---

[9]Because of the discounting by $(1 + i_1) \bullet (1 + i_2) \cdots (1 + i_{-1})$, the present value of the assets left over, $B_j/P + K_j$, tends to become negligible as j gets very large.

9 An equilibrium business-cycle model

This chapter uses the framework developed in Chapters 7 and 8 to study the short-term economic fluctuations called business cycles. A business cycle involves phases in which real gross domestic product (real GDP) is expanding or contracting. A period of expanding real GDP – a boom – is typically accompanied by increases in other macroeconomic variables, such as consumption, investment and employment, and by decreases in the unemployment rate. Conversely, a period of contraction – a recession – tends to feature decreases in consumption, investment and employment, along with rises in the unemployment rate.

The economy's total output, real GDP, is the key indicator of whether the economy is in a phase of expansion or contraction. As an example, we will look at the behaviour of Eurozone real GDP since the introduction of the euro in 1999, in order to understand the nature of economic fluctuations.

Cyclical behaviour of real GDP: Recessions and booms

The graph in Figure 9.1 shows Eurozone real GDP on a quarterly basis from 1999.1 (the first quarter of 1999) to 2015.2 (the second quarter of 2015). If we look at the graph of real GDP in Figure 9.1, we can think of the movements as reflecting two forces. First, there is the overall upward movement or *trend* in real GDP from 1999 to 2015. We think of this trend as reflecting long-term economic growth, the subject of Chapters 3–5. Second, there are shorter-term fluctuations of real GDP around its trend. We think of these economic fluctuations as stemming from the business cycle; that is, from booms and recessions. In this chapter and Chapter 10, we seek to understand these economic fluctuations.

We imagine that real GDP has two parts:

$$real\ GDP = trend\ real\ GDP + cyclical\ part\ of\ real\ GDP \tag{9.1}$$

To break down real GDP into trend and cycle, we start by estimating the trend. A good measure of the trend is a reasonably smooth curve fit to the data on real GDP. In Figure 9.2, the light blue graph shows real GDP. **Trend real GDP** is the dark blue curve.[1] This graph is a smooth curve drawn through the light blue graph.

Once we know trend real GDP, displayed in dark blue in Figure 9.2, we can calculate the deviation from the trend. If we rearrange the terms in equation (9.1), we get:

$$cyclical\ part\ of\ real\ GDP = real\ GDP - trend\ real\ GDP \tag{9.2}$$

We call the difference between real GDP and its trend the **cyclical part of real GDP**, because we view this part as coming from the business cycle; that is, from short-term economic fluctuations.

---

[1] The trend is called a Hodrick-Prescott filter (H-P filter), named after the economists Robert Hodrick and Edward Prescott. The general idea is to determine the position of the trend to fit the movements in real GDP without fluctuating too much. The procedure allows the slope of the trend to change slowly over time in response to observed changes in the growth rate of real GDP.

Figure 9.1 Eurozone real GDP, 1999–2015

The graph shows Eurozone real GDP from 1999.1 to 2015.2. The data are quarterly, seasonally adjusted, and measured in euros from the base year, 2005.

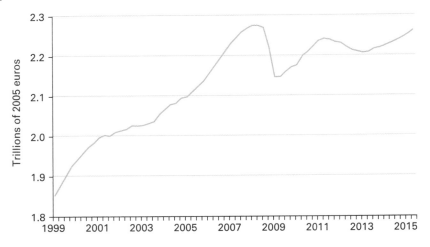

Figure 9.2 Calculating the trend of Eurozone real GDP, 1999–2015

The light blue curve shows Eurozone real GDP from Figure 9.1. The dark blue curve is a smooth trend drawn through the GDP data. We think of this trend curve as reflecting long-run economic growth.

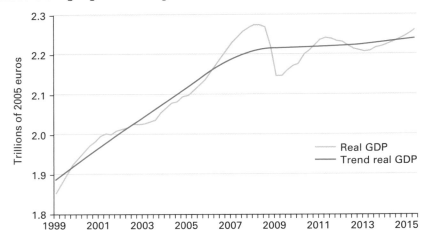

Figure 9.2 demonstrates that the most important property of Eurozone real GDP from 1999 to 2015 is the overall upward trend, shown in dark blue. In fact, it is not so easy in this graph to discern all the business cycles (i.e., the cyclical part, which is the difference between real GDP and its trend). In subsequent graphs, we magnify the cyclical part to get a clearer picture. However, we should remember that the trend in real GDP is the main determinant of how the typical person's current standard of living in the Eurozone compares with, say, ten or more years earlier. Therefore, in the long run, economic growth is more important than economic fluctuations.

Although economic fluctuations are typically small compared to long-term trends, the fluctuations do influence the typical person's well-being. For example, people are harmed during recessions because they have lower real incomes and less consumption, and often lose their jobs. Most discussions in the news media focus on fluctuations rather than trends. This focus probably exists because trends represent long-term forces that are usually not news, whereas fluctuations reflect recent events that do constitute news. In addition, it is easier (even if usually wrong) to blame economic fluctuations, especially an ongoing recession, on the current political administration. It is more difficult to assign responsibility for long-term economic growth.

Figure 9.3 shows a magnified version of the cyclical part of real GDP. This cyclical part is the difference between real GDP and its trend from Figure 9.2. By changing the scale on the vertical axis, we get a clear picture in Figure 9.3 of when real GDP was above or below its trend.

The variability of the cyclical part of real GDP is a good way to gauge the extent of economic fluctuations. To get a quantitative measure, we use a statistic called the **standard deviation**.[2] In Figure 9.3, the standard deviation of the cyclical part of real GDP is 1.3%. This value means that the typical range of fluctuation of Eurozone real GDP from 1999 to 2015 was between 1.3% below and 1.3% above trend.[3]

The general notion of a recession is a period of low economic activity, gauged by real GDP and other macroeconomic variables. In our case, we consider a more operational definition by looking at periods in which the cyclical part of real GDP was negative and reached at least 1.5% in magnitude. By this definition, a recession occurred in 2009–10. We discussed in Chapter 1 the potential causes of this Great Recession during which real GDP in the Eurozone was below trend by as much as 3% in 2009.

The semi-official arbiter of when Eurozone recessions begin and end is the Centre for Economic Policy Research (CEPR), which is a network of over 900 researchers mostly from universities throughout Europe. The definition of a recession that CEPR adopts is 'a significant decline in the level of economic activity, spread across the economy of the euro area, usually visible in two or more consecutive quarters of negative growth in GDP, employment and other measures of aggregate economic activity for the euro area as a whole'.

Figure 9.3 Cyclical part of Eurozone real GDP, 1999–2015

The graph plots the difference between real GDP (the light blue curve in Figure 9.2) and its trend (the dark blue curve in Figure 9.2). The resulting series – the cyclical part of real GDP – shows the deviations of real GDP from its trend. This cyclical part is measured in a proportionate sense; for example, 0.02 means that real GDP is 2% above trend, and –0.02 means that real GDP is 2% below trend.

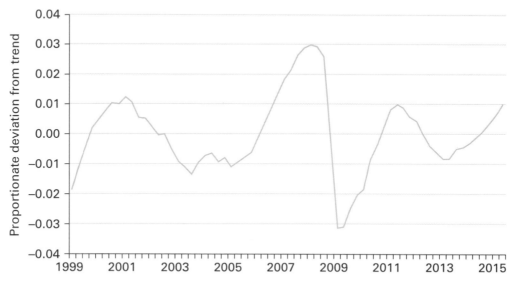

[2]The standard deviation is the square root of the variance. The variance is the average of the squared deviation of a variable from its mean. In the present case, the mean of the cyclical part of real GDP is close to zero (because of the way we constructed the trend in Figure 9.2). Therefore, the variance is just the average squared value of the cyclical part of real GDP.
[3]If a variable is normally distributed (a reasonable approximation for the cyclical part of real GDP), about 65% of the time the variable is between one standard deviation below and one standard deviation above its mean. About 95% of the time, the variable is between two standard deviations below and two standard deviations above its mean.

An equilibrium business-cycle model

CONCEPTUAL ISSUES

To model economic fluctuations, we start by assuming that these fluctuations reflect **shocks** to the economy. An example of a shock is a change in the technology level, A, which enters into the production function introduced in equation (3.1) of Chapter 3 and repeated here:

$$Y = A \bullet F(K, L) \tag{9.3}$$

An increase in A means that the economy is more productive – it can produce more output, Y, with given inputs of capital and labour, K and L. Conversely, a decrease in A means that the economy is less productive. In the present chapter, we focus on shocks to A as sources of economic fluctuations.

We call our model an **equilibrium business-cycle model** (EBC model) because it uses equilibrium conditions to determine how the shocks affect real GDP, Y, and other macroeconomic variables, such as consumption, C, investment, I, and the quantity of labour input, L. The model assumes that the supply and demand functions, such as those for labour and capital services, accord with the underlying microeconomic foundations worked out in Chapters 7 and 8. Given these functions, the key equilibrium conditions are that markets have to clear. For example, the total quantity of labour supplied equals the total quantity demanded, and the total quantity of capital services supplied equals the total quantity demanded. In Chapter 17, we explore models in which some markets do not clear.

A famous example of an equilibrium business-cycle model is the **real business-cycle model** (RBC model) developed by the 2004 Nobel Laureates Finn Kydland and Edward Prescott (1982). The RBC model emphasizes shocks to the technology level, A, and uses the same kind of equilibrium conditions that we employ. Hence, the equilibrium business-cycle model in this chapter is a real business-cycle model. However, in subsequent chapters we generalize the model to include different forms of shocks; for example, Chapters 16 and 17 consider disturbances that are monetary, rather than real. Since our basic approach remains the same, we can use the broader label, equilibrium business-cycle model, to cover these extensions as well as the model in this chapter.

Our model will predict patterns of fluctuations in real GDP and other macroeconomic variables. After working out these predictions, we compare them to macroeconomic data. Since we focus in this chapter on shocks to the technology level, A, the model will have a chance to work well only if we allow for shifts in A to be sometimes positive and sometimes negative. The positive shocks will generate booms, and the negative shocks will generate recessions.

If we think of A as the technology level, it is easy to imagine increases in A; for example, from discoveries of new goods or methods of production. Examples from our discussion of technological progress in Chapter 5 are the invention and adaptation of electric power, the transistor, computers and the Internet.[4] However, many smaller discoveries contributed to the economic booms shown in Figure 9.3.

If we view A as the technology level, it is hard to imagine important decreases in A. After all, producers would not usually forget previous technological advances. However, we mentioned in our study of the Solow growth model in Chapter 5 that events other than technological discoveries can affect productivity and, thereby, influence the economy in ways similar to changes in the technology level. Moreover, these other events can be negative – amounting to decreases in A – or positive.

Some events that resemble changes in the technology level, A, are shifts in legal and political systems, changes in the degree of competition and variations in the volume of international trade. Adverse events that have effects similar to reductions in A include harvest failures, wartime destruction, natural disasters and strikes.

Our analysis of economic fluctuations takes a broad view of A to encompass these examples. In this case, changes in A can sometimes be positive and sometimes negative. However, we shall find it convenient still to refer to A as the 'technology level'.

---

[4] For a more complete list, including innovations such as just-in-time inventory management, see the discussion in Jones (2005).

In the equilibrium business-cycle model developed in this chapter, we explain economic fluctuations as short-term responses to shocks to the technology level, A. The main feature that makes the analysis short-term is that we assume, as an approximation, that we can hold fixed the stock of capital, K. That is, in thinking about the relatively brief duration of a recession or a boom, we do not allow enough time to elapse for the changes in machines and buildings – the goods included in K – to be significant. In contrast, for long-term analyses of economic growth, as in Chapters 3–5, the changes in K are a central part of the story.

THE MODEL

Now we will work out the short-run effects from a shift in the technology level, A. Real GDP, Y, is given by the production function:

$$Y = A \bullet F(K, L) \tag{9.3}$$

In addition to treating the capital stock, K, as fixed in the short run, we also assume initially that labour input, L, is fixed. In this case, changes in Y will reflect only changes in A. When A rises, Y rises, and when A falls, Y falls. Later in this chapter, we make the model more realistic by allowing for short-run variations in L. In Chapter 10, we will extend further to allow for variations in the utilization rate of capital.

In practice, many shifts to A will not be observable; that is, we will not be able to tell what changes have occurred in the variables that influence the economy's productivity. The problem is that, if we are free to make assumptions about which unobservable changes have occurred, we will be able to match any observed fluctuations in real GDP, such as those shown in Figure 9.3. Given how easy it is to fit these data, we should not give our model any credit for 'explaining' the fluctuations in real GDP in this way. The next Extending the Model box discusses the difference between the EBC model and the Keynesian model in terms of explaining the origins of economic fluctuations.

The real challenge for the model is to predict how other macroeconomic variables move along with real GDP during economic fluctuations. As an example, we want to see what the model predicts for the changes in consumption and investment during booms and recessions. Similarly, we can assess the behaviour of the real wage rate, the real rental price of capital, and the interest rate. Later, when we drop the assumption that L is fixed, we can look at the behaviour of employment and unemployment. The general idea is that we will test our equilibrium business-cycle model by making predictions about the relationship between real GDP and other macroeconomic variables, and then looking at the data to see if these predictions are accurate. We will now start our analysis of macroeconomic variables.

Extending the Model
Adding demand shocks to the EBC Model

As discussed above, we will consider economic fluctuations originating from shocks to the technology level A in the EBC model. We refer to these disturbances as supply shocks because these shocks initially affect the supply side of the economy via the production function. In contrast, the Keynesian models presented in Chapter 6 usually focus on demand shocks, such as changes in investor sentiment and monetary disturbances. We refer to these disturbances as demand shocks because these shocks initially affect the demand side of the economy via the aggregate demand (AD) curve. In Chapters 16 and 17, we will extend the EBC model in order to explore the effects of a demand shock; namely, monetary disturbances, on the macroeconomy.

The marginal product of labour and the real wage rate

We know from the production function in equation (9.3) that an increase in the technology level, A, raises the marginal product of labour, MPL, for given inputs of capital, K, and labour, L. We show the effects from a higher schedule for the MPL in Figure 9.4. We consider two technology levels, A and A', where A' is greater than A. We assume that the capital stock is fixed at K. The downward-sloping light blue curve shows how the MPL varies with L when the technology level is A. If the real wage rate is w/P, on the vertical axis, the quantity of labour demanded is the amount L on the horizontal axis. The downward-sloping dark blue curve shows the MPL when the technology level is A'. The MPL is higher for any L on this second curve than on the first one. Therefore, at the given real wage rate, w/P, the quantity of labour demanded, $(L^d)'$ on the horizontal axis, is greater than L.

The two labour-demand curves in Figure 9.5 come from Figure 9.4. For labour supply, we assume for now that the quantity of labour supplied is fixed at the value L on the horizontal axis. That is, the labour-supply curve is a vertical line at L.

If the technology level is A, the labour-demand curve is given in Figure 9.5 by the downward-sloping light blue curve. Therefore, the labour market clears – the quantity of labour demanded equals the quantity supplied – when the real wage rate, w/P, equals the market-clearing value $(w/P)^*$, shown on the vertical axis. The real wage rate $(w/P)^*$ equals the marginal product of labour, MPL, evaluated at L (when the technology level is A and the capital stock is fixed at K).

If the technology level rises to A', the labour-demand curve is given in Figure 9.5 by the downward-sloping dark blue curve. In this case, the market-clearing real wage rate equals $[(w/P)^*]'$ on the vertical axis. Since the MPL is higher, at the given L, on the dark blue curve than on the light blue one, the market-clearing real wage rate is higher. That is, $[(w/P)^*]'$ is greater than $(w/P)^*$.

One way to think about the result is that, at the initial real wage rate, $(w/P)^*$, the rise in the MPL means that the quantity of labour demanded, $(L^d)'$, exceeds the quantity supplied, which is fixed at L. Therefore, employers (households in their role as business managers) compete for the scarce labour and drive up the real wage rate to $[(w/P)^*]'$.

We found that an increase in the technology level, A, raises the real wage rate, w/P. Hence, the model predicts that an economic boom – where real GDP is high because A is high – will have a relatively high w/P. In contrast, a recession will have a relatively low w/P.

Figure 9.4 Effect of an increase in the technology level on the demand for labour

When the technology level is A, the MPL is given by the light blue curve, labelled MPL (A). At the real wage rate w/P, shown on the vertical axis, the quantity of labour demanded is L on the horizontal axis. The technology level A' is greater than A. Therefore, the MPL, given by the dark blue curve labelled MPL (A'), is higher at any labour input than the value along the light blue curve. When the technology level is A' and the real wage rate is w/P, the quantity of labour demanded is $(L^d)'$, which is greater than L.

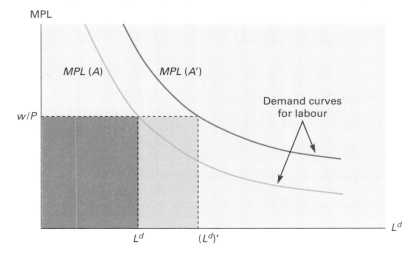

Figure 9.5 Effect of an increase in the technology level on the real wage rate

Labour supply is the given value L, shown on the horizontal axis. If the technology level is A, the schedule for the MPL determines the light blue labour-demand curve, labelled MPL (A). Therefore, the market-clearing real wage rate is $(w/P)^*$, shown on the vertical axis. The technology level A' is greater than A, as in Figure 9.4. Therefore, the schedule for the MPL is given by the dark blue labour-demand curve, labelled MPL (A'). In this case, the market-clearing real wage rate is $[(w/P)^*]'$, which is greater than $(w/P)^*$.

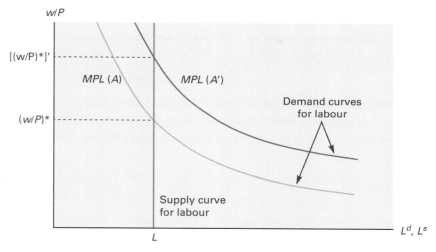

Marginal product of capital, real rental price and the interest rate

We know from the production function in equation (9.3) that an increase in the technology level, A, raises the marginal product of capital, MPK, for given inputs of capital, K, and labour, L. We show the effects of a higher MPK in Figure 9.6. This figure again considers two technology levels, A and A', where A' is greater than A. We still assume that labour input is fixed at L. The downward-sloping light blue curve shows how the MPK varies with K when the technology level is A. If the real rental price is R/P on the vertical axis, the quantity of capital demanded is the

Figure 9.6 Effect of an increase in the technology level on the demand for capital services

When the technology level is A, the MPK is given by the light blue curve, labelled MPK (A). At the real rental price R/P, shown on the vertical axis, the quantity of capital demanded is K on the horizontal axis. The technology level A' is greater than A. Therefore, the MPK, given by the dark blue curve labelled MPK (A'), is higher at any capital input than the value along the light blue curve. When the technology level is A' and the real rental price is R/P, the quantity of capital demanded is $(K^d)'$, which is greater than K^d.

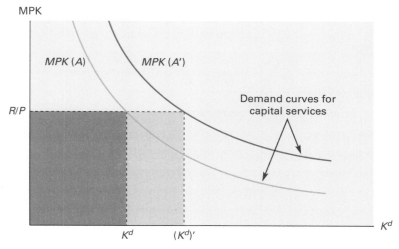

amount K on the horizontal axis. The downward-sloping light blue curve shows the MPK when the technology level is A'. The MPK is higher at any given K on this second curve than on the first one. Therefore, at the given real rental price, R/P, the quantity of capital demanded, $(K^d)'$ on the horizontal axis, is greater than K^d.

The two demand curves for capital services in Figure 9.7 come from Figure 9.6. We assume that the quantity of capital services supplied is fixed at K on the horizontal axis. That is, the supply curve is a vertical line at K.

If the technology level is A, the demand curve for capital services is given in Figure 9.7 by the downward-sloping light blue curve. Therefore, the market for capital services clears – the quantity of capital services demanded equals the quantity supplied – when the real rental price, R/P, equals the market-clearing value $(R/P)^*$ on the vertical axis. The real rental price $(R/P)^*$ equals the marginal product of capital, MPK, evaluated at K (when the technology level is A and labour input is fixed at L).

If the technology level rises to A', the demand curve for capital services is given in Figure 9.7 by the downward-sloping dark blue curve. In this case, the market-clearing real rental price equals $[(R/P)^*]'$ on the vertical axis. Since the MPK is higher, at the given K, on the dark blue curve than on the light blue one, the market-clearing real rental price is higher. That is, $[(R/P)^*]'$ is greater than $(R/P)^*$.

We conclude that an increase in the technology level, A, raises the real rental price of capital, R/P. Hence, the model predicts that an economic boom – where real GDP is high because A is high – will have a relatively high R/P. In contrast, a recession will have a relatively low R/P.

Recall from our analysis in Chapter 7 that the interest rate is given by:

$$i = R/P - \delta$$

$$\textit{rate of return on bonds} = \textit{rate of return on ownership of capital} \qquad (7.6)$$

We know from Figure 9.7 that, when the market for capital services clears, the real rental price, R/P, equals the marginal product of capital, MPK, evaluated at the given values of capital, K, and labour, L. Therefore, the interest rate is given by:

$$i = MPK\,(\textit{evaluated at given K and L}) - \delta \qquad (9.4)$$

Figure 9.7 Effect of an increase in the technology level on the real rental price of capital

The supply of capital services is the given value K, shown on the horizontal axis. If the technology level is A, the schedule for the MPK is given by the light blue curve, labelled *MPK (A)*. This curve gives the demand for capital services when the technology level is A. The market-clearing real rental price is $(R/P)^*$, shown on the vertical axis. The technology level A' is greater than A, as in Figure 9.6. Therefore, the schedule for the MPK is given by the dark blue curve, labelled *MPK (A')*. This curve gives the demand for capital services when the technology level is A'. In this case, the market-clearing real rental price is $[(R/P)^*]'$, which is greater than $(R/P)^*$.

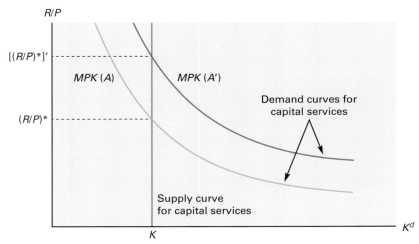

An increase in the technology level raises the marginal product of capital, MPK, at given inputs of capital, K, and labour, L. Therefore, equation (9.4) implies that the interest rate, i, rises. Hence, the model predicts that an economic boom will have a relatively high interest rate, whereas a recession will have a relatively low interest rate.

Consumption, saving and investment

Now we will use our microeconomic analysis from Chapter 8 to determine how much households consume and save. A rise in the technology level, A, raises the interest rate, i, and a higher i motivates households to defer consumption from the present to the future (the intertemporal-substitution effect). On this ground, we predict that current consumption would fall. However, our analysis is incomplete, because we have to allow for income effects.

Consider the household budget constraint at each point in time from Chapter 8:

$$C+(1/P)\bullet\Delta B+\Delta K =(w/P)\bullet L+i\bullet(B/P+K)$$
$$consumption+real\ saving=real\ income \tag{8.1}$$

Income effects enter through real wage income, $(w/P)\bullet L$, and real asset income, $i\bullet(B/P+K)$. An increase in A raises real wage income, because w/P rises and L does not change. An increase in A also raises real asset income, because i rises, B/P is unchanged (at zero in the aggregate), and K does not change in the short run. Therefore, an increase in A raises overall household real income.

Another way to see the effect on overall income is to use the aggregate household budget constraint from Chapter 8 that applies when the markets for bonds, labour, and capital services clear:

$$C+\Delta K=Y-\delta K$$
$$consumption+net\ investment=real\ GDP-depreciation$$
$$=real\ net\ domestic\ product \tag{8.13}$$

If we substitute $Y = A \bullet F(K, L)$ from the production function (equation [9.3]), we get:

$$C+\Delta K=A\bullet F(K,L)-\delta K \tag{9.5}$$

Since depreciation, δK, is fixed in the short run, the income effect from a change in A boils down to its effect on real GDP, $Y = A \bullet F(K, L)$. Since an increase in A raises real GDP for given K and L, we again see that a rise in A raises overall real income.

The increase in real income motivates households to raise current consumption (as well as future consumption). This response is the familiar income effect. This effect works against the intertemporal-substitution effect, which tends to reduce current consumption. Therefore, we are unsure whether an increase in the technology level, A, leads to more or less current consumption, C. The net change depends on whether the income effect is stronger or weaker than the intertemporal-substitution effect.

We can sharpen our prediction because the size of the income effect depends on how long the change in the technology level, A, lasts. For the rest of this section, we assume that the change in A is permanent. This situation would apply to a literal technological advance, because producers tend not to forget these advances. In this case, the increases in real income tend also to be permanent. Therefore, we should consider the case from Chapter 8 in which real income rises by similar amounts each year. The prediction for this case was that the propensity to consume out of higher income would be close to 1.0. Hence, if an increase in A raises real GDP, $Y = A \bullet F(K, L)$, by one unit, then – from the standpoint of the income effect – current consumption, C, would rise by roughly one unit.

To compute the overall effect on current consumption, we have to balance the income effect – whereby consumption rises by roughly as much as real GDP – against the intertemporal-substitution effect, which lowers current consumption. Quantitative estimates of the intertemporal-substitution effect show that it has less of an impact than this large income effect. Hence, when the increase in A is permanent, current consumption will rise. However, as long as the intertemporal-substitution operates at all, the increase in current consumption will be less than the increase in real GDP.

In equation (8.1), the change on the left-hand side in C is less than the change on the right-hand side in real income, which corresponds to the change in real GDP, Y. Therefore, household real saving must rise on the left-hand side. That is, part of the extra household real income goes to consumption and another part goes to real saving.

In the aggregate household budget constraint in equation (8.13), we found that current consumption, C, rises, but by less than the increase in real GDP, Y. Therefore, net investment, ΔK, must increase – the increase in real GDP shows up partly as more C and partly as more ΔK. Since net investment, ΔK, equals real saving, this result is consistent with our finding that real saving increased.

Matching the theory with the facts

Our equilibrium business-cycle model makes a number of predictions about how fluctuations in macroeconomic variables match up with variations in real GDP. Now, we will examine the predictions for consumption, investment, the real wage rate, the real rental price of capital, and the interest rate. We will consider Eurozone data as an example.

CONSUMPTION AND INVESTMENT

We can measure consumption, C, from the national-income accounts by real consumer expenditure. This expenditure accounted, on average, for 56% of Eurozone GDP from 1999 to 2015. We calculate the cyclical part of real consumer expenditure by using the method applied to real GDP in Figure 9.1. The result is the light blue curve in Figure 9.8. This graph shows the proportionate deviation of real consumer expenditure from its trend. We also show, as the dark blue curve, the cyclical part of real GDP (copied from Figure 9.3).

Two important findings emerge from Figure 9.8. First, real consumer expenditure typically fluctuates in the same direction as real GDP.[5] When a variable fluctuates, such as real consumer expenditure, in the same direction as real GDP, we say that the variable is **procyclical**. A procyclical variable moves in the same direction as the business cycle – it tends to be high relative to its trend in a boom and low relative to its trend in a recession. (A variable

Figure 9.8 Cyclical behaviour of Eurozone real GDP and consumer expenditure

The dark blue curve is the deviation of real GDP from its trend. The light blue curve is the deviation of real consumer expenditure from its trend. These deviations are measured in a proportionate sense. The data on GDP and consumer expenditure are quarterly and seasonally adjusted. Real consumer expenditure is procyclical – it fluctuates closely with real GDP but is less variable than real GDP.

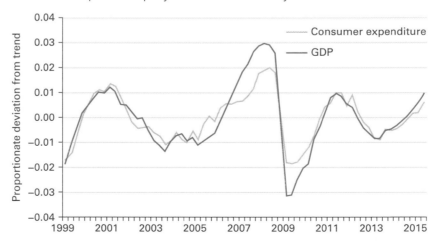

[5]From 1999.1 to 2015.2, the correlation of the cyclical part of real consumer expenditure with the cyclical part of real GDP in the Eurozone was 0.94.

that fluctuates in the opposite direction from real GDP is **countercyclical.** One that has little tendency to move in a particular direction during a business cycle is **acyclical.**) Second, real consumer expenditure fluctuates in a proportional sense by less than real GDP. From 1999.1 to 2015.2, the standard deviation of the cyclical part of real consumer expenditure was 0.9%, compared with 1.3% for the cyclical part of real GDP. Thus, in a proportionate sense, real consumer expenditure varies by less than real GDP in booms and recessions.

We can measure gross investment, I, from the national-income accounts by real gross domestic private investment. This expenditure accounted, on average, for 20% of Eurozone GDP from 1999 to 2015. We again use the method from Figure 9.3 to calculate the cyclical part of real gross investment. The result is the light blue curve in Figure 9.9. This graph shows the proportionate deviation of real investment from its trend. The cyclical part of real GDP is, again, the dark blue curve.

One finding from Figure 9.9 is that, as with real consumer expenditure, real gross investment is procyclical; that is, it typically fluctuates in the same direction as real GDP.[6] Hence, investment is high relative to its trend in a boom and low relative to its trend in a recession. Another finding is that real gross investment fluctuates, in a proportional sense, much more than real GDP. In terms of the standard deviations of the cyclical parts, the one for gross investment was 3.3%, compared to 1.3% for real GDP. Thus, in a proportionate sense, real investment fluctuates much more than real GDP in booms and recessions. The volatility of investment means that it represents far more of the fluctuations in real GDP than we would expect from the average ratio of gross investment to GDP (20%).

Figure 9.9 Cyclical behaviour of Eurozone real GDP and investment

The dark blue curve is the deviation of real GDP from its trend. The light blue curve is the deviation of real gross private domestic investment from its trend. These deviations are measured in a proportionate sense. The data on GDP and investment are quarterly and seasonally adjusted. Real gross investment is procyclical – it fluctuates closely with real GDP but is far more variable than real GDP.

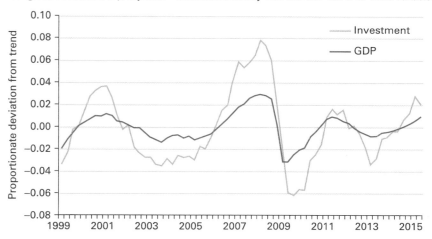

Going back to the model, permanent shifts in the technology level, A, match up with some of the empirical patterns found in Figures 9.8 and 9.9. Specifically, increases in A generate economic booms where real GDP increases, and these increases show up partly as more consumption and partly as more investment. In reverse, decreases in A create recessions, where real GDP, consumption and investment all decline.

Does the model explain why investment fluctuates proportionately far more than consumption? Recall that, because the changes in the technology level, A, are permanent, the income effects are strong. On this ground, consumption would change by roughly the same amount as real GDP. However, we also found that an increase in A led to a rise in the interest rate, which reduced current consumption and raised current real saving. This effect

---

[6]From 1999.1 to 2015.2, the correlation of the cyclical part of real gross domestic private investment with the cyclical part of real GDP in the Eurozone was 0.95.

means that, during a boom, consumption rises proportionately by less than real GDP. Analogously, during a recession, consumption falls proportionately by less than real GDP. Thus, to match the observation that consumption is less variable than real GDP, the model relies on the intertemporal-substitution effect from the interest rate. One problem, however, is that empirical studies have found evidence only for small intertemporal-substitution effects on consumption and saving. Therefore, it may be important to find additional reasons to explain why consumption is proportionately less variable than real GDP. We explore an important reason in a later section, which allows for the change in the technology level, A, to be partly temporary.

THE REAL WAGE RATE

The model predicts that the real wage rate, w/P, will be relatively high in booms and relatively low in recessions. A good measure of the nominal wage rate, w, is the average wages and salaries of workers in the private sector. We can measure the real wage rate, w/P, by dividing nominal wages and salaries by a broad measure of the price level, the deflator for the gross domestic product.

We calculate the cyclical part of the real wage rate, w/P, by the procedure used for real GDP in Figure 9.3. The result is the light blue curve in Figure 9.10. This graph shows the proportionate deviation of w/P from its trend. We again show as the dark blue curve the cyclical part of real GDP (from Figure 9.3). We see that the real wage rate tends to be procyclical (i.e., it moves in the same direction as GDP). This finding accords with the model's predictions. However, the degree of procyclicality in the real wage rate seems to be quite small in the data.[7] Our model predicts a highly procyclical real wage rate because we have so far made the assumption of a fixed labour supply (i.e., a vertical labour-supply curve). If the labour-supply curve turns out to be horizontal, then shifts in the labour-demand curve would not affect the real wage rate in equilibrium; in this case, the real wage rate becomes acyclical. Therefore, the degree of procyclicality in the real wage rate depends on the slope of the labour-supply curve. Later in this chapter, we will extend the model to allow for variable labour supply that gives rise to an upward-sloping labour supply curve.

Figure 9.10 Cyclical behaviour of Eurozone real GDP and the real wage rate

The dark blue graph is the deviation of real GDP from its trend. The light blue graph is the deviation of the real wage rate from its trend. These deviations are measured in a proportionate sense. The real wage rate is calculated by dividing wages and salaries, for which data are available from 2000.1, by the number of employed workers and then adjusted by the price deflator for the GDP. The data on GDP and wage rates are quarterly and seasonally adjusted. The real wage rate is procyclical – it fluctuates with real GDP but is not as variable as real GDP.

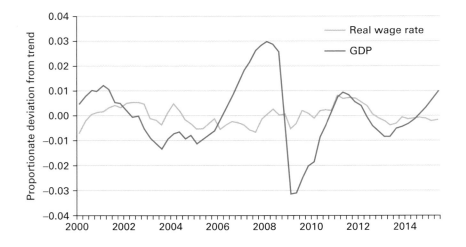

[7]From 1999.1 to 2015.2, the correlation of the cyclical part of the real wage rate with the cyclical part of real GDP in the Eurozone was 0.13.

THE REAL RENTAL PRICE

The model predicts that the real rental price of capital, R/P, will be relatively high in booms and relatively low in recessions. The main problem in testing this proposition is that the rental price is difficult to measure for the whole economy. The reason is that most forms of capital – such as structures and equipment owned by corporations – are not explicitly rented out. These types of capital are typically used by their owners. In effect, businesses rent capital to themselves, but we cannot observe the implicit rental price for this capital. Without better data, we simply divide operating surplus (i.e., capital income) from the national-income accounts by the real value of the capital stock, for which data are only available *annually* from 2000 to 2013, to obtain real capital income per unit of capital as a proxy for the capital rental price. The light blue curve in Figure 9.11 is the cyclical part of this capital rental price R/P. This graph shows the proportionate deviation of R/P from its trend. We again show as the dark blue curve the cyclical part of real GDP. We see that R/P is procyclical – it tends to be above its trend in booms and below its trend during recessions.[8] This finding fits the model's predictions.

Figure 9.11 Cyclical behaviour of Eurozone real GDP and the real rental price of capital

The dark blue curve is the deviation of real GDP from its trend (in a proportionate sense). The light blue curve is the deviation of the real capital rental price from its trend. The real rental price of capital is procyclical – it fluctuates with real GDP.

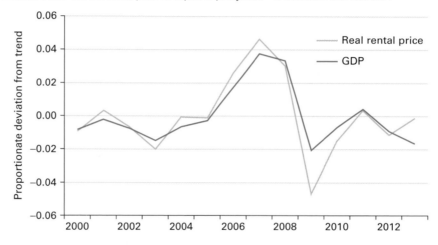

THE INTEREST RATE

The model predicts that booms will have a high interest rate, i, whereas recessions will have a low interest rate. To get a full picture, we need to distinguish between nominal and real interest rates. We will consider inflation in Chapter 12.

Temporary changes in the technology level

In our model, all changes in the technology level, A, were permanent. This assumption is reasonable for technological advances but less compelling for other interpretations of A. For example, if a decrease in A represents a harvest failure or a general strike, the change would be temporary. To allow for these cases, we now assume that the change in A is temporary. Think of the change as lasting for one year.

The change in the assumption about the technology level, A, does not affect most of our analysis. If A increases temporarily, real GDP, $A \cdot F(K, L)$, still rises for fixed values of K and L. The marginal product of capital, MPK, and the interest rate, i, also rise as before. The intertemporal-substitution effect from the higher i still motivates households to reduce current consumption, C, and raise current real saving.

[8]From 1999 to 2013, the correlation of the cyclical part of the real capital rental price with the cyclical part of real GDP was 0.92.

There are some new results about income effects. The overall change in current consumption, C, again depends on the size of the income effect. In our previous case – where the increase in the technology level, A, was permanent – the income effect raised consumption by about as much as the increase in real GDP. This change worked against the intertemporal-substitution effect, which reduced current consumption. For a permanent rise in A, the income effect more than offset the intertemporal-substitution effect, and current consumption increased.

When the increase in the technology level, A, is temporary, the income effect is weak. Therefore, the income effect now raises current consumption, C, by only a small amount. Since the income effect is weak, we can no longer be confident that it more than offsets the intertemporal-substitution effect. Hence, current consumption may rise or fall. In any event, current consumption does not rise by nearly as much as real GDP.

Consider again the aggregate budget constraint that applies when the markets for bonds, labour, and capital services clear:

$$C + \Delta K = Y - \delta K$$
$$consumption + net\ investment = real\ GDP - depreciation$$
$$= real\ net\ domestic\ product \qquad (8.13)$$

Real GDP, $Y = A \bullet F(K, L)$, rises and consumption, C, either falls or rises by a small amount. Hence, net investment, ΔK, rises by nearly as much as – or possibly by even more than – real GDP. The model therefore predicts that an economic boom would feature high real GDP and investment. However, consumption would rise by, at most, a small amount. Conversely, a recession would have low real GDP and investment, but consumption would decline by, at most, a modest amount.

These patterns conflict with the data, because consumption is clearly procyclical – it rises well above trend during booms and falls well below trend in recessions. Thus, if the underlying shocks were purely temporary changes in the technology level, A, the model would not explain the behaviour of consumption. Our conclusion is that we cannot rely solely on temporary changes in A as the main source of economic fluctuations. However, the model does work better if we allow for changes in A to be less than fully permanent, even if not purely temporary.

Consider again the empirical observation that consumption fluctuates proportionately by less than real GDP. When we assumed that the changes in the technology level, A, were permanent, the model could explain the smaller variability of consumption only if the intertemporal-substitution effect on consumption was substantial. However, if the changes in A are less than fully permanent, we have another reason why consumption is less variable than real GDP. If a change in A lasts for a long time, but not for ever, the income effect will be strong. However, the income effect will not be strong enough to raise consumption by as much as the change in real GDP. Thus, consumption can fluctuate proportionately less than real GDP even if the intertemporal-substitution effect on consumption is weak. This reasoning suggests that the model works best to fit the data when the underlying shocks to A are long lasting but less than fully permanent. This form of shock to technology has typically been assumed in real business-cycle models.

Variations in labour input

An important shortcoming of the model worked out thus far is its failure to fit the observed behaviour of labour input during economic fluctuations. Labour input, L – measured by employment or **total hours worked** – varies with the business cycle. As we detail later, L is high in booms and low in recessions; that is, it is clearly procyclical. We cannot give our model a high grade unless we can use it to explain this important phenomenon.

To fit the facts on labour input, we will now extend the model to allow for a variable supply of labour, L^s. This extension will be important for two reasons. First, we will be able to explain short-term variations in labour input, L. Second, changes in real GDP will reflect the variations in L, as well as the direct effect from changes in the technology level, A. We first extend the microeconomic foundations of the model to allow for variable L^s. Then, we will use our equilibrium business-cycle model to assess how labour input, L, moves during economic fluctuations.

LABOUR SUPPLY

Start with a modified form of the household budget constraint worked out in equation (8.1) of Chapter 8:

$$C + (1/P) \cdot \Delta B + \Delta K = (w/P) \cdot L^s + i \cdot (B/P + K)$$

$$consumption + real\ saving = real\ income \tag{9.6}$$

The left-hand side is the total of consumption, C, and real saving, $(1/P) \cdot \Delta B + \Delta K$. The right-hand side is household real income, which is the sum of real wage income, $(w/P) \cdot L^s$, and real asset income, $i \cdot (B/P + K)$. The difference from before is that we replaced L by the quantity of labour supplied, L^s, to allow for a variable labour supply.

Since each household has a fixed amount of time each year, a higher quantity of labour supplied, L^s, means a smaller amount of leisure time. From the perspective of a household, a higher L^s can mean either that working family members work more hours per year or that more members work. In the latter case, the rise in labour supply shows up as an increase in labour-force participation. Either way, more labour supplied means less leisure time for the family.

We have already assumed that households like consumption, C. Now, we assume that households also like more leisure time. To put it differently, households dislike work effort, represented by the quantity of labour supplied, L^s.

As with consumption and saving, the choice of L^s involves substitution and income effects. We start with the *substitution effect for leisure and consumption.*

The substitution effect for leisure and consumption

Consider the household budget constraint in equation (9.6). The right-hand side includes the real wage rate, w/P, and the interest rate, i, each of which an individual household takes as given. Suppose that we also hold fixed the real assets, $B/P + K$, on the right-hand side, and the real saving, $(1/P) \cdot \Delta B + \Delta K$, on the left-hand side. In this case, a household can raise or lower the quantity of labour supplied, L^s, and thereby raise or lower real wage income, $(w/P) \cdot L^s$. Since we are holding everything else fixed in equation (9.6), the higher or lower real wage income will increase or decrease consumption, C. In other words, if the household chooses to work one more hour and thereby have one less hour of leisure, the extra w/P of real wage income pays for w/P more units of consumption. Therefore, the household can substitute one less hour of leisure for w/P more units of consumption.

If the real wage rate, w/P, rises, the household gets a better deal by working more because it gets more consumption for each extra hour worked. Since the deal is better, we predict that the household responds to a higher w/P by working more. Another way to view the result is that a higher w/P makes leisure time more expensive compared to consumption: w/P tells the household how much consumption it gives up by taking an extra hour of leisure. An increase in w/P motivates the household to substitute away from the object that got more expensive – leisure time – and towards the one that got cheaper – consumption. Therefore, a higher real wage rate, w/P, raises the quantity of labour supplied, L^s.

Income effects on labour supply

As usual, we also have to consider income effects. Consider again the budget constraint:

$$C + (1/P) \cdot \Delta B + \Delta K = (w/P) \cdot L^s + i \cdot (B/P + K)$$

$$consumption + real\ saving = real\ income \tag{9.6}$$

We see from the shaded term that a change in the real wage rate, w/P, has an income effect. For a given quantity of labour supplied, L^s, a higher w/P means higher real wage income, $(w/P) \cdot L^s$. Our prediction is that the household spends the extra income on consumption and leisure time. Thus, on this ground, a higher w/P leads to a smaller quantity of labour supplied, L^s. Since the substitution effect from a higher w/P favours higher L^s, the overall effect is ambiguous. An increase in the real wage rate, w/P, raises L^s if the substitution effect is stronger than the income effect.

We may be able to resolve the ambiguity by considering whether the income effect is strong or weak. We found in Chapter 8 that the strength of the income effect depended on whether the change in income was permanent or temporary. To see how this works, consider a modified form of the multiyear budget constraint worked out in Chapter 8 in equation (8.12):

$$C_1 + C_2/(1+i_1) + C_3/[(1+i_1) \bullet (1+i_2)] + \cdots = (1+i_0) \bullet (B_0/P + K_0)$$
$$+ (w/P)_1 \bullet L_1^s + (w/P)_2 \bullet L_2^s/(1+i_1) + (w/P)_3 \bullet L_3^s/[(1+i_1) \bullet (1+i_2)] + \cdots$$

present value of consumption = value of initial assets + present value of wage incomes   (9.7)

The difference from before is that we have replaced the fixed quantity of labour, L, with the quantity of labour supplied in each year, L_t^s, where $t = 1, 2$, and so on.

When we examined income effects on consumption in Chapter 8, we found that households responded to higher real wage rates by consuming more each year. That is, the income effect was positive for each year's consumption. However, the income effect was much stronger if the change in the real wage rate was permanent and applied to $(w/P)_2$, $(w/P)_3$, and so on, rather than just to $(w/P)_1$.

The same reasoning applies to labour supply. A permanent increase in real wage rates results in a large income effect. In this case, we are unsure whether an increase in $(w/P)_1$ (accompanied by increases in future real wage rates, $[w/P]_2$, $[w/P]_3$, and so on) raises or lowers year 1's quantity of labour supplied, L_1^s. The income effect, which lowers labour supply, may be stronger or weaker than the substitution effect, which raises labour supply.

In contrast, if the change in year 1's real wage rate, $(w/P)_1$, is temporary, the income effect is small. In this case, we can be confident that the income effect will be weaker than the substitution effect. Therefore, a temporary increase in year 1's real wage rate, $(w/P)_1$ (when $[w/P]_2$, $[w/P]_3$, and so on do not change), would raise year 1's quantity of labour supplied, L_1^s.

Intertemporal-substitution effects on labour supply

We found in Chapter 8 that a change in the interest rate, i, had an intertemporal-substitution effect on consumption. Now, we will study intertemporal-substitution effects on labour supply. We will first consider effects from interest rates and then study new effects from variations over time in real wage rates.

The multiyear budget constraint is again:

$$C_1 + C_2/(1+i_1) + C_3/[(1+i_1) \bullet (1+i_2)] + \cdots = (1+i_0) \bullet (B_0/P + K_0)$$
$$+ (w/P)_1 \bullet L_1^s + (w/P)_2 \bullet L_2^s/(1+i_1) + (w/P)_3 \bullet L_3^s/[(1+i_1) \bullet (1+i_2)] + \cdots$$

(9.7)

The first shaded term show that an increase in year 1's interest rate, i_1, makes year 2's consumption, C_2, cheaper than year 1's, C_1. Therefore, an increase in i_1 has lowered C_1 and raised C_2. In other words, households substituted away from the object that got more expensive – current consumption – and towards the one that got cheaper – future consumption.

The second shaded term in equation (9.7) show that year 2's real wage income, $(w/P) \bullet L_2^s$, is discounted by $1 + i_1$ to get a present value before combining it with year 1's real wage income, $(w/P) \bullet L_1^s$. If the interest rate, i_1, rises, a unit of year 2's real wage income, $(w/P)_2 \bullet L_2^s$, becomes less valuable as a present value compared to a unit of year 1's real wage income, L_1^s. We therefore predict that the household would increase L_1^s and decrease L_2^s. This change is an intertemporal-substitution effect on labour supply – a higher interest rate favours more labour supply today and less in the future.

Another way to view this result is through leisure time. A higher interest rate, i_1, means that future consumption and leisure time are cheaper in present-value terms compared to current consumption and leisure time. Therefore, the household substitutes towards the cheaper objects – future consumption and leisure time – and away from the more expensive ones – current consumption and leisure time.

There are also intertemporal-substitution effects from variations of the real wage rate over time. Start from equal real wage rates in each year (i.e., $(w/P)_1 = (w/P)_2 = \cdots$), and assume that year 1's real wage rate, $(w/P)_1$, falls, while future real wage rates (i.e., $(w/P)_2$, $(w/P)_3$, and so on) do not change. This change motivates the household to supply less labour when the real wage rate is temporarily low (year 1) and more labour in future years. Hence, a fall in year 1's real wage rate, $(w/P)_1$, reduces year 1's quantity of labour supplied, L_1^s, because of this intertemporal-substitution effect. We can also say that current leisure time is relatively cheap when the real wage rate is temporarily low. In other words, a period of temporarily low real wage rates is a good time to take a vacation.

The next By the Numbers box summarizes empirical evidence about intertemporal-substitution effects on labour supply. These results suggest that the quantity of labour supplied responds as predicted to interest rates and to variations in real wage rates over time.

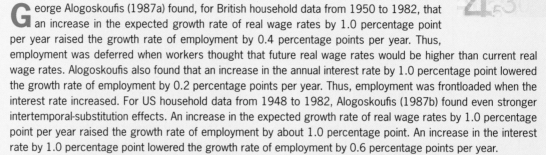

By the Numbers
Empirical evidence on intertemporal substitution of labour supply

George Alogoskoufis (1987a) found, for British household data from 1950 to 1982, that an increase in the expected growth rate of real wage rates by 1.0 percentage point per year raised the growth rate of employment by 0.4 percentage points per year. Thus, employment was deferred when workers thought that future real wage rates would be higher than current real wage rates. Alogoskoufis also found that an increase in the annual interest rate by 1.0 percentage point lowered the growth rate of employment by 0.2 percentage points per year. Thus, employment was frontloaded when the interest rate increased. For US household data from 1948 to 1982, Alogoskoufis (1987b) found even stronger intertemporal-substitution effects. An increase in the expected growth rate of real wage rates by 1.0 percentage point per year raised the growth rate of employment by about 1.0 percentage point. An increase in the interest rate by 1.0 percentage point lowered the growth rate of employment by 0.6 percentage points per year.

However, the Alogoskoufis studies found no evidence that hours worked per worker responded to time-varying real wage rates or interest rates. This pattern is surprising – one would expect workers to work extra hours, including overtime and weekends, when real wage rates are *temporarily* high. Casey Mulligan (1995) argued that it is hard to detect intertemporal-substitution effects from time-varying real wage rates in the Alogoskoufis data. One problem is that it is unclear when households perceive current real wage rates to be temporarily high or low. Therefore, Mulligan looked at unusual events for which the temporary nature of high real wage rates was clear and found that a temporary rise of real wage rates of 10% was estimated to raise average hours worked per week by 20% or more. Thus, unlike Alogoskoufis, Mulligan found a substantial response of hours worked per worker to temporarily high real wage rates.

FLUCTUATIONS IN LABOUR INPUT

We want to incorporate the new analysis of labour supply into our equilibrium business-cycle model. However, before we make this extension, let's look at the data to see what we are trying to explain.

The cyclical behaviour of labour input: empirical

We show the cyclical parts of employment as the light blue curve in Figure 9.12. This graph shows the proportionate deviation of employment from trend. As before, the dark blue curve shows the cyclical parts of real GDP. We see from the graph that labour input is procyclical: it moves in the same direction as real GDP during booms and recessions.[9] That is, employment is high relative to trend during booms and low relative to trend during recessions. The variability of labour input is not as great as that of real GDP – the standard deviation of the cyclical parts was 0.7% for employment, compared with 1.3% for real GDP. Thus, in a proportionate sense, employment varies less than real GDP during booms and recessions.

The cyclical behaviour of labour input: theory

We will now work out the equilibrium business-cycle model with variable labour supply. We assume again that economic fluctuations reflect shocks to the technology level, A. These shocks are long-lasting but not permanent.

[9]From 1999.1 to 2015.2, the correlation of the cyclical part of employment with the cyclical part of real GDP was 0.73.

Figure 9.12 Cyclical behaviour of Eurozone real GDP and employment

The dark blue curve is the deviation of real GDP from its trend. The light blue curve is the deviation of employment from its trend. These deviations are measured in a proportionate sense. The data on real GDP and employment are quarterly and seasonally adjusted. Employment is procyclical – it fluctuates closely with real GDP but it is not as variable as real GDP.

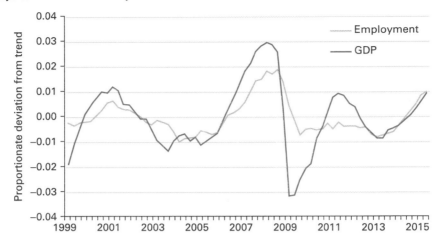

Figure 9.13 shows how an increase in the technology level, A, affects the labour market. The downward-sloping labour-demand curves come from Figure 9.4. The light blue curve shows market labour demand, L, at an initial technology level, A. This curve slopes downward, as usual, because a decrease in the real wage rate, w/P, raises the quantity of labour demanded. The downward-sloping dark blue curve is for a higher technology level, A'.

Figure 9.13 shows an upward-sloping curve for labour supply, L^s. This curve slopes upward because we assume that the substitution effect from a higher current real wage rate, w/P, dominates the income effect. We have already noted that this upward slope is likely to apply if the changes in w/P are not fully permanent. The same curve for L^s

Figure 9.13 Clearing of the labour market

At the technology level A, the demand for labour, labelled $L^d(A)$ along the light blue curve, slopes downward versus the real wage rate, w/P. At the higher technology level, A', the demand for labour, labelled $L^d(A')$ along the dark blue curve, is larger at any given w/P. These two curves are from Figure 9.4. The supply of labour, L^s, slopes upward versus w/P because we assume that the substitution effect from a change in w/P dominates the income effect. The increase in the technology level from A to A' raises the real wage rate from $(w/P)^*$ to $[(w/P)^*]'$ on the vertical axis, and increases labour input from L^* to $(L^*)'$ on the horizontal axis.

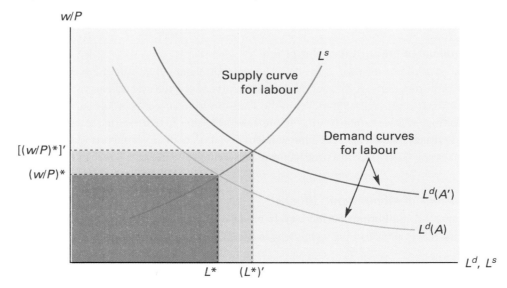

applies for the two technology levels. That is, for a given w/P, we assume that the labour-supply curve does not shift when the technology level rises from A to A'. This assumption is not fully accurate because it neglects effects on L^s from an increase in the interest rate (which occur when the technology level rises). However, the inclusion of an interest-rate effect would not change our main results.

We reach two important conclusions from Figure 9.13. First, as before, the real wage rate rises from $(w/P)^*$ to $[(w/P)^*]'$ on the vertical axis. Second, aggregate labour input increases from L^* to $(L^*)'$ on the horizontal axis. The second effect is new, and it depends on the upward slope of the labour-supply curve, L^s. If a higher current w/P induces a greater quantity of labour supplied, an increase in the technology level raises labour input, L. Hence, the model now matches the observation, from Figure 9.12, that labour input moves along with real GDP during economic fluctuations.

The increase in labour input also contributes to the rise in real GDP, $Y = A \cdot F(K, L)$. Hence, real GDP rises partly because of the direct effect from the higher technology level, A, and partly because of the increase in labour input, L.

The cyclical behaviour of labour productivity

Another important macroeconomic variable is labour productivity. The definition of labour productivity used in popular media is the average product of labour, which is the ratio of real GDP, Y, to labour input, L. In the equilibrium business-cycle model, this concept of labour productivity tends to be procyclical – high in booms and low in recessions. The reason is that the average product of labour, Y/L, typically moves in the same direction as the marginal product of labour, MPL. We already know that the MPL – which equals the real wage rate, w/P, when the labour market clears – is procyclical.

To calculate labour productivity, we can measure labour input, L, by employment or total hours worked. The first measure of labour productivity, Y/L, is real GDP per worker, and the second is real GDP per worker-hour. Labour productivity turns out to be procyclical in both cases. The model matches this feature of labour productivity. However, a more detailed analysis suggests that there may be a quantitative puzzle in that real GDP per worker-hour is less procyclical than predicted by the model.

Summing Up

An equilibrium business-cycle model can go a long way in matching observed economic fluctuations. The key assumption is that economic fluctuations originate from long-lived, but less than permanent, shifts to the technology level, A. We can interpret shocks to A as a variety of real disturbances that influence an economy's productivity. With these types of shocks, the model explains why consumption, investment, the real wage rate and the real rental price of capital are all procyclical. The model can also explain why investment fluctuates proportionately more than consumption.

With variable labour supply, the model can match the procyclical behaviour of employment and worker-hours. These results depend on a positive response of labour supply to the real wage rate. This response applies if the substitution effects from the real wage rate dominate the income effect. The cyclical variations in labour input contribute to the rise of real GDP in a boom and the decline of real GDP in a recession.

Key Terms and Concepts

acyclical	equilibrium business-cycle	real business-cycle model	total hours worked
countercyclical	model	shocks	trend real GDP
cyclical part of real GDP	procyclical	standard deviation	

Questions and Problems

A Review questions

1 Discuss the effects on this year's quantity of labour supplied, L_1^s, from the following changes:
   a An increase in the interest rate, i_1;
   b A permanent increase in the real wage rate, w/P;
   c A temporary increase in the real wage rate, w/P;
   d A one-time windfall, which raises initial real assets, $(B_0/P + K_0)$.

B Problems for discussion

2 A change in the willingness to work
   Suppose that households change their preferences so that they wish to work and consume more in each year.
   a Use a variant of Figure 9.13 to determine the effects on the labour market. What happens to labour input, L, and the real wage rate, w/P?
   b Use a variant of Figure 9.7 to determine the effects on the market for capital services. What happens to the real rental price, R/P? What happens to the interest rate, i?
   c What happens to consumption, C, and investment, I? What happens over time to the stock of capital, K?

3 A shift in desired saving
   Suppose that households change their preferences so that they wish to consume more and save less in the current year. That is, current consumption, C_1, rises for a given interest rate, and for given current and future income.
   a Use a variant of Figure 9.13 to determine the effects on the labour market. What happens to labour input, L, and the real wage rate, w/P?
   b Use a variant of Figure 9.7 to determine the effects on the market for capital services.

What happens to the real rental price, R/P? What happens to the interest rate, i?
   c What happens to consumption, C, and investment, I? What happens over time to the stock of capital, K?

4 A change in the capital stock
   Assume a one-time decrease in the capital stock, K, possibly caused by a natural disaster or an act of war. Assume that population does not change.
   a Use a variant of Figure 9.7 to determine the effects on the market for capital services. What happens to the real rental price, R/P? What happens to the interest rate, i?
   b Use a variant of Figure 9.13 to determine the effects on the labour market. What happens to labour input, L, and the real wage rate, w/P?
   c What happens to output, Y, and consumption, C? What happens to investment, I? What happens over time to the stock of capital, K?

5 A change in population
   Assume a one-time decrease in population, possibly caused by an onset of disease or a sudden out-migration.
   a Use a variant of Figure 9.13 to determine the effects on the labour market. What happens to labour input, L, and the real wage rate, w/P?
   b Use a variant of Figure 9.7 to determine the effects on the market for capital services. What happens to the real rental price, R/P? What happens to the interest rate, i?
   c What happens to output, Y, and consumption, C? What happens to investment, I? What happens over time to the stock of capital, K?

10 Capital utilization and unemployment

The equilibrium business-cycle model from Chapter 9 explains a number of features of economic fluctuations. However, an important shortcoming is that the two factor inputs, capital and labour, are always fully employed. This chapter remedies these deficiencies by allowing for a variable utilization rate for capital and a variable employment rate for labour.

For the capital stock, K, we allow for a variable supply of capital services in the short run. This extension explains why the capital-utilization rate is less than 100% and tends to be relatively high in a boom and relatively low in a recession. This pattern helps us to understand the fluctuations of real gross domestic product (real GDP).

Similarly, the model does not explain why the labour force is less than fully employed; that is, it does not explain unemployment. To study the levels and variations in the unemployment rate, we extend the model to allow workers to search for good jobs and employers to search for productive workers. This process of job matching can explain the existence and variability of unemployment and job vacancies. We can explain why the unemployment rate is low in a boom and high in a recession. This pattern helps us to understand the fluctuations of labour input and real GDP.

Capital input

In Chapter 9, we assumed that households supplied all of their given capital stock, K, to the rental market, so that the supply of capital services, K^s, was a vertical line at K in Figure 9.7. The real rental price, R/P, is adjusted to equate the quantity of capital services demanded, K^d, to the quantity supplied, K^s. Therefore, the given capital stock, K, was always fully utilized in production. To put it another way, the **capital-utilization rate** – the proportion of the capital stock used in production – was always 100%.

Now, we extend the microeconomic foundations of the model to allow for a variable capital-utilization rate and, hence, for a variable supply of capital services. Then, we use our **market-clearing approach** to the rental market to assess the determination of the quantity of capital services.

Up to now, we have not distinguished the stock of capital, K, from the quantity of capital services used in production. Think of K as the number of machines, and assume that each machine is utilized a fixed number of hours per year. For example, if businesses use each machine 8 hours per day, 5 days per week and 52 weeks per year, then each machine yields 2080 machine-hours per year. In this case, capital services – measured as machine-hours per year – would always be a fixed multiple, such as 2080, of the capital stock.

In practice, the capital-utilization rate can vary. If businesses operate each machine 16 hours per day, corresponding to two 8-hour shifts each weekday instead of one, then each machine would yield 4160 machine-hours per year, rather than 2080. Similarly, businesses can raise the utilization rate by operating at weekends.

Let the variable κ (the Greek letter kappa) represent the utilization rate for the capital stock, K. We measure κ in units of hours per year, and K as the number of machines (a stock of goods). The product of κ and K, represents the flow of capital services. The term κK has units of:

$$(hours\ per\ year) \bullet (number\ of\ machines) = machine\text{-}hours\ per\ year$$

We now modify the production function from equation (3.1) to replace the capital stock, K, by the quantity of capital services, κK:

> **Key equation (production function with variable capital utilization):**
>
> $$Y = A \cdot F(\kappa K, L) \qquad (10.1)$$

For given K, κK, rises with the utilization rate, κ. Therefore, an increase in κ raises real GDP, Y, for a given technology level, A, capital stock, K, and labour input, L. Our assumption is that production depends only on the quantity of capital services per year, κK, and not on how these services break down between the utilization rate, κ, and the number of machines, K. Running 16 machines for 8 hours per day is assumed to be just as productive as running 8 machines for 16 hours per day.

THE DEMAND FOR CAPITAL SERVICES

In Chapter 7, we worked out the demand for capital services, K^d, as an input to production. Households, as managers of family businesses, chose K to maximize real profit, given by:

$$\Pi/P = A \cdot F(K^d, L^d) - (w/P) \cdot L^d - (R/P) \cdot K^d \qquad (7.13)$$

The maximization of Π/P led to the equation of the marginal product of capital, MPK, to the real rental price of capital, R/P. An increase in R/P reduced the quantity of capital services demanded, K^d, as shown by the downward-sloping curve in Figure 7.6.

This analysis is still valid if we revise equation (7.13) to allow for a variable capital-utilization rate, κ:

$$\Pi/P = A \cdot F[(\kappa K)^d, L^d)] - (w/P) \cdot L^d - (R/P) \cdot (\kappa K)^d \qquad (10.2)$$

The real rental price, R/P, is now measured per unit of capital services. That is, since κK has units of machine-hours per year, R/P has units of goods per machine-hour.

As before, households choose the quantity of capital services demanded, now represented by $(\kappa K)^d$, to maximize real profit, Π/P. This maximization again implies that the MPK equals the real rental price, R/P. However, the MPK is now the additional goods produced by an extra machine-hour of capital services. The resulting demand curve for capital services, $(\kappa K)^d$, still looks like the one shown in Figure 7.6. We show this demand as the downward-sloping curve in Figure 10.1.

Assume that the technology level rises from A to A'. This change raises the MPK at a given quantity, κK. Figure 10.2 shows this change as the shift from the light blue curve to the dark blue one. At the given real rental price, R/P, the quantity of capital services demanded rises from $(\kappa K)^d$ to $[(\kappa K)^d]'$. These results are similar to those in Figure 9.6, which did not allow for a variable capital-utilization rate.

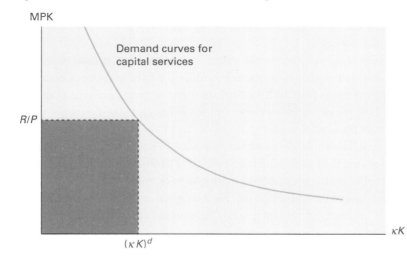

Figure 10.1 Demand for capital services

For a given technology level, A, and labour input, L, the marginal product of capital services, MPK on the vertical axis, decreases as the quantity of capital services, κK, rises on the horizontal axis. The household chooses the quantity of capital services, $(\kappa K)^d$, where the MPK equals the real rental price, R/P.

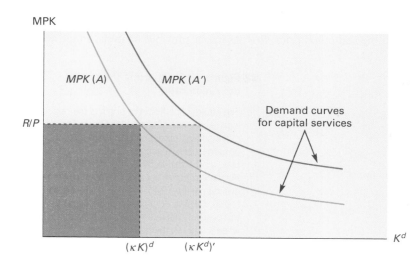

Figure 10.2 Effect of an increase in the technology level on the demand for capital services

When the technology level is A, the MPK is given by the light blue curve, labelled *MPK (A)*. At the real rental price *R/P*, shown on the vertical axis, the quantity of capital services demanded is $(\kappa K)^d$ on the horizontal axis. The technology level A' is greater than A. Therefore, the MPK, given by the dark blue curve labelled *MPK (A')*, is higher at any capital input than the value along the light blue curve. When the technology level is A' and the real rental price is *R/P*, the quantity of capital services demanded is $(\kappa K^d)'$, which is greater than $(\kappa K)^d$.

THE SUPPLY OF CAPITAL SERVICES

We assumed in Chapter 9 that owners of capital (households) supplied all of their capital, K, to the rental market. Now, we extend this analysis to allow owners to choose the capital-utilization rate, κ. For a given stock of capital, K, owners can supply more or less capital services per year by varying κ. Why would an owner ever set κ below its maximum possible value? This maximum rate, corresponding to the operation of machines 24 hours per day and 7 days per week, is 8736 hours per year.

One reason to set the utilization rate, κ, below its maximum is that increases in κ tend to raise the depreciation rate, δ. Machines wear out faster if they are used more intensively. Moreover, as κ rises, the time available for maintenance declines, thereby contributing further to a higher depreciation rate. We can capture these effects by writing the depreciation rate as an upward-sloping function of κ:[1]

$$\delta = \delta(\kappa)$$

Owners of capital choose the utilization rate, κ, to maximize their net real income from supplying capital services:

net real income from supplying capital services = real rental payments − depreciation

$$= (R/P) \bullet \kappa K - \delta(\kappa) \bullet K$$

If we take the variable K outside, we can write the result as:

net real income from supplying capital services $= K \bullet [(R/P) \bullet \kappa - \delta(\kappa)]$ (10.3)

Thus, the net real income equals the capital owned, K, multiplied by the term $(R/P) \bullet \kappa - \delta(\kappa)$. To understand this term, note that the first part, $(R/P) \bullet \kappa$, is the product of the real rental per machine-hour, R/P, and the machine-hours per year, κ, from each machine. Thus, $(R/P) \bullet \kappa$ is the real rental income per year on each unit of capital. When we subtract the depreciation rate, $\delta(\kappa)$, we get the net real rental income per unit of capital, $(R/P) \bullet \kappa - \delta(\kappa)$. This term gives the rate of return from owning capital:

Key equation (rate of return on capital):

rate of return from owning capital $= (R/P) \bullet \kappa - \delta(\kappa)$ (10.4)

For a given capital stock, K, the maximization of the net real income from supplying capital services boils down to maximizing the net real return from owning capital, $(R/P) \bullet \kappa - \delta(\kappa)$, in equation (10.4). Figure 10.3 graphs the

---

[1]This analysis was introduced by Jeremy Greenwood, Zvi Hercowitz and Gregory Huffman (1988).

two parts of this return against the capital-utilization rate, κ. The straight line shows the first part, $(R/P) \cdot \kappa$. This line starts from the origin, and its slope equals the real rental price, R/P. As in our previous analysis, an individual household takes R/P as given.

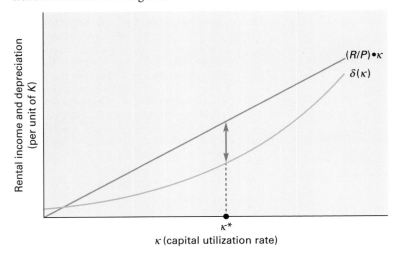

Figure 10.3 Choosing the capital-utilization rate

The straight line from the origin is the real rental income per unit of capital, $(R/P) \cdot \kappa$. The convex curve shows the depreciation rate, $\delta(\kappa)$, as an upward-sloping function of the capital-utilization rate, κ. The gap between the straight line and the convex curve equals the rate of return from owning capital, $(R/P) \cdot \kappa - \delta(\kappa)$, given in equation (10.3). Owners of capital choose κ to maximize this vertical distance – this maximization occurs when $\kappa = \kappa^*$ on the horizontal axis.

The second part of the rate of return from owning capital in equation (10.4) is the negative of the depreciation rate, $\delta(\kappa)$. We graph $\delta(\kappa)$ versus κ in Figure 10.3 as the convex curve. We assume that $\delta(\kappa)$ is greater than zero when κ equals zero; that is, capital depreciates even when it sits idle (perhaps because it gets rusty). Second, $\delta(\kappa)$ rises as κ increases above zero, so that a higher κ leads to a higher depreciation rate, $\delta(\kappa)$.[2]

The rate of return from owning capital, given by equation (10.4), equals the vertical distance between the straight line and the convex curve in Figure 10.3. Owners of capital (households) select the utilization rate, κ, that maximizes this distance. In the graph, this maximization occurs when $\kappa = \kappa^*$ on the horizontal axis. At κ^*, the vertical distance between the line and the curve is shown by the arrows. Typically, κ^* will be set below its maximum feasible value of 8,736 hours per year. Owners avoid this extremely high rate of capital utilization because it leads to rapid depreciation of the capital stock. The Economics in Practice box discusses other reasons for owners to choose a capital-utilization rate less than 100%.

Economics in Practice
Multiple shifts and overtime hours

We found that the capital-utilization rate, κ, would typically be set at less than its maximum feasible value of 8736 hours per year. We got this result by considering the positive effect of κ on the depreciation rate, $\delta(\kappa)$. We can bring in additional reasons for less than full utilization of factories and machines.

We have assumed that real GDP, Y, depends on capital services in the form κK:

$$Y = A \cdot F(\kappa K, L) \tag{10.1}$$

where K is the number of machines and κ the hours per year that each machine operates. If we start with $\kappa = 2080$ hours per year – where a business uses capital 8 hours per day on weekdays – the business could raise κ by operating more than one shift per day or by opening at weekends. However, more hours of operation per week incur additional costs, including the power needed to keep the lights on. These kinds of expenses are called **user costs** – they arise only when capital is used. We should subtract these costs from the expression for real profit in equation (10.2) to get:

$$\Pi/P = A \cdot F[(\kappa K)^d, L^d)] - (W/P) \cdot L^d - (R/P) \cdot (\kappa K)^d - user\ costs\ of\ capital$$

[2]We also assume that $\delta(\kappa)$ gets more sensitive to κ as κ increases. Graphically, the curve $\delta(\kappa)$ has a convex shape – it bows out toward the horizontal axis.

The user costs – which increase with κ – can explain why capital operates less than full time. That is, a business may prefer to have 100 machines operating half the time, rather than 50 machines operating all the time.

In addition, to raise κ, businesses typically have to operate machines and factories at less convenient times, such as evenings and weekends. Typically, these times of operation are more expensive than standard business hours because workers require higher wage rates for night shifts or overtime hours. Complementary services from other businesses, such as suppliers and transporters, may also be unavailable at these times. (Lower electricity rates and less highway congestion at off-peak hours are offsetting factors.) If we allow for high costs of operation at unusual hours, we get another reason why businesses operate their capital at less than maximal capacity.

Now, we have to work out how a change in the real rental price, R/P, changes the chosen capital-utilization rate, κ^*. Suppose that the real rental price rises from R/P to $(R/P)'$. At R/P, the real rental payments per unit of capital, $(R/P) \cdot \kappa$, are given by the blue line from the origin in Figure 10.4. At the higher real rental price, $(R/P)'$, the real rental payments per unit of capital, $(R/P)' \cdot \kappa$, are given by the black line, which is steeper than the blue line. The depreciation curve, $\delta(\kappa)$, shown as the convex curve, comes from Figure 10.3. This curve does not shift because $\delta(\kappa)$ does not depend on R/P.

When the real rental price is R/P, households maximize the vertical distance between the blue line and the convex curve by picking the capital-utilization rate κ^*, shown on the horizontal axis in Figure 10.4. When the real rental price rises to $(R/P)'$, households maximize by choosing the higher utilization rate $(\kappa^*)'$. Thus, an increase in the real rental price raises the capital-utilization rate; the higher real rental price makes it worthwhile to raise κ despite the resulting increase in the depreciation rate, $\delta(\kappa)$.

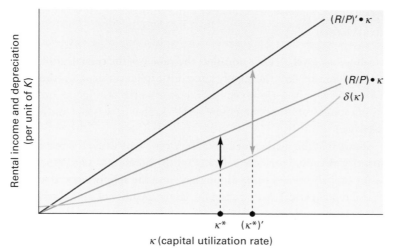

Figure 10.4 Effect of an increase in the real rental price on the capital-utilization rate

The convex curve is the depreciation rate, $\delta(\kappa)$, from Figure 10.3. The two lines from the origin are the real rental income per unit of capital. The blue line is for the real rental price R/P, and the black line is for the higher real rental price $(R/P)'$. At R/P, owners of capital maximize the difference between the rental income line and the depreciation curve by choosing the capital-utilization rate κ^* on the horizontal axis. At $(R/P)'$, they maximize the difference by choosing the higher utilization rate $(\kappa^*)'$. Therefore, an increase in R/P raises the capital-utilization rate.

MARKET CLEARING AND CAPITAL UTILIZATION

We considered in Chapter 9 the effects of an increase in the technology level, A, on real GDP, labour input and other variables. Now, we can include the effect on the capital-utilization rate, κ, and, hence, on the quantity of capital services, κK.

Figure 10.5 puts together our analyses of the demand for, and supply of, capital services. The vertical axis shows the real rental price, R/P, and the horizontal axis shows the market demand for, and supply of, capital services. The two downward-sloping demand curves come from Figure 10.2. The light blue curve corresponds to the technology level *A*, and the dark blue curve to the higher technology level *A′*. Note that the increase in the technology level raises the market demand for capital services, $(\kappa K)^d$.

The upward-sloping supply curve in Figure 10.5 comes from Figure 10.4. The supply curve slopes up because an increase in the real rental price, *R/P*, motivates a higher capital-utilization rate, *κ*. For a given stock of capital, *K*, the increase in *κ* raises the quantity of capital services supplied, $(\kappa K)^s$.

Figure 10.5 Clearing of the market for capital services

At the technology level *A*, the demand for capital services, labelled $(\kappa K)^d$ (A) along the light blue curve, slopes downward versus the real rental price, *R/P*. At the higher technology level *A′*, the demand for capital services, labelled (κK) (A′) along the dark blue curve, is larger at any given *R/P*. These curves are from Figure 10.2. The supply of capital services, $(\kappa K)^s$, slopes upward versus *R/P* because an increase in *R/P* raises the capital-utilization rate, *κ* (as in Figure 10.4). Thus, an increase in the technology level from *A* to *A′* raises the market-clearing real rental price from $(R/P)^*$ to $[(R/P)^*]'$, and the quantity of capital services from $(\kappa K)^*$ to $[(\kappa K)^*]'$. Since the stock of capital, *K*, is fixed, the increase in capital services reflects the rise in the utilization rate from *κ** to $(\kappa^*)'$, as in Figure 10.4.

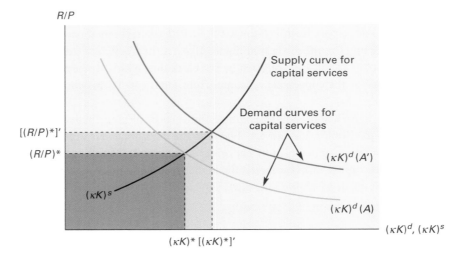

Figure 10.4 shows that, for a given *R/P*, the technology level, *A*, does not affect the choice of the capital-utilization rate, *κ*. Therefore, the increase in *A* in Figure 10.5 does not shift the supply curve for capital services. (Ultimately, a rise in *A* will increase the quantity of capital services supplied. However, this increase works through an increase in *R/P*, which determines the reward to owners of capital from supplying more services. That is, we get a movement along the given supply curve, not a shift in the curve.)

When the technology level is *A*, Figure 10.5 shows that the market for capital services clears when the real rental price is $(R/P)^*$ on the vertical axis and the quantity of capital services is $(\kappa K)^*$ on the horizontal axis. When the technology level rises to *A′*, the demand curve for capital services shifts to the right, and the supply curve does not shift. Therefore, the market clears at the higher real rental price, $[(R/P)^*]'$, and the larger quantity of capital services, $[(\kappa K)^*]'$.

We noted in Chapter 9 that an increase in the technology level raised the real rental price, *R/P*. The new effect in Figure 10.5 is the increase in the quantity of capital services, *κK*. Since the capital stock, *K*, is fixed in the short run, the increase in capital services reflects the rise in the utilization rate from *κ** to $(\kappa^*)'$. We therefore find that booms – where a high *A* causes real GDP to be high – will have a relatively high capital-utilization rate, whereas recessions – where a low *A* causes real GDP to be low – will have a relatively low utilization rate.

Recall that the production function is:

$$Y = A \bullet F(\kappa K, L) \tag{10.1}$$

We now have three reasons why real GDP rises in a boom and falls in a recession. First, a high or low technology level, *A*, causes real GDP to be correspondingly high or low. Second, as discussed in Chapter 9, a high or low

A causes *L* to be correspondingly high or low. Third, the new effect is that a high or low *A* causes the capital-utilization rate, *κ*, and, thereby, the quantity of capital services, *κK*, to be correspondingly high or low.

Recall that the rate of return on capital is given by:

$$rate\ of\ return\ from\ owning\ capital = (R/P) \bullet \kappa - \delta(\kappa) \tag{10.4}$$

For a given capital-utilization rate, *κ*, equation (10.4) shows that an increase in the real rental price, *R/P*, raises the rate of return from owning capital. This effect is the one explored in Chapter 9, where *κ* did not vary. Now, we get an additional effect from the adjustment of *κ*. We know that *κ* is chosen to maximize the rate of return shown in equation (10.4). Therefore, the change in *κ* – upward in our case, in response to the increase in *R/P* – raises the rate of return on capital. We therefore conclude, as in Chapter 9, that the rate of return from owning capital rises overall in response to an increase in the technology level, *A*.

We still have that the rate of return on bonds – the interest rate, *i* – must equal the rate of return on ownership of capital. In Chapter 7, this condition was:

$$i = R/P - \delta$$
$$rate\ of\ return\ on\ bonds = rate\ of\ return\ on\ ownership\ of\ capital \tag{7.6}$$

Now, we use equation (10.4) to measure the rate of return on ownership of capital to get:

$$i = R/P \bullet \kappa - \delta(\kappa)$$
$$rate\ of\ return\ on\ bonds = rate\ of\ return\ on\ ownership\ of\ capital \tag{10.5}$$

We find that an increase in the technology level, *A*, raises the rate of return from owning capital, which is the expression on the right-hand side of equation (10.5). Therefore, as in Chapter 9, the interest rate, *i*, increases. The interest rate is still procyclical in the model.

THE CYCLICAL BEHAVIOUR OF CAPACITY UTILIZATION

To check our prediction that the capital-utilization rate, *κ*, is procyclical, we can use the data on capacity utilization rates in manufacturing. The Business Tendency Surveys for Manufacturing collect data on capacity utilization in the Eurozone. From 1999.1 to 2013.4, the average capacity utilization rate was 81%, with a range from 69% to 85%.

The light blue graph in Figure 10.6 shows the deviation of the capacity utilization rate from its trend (using the method shown in Figure 9.2 to construct the trend). The dark blue graph is, again, the deviation of real GDP from

Figure 10.6 Cyclical behaviour of Eurozone real GDP and capacity utilization

The dark blue graph is the deviation of real GDP from its trend. The light blue graph is the deviation of the capacity utilization rate from its trend. These data are from 1999.1 to 2013.4. The data on real GDP and capacity utilization are quarterly and seasonally adjusted. The capacity-utilization rate is procyclical – it fluctuates closely with real GDP but is more variable than real GDP.

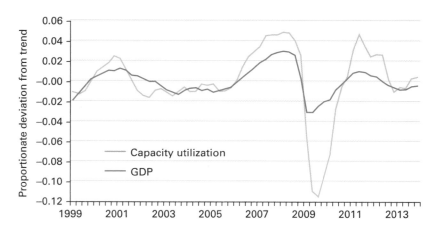

its trend. Note that the capacity utilization rate is clearly procyclical.[3] The rate is above trend in booms and below trend in recessions. Thus, the model's prediction about the cyclical behaviour of the capital-utilization rate matches up with the data on capacity utilization rates.

The labour force, employment and unemployment

We now explore how observed fluctuations in labour input, L, relate to variations in the labour force, employment and hours worked per worker. First, we look at empirical patterns in the Eurozone. Then, we will extend our equilibrium business-cycle model to explain some puzzles, especially the fluctuations in the employment rate.

BASIC CONCEPTS AND EMPIRICAL PATTERNS

Data from the Eurozone show that labour input, L, is procyclical; that is, it moves during economic fluctuations in the same direction as real GDP. For example, in Figure 9.12, we measured L by employment (i.e., the number of persons with jobs). This concept of L is strongly procyclical – from 1999 to 2015, the correlation of the cyclical part of employment with the cyclical part of real GDP was 0.73.

In Chapter 9, we allowed L to change by introducing variable labour supply. To get the right cyclical pattern, we relied on a positive response of the quantity of labour supplied, L^s, to the real wage rate, w/P. A high w/P in economic booms motivated households to raise L^s, and this response allowed L to expand.

Our analysis did not specify whether the changes in L resulted from shifts in the labour force, from changes in the employment rate or from changes in hours worked per worker. Suppose, for now, that we continue to neglect variations in hours worked per worker, so that each job comes with a standard number of hours worked per year. Changes in total hours worked, then, reflect only changes in employment – the number of persons with jobs. In this environment, the quantity of labour supplied, L^s, is the number of persons who offer themselves for work, given the real wage rate, w/P. This concept of labour supply fits with Eurostat's measure of the civilian labour force – the sum of persons with jobs plus persons self-described as looking for work. We can think of the quantity of labour demanded, L^d, as the number of jobs that employers want filled, given w/P.

In a market-clearing setting, the real wage rate, w/P, is determined, as usual, to equate the quantity of labour supplied, L^s, to the quantity demanded, L^d. Thus, the market-clearing employment, L, equals the labour force, L^s, and also equals the number of jobs that employers want filled, L^d. The real world departs from this environment in two major respects. First, the labour force is always greater than employment, and the difference between the two equals the number of persons unemployed. Second, the number of jobs that employers want filled is always greater than employment, and the difference between these two equals the number of job **vacancies**.

One important variable from the supply side of the labour market is the *unemployment rate*, which equals the ratio of the number of persons unemployed to the labour force. Conversely, the **employment rate** is the ratio of the number of persons employed to the labour force. If we let u be the unemployment rate, we have:

$$u = number\ unemployed/labour\ force$$
$$= (labour\ force - number\ employed)/labour\ force$$
$$= 1 - (number\ employed/labour\ force)$$
$$= 1 - employment\ rate$$

Thus, if we rearrange terms, we get:

$$employment\ rate = 1 - u$$

[3] From 1999.1 to 2013.4, the correlation of the cyclical part of the capacity utilization rate with the cyclical part of real GDP was 0.86.

On the demand side of the labour market, the **vacancy rate** is the ratio of the number of job vacancies to the total number of jobs that employers want occupied. The employment rate from the employer perspective is the ratio of employment to the total number of jobs that employers want occupied. One reason that this side of the market is less emphasized is that data on job vacancies are not as accurate as data on unemployment. Typically, economists have relied on incomplete information on **help-wanted advertising** in newspapers. Recently, however, Eurostat has improved its measures of job vacancies.

From the labour-supply side, we can think of employment as determined by:

$$employment = labour\ force \bullet (employment / labour\ force)$$
$$= labour\ force \bullet employment\ rate$$
$$= labour\ force \bullet (1 - u)$$

Our previous analysis assumed that the unemployment rate, u, was zero, so that variations in employment coincided with variations in the labour force. Now, changes in employment can also reflect changes in u.

We saw in Figure 9.12 that employment is quite variable, although not as variable as real GDP – from 1999 to 2015, the standard deviations of the cyclical parts were 0.7% for employment and 1.3% for real GDP. In addition, these cyclical parts were strongly positively correlated – the correlation was 0.73 – so that employment is clearly procyclical.

Figures 10.7 and 10.8 show how the two variables that determine employment – the labour force and the employment rate, $1 - u$, – contribute to the variations in employment in the Eurozone from 1999 to 2015. Figure 10.7 shows that the labour force is relatively stable – from 1999 to 2015, the standard deviation of the cyclical part was 0.3%. Moreover, the correlation with the cyclical part of real GDP was practically zero.[4] In contrast, the employment rate shown in Figure 10.8 is more variable – the standard deviation of the cyclical part was 0.6% – and much more correlated with the cyclical part of real GDP – this correlation was 0.82. Thus, the procyclical variations in employment have more to do with changes in the employment rate than with changes in the labour force. This finding means that our previous analysis – which focused on fluctuations in the labour force (a proxy for labour supply) – is missing something important.

Figures 10.7 and 10.8 consider the two variables that determine employment: the labour force and the employment rate. We can also allow for variations in hours worked per worker. We can write:

$$total\ hours\ worked = employment \bullet (hours\ worked\ per\ worker)$$

Figure 10.7 Cyclical behaviour of Eurozone real GDP and the labour force

The dark blue graph is the deviation of real GDP from its trend. The light blue graph is the deviation of the civilian labour force from its trend. The civilian labour force – the number of persons employed or seeking employment – comes from Eurostat (http://ec.europa.eu/eurostat/data/database). The data on real GDP and the labour force are quarterly and seasonally adjusted. The labour force is, on average, acyclical and is less variable than real GDP.

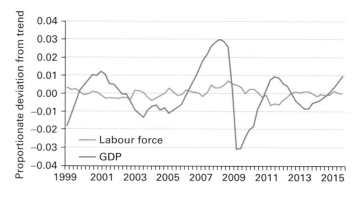

[4]From 1999.1 to 2015.2, the correlation of the cyclical part of the labour force with the cyclical part of real GDP was -0.02.

Figure 10.8 Cyclical behaviour of Eurozone real GDP and the employment rate

The dark blue graph is the proportionate deviation of real GDP from its trend. The light blue graph is the deviation of the employment rate from its trend. The employment rate is the ratio of the number employed to the labour force. The measures of employment and labour force come from Eurostat. The data on real GDP and the employment rate are quarterly and seasonally adjusted. The employment rate is strongly procyclical – it fluctuates in the same direction as real GDP.

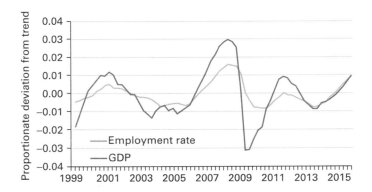

Figure 10.9 shows the additional variable, hours worked per worker. From 2005 to 2015, the standard deviation of the cyclical part of hours worked per worker was 0.1%, and the correlation with the cyclical part of real GDP was 0.46. Thus, from the standpoint of accounting for the overall procyclicality of total hours worked, hours worked per worker is less important than the employment rate and more important than the labour force.

Figure 10.9 Cyclical behaviour of Eurozone real GDP and average weekly hours

The dark blue graph is the deviation of real GDP from its trend. The light blue graph is the deviation of average weekly hours worked from its trend. The data for weekly hours come from Eurostat. The data on real GDP and weekly hours are quarterly and seasonally adjusted. Average weekly hours are procyclical – they fluctuate with real GDP but are much less variable than real GDP.

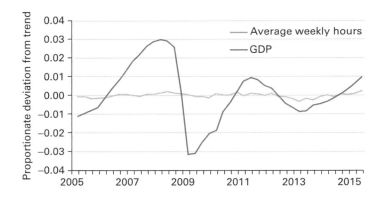

Our equilibrium business-cycle model from Chapter 9 is probably satisfactory for understanding fluctuations in the labour force and hours worked per worker. In these cases, we can think of the real wage rate, w/P, as adjusting to equate the quantity of labour supplied, L^s, to the quantity demanded, L^d. However, this approach leaves unexplained the most important factor – the fluctuations in the employment rate or, equivalently, in the unemployment rate.

To explain unemployment and vacancies, we have to introduce some 'friction' into the workings of the labour market. That is, we have to explain why persons in the labour force who lack jobs take some time to find them, and why businesses with unfilled jobs take some time to fill them. Thus, the key to unemployment and vacancies is the process of persons searching for jobs and businesses searching for workers.

In our previous discussions of the labour market, we simplified by treating all workers and jobs as identical. However, in this world, the search process among workers and businesses would be trivial. Thus, for the analysis to be realistic, we have to allow for differences among workers and jobs. Then, we can think of the labour market as operating to find good matches between jobs and workers. Because jobs and workers differ, this matching process is difficult and time consuming; unemployment and vacancies arise as parts of this process.

The next section extends our equilibrium business-cycle model to include a simple model of job matching. This extension has two main objectives. First, we want to explain why the levels of unemployment and vacancies are greater than zero. Second, we want to understand how unemployment and vacancies vary over time – in particular, why the employment rate is procyclical and the unemployment rate is countercyclical.

A MODEL OF JOB FINDING

Consider a person, call her Hillary, who has just entered the labour force and is not yet employed. Hillary might be a student who has just graduated from school or just re-entered the labour force after raising a family. Suppose that Hillary searches for a position by visiting firms. Each firm interviews job candidates to assess their likely qualifications for a position. As a result of each inspection, the firm estimates the value of a candidate's potential marginal product, MPL. To keep things simple, assume that the firm offers Hillary a job with a real wage rate, w/P, equal to the estimated marginal product. We assume, only for simplicity, that each job entails a standard number of hours worked per week. In this case, w/P determines the real income received while employed (equal to the product of w/P and the number of hours worked per week).

Hillary decides whether to accept the job at the offered real wage rate, w/P. The alternative is to remain unemployed and continue to search. We assume that it does not pay to accept a job and nevertheless keep searching. This assumption is reasonable because the costs of getting set up in a new job usually make it undesirable to take positions with short expected durations. Furthermore, it is likely to be easier to search for jobs while unemployed.

More search pays off if a subsequent wage offer exceeds the initial one. One cost of rejecting an offer is the income foregone while not working. This income must, however, be balanced against any income that people receive because they are unemployed. We denote by ω (the Greek letter omega) the effective real income while unemployed. The amount ω includes **unemployment insurance** payments from the government and any value that Hillary attaches to time spent not working, rather than on the job.

In evaluating an offer, the first consideration is how it compares with others that may be available. In making this comparison, Hillary has in mind a distribution of likely wage offers, given her education, experience, and so on. We are assuming that the attractiveness of a job depends only on the real wage rate. The main results would not change if we extended the model to take into account the work location and working conditions.

Figure 10.10 shows a typical shape for the distribution of wage offers. For each real wage rate, w/P, on the horizontal axis, the value on the vertical axis shows the probability of receiving that offer. For the curve shown, offers usually fall in a middle range of w/P. There is, however, a small chance of getting a very high offer (in the right tail of the distribution) or a very low offer (in the left tail of the distribution).

Figure 10.10 shows the value ω, which is the effective real income received while unemployed. We know that Hillary would reject any offer that paid less than ω. For the case in the graph, ω lies towards the left end of the distribution of wage offers. This construction implies that most – but not all – offers exceed ω. Given the position of ω, Hillary's key decision is whether to accept a real wage, w/P, when it is greater than ω.

She may refuse a real wage rate, w/P, that exceeds ω, to preserve her chance of getting a still better offer. However, there is a trade-off, because she then foregoes real income while not working. The balancing of these forces generates what economists call a **reservation real wage**, denoted by $(w/P)'$. Offers below $(w/P)'$ are rejected, and those above $(w/P)'$ are accepted. If Hillary sets a high value of $(w/P)'$, she will probably spend a long time unemployed and seeking work. Conversely, a low $(w/P)'$ means that the time spent unemployed will usually be brief. However, a low $(w/P)'$ also means that Hillary will likely end up in a job with a low w/P.

The optimal reservation real wage, $(w/P)'$, depends on the shape of the wage-offer distribution in Figure 10.10, as well as the effective real income while unemployed, ω, and the expected duration of a job.[5] For our purposes, we

---

[5]For a discussion of job search models that involve a reservation wage, see Belton Fleisher and Thomas Kniesner (1984, pp. 477–507).

do not have to go through the details of the determination of the optimal $(w/P)'$. We can get the main results by describing the important properties that come out of this analysis.

Figure 10.10 Distribution of real wage offers

The curve shows the chances of receiving offers of real wages, w/P, of different sizes. The higher the curve, the more likely that real wage offers of that size will be received. On the horizontal axis, ω is the effective real income received while unemployed, and $(w/P)'$ is the reservation real wage. Job offers are accepted if they pay at least as much as $(w/P)'$, and are otherwise rejected.

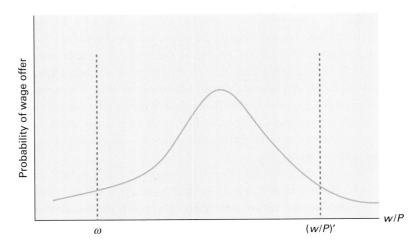

Since some job offers are unacceptable – that is, $w/P < (w/P)'$ for some offers – it typically takes time for Hillary to find an acceptable position. In the interim, she is 'unemployed', although engaged in job search. Thus, incomplete information about where to find the best job can explain why unemployment is greater than zero.

An increase in the effective real income while unemployed, ω, motivates Hillary to raise her standards for job acceptance; that is, $(w/P)'$ increases. This effect is particularly strong if Hillary's likely offers of real wages, w/P, are not much above ω. For example, an increase in ω caused by a rise in unemployment insurance benefits will have a strong impact on $(w/P)'$ if the benefits are high compared to usual wage offers. In the United States, where unemployment insurance benefits are not so high, a small increase in benefits would not have a major effect on $(w/P)'$ for the typical job seeker. In contrast, in countries such as France and Germany, which have very generous unemployment insurance programmes, a rise in benefits would have a much greater impact on the typical $(w/P)'$.

For a given distribution of wage offers in Figure 10.10, an increase in ω makes it more likely that $w/P < (w/P)'$ will apply, because $(w/P)'$ increases. Hence, job offers will be rejected more often. It follows that job searchers, such as Hillary, tend to take longer to find a position when ω increases. For a group of persons, we therefore predict that a rise in ω reduces the **job-finding rate**, which is the rate at which job seekers find positions. Correspondingly, a rise in ω raises the expected **duration of unemployment**, which is the amount of time that the typical unemployed person stays unemployed.

Suppose that the entire distribution of wage offers improves. For example, a favourable shock to the technology level, A, could raise the MPL of all workers – say, by 10%. Since each real wage offer, w/P, equals the value of a worker's potential marginal product, the distribution of real wage offers in Figure 10.10 shifts to the right – the typical real wage offer, w/P, rises by 10%. Therefore, if the reservation real wage, $(w/P)'$, does not change, job offers fall more often in the acceptable range, where $w/P > (w/P)'$. Hence, the job-finding rate rises and the expected duration of unemployment falls.

We have to consider, however, that a better distribution of wage offers tends to raise the reservation real wage, $(w/P)'$. Job seekers, such as Hillary, become more selective – raise $(w/P)'$ – if they anticipate that the better distribution of real wage offers will persist into the future. For example, a permanent improvement in technology would tend to have a long-run impact on real wage offers. In this case, $(w/P)'$ would rise. The increase in $(w/P)'$ works against our predicted rise in the job-finding rate. In the example where all real wage offers, w/P, increase by 10%, the job-finding rate will rise only if the increase in $(w/P)'$ is by less than 10%.

There are two reasons why the increase in the reservation real wage, $(w/P)'$, tends to be relatively smaller than the rise in the typical real wage offer, w/P. First, if the rise in workers' MPL is not permanent, future real wage offers will tend to rise by less than current offers. In this case, $(w/P)'$ will also rise proportionately less than the typical real wage, w/P, offered currently to job searchers.

Second, even if the improvement in real wage offers is permanent, $(w/P)'$ will rise proportionately by less than the typical real wage offer, w/P, if the effective real income received while unemployed, ω, does not change. To see why, we can compare three scenarios, as follows:

- Scenario 1 is the initial situation, where offers of real wage rates, w/P, are given by the distribution in Figure 10.10, and the effective real income received while unemployed is ω.
- Scenario 2 is the new situation, where the typical real wage offer, w/P, is permanently higher by 10%, and ω is unchanged.
- Scenario 3 is a hypothetical situation, where the typical real wage offer, w/P, is permanently higher by 10%, and ω is also permanently higher by 10%.

Compare Scenario 1 with Scenario 3: the only difference is that everything is scaled upward by 10% in Scenario 3. Therefore, in weighing up the trade-off between accepting or rejecting a job offer, it seems reasonable (and is, in fact, optimal) that a person would set the reservation real wage, $(w/P)'$, 10% higher in Scenario 3. Therefore, the probability of receiving an acceptable job offer is the same in Scenario 3 as in Scenario 1. Hence, the job-finding rate is the same in these two cases.

Now, compare Scenario 3 with Scenario 2. The only difference is that the real income received while unemployed, ω, is higher by 10% in Scenario 3. Therefore, a job seeker would set the reservation real wage, $(w/P)'$, higher in Scenario 3 than in Scenario 2, and the job-finding rate is lower in Scenario 3 than in Scenario 2.

Now, put the results together. Scenario 3 has the same job-finding rate as Scenario 1. Scenario 2 has a higher job-finding rate than Scenario 3. We have therefore shown that the job-finding rate is higher in Scenario 2 than in Scenario 1. Thus, as claimed, a permanent improvement in real wage offers, w/P, raises the job-finding rate if the real income while unemployed, ω, does not change.

In our model, the increase in real wage offers could come from an improvement in the technology level, A. However, in a richer model, technological change might make some skills obsolete. For example, electric lights made worthless the value of the output of lamplighters, and the motor car lowered the value of the output of blacksmiths. Therefore, technological change can reduce the value of the MPL – and, hence, the real wage offered – for workers with obsolete skills. Nevertheless, it is still reasonable for the economy as a whole that an improvement in technology would raise the value of the MPL and, therefore, the real wage offered to the typical job seeker.

SEARCH BY FIRMS

Thus far, we have taken an unrealistic view of how firms participate in the job-search process. Firms received applications, evaluated candidates in terms of the likely value of their MPL, and then expressed real wage offers, w/P, that equalled these marginal products. This model does not allow firms to utilize their information about the characteristics of jobs, the traits of workers who tend to be productive in these jobs, and the real wages that typically have to be paid for such workers. Firms would communicate this information by advertising job openings that specify ranges of requirements for education, work experience, and so on, and also indicate a salary range. Such advertisements appropriately screen out most potential applicants and generate more rapid and better matches of workers to jobs.

Although search by firms is important in a well-functioning labour market, the allowance for this search does not change our major conclusions. In particular:

- It still takes time for workers to match with jobs, so that the expected durations of unemployment and vacancies are greater than zero.
- An increase in workers' effective real incomes while unemployed, ω, lowers the job-finding rate and raises the expected duration of unemployment.
- A favourable shock to productivity raises the job-finding rate and lowers the expected duration of unemployment.

JOB SEPARATIONS

Workers search for jobs that offer high real wages, and employers search for workers with high productivity. Although workers and firms evaluate each other as efficiently as possible, they often find out later that they have made mistakes. An employer may learn that a worker is less productive than anticipated, or a worker may discover that they dislike the job. When a job match looks significantly poorer than it did initially, firms are motivated to discharge the worker, or the worker is motivated to quit.

Separations arise because of changed circumstances, even when firms and workers have accurately assessed each other at the outset. For example, an adverse shock to a firm's production function may lower a worker's MPL and lead to a discharge. If we distinguish the goods produced by different firms, we get a similar effect from a decline in the demand for a firm's goods. That is, the value of a worker's MPL would fall if the real value attached to each unit of output declined. For example, a blacksmith's physical marginal product might not change, but the advent of the car lowered the value attached to fitting a horse with a shoe.

Workers also experience changed circumstances – for example, in family status, schooling, location and retirement, as well as alternative job prospects. Some of these shifts are surprises, whereas others are predictable. The important point is that these changes can induce workers to quit jobs.

The tendency for a job match to break up is sensitive to how good the match was at the outset. If the match was borderline, small changes in production conditions or worker circumstances are sufficient to make the match mutually unattractive. Separations also occur because jobs were known to be temporary at the outset. Examples include seasonal workers in agriculture or at sports stadiums, or working for the Royal Mail (which has high demand before Christmas of each year).

We conclude that job separations take place for a variety of reasons. For a group of workers, we can identify determinants of the **job-separation rate**, the rate at which job matches dissolve. This rate is high, for example, among inexperienced workers who are hard to evaluate, or among young persons who are likely to experience changes in family size or job preferences. The separation rate is also high in industries that are subject to frequent shocks to technology or product demand.

If there were no job separations, no new persons entering the labour force and no new jobs, the search process would eventually eliminate unemployment and vacancies. But separations, new job seekers and new positions mean that the finding of jobs is continually offset by the creation of new unemployment and vacancies. We will now illustrate this process with a simple example.

JOB SEPARATIONS, JOB FINDING AND THE NATURAL UNEMPLOYMENT RATE

In Figure 10.11, the square labelled L denotes the number of persons employed, and the square labelled U shows the number unemployed. To simplify, assume that the labour force, $L + U$, does not change over time. To understand economic fluctuations, the assumption of a constant labour force may be satisfactory because, empirically, variations in the labour force are a small part of short-run changes in labour input.

Some proportion of employed persons experiences a job separation each period – say, one month. In Figure 10.11, the arrow from L to U represents the number of job separations per month. Since the labour force is constant, all those who lose jobs move from category L to category U. We are ignoring the fact that many job losers find new jobs immediately, without ever becoming unemployed.

Figure 10.11 Movements between employment and unemployment

In this example, 3% of those employed, L, lose their jobs each month, and 50% of those unemployed, U, find jobs. The net change in employment, ΔL, is $0.5 \cdot U - 0.03 \cdot L$. The change in unemployment, ΔU, is the negative of ΔL.

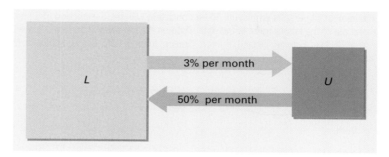

The job-separation rate is the ratio of job separations over one quarter to civilian employment. From 2010 to 2015, the separation rate in the Eurozone averaged 2.3% per quarter. Figure 10.12 shows how the job-separation rate varied from 2010 to 2015. The light blue graph in Figure 10.12 shows that the job-separation rate did not vary much from 2010 to 2015 – only between 2.1% and 2.5% per quarter. In particular, the job-separation rate changed little between 2011 and 2013. In contrast, the dark blue graph in Figure 10.12 shows that the unemployment rate rose from 8.8% in 2011 to a peak of 10.8% in 2013. Thus, these data – though available only for several years – suggest that the job-separation rate may not have a strong association with economic fluctuations.[6]

The other part of the story is the rate at which people find jobs. In Figure 10.11, the arrow pointing from U to L represents the number of unemployed persons who find jobs during one month. We are again not being completely realistic, because we are ignoring movements out of and into the labour force. Some of the unemployed, U, may become discouraged about job prospects during a recession and therefore drop out of the labour force. This phenomenon is called **discouraged workers**. However, we are also neglecting opposing forces that motivate people to intensify their job search during a recession. For example, if a person loses his or her job, the person's spouse might enter the labour force. As already mentioned, we know that variations in the labour force are a small part of short-run fluctuations in labour input. Therefore, the assumption of a constant labour force may be a satisfactory approximation.

We can again use the data from Eurostat to gauge the job-finding rate. To measure the job-finding rate, we have to express the number of jobs found by the unemployed in relation to the number of persons seeking jobs – that is, the number of persons unemployed, U. Thus, we have:

$$job\text{-}finding\ rate = (number\ of\ hires\ per\ month)/U$$

When defined this way, the job-finding rate measured by the Labour Force Survey in Eurostat averaged 19.6% per quarter from 2010 to 2015 – roughly one-fifth of the unemployed persons found a job within one quarter. In other words, while 2.3% of the employed workers are separated from their jobs each quarter, 19.6% of the unemployed job seekers are hired each quarter. Thus, there are tremendous gross flows of persons out of and into employment.

The light blue graph in Figure 10.13 shows the pattern of the calculated job-finding rate from 2010 to 2015. By comparing this with the dark blue graph, we see that the job-finding rate mirrored the unemployment rate. The job-finding rate fell from a peak of 22.3% in 2011 to a low point of 17.3% in 2013, then recovered along with a fall in the unemployment rate. Thus, the data show clearly that the job-finding rate falls when unemployment rises (and rises when unemployment falls).

The job-separation and job-finding rates determine the dynamics of persons employed and unemployed. We consider some specific numbers for the job-separation and job-finding rates as an illustrative example. As shown in

---

[6]For a discussion of this behaviour of the job-separation rate, see Robert Hall (2005).

Figure 9.11, we assume that the job-separation rate is 0.03 per month and the job-finding rate is 0.5 per month.[7] We assume, for now, that these rates are constant. This assumption may be satisfactory for the job-separation rate but not for the job-finding rate, which tends to fall below average during a recession and rise above average during a boom.

Figure 10.12 Job-separation rate and the unemployment rate, 2010–2015

The graph covers the period of data availability for the Labour Force Survey from Eurostat (http://ec.europa.eu/eurostat/data/database). The dark blue graph is the unemployment rate. The light blue graph is the job-separation rate, calculated as the ratio of quarterly job separations to the number of persons employed. To be consistent with the assumption of a constant labour force, we have neglected the flows into and out of the labour force in the data. Data on the job-separation rate are available only for the following countries in the Eurozone: Austria, Cyprus, Estonia, Finland, France, Greece, Ireland, Italy, Latvia, Lithuania, Malta, Netherlands, Portugal, Slovakia, Slovenia and Spain.

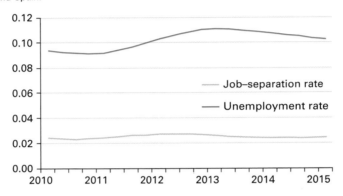

Figure 10.13 Job-finding rate and the unemployment rate, 2010–2015

The graph covers the period of data availability for the Labour Force Survey from Eurostat (http://ec.europa.eu/eurostat/data/database). The dark blue graph is the unemployment rate. The light blue graph is the job-finding rate, calculated as the ratio of quarterly job hires (from the pool of persons unemployed) to the number of persons unemployed. To be consistent with the assumption of a constant labour force, we have neglected the flows into and out of the labour force in the data. Data on the job-finding rate are available only for the following countries in the Eurozone: Austria, Cyprus, Estonia, Finland, France, Greece, Ireland, Italy, Latvia, Lithuania, Malta, Netherlands, Portugal, Slovakia, Slovenia and Spain.

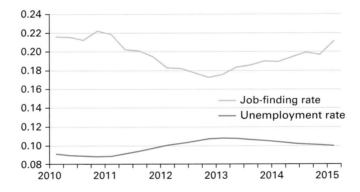

Table 10.1 assumes that the labour force is fixed at 150 million people. Suppose that the economy starts in month 1 with an unemployment rate, u, of 10%, indicating a recession. Employment, L, starts at 135 million and unemployment, U, starts at 15 million.

We can work through the process of job separation and finding to determine the time paths of employment and unemployment. In the first month, 3% of the 135 million employed – 4 million persons – lose their jobs. At the same

[7]Later, we will assume that a person who finds a job stays employed for at least one month, and that a person who loses a job takes at least one month to find a new one. If we consider quarterly frequency as in the data, we would have to make a more unrealistic assumption that a person who finds a job stays employed for at least one quarter, and that a person who loses a job takes at least one quarter to find a new one.

time, 50% of the 15 million unemployed – 7.5 million persons – find jobs. Hence, the net increase in employment during the month is 3.5 million – an enormous number that is not realistic. Correspondingly, unemployment falls by 3.5 million, and the unemployment rate declines to 7.7%.

Table 10.1 Dynamics of employment and unemployment

	Start of month			During month			
Month	Number employed (L) (millions)	Number unemployed (U) (millions)	Unemployment rate (u)	Number who lose jobs (millions)	Number who find jobs (millions)	Change in L (ΔL) (millions)	Change in U (ΔU) (millions)
1	135.0	15.0	0.100	4.0	7.5	3.5	–3.5
2	138.5	11.5	0.077	4.2	5.8	1.6	–1.6
3	140.1	9.9	0.066	4.2	5.0	0.8	– 0.8
4	140.9	9.1	0.061	4.2	4.6	0.4	– 0.4
5	141.3	8.7	0.058	4.2	4.4	0.2	– 0.2
6	141.5	8.5	0.057	4.2	4.2	0.0	0.0
∞	141.5	8.5	0.057	4.2	4.2	0.0	0.0

Note: This example assumes that the economy starts with 135 million people employed, L, and 15 million unemployed, U. The labour force, $L + U$, is fixed at 150 million. The unemployment rate is $u = U/(L + U) = U/150$. As in Figure 9.11, 3% of those employed lose jobs each month, and 50% of those unemployed find jobs. The net change in employment, ΔL, is $0.5 \cdot U - 0.03 \cdot L$. The net change in unemployment, ΔU, is the negative of ΔL. When L reaches 141.5 million and U reaches 8.5 million, ΔL and ΔU equal zero. Thus, the natural unemployment rate *is* $u^n = 8.5/150 = 5.7\%$.

As the number employed rises, job separations increase, but only slightly – to 4.2 million in the second month. As the number unemployed falls, job findings fall – to 5.8 million in the second month. Therefore, in month 2, net employment rises by 1.6 million, and unemployment falls by 1.6 million. The unemployment rate is now down to 6.6%.

This process continues until the numbers of job separations and findings are the same. In our example, the economy gets close to this balance in month 6 – when employment reaches 141.5 million and unemployment equals 8.5 million. The corresponding unemployment rate is 5.7%. Therefore, the **natural unemployment rate** is 5.7%. By natural, we mean that the economy tends towards this value automatically, given the rates at which people lose and find jobs.

This model, although not fully realistic, brings out some important points about the unemployment rate. First, although the unemployment rate eventually stays constant at the natural rate, there is still a large amount of job turnover. In the model, about 4 million people lose and find jobs each month when the unemployment rate equals its natural value of 5.7%. These large flows out of and into jobs are a normal part of the operation of a fluid labour market.

Second, the keys to the dynamics of employment and unemployment are the rates of job separation and finding. In our example, we assumed that these rates were fixed at 3% and 50%, respectively. Our earlier discussion suggested that these rates would depend on characteristics of workers and jobs. For example, we discussed effects from a person's age and job experience, from the effective real income while unemployed, ω, and from the variability of an industry's supply-and-demand conditions. The rates of job separation and finding depend also on shifts to economy-wide productivity; for example, shocks to the technology level, A.

We now generalize the model to bring out the roles of the job-separation and job-finding rates. Let σ (the Greek letter sigma) be the job-separation rate and φ (the Greek letter phi) the job-finding rate. The change in the number of persons employed over a month, ΔL, is given by:

$$\Delta L = \varphi U - \sigma L$$
$$= \textit{job findings} - \textit{job separations} \tag{10.6}$$

The first term, φU, is the number of unemployed persons who find jobs over a month, and the second term, σL, is the number of employed persons who lose jobs over a month. (We assume that a person who finds a job stays employed for at least one month, and that a person who loses a job takes at least one month to find a new one.)

Equation (10.6) implies that employment, L, increases and unemployment, U, decreases if job findings, φU, are greater than job separations, σL. In the reverse case, L decreases and U increases. To determine the long-run levels of L and U, we have to find the situation where L and U are constant. This constancy requires $\Delta L = 0$, and equation (10.6) says that $\Delta L = 0$ when job findings equal job separations:

$$\varphi U = \sigma L$$

job findings = job separations

To find the long-run L and U, we use our assumption that the labour force, $L + U$, is constant at 150 million. Hence, we can substitute $L = 150 - U$ in the last equation to get:

$$\varphi U = \sigma \bullet (150 - U)$$

If we combine the terms involving U and put them on the left-hand side, we get:

$$U \bullet (\varphi + \sigma) = 150 \bullet \sigma$$

Therefore, the long-run number unemployed is given by:

$$U = 150 \bullet \sigma / (\varphi + \sigma)$$

The natural unemployment rate, $u^n = U/150$, is therefore:

> Key equation (natural unemployment rate):
> $$u^n = \sigma / (\varphi + \sigma) \qquad (10.7)$$

Equation (10.7) shows that a higher job-separation rate, σ, raises the natural unemployment rate, u^n, whereas a higher job-finding rate, φ, lowers u^n.[8] For example, an increase in the effective real income while unemployed, ω, lowers φ, and thereby raises u^n. Thus, more generous unemployment insurance programmes increase the long-run unemployment rate. The Internet assists in the process of job matching, probably raising φ. Hence, the Internet would lower u^n.

ECONOMIC FLUCTUATIONS, EMPLOYMENT AND UNEMPLOYMENT

We now combine the model of job search with our equilibrium business-cycle model to see how employment and unemployment behave during recessions and booms. Assume, as usual, that economic fluctuations result from shocks to the technology level, A. Suppose, as in Table 10.1, that the labour force is fixed at 150 million; the job-separation rate, σ, is 0.03 per month; and the job-finding rate, φ, is 0.50 per month. Employment, L, starts at 141.5 million; unemployment, U, at 8.5 million; and the unemployment rate, u, at 5.7%.

Suppose that an adverse shock to the technology level, A, reduces the marginal product of labour for the typical worker and job. The job-finding rate, φ, falls because market opportunities became poorer – probably temporarily – relative to the real income received while unemployed, ω. Figure 10.13 suggests that the decline in the job-finding rate during a recession is quantitatively important. We assume, for example purposes, that φ falls from 0.50 per month to 0.40.

Figure 10.12 shows that the job-separation rate, σ, did not change a great deal as the economy moved from boom to recession to recovery. Therefore, we assume that σ stays fixed at 0.03 per month.

Table 10.2 shows that the drop in the job-finding rate, φ, causes employment, L, to fall gradually and unemployment, U, to rise gradually. In month 1, job finding falls to 3.4 million – still a large number, but more than offset by the 4.2 million job loss. Hence, L falls during the month by 0.8 million, and U expands accordingly. This process

[8]For analyses of this type of model, see Robert Hall (1979), Chitra Ramaswami (1983), and Michael Darby, John Haltiwanger, and Mark Plant (1985).

continues through month 5, when the cumulative fall in employment is 1.8 million, and the unemployment rate, u, reaches 6.9%.

Table 10.2 assumes that the job-finding rate, φ, returns to its normal value, 0.50, in month 5. In response, employment, L, and unemployment, U, return gradually to their long-run values. Since φ and σ now take on the values assumed in Table 10.1, the economy approaches the long-run position where $L= 141.5$ million and $U= 8.5$ million. By month 9, L and U are close to their long-run values, and the unemployment rate, u, is near the natural rate, 5.7%.

Although the example in Table 10.2 is not fully realistic, it brings out several features of real-world recessions. First, the build-up of a recession involves a period of gradually falling employment and rising unemployment. Second, even after an economic recovery begins, it takes a while for employment and unemployment to return to their pre-recession levels. Third, even during a recession, large numbers of jobs are created each month – they are just outnumbered by jobs lost.

Table 10.2 Dynamics of employment and unemployment during a recession

	Start of month			During month			
Month	Number employed (L) (millions)	Number unemployed (U) (millions)	Unemployment rate (u)	Job-finding rate (ϕ) (monthly)	Number who lose jobs (millions)	Number who find jobs (millions)	Change in L (ΔL) (millions)
1	141.5	8.5	0.057	0.40	4.2	3.4	−0.8
2	140.7	9.3	0.062	0.40	4.2	3.7	−0.5
3	140.2	9.8	0.065	0.40	4.2	3.9	−0.3
4	139.9	10.1	0.067	0.40	4.2	4.0	−0.2
5	139.7	10.3	0.069	0.50	4.2	5.2	1.0
6	140.7	9.3	0.062	0.50	4.2	4.6	0.4
7	141.1	8.9	0.059	0.50	4.2	4.4	0.2
8	141.3	8.7	0.058	0.50	4.2	4.4	0.2
9	141.5	8.5	0.057	0.50	4.2	4.2	0.0
∞	141.5	8.5	0.057	0.50	4.2	4.2	0.0

Note: In this example, the labour force is fixed at 150 million. The economy starts from the long-run position of Table 10.1, with employment, L, of 141.5 million; unemployment, U, of 8.5 million; and an unemployment rate, u, of 5.7%. These values correspond to a job-separation rate, σ, of 0.03 per month and a job-finding rate, ϕ, of 0.50 per month. In month 1, the start of a recession is assumed to lower ϕ to 0.40 but to leave σ unchanged at 0.03. These values generate a gradual decline in L and a gradual rise in U. In month 5, we assume that ϕ returns to 0.50. This change generates a gradual return of L towards 141.5 million and of U towards 8.5 million.

VACANCIES

We can extend the model to allow for job vacancies. Suppose that firms have some idea about potential workers in the sense of the value of their MPL. Firms also have a sense of the real wage rate, w/P, needed to induce the typical qualified applicant to accept a job. Finally, there are costs for posting job openings and interviewing applicants. Given these considerations, firms determine how many job openings to advertise.

For our purposes, we do not have to work through a detailed model of job openings. We can just note some important properties that emerge from such a model. One result is that an increase in the value of prospective marginal products, MPL, raises the number of job openings. A second result is that an increase in the real wage rate, w/P, required to get workers to accept jobs lowers the number of job openings. Finally, a reduction in costs of posting jobs and processing applications – caused, for example, by the rise of the Internet – raises the number of job openings.

Suppose that an increase in the technology level, A, raises the MPL. For given real wage rates, w/P, firms post more job openings. Therefore, job vacancies increase. Conversely, an unfavourable shock reduces vacancies. Thus, our prediction is that vacancies are procyclical – high in booms and low in recessions.

The light blue graph in Figure 10.14 shows the cyclical part of job vacancies from 2009 to 2015. This variable is constructed by the method used for real GDP in Figure 9.3. The dark blue graph is the cyclical part of real GDP. The main finding is that, as predicted, the number of job vacancies is procyclical – the correlation with the cyclical part of real GDP was 0.82.

The procyclical pattern for vacancies helps to explain why the job-finding rate is high in a boom and low in a recession. In our previous analysis, we argued that job seekers would be more likely to accept job offers in a boom because of the increase in the real wage rate, w/P. The increase in vacancies reinforces this response, because the greater availability of jobs makes it easier for workers to locate positions that look like good matches. Thus, in a boom, the rate of job acceptance increases partly because the wage offers are better and partly because good jobs are easier to find. Conversely, in a recession, the rate of job acceptance decreases because the pay is worse and attractive positions are harder to find.

We know, from Figure 10.8, that the employment rate is procyclical and, hence, that the unemployment rate is countercyclical. Thus, vacancies and unemployment move in opposite directions. Figure 10.15 describes this relation with a scatter plot for Eurozone data from 2009 to 2015 between the cyclical parts of the unemployment rate

Figure 10.14 Cyclical behaviour of Eurozone real GDP and job vacancies

The dark blue graph is the deviation of real GDP from its trend. The light blue graph is the deviation of the number of job vacancies from its trend. Data on the number of job vacancies are available only for the following countries in the Eurozone: Estonia, Germany, Latvia, Lithuania, Luxembourg, Netherlands, Portugal, Slovakia and Slovenia. The data on real GDP and job vacancies are quarterly and seasonally adjusted. The number of job vacancies is procyclical – it fluctuates with real GDP and is much more variable than real GDP.

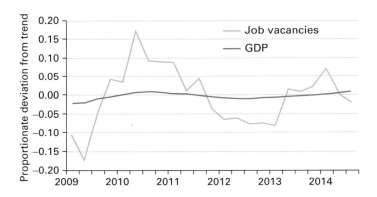

Figure 10.15   The unemployment rate and job vacancies: a Beveridge curve

The horizontal axis is the deviation of the unemployment rate from its trend. This variable is the same, except for a minus sign, as the deviation of the employment rate from its trend, shown in Figure 10.8. The vertical axis is the proportionate deviation of the number of job vacancies from its trend (from Figure 10.14). The plots use quarterly, seasonally adjusted data from 2009.4 to 2015.2.

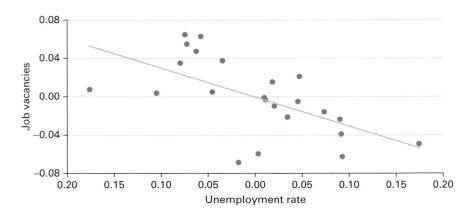

and the number of job vacancies. This plot is called a *Beveridge curve*, named after the British economist William Beveridge. For a discussion, see Robert Shimer (2003).

The horizontal axis in Figure 10.15 shows the cyclical part of the unemployment rate, u. The vertical axis shows the cyclical part of the number of job vacancies. Note the clear downward slope – the correlation between the two series is −0.61. Thus, the data confirm that a low unemployment rate matches up with high vacancies, whereas a high unemployment rate matches up with low vacancies.

Economics in Practice
Seasonal fluctuations

Our analysis views economic fluctuations as resulting from shocks to the technology level, *A*. Shocks other than technological changes, such as harvest failures and strikes, have effects that resemble those from changes in *A*. Seasonal changes also resemble shifts to the technology.

As noted in Chapter 2, economists usually use seasonally adjusted data to study economic fluctuations. The seasonal adjustment eliminates the normal change in a variable, such as real GDP, from winter (the first quarter) to spring (the second quarter), and so on. In the unadjusted data, real GDP tends to rise each year towards a peak in the fourth quarter. This systematic quarter-to-quarter pattern does not appear in the seasonally adjusted numbers.

Robert Barsky and Jeffrey Miron (1989) studied the seasonally unadjusted numbers. They found that the seasonal fluctuations in quantities – real GDP, consumption, investment, employment and unemployment – are larger than the variations associated with typical recessions and booms. From 1948 to 1985, over 80% of the quarterly fluctuations in real GDP and over 60% of those in the unemployment rate reflected seasonal factors (Barsky and Miron, 1989, table 1). Further, the seasonal patterns of co-movement among real GDP and its major components and between real GDP and employment look similar to those found in economic fluctuations (*ibid.*, table 2). For example, in the seasonal pattern, investment and consumption move along with real GDP, and investment fluctuates much more than consumption. J. Joseph Beaulieu and Jeffrey Miron (1992) show that the above findings in the US apply also to 25 industrialized or semi-industrialized countries.

Seasonal fluctuations reflect influences of weather and holidays. We can think of some of these effects as variations in technology, such as the adverse impact of winter on the construction industry. Other effects correspond to variations in household preferences, such as the positive impact of Christmas on consumer demand and the negative impact of summer vacations on labour supply. The magnitude of the seasonal fluctuations shows that these kinds of disturbances can be quantitatively important in the short run. That is, the seasonal evidence weakens the argument made by some economists that shocks to technology and preferences are not large enough to account for the observed magnitude of recessions and booms.

Summing Up

We began by extending the equilibrium business-cycle model to allow for variable capital utilization and, therefore, for a variable supply of capital services in the short run. This extension predicts that the capital-utilization rate will be procyclical – high in booms and low in recessions. The data on capacity utilization accord with this prediction.

In the data, labour input – measured, for example, by total worker-hours – is strongly procyclical. Worker-hours can be broken down into three components: the labour force, the employment rate (the proportion of the labour force with jobs) and the average hours worked per worker. The most important part of the fluctuations in worker-hours is the employment rate. Changes in average hours worked rank second in importance, and movements in the labour force rank third. Our analysis in Chapter 9 applies to the last two of these components but does not explain the most important part: the fluctuations in the employment rate.

This chapter extends the equilibrium business-cycle model to allow workers to search for good jobs and employers to search for productive workers. This extension explains why the unemployment rate would be greater than zero; that is, why the employment rate would be less than 100%. The analysis shows why the unemployment rate would be countercyclical, so that the employment rate would be procyclical. In addition, the model predicts that the job vacancy rate would move opposite to the unemployment rate; that is, job vacancies are procyclical. Overall, this extended version of the equilibrium business-cycle model gives us a better understanding of why labour input is high in booms and low in recessions.

Key Terms and Concepts

capital-utilization rate	help-wanted advertising	natural unemployment rate	vacancies
discouraged workers	job-finding rate	reservation real wage	vacancy rate
duration of unemployment	job-separation rate	unemployment insurance	
employment rate	market-clearing approach	user costs	

Questions and Problems

A   Review questions

1   What is the natural rate of unemployment, u^n? Why might the unemployment rate, u, differ from u^n? Can u^n change over time?

2   Once a job seeker and a firm find a job match, why might they choose subsequently to end the match? List some influences on the job-separation rate.

3   Suppose that a job seeker receives a real wage offer, w/P, that exceeds his or her effective real income while unemployed, ω. Why might the person reject the offer?

4   Use Figure 10.4 to study the capital-utilization rate, κ. How does κ change when
   a   the real rental price, R/P, rises?
   b   the depreciation rate, $\delta(\kappa)$, rises for each value of κ?

5   Explain how the quantity of capital services depends on the stock of capital, K, and the capital-utilization rate, κ. Why is the rate of return on capital given by equation (10.4)?

6   What is the definition of the unemployment rate? Since it does not include persons who are 'out of the labour force', does it underestimate the true unemployment rate? Can you think of reasons why the reported numbers may overestimate the true unemployment rate?

B   Problems for discussion

7   The job-finding rate, the job-separation rate and the dynamics of the unemployment rate
   Suppose that the labour force is fixed at 100 million people, of whom 92 million initially have jobs and 8 million are unemployed. Assume that the job-separation rate is 2% per month and the job-finding rate is 40% per month. Trace out the time paths of employment and unemployment. What is the natural unemployment rate?

8   Cyclical behaviour of the labour force
   Figure 10.7 shows that the labour force is acyclical. What pattern would you predict on theoretical grounds? (Hint: think first about

people's incentives to leave the labour force – that is, to stop looking for work – during a recession. Are there also incentives for people to enter the labour force during a recession?)

9 Job vacancies

Suppose that economic fluctuations are caused by shocks to the technology level, A. What do you predict for the cyclical behaviour of job vacancies? How then would fluctuations in vacancies relate to fluctuations in the unemployment rate? How does your answer relate to the Beveridge curve shown in Figure 10.15?

10 The job-finding rate

Discuss the effects on the job-finding rate and the expected duration of unemployment from the following:

a an increase in unemployment insurance benefits;

b an increase in the allowable duration of unemployment insurance benefits;

c a technological change, such as the Internet, that improves the matching of workers and jobs.

Money and prices

PART IV

11 The demand for money and the price level

Our model has three forms of assets: money, bonds and ownership of capital. So far, we have not analyzed how much money households hold or how these holdings change over time. Our analysis in Chapters 7 to 10 was therefore carried out under the assumption that each household held a constant stock of money, *M*. Now, we extend the microeconomic foundations of the model to explain why a household holds part of its assets as money; that is, we explain the **demand for money**. By demand for money, we refer to the quantity of money that a household decides to hold as a function of the price level, *P*, the interest rate, *i*, and other variables.

As mentioned in Chapter 7, we assume in the model that money is the sole medium of exchange in the economy. Households exchange money for goods on the goods market, money for labour on the labour market, money for capital services on the rental market and money for bonds on the bond market. However, households do not directly exchange goods for goods (a process called **barter**), bonds for goods, and so on.

Concepts of money

The money in our model matches up with paper currency issued by a government. For example, the money could be British pound notes issued by the Bank of England, euro notes issued by the European Central Bank and almost 170 other forms of paper currency issued by the world's governments. These currencies are sometimes called **fiat money** because they have value due to government fiat, rather than through intrinsic value. In earlier times, societies tended to rely more on **commodity money**, such as gold and silver coins, which do have intrinsic value. These coins are valued, in part, for their content of gold or silver. In the box below, we discuss how another commodity, the cigarette, served as money in a prisoner-of-war camp. In our model, money has no intrinsic value; it is just a piece of paper issued by the government. Therefore, we do not have to consider any resources used up when intrinsically valuable goods serve as money.

Economics in Practice
Money in a prisoner-of-war camp

R.A. Radford (1945) described his experience with the economy of a German prisoner-of-war (POW) camp during World War II. He observed that cigarettes became the primary medium of exchange, with many goods being exchanged for cigarettes, which were then used to buy other goods. In addition, most prices were expressed in units of cigarettes; for example, as four cigarettes per ration of treacle (a form of syrup).

Radford noted that cigarettes had several attractive characteristics as money (p. 194): 'homogeneous, reasonably durable, and of convenient size for the smallest or, in packets, for the largest transactions'. One drawback, applicable also to other commodity moneys, was the resource cost of using cigarettes as a medium of exchange. That is, the cigarettes used as money could not simultaneously be smoked and, worse yet, might deteriorate physically over time.

Radford discussed an attempt to introduce paper money as an alternative medium of exchange. This money was issued by the camp restaurant and was supposed to be redeemable for a fixed quantity of food. However, problems arose with respect to the credibility of the promised food value of the paper money, and cigarettes remained the primary medium of exchange. For our purposes, an interesting lesson from Radford's story is that a medium of exchange is important in any economy, even a POW camp.

If we think of money as paper currency issued by the government, there are several reasons why this money might occupy the dominant position as an economy's medium of exchange. First, the government may impose legal restrictions that prevent private parties, such as Microsoft Corporation, from issuing small-size, interest-bearing bonds that could serve conveniently as hand-to-hand currency. Further, the government may enact statutes that reinforce the use of its money. As an example, there is the proclamation that the euro is '**legal tender** for all debts public and private'. The term 'legal tender' means that euro currency has to be accepted in some forms of trade, such as payments of taxes to the government. However, since the legal-tender requirement does not specify the price, P, at which exchanges have to occur, the content of the legal-tender provision is unclear – what would legal tender mean if P were infinity?

Another consideration is the cost of establishing one's money as reliable and convenient. These costs include prevention of counterfeiting, replacement of worn-out notes, willingness to convert notes into different denominations, and so on. Because of these costs, money would always tend to bear interest at a rate lower than bonds. In fact, because of the inconvenience of paying interest on hand-to-hand currency, the interest rate on currency is typically zero. That is, if one holds €1 of currency and does not lose it, one will still have €1 of currency in the future.

We can relate our abstract concept of money to conventional measures of the money stock. The theoretical construct corresponds most closely to currency held by the public. In the real world, currency held by the public differs from *total currency in circulation*, which includes currency held in the vaults of banks and other depository institutions. (Currency in circulation does not include amounts held by central banks.) A further distinction is between total currency in circulation and **high-powered money**, which adds the deposits held by banks and other depository institutions at central banks. Another name for high-powered money is the **monetary base**. In the following, we first discuss the US dollar, which is the world's most dominant reserve currency, and then other currencies in a number of countries.

Economics in Practice
Where is all the currency?

In December 2015, the amount of US currency held by the public was about $4200 per person in the United States. To understand this surprisingly large number, start with the observation that, at the end of 2015, much of the 78% of currency in circulation was in $100 bills, although this percentage also includes coins. (The data on currency by denomination are from the Federal Reserve Board.) Thus, much of the currency is probably not used for ordinary transactions. Because currency is anonymous, it is attractive for illegal activities, such as the drug trade. Currency transactions also facilitate tax evasion. However, the amount of US currency held for these purposes is unknown.

More is known about the amounts of US currency held abroad, mostly in the form of $100 bills. Foreigners like US money as a store of value and a medium of exchange because the money has a reasonably stable value and can readily be exchanged for goods or other assets. In addition, transactions carried out in currency can usually be hidden from local governments, and this secrecy is particularly attractive when the government is oppressive. The foreign demand for US currency is especially high in countries experiencing economic and political turmoil. A joint study by the Federal Reserve and the US Treasury estimated that 55–60% of the total US currency in circulation in 2002 was held abroad. Recent updates by economist Ruth Judson of the Federal Reserve estimated the figure to be closer to 50% in 2011. The geographical division was estimated as of 2002 to be 25% in Latin America (with Argentina the highest demander), 20% in the Middle East and Africa, 15% in Asia and 40% in Europe (with Russia and other former Soviet republics as particularly high users). For additional discussion, see Richard Porter and Ruth Judson (2001), Board of Governors of the Federal Reserve System (2003) and Ruth Judson (2012).

In December 2015, the amount of (seasonally adjusted) currency held by the public in the United States was $1338 billion, which amounted to 7.4% of nominal gross domestic product (GDP). This amount of currency is surprisingly large – about $4200 per US resident. In the box above, we note that much of the currency is in $100 bills, many of which are held abroad, rather than by US residents.

The term 'money' often refers to a **monetary aggregate** that is broader than currency. A monetary aggregate is the total dollar stock of a group of financial assets defined to be money. The most common definition, called **M1**, attempts to classify as money the assets that serve regularly as media of exchange. This concept adds to currency held by the public the **checkable deposits** issued by banks and other financial institutions. Checkable deposits are deposits held at financial institutions that can be withdrawn by writing a cheque. The amount of these checkable deposits (including travellers' cheques) in the United States in December 2015 was $1744 billion, or 9.6% of nominal GDP.[1] Therefore, M1 – the sum of currency and checkable deposits – was $3082 billion, or 17% of nominal GDP. The total M1 was 43% in currency and 57% in checkable deposits (including travellers' cheques). In earlier times, a much smaller proportion of M1 was in currency and a much larger proportion was in checkable deposits. For example, in 1960, only 19% of M1 was in currency, whereas 81% was in checkable deposits. This change illustrates the declining importance of checkable deposits held at banks and other financial institutions. These types of account have been replaced to a considerable extent by other forms of financial assets, such as money-market accounts, which have become much easier to access.

Table 11.1 shows ratios of currency to nominal GDP for OECD countries (the rich countries in the Organisation for Economic Cooperation and Development), plus China, in 1960, 1980, 2000 and 2012. Notice that the ratio of currency to GDP has declined over time in most countries – a typical case, for France, showed a decrease from 0.133 in 1960 to 0.052 in 1980 and 0.035 in 2000. Data for 2012 for countries that have adopted the euro since 2000 are included in the ratio of currency to nominal GDP of 0.095 for the Euro area. In some countries, the ratio levelled off, or even rose, from 1980 to 2012 – this pattern applied to Canada, Japan and the United States. For countries with data available in 2012, the highest currency ratio was 0.187 in Japan, and the lowest was 0.025 in Sweden. The United States, at 0.065, was close to the average of 0.069. Table 11.2 shows comparable figures with money defined to be M1.

Still broader definitions of money add in other kinds of deposits held at financial institutions. For example, M2 ($12 299 billion in the United States in December 2015) includes household holdings of savings deposits, small-time deposits and retail money-market mutual funds. However, the M2 definition goes beyond the concept of money as a medium of exchange. In our model, it is best to use a narrower definition of money; for example, as currency held by the public.

---

[1]The standard definition of checkable deposits includes travellers' cheques issued by banks and other depository institutions. Other travellers' cheques, amounting to $2.6 billion in December 2015, are included separately in M1, not as part of checkable deposits. Our measure of checkable deposits departs from the standard definition by including all travellers' cheques.

Table 11.1 Ratios of currency to nominal GDP

Country	1960	1980	2000	2012
Australia	0.054	0.036	0.041	0.037
Austria	0.119	0.078	0.071	–
Belgium	0.220	0.110	0.054	–
Canada	0.046	0.034	0.034	0.032
China	–	–	0.072	0.086
Denmark	0.068	0.032	0.029	0.034
Euro area	–	–	–	0.095
Finland	0.036	0.025	0.025	–
France	0.133	0.052	0.035	–
Germany	0.072	0.062	0.070	–
Greece	0.103	0.130	–	–
Ireland	0.117	0.077	0.052	–
Italy	–	0.070	0.066	–
Japan	0.069	0.072	0.121	0.187
Netherlands	0.125	0.064	0.047	–
New Zealand	0.061	0.025	0.019	–
Norway	0.112	0.060	0.030	–
Portugal	0.177	0.131	0.057	–
South Korea	0.059	0.049	0.034	0.037
Spain	0.120	0.083	0.099	–
Sweden	0.090	0.064	0.043	0.025
Switzerland	0.197	0.141	0.093	0.092
United Kingdom	0.081	0.044	0.025	–
United States	0.056	0.042	0.059	0.065

Note: The table shows the ratio of currency held by the public to nominal GDP up to 2000. Thereafter, the data reflects total currency in circulation due to data availability. The data are from International Monetary Fund, *International Financial Statistics*. Data for Switzerland taken from Swiss National Bank.

Table 11.2 Ratios of M1 to nominal GDP

Country	1960	1980	2000	2012
Australia	0.228	0.126	0.211	0.181
Austria	0.197	0.151	0.280	–
Belgium	0.322	0.192	0.271	–
Canada	0.152	0.112	0.213	0.343
China	–	–	0.536	0.594
Denmark	0.246	0.201	0.291	0.445
Euro area	–	–	0.307	0.545
Finland	–	0.080	0.307	–
France	0.468	0.280	0.224	–
Germany	0.160	0.170	0.288	–
Greece	0.151	0.196	0.288	–
Ireland	–	–	0.197	–
Italy	–	0.442	0.416	–
Japan	0.265	0.286	0.582	1.149
Netherlands	0.274	0.187	0.367	–
New Zealand	0.279	0.110	0.141	0.156
Norway	0.235	0.145	0.135	0.170

Table 11.2 *Continued*

Country	1960	1980	2000	2012
Portugal	–	0.390	0.427	–
South Korea	0.104	0.102	0.286	0.322
Spain	0.327	–	0.338	–
Sweden	–	–	0.324	0.459
Switzerland	0.360	0.278	0.444	0.818
United Kingdom	–	–	0.448	0.695
United States	0.258	0.138	0.107	0.143

Note: The table shows the ratio of M1 (currency held by the public plus checkable deposits) to nominal GDP. The data are from the Organization for Economic Cooperation and Development, and International Monetary Fund, *International Financial Statistics.* Data for countries adopting the euro after 2000 are included in ratio for Euro area.

The demand for money

We will now extend the microeconomic foundations of our model to consider the demand for money. Since we identify money with hand-to-hand currency, we assume that the interest rate paid on money is zero. In contrast, the rate of return on bonds and ownership of capital equals the interest rate, i, which we assume is greater than zero. Henceforth, we refer to bonds and ownership of capital as **interest-bearing assets**, because these assets pay a positive return to the holder. The important point is that these assets yield a higher rate of return than money and are therefore better than money as long-term **stores of value**. Nevertheless, since households use money to make exchanges, households will hold some money for convenience, rather than always cashing in earning assets immediately prior to each exchange. That is, the demand for money will be greater than zero.

In Chapter 7, we wrote the household budget constraint in nominal terms in equation (7.11), which we repeat here:

$$PC + \Delta B + P \bullet \Delta K = \prod + wL + i \bullet (B + PK)$$
$$nominal\,consumption + nominal\,saving = nominal\,income \tag{11.1}$$

On the right-hand side, the household receives nominal profit, $\prod$ (which is zero in equilibrium), nominal wage income, wL, and nominal asset income, $i \bullet (B + PK)$, all in the form of money. On the left-hand side, the household uses money to buy consumption goods, in the nominal amount PC, and to add to interest-bearing assets (that is, to save), in the nominal amount $\Delta B + P \bullet \Delta K$.

Although all of the income and spending terms in equation (11.1) use money, it would be possible for the household to hold little or no money at every point in time. If each inflow of income were perfectly synchronized with an equal outflow of expenditure on goods or purchases of interest-bearing assets, each household's money balance could always be close to zero. However, this synchronization would require a great deal of effort and planning. We assume, as a general matter, that the household can reduce its average money balance by incurring more **transaction costs**. By transaction costs, we mean any expenses of time or goods related to the timing and form of various exchanges. In the real world, examples of transaction costs are the time spent going to the bank or an automatic teller machine (ATM), and brokerage fees.

One way to maintain a low average money balance is to rush off to the store as soon as money wages are paid to spend one's entire weekly or monthly pay on goods. Another method would be to go immediately to a financial institution to convert all of one's wage income into interest-bearing assets. More realistically, a household might immediately deposit its pay cheque into a bank account (or might arrange for the pay to be deposited directly into an account). In addition, if workers were paid wages more frequently – say, weekly rather than monthly – it would be easier for workers to maintain a lower average money balance.

The general idea is that, by putting more effort into money management and, thereby, incurring more transaction costs, the household can reduce its average holding of money, M. For a given total of nominal assets, $M + B + PK$, a reduction in the average level of M raises the average holding of interest-bearing assets, $B + PK$. Since asset income is $i \cdot (B + PK)$, the rise in $B + PK$ raises asset income. Thus, a household's average holding of money, M, emerges from a trade-off. With a frequent transaction strategy, M will be low and asset income will be high, but transaction costs will be high. With an infrequent transaction strategy, M will be high and asset income will be low, but transaction costs will be low. The household's choice of average money holdings entails finding the right balance between additional asset income and added transaction costs.

We use the term 'demand for money', labelled M^d, to describe the average holding of money that results from the household's optimal strategy for money management. Many formal models of money management have been developed to assess this demand for money. For our purposes, we do not have to go through these models. Rather, we are mainly interested in how some key variables affect the quantity of money demanded, M^d. Specifically, we want to know how M^d depends on the price level, P, the interest rate, i, and real GDP, Y.

THE INTEREST RATE AND THE DEMAND FOR MONEY

A higher interest rate, i, provides a greater incentive to hold down average holdings of money, M, in order to raise average holdings of interest-bearing assets, $B + PK$. That is, with a higher i, households are more willing to incur transaction costs in order to reduce M. For example, households respond to a higher i by transacting more frequently between money and interest-bearing assets. We predict, accordingly, that an increase in i reduces the nominal demand for money, M^d. For a given price level, P, we can also say that a higher i lowers the real demand for money, M/P.

THE PRICE LEVEL AND THE DEMAND FOR MONEY

Suppose that the price level, P, doubles. Assume that the nominal wage rate, w, and the nominal rental price, R, also double, so that the real wage rate, w/P, and the real rental price, R/P, do not change. In this case, the household's nominal income, $\Pi + wL + i \cdot (B + PK)$ on the right-hand side of the budget constraint in equation (11.1), is twice as high as before.[2] However, the real value of this income, $\Pi/P + (w/P) \cdot L + i \cdot (B/P + K)$, is unchanged. Thus, we are considering a doubling of the nominal values of all variables, with no changes in the real values. In this circumstance, the household would want to double the average nominal quantity of money, M, held. This doubling of M means that the average real money balance, M/P, does not change.

To think about this result, suppose that a household's nominal income is €500 per week. Suppose that the initial plan for money management – involving some frequency of exchange between money and interest-bearing assets – dictates holding half a week's worth of income, on average, in the form of money. In this case, the household's average holding of money, M, is €250. After the doubling of the price level, P (along with the doubling of the nominal wage rate, w, and rental price, R), the household's nominal income is €1000 per week. The household would not change its frequency of exchange between money and interest-bearing assets, because the trade-off for optimal money management – interest income versus transaction costs – is the same as before. Therefore, the household still holds half a week's worth of income in the form of money. With twice as much nominal income, half a week's worth of income is twice as much money in nominal terms – €500 instead of €250. Hence, the nominal demand for money, M^d, doubles. Since M^d and P have both doubled, the ratio, M/P, is the same. The result is that the **real demand for money**, M/P, does not change when P changes.

REAL GDP AND THE DEMAND FOR MONEY

Suppose again that the initial plan for money management dictates holding half a week's worth of income, on average, in the form of money. Hence, when nominal income is €500, the household's average holding of money, M, is €250. Assume now that nominal income doubles to €1000, while the price level, P, is unchanged. Therefore, real

---

[2]We are assuming that $\Pi = 0$ and that L, K and i are unchanged. We are also considering the average household, so that $B = 0$.

income, $\Pi/P + (w/P) \cdot L + i \cdot (B/P + K)$, doubles. If its money-management plan were unchanged, each household would still hold half a week's worth of nominal income as money. However, half a week's worth of income is now twice as much money – €500 instead of €250. Thus, households would double their nominal demand for money, M^d. Since P is constant, the real demand for money, M/P, also doubles.

This result has to be modified because higher real income shifts the trade-off between interest income and transaction costs. Specifically, the larger real money balance, M/P, means that more real income on assets, $i \cdot (B/P + K)$, could be gained by spending additional effort on money management. The key point is that the real transaction costs for economizing on money have not changed. Thus, when real income doubles, households are motivated to incur more transaction costs to reduce their average money holding. For example, instead of holding 0.5 weeks' worth of income as money, households might hold only 0.4 weeks' worth of income as money. In this case, nominal money demand, M^d, rises from €250 to €400, rather than €500. That is, a doubling of real income raises M^d, but by less than 100%. The response of M^d is, in proportional terms, smaller than the change in real income. (This result is called **economies of scale in cash management**, because higher-income households hold less money in proportion to their income.) Since the price level, P, is unchanged, the real demand for money, M/P, rises, but less than proportionately, with real income.

In the aggregate, household real income moves along with real GDP, Y. That is, from Chapter 8, the aggregate form of the household budget constraint is:

$$C + \Delta K = Y - \delta K$$
$$consumption + net\,investment = real\,GDP - depreciation$$
$$= real\,net\,domestic\,product \tag{8.13}$$

For given depreciation, δK, the aggregate of household real income is determined on the right-hand side of equation (8.13) by real GDP, Y. We therefore have that the aggregate real demand for money, M/P, rises, but less than proportionately, with Y.

OTHER INFLUENCES ON THE DEMAND FOR MONEY

For given values of the interest rate, i, the price level, P, and real GDP, Y, money demand depends on the payments technology and the level of transaction costs. As examples, increased use of credit cards and other electronic payment systems and greater convenience of checkable deposits reduce the demand for currency. Expanded use of ATM machines makes currency easier to obtain but has an uncertain impact on the demand for currency; the machines make currency more attractive for payments but also make it easier to hold a smaller average currency balance by going more often to the ATM.

THE MONEY-DEMAND FUNCTION

We can summarize the discussion by writing down a formula for nominal money demand for the aggregate of households:

> Key equation (money-demand function):
> $$M^d = P \cdot D(Y, i) \tag{11.2}$$

We get the aggregate money-demand function in equation (11.2) by adding up the demands from individual households. We assume that the form of the aggregate money-demand function comes from the effect of each right-hand-side variable, such as the interest rate, i, on the average money held by each household.

Economics in Practice
The payments period and the demand for money

Irving Fisher (1926) stressed the dependence of the demand for money on the period between payments of wages. The general idea is that a shorter period makes it easier for workers to maintain a low average money balance. This effect is particularly important during extreme inflations; for example, the German hyperinflation after World War I. In such circumstances, the cost of holding money becomes very high – we can represent this effect in our model by a high interest rate, i. Because of the high cost of holding money, workers and firms are willing to incur more transaction costs – such as the costs of making more frequent wage payments – to reduce their average holdings of money. In 1923, the final year of the German hyperinflation, an observer reported: 'It became the custom to make an advance of wages on Tuesday, the balance being paid on Friday. Later, some firms used to pay wages three times a week or even daily' (Costantino Bresciani-Turroni, 1937, p. 303). Similarly, during the Austrian hyperinflation after World War I: 'The salaries of the state officials, which used to be issued at the end of the month, were paid to them during 1922 in installments three times per month' (J. van Walre de Bordes, 1927, p. 163).

We assume in equation (11.2) that the nature of the transactions technology is given. Then, for given real GDP, Y, and interest rate, i, the nominal money demand, M^d, is proportional to the price level, P. For given P, M^d increases with Y (though less than proportionately) and decreases with i. This dependence is summarized by the function $D(\bullet)$. Note that if we divide both sides of equation (11.2) by P, we get the real demand for money:

$$M^d/P = D(Y, i) \tag{11.3}$$

We call $D(\bullet)$ the real money-demand function. From this perspective, equation (11.2) says:

$$nominal\ demand\ for\ money = price\ level \bullet (real\ demand\ for\ money)$$

EMPIRICAL EVIDENCE ON THE DEMAND FOR MONEY

Many statistical studies have analyzed the determinants of the demand for money. Most of these studies focus on M1, the monetary aggregate that comprises currency held by the public plus checkable deposits. However, some studies have examined separately the demand for currency.

The empirical results confirm the negative effects of interest rates on the demand for money, whether money is measured by M1 or currency. For example, in his classic empirical studies, Steven Goldfeld (1973, 1976) found that a 10% increase in interest rates (e.g., a rise from 5% to 5.5%) reduces the demand for M1 in the long run by about 3% for the United States. Goldfeld and Daniel Sichel (1990) and Ray Fair (1987) reported similar findings for a number of OECD countries. Jack Ochs and Mark Rush (1983) showed that the negative effect of interest rates on the demand for M1 reflect similar proportionate effects on currency and checkable deposits.

Casey Mulligan and Xavier Sala-i-Martin (2000) showed that money demand becomes more sensitive to changes in interest rates when the level of interest rates rises. At low rates – say, 2% – an increase in the interest rate by 10% (to 2.2%) lowers money demand by 2%. However, at an interest rate of 6%, an increase by 10% (to 6.6%) reduces money demand by 5%.

There is strong evidence for a positive effect of real GDP on real money demand and weaker evidence for economies of scale in this relation. Goldfeld (1973, 1976) found that an increase in real GDP by 10% leads, in the long run, to an increase by about 7% in the real demand for M1. The change in M1 breaks down into an increase of checkable deposits by around 6% and an increase in currency by about 10%. Therefore, economies of scale in the demand for M1 apply to checkable deposits but not to currency.

Our analysis predicted that an increase in the price level would raise the nominal demand for money in the same proportion. This proposition receives strong empirical support. For example, Goldfeld (1973, 1976) found that an increase in the price level by 10% leads to a 10% increase in the nominal demand for M1.

We have noted that changes in transactions technology can have important influences on the demand for money. This effect has been important since the early 1970s because of a variety of financial innovations. The innovations include the expanded use of credit cards, the development of money-market accounts that are convenient alternatives to checkable deposits held at banks, the introduction of ATM machines and the widespread use of electronic funds transfers.

Before the 1980s, economists ignored financial innovations when fitting equations for money demand. The estimated equations worked well up to the mid-1970s, in the sense that their predictions of the demand for money were fairly accurate. However, after the mid-1970s, estimates that ignored financial innovations started to fail. In particular, the actual amount of M1 – especially checkable deposits – that people held fell well short of the amount predicted from earlier empirical relationships. Michael Dotsey (1985) showed that the volume of electronic funds transfers was a good measure of the extent of financial innovation. He found, first, that the spread of electronic funds transfers led to a substantial decline in the real demand for M1. Second, when the volume of electronic funds transfers was held constant, the demand for M1 became stable over time. In particular, the fitted equation showed effects from interest rates and real GDP that were similar to those, such as Goldfeld's, that ignored financial innovations but included data only up to the early 1970s.

Determination of the price level

We now extend the equilibrium business-cycle model to determine the price level, P. The central idea is to add a new equilibrium condition: the nominal quantity of money equals the nominal quantity demanded.

THE NOMINAL QUANTITY OF MONEY SUPPLIED EQUALS THE NOMINAL QUANTITY DEMANDED

We assume that money takes the form of currency and that the nominal quantity of money is determined by the monetary authority; for example, the Federal Reserve in the United States, or the European Central Bank in the Eurozone. Thus, the nominal quantity of money supplied, M^s, is a given amount, M.

The aggregate demand for nominal money is given from the function we worked out before:

$$M^d = P \bullet D(Y, i) \tag{11.2}$$

This equation gives the nominal quantity of money, M^d, that households want to hold, whereas M^s is the actual amount of nominal money outstanding. We propose as another equilibrium condition for our model an equality between M^s and M^d:

$$M^s = M^d$$

nominal quantity of money supplied = nominal quantity of money demanded (11.4)

If we substitute for M^d the form of the nominal demand-for-money function from equation (11.2), we can write the result as:

> Key equation (nominal quantity of money supplied equals nominal quantity demanded):
> $$M^s = P \bullet D(Y, i) \tag{11.5}$$

To see why we expect $M^s = M^d$ to hold in equation (11.4), consider what happens when M^s – the given quantity of money supplied – differs from M^d. If M^s is greater than M^d, households have more money than they want to hold. Therefore, they try to spend their excess money; for example, on goods.[3] We anticipate that the increased desire to

---

[3] Another possibility is that households buy bonds, thereby affecting the interest rate, i, paid on bonds. However, in the present setting, i turns out not to change in a full equilibrium. The result is different – that is, the interest rate may change – if we do not allow for full flexibility of the price level, P. We consider this possibility in Chapter 17.

buy goods would raise the price level, P. This process continues until P rises enough to equate the nominal quantity of money demanded, M^d, on the right-hand side of equation (11.4) to the nominal quantity supplied, M^s, on the left-hand side. That is, the equilibrium price level is sufficiently high for households to be willing to hold the nominal quantity of money supplied, M^s.

The same process works in reverse if M^s is less than M^d. In that case, households try to rebuild their money balances; for example, by reducing their spending on goods. In this case, P falls enough to equate the nominal quantity of money demanded, M^d on the right-hand side of equation (11.4), to the nominal quantity supplied, M^s on the left-hand side.

One important point is that we are assuming that goods prices are flexible, so that the price level, P, adjusts rapidly to ensure equality between the nominal quantity of money supplied, M^s, and the nominal quantity demanded, M^d. This assumption about price flexibility parallels our previous assumptions about market-clearing conditions in the markets for labour and capital services. For the labour market, we assumed that the real wage rate, w/P, adjusted to ensure equality between the quantities of labour supplied, L^s, and demanded, L^d. For the rental market, we assumed that the real rental price, R/P, adjusted to ensure equality between the quantities of capital services supplied, $(\kappa K)^s$, and demanded, $(\kappa K)^d$. If we put the equations together, we have that the three nominal prices – P, w and R – adjust rapidly to ensure that three equilibrium conditions hold simultaneously: first, $M^s = M^d$; second, $L^s = L^d$; and third, $(\kappa K)^s = (\kappa K)^d$. Economists refer to this situation as one of **general equilibrium**. The word 'general' in this expression means that the equilibrium conditions – supply equals demand – apply simultaneously in all the markets.

Figure 11.1 shows graphically the equation of the nominal quantity of money demanded, M^d, to the nominal quantity supplied, M^s. The vertical axis shows the price level, P. The nominal quantity of money demanded, M^d, is the product of P and the real quantity of money demanded, $D(Y, i)$ – see equation (11.2). Recall that the real quantity of money demanded, $D(Y, i)$, is determined, for a given transactions technology, by real GDP, Y, and the interest rate, i. Hence, for given Y and i (and a given transactions technology), the nominal quantity of money demanded, M^d, is proportional to P. We graph M^d accordingly in Figure 11.1 as the upward-sloping line, which starts from the origin.[4] It is important to realize that this graph applies for given determinants of the real demand for money, $D(Y, i)$. The nominal quantity of money supplied, M^s, is shown by the vertical line at the value M.

The equilibrium condition, $M^s = M^d$ in Figure 11.1, corresponds to equations (11.4) and (11.5). The graph for M^d applies for given determinants of the real demand for money, $D(Y, i)$. That is, we are taking as given real GDP, Y, the

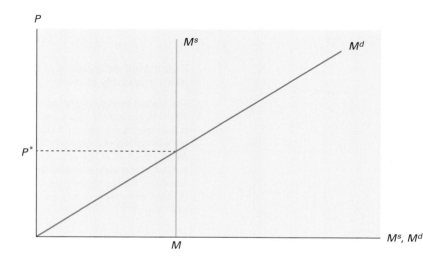

Figure 11.1 The nominal quantity of money supplied equals the nominal quantity demanded

The nominal quantity of money demanded is given by $M^d = P \cdot D(Y, i)$ from equation (11.2). For a given real quantity of money demanded, $D(Y, i)$, M^d is proportional to the price level, P. Therefore, the nominal quantity demanded, M^d, is given by the upward-sloping line, which starts from the origin. The nominal quantity of money supplied is the constant $M^s = M$, shown by the vertical line. The equilibrium condition $M^s = M^d$ holds when the price level is P^* on the vertical axis. Thus, P^* is the equilibrium value of P.

[4]It may seem puzzling to have a demand curve with an upward slope, since economists are used to having demand curves with a downward slope. However, P is the price of a unit of goods in terms of money (euros per good). The price of a unit of money in terms of goods is $1/P$ (goods per euro). If we had placed $1/P$, rather than P, on the vertical axis, the money-demand function would have the conventional negative slope. However, since we want to think about the determinants of the price level, it is more convenient to have P on the vertical axis.

interest rate, i, and any other determinants of the real demand for money. We can then use Figure 11.1 to find the equilibrium price level, which is the value P^* shown on the vertical axis. At P^*, the upward-sloping M^d line intersects the vertical M^s line. That is, P^* is the price level, P, that equates the nominal quantity of money demanded, M^d, to the nominal quantity supplied, M^s.

A CHANGE IN THE NOMINAL QUANTITY OF MONEY

We now study the effects from a one-time change in the nominal quantity of money supplied, M^s. To be concrete, suppose that M^s doubles from M to $2M$. The simplest way this could happen is for the monetary authority, on a one-time basis, to print up a great deal of extra currency and give it to people.

Figure 11.2 shows the effect from an increase in the nominal quantity of money supplied, M^s, from M to $2M$. Suppose that the money-demand line, M^d, does not shift. In this case, we can determine the change in the equilibrium price level, P^*, by looking at the intersections with the M^d line. The figure shows that the increase in M^s from M to $2M$ raises the equilibrium price level from P^* to $2P^*$ on the vertical axis.

We can verify the result from equation (11.5):

$$M^s = P \bullet D(Y, i) \tag{11.5}$$

The nominal quantity of money supplied, M^s, doubles on the left-hand side. If the real quantity of money demanded, $D(Y, i)$, does not change, the doubling of the price level, P, doubles the nominal quantity of money demanded, $M^d = P \bullet D(Y, i)$ on the right-hand side. Thus, equation (11.5) still holds with M^s and P twice as high as they were initially.

Consider now how the doubling of M^s affects the labour market described in Figure 9.13. Since the technology level, A, has not changed, the real wage rate, w/P, and labour input, L, do not change. Therefore, the price level, P, is twice as high, and w/P is unchanged. We conclude that, in general equilibrium, the nominal wage rate, w, has to double.

Consider next how the doubling of M^s affects the rental market for capital services, described in Figure 10.5. As in the labour market, the unchanged technology level, A, means that the real rental price, R/P, and the quantity of capital services, κK, do not change. The fixed κK corresponds to a given capital stock, K, and an unchanged capital utilization rate, κ. Thus, the price level, P, is twice as high and R/P is unchanged. We must have, in general equilibrium, that the nominal rental price, R, doubles.

Remember from Chapter 10 that the interest rate, i, has to equal the rate of return on ownership of capital:

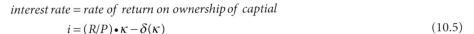

$$interest\ rate = rate\ of\ return\ on\ ownership\ of\ captial$$
$$i = (R/P) \bullet \kappa - \delta(\kappa) \tag{10.5}$$

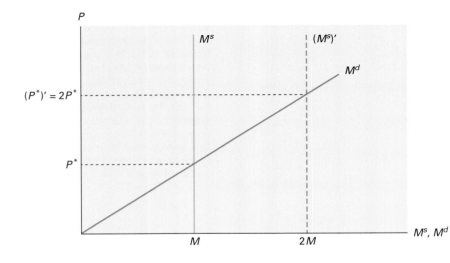

Figure 11.2 An increase in the nominal quantity of money

The nominal demand for money, M^d, shown by the upward-sloping line, is the same as in Figure 11.1. The nominal quantity of money supplied, M^s, doubles from M (the vertical solid line) to $2M$ (the vertical dashed line). Therefore, the equilibrium price level doubles, on the vertical axis, from P^* to $(P^*)' = 2P^*$.

Since the doubling of M^s does not change the real rental price, R/P, and the capital utilization rate, κ, the rate of return on ownership of capital does not change on the right-hand side of equation (10.5). Therefore, the interest rate, i, is also unchanged on the left-hand side of the equation. This result is important – in general equilibrium, with full adjustment of the price level, P, a one-time increase in the nominal quantity of money supplied, M^s, does not affect the interest rate.

Recall that real GDP, Y, is given from the production function used in Chapter 10:

$$Y = A \bullet F(\kappa K, L) \tag{10.1}$$

The technology level, A, is fixed, and we have shown that a doubling of M^s does not affect the quantities of capital services, κK, and labour, L. Therefore, equation (10.1) implies that Y is unchanged. In other words, in general equilibrium, a one-time increase in the nominal quantity of money supplied, M^s, does not affect real GDP.

We have verified that a doubling of M^s does not affect real GDP, Y, and the interest rate, i. These two variables are the determinants of real money demand, given by $D(Y, i)$ in equation (11.3). This result validates our assumption in Figure 11.2 that the money-demand line, $M^d = P \bullet D(Y, i)$, does not shift when M^s doubles. We conclude that our previous result – a doubling of M^s leads to a doubling of the price level, P – is correct.

To sum up, a doubling of the nominal quantity of money supplied, M^s, leads to a doubling of all of the nominal prices – the price level, P; the nominal wage rate, w; and the nominal rental price, R. There are no changes in real money balances, M/P; the real wage rate, w/P; and the real rental price, R/P. We also conclude that the determinants of the real demand for money, $D(Y, i)$, remain the same – the increase in M^s has no effect on real GDP, Y, or the interest rate, i. Note, however, that nominal GDP equals PY. Since P doubles and Y is unchanged, nominal GDP doubles.

The analogous conclusions hold for a decrease in the nominal quantity of money supplied, M^s. If M^s halved, going from M to $M/2$, P would halve and real money balances, M/P, would again be unchanged. The nominal wage rate, w, and the nominal rental price, R, would halve, so that the real wage rate, w/P, and the real rental price, R/P, would stay the same. As before, the decrease in M^s has no effect on real GDP, Y. Hence, nominal GDP, PY, falls to half its initial value.

THE NEUTRALITY OF MONEY

The results in the previous section exhibit a property called the **neutrality of money**. One-time changes in the nominal quantity of money supplied, M^s, affect nominal variables but leave real variables unchanged. Money is neutral in the sense of not affecting real variables. The real variables include real GDP, Y; the real wage rate, w/P; the real rental price, R/P; and the quantity of real money balances, M/P. The interest rate, i, also does not change. We should think of i as a real variable because it governs intertemporal-substitution effects for consumption and work. In Chapter 12, which introduces inflation, we distinguish the nominal interest rate from the real interest rate.

Almost all economists accept the neutrality of money as a valid long-run proposition. That is, in the long run, an increase or decrease in the nominal quantity of money supplied, M^s, influences nominal variables but not real ones. However, many economists believe that money is not neutral in the short run. In the short run, increases in M^s are usually thought to increase real GDP, Y, whereas decreases in M^s are thought to decrease Y. The main source of the difference in conclusions involves the flexibility of nominal prices – notably, the price level, P, and the nominal wage rate, w. These nominal prices are thought to be flexible up or down in the long run in response to increases or decreases in M^s. However, P and w are often viewed as less flexible in the short run, especially when decreases in M^s mean that P and w have to decrease. In some models, the assumption of price flexibility is replaced by an assumption that P or w is *sticky* in the short run. We introduce sticky prices and sticky wages to the equilibrium business-cycle model in Chapter 17.

A CHANGE IN THE DEMAND FOR MONEY

We mentioned that financial innovations could affect the real demand for money. To explore these effects, suppose that the nominal demand for money is again given initially by:

$$M^d = P \cdot D(Y, i) \qquad (11.2)$$

where $D(Y, i)$ is the real demand for money. As before, the nominal money demand, M^d, is graphed versus the price level, P, as the upward-sloping solid line in Figure 11.3.

Suppose now that an improvement in the technology for making financial transactions – perhaps increased use of credit cards or ATM machines – decreases the real demand for money to $[D(Y, i)]'$, so that the nominal demand becomes:

$$(M^d)' = P \cdot [D(Y, i)]'$$

We graph the new nominal money demand, $(M^d)'$, as the upward-sloping dashed line in Figure 11.3. At any price level, P, the nominal quantity of money demanded is smaller along the dashed line than along the solid line.

We assume that the nominal quantity of money supplied, M^s, is fixed at M, shown by the vertical line in Figure 11.3. Therefore, the initial equilibrium price level is P^* on the vertical axis. At this point, M^s equals the nominal quantity of money demanded, M^d. After the fall in the real demand for money, the equilibrium price level is $(P^*)'$ on the vertical axis. At this point, M^s equals the new nominal quantity of money demanded, $(M^d)'$. Note that the decrease in the real demand for money leads to a higher price level; that is, $(P^*)'$ is above P^*. (As before, we assume that the price level adjusts rapidly to its equilibrium level.)

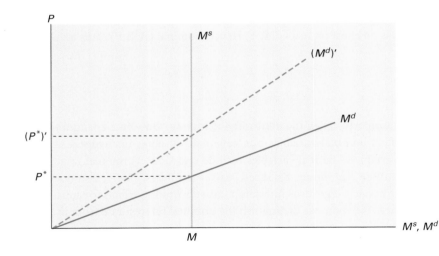

Figure 11.3 A change in the demand for money

The nominal demand for money is initially given by the upward-sloping solid line, $M^d = P \cdot D(Y, i)$. We consider a decrease in the real demand for money, $D(Y, i)$. This real demand is lower along the dashed upward-sloping dashed line, $(M^d)'$, than along the upward-sloping solid line. The nominal quantity of money supplied, M^s, is the constant M, shown by the vertical line. The decrease in the real demand for money raises the equilibrium price level from P^* to $(P^*)'$ on the vertical axis.

A decrease in the real demand for money is similar to an increase in the nominal quantity of money supplied, M^s, in that the price level, P, rises in each case. However, one difference is that a change in M^s is fully neutral, whereas a change in the real demand for money is not fully neutral. To see why, note that the decrease in the real demand for money led to a rise in P, while M^s was fixed at M. Therefore, the real quantity of money, M/P, decreased. In addition, the change in transactions technology that led to the decline in the real demand for money – such as expanded use of credit cards or ATM machines – would itself have real effects. For example, the resources used up in transaction costs would change. However, in most cases, the effects on macroeconomic variables, such as real GDP, will be small enough to neglect.

THE CYCLICAL BEHAVIOUR OF THE PRICE LEVEL

In Chapters 9 and 10, we used our equilibrium business-cycle model to study how shifts to the technology level, A, create economic fluctuations. Now, we can use our analysis of the demand for money to determine how the price level, P, moves during economic fluctuations.

Recall that the nominal demand for money is given by:

$$M^d = P \bullet D(Y, i) \tag{11.2}$$

Think about a recession, in which real GDP, Y, falls. The decline in Y reduces the real quantity of money demanded, given by $D(Y, i)$ on the right-hand side of equation (11.2). However, we also found that the interest rate, i, tends to fall in a recession. The decrease in i raises the real quantity of money demanded, $D(Y, i)$. The overall change depends on the magnitudes of the decreases in Y and i, and on the sensitivity of $D(Y, i)$ to Y and i. Typical estimates indicate that the real quantity of money demanded, $D(Y, i)$, declines overall in this situation; the fall in i tends to be small, and $D(Y, i)$ is not very responsive to changes in i. Therefore, we assume that, in a recession, the real quantity of money demanded, given by $D(Y, i)$, decreases overall.

Economics in Practice
The quantity theory of money

The **quantity theory of money** refers to a body of thinking about the relation between money and prices. This viewpoint goes back hundreds of years, with some of the more important statements coming from David Hume, Henry Thornton and Irving Fisher.[5] There are two common elements in these analyses. First, increases in the nominal quantity of money raise the general level of prices. Second, as an empirical matter, movements in the nominal quantity of money account for the bulk of long-run changes in the price level.

Some economists have refined the quantity theory to apply to changes in the nominal quantity of money measured relative to changes in the quantity of goods and services – real GDP – on which people have spent their money. However, real GDP is only one variable that affects the real demand for money. Therefore, quantity theorists went further to argue that prices rose only when the nominal quantity of money expanded in relation to the real money balances that people wanted to hold. Hence, most variations in the price level would reflect movements in the nominal quantity of money if the fluctuations in this quantity were much greater than the fluctuations in the real quantity of money demanded. Milton Friedman (1956) stressed the stability of the real demand for money as the hallmark of a modern quantity theorist.

Sometimes economists identify the quantity theory of money with the proposition that changes in the nominal quantity of money are neutral. This idea corresponds to our previous result that changes in nominal money have no effects on real variables. Many quantity theorists regard this result as valid in the long run but not for short-run variations in the nominal quantity of money. Thus, in some versions of the quantity theory, changes in the nominal quantity of money have temporary effects on real variables, such as real GDP.

We can use Figure 11.3 to determine the effect of an economic contraction on the price level, P. Recall that this figure applied to a decrease in the real demand for money, $D(Y, i)$, caused by a change in transactions technology. However, the same construction applies if $D(Y, i)$ decreases for other reasons. In the present case, the real quantity of money demanded, $D(Y, i)$, falls overall because of the decreases in real GDP, Y, and the interest rate, i. Thus, we can use Figure 11.3 to study how the price level, P, changes during a recession.

We see from Figure 11.3 that, for a given nominal quantity of money supplied, M^s, the decrease in the real quantity of money demanded, $D(Y, i)$, raises the price level, P. Hence, in a recession, a relatively high P tends to accompany the

[5]See Hume's essay, 'Of Money', in Eugene Rotwein (1970), Thornton (1802) and Fisher (1926).

decrease in real GDP, Y. If we had done the analysis in reverse – to consider a boom in which the real quantity of money demanded, $D(Y, i)$, increased – we would get the opposite conclusion. That is, the price level, P, would fall. Thus, our model has a new prediction: if the nominal quantity of money supplied, M^s, does not vary, the price level, P, will be relatively high in recessions and relatively low in booms. That is, we predict that P will be countercyclical.[6]

The result that the price level, P, is countercyclical may be counterintuitive. One might guess that, since real GDP is low in a recession, the low real income would lead to low consumer demand and tend thereby to reduce P. However, in our equilibrium business-cycle model, the underlying shocks come from the supply side, not the demand side. For example, a low technology level, A – the source of a recession in the model – means that goods and services are in low supply. When looked at this way, it makes sense that P would tend to be high in a recession.

Now, we will consider how the model's predictions about the price level, P, match up with data in the Eurozone. We measure P by the deflator for the gross domestic product. We calculate the cyclical part of P by using the method applied to real GDP in Figure 9.2. The result is the light blue graph in Figure 11.4. This graph shows the proportionate deviation of P from its trend. We also show as the dark blue graph the cyclical part of real GDP (from Figure 9.3). We can see from Figure 11.4 that P typically fluctuates in the direction opposite to real GDP except for the years between 2007 and 2008. Therefore, normally the price level is high – relative to trend – in recessions, and low – relative to trend – in booms, as predicted by our model. In the case of the Great Recession, the underlying disturbances are likely to be in the form of demand shocks such that the correlation of the cyclical part of the GDP deflator with the cyclical part of real GDP became positive during this period. The main difference in this period is the high frequency of banking panics, which tended to reduce broad monetary aggregates, such as M1, and the price level, along with output. This effect was also important from 1931 to 1934, during the Great Depression.

Figure 11.4 Cyclical behaviour of Eurozone real GDP and the price level

The dark blue graph is the deviation of real GDP from its trend. The light blue graph is the deviation of the GDP deflator from its trend. These deviations are measured in a proportionate sense. The GDP deflator is overall acyclical and is less variable than real GDP. If we remove the data in 2007–08, the beginning of the Great Recession, the correlation of the cyclical part of the GDP deflator with the cyclical part of real GDP was −0.65.

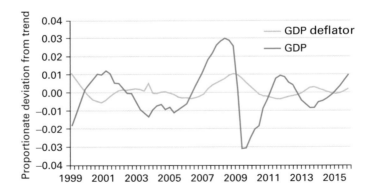

PRICE-LEVEL TARGETING AND ENDOGENOUS MONEY

A key assumption in our model is that the nominal quantity of money supplied, M^s, is independent of the nominal demand for money, $M^d = P \cdot D(Y, i)$. In other words, the monetary authority decides how much nominal money, M, to provide and sticks with this quantity no matter what happens to nominal money demand, M^d. A formal way to say this is that the money-supply function, given in our case by $M^s = M$, is independent of the money-demand function.

This formulation is useful for studying exogenous changes in the nominal quantity of money supplied, M^s. By exogenous, we mean that the change comes from out of the blue, or at least from outside of the model. The trouble is that most changes in money supply are not like this in the real world. The head of the central bank does not just wake up in

---

[6]This result was first emphasized by Finn Kydland and Edward Prescott (1990).

the morning and happen to think that it would be nice if the nominal quantity of money were higher or lower by 10%. Usually, the changes in M^s are responses to economic events; the changes happen because the monetary authority is trying to accomplish some important economic objective. One common objective is to achieve a desired or *target* value of the price level, P. Related objectives, considered in later chapters, are to target the inflation rate and the nominal interest rate.

When the monetary authority seeks to attain a specified price level, P, it typically has to adjust the nominal quantity of money, M, in response to changes in the nominal quantity demanded, M^d. Another way to say this is that M will be endogenous, or determined within the model. We therefore have a setting of **endogenous money**. To see how this works, we now assume that the monetary authority wants the price level, P, to equal a target level, which we call $\bar{P}$. This objective is called **price-level targeting**.

For present purposes, we assume that the monetary authority can determine the path of the nominal quantity of money, M, possibly subject to minor random errors. This assumption is reasonable in our model because we are taking a narrow view of money as currency. However, the assumption would be less satisfactory if we took a broader view of M; for example, to add the deposit accounts included in broader monetary aggregates, such as M1 and M2. Another reasonable assumption is that the monetary authority can control a monetary aggregate that is slightly broader than currency: the monetary base. This aggregate adds to total currency outstanding the reserves of financial institutions held at the central bank.

Since we assume that the monetary authority has no technical problems in controlling the quantity of nominal money, the changes in M will reflect only intentional policy, not technical errors. In particular, changes in M will occur because the underlying objective of price-level targeting, $P = \bar{P}$, dictates changes in M.

We still have equality at every point in time between the nominal quantity of money, M, and the nominal quantity demanded, M^d:

$$M^d = P \bullet D(Y, i) \tag{11.6}$$

Before, we thought of M as equal to an arbitrary quantity supplied, M^s. Now, we will let M be endogenous – determined by equation (11.6) – and assume that the monetary authority allows M to adjust to achieve its price-level target:

$$P = \bar{P} \tag{11.7}$$

If we substitute $P = \bar{P}$ from equation (11.7) into equation (11.6), we get a condition for determining the nominal quantity of money:

Key equation (endogenous determination of money):

$$M = \bar{P} \bullet D(Y, i)$$

nominal quantity of money = price-level target • real quantity of money demanded

$$\tag{11.8}$$

The idea in equation (11.8) is that the price level, P, can be constant at its target value $\bar{P}$ only if the nominal quantity of money, M, varies on the left-hand side to compensate for changes in the real quantity of money demanded, $D(Y, i)$, on the right-hand side. For example, if $D(Y, i)$ doubles but M stays the same, P would have to fall to satisfy equation (11.6). Alternatively, if $D(Y, i)$ stays the same but M doubles, P would have to rise. To keep P fixed at $\bar{P}$, proportionate changes in the real quantity of money demanded, $D(Y, i)$, have to be matched by equal proportionate changes in M. This condition tells us how price-level targeting determines the behaviour of M in equation (11.8). The general point is that the nominal quantity of money, M, will be endogenous and will react to changes in variables that affect the real quantity of money demanded, $D(Y, i)$. We now apply this analysis to determine M in three settings: long-term growth, cyclical fluctuations and seasonal movements.

Trend growth of money

To determine the trend in the nominal quantity of money, M, we have to allow for a long-run trend in the real quantity of money demanded, $D(Y, i)$, on the right-hand side of equation (11.8). The most important source of this trend is long-run economic growth; that is, an upward trend in real GDP, Y. We can use the Solow growth model from Chapter 5 to understand this trend. In the long-run or steady-state situation, real GDP, Y, grows at a constant rate due to technological progress and population growth.[7] This growth of Y produces a continuing rise in the real quantity of money demanded, $D(Y, i)$. If we think of money as currency, the empirical estimates of money demand suggest that the growth rate of $D(Y, i)$ will be about the same as the growth rate of Y.[8]

Consider our condition for determining the nominal quantity of money, M:

$$M = \bar{P} \bullet D(Y, i) \tag{11.8}$$

Since the price-level target, $\bar{P}$, is constant, continuing growth of the real quantity of money demanded, $D(Y, i)$, on the right-hand side requires M to grow at the same rate on the left-hand side. Since $D(Y, i)$ grows at the same rate as real GDP, Y, we conclude that M must grow at the same rate as Y. Thereby, the growth rate of the nominal quantity of money, M, matches the growth rate of the real quantity demanded, $D(Y, i)$, and allows the price level, P, to remain constant at its target level, $\bar{P}$.

The important conclusion is that a growing economy will have growth in its nominal quantity of money, M, assuming that the monetary authority seeks to stabilize the price level, P. This result accords with data considered in Chapter 12. We shall see there that growing M applies to almost all countries in the world. However, we also allow in Chapter 12 for inflation; that is, for a continual upward movement in P.

Cyclical behaviour of money

To study the cyclical behaviour of money, we again use the condition for determining the nominal quantity of money, M:

$$M = \bar{P} \bullet D(Y, i) \tag{11.8}$$

We know that the real quantity of money demanded, $D(Y, i)$, is high in a boom and low in a recession; this is because a change in real GDP, Y, moves $D(Y, i)$ in the same direction. (We assume that this effect dominates the impact from a change in the interest rate, i.) We also know that, if M did not fluctuate, the price level, P, would fall in a boom and rise in a recession. That is, P would be countercyclical – low relative to trend in booms and high relative to trend in recessions.

If the monetary authority wants to keep the price level, P, fixed at its target, $\bar{P}$, during economic fluctuations, it has to introduce a cyclical pattern into the nominal quantity of money, M. In particular, in equation (11.8), the cyclical fluctuations in M on the left-hand side have to match the cyclical fluctuations in the real quantity of money demanded, $D(Y, i)$, on the right-hand side. Thus, M will have to rise in a boom (along with the rise in $D[Y, i]$) and fall in a recession (along with the fall in $D[Y, i]$). In other words, M should be procyclical.

Recall that we found that the price level, P, is countercyclical in the data. This pattern fits with our equilibrium business-cycle model when we assumed that the nominal quantity of money, M, did not vary over the business cycle. In other words, the monetary authority (e.g., the European Central Bank) has not pursued a monetary policy that completely eliminated the countercyclical behaviour of P: M has not been sufficiently procyclical to avoid a counter-cyclical price level. Nevertheless, we would like to know whether the monetary authority has followed a policy that is somewhat procyclical; that is, whether nominal money, M, is high relative to trend during booms and low relative to trend during recessions. If so, this policy would have moderated the countercyclical pattern for P.

Empirically, the nominal quantity of money, M, is weakly procyclical. This weak procyclical pattern in monetary aggregates is consistent with our finding that the price level, P, is countercyclical. The monetary aggregates would have had to be more procyclical to eliminate the countercyclical pattern in P.

---

[7] The interest rate, i, will be constant in this situation, because the marginal product of capital, MPK, will not be changing. Therefore, at least if we neglect financial innovations, the real quantity of money demanded, $D(Y, i)$, will be changing only because of the growth of real GDP, Y.
[8] With economies of scale in money demand, the real quantity of money demanded would grow at a slower rate than real GDP. As discussed before, the empirical evidence suggests that these economies of scale are important for checkable deposits but not for currency. We are also neglecting the possibility that continuing financial innovations affect the real demand for money.

Seasonal variations in money

We have argued that, to achieve price-level stability, the monetary authority has to vary the nominal quantity of money, M, to match the changes in the real quantity demanded, $D(Y, i)$, that occur because of economic growth or fluctuations. An analogous argument applies to the variations in $D(Y, i)$ associated with the seasons.

Because the US dollar, being the dominant international reserve currency, has experienced a significant change in its seasonal variations, we discuss the US dollar currency here. Until the mid-1980s, the quantity of real currency held in December was about 2.6% higher than the average for the year, whereas the amount held in February was about 1.7% lower than average. If the monetary authority had kept the nominal quantity of currency, M, constant over the year, the price level, P, would have had the reverse seasonal pattern – low in December and high in February. To see how the monetary authority avoided this outcome, we can again use our condition for determining the nominal quantity of money, M:

$$M = \bar{P} \bullet D(Y, i) \tag{11.8}$$

To avoid a seasonal pattern in the price level, P, the Federal Reserve engineered a relatively high nominal quantity of currency, M, when the real quantity of money demanded, $D(Y, i)$, was high – for example, December – and a relatively low nominal quantity when $D(Y, i)$ was low – for example, February. Thus, the nominal quantity of currency, M, has a pronounced seasonal pattern, whereas the price level, P, does not have a substantial seasonal pattern. (That is, before seasonal adjustments, P has little seasonal variation.)

The seasonal variations in the real demand for US currency have declined since the 1990s. For example, the December excess of real currency over the average for the year was on average 2.6% from 1959 to 1984, but then increased to an average of 3.6% in the 1990s and declined to an average of 2.4% from 2000 to 2015. A study by the Federal Reserve and the US Treasury (Board of Governors of the Federal Reserve System, 2003) suggests that this change relates to the increased use of US currency in foreign countries. The foreign demand for US currency has less of a seasonal pattern than that found in domestic demand. Therefore, the full seasonal variation weakened when more of the currency was held by foreigners.

The pattern is different if we look at checkable deposits, the other main part of M1. The seasonal variations in the US real demand for checkable deposits declined after 1990 but have risen since the financial crisis. For example, the December excess of real checkable deposits over the average for the year was on average 3.2% from 1959 to 1990, then fell to an average of 2.0% from 1990 to 2008 and rose significantly from 2008 to 2015 to an average of 6.9%. The difference from currency probably arises because the foreign demand for US checkable deposits is not nearly as important as the foreign demand for US currency.

Summing Up

We extended our macroeconomic model to add another equilibrium condition: the nominal quantity of money supplied, M^s, equals the nominal quantity demanded, M^d. We then have a general-equilibrium model that determines the price level, P, the nominal wage rate, w, and the nominal rental price, R. The three nominal prices are flexible and adjust rapidly to ensure that three equilibrium conditions hold: $M^s = M^d$, $L^s = L^d$ (clearing of the labour market), and $(\kappa K)^s = (\kappa K)^d$ (clearing of the market for capital services).

We extended the microeconomic foundations of the model to consider the determinants of the nominal demand for money, $M^d = P \bullet D(Y, i)$, where the function $D(Y, i)$ gives the quantity of money demanded in real terms, M^d/P. The real quantity demanded, $D(Y, i)$, rises with real GDP, Y, and falls with the interest rate, i. Shifts in financial technology also affect $D(Y, i)$.

An increase in the nominal quantity of money supplied, M^s, raises nominal variables – such as the price level, P; the nominal wage rate, w; and the nominal rental price, R – in the same proportion. Real variables – such as w/P, R/P, and real GDP, Y – do not change. This property is called neutrality of money. An increase in the real quantity of money demanded, $D(Y, i)$, lowers P if M^s is fixed. Therefore, the model predicts that P would be countercyclical, as found in the data.

If the monetary authority seeks to keep the price level, P, equal to a fixed target, $\bar{P}$, the nominal quantity of money, M, becomes endogenous. In particular, shifts in the real quantity of money demanded, $D(Y, i)$, affect M in the same direction. We applied this result in three contexts: long-term growth, economic fluctuations and seasonal movements. With long-term growth in real GDP, M is predicted to trend upward. In a cyclical context, M has to be procyclical to avoid countercyclical fluctuations in the price level, P. However, empirically, M has not been sufficiently procyclical to eliminate the countercyclical behaviour of P. In a seasonal setting, M would have to vary seasonally to avoid a seasonal pattern in P. We found evidence for this seasonal behaviour of M.

Key Terms and Concepts

barter	endogenous money	M1 M2	real demand for money
checkable deposits	fiat money	monetary aggregate	stores of value
commodity money	general equilibrium	monetary base	transaction costs
demand for money	high-powered money	neutrality of money	
economies of scale in cash	interest-bearing assets	price-level targeting	
management	legal tender	quantity theory of money	

Questions and Problems

A Review questions

1 Explain why it is important to distinguish between shifts in the nominal quantity of money, M, and shifts in the nominal demand for money, M^d. What association would we expect between the price level, P, and real GDP, Y, for periods in which both types of monetary shifts occurred?

2 Explain why a favourable shock to the production function tends to reduce the price level, P. How could the monetary authority prevent this fall in P?

3 What is the meaning of the term 'endogenous money'? Under what circumstances would endogenous money generate a positive association between nominal money, M, and real GDP, Y?

4 Consider the following changes and state whether the effect on the real quantity of money demanded is an increase, decrease, or no change:

a an increase in the nominal interest rate, i;

b an increase in real transaction costs;

c an increase in real GDP, Y, caused by a rise in per capita real GDP with population held constant;

d an increase in real GDP, Y, caused by a rise in population with per capita real GDP held constant;

e an increase in the price level, P.

5 What are the costs of transacting between money and alternative financial assets? You might make a list and include such items as the time spent going to the bank or waiting in line. How were these costs affected by the development of automatic teller machines (ATMs)?

6 Suppose that the nominal quantity of money, M, doubles once and for all.

a The rise in the price level, P, suggests that workers will be worse off. Is this correct?

b The rise in the nominal wage rate, w, suggests that workers will be better off. Is this correct?

c How do your results relate to the concept of the neutrality of money?

7 Economists who subscribe to the quantity theory of money believe that changes in the price level, P, are primarily the result of changes in the nominal quantity of money, M. Can this conclusion be based solely on theoretical reasoning?

B Problems for discussion

8 Shopping trips and the demand for money
Suppose that a worker has an annual income of €60 000. Assume that the worker receives wage payments once per month. The worker makes periodic shopping trips. During each trip, enough goods (e.g., groceries) are bought to last until the next trip.

a If the worker shops four times per month, what is the average money balance?

b What happens if the worker shops only twice per month?

c What is the general relation between the frequency of shopping trips and the demand for money?

d   Suppose that the cost of a shopping trip rises, perhaps because of an increase in the price of petrol. What would happen to the frequency of shopping trips? What would happen to the demand for money?

9   Denominations of currency

Consider how people divide their holdings of currency between large bills (say, €100 bills) versus small ones. How would the dollar proportion of currency held in large bills depend on the following:

a   the price level, P?

b   real per capita GDP?

c   population?

d   incentives to avoid records of payments; for example, for tax evasion or to disguise illegal activities, such as the drug trade?

10   Transaction costs and households' budget constraints

In our model, we neglected the resources that households use up in transaction costs. Suppose that these costs take the form of purchases of goods and services (such as fees paid to banks or brokers). Assume that real transaction costs decline because of the expansion of ATM machines.

a   How does this change show up in households' budget constraints?

b   What is the income effect on consumption and leisure?

c   Suppose that transaction costs represent the time required to go to a bank, rather than a purchase of goods and services. Is there a change in the results for questions a and b?

11   Transaction frequency and the demand for money

Suppose that a household's consumption expenditure is €60 000 per year and is financed by monthly withdrawals from a savings account.

a   Show on a graph the pattern of the household's money holding over a year. What is the average money balance? Should we identify this average balance with the quantity of money demanded in our model?

b   Suppose now that the frequency of withdrawals from the savings account rises to two per month. What happens to the average money balance?

c   Return to question a, but assume now that consumption expenditure is €120 000

per year. If withdrawals from the savings account are still made monthly, what is the average money balance? How does this average compare to the average in question a? Is it optimal for the frequency of withdrawals to remain the same when consumption expenditure increases? Explain.

12   A currency reform

Suppose that the government replaces the existing monetary unit with a new one. For example, Britain might shift from the old British pound to the new British pound, defined to equal 10 old pounds. People would be able to exchange their old currency for the new currency at the ratio of 10 to 1. Also, any contracts that were written in terms of old dollars are reinterpreted in the new British pounds at the ratio 10 to 1.

a   What happens to the price level, P, and the interest rate, i?

b   What happens to real GDP, Y; consumption, C; and labour, L?

c   Do the results exhibit the neutrality of money?

13   Velocity of money

The velocity of money is the ratio of the nominal volume of transactions – say, nominal GDP – divided by the nominal quantity of money. How is the velocity of money affected by:

a   an increase in the nominal interest rate, i?

b   an increase in real GDP, Y, caused by a rise in per capita real GDP with population held constant?

c   an increase in real GDP, Y, caused by a rise in population with per capita real GDP held constant?

d   an increase in the price level, P?

e   Why might nominal GDP not be the correct measure of transactions?

f   What do you predict happens to the velocity of money as an economy develops?

14   Effects of other variables on the demand for money

Assume given values of real GDP, Y; population; the nominal interest rate, i; and real transaction costs. If these variables are given, would you say that the following statements about the real demand for money are true, false or uncertain?

a   Agricultural societies have lower real money demand than industrial societies.

b Dictatorships have higher real money demand than democracies.

c Countries with a larger proportion of persons who are elderly have higher real money demand.

d Countries with a higher literacy rate have lower real money demand.

For empirical evidence on these effects, see the study by Lawrence Kenny (1991).

15 **The payments period and the demand for money**
Suppose again that a worker has an annual income of €60 000. Assume that the worker receives wage payments twice per month. The worker keeps all of these payments in money, does not use any alternative financial assets, and pays for consumption expenditure of €60 000 per year from money holdings.

a What is the worker's average money balance?

b What would the average money balance be if the worker were paid monthly, rather than twice per month?

c What is the general relation between the payments period and the demand for money?

d How do the results change if the worker puts part of their monthly wage payments into a savings account and then makes withdrawals as needed from this account?

12 Inflation, money growth and interest rates

In Chapter 11, we studied the determination of the price level, P. Now, we will consider inflation, by which we mean a continuing upward movement in P. Our previous analysis suggests possible sources of inflation. Start with the equality between the nominal quantity of money supplied, M^s, and the nominal quantity demanded:

$$M^s = P \bullet D(Y, i)$$
nominal quantity of money supplied = nominal quantity of money demanded (12.1)

We assume again that M^s is set exogenously by the monetary authority to equal a given quantity M. Therefore, we can write equation (11.5) as:

$$M = P \bullet D(Y, i)$$
nominal quantity of money = nominal quantity of money demanded (12.2)

We can divide by the price level, P, to express the equation in real terms:

$$M/P = D(Y, i)$$
real quantity of money = real quantity of money demanded (12.3)

Suppose that the real quantity of money demanded, $D(Y, i)$, decreases. The decrease in $D(Y, i)$ could reflect a financial innovation, such as increased use of credit cards, or a reduction in real gross domestic product (real GDP), Y. Since $D(Y, i)$ falls on the right-hand side of equation (12.2), M/P has to fall on the left-hand side. For given M, a fall in M/P requires P to increase. Therefore, it seems that declines in the real quantity of money demanded could be sources of inflation.

Notice, however, that each decrease in the real quantity of money demanded, $D(Y, i)$, creates a single increase in P, rather than a continuing series of increases in P. To generate inflation along these lines, we would need a succession of reductions in $D(Y, i)$. Although theoretically possible, this pattern is not realistic. Most countries experience long-term increases in real GDP, Y, which continually raise $D(Y, i)$ on the right-hand side of equation (12.2). Therefore, M/P trends upward on the left-hand side of the equation, and P would trend downward if M did not change. Thus, we cannot explain inflation this way.

Look again at equation (12.2). Since we are ruling out a continuing series of decreases in the real quantity of money demanded as the cause of inflation, we are left with only one other possible explanation. The nominal quantity of money, M, must continually increase in order for P to rise continually. Our analysis from Chapter 11 already noted a link between increases in the nominal quantity of money, M, and expansions of the price level, P. Empirically, it is clear that M – measured as currency or as broader aggregates such as M1 – typically grows over time. Moreover, the **money growth rate** – the rate at which M is increasing – varies substantially across countries and over time. Therefore, variations in money-growth rates are good candidates for explaining inflation. To assess this linkage, we begin by considering international data on inflation and money growth.

Cross-country data on inflation and money growth

Table 12.1 shows inflation rates and money growth rates for 57 countries with available data starting in 1960 to 2011. We measure the price level, P, by the consumer price index (CPI). We use the CPI, rather than the GDP deflator, because of data availability. However, results with the GDP deflator are similar for countries that have these data.

The inflation rate, shown in column 2 of Table 12.1, is the annual growth rate of the price level, P, starting from 1960 to 2011. Due to data availability, the countries included in the table are those that have at least 15 years of available data. The years for which data are available are shown in column 1 of the table. The countries appear in descending order of the inflation rate. Column 3 shows the growth rate of nominal money, M, defined as M1. Column 4 shows the difference between the growth rate of currency and the inflation rate. This difference tells us the growth rate of real money; that is, of M/P. Column 5 has the growth rate of real GDP.

- The inflation rate was greater than zero for all countries from 1960 to 2011. That is, all countries had some degree of inflation. Falling prices – called **deflation** – did not apply to any country, at least in terms of the overall experience since 1960. The lowest inflation rate was 1.7% per year, for Singapore from 1991 to 2011. Japan has experienced deflation over the period from 2000 to 2013 at an average rate of −0.14%; however, in 2014, prices in Japan were again rising.
- The growth rate of nominal currency (column 3) was greater than zero for all countries.
- The median inflation rate was 7.3% per year, with 23 countries exceeding 10%. For the growth rate of nominal currency, the median was 13.6% per year, with 30 countries above 10%.
- There is a broad cross-sectional range for the inflation rates and the growth rates of money. The inflation rates varied from 83% for Brazil to 1.7% for Singapore. The growth rates of currency varied from 87% for Brazil to 4.6% for Luxembourg and 5.2% for the United States.
- In most countries, the growth rate of nominal currency, M, exceeded the growth rate of prices, P (the inflation rate). Therefore, the growth rate of real money balances, M/P, shown in column 4, was greater than zero in most countries. The median growth rate of real currency from 1960 to 2011 was 4.6% per year.

Table 12.1 Inflation rates and money growth rates for 57 countries

Country	Years (1)	Inflation rate (2)	Growth rate of money (3)	Growth rate of real money (4)	Growth rate of real GDP (5)
Brazil	1980–2011	0.852	0.871	0.018	0.025
Ukraine	1992–2011	0.535	0.505	−0.029	−0.009
Bolivia	1977–2011	0.406	0.452	0.046	0.024
Uruguay	1972–2011	0.327	0.336	0.009	0.026
Turkey	1960–2011	0.279	0.319	0.041	0.045
Bulgaria	1995–2011	0.260	0.306	0.046	0.024
Israel	1981–2011	0.229	0.304	0.075	0.041
Mexico	1977–2011	0.228	0.273	0.045	0.029
Mongolia	1992–2011	0.201	0.286	0.084	0.052
Russia	1995–2011	0.178	0.269	0.091	0.037
Sao Tome and Principe	1996–2011	0.172	0.214	0.042	0.042
Tanzania	1967–2011	0.155	0.192	0.036	0.042
Iceland	1960–2011	0.153	0.210	0.058	0.036
Colombia	1960–2011	0.147	0.191	0.044	0.041

Table 12.1 *Continued*

Moldova	1994–2011	0.132	0.206	0.074	0.025
Poland	1990–2011	0.129	0.166	0.037	0.038
Paraguay	1985–2011	0.128	0.190	0.063	0.030
Costa Rica	1987–2011	0.126	0.157	0.031	0.046
Hungary	1990–2011	0.115	0.126	0.011	0.011
Portugal	1979–2011	0.114	0.141	0.028	0.031
Honduras	1980–2011	0.104	0.136	0.032	0.032
Swaziland	1974–2011	0.102	0.139	0.037	0.041
Indonesia	1990–2011	0.101	0.163	0.062	0.047
Estonia	1993–2010	0.089	0.152	0.063	0.039
Spain	1962–1998	0.088	0.126	0.039	0.037
South Africa	1965–2011	0.087	0.139	0.051	0.028
Botswana	1994–2011	0.083	0.141	0.059	0.054
South Korea	1966–2011	0.076	0.192	0.116	0.072
India	1960–2011	0.073	0.126	0.053	0.051
Croatia	1993–2011	0.072	0.152	0.080	0.030
New Zealand	1965–2011	0.063	0.082	0.019	0.022
Trinidad and Tobago	1991–2011	0.061	0.136	0.075	0.048
France	1977–1998	0.051	0.057	0.006	0.021
Australia	1960–2011	0.050	0.084	0.034	0.035
Denmark	1970–2011	0.048	0.087	0.039	0.018
Czech Republic	1993–2011	0.043	0.094	0.051	0.030
Luxembourg	1974–1997	0.043	0.046	0.002	0.035
Austria	1963–1997	0.041	0.068	0.027	0.032
Canada	1960–2011	0.040	0.080	0.040	0.033
United States	1960–2011	0.040	0.052	0.012	0.030
Jordan	1990–2011	0.038	0.077	0.039	0.052
Malaysia	1969–2011	0.036	0.117	0.081	0.065
Qatar	1982–2011	0.034	0.106	0.072	0.076
Japan	1960–2011	0.033	0.090	0.058	0.040
Lithuania	1996–2011	0.033	0.144	0.111	0.044
St. Kitts and Nevis	1984–2011	0.031	0.111	0.079	0.038
Cabo Verde	1995–2011	0.030	0.074	0.043	0.065
St. Lucia	1984–2011	0.029	0.090	0.061	0.036
Switzerland	1960–2011	0.028	0.066	0.038	0.022
United Kingdom	1988–2011	0.028	0.093	0.065	0.020
St. Vincent and the Grenadines	1984–2011	0.028	0.079	0.052	0.036
Grenada	1984–2011	0.025	0.078	0.052	0.033
Dominica	1984–2011	0.025	0.068	0.043	0.028
Malta	1980–2007	0.025	0.069	0.044	0.037
Norway	1992–2011	0.020	0.078	0.058	0.024
Saudi Arabia	1993–2011	0.020	0.102	0.082	0.030
Singapore	1991–2011	0.017	0.104	0.086	0.061

Figure 12.1 Inflation rate and growth rate of nominal currency for 57 countries, 1960–2011

This graph uses the data from Table 12.1. The vertical axis plots the inflation rate from based on consumer price indices. The horizontal axis plots the growth rate of nominal money. The two variables have a strong positive association; the correlation is 0.92. The slope of the relation is close to 1.0; that is, an increase in the growth rate of nominal currency by 1% per year is associated with an increase in the inflation rate by about 1% per year.

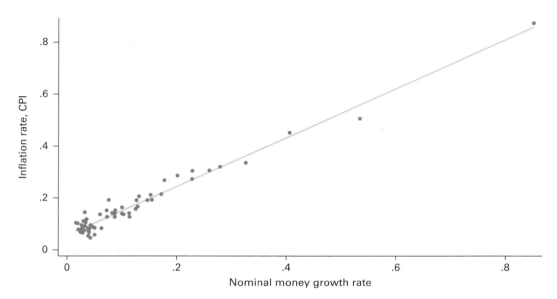

- To understand inflation, the most important observation from the cross-country data is the strong positive association between the inflation rate and the growth rate of nominal currency. Figure 12.1 displays this relationship using data from 1960 to 2011. The vertical axis plots a country's inflation rate (column 2 of the table), and the horizontal axis plots the growth rate of currency (column 3). The graph shows that a country with a great deal of inflation also had a high money growth rate; the correlation between the two variables is remarkably high, at 0.92. The slope is close to 1.0, so that an increase in the growth rate of nominal currency by 1% per year is associated with an increase in the inflation rate by around 1% per year. This strong association does not, however, tell us the direction of causation between inflation and money growth. That is, we cannot say whether a country had a high inflation rate because it had a high money growth rate, or vice versa. However, we can be sure that a country cannot have a high inflation rate over 40 years unless it also has a high money growth rate.

One lesson from the cross-country data is that, to understand inflation, we have to include money growth as a central part of the analysis. That is, we have to take seriously Milton Friedman's (1968b, p. 29) famous dictum: 'Inflation is always and everywhere a monetary phenomenon'. We will now extend our equilibrium business-cycle model to allow for inflation and money growth.

Inflation and interest rates

We now begin to incorporate inflation into our equilibrium business-cycle model. We will start by considering actual and expected inflation rates.

ACTUAL AND EXPECTED INFLATION

Let the price level in year 1 be P_1 and that in year 2 be P_2. The change in the price level from year 1 to year 2 is $\Delta P_1 = P_2 - P_1$. Let π be the inflation rate. The inflation rate from year 1 to year 2, π_1, is the ratio of the change in the price level to the initial price level:

$$\pi_1 = (P_2 - P_1)/P_1$$
$$\pi_1 = \Delta P_1/P_1 \qquad (12.3)$$

For example, if $P_1 = 100$ and $P_2 = 105$, the inflation rate from year 1 to year 2 is:

$$\pi_1 = (105 - 100)/100$$
$$= 0.05 \text{ or } 5\% \text{ per year}$$

Table 12.1 showed that inflation rates, π, are typically greater than zero. Therefore, we usually consider cases where prices are rising, so that $P_2 > P_1$ and, hence, $\pi_1 > 0$. We can, however, study falling prices, where $P_2 < P_1$ and, hence, $\pi_1 < 0$. These cases are called *deflations*. Economists have become more interested in deflations because the recent experiences of a few countries, notably Japan, suggest that deflations may become empirically relevant in the future.

We can rearrange equation (12.3) to solve for year 2's price level, P_2. First, multiply through by P_1 to get:

$$\pi_1 \bullet P_1 = P_2 - P_1$$

Then, add P_1 to both sides, combine the two terms that have P_1 on the left, and swap the left- and right-hand sides to get:

$$P_2 = (1 + \pi_1) \bullet P_1 \qquad (12.4)$$

Over one year, the price level rises by the factor $1 + \pi_1$. If $P_1 = 100$ and $\pi_1 = 0.05$, then:

$$P_2 = (1.05) \bullet 100 = 105$$

In making choices, such as whether to consume this year or next year, households want to know how prices will change over time. Since the future is unknown, households have to form forecasts or **expectations of inflation.** Denote by π_1^e the expectation of the inflation rate π_1. If households know year 1's price level, P_1, equation (12.3) shows that the prediction for π_1 corresponds to a forecast of next year's price level, P_2.

Since future price levels are unknown, forecasts of inflation will be imperfect. Therefore, the actual inflation rate, π_1, will usually deviate from its expectation, π_1^e, and the forecast error – or **unexpected inflation** – will be nonzero. Sometimes unexpected inflation is greater than zero and sometimes it is less than zero. Although these errors are unavoidable, households try to keep the errors as small as possible. Therefore, they use available information on past inflation and other variables to avoid systematic mistakes. Expectations formed this way are called **rational expectations.**[1] This rationality implies that unexpected inflation would not exhibit a systematic pattern of errors over time. For example, if unexpected inflation is greater than zero this year, this mistake will be factored into the calculation for next year.

REAL AND NOMINAL INTEREST RATES

In previous chapters, we assumed that the inflation rate was zero. Therefore, we did not have to distinguish between the *real interest rate* and the *nominal interest rate*. Now, we make this distinction when the inflation rate is not zero.

Let i_1 be the interest rate on bonds in year 1. Suppose, for example, that $i_1 = 0.05$, or 5%, per year. If a household holds €1000 of bonds in year 1, how much in assets would the household have in year 2? First, the household still

[1] The idea of rational expectations comes from John Muth (1961). For applications to macroeconomics, see Robert Lucas (1977).

has the principal of €1000. Second, the household has interest income equal to €1000 • 0.05 = €50. Therefore, the total of assets in year 2 is:

$$principal(€1000) + interest(€50) = assets\,in\,year\,2(€1000 + €50)$$
$$= €1050$$

Now, we generalize to allow for any interest rate, i_1. The principal carried over to year 2 is still €1000. The interest income equals €1000 • i_1. Therefore, we have:

$$principal(€1000) + interest(€1000 • i_1) = assets\,in\,year\,2(€1000 + €1000 • i_1)$$
$$= €1000 • (1 + i_1)$$

Thus, the nominal value of assets held as bonds rises over the year by the factor $1 + i_1$. The interest rate i_1 is the **nominal interest rate** because i_1 determines the change over time in the nominal value of assets held as bonds.

We have learned how the household's nominal assets change over time. However, the household does not care about the nominal value of assets. What it cares about are the goods that can be bought with these assets; that is, the real value of assets. Thus, we have to figure out what happens over time to the real value of assets.

Suppose that the inflation rate is $\pi_1 = 0.01$, or 1%, per year, as shown in row 1 of Table 12.2. Equation (12.4) shows that the price level rises over one year by the factor $1 + \pi_1$. Thus, the price level increases from $P_1 = 100$ in year 1 to $P_2 = 100 • (1.01) = 101$ in year 2. These values appear in row 2 of the table. If the nominal interest rate is $i_1 = 0.05$, or 5%, per year, as in row 3 of Table 12.2, nominal assets still grow from €1000 in year 1 to €1050 in year 2, as shown in row 4.

What happens to real assets? In year 1, real assets are:

$$year\,1\,real\,assets = 1000 / 100 = 10\,goods$$

In year 2, real assets are:

$$year\,2\,real\,assets = 1050 / 101 = 10.4\,goods$$

(We rounded off the result to one digit to get 10.4 as an approximation.) These values appear in row 5 of Table 12.2. Real assets rose by the proportion:

$$(10.4 - 10) / 10$$
$$= 0.4 / 10$$
$$= 0.04$$

Define the **real interest rate** to be the rate at which the real value of assets held as bonds changes over time. Therefore, as shown in row 6, the real interest rate in this example is 0.04, or 4%, per year. Notice that the real interest rate, 4%, falls short of the nominal interest rate, 5%, by the inflation rate, 1%.

Table 12.2 Nominal and real interest rates

		Year 1	Year 2
(1)	Inflation rate	0.01	
(2)	Price level	100	101.0
(3)	Nominal interest rate	0.05	
(4)	Nominal assets	1000	1050.0
(5)	Real assets	10	10.4
(6)	Real interest rate	0.04	

Note: Lines 1 and 2 show the effect of the inflation rate on the price level. Lines 3 and 4 show the effect of the nominal interest rate on the change over time in the nominal value of assets. Lines 5 and 6 show the effects of the nominal interest rate and the inflation rate on the change over time in the real value of assets. The change in the real value of assets depends on the real interest rate, which equals the difference between the nominal interest rate and the inflation rate.

Now, we generalize to allow for any nominal interest rate, i_1, and inflation rate, π_1. Since the nominal interest rate is i_1, nominal assets rise by the factor $1 + i_1$:

$$nominal\,assets\,in\,year\,2 = (nominal\,assets\,in\,year\,1) \bullet (1 + i_1)$$

Since the inflation rate is π_1, the price level rises by the factor $1 + \pi_1$ (see equation [12.4]):

$$P_2 = P_1 \bullet (1 + \pi_1)$$

Since real assets are the ratio of nominal assets to the price level, we can get an expression for real assets by dividing the first equation by the second one:

$$\frac{nominal\,assets\,in\,year\,2}{P_2} = \left(\frac{nominal\,assets\,in\,year\,1}{P_1} \right) \bullet \frac{(1 + i_1)}{(1 + \pi_1)}$$

$$real\,assets\,in\,year\,2 = (real\,assets\,in\,year\,1) \bullet (1 + i_1) / (1 + \pi_1)$$

Thus, real assets rise by the factor $(1 + i_1)/(1 + \pi_1)$.

Since the real interest rate, denoted by r_1, is the rate at which assets held as bonds change in real value, we have:

$$(1 + r_1) = (1 + i_1) / (1 + \pi_1) \tag{12.5}$$

For the example in Table 12.2, we had:

$$1.04 \approx 1.05 / 1.01$$

so that the real interest rate was $r_1 \approx 0.04$.

In the general case, we can get a useful formula for the real interest rate, r_1, if we manipulate equation (12.5). Multiply through on both sides by $1 + \pi_1$ to get:

$$(1 + r_1) \bullet (1 + \pi_1) = 1 + i_1$$

If we multiply out the two terms on the left-hand side, we get:

$$1 + r_1 + \pi_1 + r_1 \bullet \pi_1 = 1 + i_1$$

If we cancel the '1' on each side and place all terms except for r_1 on the right-hand side, we get:

$$r_1 = i_1 - \pi_1 - r_1 \bullet \pi_1$$

The right-hand side has the cross term, $r_1 \bullet \pi_1$, which tends to be small; for example, if $r_1 = 0.04$ and $\pi_1 = 0.01$, the term is 0.0004. In fact, this cross term appears only because we allowed interest rates and inflation rates to be compounded just once per year. A more accurate procedure would be to compound these rates continuously. In that case, the cross term disappears, and we get the simpler formula for the real interest rate:

Key equation:

$$r_1 = i_1 - \pi_1 \tag{12.6}$$

Henceforth, we use equation (12.6) to compute the real interest rate.

THE REAL INTEREST RATE AND INTERTEMPORAL SUBSTITUTION

We discussed intertemporal-substitution effects on consumption in Chapter 8. A higher interest rate, i_1, motivated the household to reduce year 1's consumption, C_1, compared to year 2's, C_2. When the inflation rate, π_1, is not zero, it is the real interest rate, r_1, rather than the nominal rate, i_1, that matters for intertemporal substitution.

To see why, assume that i_1 is 5% per year and π_1 is 2% per year, so that r_1 is 3% per year. Suppose that the household reduces C_1 by one unit and thereby raises real assets held as bonds or capital by one unit. These extra real assets become 1.03 additional real assets in year 2 (because r_1 is 3%). Therefore, the household can raise C_2 by 1.03 units. Thus, one unit less of C_1 can be transformed into 1.03 units more of C_2. If r_1 rises, the incentive to defer consumption increases, and the household reduces C_1 and raises C_2.

The nominal interest rate, i_1, is not the right variable for intertemporal substitution. If i_1 is 5% per year, the household can reduce year 1's nominal spending on C_1 by €1.00 and raise year 2's nominal spending on C_2 by €1.05. However, the extra €1.05 of spending in year 2 buys only 1.03 additional units of goods (if the inflation rate is $\pi_1 =$ 2% per year). Thus, the correct variable for intertemporal substitution is the real interest rate, $r_1 = 3\%$ per year. The same conclusion holds for intertemporal-substitution effects on labour supply: the real interest rate, r_1, matters.

ACTUAL AND EXPECTED REAL INTEREST RATES

When we refer to bonds, we usually have in mind assets such as UK Treasury bills that specify in advance the nominal interest rate, i. For example, a newly issued three-month UK Treasury bill (a T-bill) guarantees the nominal interest rate when held for three months. The real interest rate on the T-bill depends on the inflation rate over the three months.

As an example, during year t, the real interest rate on a 3-month T-bill is:

$$r_t = i_t - \pi_t \tag{12.7}$$

We can think of i_t as the nominal interest rate on a three-month T-bill issued on 1 January of year t. The rate i_t is expressed at an annual rate, such as 0.02, or 2%, per year. The variable π_t is the inflation rate, also expressed at an annual rate, from January to April. The problem is that this inflation rate is unknown in January, when the household buys the T-bill. The real interest rate, r_t, becomes known only later, when π_t is observed.

Suppose that, in January, households expect the inflation rate from January to April to be π_t^e. This expected inflation rate determines the **expected real interest rate**, r_t^e, on the T-bill from equation (12.7):

$$r_t^e = i_t - \pi_t^e$$
$$\textit{expected real interest rate} = \textit{nominal interest rate} - \textit{expected inflation rate} \tag{12.8}$$

For example, if $i_t = 0.03$ per year and $\pi_t^e = 0.01$ per year, then $r_t^e = 0.02$ per year. Formally, the expected real interest rate is the expectation, formed at the beginning of year t, of the real interest rate, r_t, over a period such as the next three months.

When households choose today's consumption and labour supply, they know the expected real interest rate, r_t^e, not the actual rate, r_t. Thus, intertemporal-substitution effects depend on r_t^e, which we would like to measure. To do so, we have to calculate the expected inflation rate, π_t^e.

Measuring expected inflation

Economists have used three methods to measure the expected inflation rate:

1 Ask a sample of people about their expectations;
2 Use the hypothesis of rational expectations, which says that expectations correspond to optimal forecasts, given the available information; then use statistical techniques to gauge these optimal forecasts;
3 Use market data to infer expectations of inflation.

The main shortcoming of the first approach is that the sample may not be representative of the whole economy. Also, economists have better theories of how households take actions than of how they answer survey questions. Nevertheless, surveys can be useful, and we discuss applications to expected inflation in the next section.

The second approach, based on rational expectations, has produced both successes and failures. One challenge is to figure out what information households possess when they form expectations. Another issue is the choice among statistical models to generate forecasts of inflation.

The third approach has become especially useful since, in the 1980s and 1990s, the governments of many advanced countries began to issue **indexed bonds**. Unlike more familiar nominal bonds, which specify the nominal interest rate, indexed bonds prescribe the real interest rate. For example, a 10-year indexed bond adjusts nominal payouts of interest and principal in response to inflation to ensure the promised real rate of return over 10 years. We discuss later how to use these data to infer expected inflation rates, π_t^e.

Expected inflation and interest rates

A classic example of survey measure of expected inflation is the one initiated in 1946 by Joseph Livingston, a Philadelphia journalist in the United States. Therefore, we consider these data in this section. The survey asks around 50 economists for their forecasts of the US CPI 6 and 12 months in the future.[2] These forecasts allow us to construct expected inflation rates. The 6-month-ahead forecasts of inflation are shown as the dark blue graph in Figure 12.2. The figure also shows as the light blue graph the actual inflation rate over the previous 12 months. These inflation rates were known to the survey respondents when they made their forecasts.

Figure 12.2 shows that actual and expected inflation rates tended to move together from 1950 to 2015. Inflation rates were low from the mid-1950s to the mid-1960s, rose until the start of the 1980s, then fell sharply in the early 1980s. Inflation rates were low and fairly stable following the mid-1980s. In December 2015, the expected inflation rate for the next six months was 1.6%.

Figure 12.3 shows as the light blue graph the nominal interest rate, i_t, on three-month US Treasury bills. The dark blue graph is the expected real interest rate, r_t^e, calculated by subtracting the Livingston expected inflation rate, π_t^e, shown in Figure 12.2, from i_t:

$$r_t^e = i_t - \pi_t^e \tag{12.8}$$

The nominal interest rate, i_t, moved upward from the mid-1950s to the early 1980s. However, because the expected inflation rate, π_t^e, rose in a similar way, the expected real interest rate, r_t^e, did not have this upward trend.

Figure 12.2 Actual and expected inflation rates

The light blue graph shows the inflation rate over the prior 12 months, computed from the US consumer price index (CPI). The dark blue graph shows the expected CPI inflation rate. These expectations, formed six to eight months in advance, are from the Livingston survey, available from the Federal Reserve Bank of Philadelphia.

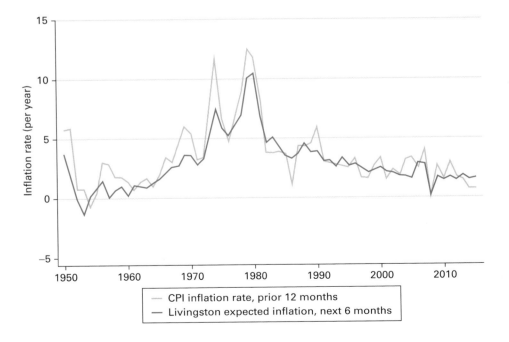

[2]For a discussion of the Livingston survey, see John Carlson (1977).

Figure 12.3 Nominal and expected real interest rates

The three-month US Treasury bill rate, shown as the light blue graph, is a nominal interest rate. We compute the expected real interest rate by subtracting the expected CPI inflation rate given by the Livingston survey measure shown in Figure 12.2. The resulting expected real interest rate is the dark blue graph.

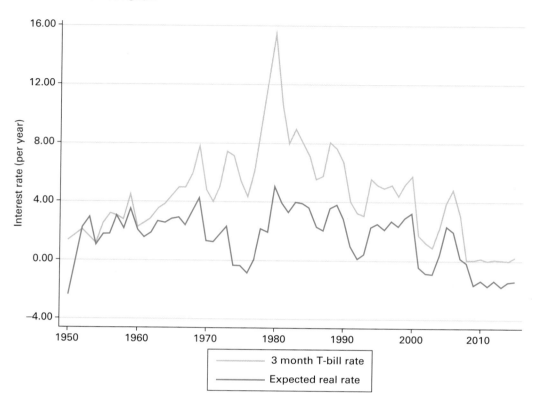

This tendency for i_t and π_t^e to move together is a typical long-run pattern. Therefore, we will want to explain this pattern with our model.

The expected real interest rate, r_t^e, was fairly stable at 2–3% from the mid-1950s until the early 1970s. Then r_t^e fell to near zero for much of the 1970s, before rising to around 4% in the 1980s. The rate r_t^e was, again, near zero in 1992–93, rose back to 3–4% for the rest of the 1990s, fell to near zero from mid-2001 to 2004, then rose to 2.4% in mid-2006. After the financial crisis, the nominal interest rate fell to around 0%, which induced, given positive inflation expectations, a negative expected real interest rate of around −1.5%.

Indexed bonds, real interest rates and expected inflation rates

More reliable measures of real interest rates and expected inflation rates became available in the 1980s and 1990s from data on indexed government bonds, which adjust nominal payouts of interest and principal for changes in consumer price indices. These bonds guarantee the real interest rate over the maturity of each issue. The UK government first issued these types of bonds in 1981. Subsequently, indexed bonds were issued by the governments of Australia (1985), Canada (1991), Iceland (1992), New Zealand (1995), Israel (1995), the United States (1997), Sweden (1997), France (1998), Greece and Italy (2003), and Japan (2004).

Since the real interest rates on indexed bonds are guaranteed, the expected real interest rate equals the actual rate. Figure 12.4 shows the real interest rate since 1998 for US indexed bonds of 30-year maturity (the black graph), since 2003 for 10-year maturity (the dark blue graph), and for 5-year maturity (the light blue graph). For the 10-year bonds, the real interest rate fluctuated around 2% from 2003 to 2010, falling into negative territory from 2011 to 2013 and returning to around 1% starting in 2013. This pattern is similar to that shown for the estimated expected real interest rate on three-month T-bills in Figure 12.3.

Figure 12.4 Real interest rates on indexed bonds

The graphs show the real interest rate on inflation-protected US Treasury bonds (indexed bonds). The light blue graph is for 5-year maturity, the dark blue graph for 10-year maturity, and the black graph for 30-year maturity. Data are from US Federal Reserve Board.

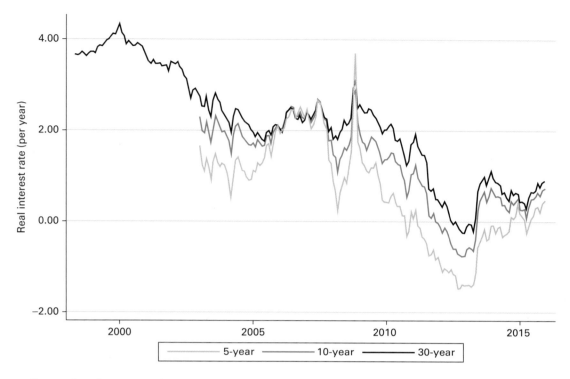

We will now show how to use the indexed-bonds data to measure the expected inflation rate. The basic principle that we use is that the prospective real returns on nominal bonds must be close to the guaranteed real returns on indexed bonds – otherwise, households would be unwilling to hold both types of bonds. We can use Figure 12.4 to get a time series on real interest rates, r_t, for indexed bonds of varying maturity. We can use data on nominal bonds to measure the nominal interest rate, i_t, for the same maturities. Remember that the expected real interest rate on nominal bonds is given from equation (12.8) by:

$$r_t^e\,(on\ nominal\ bonds) = i_t\,(on\ nominal\ bonds) - \pi_t^e$$

If the expected real interest rate on nominal bonds, r_t^e, equals the guaranteed real rate, r_t, on indexed bonds,[3] we can substitute r_t on the indexed bonds for r_t^e on the nominal bonds to get:

$$r_t^e\,(on\ indexed\ bonds) = i_t\,(on\ nominal\ bonds) - \pi_t^e$$

We can then rearrange terms to get the expected inflation rate, π_t^e, on the left-hand side:

$$\pi_t^e = i_t\,(on\ nominal\ bonds) - r_t^e\,(on\ indexed\ bonds) \tag{12.9}$$

Thus, we can calculate π_t^e from data on the interest rates on the right-hand side.

Figure 12.5 shows the expected inflation rate, π_t^e, computed from equation (12.9), for bonds of 10-year maturity (the dark blue graph), 30-year maturity (the black graph), and 5-year maturity (the light blue graph). In 2015, π_t^e was between 1% and 2%. These measures of π_t^e match up reasonably well with the 6-month-ahead expected inflation rate from the Livingston survey, shown by the dark blue graph in Figure 12.2. The values in Figure 12.5 are more variable – and probably more accurate – than the Livingston numbers. However, the Livingston survey has the advantage of being available since the late 1940s.

[3]Uncertainty about the real interest rate on nominal bonds means that the expected real interest rate on these bonds could differ from the guaranteed real interest rate on indexed bonds. Nevertheless, equation (12.9) provides a reasonable approximation to the expected inflation rate π_t^e.

Figure 12.5 Expected inflation rates, based on indexed bond yields

We compute expected CPI inflation rates by taking the nominal interest rate on nominal US Treasury bonds and subtracting the real interest rate on indexed US Treasury bonds (from Figure 12.4). See equation (12.9). The light blue graph is based on 5-year bonds, the dark blue graph on 10-year bonds and the black graph on 30-year bonds. Thus, the graphs measure expected CPI inflation rates over 5 years, 10 years and 30 years, respectively. The comparable measure for nominal yields on 30-year bonds is missing from February 2002 to February 2006.

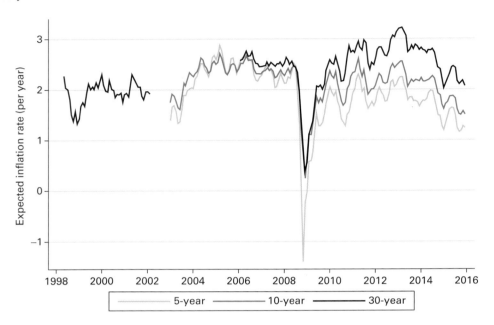

INTEREST RATES ON MONEY

Our analysis of nominal and real interest rates applies to money (currency), once we recognize that the nominal interest rate on money is zero. The real interest rate on money is:

$$real\ interest\ rate\ on\ money = nominal\ interest\ rate\ on\ money - \pi_t$$

$$real\ interest\ rate\ on\ money = -\pi_t$$

Thus, if π_t is greater than zero, the real interest rate on money is less than zero; the real value of money erodes over time because of increases in the price level.

Inflation in the equilibrium business-cycle model

We now extend the equilibrium business-cycle model to allow for inflation. In making this extension, we have two major objectives. First, we want to see how inflation affects our conclusions about the determination of real variables, including real GDP, consumption and investment, quantities of labour and capital services, the real wage rate and the real rental price. The real interest rate is another real variable that can be added to this list. Second, we want to understand the causes of inflation.

In the rest of this chapter, we study fully anticipated inflation, so that the inflation rate, π_t, equals the expected rate, π_t^e. This analysis applies to long-lasting changes in inflation, because households would adjust to a changed inflation environment and, therefore, factor these changes into their expectations. When the actual inflation rate equals the expected inflation rate, the real interest rate, r_t, equals the expected real interest rate, r_t^e. Chapter 16 considers unexpected inflation.

The cross-country data suggest that inflation is closely related to money growth. Therefore, we now extend the equilibrium business-cycle model to allow for money growth. In the simplest setting, the government prints new currency and gives it to people. In an imaginary story by Milton Friedman (1969, pp. 4–5), public officials stuff a helicopter full of paper money and fly around, dropping money randomly over the countryside. When people pick up the money, they receive a **transfer payment** from the government. Although the story is unrealistic, it provides a simple device for introducing new money into the economy. The important assumption is that the payments are **lump-sum transfers**, meaning that the amount received is independent of how much the household consumes and works, how much money the household holds, and so on. Therefore, we do not have to analyze how people adjust their behaviour to attract more transfers. We will find that more realistic forms of money creation yield similar results.

Now, we will consider various ways in which inflation affects real variables in the equilibrium business-cycle model.

INTERTEMPORAL-SUBSTITUTION EFFECTS

For a given nominal interest rate, i_t, a change in the inflation rate, π_t, affects the real interest rate, $r_t = i_t - \pi_t$. Moreover, we are assuming that the expected inflation rate, π_t^e, equals the actual rate, π_t, so that the expected real interest rate, r_t^e, equals the actual rate, r_t. We know that the expected real interest rate, r_t^e, has intertemporal-substitution effects on consumption and labour supply. Therefore, for given i_t, a change in π_t will have these intertemporal-substitution effects.

BONDS AND CAPITAL

Households still hold two forms of earning assets: bonds and ownership of capital. We know from Chapter 10 that the rates of return on these two assets have to be equal; otherwise, households would be unwilling to hold both types. Therefore, when the inflation rate, π, was zero, we got the condition:

$$i = (R/P) \bullet \kappa - \delta(\kappa)$$

rate of return on bonds = rate of return from owning capital   (10.5)

The rate of return on capital on the right-hand side, $(R/P) \bullet \kappa - \delta(\kappa)$, depends on the real rental price, R/P, the utilization rate for capital, κ, and the depreciation rate, $\delta(\kappa)$.

When the inflation rate, π, is nonzero, the expression $(R/P) \bullet \kappa - \delta(\kappa)$ on the right-hand side of equation (10.5) still gives the real rate of return from owning capital. (All parts of this expression are in real terms.) However, we have to modify the left-hand side of equation (10.5) to replace the nominal interest rate on bonds, i, by the real rate, r, to get:

Key equation (equality of real rates of return):

$$r = (R/P) \bullet \kappa - \delta(\kappa)$$

real rate of return on bonds = real rate of return from owning capital   (12.10)

INTEREST RATES AND THE DEMAND FOR MONEY

In Chapter 11, we discussed how the demand for money came from balancing transaction costs and asset income. By incurring more transaction costs, the household could hold less real money balances, M/P, and thereby more real earning assets, $(B/P + K)$. The nominal interest rate on earning assets was i, whereas that on money was zero. Therefore, i determined how much interest income was lost by holding money rather than earning assets. An increase in i made the potential loss of interest income more significant and, therefore, motivated households to incur more transaction costs to reduce M/P.

This analysis still applies when the inflation rate, π, differs from zero. The real interest rate on earning assets is $r = i - \pi$, and the real interest rate on money is $-\pi$. The difference between the two real interest rates is:

$$(i - \pi) - (-\pi) = i$$

Therefore, the nominal interest rate, i, still determines the cost of holding money rather than earning assets. We can therefore still describe real money demand by the function used in Chapter 11:

$$M^d / P = D(Y, i) \qquad (11.2)$$

Notice an important point: *it is the real interest rate, r, that has intertemporal-substitution effects on consumption and labour supply. However, it is the nominal interest, i, that influences the real demand for money, M^d/P.*

INFLATION AND THE REAL ECONOMY

We found in Chapter 11 that a change in the nominal quantity of money, M, was neutral. A doubling of M led to a doubling of the price level, P, and to no changes in real variables, such as real GDP. If we allow M to grow over time, we will find that P also grows. That is, money growth creates inflation – the inflation rate, π, will be greater than zero. We study in this section the effects of money growth and inflation on real GDP and other real variables.

Figure 10.5 in Chapter 10 analyzed the demand and supply of capital services, $(\kappa K)^d$ and $(\kappa K)^s$, where κ is the capital utilization rate and K is the capital stock. Figure 12.6 shows these demand and supply curves. A change in π does not shift $(\kappa K)^d$, because π does not affect the marginal product of capital services, MPK. (The demand, $(\kappa K)^d$, does not shift if labour input, L, is unchanged, as we will soon verify.) A change in π does not shift $(\kappa K)^s$, because K is fixed in the short run and π does not alter the optimal κ (for a given real rental price, R/P). Since the demand and supply curves do not shift, a change in π does not affect the market-clearing real rental price, $(R/P)^*$, and quantity of capital services, $(\kappa K)^*$.

Figure 9.13 analyzed the demand and supply of labour, L^d and L^s. Figure 12.7 shows these demand and supply curves. A change in π does not shift L^d, because π does not affect the marginal product of labour, MPL. However, L^s would shift if a change in π had an income effect. We assume that this income effect is small enough to ignore. In that case, a change in π does not shift L^s and, therefore, does not affect the market-clearing real wage rate, $(w/P)^*$, and quantity of labour input, L^*.

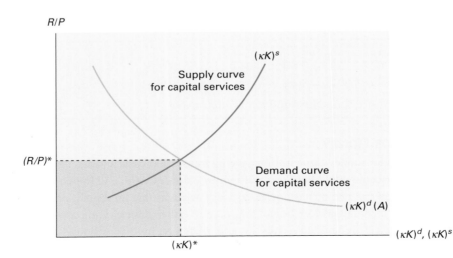

Figure 12.6 Clearing of the market for capital services

A change in the inflation rate, π, does not shift the demand or supply curve for capital services. Therefore, $(R/P)^*$ and $(\kappa K)^*$ do not change.

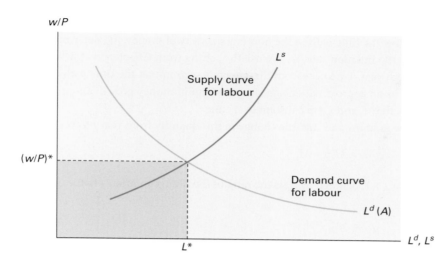

Figure 12.7 Clearing of the labour market

A change in the inflation rate, π, does not shift the demand or supply curve for labour. Therefore, $(w/P)^*$ and L^* do not change.

Why might a change in the inflation rate, π, have an income effect? The reason is that π will turn out to affect real money balances, M/P, and the transaction costs associated with money management. However, in normal times, these income effects are minor, and we can ignore them as a reasonable approximation. In this case, we are correct in our assumption in Figure 12.7 that a change in π does not shift the labour supply curve, L^s. We then conclude that a change in π does not influence labour and capital input, L and κK; the real wage rate, w/P; and the real rental price, R/P.

Real GDP, Y, is determined by the production function from Chapter 10:

$$Y = A \cdot F(\kappa K, L) \tag{10.1}$$

We know that a change in the inflation rate, π, does not affect the inputs of capital services and labour, κK and L. Since the technology level, A, is fixed, we conclude that a change in π does not influence real GDP, Y.

The real rental price, R/P, and the capital utilization rate, κ, determine the real rate of return from owning capital, $(R/P) \cdot \kappa - \delta(\kappa)$, and therefore the real interest rate, r, from the formula worked out before:

$$r = (R/P) \cdot \kappa - \delta(\kappa) \tag{12.10}$$

Since R/P and κ are unchanged, we find that a change in the inflation rate, π, does not affect the real interest rate, r.

Finally, we can use our analysis from Chapters 9 and 10 to study the division of real GDP, Y, between consumption, C, and gross investment, I. If we continue to ignore income effects from inflation, π, we know that C does not change. (No substitution effects arise, because the real interest rate, r, and the real wage rate, w/P, are unchanged.) Since Y is fixed, we conclude that I does not change. Therefore, we can add C and I to the list of unchanged real variables.

We have found that – as an approximation when we ignore income effects – the time paths of money growth and inflation do not affect a group of real variables. This group comprises real GDP, Y; inputs of labour and capital services, L and κK; consumption and investment, C and I; the real wage rate, w/P; the real rental price, R/P; and the real interest rate, r. Therefore, our earlier results on the neutrality of money – which referred to a one-time change in the nominal quantity, M – apply, as an approximation, to the entire path of money growth. The approximate independence of real variables from money growth is an important result. Moreover, this independence simplifies our next topic – the linkages between money growth, inflation and the nominal interest rate.

MONEY GROWTH, INFLATION AND THE NOMINAL INTEREST RATE

Our objective in this section is to analyze how the time path of the nominal quantity of money, M_t, determines the time path of the price level, P_t, and, hence, the inflation rate, π_t. We use the setting from Chapter 11 in which the monetary authority exogenously sets M_t each year. We know from the previous section that the time paths of real GDP, Y_t, and the real interest rate, r_t, will – as an approximation – be independent of money growth and inflation. To simplify further, we also assume for now that Y_t and r_t are constant over time.

Let M_t be the nominal quantity of money in year t and ΔM_t the change in this quantity from year t to year $t + 1$:

$$\Delta M_t = M_{t+1} - M_t$$

The growth rate of money from year t to year $t + 1$, denoted by μ_t, is the ratio of the change in money to the quantity of money:

$$\mu_t = \Delta M_t / M_t \tag{12.11}$$

For example, if $M_t = 100$ and $\Delta M_t = 5$, the growth rate of money is:

$$\mu_t = 5/100$$
$$= 0.05, or\ 5\% \ per\ year$$

If we multiply through equation (12.11) by M_t, we get:

$$\mu_t M_t = M_{t+1} - M_t$$

If we move M_t from the right-hand side to the left-hand side, combine the terms involving M_t, and then switch the right- and left-hand sides, we get:

$$M_{t+1} = (1 + \mu_t) \bullet M_t \tag{12.12}$$

Thus, the nominal quantity of money rises from year t to year $t + 1$ by the factor $1 + \mu_t$. For example, if $M_t = 100$ and $\mu_t = 0.05$, $M_{t+1} = 1.05 \bullet 100 = 105$.

Now, we consider inflation. The inflation rate, π_t, for year t is:

$$\pi_t = \Delta P_t / P_t$$
$$= (P_{t+1} - P_t) / P_t$$

If we multiply through by P_t, we get:

$$\pi_t P_t = P_{t+1} - P_t$$

If we move P_t from the right-hand side to the left-hand side, combine the terms involving P_t, and then switch the right- and left-hand sides, we get:

$$P_{t+1} = (1 + \pi_t) \bullet P_t \tag{12.13}$$

Thus, the price level rises from year t to year $t + 1$ by the factor $1 + \pi_t$. For example, if $P_t = 100$ and $\pi_t = 0.05$, $P_{t+1} = 1.05 \bullet 100 = 105$.

We now link inflation to money growth. Suppose that the growth rate of money is the constant $\mu_t = \mu$. In Chapter 11, we found that a once-and-for-all increase in the nominal quantity of money, M, raised the price level, P, in the same proportion. By analogy to this result, we now make a key conjecture: *when M_t grows steadily at the rate μ, the price level, P_t, will also grow steadily at the rate μ.* That is, the inflation rate, π_t, will be the constant $\pi = \mu$. As we move through the steps of our analysis, we will verify that this conjecture is correct.

If the inflation rate, π, equals the money growth rate, μ, the level of real money balances, M_t/P_t, does not change over time. In Chapter 11, we used the equilibrium condition that the quantity of money supplied equalled the quantity of money demanded. We use the same condition here, but we have to ensure that this condition holds for every year t. Since real money balances, M_t/P_t, do not change over time, equilibrium requires that:

- The real quantity of money demanded, $D(Y, i)$, does not vary over time;
- The level of real money demanded, $D(Y, i)$, equals the unchanging level of real money balances, M_t/P_t.

The first condition is easy to satisfy, because we assumed that real GDP, Y, is fixed. Therefore, we require only that the nominal interest rate, i, be unchanging. Recall that i is the sum of the real interest rate, r, and the inflation rate, π. Moreover, our conjecture is that π equals the money growth rate, μ. Therefore, we have:

$$i = r + \pi$$
$$i = r + \mu \tag{12.14}$$

Since we assumed that r and μ are fixed, i is unchanging. Since Y and i are fixed, we have verified that the real quantity of money demanded, $D(Y, i)$, is unchanging.

Now, we have to ensure that the level of real money demanded, $D(Y, i)$, equals the level of real money balances, M_t/P_t, in each year. Note that $D(Y, i)$ and M_t/P_t are both fixed over time. Therefore, if the levels of the two variables are equal in the current year, year 1, they will remain equal in every future year. Thus, the final equilibrium condition is that year 1's real quantity of money, M_1/P_1, equals the real quantity demanded, $D(Y, i)$:

$$M_1 / P_1 = D(Y, i) \tag{12.15}$$

This condition is just like those we studied in Chapter 11. The key insight there was that, in equilibrium, the price level, P_1, adjusted so that the real quantity of money, M_1/P_1 on the left-hand side of equation (12.15), equalled the real quantity demanded, $D(Y, i)$, on the right-hand side. We can rearrange the terms to solve out for the equilibrium price level, P_1:

> **Key equation (determination of price level):**
>
> $$P_1 = M_1/D(Y, i)$$
>
> *price level = nominal quantity of money/real quantity of money demanded* $\qquad$ (12.16)

We know everything on the right-hand side of equation (12.16) because the nominal quantity of money, M_1, is given, and Y and i are known. In particular, equation (12.14) implies $i = r + \mu$. Thus, equation (12.16) determines year 1's price level, P_1.

After year 1, the nominal quantity of money, M_t, and the price level, P_t, grow at the same rate, μ. Therefore, real money balances, M_t/P_t, do not change. Hence, for any year t, M_t/P_t equals M_1/P_1, which appears on the left-hand side of equation (12.15). The right-hand side of this equation, $D(Y, i)$, does not vary over time. We conclude that real money balances, M_t/P_t, equal the real quantity demanded, $D(Y, i)$, in every year t.

Notice that the solution verifies our conjecture that the inflation rate, μ_t, is the constant $\pi = \mu$. The full set of results is as follows:

- The inflation rate, π, equals the unchanging growth rate of money, μ.
- Real money balances, M_t/P_t, are fixed over time.
- The nominal interest rate, i, equals $r + \mu$, where r is the unchanging real interest rate, determined as in the equilibrium business-cycle model of Chapter 10.
- The real quantity of money demanded, $D(Y, i)$, is fixed over time, where Y is the unchanging real GDP, determined as in Chapter 10.
- Year 1's price level, P_1, is determined from equation (12.16) to equate year 1's real money balances, M_1/P_1, to the real quantity demanded, $D(Y, i)$.

A TREND IN THE REAL DEMAND FOR MONEY

A simplifying assumption in the previous section was that the real quantity of money demanded, $D(Y, i)$, did not change over time. This assumption is unrealistic, particularly because growth of real GDP, Y, generates growth of $D(Y, i)$. We show in this section how to extend our results to allow for changes over time in $D(Y, i)$.

Assume that the real quantity of money demanded, $D(Y, i)$, grows steadily at the constant rate γ. This growth might reflect long-term growth of real GDP, Y; for example, in the steady state of the Solow model with technological progress from Chapter 5, Y grows at a constant rate. In equilibrium, the growth rate of real money balances, M_t/P_t, has to equal the growth rate, γ, of the real quantity demanded. To use this condition, we have to recalculate the rate at which real money balances, M_t/P_t, are growing.

We still assume that the nominal quantity of money, M_t, grows at the constant rate μ. The inflation rate, π, will turn out to be constant but less than μ if the growth rate of real money demanded, γ, is greater than zero. The reason that π is less than μ is that the rising real money demanded holds down the inflation rate. This result accords with our finding from Chapter 11 that a one-time increase in real money demand reduces the price level.

Real money balances, M_t/P_t, increase because of growth in the numerator, M_t, at the rate μ, but decrease because of growth in the denominator, P_t, at the rate π. We can show with a little algebra that the growth rate of M_t/P_t is given by:

$$\text{growth rate of } M_t/P_t = \mu - \pi$$
$$\text{growth rate of real money balances} = \text{growth rate of nominal money} - \text{inflation rate} \qquad (12.17)$$

Thus, if μ is greater than π, M_t/P_t rises over time.

The equilibrium condition is, again, that real money balances, M_t/P_t, equal the real quantity of money demanded, $D(Y, i)$, each year. Thus, if $D(Y, i)$ grows at rate γ, M_t/P_t must also grow at rate γ. If we substitute this result for the left-hand side of equation (12.17), we get:

$$\gamma = \mu - \pi$$

Therefore, if we rearrange terms, the inflation rate is:

$$\pi = \mu - \gamma \qquad (12.18)$$

Thus, if y is greater than zero, π is less than μ. However, an increase in μ of 1% per year still leads, for given γ, to a rise in π of 1% per year. Hence, as in Figure 12.1, variations in money growth rates across countries can still account for differences in inflation rates. The new result from equation (12.18) is that variations in the growth rate, γ, of the real quantity of money demanded affect the relationship between the growth rates of money, μ, and prices, π. A higher y raises $\mu - \pi$ and, therefore, increases the growth rate of real money balances, M_t/P_t.

Figure 12.8 uses information for 57 countries from Table 12.1 to check our prediction for the growth rate of real money balances. We assume that growth of real GDP is the main source of growth in the real quantity of money demanded. Thus, the horizontal axis plots the growth rate of real GDP, from column 5 of the table. The vertical axis plots the growth rate of real money, from column 4. The graph shows that a higher growth rate of real GDP matches up with a higher growth rate of real currency. The correlation between the two variables is high: 0.60. The slope of the relation is roughly close to 1.0; that is, if the growth rate of real GDP is higher by 1% per year, the growth rate of real currency is higher by about 1% per year. Therefore, if the real GDP growth rate is higher by 1% per year, the inflation rate, π, is lower by 1% per year for a given money growth rate, μ.

A SHIFT IN THE MONEY GROWTH RATE

In this section, we study the effects of a change in the money growth rate, μ, on the inflation rate, π, and the nominal interest rate, i. To simplify, return to the setting with no trend in the real quantity of money demanded, $D(Y, i)$. In particular, real GDP, Y, is fixed. Suppose that the nominal quantity of money, M_t, has been growing for a long time at the constant rate μ. Thus, M_t is given by the dark blue line on the left-hand side of Figure 12.9. Since the graph uses a proportionate scale, the slope of the line equals μ.

Suppose that households initially expect the monetary authority to keep the nominal quantity of money, M_t, growing forever at the rate μ. In this case, our previous analysis applies, and the inflation rate is the constant

$\pi = \mu$. We show the price level, P_t, as the light blue line on the left-hand side of Figure 12.9. The slope of this line equals the inflation rate, $\pi = \mu$, which equals the slope of the dark blue line.

Figure 12.8 Growth rate of real currency and growth rate of real GDP for 57 countries, 1960–2011

This graph uses the data from Table 12.1. The horizontal axis has the growth rate of real GDP from 1960 to 2011. The vertical axis has the growth rate of real money (nominal money divided by the CPI) from 1960 to 2011. The two variables have a correlation of 0.60.

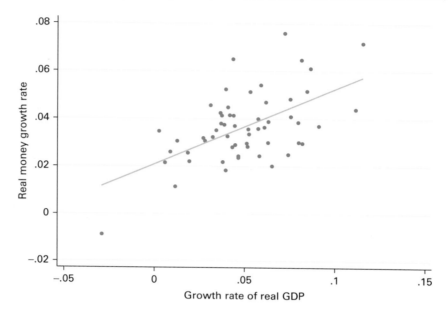

Figure 12.9 Effect of an increase in the money growth rate on the price level

The dark blue line shows that the nominal quantity of money, M_t, grows at the constant rate μ before year T. After year T, M_t grows along the black line at the higher rate μ'. The light blue line shows that the price level, P_t, grows at the same rate as money, μ, before year T. After year T, P_t grows along the light blue line at the same rate as money, μ'. The price level, P_t, jumps upward during year T. This jump reduces real money balances, M_t/P_t, from the level prevailing before year T to that prevailing after year T.

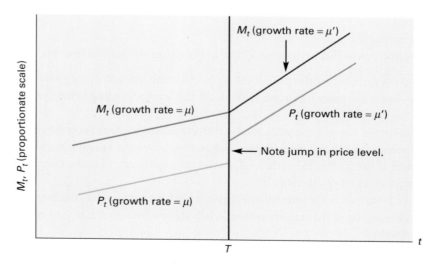

Now, suppose that the monetary authority raises the money growth rate from μ to μ' in year T. The right-hand side of Figure 12.9 shows that the nominal quantity of money, M_t, follows the black line after year T. This line has slope μ' and is steeper than the red line. We assume that the change in the money growth rate in year T is a surprise. However, once the change occurs, we assume that households expect the new growth rate of money, μ', to prevail forever. Therefore, after year T, the economy is in the same situation as before, except that the money growth rate is μ', rather than μ, and the inflation rate is $\pi' = \mu'$. The right-hand side of Figure 12.9 shows that the price level, P_t, follows the light blue line, which has the slope $\pi' = \mu'$, which equals the slope of the black line.

The inflation rate after year T, π', is greater than the inflation rate, π, before year T. Therefore, the light blue line on the right-hand side of Figure 12.9 is steeper than the light blue line on the left-hand side. Notice an important complication in the graph of P_t. The two lines do not intersect. Instead, *the figure shows an upward jump in the price level in year T.* To see why, we have to consider the real quantity of money demanded.

Before year T, the nominal interest rate, i, is given by $i = r + \pi$, where r is the real interest rate and π is the inflation rate. Since $\pi = \mu$, we have:

$$i = r + \mu \tag{12.19}$$

Recall that a change in the money growth rate does not change the real interest rate, which remains at r. Therefore, the nominal interest rate after year T will be $i' = r + \pi'$, where π' is the inflation rate after year T. If we substitute μ' for π', we have:

$$i' = r + \mu' \tag{12.20}$$

If we subtract equation (12.19) from equation (12.20), we can calculate the increase in the nominal interest rate:

$$i' - i = \mu' - \mu$$

increase in nominal interest rate = increase in money growth rate (12.21)

A key property of the demand for money, $D(Y, i)$, is that a rise in the nominal interest rate, i, lowers the real quantity of money demanded. Therefore, $D(Y, i)$ must be lower after year T than before. We still have the equilibrium condition that the real quantity of money, M_t/P_t, always equals $D(Y, i)$. Therefore, the real quantity of money, M_t/P_t, must be lower after year T.

The left-hand side of Figure 12.9 shows that, before year T, the nominal quantity of money, M_t, grows at the same rate, μ, as the price level, P_t. Therefore, the real quantity of money, M_t/P_t, is constant. The right-hand side shows that, after year T, M_t grows at the same rate, μ', as P_t. Hence, M_t/P_t is, again, constant. We therefore have three facts:

- M_t/P_t is constant before year T.
- M_t/P_t is constant after year T.
- M_t/P_t after year T is lower than that before year T (due to the rise in the nominal interest rate from i to i').

The way to reconcile these facts is that the price level, P_t, has to jump upward during year T, as shown in Figure 12.9. This rise in P_t lowers real money balances, M_t/P_t, from the level prevailing before year T to that prevailing after year T.

One way to think about the jump in the price level is that the inflation rate is exceptionally high during year T. Specifically, when the money growth rate rises in year T from μ to μ', the inflation rate, π_t, rises above μ' in the short run. The excess of π_t over μ' means that the price level, P_t, rises at a faster rate than the nominal quantity of money, M_t, so that real money balances, M_t/P_t, decline.

In the case shown in Figure 12.9, the interval of exceptionally high inflation is concentrated in a short period, essentially an instant of time. Thus, the transition from relatively low inflation, $\pi = \mu$, to relatively high inflation, $\pi' = \mu'$, takes place overnight.

The more general result is that real money balances, M_t/P_t, decrease during a transition interval, because the higher nominal interest rate reduces the real quantity of money demanded. During the transition, the inflation rate, π_t, exceeds the money growth rate, μ_t. The exact nature of the transition depends on the details of the model – it is not necessarily limited to a single year or an instant of time.

In one modification of the model, households adjust their real quantity of money demanded downward only gradually in response to an increase in the nominal interest rate, i_t. This gradual adjustment makes sense if households have to change their underlying cash-management plans to hold lower real money balances. In this case, the transition to a lower real money balance, M_t/P_t, is stretched out. As the real quantity of money demanded falls gradually, M_t/P_t also decreases gradually. The period of falling M_t/P_t corresponds to an extended transition in which the inflation rate, π_t, exceeds the growth rate of money, μ_t.

As another example, households may know in advance that the monetary authority is planning to shift from relatively low money growth, μ, to relatively high money growth, μ'. Households may expect, before year T, that money growth and inflation will be higher from year T onward. In this case, some of the unusually high short-run inflation occurs *before* year T. That is, the expectation of higher inflation in the future leads to higher inflation today – before the rise in the money growth rate occurs. The higher short-run inflation arises because the anticipated future inflation decreases the real quantity of money demanded before year T.

Expectations about future changes in money growth rates and inflation have sometimes been at the centre of political campaigns. An example is the post-World War I German *hyperinflation*, examined in the By the Numbers box 'Money and prices during the German hyperinflation'. The end of the hyperinflation occurred in November 1923. However, people anticipated prior to November that a monetary reform was coming and that this reform would entail lower money growth rates, μ, and inflation rates, π. Empirical studies show that this anticipation reduced π before November 1923, even though the reduction in μ had not yet occurred.[4]

GOVERNMENT REVENUE FROM PRINTING MONEY

We have assumed, thus far, that the monetary authority prints new money (currency) and gives it to households as transfer payments. More realistically, governments get **revenue from printing money** and can use this revenue to pay for a variety of expenditures. Governments do not usually use this revenue to finance Milton Friedman's imaginary helicopter drops of cash!

The government's nominal revenue from printing money between years t and $t + 1$ equals the change in the nominal quantity of money:

$$nominal\,revenue\,from\,printing\,money = M_{t+1} - M_t$$
$$= \Delta M_t$$

To calculate the real value of revenue, divide ΔM_t by P_{t+1}, the price level for year $t + 1$:

$$real\,revenue\,from\,printing\,money = \Delta M_t/P_{t+1}$$

We want to relate this real revenue to the money growth rate, μ_t, which is given by:

$$\mu_t = \Delta M_t/M_t \tag{12.11}$$

We can use equation (12.11) to substitute $\mu_t \bullet M_t$ for ΔM_t in the formula for real revenue:

$$real\,revenue\,from\,printing\,money = \mu_t \bullet (M_t/P_{t+1})$$

The term on the far right-hand side, M_t/P_{t+1}, is approximately the level of real money balances, M_t/P_t. Therefore, the real revenue from printing money is:

$$real\,revenue\,from\,printing\,money \approx \mu_t \bullet (M_t/P_{t+1})$$
$$= (money\,growth\,rate) \bullet (level\,of\,real\,money\,balances) \tag{12.22}$$

We know that a higher money growth rate, μ, leads to a higher inflation rate, π, and a higher nominal interest rate, i. We also know that the higher i reduces the real quantity of money demanded, $D(Y, i)$, and, therefore, lowers real money balances, M_t/P_t. Thus, an increase in μ, has two opposing effects on the real revenue from printing

[4]See Robert Flood and Peter Garber (1980) and Laura Lahaye (1985).

money in equation (12.22): the rise in μ_t raises real revenue, but the decrease in M_t/P_t reduces real revenue. The net effect depends on how much $D(Y, i)$ falls in response to a rise in i.

As an example, suppose that real money balances, M_t/P_t, were initially equal to 100, and that μ_t then doubled from 5% to 10% per year. The net real revenue from printing money would rise unless M_t/P_t fell below 50; that is, by more than 50%. More generally, the real revenue rises unless the decrease in the quantity of real money demanded is proportionately larger than the increase in the money growth rate. This condition holds empirically except for the most extreme cases. For example, during the German hyperinflation, the condition was violated only when μ_t approached 100% per month between July and August 1923. Until then, the government extracted more real revenue by printing money at a faster rate.

In normal times for most countries, the government obtains only a small portion of its revenue from printing money. Considering the continued expansionary monetary policy carried out after the financial crisis in 2014, the Federal Reserve obtained $97 billion from this source, a significant increase of $24 billion over the 2005 figure prior to the financial crisis. This amount constituted 3.2% of total federal receipts and 0.5% of GDP. Slightly lower figures are typical for most developed countries.

In a few high-inflation countries, the revenue from printing money became much more important. For example, in Argentina from 1960 to 1975, money creation accounted for nearly half of government revenue and about 6% of GDP. Some other countries in which the revenue from printing money was important were Chile (5% of GDP from 1960 to 1977), Libya (3% of GDP from 1960 to 1977) and Brazil (3% of GDP from 1960 to 1978).

John Maynard Keynes (1923, p. 41) observed that money creation became the main source of government receipts during the German and Russian hyperinflations after World War I: 'A Government can live for a long time, even the German Government or the Russian Government, by printing paper money. That is to say, it can by this means secure the command over real resources – resources just as real as those obtained by taxation.' In some hyperinflations, the revenue approached 10% of GDP, which seems to be about the maximum attainable from printing money. In Germany, from 1920 to 1923, a close connection existed between real government spending and the money growth rate.[5] Much of this spending went towards reparations payments to the victors in World War I. Therefore, the reduction in these payments after November 1923 was a major factor in ending the German hyperinflation.

By the Numbers
Money and prices during the German hyperinflation

A hyperinflation is a sustained period of super-high inflation rates. The post-World War I German hyperinflation provides a great laboratory experiment for studying the interplay between money growth rates and inflation.[6] From 1920 to 1923, inflation rates ranged from near zero to over 500% per month! Despite the extreme inflation, comparatively small changes occurred in real GDP.

When inflation rates are volatile, as in post-World War I Germany, it is impossible to predict accurately the real interest rate on loans that prescribe nominal interest rates. Therefore, this type of lending tends to disappear. For this reason, we have no good measures of the nominal interest rate during the German hyperinflation, and the best measure of the cost of holding money is the expected inflation rate, π_t^e. This rate determined how much income people lost by holding money, rather than by consuming or holding a durable good that maintained its real value over time. Empirical studies have estimated π_t^e by assuming that it adjusted gradually to changes in the actual inflation rate, π_t.

[5]See Zvi Hercowitz (1981) for a detailed analysis.
[6]This episode has fascinated many economists, starting with the classic study by Costantino Bresciani-Turroni (1937). Phillip Cagan (1956) studied the German hyperinflation along with six others: Austria, Hungary, Poland, and Russia after World War I, and Greece and Hungary after World War II. The Hungarian experience after World War II seems to be the all-time record: the price level rose by a factor of 3×1025 from July 1945 to August 1946. See William Bomberger and Gail Makinen (1983).

Table 12.3 shows the money growth rate, μ_t (based on currency in circulation), the inflation rate, π_t, and real money balances, M_t/P_t, in Germany from 1920 to 1925. In most cases, the table shows μ_t and π_t over six-month intervals. The level of M_t/P_t pertains to the ends of these intervals.

At the beginning of 1920, the money growth rate, μ_t, and the inflation rate, π_t, were already at 6% per month. Then μ_t declined in early 1921 to less than 1% per month. As our model predicts, π_t fell by more than μ_t, so that real money balances, M_t/P_t, rose by about 20% from early 1920 to early 1921.

From late 1921 through to the end of 1922, the money growth rate, μ_t, rose to 30% per month. Since the inflation rate, π_t, exceeded μ_t, real money balances, M_t/P_t, fell to 25% of the early-1920 level by the end of 1922. From the end of 1922 through to mid-1923, the money growth rate, μ_t, was extremely high but no longer trending upward; it averaged around 40% per month. Since the inflation rate, π_t, was also about 40% per month, real money balances, M_t/P_t, remained at 25% of the early-1920 level. However, in late 1923, the hyperinflation built to its climax, with π_t reaching 300–600% per month in October and November. Since π_t exceeded μ_t, M_t/P_t, fell to its low point in October of about 3% of the 1920 level.

A monetary reform occurred in November 1923. The reform included a new type of currency, a promise not to print new money beyond a specified limit to finance government expenditures, reductions in real government spending, reform of the tax system and a commitment to back the value of the new currency by gold.[1] These changes led to sharp cutbacks in the money growth rate, μ_t, and the inflation rate, π_t, after December 1923. During 1924, μ_t averaged 5% per month, and π_t was less than 1% per month. The excess of μ_t over π_t allowed for the rebuilding of real money balances, M_t/P_t, which increased from 3% of the early-1920 level in October 1923 to 56% of that level by December 1924. Although π_t remained low for the rest of the 1920s, M_t/P_t did not re-attain its early-1920 level. Perhaps this gap reflected a long-lasting negative influence of the hyperinflation on the real demand for money.

Table 12.3 **Money growth and inflation during the German hyperinflation**

Period	μ_t	π_t	M_t/P_t (end of period)
2/20–6/20	5.7	6.0	1.01
6/20–12/20	3.0	1.1	1.13
12/20–6/21	0.8	0.1	1.18
6/21–12/21	5.5	8.4	0.99
12/21–6/22	6.5	12.8	0.68
6/22–12/22	29.4	46.7	0.24
12/22–6/23	40.0	40.0	0.24
6/23–10/23	233.0	286.0	0.03
Reform period			
12/23–6/24	5.9	−0.6	0.44
6/24–12/24	5.3	1.4	0.56
12/24–6/25	2.0	1.6	0.57
6/25–12/25	1.2	0.4	0.60

Note: The nominal quantity of money, M_t, is an estimate of the total circulation of currency. Until late 1923, the figures refer to total legal tender, most of which constituted notes issued by the Reichsbank. Later, the data include issues of the Rentenbank, private bank notes, and various 'emergency moneys'. Unofficial emergency currencies, as well as circulating foreign currencies, are not counted. The numbers are normalized so that M_t in 1913 is set to 1.0. The price level, P_t, is an index of the cost of living, based on 1913 = 1.0. Column 1 shows the period for the data. Column 2, in per cent per month, is the money growth rate, μ_t, over the period shown. Column 3, also in per cent per month, is the inflation rate, μ_t, over the period shown. Column 4 is the level of real money balances, M_t/P_t, at the end of each period. Since the value of M_t/P_t for 1913 is 1.0, the values shown for M_t/P_t are relative to the level in 1913.
Source: *Sonderhefte zür Wirtschaft und Statistik*, Berlin, 1929.

[1]For discussions of the reform, see Bresciani-Turroni (1937), Thomas Sargent (1982), and Peter Garber (1982). Sargent's analysis stresses the rapidity with which inflations can be ended once the government makes a credible commitment to limit money creation.

Summing Up

Sustained inflation requires persistent money growth, and we found this pattern in the cross-country data. An increase in the money growth rate of 1% per year is associated with an increase in the inflation rate of 1% per year. An increase in the growth rate of real GDP of 1% per year is associated with an increase of 1% per year in the growth rate of real money balances. Hence, a higher growth rate of real GDP lowers the inflation rate for a given growth rate of money.

The nominal interest rate exceeds the real interest rate by the rate of inflation. Conventional nominal bonds specify in advance the nominal interest rate, whereas indexed bonds specify the real interest rate. Data on indexed bonds allow us to measure the expected real interest rate and the expected inflation rate.

Intertemporal-substitution effects depend on the real interest rate, whereas the demand for money depends on the nominal interest rate. We extended the equilibrium business-cycle model to show how an increase in the money growth rate leads, one for one, to a higher inflation rate and a higher nominal interest rate. As an approximation, a change in the money growth rate does not affect a group of real variables that includes real GDP, consumption, investment, the real wage rate, the real rental price and the real interest rate. However, a higher money growth rate leads to lower real money balances and, typically, to greater real revenue for the government.

Key Terms and Concepts

deflation	indexed bonds	rational expectations	transfer payment
expectations of inflation	lump-sum transfers	real interest rate	unexpected inflation
expected real interest rate	money growth rate	revenue from printing	
hyperinflation	nominal interest rate	money	

Questions and Problems

A Review questions

1   Why does the real interest rate, not the nominal interest rate, have intertemporal-substitution effects on consumption and saving? Does the same result apply for intertemporal substitution of labour supply?

2   What is the Livingston survey of inflationary expectations? What are the pluses and minuses of using this type of information to measure the expected inflation rate, π_t^e?

3   Which of the following statements is correct?

   a   A constant rate of increase in the price level, P, will lead to a continuous rise in the nominal interest rate, i.

   b   A continuous increase in the inflation rate, π, will lead to a continuous rise in the nominal interest rate, i.

4   Why does the actual real interest rate, r, generally differ from the expected real interest rate, r_t^e? How does this relation depend on whether bonds prescribe the nominal or real interest rate?

5   Define the real interest rate, r. Why does it differ from the nominal interest rate, i, in the presence of inflation?

B Problems for discussion

6   Money growth and government revenue

   Can the government always increase its real revenue from printing money by raising the money growth rate, μ? How does the answer depend on the responsiveness of real money demand, M^d/P, to the nominal interest rate, i?

7   A case of counterfeiting

   In 1925, a group of swindlers induced the Waterlow Company, a British manufacturer of bank notes, to print and deliver to them £3 million worth of Portuguese currency (escudos). Since the company also printed the legitimate notes for the Bank of Portugal, the counterfeit notes were indistinguishable from the real thing (except that the serial numbers were duplicates of those from a previous series of legitimate notes). Before the fraud was discovered, £1 million worth of the fraudulent notes had been introduced into circulation in Portugal. After the scheme unravelled (because someone noticed the duplication of serial numbers), the Bank of Portugal made good on the fraudulent notes by exchanging them for newly printed, valid notes. The Bank subsequently sued the Waterlow Company for damages. The company was found liable, but the key question was the amount of damages. The Bank argued that the damages were £1 million (less funds collected from the swindlers). The other side contended that the Bank suffered only negligible real costs in having to issue an additional £1 million worth of money to redeem the fraudulent notes. (Note that the currency was purely a paper issue, with no convertibility into gold or anything else.) Thus, the argument was that the only true costs to the Bank were the expenses for paper and printing. Which side do you think was correct? (The House of Lords determined in 1932 that £1 million was the correct measure. For discussions of this fascinating episode in monetary economics, see Ralph Hawtrey, 1932, and Murray Bloom, 1966.)

8 Interest-rate targeting

Suppose that the monetary authority wants to keep the nominal interest rate, i, constant. Assume that the real interest rate, r, is fixed. However, the real demand for money, M^d/P, shifts around a great deal.

a How should the monetary authority vary the nominal quantity of money, M, if the real demand for money, M^d/P, increases temporarily? What if the real demand increases permanently?

b How does the price level, P, behave in your answers to question a? What should the monetary authority do if it wants to dampen fluctuations of P, as well as maintain a constant nominal interest rate, i?

9 Indexed bonds

a Consider a one-year nominal bond that costs €1000. After one year, the bond pays the principal of €1000 plus an interest payment of €50. What is the one-year nominal interest rate on the bond? What are the actual and expected one-year real interest rates on the bond? Why is the nominal interest rate known but the real rate uncertain?

b Consider now a one-year indexed bond. Suppose that the bond costs €1000. One year later, the nominal principal of the bond is

adjusted to be €1000 • $(1 + \pi)$, where π is the actual inflation rate over the year. Then the bond pays off the adjusted principal of €1000 • $(1 + \pi)$ plus an interest payment of, say, 3% of the adjusted principal. What is the one-year real interest rate on the indexed bond? What are the actual and expected one-year nominal interest rates on the bond? Why is the real rate known but the nominal rate uncertain?

c Can you think of other ways to design indexed bonds? Are the nominal and real interest rates both uncertain in some cases?

10 Effects on the nominal interest rate

What are the effects on the price level, P, and the nominal interest rate, i, from the following events?

a A once-and-for-all increase in the nominal quantity of money, M;

b A once-and-for-all increase in the money growth rate, μ;

c A credible announcement that the money growth rate, μ, will rise beginning one year in the future.

11 Rational expectations and measures of expected inflation

How would the hypothesis of rational expectations help us to measure the expected inflation rate, π_t^e? What seem to be the pluses and minuses of this approach?

12 Seasonal variations in money

Suppose that the real quantity of money demanded is relatively high in the fourth quarter of each year and relatively low in the first quarter. Assume that there is no seasonal pattern in real interest rates.

a Suppose that there were no seasonal pattern in the nominal quantity of money, M. What would the seasonal pattern be for the price level, P, the inflation rate, π, and the nominal interest rate, i?

b What seasonal behaviour for the nominal quantity of money, M, would eliminate the seasonal variations in P, π and i?

13 Statistical relations between money growth and inflation

Students who have studied econometrics and have access to a statistical package can do the following exercise.

a   Use the data in Table 12.1 to run a regression of the inflation rate, π, on a constant and the growth rate of money (currency), μ. What is the estimated coefficient on μ, and how should we interpret it? What is the meaning of the constant term?

b   Run a regression of the growth rate of real money balances, $\mu - \pi$, on the growth rate of real GDP, $\Delta Y/Y$, and a constant. What is the estimated coefficient on $\Delta Y/Y$, and how should we interpret it?

c   Suppose that we add the variable $\Delta Y/Y$ to the regression run in question a. What is the estimated coefficient on $\Delta Y/Y$, and how should we interpret it?

14 Money growth and inflation
      Suppose that the money-demand function takes the form:

$$M^d/P = D(Y, i) = Y \cdot \psi(i)$$

That is, for a given nominal interest rate, i, a doubling of real GDP, Y, doubles the real quantity of money demanded, M^d/P.

a   Consider the relation across countries between the growth rate of money (currency), μ, and the inflation rate, π, as shown in Figure 12.1. How does the growth rate of real GDP, $\Delta Y/Y$, affect the relationship between μ and π?

b   What is the relation between μ and π for a country in which the nominal interest rate, i, has increased?

c   Suppose that the expected real interest rate, r_t^e, is given. What is the relation between μ and π for a country in which the expected inflation rate, π_t^e, has increased?

15 Prepayment of mortgages and callability of bonds
      Mortgages typically allow the borrower to make early payments ('prepayments') of principal. Sometimes, the mortgage contract specifies a prepayment penalty and, sometimes, there is no penalty. Similarly, long-term bonds sometimes allow the issuer to prepay the principal after a prescribed date, with a specified penalty. When the bond issuer exercises this option to prepay, they are said to 'call' the bond. Bonds that allow this prepayment are said to be 'callable' or to have a 'call provision'.

a   When would a borrower want to prepay (or call) their mortgage or bond? Would we see more prepayments when the nominal interest rate, i, unexpectedly increased or decreased?

b   From the late 1970s until 1982, banks and savings and loan associations were eager for customers to prepay their mortgages. Why was this the case? Later on, customers wanted to prepay. Why did they want to do so?

c   Suppose that the year-to-year fluctuations in nominal interest rates become larger. (These fluctuations – or volatility – were particularly great from the mid-1970s to the early 1980s.) From the standpoint of a borrower, how does this change affect the value of having a prepayment option – that is, callability – in their mortgage or bond?

The government sector

PART V

13 Government expenditure

Up to now, the government has had very limited functions in our model. We have considered only lump-sum transfers financed by money creation. Now, we will allow for the government purchases of goods and services. In the national accounts, these purchases are called government consumption and investment.[1] We assume in this chapter that government expenditures are financed by *lump-sum taxes*, which are analogous to the lump-sum transfers that we considered before. We also continue to assume that the transfers are lump-sum. In Chapter 14, we will allow for more realistic systems of taxes and transfers. It is useful to start with data on government expenditure for the Eurozone and other countries.

Data on government expenditure

General government expenditure is the amount of money spent at all levels of government for purchases of goods and services, transfer payments (amounts given to households and businesses) and interest payments. (We defer a discussion of interest payments until Chapter 15.) Figure 13.1 shows general government expenditure as a ratio to gross domestic product (GDP) in the Eurozone. From 1999 to 2014, general government expenditure was about half of GDP. Figure 13.1 shows that the two largest components of general government expenditure were the purchases of goods/services and transfers payments. From 1999 to 2014, out of the 48% of GDP represented by total general government expenditure, 23% of GDP went for purchases and 21% went for transfers. (The other 3% went for interest payments.)

Figure 13.2 shows the breakdown of general government purchases into the parts that can be attributed to purchases by central governments and purchases by state/local governments. From 1999 to 2014, purchases by central governments were 7% of GDP, whereas purchases by state and local governments were 11%. Since the Great Recession in 2008–09, purchases by all levels of governments have been slightly trending downwards.

Figure 13.3 shows the breakdown of government transfer payments into the parts that can be attributed to transfer payments by central governments and transfers payments by state/local governments. From 1999 to 2014, transfer payments by central governments were 13% of GDP, whereas transfer payments by state and local governments were about 5%. Since the Great Recession in 2008–09, transfer payments by central government have increased from 12% to 14%.

General government expenditure can be split into ten functional classes: general public services; defence; public order and safety; economic affairs; environmental protection; housing and community amenities; health; recreation, culture and religion; education; and social protection. Figure 13.4 shows the breakdown of total general government expenditure into these functional classes in the Eurozone from 2006 to 2013. The

---

[1]The difference between government consumption and investment and government purchases is that the former category includes the implicit rental income on the government's capital stock. In practice, in the national accounts, this rental income is assumed to equal the estimated depreciation of government capital. In the model, the government owns no capital. Hence, depreciation of the government's capital stock is zero, and government investment is also zero. Therefore, in the model, government purchases are the same as government consumption.

largest components of total general government expenditure were social protection, health and general public services.

Figure 13.1 Total government expenditure, purchases, transfers and interest payments

The graphs refer to total general government expenditure and show ratios of each nominal expenditure component to nominal GDP. Purchases of goods and services are the outlays for consumption and investment. In the national accounts, purchases equal government consumption and investment less depreciation of public capital stocks. Data are from the Eurostat: Government Finance Statistics.

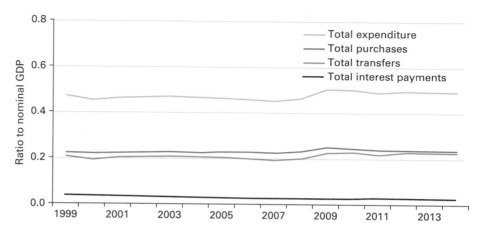

Figure 13.2 Breakdown of government purchases

The graphs show the ratio of different levels of government purchases to nominal GDP. Government purchases are broken down into those by central governments and those by state and local governments.

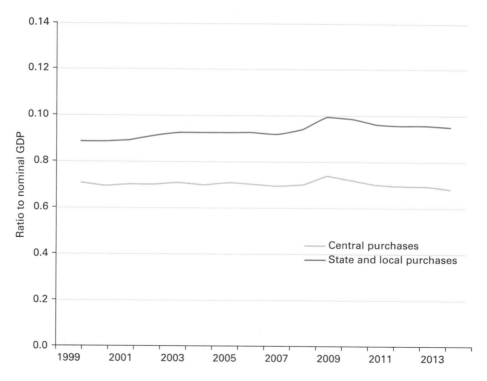

   Table 13.1 shows ratios of total general government expenditure to GDP for 156 countries in 2013. The countries listed are those for which data are available on a broad concept of government expenditure. This concept includes expenditure by all levels of government for purchases, transfers and interest payments. The ratios shown

range from 13% at the low end for Guinea-Bissau, Nigeria and Sudan to 57%–58% at the high end for Denmark, Finland and France. The median, or middle, position is 31%. Most European countries are above the median. Similarly, most Middle Eastern countries are also above the median, with Iran being a notable exception at 15%. In contrast, many African countries are below the median in terms of general government expenditure as a percentage of GDP.

Figure 13.3 Breakdown of government transfer payments

The graphs show the ratio of different levels of government transfer payments to nominal GDP. Transfer payments include subsidies.

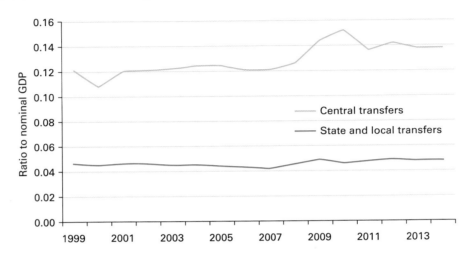

Figure 13.4 Breakdown of government expenditure by function, 2006–13

The graphs show the breakdown of total general government expenditure into ten functional classes.

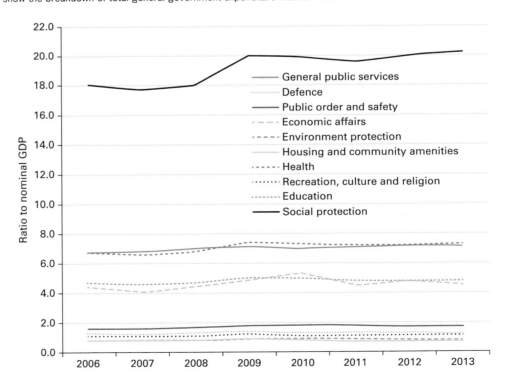

Table 13.1 General government expenditure as a ratio to GDP in a sample of countries, 2013

Country	Spending ratio	Country	Spending ratio
Afghanistan	0.25	Lebanon	0.28
Albania	0.29	Liberia	0.33
Algeria	0.36	Lithuania	0.35
Angola	0.41	Luxembourg	0.43
Argentina	0.35	Macedonia	0.32
Armenia	0.24	Madagascar	0.15
Australia	0.37	Malawi	0.35
Austria	0.51	Malaysia	0.28
Azerbaijan	0.38	Mali	0.24
Bangladesh	0.15	Mauritania	0.29
Belarus	0.42	Mexico	0.28
Belgium	0.54	Moldova	0.38
Belize	0.31	Mongolia	0.40
Benin	0.22	Montenegro	0.47
Bhutan	0.33	Morocco	0.33
Bolivia	0.38	Mozambique	0.35
Bosnia and Herzegovina	0.47	Myanmar	0.25
Botswana	0.32	Namibia	0.35
Brazil	0.39	Nepal	0.17
Brunei	0.34	Netherlands	0.46
Bulgaria	0.36	New Zealand	0.36
Burkina Faso	0.28	Nicaragua	0.25
Burundi	0.31	Niger	0.28
Cambodia	0.21	Nigeria	0.13
Cameroon	0.22	Norway	0.43
Canada	0.41	Oman	0.46
Central African Republic	0.15	Pakistan	0.22
Chad	0.23	Panama	0.27
Chile	0.24	Papua New Guinea	0.36
China	0.29	Paraguay	0.24
Colombia	0.29	Peru	0.22
Costa Rica	0.19	Philippines	0.19
Côte d'Ivoire	0.22	Poland	0.42
Croatia	0.48	Portugal	0.50
Cyprus	0.42	Qatar	0.32
Czech Republic	0.42	Romania	0.34
Denmark	0.57	Russia	0.38
Djibouti	0.38	Rwanda	0.28
Dominican Republic	0.18	Saudi Arabia	0.36
Ecuador	0.44	Senegal	0.28
Egypt	0.37	Serbia	0.43
El Salvador	0.22	Sierra Leone	0.16
Equatorial Guinea	0.39	Slovakia	0.41
Eritrea	0.30	Slovenia	0.55

(continued)

Table 13.1 *Continued*

Country	Spending ratio	Country	Spending ratio
Estonia	0.38	Solomon Islands	0.50
Ethiopia	0.18	South Africa	0.32
Fiji	0.29	South Korea	0.21
Finland	0.58	South Sudan	0.26
France	0.57	Spain	0.44
Gabon	0.28	Sri Lanka	0.18
Georgia	0.29	Sudan	0.13
Germany	0.44	Suriname	0.31
Ghana	0.28	Swaziland	0.29
Greece	0.49	Sweden	0.51
Guatemala	0.14	Switzerland	0.31
Guinea	0.25	Tajikistan	0.28
Guinea-Bissau	0.13	Tanzania	0.19
Guyana	0.30	Thailand	0.22
Haiti	0.28	The Bahamas	0.22
Honduras	0.31	The Gambia	0.27
Hungary	0.50	Timor-Leste	0.19
Iceland	0.44	Togo	0.26
India	0.27	Trinidad and Tobago	0.35
Indonesia	0.19	Tunisia	0.30
Iran	0.15	Turkey	0.38
Iraq	0.48	Turkmenistan	0.16
Ireland	0.39	Uganda	0.17
Israel	0.41	Ukraine	0.48
Italy	0.51	United Arab Emirates	0.31
Jamaica	0.27	United Kingdom	0.42
Japan	0.41	United States	0.36
Jordan	0.36	Uruguay	0.32
Kazakhstan	0.20	Uzbekistan	0.34
Kenya	0.25	Vanuatu	0.22
Kosovo	0.28	Venezuela	0.38
Kuwait	0.38	Vietnam	0.30
Kyrgyzstan	0.38	Yemen	0.31
Laos	0.30	Zambia	0.25
Latvia	0.37	Zimbabwe	0.30

Note: The table shows the ratio of general government expenditure to GDP for 2013. Countries are included only when data are available for general government expenditure. Data are from the International Monetary Fund.

The government's budget constraint

Now, we extend our equilibrium business-cycle model to allow for government purchases of goods and services, and transfer payments. Let G_t represent government purchases in real terms for year t. In our previous analysis, we considered two forms of private real spending on goods and services: consumption, C_t, and gross investment, I_t. The total of the three terms, $C_t + I_t + G_t$, is the aggregate real spending on goods and services in year t. Let V_t represent the government's real expenditure on transfers. Unlike G_t, real transfers, V_t, are not spending on goods and services.

A transfer just represents the government shuffling income around, taking from one group of people (through taxes) and giving to another (through transfers).

In Chapter 12, the government's only revenue came from printing money. The real value of this revenue for year t is $(M_t - M_{t-1})/P_t$, where M_t is the nominal quantity of money in year t, and M_{t-1} is the quantity one year earlier. In the Eurozone, the revenue from printing money accrues directly to the central bank, which is the European Central Bank. In the model, we consolidate the central bank with the government. Now, we assume that the government also levies taxes on households. These taxes might apply to businesses, but remember that the households own and run the businesses. Let T_t be the total real taxes collected by the government in year t.

The **government's budget constraint** says that its total uses of funds must equal its total sources of funds. The uses are for purchases of goods and services and transfer payments. The sources are taxes and money creation. Therefore, we can write the government's budget constraint in real terms for year t as:

Key equation (government budget constraint):

$$total\ uses\ of\ funds = total\ sources\ of\ funds$$
$$G_t + V_t = T_t + (M_t - M_{t-1})/P_t$$
$$real\ purchase + real\ transfers = real\ taxes + real\ revenue\ from\ money\ creation \qquad (13.1)$$

Note that we have not introduced public debt in the model. Therefore, the government's uses of funds on the left-hand side do not include interest payments, and the government's sources of funds on the right-hand side do not include the proceeds from issue of public debt. We will make the extensions to include interest payments and public-debt issue in Chapter 15.

We mentioned in Chapter 12 that the real revenue from printing money, $(M_t - M_{t-1})/P_t$, is normally a minor part of overall government revenue. We shall find it convenient to ignore the revenue from printing money, and we can do this by returning to the case in which the nominal quantity of money, M_t, is constant. In this case, we can substitute $M_t - M_{t-1} = 0$ in equation (13.1) to get:

$$G_t + V_t = T_t$$
$$real\ purchase + real\ transfers = real\ taxes \qquad (13.2)$$

In Chapter 12, transfer payments took the form of helicopter drops of cash that households picked up. The important assumption was that these transfers were lump-sum – the amount the household received did not depend on the household's income, money holdings, and so on. We continue to assume that the real transfers, V_t, are lump-sum. That is, the household's transfers do not depend on its decisions.

We also assume **lump-sum taxes** in this chapter. That is, the real taxes, T_t, that the household pays are independent of its income, consumption, and so on. This assumption is unrealistic. In the real world, elaborate tax laws specify how a household's taxes depend on its income, consumption, and so on. There are many things a household can do to lower its taxes, including hiring accountants, working less, under-reporting income and exploiting tax loopholes. These possibilities imply substitution effects from the tax system on labour supply, consumption, and even the number of children. Although we want to study these substitution effects, we shall find it convenient to ignore them provisionally to isolate the effects from government expenditure. That is why we assume lump-sum taxes in this chapter. In Chapter 14, we will allow for substitution effects from realistic types of taxes. That analysis also brings in substitution effects from transfer programmes.

Public production

We assume that the government uses its real purchases of goods and services, G_t, to provide services to households and businesses, and that the government delivers these services free of charge to the users. In most countries, public services include national defence, enforcement of laws and private contracts, police and fire protection, primary and secondary schooling and some portions of higher education, parts of health services, highways, parks, and so on. The range of governmental activities has expanded over time, although this range varies from one country or locality to another.

We could model public services as the output from the government's production function. The inputs to this function would be the government-owned stock of capital, labour services from public employees and materials that the government buys from the private sector. To simplify, we ignore government production and assume, instead, that the government buys final goods and services from private producers. That is, the government's purchases, G_t, add to the demand for goods and services by private consumers, C_t, and investors, I_t.

In effect, we are assuming that the government subcontracts all of its production to the private sector. In this set-up, public investment, publicly owned capital and government employment are zero. Ultimately, we would get different answers by allowing for public production only if the government's production function – that is, its technology and management capability – differed from that of the private sector. Otherwise, it would not matter whether the government buys final goods and services, as we assume, or, instead, buys capital and labour inputs to produce things itself.

Public services

We have to take a position on the uses of the services that the government provides. One possibility is that these services yield utility for households. Examples are parks, libraries, school lunch programmes, subsidized health care and transportation, and the entertaining parts of the space programme. These public services may substitute for private consumption. For example, if the government buys a student's lunch at school, the student does not have to buy their own lunch.

Another possibility is that public services are inputs to private production. Examples include the provision and enforcement of laws and contracts, aspects of national defence, government-sponsored research and development programmes, the technologically valuable parts of the space programme, fire and police services, and regulatory activities. In some cases, public services substitute for private inputs of labour and capital services. For example, the government's police services may substitute for guards hired by a private company. In other cases – including infrastructure activities such as the provision of a legal system, national defence, and perhaps public transport – the public services are likely to raise the marginal products of private inputs.

We shall find it convenient to begin with the hypothetical case in which public services have zero effect on utility and production. This set-up is akin to assuming that the government buys goods and services and then throws them into the ocean. We will consider later how the conclusions change if we allow public services to be useful.

The household's budget constraint

The government's taxes and transfers affect each household's budget constraint. To see how, start with the household budget constraint from Chapter 9:

$$C + (1/P) \bullet \Delta B + \Delta K = (w/P) \bullet L^s + i \bullet (B/P + k)$$

$$consumption + real\, saving = real\, income \tag{9.6}$$

The analysis in Chapter 9 neglected inflation; that is, the price level, P_t, was constant over time. We simplify by returning to this case. Note that our assumption of a constant P_t is consistent with our assumption of a constant nominal quantity of money, M_t. Neither of these unrealistic assumptions affects our analysis of government purchases.

The right-hand side of equation (9.6) includes real asset income, $i \bullet (B/P + K)$, which depends on the nominal interest rate, i. However, since we are assuming that the inflation rate, π, is zero, the real interest rate, r, equals the nominal rate, i. We shall find it useful to replace i by r, because then the analysis will be valid when we allow π to be nonzero. If we apply equation (9.6) to year t and replace i by r, we get:

$$C_t + (1/P) \cdot \Delta B_t + \Delta K_t = (w/P)_t \cdot L_t^s + r_{t-1} \cdot (B_{t-1}/P + k_{t-1})$$
$$consumption + real\,saving = real\,income,$$
(13.3)

where $\Delta B_t = B_t - B_{t-1}$ and $\Delta K_t = K_t - K_{t-1}$.

The existence of the government leads to two modifications of the household's budget constraint in equation (13.3). First, year t's real taxes, T_t, subtract from real income on the right-hand side. One unit more of real taxes means one unit less of **real disposable income**, which is the real income available after taxes. Second, year t's real transfers, V_t, add to real income on the right-hand side. Therefore, the household's budget constraint becomes:

$$C_t + (1/P) \cdot \Delta B_t + \Delta K_t = (w/P)_t \cdot L_t^s + r_{t-1} \cdot (B_{t-1}/P + K_{t-1}) + V_t - T_t$$
$$consumption + real\,saving = real\,disposable\,income$$
(13.4)

The shaded new term on the right-hand side is the difference between real transfers and real taxes, $V_t - T_t$.

We showed in Chapters 8 and 9 how to extend the household's one-year budget constraint to many years. The result, when we modify equation (9.7) to replace the nominal interest rate, i_t, by the real interest rate, r_t, is:

$$C_1 + C_2(1/r_1) + C_3[(1+r_1) \cdot (1+r_2)] + \cdots = (1/r_0) \cdot (B_0/P + K_0)$$
$$+ (w/P)_1 \cdot L_1^s + (w/P)_2 \cdot L_2^s/(1+r_1) + (w/P)_3 \cdot L_3^s/[(1+r_1) \cdot (1+r_2)] + \cdots$$
$$present\,value\,of\,consumption = value\,of\,initial\,assets + present\,value\,of\,wage\,incomes$$
(13.5)

When we allow for taxes and transfers, as we did in going from equation (13.3) to equation (13.4), we get an extension to the multiyear budget constraint from equation (13.5). The extended version is:

> Key equation (multiyear household budget constraint with transfers and taxes):
> $$C_1 + C_2(1/r_1) + \cdots = (1/r_0) \cdot (B_0/P + K_0) + (w/P)_1 \cdot L_1^s + (w/P)_2 \cdot L_2^s/(1+r_1) + \cdots$$
> $$+ (V_1 - T_1) + (V_2 - T_2)/(1+r_1) + (V_3 - T_3)/[(1+r_1) \cdot (1+r_2)] + \cdots$$
> $$present\,value\,of\,consumption = value\,of\,initial\,assets + present\,value\,of\,wage\,incomes$$
> $$+ present\,value\,of\,transfers\,net\,of\,taxes$$
> (13.6)

The shaded new term on the right-hand side is the present value of real transfers net of real taxes:

$$(V_1 - T_1) + (V_2 - T_2)/(1+r_1) + (V_3 - T_3)/[(1+r_1) \cdot (1+r_2)] +$$
$$= present\,value\,of\,real\,transfers\,net\,of\,real\,taxes$$
(13.7)

A lower present value of real transfers net of real taxes lowers the overall sources of funds for the household. Our analysis from Chapter 8 predicts that the household would react just as it would to any other loss of income. In particular, the income effects predict reductions in consumption, C_t, and leisure in each year. The decrease in leisure implies an increase in labour supply, L_t^s, in each year.

Our analysis from Chapter 8 tells us that the strength of the income effect depends on whether a change in real transfers net of real taxes is temporary or permanent. For a temporary change, we can consider a decrease in real transfers net of real taxes for year 1, $V_1 - T_1$, while holding fixed the terms $V_t - T_t$ for other years t. In this case, the present value of real transfers net of real taxes falls in equation (13.7), but only by a small amount. Therefore, we predict small decreases in C_t and small increases in L_t^s for each year. In contrast, if the decline in $V_t - T_t$ applies for all years t, the present value of real transfers net of real taxes falls in equation (13.7) by a large amount. Therefore, we predict large decreases in C_t and large increases in L_t^s for each year.

Permanent changes in government purchases

We now turn our attention to government purchases. We begin by considering the economic effects of a permanent change in government purchases. Recall that Figure 13.1 showed the Eurozone data on total government purchases, expressed as a ratio to GDP. The present analysis does not apply to large temporary changes, such as surges in defence purchases during wartime. The analysis does apply to most other variations in government purchases; empirically, most changes in the ratio of government purchases to GDP have been long-lasting.

A PERMANENT CHANGE IN GOVERNMENT PURCHASES: THEORY

Suppose that government purchases, G_t, rise by one unit each year. Since we are considering the same change each year, we can simplify by dropping the year subscript, t. In this case, the government's budget constraint from equation (13.2) is:

$$G + V = T$$

Therefore, we can rearrange the terms to get a formula for real transfers net of real taxes:

$$V - T = -G \qquad (13.8)$$

If G rises by one unit each year, $V - T$ falls by one unit each year. Hence, the typical household's disposable real income falls by one unit each year. The income effects predict, accordingly, a decrease in each year's consumption, C, and an increase in each year's labour supply, L^s.

We can get the main results by ignoring for now the changes in labour supply, L^s. That is, we assume that each year's L^s equals a constant, L. We reconsider this assumption later in this chapter and in Chapter 14, where we allow also for the substitution effects from realistic forms of taxes.

Consider the income effect on consumption, C. Since the typical household has one less unit of real disposable income each year, we predict that the decrease in C each year will be roughly by one unit. This prediction follows from the result in Chapter 8 that the propensity to consume out of a permanent change in income would be close to 1.0.

Now, let's consider how the increase in government purchases affects the demand and supply of capital services and real GDP. Recall that real GDP, Y, is given by the production function from Chapter 10:

$$Y = A \bullet F(\kappa K, L) \qquad (10.1)$$

This formulation allows for a variable capital utilization rate, κ, so that κK is the quantity of capital services. We are assuming that the capital stock, K, is fixed in the short run. We are also assuming that the technology level, A, and the quantity of labour input, L, are fixed.

As in Chapter 10, the quantity of capital services demanded, $(\kappa K)^d$, comes from the equation of the marginal product of capital services, MPK, to the real rental price, R/P. This condition determined a downward-sloping demand curve for capital services, as shown in Figure 10.5. We reproduce this demand curve as the dark blue graph in Figure 13.5.

Since the capital stock, K, is given, the quantity of capital services supplied, $(\kappa K)^s$, varies only because of changes in the capital utilization rate, κ. As in Figure 10.5 in Chapter 10, the chosen κ and, hence, the quantity of capital services supplied, $(\kappa K)^s$, is an upward-sloping function of the real rental price, R/P. We show this supply curve as the light blue graph in Figure 13.5.

The important observation is that an increase in government purchases, G, does not shift the curves for the demand or supply of capital services. The demand curve does not shift because the rise in G does not affect the MPK (for a given input of capital services, κK). The supply curve does not shift because, first, K is given, and, second, the change in G does not affect the choice of the capital utilization rate, κ (as worked out in Figure 10.3 in Chapter 10). Because the demand and supply curves do not shift in Figure 13.5, we conclude that the market-clearing real rental price, $(R/P)^*$, and quantity of capital services, $(\kappa K)^*$, do not change.

Figure 13.5 Clearing of the market for capital services

This construction comes from Figure 10.5. The demand curve for capital services, $(\kappa K)^d$, comes from the equation of the marginal product of capital services, MPK, to the real rental price, R/P. When R/P rises, the quantity of capital services demanded falls. The supply of capital services, $(\kappa K)^s$, applies for a given capital stock, K. If R/P rises, owners of capital raise the capital utilization rate, κ. Therefore, the quantity of capital services supplied rises. The market clears where the quantity of capital services supplied equals the quantity demanded. At this point, R/P equals $(R/P)^*$ on the vertical axis, and κK equals $(\kappa K)^*$ on the horizontal axis.

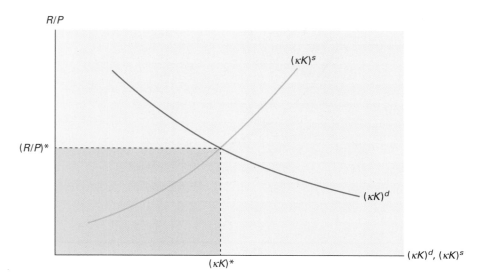

Real GDP, Y, is given from the production function in equation (10.1) as $Y = A \bullet F(\kappa K, L)$. We found that the quantity of capital services, κK, is unchanged, and we assumed that the technology level, A, and the quantity of labour input, L, are fixed. Therefore, Y is unchanged. Thus, *we have the important conclusion that a permanent increase in government purchases does not affect real GDP when labour supply is fixed.*

Consider the real interest rate, r. We know from Chapter 12 that r is given by:

$$r = (R/P) \bullet \kappa - \delta(\kappa)$$

real rate of return on bonds = real rate of return from owning capital   (12.10)

where R/P is the real rental price and κ is the capital utilization rate. The term $(R/P) \bullet \kappa$ is the real rental income per unit of capital. We have found that a permanent increase in government purchases, G, does not affect R/P or κ. Therefore, equation (12.8) implies that the real interest rate, r, does not change. Thus, we have another important result: *a permanent increase in government purchases does not affect the real interest rate when labour supply is fixed.*

Now, we turn to the labour market. As we saw in Chapters 7 and 9, the quantity of labour demanded, L^d, comes from the equation of the marginal product of labour, MPL, to the real wage rate, w/P. This condition determines a downward-sloping demand curve for labour, as shown in Figures 7.4 and 9.5. We reproduce this demand curve as the dark blue graph in Figure 13.6.

We discussed in Chapter 9 how an increase in the real wage rate, w/P, motivates households to increase the quantity of labour supplied, L^s. However, we are assuming for now that labour supply, L^s, is a constant, L. Therefore, Figure 13.6 shows L^s as a vertical line at L. We assume that the increase in government purchases, G, does not change L.

The permanent increase in government purchases, G, does not shift the labour-demand curve, L^d, in Figure 13.6. The reason is that the rise in G does not affect the MPL (for given input of labour, L). To get this answer, we use the result from Figure 13.5 that the quantity of capital services, κK, is unchanged. If capital services had changed, the MPL would be different (at a given L), and the L^d curve would shift in Figure 13.6.

Figure 13.6 Clearing of the labour market

This construction comes from Figure 9.5. The demand curve for labour, L^d, shown in dark blue, comes from the equation of the marginal product of labour, MPL, to the real wage rate, w/P. When w/P rises, the quantity of labour demanded falls. We assume here that labour supply, L^s, shown in light blue, equals the constant L. The market clears where $w/P = (w/P)^*$ on the vertical axis, so that the quantity of labour demanded equals L.

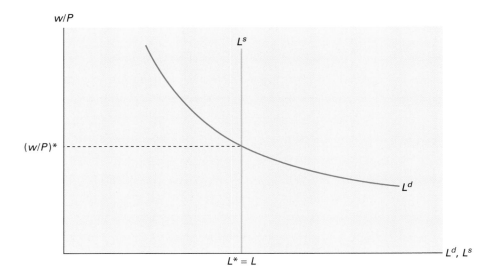

The increase in government purchases, G, does not shift labour supply, L^s, which is fixed at L, and does not shift the labour-demand curve, L^d. Therefore, the increase in G changes nothing in Figure 13.6. Hence, the market-clearing real wage rate, $(w/P)^*$, does not change. We conclude that *a permanent increase in government purchases does not affect the real wage rate when labour supply is fixed*

Now, we return to the behaviour of consumption, C. We know from our analysis of income effects that a permanent rise in government purchases, G, by one unit reduces C in each year by roughly one unit. To find the full effect on current consumption, we have to consider whether any substitution effects apply. The intertemporal-substitution effect depends on the real interest rate, r. Since r does not change, the intertemporal-substitution effect does not operate. Another substitution effect involves consumption and leisure, but we have assumed that the quantity of labour and, hence, the quantity of leisure, is fixed. In any event, this substitution effect depends on the real wage rate, w/P, which does not change.

Since no substitution effects arise, we can determine the change in current consumption, C, solely from the income effect. As already noted, the income effect causes C to decline by roughly one unit. Therefore, *our prediction is that when labour supply is fixed, a permanent increase in government purchases by one unit causes consumption to decrease by about one unit*.

To find the response of gross investment, I, recall that real GDP, Y, equals the sum of consumption, C, gross investment, I, and government purchases, G:

$$Y = C + I + G \tag{13.9}$$

In the present case, Y is unchanged, G rises by one unit, and C falls by one unit. Therefore, equation (13.9) tells us that the changes in C and G fully offset each other and, thereby, allow I to remain unchanged. We conclude that *when labour supply is fixed, a permanent increase in government purchases does not affect gross investment*.

To sum up, we predict that a permanent increase in government purchases, G, reduces consumption, C, roughly one to one. The variables that do not change include real GDP, Y; gross investment, I; the quantity of capital services, κK; the real rental price, R/P; the real interest rate, r; and the real wage rate, w/P.

Extending the Model
Useful public services

We did not consider that the government may use its purchases, G, to provide useful public services. We study here the case in which these services provide utility for households. As examples, the government might provide free or subsidized school lunches or transport, or concerts in the park. We assume that these publicly provided services combine with private consumer expenditure to determine overall household utility. For example, utility depends on transport, one part of which is provided by the government.

Suppose that each household views a unit of government purchases, G, as equivalent in utility to λ units of private consumption, C. We assume that $\lambda \geq 0$ applies. Differences of opinion about the size of λ are at the heart of debates about the desirable size of government. The case $\lambda = 1$ means that one unit of G is equivalent in utility to one unit of C. The case $\lambda < 1$ means that a unit of resources that goes through the government provides less utility than a unit of private consumer spending. This case might apply because the lack of market incentives makes government operations relatively inefficient. We could, instead, have $\lambda > 1$, if there are scale benefits in the provision of public goods.

Recall from equation (13.4) that the household budget constraint, when written without year subscripts, is:

$$C + (1/P) \bullet \Delta B + \Delta K = (w/P) \bullet L^s + r \bullet (B/P + K) + V - T$$
$$consumption + real\ saving = real\ disposable\ income$$

We can add λG to each side of the equation to get:

$$(C + \lambda G) + (1/P) \bullet \Delta B + \Delta K = (w/P) \bullet L^s + r \bullet (B/P + K) + V - T + \lambda G$$
$$effective\ consumption + real\ saving = effective\ real\ disposable\ income \qquad (13.10)$$

The two new terms are shaded in yellow. This specification is useful because $C + \lambda G$ on the left-hand side can be thought of as *effective consumption*: the sum of private consumption, C, and the utility received from public services, λG. The new term on the right-hand side, λG, is the implicit value of the free or subsidized public services. Thus, we can think of the right-hand side as *effective real disposable income*, the sum of real disposable income and the implicit value of public services, λG.

Consider the case in which government purchases, G, rise by one unit each year. The government's budget constraint in equation (13.8) says that the difference between real transfers and real taxes, $V - T$, falls by one unit each year. Therefore, an increase in G by one unit changes the combination of the last three terms on the right-hand side of equation (13.10) by:

$$\Delta(V - T + \lambda G) = \Delta(V - T) + \Delta(\lambda G)$$
$$= -1 + \lambda$$

where we used the conditions $\Delta(V - T) = -1$ and $\Delta(\lambda G) = \lambda$. Thus, the change in effective real disposable income depends on whether λ is less than, equal to or greater than 1. If $\lambda < 1$, effective real disposable income declines by $1 - \lambda$ units when G rises by one unit, but if $\lambda > 1$, effective real disposable income rises by $\lambda - 1$ units when G increases by one unit. In the main text, we assumed $\lambda = 0$, so that effective real disposable income fell by one unit when G rose by one unit.

To fix ideas, consider the case in which $\lambda < 1$. (However, the analysis also applies if $\lambda = 1$ or $\lambda > 1$.) Since effective real disposable income falls by $1 - \lambda$ units each year, we predict that the household's effective consumption, $C + \lambda G$, would fall by about $1 - \lambda$ units each year. That is, the change in effective consumption will be close to the change in effective real disposable income. To determine the change in C, use the condition:

$$\Delta(C + \lambda G) = -1 + \lambda$$

If we separate out the two changes on the left-hand side, we get:

$$\Delta C + \lambda \bullet \Delta G = -1 + \lambda$$

If we substitute $\Delta G = 1$ and cancel out λ on each side, we get:

$$\Delta C = -1$$

The result $\Delta C = -1$ means that a permanent increase in G by one unit crowds out private consumption, C, by one unit. We have found that this result holds for any value of λ. It works for the case in the main text in which public services are useless ($\lambda = 0$), when a unit of public services provides less utility than a unit of private consumption ($0 < \lambda < 1$), when public and private services are viewed equally ($\lambda = 1$) and when public services are valued more highly ($\lambda > 1$). The only difference between the cases – but an important difference – is that the higher λ, the happier households are when the government expands G.

THE CYCLICAL BEHAVIOUR OF GOVERNMENT PURCHASES

One prediction from the equilibrium business-cycle model is that long-lasting changes in real government purchases would not have much impact on real GDP. We mentioned that many changes in real government purchases fit the assumption of being long-lasting. Therefore, the model predicts that the fluctuations in real government purchases should bear little relation to the fluctuations in real GDP.

To test this proposition, Figure 13.7 uses our standard approach of comparing the cyclical part of a variable — in this case, real government purchases – with the cyclical part of real GDP. The variability of real government purchases from 1999 to 2015 is about half of that of real GDP. Figure 13.7 shows that the cyclical parts of the two variables were sometimes positively correlated and sometimes negatively correlated, with an overall correlation of −0.21. This result contradicts our equilibrium business-cycle model. In the rest of this chapter and in Chapter 14, we will generalize the model in order to allow it to generate the different relationships shown in Figure 13.7. As we will see later in this chapter, introducing variable labour supply would allow the equilibrium business-cycle model to deliver a positive relationship between real GDP and government purchases, as in the IS-LM/AS-AD model but via a different channel to be discussed later in this chapter. As we will show in Chapter 14, considering a wage-income

Figure 13.7 Cyclical behaviour of Eurozone real GDP and government purchases

The dark blue graph is the deviation of real GDP from its trend. The light blue graph is the deviation of real government purchases from its trend. (We measure government purchases by the national-accounts data on government consumption due to data availability. This treatment is also consistent with the model; see footnote 1.) The deviations are measured in a proportionate sense. The data on GDP and government purchases are quarterly and seasonally adjusted. Government purchases are about half as variable as GDP. The overall correlation of the cyclical part of real government purchases with the cyclical part of real GDP was −0.21.

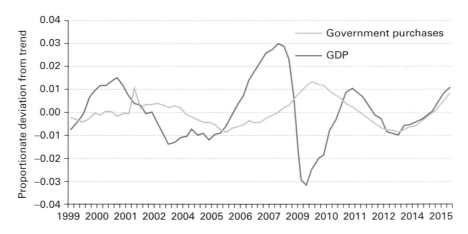

tax, instead of a lump-sum tax, could allow the model to deliver a negative relationship between real GDP and government purchases. Note also that the pattern for government purchases is very different from the ones we found for consumer expenditure and investment (Figures 9.8 and 9.9), each of which was strongly procyclical.

Temporary changes in government purchases

Now, we will analyze temporary changes in real government purchases. We begin by extending the equilibrium business-cycle model to include temporary variations in government purchases. Then, we apply the extended model to wartime experiences.

A TEMPORARY CHANGE IN GOVERNMENT PURCHASES: THEORY

Assume now that year 1's real government purchases, G_1, rise by one unit, while those for other years, G_t, do not change. That is, everyone expects that G_t in future years will return to the original level. We can think of this case as representing a war that begins at the start of year 1 and is expected to last one year. Of course, this description is a simplification, intended to capture the main features of temporarily high government purchases. In reality, the durations of wars vary, and the interval of heightened government purchases might be greater or less than one year.

The government's budget constraint from equation (13.8) implies for year t:

$$V_t - T_t = -G_t \qquad (13.11)$$

Therefore, in year 1, the net of real transfers over real taxes, $V_1 - T_1$, falls by one unit and households have one unit less of real disposable income. In subsequent years, $V_t - T_t$ and, hence, real disposable incomes return to their original levels. Thus, the difference from a permanent rise in government purchases is that the expected real disposable income in future years is unchanged. Our analysis from Chapter 8 predicts that households would spread their reduced disposable income in year 1 over reduced consumption, C_t, in all years t. Therefore, the effect on year 1's consumption, C_1, will be relatively small. The propensity to consume out of a temporary change in income is greater than zero but much less than 1.0.

Now, to simplify the notation, we again drop the time subscripts, with each variable implicitly applying to the current year, year 1. Much of the analysis of a temporary change in government purchases is the same as that worked out for a permanent change. As before, we ignore any changes in labour supply, so that $L^s = L$. In Figure 13.5, the change in government purchases still does not affect the MPK (for a given quantity of capital services, κK) and, therefore, does not shift the demand curve for capital services, $(\kappa K)^d$. The change in government purchases also does not affect the way that suppliers of capital services choose their utilization rate, κ (for a given real rental price, R/P). Therefore, with a fixed stock of capital, K, the supply curve for capital services, $(\kappa K)^s$, does not shift. Since neither curve shifts in Figure 13.5, we conclude, as before, that the real rental price, R/P, and the quantity of capital services, κK, do not change.

Since capital services, κK, do not change and labour is fixed at L, we know from the production function:

$$Y = A \bullet F(\kappa K, L) \qquad (10.1)$$

that real GDP, Y, does not change. Since the real rental price, R/P, and the capital utilization rate, κ, do not change, we also have that the real interest rate, r, stays the same. This result follows from the formula:

$$r = (R/P) \bullet \kappa - \delta(\kappa)$$
$$\textit{real rate of return on bonds} = \textit{real rate of return from owning capital} \qquad (12.10)$$

In Figure 13.6, the change in government purchases still does not affect the MPL (for a given labour input, L) and, therefore, does not shift the labour demand curve, L^d. Since labour supply, L^s, is fixed at L, the change in government purchases also does not shift the labour-supply curve. Since neither curve shifts, the real wage rate, w/P, does not change.

New results come when we consider consumption and investment. Consider again the expression for real GDP:

$$Y = C + I + G \tag{13.9}$$

Real GDP, Y, is unchanged; real government purchases, G, are higher in year 1 by one unit; and consumption, C, is lower, but by much less than one unit. Consequently, equation (13.9) implies that gross investment, I, must fall. In fact, since the decrease in C is relatively small, the decline in I is large. That is, year 1's extra G comes mainly at the expense of I, rather than C. In contrast, when the change in G was permanent, we predicted that most or all of the extra G came at the expense of C.

Extending the Model
Effects on the term structure of interest rates

We found that a temporary increase in government purchases, G, did not affect the real interest rate, r. We also found that investment, I, declined. For example, I would be depressed during a war, which might last several years. Over time, the decline in investment means that the stock of capital, K, will be lower than it otherwise would have been; in particular, K will be lower at the end of the war. The decrease in K reduces the supply of capital services, leading to an increase in the market-clearing real rental price, R/P. The rise in R/P leads to an increase in r, in accordance with equation (12.8), $r = (R/P) \cdot \kappa - \delta(\kappa)$. Hence, although the current real interest rate does not change, future real interest rates rise.

In our model, the real interest rate, r, is a short-term real rate. In the real world, bonds are traded with varying maturities. For example, a one-year bond might pay the real rate of return $r(1)$, a five-year bond the real rate of return $r(5)$, and so on. The **term structure of real interest rates** is the relation between the real rate of return, $r(j)$, and the maturity, j. If $r(j)$ increases with j, the term structure is upward sloping; otherwise, it is flat or downward sloping.

If we consider, say, a five-year horizon, an individual can hold to maturity a five-year indexed government bond or can, instead, hold a sequence of five one-year indexed bonds. In the first case, the real rate of return is $r(5)$. In the second, the real rate of return is an average of the five one-year returns, $r(1)$. Competition in the financial markets will work to equate the anticipated rates of return from the two options. Hence, $r(5)$ will be an average of the $r(1)s$ expected to prevail over the next five years.

In the case of a temporary increase in government purchases, short-term real interest rates, such as $r(1)$, did not change initially. However, anticipated future values of $r(1)$ increased. Therefore, the average of the $r(1)s$ expected to prevail over the next five years rose. Since $r(5)$ equals the average of the expected $r(1)s$, it follows that $r(5)$ rises immediately when government purchases increase. In other words, the model predicts an effect on the term structure of real interest rates. Short-term rates do not change immediately, but longer-term rates increase. Hence, the term structure becomes more upward sloping.

GOVERNMENT PURCHASES AND REAL GDP DURING WARTIME: EMPIRICAL

We will now evaluate the equilibrium business-cycle model's predictions for the effects of a temporary change in real government purchases. We test the model by studying the response of the economy to the temporary changes in government purchases that have accompanied wars. To ensure that these wartime purchases were the major influence on the economy, we consider major wars in the last century. Due to data availability, we consider wartime data in the US as an example.

Table 13.2 covers World War I, World War II, the Korean War and the Vietnam War. We can measure the temporary part of real defence purchases by the difference between actual purchases and an estimated trend. The trend is calculated in our usual manner by fitting a line through the historical data. We focus on the peaks of wartime purchases: 1918, 1943–44, 1952–53 and 1967–68. The values of temporary real purchases, in 1996 prices, were $84 billion, or 16% of trend real GDP, in 1918; $537 billion, or 44% of trend real GDP, in 1943–44; $56 billion, or 3% of trend real GDP, in 1952–53; and $46 billion, or 1.4% of trend real GDP, in 1967–68. Based on these numbers, we can be confident that wartime purchases, and possibly other effects from war, were the major influences on the economy during World Wars I and II. That is, we do not have to worry about holding constant other factors. Wartime purchases would also be a major influence during the Korean War, though not necessarily the dominant force. In the Vietnam War, the temporary military purchases of only 1.4% of real GDP were unlikely to be the overriding factor; other disturbances were likely of comparable or greater significance.

Table 13.2 US wartime spending, real GDP and employment

I: Real GDP and components. Each entry is the deviation from trend in billions of 1996 prices. Values in parentheses are percentage of own trend.

| Category of GDP: | Wartime years | | | |
	1918 (WW I)	1943–44 (WW II)	1952–53 (Korea)	1967–68 (Vietnam)
Defence purchases	84 (679)	537 (317)	56 (25)	46 (15)
% of trend real GDP	16	44	3	1
Real GDP	42 (8)	433 (36)	49 (3)	81 (2)
Consumption	−21 (−5)	−1 (0)	0 (0)	31 (1)
Gross investment	−21 (−28)	−58 (−51)	0 (0)	5 (1)
Non-defence government	(0)	−20 (−19)	5 (3)	5 (1)
Net exports	0	−23	−11	−5

II: Employment. Each entry is the deviation from trend in millions. Values in parentheses are percentage of own trend.

Category of employment:				
Total employment	3.0 (8)	9.1 (17)	0.9 (1)	1.0 (1)
Civilian employment	0.5 (1)	1.5 (3)	0.2 (0)	0.4 (1)
Military personnel	2.5 (566)	7.7 (296)	0.7 (24)	0.6 (19)

Notes: In part I, each cell shows the deviation of a real expenditure component from its estimated trend in billions of 1996 prices per year. The values in parentheses express the deviations as a percentage of the trend. For example, as an average for 1943 and 1944, defence purchases were $537 billion, or 317% above trend; real GDP was $433 billion, or 36% above trend; and so on. Each real expenditure component is the nominal value divided by the deflator for the GDP. (The trend for real GDP was constrained to equal the sum of the trends estimated for the components of GDP.) In part II, total employment is the sum of civilian employment and military personnel. Each entry shows the deviation of a component of employment from its own trend in millions. For example, as an average for 1943 and 1944, total employment was 9.1 million, or 17% above its own trend; civilian employment was 1.5 million, or 3% above its own trend; and military personnel was 7.7 million, or 296% above its own trend. (The trend for total employment was constrained to equal the sum of the trends estimated for its two parts, civilian employment and military personnel.) Data for the last three wars are from Bureau of Economic Analysis (http://www.bea.gov). Data for 1918 are from John Kendrick (1961), Christina Romer (1988), and U.S. Department of Commerce (1975).

To illustrate the main results, we focus in Table 13.2 on World War II and the Korean War. In each case, real GDP was above its trend, but by less than the excess of real defence purchases from its trend. For example, in 1943–44, the excess for real defence purchases of $537 billion was matched by an excess for real GDP of $433 billion. For 1952–53, the numbers were $56 billion and $49 billion, respectively.

Since real GDP was up by less than defence purchases, the other components of GDP had to be below trend overall. In 1943–44, the shortfalls from trend were $58 billion in gross investment and $20 billion in non-defence forms of government consumption and investment. Consumption was about equal to trend, and net exports of goods and services were $23 billion below trend. (We will study net exports in Chapter 18.) In 1952–53, gross investment and consumption were each about equal to trend, non-defence government consumption was $5 billion above trend, and net exports were $11 billion below trend.

Consider how the equilibrium business-cycle model relates to these wartime observations. The main discrepancy is that the model predicted no change in real GDP, whereas the data reveal substantial increases in real GDP. The data also show that the rises in real GDP are by less than the increases in government purchases. That is, aside from military purchases, the totals of the other components of real GDP are down during wartime. The model accords with this pattern. However, the components of real GDP other than military purchases do not fall nearly as much as predicted by the model.

WARTIME EFFECTS ON THE ECONOMY

The main failing of the model – and quite a striking one – is its prediction that real GDP would be unchanged during wartime. The source of this prediction is our assumption that labour input, L, is fixed. Therefore, it is worthwhile to reconsider this assumption. We begin by looking at the data on employment during wartime.

Employment during wartime

We can illustrate the main pattern from World War II. The number of persons in the military soared – in 1943–44, military personnel reached 7.7 million persons above its estimated trend. But surprisingly, civilian employment also increased, rising by 1.5 million or 3% above its estimated trend. Putting the two parts together, total employment – civilian plus military – was 9.1 million or 17% above trend. The basic pattern is that the military took in a significant number of persons – primarily through the military draft in the wars up to Vietnam – and total employment expanded a little more. To do better with our predictions, we have to explain why the total quantity of labour supplied increased so much.

Effects of war on labour supply

At this point, there is no settled view among economists about the best way to understand labour supply during wartime. Thus, we consider a number of possibilities and will not be able to reach a definitive explanation. Here are some ideas that have been advanced.

- A large expansion of real government purchases, G, means that households have less real disposable income. The negative income effect predicts reductions in consumption and leisure and, hence, an increase in labour supply, L^s. Several considerations influence the size of the income effect. For one thing, we have stressed that the increase in G is likely to be temporary, at least if the wars are expected to last no more than a few years and if no major destruction of capital stock and population is anticipated. This consideration makes the income effects on consumption and leisure relatively small. On the other hand, military outlays would not substitute for private consumption in the provision of utility; that is, the parameter λ introduced in the Extending the Model box 'Useful public services' would be zero. This consideration makes the income effects large in comparison with those from non-military government purchases. Overall, the income effect predicts an increase in labour supply, L^s. The problem, however, is that the same argument predicts a decrease in consumption, C. This prediction conflicts with the finding in Table 13.2 that C did not decrease much during the wars.
- Casey Mulligan (1998) argues that labour supply, L^s, increases during wartime because of patriotism. That is, for a given real wage rate, w/P, and for given total real income, people are willing to work more as part of the war effort. The attraction of this argument is that it does not rely on a negative income effect and can, therefore, explain why consumption does not fall much during wartime. However, it may be that the effect of patriotism is more important during a popular war, such as World War II, than in other conflicts.
- From the standpoint of families, we want to understand how the military draft's forced removal of many men would influence the labour supply of those not drafted, especially women. One part of this analysis involves married couples, with the man drafted into the military. In these cases, the postponement of having children would be an important part of the story. Thus, women might participate more in the labour force as a temporary alternative to raising a family or having a larger family. Another consideration involves the postponement of marriage. Through this channel, the military draft would affect the labour supply of single women. That is, women who would otherwise have married and had children found market work to be an attractive, temporary alternative.

The upshot of these arguments is that wartime probably entails an increase in labour supply, L^s. Thus, we now assume that the occurrence of a war shifts the labour-supply curve, L^s, as shown in Figure 13.8. Unlike in Figure 13.6, we now allow for a positive effect of the real wage rate, w/P, on L^s. Thus, before the war, the labour-supply curve, shown in light blue, slopes upward versus w/P. The war shifts the curve to the right to the dark blue one, denoted $(L^s)'$. At any w/P, the quantity of labour supplied is larger along the dark blue curve than along the light blue one'.

Figure 13.8 Effect of a wartime increase in labour supply on the labour market

The downward-sloping labour-demand curve, L^d, comes from Figure 13.6. We now allow the real wage rate, w/P, to have a positive effect on labour supply, L^s, shown by the light blue curve. We assume that the occurrence of a war shifts the labour-supply curve rightward from L^s to $(L^s)'$, shown in dark blue. The quantity of labour input rises from L^* to $(L^*)'$ on the horizontal axis, and the real wage rate falls from $(w/P)^*$ to $[(w/P)^*]'$ on the vertical axis.

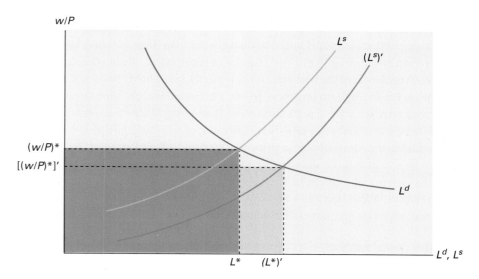

The labour-demand curve, denoted by L^d in Figure 13.8, slopes downward versus w/P. This curve is the same as the one in Figure 13.6. We still assume that the occurrence of a war does not shift the labour-demand curve (because the change in government purchases, G, does not affect the MPL).

Before the war, the labour market clears at the quantity of labour, L^*, and real wage rate, $(w/P)^*$, shown in Figure 13.8. During the war, the quantity of labour rises to $(L^*)'$ on the horizontal axis, and the real wage rate falls to $[(w/P)^*]'$ on the vertical axis. Thus, when we allow for an increase in labour supply, the model can explain a rise in total employment, as observed in Table 13.2. A new prediction is that the occurrence of war lowers the real wage rate, w/P.

Extending the Model
Adding a demand effect of government purchases to the equilibrium business-cycle model

In our equilibrium business-cycle model, a rise in government purchases increases the level of output in the economy through an increase in labour supply. We refer to this effect as a supply effect of government purchases because this effect initially affects the supply side of the economy via labour input in the production function. In the Keynesian models, presented in Chapter 6, although a rise in government purchases also increases the level of output, this effect works though the demand side of the economy via the aggregate demand (AD) curve. This demand effect relies on nominal rigidity in prices and/or wages. To capture both the demand and supply effects of government purchases, one can explore these effects in an equilibrium business-cycle model with sticky prices and/or sticky wages. In Chapter 17, we will present such a so-called New Keynesian model but will use it to explore monetary policy, instead of fiscal policy. See Galí et al. (2007), for an analysis of both the empirical and theoretical effects of government spending in the New Keynesian model.

Effects of war on the real wage rate

We now consider the prediction from Figure 13.8 that a war reduces the real wage rate, w/P. This proposition receives a mixed verdict from the main wartime experiences. If we compute the average percentage deviation of the real wage rate from its trend during the years of the main wars, we get the following:[2]

- World War I (1917–18):–4.0%,
- World War II (1942–45): +3.1%,
- Korean War (1951–53): 0.0%.

Thus, the predicted negative effect on w/P shows up only for World War I. The excess of w/P from trend during World War II conflicts with our prediction. For the Korean War, w/P deviates negligibly from its trend.

A further analysis suggests that the model might be doing better than these numbers indicate. Price controls and rationing of goods were imposed during World War II and, to a lesser extent, during the Korean War. Consequently, the reported price level, P, understated the true price level; typically, households could not buy additional goods just by paying the stated price. For example, to buy more goods, a household might have to pay the black-market price, which exceeded the stated price at a time of price controls and rationing. Since P was understated, the measured real wage rate, w/P, overstated the true real wage rate. That is, because of rationing, households could not buy w/P additional goods with an additional hour of labour. In principle, we could adjust P upward (by an unknown amount) to calculate the true price level, which is the amount that a household would actually have to pay on the black market to buy more goods. The upward adjustment in P means that the adjusted real wage rate would be lower than the measured rate during World War II and the Korean War. With this amendment, the model would work better, because the adjusted real wage rate may have fallen below trend during World War II and the Korean War.

Effects of war on the rental market

We learned from Figure 13.8 that a wartime increase in labour supply, L^s, led to an increase in labour input, L. This change affects the rental market, because the rise in L tends to increase the MPK (for a given quantity of capital services, κK).

In the pre-war environment, the demand for capital services, $(\kappa K)^d$, slopes downward versus the real rental price, R/P, as shown by the light blue curve in Figure 13.9. The war shifts this demand to the right to the curve $[(\kappa K)^d]'$, shown in dark blue. The demand curve shifts to the right because the higher quantity of labour, L, raises the MPK for a given quantity of capital services, κK. We still have that the war does not shift the supply curve for capital services, $(\kappa K)^s$.

We see from Figure 13.9 that the real rental price, R/P, and the quantity of capital services, κK, increase. For a given capital stock, K, the rise in κK corresponds to an increase in the capital utilization rate, κ. Recall that the real interest rate is given by:

$$r = (R/P) \bullet \kappa - \delta(\kappa) \tag{12.10}$$

The increases in R/P and κ imply that r increases. Therefore, we have two new predictions about wartime. The capital utilization rate, κ, and the real interest rate, r, increase.

We looked before at data on capacity utilization rates. These numbers show that the utilization rate, κ, rose significantly above trend during the Korean War – the average for 1952–53 was 0.025. These data are unavailable before 1948, but another series reveals a sharp rise in capital utilization rates in manufacturing during World War II.[3] Thus, the model's prediction for higher capital utilization during wartime accords with the facts.

The predictions for higher real interest rates during wartime conflict with the data. During the Korean War (1951–53), the real interest rate on three-month US Treasury bills was, on average, about equal to its trend value.

---

[2]The nominal wage rate is the average hourly earnings of production workers in manufacturing. The real wage rate is the nominal wage rate divided by the GDP deflator. The trend for the real wage rate is calculated in our usual manner. The results for the Korean War come from quarterly data since 1947. The results for World Wars I and II come from annual data since 1889.

[3]This series, constructed by the Federal Reserve and the Bureau of Economic Analysis, is for manufacturing production per unit of installed equipment. These data start in 1925 and are therefore unavailable for World War I.

Figure 13.9 Effect of a wartime increase in labour input on the market for capital services

The increase in employment from L^* to $(L^*)'$, shown in Figure 13.8, raises the MPK (for a given quantity of capital services, κK). Therefore, the demand curve for capital services shifts rightward, from $(\kappa K)^d$, shown in light blue, to $[(\kappa K)^d]'$, shown in dark blue. The market-clearing real rental price of capital rises from $(R/P)^*$ to $[(R/P)^*]'$ on the vertical axis. The quantity of capital services expands from $(\kappa K)^*$ to $[(\kappa K)^*]'$ on the horizontal axis. This increase in capital services corresponds, for a given capital stock, K, to a rise in the capital utilization rate, κ.

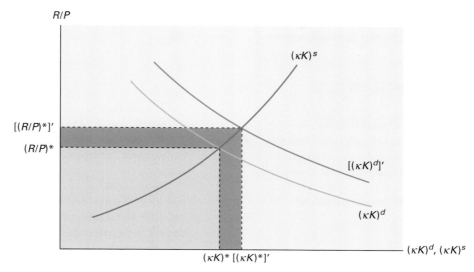

During World War II (1942–45), the nominal three-month T-bill rates were extremely low – less than 1% – and inflation rates averaged 5%. Therefore, real interest rates were negative.[4] In World War I, short-term nominal interest rates rose from 3% in 1916 to 6% in 1918, but the inflation rate soared to as high as 16%. Hence, real interest rates were again negative.

The occurrences of extremely low real interest rates during wartime are not well understood. One promising idea for explaining this puzzle involves the different amounts of uncertainty in the returns on alternative forms of assets. Wartime probably raises the perceived probability of global disaster and tends, thereby, to raise the demand for comparatively safe assets, such as government bills. This heightened demand might explain why the real interest rate paid on such assets is relatively low during wartime.

Summing Up

We extended the equilibrium business-cycle model to include government purchases of goods and services. These purchases were added to the government's budget constraint and were financed by lump-sum taxes net of lump-sum transfers.

A permanent rise in government purchases leads to a long-lasting increase in taxes net of transfers and, hence, to a long-lasting decrease in households' real disposable income. The strong income effect causes a roughly one-to-one decline in consumption. In contrast, a temporary rise in government purchases has only a weak income effect. Therefore, consumption reacts relatively little and investment falls substantially. We checked out these predictions by studying the temporary expansions of military purchases during major wars in the past century. The evidence brought out a number of unresolved puzzles, including the large wartime expansions of total employment (including the military) and the failure of real interest rates to rise systematically during wartime. Some of the observations could be explained by positive effects of patriotism on wartime labour supply. A promising idea is that wartime

---

[4] The 5% average inflation rate is based on the reported consumer price index. Because of price controls, the true inflation rates were probably higher during the war, so that the true real interest rates were even more negative than the measured ones.

raises the perceived probability of global disaster and tends, thereby, to increase the demand for comparatively safe assets. This shift in demand may explain the low real interest rates during major wars.

Key Terms and Concepts

government's budget constraint

lump-sum taxes

real disposable income

term structure of real interest rates

Questions and Problems

A Review questions

1 Derive the households' multiyear budget constraint in equation (13.6). Explain how real transfers and real taxes enter into this equation.

2 What are the economic differences between the government's purchases of goods and services and the government's transfer payments?

B Problems for discussion

3 The role of public services

The Useful Public Services box discusses the role of public services in providing utility to households. We assumed that each unit of government purchases, G, was equivalent to λ units of private consumption, C, in terms of household utility.

  a Consider various categories of government expenditure, such as military spending, police, highways, public transport, and research and development. How do you think the coefficient λ varies across these categories?

  b Suppose that G rises permanently by one unit. What are the responses of real GDP, Y, consumption, C, and investment, I? How do the results depend on the size of the coefficient λ?

4 Public ownership of capital and the national accounts

In the past, the national accounts included in GDP the government's purchases of goods and services but took no account of the flow of services on government-owned capital. The accounts also did not subtract depreciation of this capital to calculate net domestic product.

  a In this old system, what happened to GDP if the government gave its capital to a private business and then bought the final goods from that business?

  b In the current system of national accounts, the GDP includes an estimate of the flow of implicit rental income generated by public capital. However, this income flow is assumed to equal the estimated depreciation of the public capital. Redo question a in the context of this system.

5 Government consumption in the national accounts

The national accounts treat all government purchases of goods and services, G, as part of real GDP. But suppose that the public services derived from government purchases are an input to private production, say:

$$Y = F(\kappa K, L, G)$$

In this case, public services are an intermediate product – a good that enters into a later stage of production. Hence, we ought not to include these services twice in real GDP – once when the government buys them and, again, when the services contribute to private production.

  a Suppose that businesses initially hire private guards. Subsequently, the government provides free police protection, which substitutes for the private guards. Assume that the private guards and public police are equally efficient and receive the same wage rates. How does the switch from private to public protection affect measured real GDP?

  b How would you change the national accounts to get a more accurate treatment of government purchases of goods and services? Is your proposal practical? (These issues are discussed by Simon Kuznets, 1948, pp. 156–157, and Richard Musgrave, 1959, pp. 186–188.)

6 A prospective change in government purchases

Suppose that people learn in the current year that government purchases, Gt, will increase in some future year. Current government purchases, G_1, do not change.

  a What happens in the current year to real GDP, Y, consumption, C, and investment, I?

  b Can you think of some real-world cases to which this question applies?

14 Taxes

In Chapter 13, we extended the equilibrium business-cycle model to include government expenditure. However, we took an unrealistic view of government by assuming lump-sum taxes and transfers. The amount that a household paid as taxes or received as transfers did not depend on the household's income or other characteristics. In the real world, governments levy a variety of taxes and pay out a variety of transfers, but none of these look like the lump-sum taxes and transfers in our model.

Usually, a household's taxes and transfers depend on its choices. This dependence motivates changes in behaviour. For example, taxes on labour income discourage households from working and earning income. Transfers to the unemployed motivate people not to be employed. Taxes on asset income discourage saving. Overall, the systems of taxes and transfers create substitution effects that influence labour supply, production, consumption and investment. In this section, we extend the equilibrium business-cycle model to incorporate some of these effects. However, before we extend the theory, it is useful to have an overview of government revenue.

Government revenue in the Eurozone

The light blue graph in Figure 14.1 shows the ratio of total government revenue to gross domestic product (GDP) in the Eurozone from 1999 to 2014. The dark blue graph shows the part that can attributed to central governments, and the grey graph shows the part that can be attributed to state and local governments. Total government revenue remained close to 45% for most of the period and then rose slightly to 47% towards the end of the period. The ratio of central government revenue to GDP was reasonably stable throughout the period at 20%. Similarly, the ratio of state and local government revenue to GDP also remained fairly stable at 16%. The remaining part of the total government revenue comes from **social security** funds.

Figure 14.2 gives a breakdown of total tax revenue, which is about 90% of total government revenue, by main categories. The first category is taxes on production and imports, which include taxes levied on products/services produced or transacted and other taxes on production. The most important type of taxes in this category is value added-type taxes. Taxes on production and imports have been about 32% of total tax revenue.

The second category is current taxes on income and wealth, which include taxes on individual/household income and profits of corporations. The most important type of taxes in this category is taxes on individual/household income. Current taxes on income and wealth have been about 30% of total tax revenue.

The third category is net social contributions, in which the main component is actual social contributions. Actual social contributions include the compulsory and voluntary contributions paid by employers, employees, self-employed and non-employed persons. Net social contributions have been about 38% of total tax revenue.

Finally, there is also a minor component of government tax revenue. This category is called capital taxes, which are taxes levied at irregular/infrequent intervals on the net worth/value of assets owned or transferred in the form of legacies or gifts. Capital taxes have been less than 1% of total tax revenue.

Figure 14.1 Government revenue in the Eurozone

The light blue graph shows total government revenue as a ratio to GDP. The dark blue graph is for central government revenue, and the grey graph is for state and local government revenue.

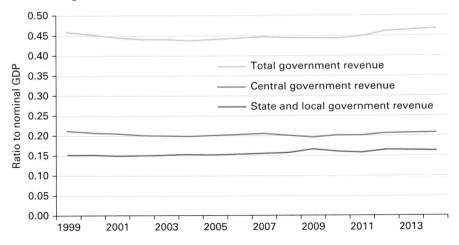

Figure 14.2 Breakdown of total tax revenue in the Eurozone

The figure shows taxes, in four categories, as ratios to total tax revenue. The categories are taxes on production and imports; current taxes on income and wealth; net social contributions; and capital taxes.

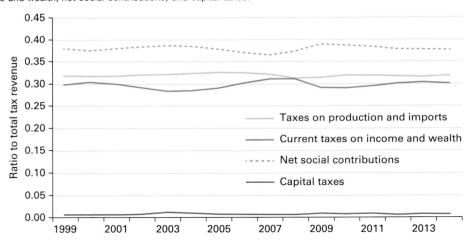

Types of taxes

Some taxes fall on forms of income: individual income taxes, corporate profits taxes and social security contributions. Social security contributions are collected from a payroll tax on wage earnings. Other taxes are based on expenditures: sales taxes, excise taxes and customs duties. Many countries use value-added taxes (VAT), which are like sales taxes but are assessed at various stages of production. Still other forms of taxes are based on ownership of property and are, therefore, forms of wealth taxes. An important point is that, for all of these taxes, the amount that a household or business pays depends on its economic activity. None of these taxes look like the lump-sum taxes in our model.

Given the importance of income taxes, it is worthwhile incorporating them into our equilibrium business-cycle model. A key point is the distinction between the **marginal tax rate** and the **average tax rate**. The marginal tax rate is the additional tax paid on an additional unit of income. The average tax rate is the ratio of total taxes paid to total income. The marginal tax rate will turn out to have substitution effects that influence the behaviour of households and businesses. The average tax rate will determine the government's revenue, which equals the average tax rate multiplied by income.

An important property of individual income tax is that the marginal tax rate normally rises with income. Table 14.1 illustrates the nature of marginal and average income tax rates with numbers that capture the individual income tax system in the United Kingdom in 2015. The first £10 600 of income is tax exempt, and this is known as the personal allowance. Income in excess of £10 600 is taxed at a 20% rate. Therefore, at an income of £10 600, the marginal income tax rate becomes 20%. However, the average income tax rate is still zero, because no taxes have yet been paid. At an income of £42 385, taxes reach £6357, so that the average tax rate is 15% (6357/42 385). At this point, the marginal income tax rate rises to 40% for the next £118 215 of income. Therefore, at £160 600, the taxes paid are £53 643, and the average tax rate is 33%. Then the marginal income tax rate rises to 45%. Notice that the marginal income tax rate does not rise with income once income exceeds £160 600.

Table 14.1 illustrates two points about the UK individual income tax, and they also apply to many other countries. First, the marginal income tax rate rises with income, until income reaches £160 600. That is why the system is said to have a **graduated-rate tax** structure (sometimes called a progressive-rate structure). However, after £160 600, the marginal tax rate schedule is *flat*, rather than graduated. Second, the marginal tax rate is always higher than the average tax rate. That is because the average tax rate incorporates the low taxes paid on early portions of income, including the zero tax paid on the first £10 600 of income. However, as income becomes very high – for example, above the £1 million shown in the table – the average tax rate approaches the top marginal tax rate of 45%.

Table 14.1 is a simplification of the more complicated individual income tax system that prevails in the United Kingdom. For example, the calculations ignore many legal actions that reduce a household's taxes. These actions include income tax reliefs (for charitable contributions, and maintenance payments to ex-spouses or civil partners) and various benefits (such as child benefit, heating and housing benefits, and low-income benefits, and so on). Some fringe benefits paid by employers, notably for child care and pensions, also escape or defer taxation.

Another important form of income tax in the United Kingdom is National Insurance contribution to finance state pension and other allowances/benefits, such as job-seeker and maternity allowances. Although the government calls these levies a contribution, they are more like taxes because the benefits that individuals get do not depend very much on the amount that an individual pays. Hence, the payments are partly a tax and partly a contribution.

The tax for National Insurance is simpler than individual income tax. In 2015, the rate for National Insurance contribution was zero for a weekly income of less than £155, 0.12 for the next £660 of weekly income, and 0.02 on all additional weekly income. Thus, the marginal tax rate is 0% for weekly earnings of less than £155, 12% for weekly earnings between £155 and £815, and 2% thereafter. Employers paid an equal amount.

Notice that, for weekly incomes between £0 and £155, the average tax rate equals the marginal tax rate of zero. This property applies to a **flat-rate tax** system. However, at £155, the system has a sharp increase in the marginal tax rate to 12%. As income rises above £815, the average tax rate falls gradually from 9.7% to 2%. Therefore, in this range, the marginal tax rate is *less* than the average tax rate. This pattern is the opposite of the one that applies to individual income tax.

Table 14.1 The UK graduated-rate income tax in 2015

Income level (£)	Taxes (£)	Marginal tax rate	Average tax rate
0	0	0	0
10 600	0	0.20	0
42 385	6357	0.40	0.15
160 600	53 643	0.45	0.33
1 000 000	431 373	0.45	0.43

Note: This table applies to an individual who takes the standard personal allowance in 2015 in the United Kingdom. The income tax rate is zero for the first £10 600 of income, 0.20 for the next £31 785 of income, 0.40 for the next £118 215 of income, and 0.45 on all additional income.

Empirically, it is difficult to measure an average marginal income tax rate for the economy, because these rates differ across persons and types of income. The graph in Figure 14.3 plots the top marginal income tax rate from individual income tax in the United Kingdom. Figure 14.3 shows that the top marginal income tax rate was very high at 83% in 1978. Then, between 1979 and 1988, the government drastically cut the top marginal income tax rate from 83% to 40%. The income-tax system remained progressive but became much less so than before. The top marginal income-tax rate remained at 40% until 2010, when it was raised to 50%. In 2013, the government lowered the top marginal income-tax rate to 45%.

Figure 14.3 Top marginal income-tax rate in the UK

The graph shows the top marginal income tax rate from individual income tax in the United Kingdom.

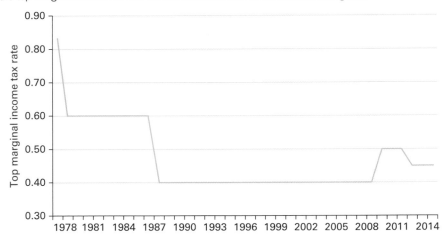

Taxes in the model

To incorporate tax rates into the equilibrium business-cycle model, start with the household budget constraint from equation (13.4). When written without year subscripts, the budget constraint is:

$$C+(1/P)\bullet \Delta B+\Delta K =(w/P)\bullet L^{s} +r\bullet (B/P+K)+V-T$$
$$consumption+real\,saving = real\,disposable\,income \qquad (14.1)$$

Up to now, we have regarded real transfers, V, and real taxes, T, as lump sums. Therefore, the household's real transfers net of real taxes, $V-T$, did not depend on the household's characteristics, including its income and consumption. Now, we allow a household's real taxes, T, to depend on some of its characteristics. Analogous considerations enter into an analysis of real transfers, V.

The various taxes that exist in the tax system can be represented as levies on the terms that appear on the two sides of equation (14.1). Sales, excise and value-added taxes depend on consumption, C. Labour-income taxes – for example, from individual income tax and social security contributions – depend on real labour income, $(w/P) \bullet L^{s}$. Taxes on asset income, a part of individual income tax, depend on real asset income, $r \bullet (B/P + K)$.[1] In the real world, the income base for this tax includes interest, dividends and capital gains.[2]

[1]Taxes are usually levied on nominal interest payments, $i \bullet (B/P)$, which are computed from the nominal interest rate, i, rather than the real rate, r. This treatment of interest income leads to an effect of the inflation rate, π, on real taxes. Another real-world complication is that parts of household interest expenses are sometimes allowed as deductions from income for tax purposes.
[2]To consider a tax on corporate profit, we could reintroduce real business profit, Π, as a form of household income. We dropped Π before because it equalled zero in equilibrium. However, in most tax systems, the definition of profit differs from the one in our model. The most important difference is that our definition includes the real rental payments to capital, $(R/P) \bullet K$, as a negative item. In the real world, only parts of this rental income – depreciation and interest expenses – are allowed as deductions from income in the computation of corporate profits taxes. With this real-world definition of profit, the corporate profits tax amounts to another levy on the income from capital. Since the income from capital is also taxed at the household level, the corporate profits tax is often described appropriately as **double taxation** of income from capital.

We will now assess the economic effects of taxation. In order to affect real GDP, a tax has to influence the quantities of one of the factors of production: labour or capital services. Therefore, the various taxes can be broken down into whether they affect labour or capital services, or both. We get the main results by considering two types of taxes – one that depends on labour income and another that depends on asset income.

A TAX ON LABOUR INCOME

We start with a tax on labour income, such as individual income tax. Let τ_w be the marginal tax rate on labour income. To simplify, we do not allow for a graduated-rate structure for τ_w, as in the individual income-tax system of most countries. Rather, we assume that τ_w is the same at all levels of income. Our main results will apply to the real world if we think of τ_w as the average of the marginal income-tax rates across households.

We assume that the marginal income-tax rate, τ_w, does not change over time – at least, households do not anticipate that future tax rates will differ from the current rate. Anticipated differences between today's tax rate and future tax rates would motivate households to work more in years with relatively low tax rates and less in years with relatively high tax rates. That is, anticipated changes in τ_w over time have intertemporal-substitution effects on labour supply. Since we treat τ_w as unchanging, we are ignoring these intertemporal-substitution effects.

Households may be eligible for deductions and credits that reduce the amount of taxes paid. These deductions create a gap between the average and marginal income tax rates; the average rate is less than the marginal rate because of the deductions. If the deductions are the same for everyone, the average tax rate will be lower for low-income households than for high-income households. (Recall our assumption that the marginal tax rate, τ_w, is the same for all households.) In some cases, a household's tax payment would be negative, amounting to a transfer from the government. In the real world, these negative taxes arise because of 'refundable' tax credits, which are credits that not only reduce taxes, but also allow for cash payments when the computed taxes are less than zero.

The real taxes paid by a household equal the average tax rate multiplied by labour income. The average tax rate depends on the marginal income-tax rate, τ_w, and on the available deductions. If we hold constant the structure of deductions, a higher τ_w implies a higher average tax rate. Therefore, for given deductions, a higher τ_w will generate more tax revenue for the government unless the amount of labour income falls sharply.

To assess the economic effects of a tax on labour income, we have to extend our analysis of household labour supply. The key force is the substitution effect between leisure and consumption. Without taxation of labour income, this substitution effect depended on the real wage rate, w/P. If a household raised the quantity of labour supplied, L^s, by one unit of time, it raised real labour income, $(w/P) \bullet L^s$, by w/P units. This extra income enabled the household to increase consumption by w/P units. At the same time, the rise in L^s by one unit of time meant that leisure time fell by one unit. Therefore, the household could substitute w/P units of consumption for one unit of leisure time. If w/P rose, this deal became more favourable. Hence, we predicted that the household would raise the quantity of labour supplied, enjoy less leisure time and consume more.

The new consideration is that an extra unit of labour income is taxed at the marginal income tax rate, τ_w. If the household raises the quantity of labour supplied, L^s, by one unit of time, it again raises pre-tax real labour income, $(w/P) \bullet L^s$, by w/P units. This extra income enters as the first shaded term on the right-hand side of the budget constraint in equation (14.1):

$$C + (1/P) \bullet \Delta B + \Delta K = (w/P) \bullet L^s + r \bullet (B/P + K) + V - T. \tag{14.1}$$

The additional labour income raises the household's real taxes, T, by τ_w units. These taxes also appear on the right-hand side of the equation – the second shaded term – but with a negative sign. Overall, the right-hand side of the equation rises by $(1 - \tau_w) \bullet (w/P)$ units. That is, after-tax real labour income rises by this amount. We also see from the equation that the household can use this additional after-tax real income to increase consumption, C – the shaded term on the left-hand side – by $(1 - \tau_w) \bullet (w/P)$ units.

We found that, by working one more unit of time, the household can raise consumption, C, by $(1 - \tau_w) \cdot (w/P)$ units. The increase in work by one unit of time still means that leisure time falls by one unit. Therefore, households can substitute $(1 - \tau_w) \cdot (w/P)$ units of C for one unit of leisure time. Another way to say this is that, with a labour income tax, the substitution effect on labour supply depends on the **after-tax real wage rate**, $(1 - \tau_w) \cdot (w/P)$, rather than the pre-tax real wage rate, w/P. If the marginal tax rate, τ_w, rises, for a given w/P, $(1 - \tau_w) \cdot (w/P)$ falls. Hence, we predict that the household would reduce the quantity of labour supplied, take more leisure time and consume less.

We stressed before that labour supply depends also on income effects. We predicted that more household income would lead to more consumption and more leisure – hence, less work. What income effects arise when the marginal income tax rate, τ_w, increases? Equation (14.1) shows that a household's real income on the right-hand side depends on real transfers net of real taxes, $V - T$. Recall also from Chapter 13 that the government's budget constraint requires:

$$V - T = -G. \tag{13.8}$$

Therefore, if government purchases, G, are unchanged, equation (13.8) implies that real transfers net of real taxes, $V - T$, must also be unchanged. Hence, for given G, we do not get any changes in household real income through the term $V - T$. In other words, if G is fixed, there are no income effects from a change in τ_w.

We need to explore this result further, because it seems that a rise in the marginal income-tax rate, τ_w, should have a negative income effect. The results depend on what else changes when the marginal income-tax rate, τ_w, rises. One possibility is that the government adjusts other features of the tax system to keep the total real taxes collected, T, unchanged. For example, marginal income-tax rates, τ_w, might rise in the individual income tax, but deductions also rise to keep T fixed. Another possibility is that the government shifts away from collecting revenue through a tax that has a relatively low marginal income-tax rate – for example, social security contributions – towards one that has a relatively high marginal rate – such as individual income tax. Shifts of this kind raise the marginal tax rate on labour income, τ_w, for a given total of real taxes collected, T.

Another possibility is that real tax revenue, T, rises along with the increase in τ_w, and all of the extra revenue pays for added real transfers, V. In that case, the term $V - T$ is again unchanged, and there is still no income effect.

Finally, we could have that real tax revenue, T, rises along with the increase in τ_w, and the extra revenue pays for added government purchases, G. In this case, the economic effects combine two forces: the rise in τ_w, which we are now studying, and the rise in G, which we considered in Chapter 13. Recall that the rise in G did have a negative income effect. To keep things straight, it is best to analyze the effects from τ_w and G separately. We are now assessing the effects from an increase in τ_w for given G. In this case, there are no income effects on labour supply. We can therefore be confident that, for a given real wage rate, w/P, a rise in τ_w reduces the quantity of labour supplied, L^s, through the substitution effect from a lower after-tax real wage rate, $(1 - \tau_w) \cdot (w/P)$.

Figure 14.4 shows the effects on the labour market from an increase in the marginal tax rate on labour income, τ_w. We use the construction from Figure 9.13 in Chapter 9. We plot the pre-tax real wage rate, w/P, on the vertical axis. As before, a lower w/P raises the quantity of labour demanded, L^d, along the downward-sloping curve. Unlike in Chapter 13, we also allow for a positive effect of w/P on the quantity of labour supplied, L^s, along the light blue curve. This positive slope applies if the substitution effect from a higher w/P dominates the income effect.

For a given pre-tax real wage rate, w/P, a higher τ_w implies a lower after-tax real wage rate, $(1 - \tau_w) \cdot (w/P)$. Therefore, in Figure 14.4, a rise in τ_w shifts the labour supply curve to the left from the light blue one labelled L^s to the dark blue one labelled $(L^s)'$. This decrease in labour supply reflects the substitution effect from the higher labour-income tax rate, τ_w.

The tax on labour income does not affect the labour demand curve, L^d, in Figure 14.4. The reason is that businesses (run by households) still maximize profit by equating the marginal product of labour, MPL, to the real wage rate, w/P. For a given w/P, the labour-income tax rate, τ_w, does not affect the profit-maximizing choice of the quantity of labour input, L^d.

We can see from Figure 14.4 that the market-clearing real wage rate rises from $(w/P)^*$ to $[(w/P)^*]'$ on the vertical axis. The market-clearing quantity of labour declines from L^* to $(L^*)'$ on the horizontal axis.

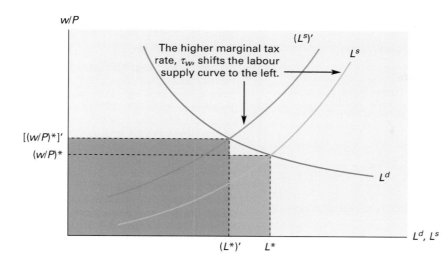

Figure 14.4 Effect of an increase in the labour-income tax rate on the labour market

The downward-sloping labour demand curve, L^d, comes from Figure 9.13. The upward-sloping labour supply curve, L^s, shown in light blue, also comes from Figure 9.13. An increase in the marginal tax rate on labour income, τ_w, shifts the labour supply curve to the left to the dark blue one, $(L^s)'$. Consequently, the market-clearing, before-tax real wage rate rises from $(w/P)^*$ to $[(w/P)^*]'$ on the vertical axis. The market-clearing quantity of labour input falls from L^* to $(L^*)'$ on the horizontal axis.

We also know that the after-tax real wage rate, $(1 - \tau_w) \cdot (w/P)$, must fall overall. That is, the rise in w/P less than fully compensates for the decrease in $1 - \tau_w$ due to the rise in τ_w. To see why, note from Figure 14.4 that L is lower (because the labour demand curve does not shift, and the labour supply curve shifts to the left). However, for L to be lower, the quantity of labour supplied, L^s, must be lower. The only way that L^s falls is that $(1 - \tau_w) \cdot (w/P)$ declines.

We found from our analysis of the labour market that a higher marginal tax rate on labour income, τ_w, lowers the quantity of labour input, L. This effect will spill over to the market for capital services because the reduction in L tends to reduce the marginal product of capital services, MPK.

Figure 14.5 shows the effects on the market for capital services. As in Figure 13.5, we plot the real rental price, R/P, on the vertical axis. The reduction in labour input, L, reduces the MPK (at a given quantity of capital services, κK). The demand for capital services decreases accordingly from the light blue curve, labelled $(\kappa K)^d$, to the dark blue one, labelled $[(\kappa K)^d]'$. The supply curve for capital services, $(\kappa K)^s$ does not shift. That is, the stock of capital, K, is given, and, for a given real rental price, R/P, suppliers of capital services have no reason to change the capital utilization rate, κ.

Figure 14.5 shows that the market-clearing real rental price falls from $(R/P)^*$ to $[(R/P)^*]'$ on the vertical axis. The quantity of capital services falls because of a decrease in the utilization rate, κ, from $(\kappa K)^*$ to $[(\kappa K)^*]'$ on the horizontal axis. Thus, although the tax rate on labour income, τ_w, does not directly affect the market for capital services, it has an indirect effect on this market. By reducing labour input, L, and thereby decreasing the MPK, an increase in τ_w reduces the quantity of capital services, κK.[3]

Recall that real GDP, Y, is given by the production function from Chapter 10:

$$Y = A \cdot F(\kappa K, L) \tag{10.1}$$

In the present case, the technology level, A, does not change. However, we found that a rise in the labour-income tax rate, τ_w, reduced the quantities of labour, L, and capital services, κK. Therefore, Y declines.[4] Thus, our conclusion is that a higher marginal tax rate on labour income, τ_w, leads to a reduction in overall market activity, as gauged by real GDP, Y.

---

[3]The decrease in κK lowers the MPL, and leads thereby to a shift to the left in the labour demand curve, L^d, in Figure 14.4. This shift leads to a further decrease in L.

[4]We can work out how the decrease in real GDP, Y, divides up between consumption, C, and gross investment, I. We know from Chapter 8 that a fall in Y by one unit corresponds to a decrease in real household income by one unit. Since the decrease in income is long-lasting, we predict that the propensity to consume would be close to 1.0. Hence, C would fall by roughly 1.0 unit. However, the decrease in R/P implies a fall in the real interest rate, r. This change has an intertemporal-substitution effect, which raises current consumption compared to future consumption. This effect offsets the decrease in C by one unit. Hence, we find that current consumption would decrease overall by less than Y. Since $Y = C + I + G$ and G is fixed, I must decline.

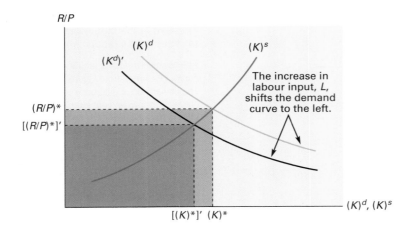

R/P

(K)^d
(K^d)'
(K)^s

The increase in
labour input, L,
shifts the demand
curve to the left.

(R/P)*
[(R/P)*]'

(K)^d, (K)^s

[(K)*]' (K)*

Figure 14.5 Effect of an increase in the labour-income tax rate on the market for capital services

This construction comes from Figure 13.5. The reduction in employment from L^* to $(L^*)'$, shown in Figure 14.4, reduces the marginal product of capital services, MPK (at a given quantity of capital services, $\kappa \cdot K$). Therefore, the demand curve for capital services shifts to the left, from $(\kappa K)^d$, shown in light blue, to $[(\kappa K)^d]'$, shown in dark blue. The supply curve for capital services, $(\kappa K)^s$, does not shift. Consequently, the market-clearing real rental price of capital falls from $(R/P)^*$ to $[(R/P)^*]'$ on the vertical axis. The quantity of capital services declines from $(\kappa K)^*$ to $[(\kappa K)^*]'$ on the horizontal axis. This decrease in capital services corresponds, for a given capital stock, K, to a reduction in the capital utilization rate, κ.

A TAX ON ASSET INCOME

Now, we will consider a tax on asset income. Go back to the household's budget constraint:

$$C + (1/P) \cdot \Delta B + \Delta K = (w/P) \cdot L^s + r \cdot (B/P + K) + V - T \qquad (14.1)$$

Suppose now that real taxes, T, depend on a household's real asset income, $r \cdot (B/P + K)$, the first shaded term. Note that this part of income equals the real interest payments on bonds, $r \cdot (B/P)$, plus the return on ownership of capital, rK. The term rK equals the net real rental payments on capital, $[(R/P) \cdot \kappa - \delta(\kappa)] \cdot K$, because of the condition from Chapter 12 that the real rates of return on bonds and capital are the same:

$$r = (R/P) \cdot \kappa - \delta(\kappa)$$

real rate of return on bonds = real rate of return from owning captial $\qquad (12.10)$

Let τ_r be the marginal tax rate on asset income. We assume that all forms of asset income are taxed at the same rate. In reality, tax systems treat differently various forms of asset income, which include interest, dividends, capital gains and parts of self-employment income. However, the simplifying assumption that all forms of asset income are treated the same will give us the main effects from taxation of asset income. Since the tax rate, τ_r, is the same for interest income as for income on ownership of capital, the equality between the two rates of return still holds in equation (12.10).

We know that the real interest rate, r, has an intertemporal-substitution effect on consumption. A reduction in year 1's consumption, C_1, by one unit allowed the household to raise year 2's consumption, C_2, by $1 + r$ units. Therefore, an increase in r motivated the household to lower C_1 compared to C_2. The difference now is that the additional r units of asset income in year 2 are taxed at the rate τ_r. This taxation means that the added r units of income are offset by an added $\tau_r \cdot r$ units of taxes; that is, the second shaded term, T, in equation (14.1) rises by $\tau_r \cdot r$. Thus, if the household reduces C_1 by one unit, it can raise C_2 by the amount:

$$\Delta C_2 = 1 + r - \tau_r \cdot r$$
$$\Delta C_2 = 1 + (1 - \tau_r) \cdot r$$

What matters, therefore, for the choice between C_1 and C_2 is the **after-tax real interest rate**, $(1 - \tau_r) \cdot r$. If τ_r rises, for given r, $(1 - \tau_r) \cdot r$ declines. Therefore, the household has less incentive to defer consumption, and it reacts by increasing C_1 compared to C_2. For given real income in year 1, an increase in τ_r motivates the household to consume more and save less in year 1.

If we multiply both sides of equation (12.10) by $(1 - \tau_r)$, we can relate the after-tax real interest rate to the after-tax return on ownership of capital:

$$(1 - \tau_r) \bullet r = (1 - \tau_r) \bullet [(R/P) \bullet \kappa - \delta(\kappa)]$$

after-tax real interest rate = after-tax rate of return on ownership of capital   (14.2)

Thus, we can calculate $(1 - \tau_r) \bullet r$ if we know – on the right-hand side of equation (14.2) – the real rental price, R/P, and the capital utilization rate, κ. These values are determined, as before, by the clearing of the market for capital services.

Refer back to Figure 14.5, which considered the demand for and supply of capital services. The marginal tax rate on asset income, τ_r, does not affect the demand curve for capital services, $(\kappa K)^d$, which is shown in light blue. Since business profit, Π, is not taxed, this curve still comes from equating the MPK to R/P.[5] Therefore, a change in τ_r does not shift the demand curve, $(\kappa K)^d$.

In Chapter 10, we worked out the supply curve for capital services, $(\kappa K)^s$. For a given stock of capital, K, owners of capital chose the utilization rate, κ, to maximize the net rental income:

$$[(R/P) \bullet \kappa - \delta(\kappa)] \bullet K$$

We assumed that a higher κ resulted in a higher depreciation rate, as represented by the function $\delta(\kappa)$. From this formulation, we found that an increase in the real rental price, R/P, raised the utilization rate, κ, and thereby increased the quantity of capital services supplied, $(\kappa K)^s$. That is why the curve $(\kappa K)^s$, in Figure 14.5, slopes upwards.

With a tax on income from capital at the rate τ_r, owners of capital would seek to maximize their after-tax net rental income, given by:

$$(1 - \tau_r) \bullet [(R/P) \bullet \kappa - \delta(\kappa)] \bullet K$$

For any τ_r, this maximization is equivalent to the maximization of $[(R/P) \bullet \kappa - \delta(\kappa)] \bullet K$; that is, the same expression as before. Therefore, for a given real rental price, R/P, the chosen utilization rate, κ, does not depend on the tax rate, τ_r.[6] Since the capital stock, K, is fixed, and τ_r does not affect κ, we conclude that τ_r does not affect the supply of capital services, $(\kappa K)^s$. Therefore, a change in τ_r does not shift the supply curve, $(\kappa K)^s$, in Figure 14.5.

Since a change in τ_r does not affect the demand and supply curves in Figure 14.5, it does not affect the market-clearing real rental price, $(R/P)^*$, and the quantity of capital services, $(\kappa K)^*$. That is, the capital stock, K, is fixed, and the capital utilization rate, κ, does not change.

Since the quantity of capital services, κK, does not change, there is no effect on the demand curve for labour, L^d, in Figure 14.4. The supply curve for labour, L^s, shown in light blue, also does not shift. Therefore, the market-clearing real wage rate, $(w/P)^*$, and the quantity of labour, L^*, do not change. Since κK and L are the same, we have from the production function, $Y = A \bullet F(\kappa K, L)$, that real GDP, Y, does not change. Thus, our conclusion is that a change in the marginal tax rate on asset income, τ_r, does not affect real GDP. We should stress, however, that this result applies in the short run, when the stock of capital, K, is given.

Since the real rental price, R/P, and the capital utilization rate, κ, are unchanged, the pre-tax rate of return on ownership of capital, $(R/P) \bullet \kappa - \delta(\kappa)$, does not change. But then, the increase in τ_r implies that the after-tax rate of return, $(1 - \tau_r) \bullet [(R/P) \bullet \kappa - \delta(\kappa)]$, falls. Equation (14.2) tells us that the after-tax real interest rate, $(1 - \tau_r) \bullet r$, equals the after-tax rate of return on ownership of capital:

$$(1 - \tau_r) \bullet r = (1 - \tau_r) \bullet [(R/P) \bullet \kappa - \delta(\kappa)]$$ (14.2)

Therefore, the increase in τ_r lowers the after-tax real interest rate, $(1 - \tau_r) \bullet r$.

---

[5] A tax on business profit tends to affect the demand for capital services. For example, in the system of corporate profits taxation described before, an increase in the tax rate on corporate profits would reduce this demand.

[6] An implicit assumption behind this neutrality result is that capital depreciation is tax deductible. If capital depreciation is not tax deductible, then the after-tax net rental income would become $[(1 - \tau_r)(R/P) \bullet \kappa - \delta(\kappa)] \bullet K$. In this case, an increase in τ_r reduces the capital utilization rate, κ.

We know that a decrease in $(1 - \tau_r) \cdot r$ has intertemporal-substitution effects on consumption. The household raises year 1's consumption, C_1, compared to year 2's, C_2. Hence, for given real income in year 1, the household consumes more and saves less in year 1. Recall, however, that year 1's real GDP, Y_1, does not change, and that $Y_1 = C_1 + I_1 + G_1$. We are assuming that government purchases, G_1, are unchanged. Therefore, the increase in C_1 must correspond to an equal-sized reduction in year 1's gross investment, I_1. Thus, the key result is that a higher tax rate, τ_r, on asset income leads to higher C_1 and lower I_1.

In the long run, the reduction in gross investment, I, means that the stock of capital, K, is smaller than it otherwise would have been. This reduced K will lead to a lower real GDP, Y. Therefore, although an increase in the tax rate on asset income, τ_r, does not affect real GDP in the short run, it decreases real GDP in the long run.[7]

Extending the Model
A consumption tax

We show here that a consumption tax has the same effects as the labour income tax that we studied in the main text. Suppose that real labour income, $(w/P) \cdot L^s$, is untaxed, but an increase in consumption, C, by one unit raises each household's real taxes, T, by τ_c units. This tax could be a sales tax, an excise tax or a value-added tax. We assume that the consumption tax is proportional to C, so that the marginal tax rate, τ_c, equals the average tax rate. We also assume that τ_c is the same for all households and does not vary over time.

If a household works one more unit of time, it again gets w/P additional units of real labour income. Our assumption now is that this additional labour income is untaxed. Suppose that the household raises consumption by ΔC units. This change raises consumption taxes by $\tau_c \cdot \Delta C$. Therefore, the extra income of w/P units must cover the added consumption, ΔC, plus the added taxes, $\tau_c \cdot \Delta C$:

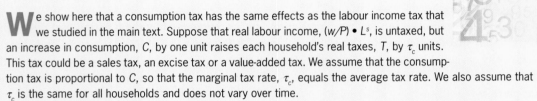

$$w/P = \Delta C + \tau_c \cdot \Delta C$$
$$w/P = \Delta C \cdot (1 + \tau_c)$$

If we divide through by $1 + \tau_c$, we can solve out for the additional consumption:

$$\Delta C = (w/P)/(1 + \tau_c) \tag{14.3}$$

Hence, for each unit more of labour – and, therefore, each unit less of leisure time – a household gets $(w/P)/(1 + \tau_c)$ units more of consumption. For example, if $\tau_c = 0.10$, the household gets about $0.9 \cdot (w/P)$ extra units of consumption. The important point is that the higher the τ_c, the worse the deal. Therefore, if τ_c rises, we predict that the household would work less, enjoy more leisure time and consume less.

With a labour-income tax at the marginal rate τ_w, a household's labour supply, L^s, depended on the after-tax real wage rate, $(1 - \tau_w) \cdot (w/P)$. With a consumption tax at the marginal rate τ_c, equation (14.3) shows that the after-tax real wage rate – in terms of the extra consumption that can be bought with an additional unit of labour – is $(w/P)/(1 + \tau_c)$. Therefore, L^s depends on $(w/P)/(1 + \tau_c)$. Thus, increases in τ_w and τ_c have analogous negative effects on L^s. The conclusion is that consumption taxation has the same economic effects that we found for labour income taxation.

The results are different if tax rates vary over time. If the consumption tax rate, τ_c, varies predictably, households would consume a great deal in years when τ_c is relatively low. In contrast, if the labour-income tax rate, τ_w, varies predictably, households would work a great deal when τ_w was relatively low.

---

[7] A tax on asset income is equivalent to a consumption tax that taxes future consumption more heavily than current consumption. Most economists agree that the economy does better if the government raises a given total of revenue through a consumption tax that is uniform over time, rather than time-varying. Therefore, from the standpoint of optimal taxation, a constant tax rate on consumption, τ_c, tends to be preferred to a tax on asset income, τ_r (which is equivalent to a time-varying consumption tax).

An increase in government purchases financed by a labour-income tax

In Chapter 13, we studied the effects of a permanent increase in government purchases, G. We assumed, unrealistically, that the increase in G was financed by lump-sum taxes. Our finding was that an increase in G by one unit left real GDP, Y, unchanged and reduced consumption, C, by about one unit. Hence, gross investment, I, was unchanged. Also unchanged were the real wage rate, w/P, the real rental price, R/P, and the real interest rate, r.

These results depended on the assumption that the quantity of labour supplied, L^s, was fixed. Now, we reconsider this assumption while also allowing the additional government purchases, G, to be financed by a tax on real labour income, $(w/P) \cdot L$. In particular, we assume that an increase in the marginal income-tax rate on labour income, τ_w, accompanies the permanent rise in G.

We will get different results from those in Chapter 13 if the combination of permanently increased government purchases, G, and the higher marginal income-tax rate, τ_w, affects the quantity of labour supplied, L^s. Therefore, we have to consider the various forces that affect L^s.

- We observed from the government's budget constraint in Chapter 13 that an increase by one unit in each year's government purchases, G, required real taxes less real transfers, $T - V$, to rise by one unit in each year. Therefore, the household has one unit less of real disposable income each year. In response to the negative income effect, the household would raise the quantity of labour supplied, L^s, each year.
- In the Extending the Model box 'Useful public services' in Chapter 13, we assumed that government purchases, G, provided public services that yield utility for households. We assumed that each unit of G was equivalent, in terms of utility, to λ units of consumption, C, where λ is greater than zero. When we include the service value of government purchases in the household's effective disposable income, we get that an increase in G by one unit raises effective disposable income by λ units. (See equation (13.10) in Chapter 13.) The combination of this effect with the rise in real taxes less real transfers, $T - V$, by one unit implies that the household's effective disposable income falls by $1 - \lambda$ units. If λ is less than 1.0, we still get that effective disposable income falls when G rises. Therefore, the negative income effect still predicts that the quantity of labour supplied, L^s, rises each year. However, the higher λ, the weaker is this effect.
- We have found in this chapter that the substitution effect from a higher marginal tax rate, τ_w, on labour income reduces the quantity of labour supplied, L^s. Figure 14.4 shows this effect. Recall that this analysis ignored any income effects.

We see that the overall effect from a rise in government purchases, G, on the quantity of labour supplied, L^s, depends on the offsetting influences from an income effect and a substitution effect. The income effect predicts that L^s would rise. The substitution effect predicts that L^s would fall. The overall effect on L^s is uncertain, which, in turn, implies that the overall effect on real GDP is also uncertain.

Figure 13.7 in Chapter 13 shows that the overall effect from permanently increased government purchases, G, on real GDP is ambiguous. The fluctuations in government purchases can be positively or negatively related to the fluctuations in real GDP. Therefore, the theoretical finding of an ambiguous effect of government purchases on real GDP is consistent with Figure 13.7. We found unambiguously positive effects on real GDP only when we looked at the temporary increases in G during major wars, notably World Wars I and II and the Korean War.

Economics in Practice
The Laffer curve

A permanent increase in government purchases, G, requires a permanent increase in real taxes, T. We assumed in the previous section that a rise in T went along with an increase in the marginal income tax rate, τ_w, on labour income. We can think of the higher τ_w as taking the form of increases in marginal tax rates at all levels of labour income in individual income tax. We explore here the relation between T and τ_w. This relation is called a **Laffer curve** after the economist Arthur Laffer.[8]

The real taxes, T, collected from a tax on labour income can be written as:

$$T = \left[\frac{T}{(w/P)\bullet L}\right]\bullet(w/P)\bullet L$$

real taxes = (average tax rate) • (real tax base)

The real tax base for a labour-income tax is real labour income, $(w/P)\bullet L$. The average tax rate is the ratio of T to $(w/P)\bullet L$.

For given deductions and other features of the tax system, a higher marginal income tax rate, τ_w, goes along with a higher average tax rate. Thus, the overall response of real taxes collected, T, to an increase in τ_w depends on the reaction of the tax base, $(w/P)\bullet L$, to an increase in τ_w. In the example discussed in the previous section, $(w/P)\bullet L$ did not change much when τ_w increased, accompanied by a permanent rise in government purchases, G. The reason was that the substitution effect from a higher τ_w, which lowered labour supply, was partly offset by the income effect from a higher G, which raised labour supply.

The key idea behind the Laffer curve is that the substitution effect from a higher marginal tax rate, τ_w, becomes stronger as τ_w rises. Therefore, for high enough τ_w, the response of $(w/P)\bullet L$ to a further increase in τ_w becomes negative (because the substitution effect on labour supply more than offsets the income effect). Moreover, the substitution effect eventually becomes so strong that T falls when τ_w rises.

To understand the argument about substitution effects, start with a zero tax rate, τ_w. If τ_w is zero at all levels of income, the real taxes collected, T, are also zero. Therefore, the Laffer curve, shown in Figure 14.6, begins at the origin. If τ_w rises above zero, T becomes positive. Therefore, the Laffer curve has a positive slope when τ_w is small.

The substitution effect of τ_w on labour supply works through the after-tax real wage rate, $(1 - \tau_w)\bullet(w/P)$. Think about the term $1 - \tau_w$. If $\tau_w = 0$, an increase in τ_w by, say, 0.1 has a relatively small proportionate effect on $1 - \tau_w$. This term falls from 1 to 0.9, or by 10%. However, if $\tau_w = 0.5$, an increase in τ_w by 0.1 decreases $1 - \tau_w$ from 0.5 to 0.4, or by 20%. When $\tau_w = 0.8$, the corresponding decrease is 50% (from 0.2 to 0.1), and when $\tau_w = 0.9$, it is 100% (from 0.1 to 0). This arithmetic suggests that the strength of the substitution effect of τ_w on labour supply becomes greater as τ_w increases. Therefore, the quantity of labour supplied, L^s, would fall eventually as τ_w rose higher and higher. Eventually, this effect means that the tax base, $(w/P)\bullet L$, would fall enough to more than offset the rise in the average tax rate. At that point, real taxes, T, would decline with a further rise in τ_w.

The graph in Figure 14.6 reflects this discussion. The slope of the relation between real taxes, T, and the marginal tax rate, τ_w, is positive at the origin but becomes flatter as τ_w rises. Eventually, T reaches a peak, when τ_w attains the value denoted $(\tau_w)^*$ on the horizontal axis. For still higher marginal tax rates, T falls as τ_w rises. The graph assumes that, at a tax rate of 100%, real labour income, $(w/P)\bullet L$ – at least the part reported to the tax authorities – declines to zero, so that T is zero.

[8]For a discussion of the Laffer curve, see Don Fullerton (1982).

A study by Charles Stuart (1981) estimated that the maximum of real tax revenue occurred in Sweden at an average marginal tax rate of 70%. That is, he estimated $(\tau_w)^*$ in Figure 14.6 to be about 70%. The actual average marginal tax rate in Sweden reached 70% in the early 1970s and rose subsequently to about 80%. (These estimates of marginal tax rates include consumption taxes as well as income taxes.) Therefore, Sweden was operating on the falling portion of the Laffer curve during the 1970s. A similar study by A. Van Ravestein and H. Vijlbrief (1988) estimated that $(\tau_w)^*$ was also about 70% in the Netherlands. They found that the actual marginal tax rate in the Netherlands reached 67% in 1985 – close to, but not quite as high as, the estimated $(\tau_w)^*$.

Figure 14.6 The relation between real tax revenue and the marginal income-tax rate (a Laffer Curve)

The horizontal axis shows the marginal tax rate on labour income, τ_w. The vertical axis has real tax revenue, T. Starting from zero, an increase in τ_w raises T. However, as τ_w rises, the slope gets less steep. Eventually, T reaches its peak when τ_w reaches $(\tau_w)^*$ on the horizontal axis. Beyond that point, T falls towards zero as τ_w rises towards 100%.

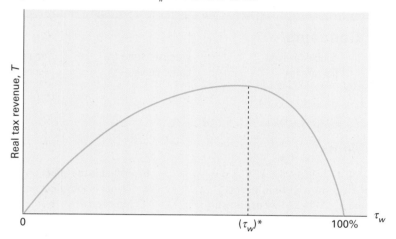

Transfer payments

We assumed, thus far, that real transfer payments, V, were lump sums. But, as with taxes, transfers are not lump sums in the real world. Rather, most transfer programmes relate an individual's payments to the individual's characteristics. For example, welfare programmes give money or services such as healthcare to poor persons and then reduce or eliminate the transfers if a person's income rises. To qualify for unemployment insurance, a recipient must not be working. Similarly, pension payments to an elderly person may be reduced if that person receives labour income above a specified amount.

The point is that an income-tested transfer programme – one that reduces transfers when labour income rises – effectively imposes a positive marginal income tax rate on labour income. An increase in the scale of a transfer programme – for example, an expansion of the welfare system – raises the marginal income tax rate, τ_w, implied by the programme. Therefore, to analyze the economic effects of increased real transfers, V, we have to take account of this increase in τ_w.

Suppose that the government increases real transfers, V, and finances these expenditures with increased real taxes, T, collected by a tax on labour income. In this case, marginal income-tax rates, τ_w, rise for two reasons. First, the rise in T goes along with a higher τ_w for households that pay individual income taxes. Second, for households that are receiving transfers – such as poor welfare recipients – the expansion of the transfer programme raises the implicit marginal income tax rate, τ_w, because of the income testing for benefits. In other words, we get an increase in τ_w from both sides. We therefore predict even stronger effects of the sort analyzed in Figures 14.4 and 14.5. In particular, labour input, L, capital services, κK, and real GDP, Y, tend to decline.

Summing Up

This chapter introduces realistic forms of taxes, which affect incentives to work and save. A tax on labour income has a substitution effect that discourages labour supply. An increase in the marginal tax rate on labour income reduces the after-tax real wage rate and the quantity of labour. Therefore, real GDP declines. An increase in the marginal tax rate on asset income does not affect real GDP in the short run. However, the decrease in the after-tax real interest rate causes a shift towards consumption and away from investment. Consequently, in the long run, the capital stock and real GDP decline.

We studied a permanent increase in government purchases, accompanied by a rise in the marginal tax rate on labour income. The overall effect on labour supply is ambiguous – the income effect suggests higher labour supply, but the substitution effect from the higher tax rate suggests lower labour supply. The evidence is consistent with the ambiguous relationship between fluctuations in government expenditures and fluctuations in real GDP, documented in Figure 13.7.

Key Terms and Concepts

after-tax real interest rate   double taxation   graduated-rate tax   marginal tax rate
after-tax real wage rate   flat-rate tax   Laffer curve   social security
average tax rate

Questions and Problems

A   Review questions

1   What is the income effect from a rise in the tax rate on labour income, τ_w? Why did we assume no income effect in part of our analysis?

2   Distinguish between the average tax rate and the marginal tax rate. Must the two be equal for a flat-rate tax?

3   Could an increase in the tax rate on labour income reduce real tax revenue? How does the answer depend on the responsiveness of labour supply to the after-tax real wage rate?

B   Problems for discussion

4   Inflation and taxes on asset income

Suppose that the tax rate on asset income is τ_r. Suppose (as is often true in the real world) that the tax is levied on nominal interest income. Assume (as is not entirely accurate) that the tax applies to the real returns on capital.

a   What is the after-tax real interest rate on bonds? Consider a permanent, unanticipated increase in the money growth rate from μ to μ', as studied in Chapter 12. Assume that τ_r does not change.

b   What is the effect on the inflation rate, π?

c   What is the effect on the after-tax real return on capital?

d   What is the effect on the after-tax real interest rate on bonds? What happens to the nominal interest rate, i? Does it move one-for-one with π?

5   Effects of inflation on a graduated-rate income tax

Consider an individual income-tax system that had many different tax-rate brackets. A married couple paid individual income tax on labour income in accordance with the table on the next page.

a   Suppose that each person's real income stays constant over time, so that inflation steadily raises each person's nominal income. If the tax schedule shown in the table had remained unchanged, what would have happened over time to each couple's marginal income tax rate?

b   Assume now that the income bracket limits shown in the left column of the table are adjusted proportionally (or 'indexed') over time for changes in the price level. That is, if the price level rises by 5%, each income bracket rises by 5%. What, then, is the effect of inflation on each couple's marginal income tax rate?

Range of taxable income (€)	Marginal income tax rate (%)
3 540–5 719	11
5 720–7 919	12
7 920–12 389	13
12 390–16 649	16
16 650–21 019	18
21 020–25 599	22
25 600–31 119	25
31 120–36 629	28
36 630–47 669	33
47 670–62 449	38
62 450–89 089	42
89 090–113 859	45
113 860–169 019	49
169 020–	50

6   A consumption tax

Suppose that consumption is taxed in each year at the constant rate τ_c.

a   What is the household budget constraint?

b   What are the effects of an increase in τ_c on the labour market? How do the results compare with those shown for an increase in the tax rate on labour income, τ_w, in Figure 14.4?

c   What are the effects of an increase in τ_c on the market for capital services? How do the results compare with those shown for an increase in the tax rate on labour income, τ_w, in Figure 14.5?

d   Suppose now that τ_c falls in year 1 but does not change in future years. How does this change affect the choice of consumption over time? How would the effects resemble those from an increase in the tax rate on asset income, τ_r? In what ways do the effects differ from those from a change in the tax rate on asset income, τ_r?

7   The flat-rate tax

Some economists advocate shifting from the graduated individual income tax to a flat-rate tax. Under the new system, there would be few deductions from taxable income, and the marginal tax rate would be constant. Because of the elimination of the deductions, the average marginal tax rate would be lower than that under the current system. What are the economic effects from a shift to a flat-rate tax on labour income?

15 Public debt

One of the most controversial economic issues is the *government's budget deficit*. The news media suggest that the economy suffers greatly when the government runs a budget deficit. The most important task in this chapter will be to evaluate this view. As we shall see, the conclusions from the equilibrium business-cycle model depart substantially from those in the newspapers.

A **budget deficit** occurs when the government's tax revenue falls short of its expenditure. The government finances this shortfall by issuing interest-bearing government bonds – **public debt**. When the budget deficit is greater than zero, the quantity of public debt increases over time.

We consider first the history of the public debt in the United Kingdom. With these facts as a background, we extend the equilibrium business-cycle model to allow for public debt. We use the model to assess the effects of budget deficits and public debt on economic variables, including real gross domestic product (GDP), saving, investment and the real interest rate.

The history of UK public debt

Table 15.1 shows the history of the public debt in the United Kingdom. The table shows the nominal quantity of interest-bearing debt and the ratio of this debt to nominal GDP (gross national product, or GNP, in earlier years).[1] Figure 15.1 shows the debt–GDP ratio for the United Kingdom from 1700 to 2005.

The major peaks in the debt–GDP ratio of the United Kingdom were associated with wartime: 0.50 after the Wars of Spanish and Austrian Succession in 1722, 1.1 at the end of the Seven Years' War in 1764, 1.2 after the War of American Independence in 1785, 1.3 after the Napoleonic Wars in 1816, 1.4 at the end of World War I in 1919, and 2.6 after World War II in 1946. The high points for UK debt in relation to GDP were more than twice as great as those for the United States. It is worth noting that the UK public debt constituted more than 100% of GDP in the 1760s – large amounts of public debt are not a modern invention!

Some researchers argue that Britain gained credibility in public-debt management with the expanded role of Parliament after the Glorious Revolution of 1688 (see Douglas North and Barry Weingast, 1989, and Thomas Sargent and Francois Velde, 1995). The availability of debt finance may have given Britain a great advantage over France in the fighting of numerous wars up to the Napoleonic conflicts that ended in 1815.

Recessions raised the UK debt–GDP ratio; for example, from 1920 to 1923 and 1929 to 1933. Declining debt–GDP ratios were typically not a feature of periods of war or recession. For example, the ratio declined from 2.57 in 1946 to 0.35 in 1990.

---

[1] The UK debt figures are the gross sterling debt of the central government. Net numbers are unavailable for the long-term history. In March 2004, the gross sterling debt of £428 billion corresponded to a public sector net debt of £376 billion.

Table 15.1 Public debt in the United Kingdom

Year	UK debt (£ billion)	UK debt–GDP ratio
1700	0.014	0.20
1710	0.030	0.31
1720	0.039	0.49
1730	0.037	0.49
1740	0.033	0.40
1750	0.059	0.68
1760	0.083	0.79
1770	0.106	1.01
1780	0.135	1.01
1790	0.179	1.05
1800	0.304	0.79
1810	0.436	0.96
1820	0.568	1.37
1830	0.544	1.12
1840	0.562	1.01
1850	0.557	0.94
1860	0.589	0.69
1870	0.593	0.51
1880	0.591	0.43
1890	0.578	0.37
1900	0.628	0.31
1910	0.665	0.28
1920	7.620	1.22
1930	7.580	1.55
1940	10.500	1.37
1950	26.100	1.77
1960	28.400	1.09
1970	33.400	0.64
1980	113.000	0.49
1990	190.000	0.35
2000	369.000	0.39
2005	473.000	0.41

Note: The public debt since 1917 is the central government's gross sterling debt in billions of pounds at nominal par value. Before 1917, the figures are the accumulation of the central government's budget deficit, starting from a benchmark stock of public debt in 1700. For discussions of the data, see Barro (1987). The underlying data are from the Central Statistical Office, *Annual Abstract of Statistics,* various issues; Mitchell and Deane (1962); and Mitchell and Jones (1971). Data on nominal GDP or GNP are from the preceding and also from Deane and Cole (1969) and Feinstein (1972). Before 1830, nominal GNP is estimated from rough estimates of real GNP multiplied by a price index based on wholesale prices.

Characteristics of government bonds

We will now expand the equilibrium business-cycle model to allow the government to issue interest-bearing bonds. We assume that government bonds pay interest and principal in the same way as private bonds. We still assume that all bonds have very short maturity[2] and that bonds specify nominal amounts of principal and interest. That is, we do not consider indexed bonds, which we discussed in Chapter 12.[3]

[2]In the United Kingdom, in 2003, 36% of marketable government bonds had a maturity of up to 5 years, 35% were between 5 and 15 years, and 29% were greater than 15 years.
[3]In the United Kingdom, in 2004, indexed bonds were 18% of the outstanding gross sterling debt of the central government.

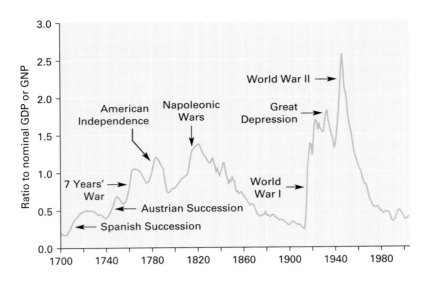

Figure 15.1 Ratio of UK public debt to GDP, 1700–2004

The graph shows the ratio of UK nominal public debt to nominal GDP or GNP, using the data given in Table 15.1.

Economics in Practice
The European sovereign debt crisis

The European sovereign debt crisis began in 2009. At that time, several Eurozone countries (Cyprus, Greece, Portugal, Ireland and Spain) experienced inability to repay/refinance their government debts or to bail out banks that were in financial trouble. This debt crisis was caused by several factors.[4] First, as a result of bank bailouts caused by real-estate bubbles in several European countries, a large amount of private debt was transferred to government debt. Second, given that the Eurozone is not a fiscal union (i.e., each national government has its own fiscal budget and is responsible for its own fiscal revenue and expenditure), European leaders had limited ability to assist the financially troubled member states. Third, the fact that a large amount of sovereign debt was owned by European banks made the crisis contagious across European countries. In response to this crisis, the European Union implemented a number of emergency measures, such as the European Financial Stability Facility (EFSF) in 2010 and the European Stability Mechanism (ESM) in 2012. Furthermore, the European Central Bank lowered interest rates, provided cheap loans to European banks, and announced unlimited support for all member states that were involved in a bailout or precautionary programme from the EFSF/ESM. These policy responses helped to calm the financial market. By 2014, Ireland and Portugal exited their bailout programmes, and Greece and Cyprus partly regained access to the financial market.

To simplify our analysis, we assume that bondholders (households in our model) regard government bonds as equivalent to private bonds. Specifically, we do not allow for the possibility that private bonds are riskier than government bonds in terms of the probability of default. Given our assumption, households would hold the two kinds of bonds only if they paid the same nominal interest rate, i. Therefore, our model has only one nominal interest rate, i, paid on all bonds.

Denote by B_t^g the nominal amount of government bonds outstanding at the end of year t. We still use the symbol B_t for private bonds (issued by households in our model). Thus, the household's total holding of bonds at the end of year t is:

$$total\,bond\,holdings = B_t + B_t^g$$
$$total\,bond\,holdings = private\,bonds + government\,bonds$$

[4]See Philip Lane (2012), for a detailed discussion on the origins of this crisis.

The quantity of private bonds held by all households is still zero, because the positive amount held by one household must correspond to the debt of another household. Therefore, $B_t = 0$ still holds in the aggregate. This result means that the total quantity of bonds held by all households equals the public debt, B_t^g:

$$total\,bond\,holdings\,of\,all\,households = B_t^g$$

We usually think of the government as a net debtor to the private sector, so that B_t is greater than zero. However, the government could be a creditor, in which case B_t^g would be less than zero.

Budget constraints and budget deficits

To consider budget deficits and public debt, we have to see how they fit into the government's budget constraint. We begin by extending the government's budget constraint.

THE GOVERNMENT'S BUDGET CONSTRAINT

We introduced the government's budget constraint for year t in Chapter 13:

$$G_t + V_t = T_t + (M_t - M_{t-1})/P_t$$

$$real\,purchases + real\,transfers = real\,taxes + real\,revenue\,from\,money\,creation \tag{13.1}$$

The first new term that we have to add is the government's interest payments, which are $i_{t-1} \bullet B_{t-1}^g$ in nominal units. The real value of these interest payments, $i_{t-1} \bullet (B_{t-1}^g/P_t)$, adds to the government's expenditure or uses of funds on the left-hand side of equation (13.1).

The second new term is the debt issue during year t. The nominal amount of this debt issue is $B_t^g - B_{t-1}^g$. Note that the reissue of bonds as they come due is not a net source of funds for the government. What matters is the difference between the stock outstanding at the end of the year, B_t^g, and the amount outstanding at the end of the previous year, B_{t-1}^g. The real value of the debt issue, $(B_t^g - B_{t-1}^g)/P_t$, adds to the government's sources of funds on the right-hand side of equation (13.1).

When we introduce the two new terms into equation (13.1), we get an expanded version of the government budget constraint:

Key equation (expanded government budget constraint):

$$G_t + V_t + i_{t-1} \bullet (B_{t-1}^g/P_t) = T_t + (B_t^g - B_{t-1}^g)/P_t + (M_t - M_{t-1})/P_t$$

$$real\,purchases + real\,transfers + real\,interest\,payments = real\,taxes + real\,debt\,issue$$
$$+\,real\,revenue\,from\,money\,creation \tag{15.1}$$

The two new terms are the real interest payments, $i_{t-1} \bullet (B_{t-1}^g/P_t)$, on the left-hand side, and the real debt issue, $(B_t^g - B_{t-1}^g)/P_t$, on the right-hand side.

To analyze budget deficits, we will find it convenient to reintroduce two simplifying assumptions from Chapters 13 and 14. Assume, first, that the nominal quantity of money, M_t, equals a constant, M. In this case, the revenue from money creation, $(M_t - M_{t-1})/P_t$, is zero on the right-hand side of equation (15.1). Second, ignore inflation, so that the price level, P_t, equals the constant P. In this case, the nominal interest rate, i_t, equals the real interest rate, r_t. These assumptions simplify the analysis without affecting our main conclusions about public debt and budget deficits.

When nominal money, M_t, and the price level, P_t, do not change over time, the government's budget constraint simplifies from equation (15.1) to:

$$G_t + V_t + r_{t-1} \bullet (B_{t-1}^g/P_t) = T_t + (B_t^g - B_{t-1}^g)/P \tag{15.2}$$

Starting from equation (15.1), we replaced P_t by P and i_{t-1} by r_{t-1}, and we eliminated the term $(M_t - M_{t-1})/P_t$.

THE BUDGET DEFICIT

To define and calculate the government's budget deficit, it is helpful to think about how much the government saves or dissaves. We define real saving for the government in the same way as for a household. If the government saves, its net real assets rise; if the government dissaves, its net real assets fall. To use these ideas, we have to define the government's net real assets.

The real public debt, B_t^g/P, is a liability of the government. When B_t^g/P rises, the government owes more and, as a result, has more liabilities and fewer net real assets. Therefore, an increase in the real public debt, $(B_t^g - B_{t-1}^g)/P$, signifies that the government is saving less or dissaving more in real terms.

If the government owned capital, its net real assets would include this capital. In that case, an increase in government-owned capital stock – called net **public investment** – would mean that the government had more net real assets. Thus, an increase in net public investment means that the government is saving more or dissaving less in real terms. However, in our model, the government does not own capital, and net public investment is zero.

Since the money stock is constant and the government owns no capital, the government's real saving or dissaving equals the negative of the change in the real public debt. If the real public debt increases, the government's real saving is less than zero, and the government is dissaving. If the real public debt decreases, the government's real saving is greater than zero. Therefore, we have:

$$real\ government\ saving = -(B_t^g - B_{t-1}^g)/P \qquad (15.3)$$

We can rearrange the government's budget constraint in equation (15.2) to relate real government saving, $-(B_t^g - B_{t-1}^g)/P$, to real expenditure and taxes:

$$-(B_t^g - B_{t-1}^g)/P = T_t - [G_t + V_t + r_{t-1} \cdot (B_{t-1}^g/P)]$$
$$real\ government\ saving = real\ taxes - real\ government\ expenditure \qquad (15.4)$$

Note that real government expenditure is the sum of real purchases, G_t, real transfers, V_t, and real interest payments, $r_{t-1} \cdot (B_{t-1}^g/P)$. When real taxes are greater than real government expenditure, real government saving is greater than zero, and the real public debt falls over time.

If the right-hand side of equation (15.4) is greater than zero, the government's revenue exceeds its expenditure, and the government has a **budget surplus**. Thus, the real surplus is the same as the government's real saving. Conversely, if the right-hand side is less than zero, the government has a budget deficit. The real deficit is the same as the government's real dissaving. If the right-hand side of equation (15.4) is zero, the government has a **balanced budget**, and the government's real saving is zero.

PUBLIC SAVING, PRIVATE SAVING AND NATIONAL SAVING

To assess the economic effects of budget deficits, it is useful to organize our discussion around three concepts of saving: government (or public) saving, household (or private) saving and national (or total) saving. Real government saving is given from equation (15.3):

$$real\ government\ saving = -(B_t^g - B_{t-1}^g)/P \qquad (15.3)$$

If the government runs a real budget deficit, so that $(B_t^g - B_{t-1}^g)/P$ is greater than zero, real government saving is less than zero. Recall that, if the government owned capital, the change in this capital stock would add to government saving.

We know from Chapter 7 that the household's real saving equals the change in the household's real assets. In our previous analysis, these real assets consisted of private bonds, B_t/P_t; money, M_t/P_t; and capital, K_t. Now, we have to add real assets held as government bonds, B_t^g/P_t. The economy-wide total of private bonds, B_t, still equals zero. Therefore, when we add up over all households, the change in these bonds equals zero. Also, we are assuming that

M_t and P_t do not change over time. Therefore, the economy-wide total of household real saving equals the change in the capital stock plus the change in real government bonds:

$$real\ household\ saving\ (economy\text{-}wide) = K_t - K_{t-1} + (B_t^g - B_{t-1}^g)/P \qquad (15.5)$$

The sum of real government saving and economy-wide real household saving equals real **national saving** – the saving of the whole nation. We can see from equations (15.3) and (15.5) that, when we combine government and household saving, the change in real government bonds, $(B_t^g - B_{t-1}^g)/P$, cancels out. An increase in real government bonds means that the government is saving less and that households are saving correspondingly more. Therefore, we get:

$$real\ national\ saving = K_t - K_{t-1} \qquad (15.6)$$

Real national saving equals the change in the capital stock, which is net investment. This result still holds if the government owns capital. In that case, K_t is the economy's total capital stock – the sum of private and public capital; and net investment, $K_t - K_{t-1}$, is the sum of private and public net investment.

Public debt and households' budget constraints

We found in Chapter 13 that the household's multiyear budget constraint included the present value of real transfers net of real taxes, $V_t - T_t$:

$$C_1 + C_2/(1+r_1) + \cdots = (1+r_0) \bullet (B_0/P + K_0)$$
$$+ (w/P)_1 \bullet L_1^s + (w/P)_2 \bullet L_2^s/(1+r_1) + \cdots$$
$$+ (V_1 - T_1) + (V_2 - T_2)/(1+r_1) + (V_3 - T_3)/[(1+r_1) \bullet (1+r_2)] + \cdots$$

$$present\ value\ of\ consumption = value\ of\ initial\ assets$$
$$+\ present\ value\ of\ wage\ incomes$$
$$+\ present\ value\ of\ transfers\ net\ of\ taxes \qquad (13.6)$$

Now, we have to modify equation (13.6) to include the household's initial holdings of real government bonds, B_0^g/P. When we make this change, the multiyear household budget constraint becomes:

$$C_1 + C_2/(1+r_1) + \cdots = (1+r_0) \bullet (B_0/P + B_0^g/P + K_0) + (w/P)_1 \bullet L_1^s$$
$$+ (w/P)_2 \bullet L_2^s/(1+r_1) + \cdots + (V_1 - T_1)$$
$$+ (V_2 - T_2)/(1+r_1) + (V_3 - T_3)/[(1+r_1) \bullet (1+r_2)] + \cdots \qquad (15.7)$$

Any income effects on households from the government's budget have to involve either the initial real government bonds, B_0^g/P, or the present value of real transfers net of real taxes, $(V_1 - T_1) + (V_2 - T_2)/(1+r_1) + (V_3 - T_3)/[(1+r_1) \bullet (1+r_2)] + \cdots$. To illustrate the results, it is convenient to begin with some simplifying assumptions.

A SIMPLE CASE OF RICARDIAN EQUIVALENCE

Start with some unrealistic assumptions, which can then be relaxed:

- The real interest rate, r_t, is the same each year: $r_0 = r_1 = r_2 = \cdots = r$.
- As already assumed, the money stock, M_t, and the price level, P_t, do not change over time. With a zero inflation rate, π, the real interest rate, r, equals the nominal rate, i.
- Real transfers, V_t, are zero each year.
- The government starts with no debt, so that $B_0^g = 0$.
- Finally, the most important assumption: *the government has a given time path of purchases, G_t*. We are *not* assuming here that G_t is unchanging over time. Rather, we are assuming that, whatever complicated path G_t takes, this whole path stays the same when we consider different choices of budget deficits or different starting levels of public debt.

Since real transfers, V_t, are zero each year, the government's budget constraint for year t simplifies from equation (15.2) to:

$$G_t + r \bullet (B^g_{t-1}/P) = T_t + (B^g_t - B^g_{t-1})/P \qquad (15.8)$$

Since the government starts with zero debt, we have $B^g_0/P = 0$. Therefore, in year 1, the government's real interest payments, $r \bullet (B^g_0/P)$, are zero, and the budget constraint is:

$$G_1 = T_1 + B^g_1/P$$

government purchases in year 1 = real taxes in year 1 + real debt at end of year 1 $\qquad (15.9)$

Suppose, to begin, that the government balances its budget each year. Then, in year 1, real purchases, G_1, equal real taxes, T_1. In that case, equation (15.9) implies that the real public debt remains at zero at the end of year 1; that is, $B^g_1/P = 0$. Continuing on, if the government balances its budget every year, the real public debt, B^g_t/P, is zero in every year t.

What happens if, instead of balancing its budget in year 1, the government runs a real budget deficit of one unit? Since we are assuming that the path of government purchases stays the same, year 1's real purchases, G_1, do not change. Therefore, the deficit must come from a cut in real taxes, T_1, by one unit. Equation (15.9) implies that the real deficit of one unit requires the government to issue one unit of real public debt at the end of year 1, so that $B^g_1/P = 1$.

Assume that the government decides to restore the public debt to zero from year 2 onward, so that $B^g_2/P = B^g_3/P = \cdots = 0$. We have to figure out what this policy requires for year 2's real taxes, T_2. To calculate T_2, we use the government's budget constraint for year 2. This constraint is given from equation (15.8) as:

$$G_2 + r \bullet (B^g_1/P) = T_2 + (B^g_2 - B^g_1)/P$$

government purchases in year 2 + real interest payments in year 2

= real taxes in year 2 + real budget deficit in year 2 $\qquad (15.10)$

If we substitute $B^g_1/P = 1$ and $B^g_2/P = 0$ in equation (15.10), the constraint simplifies to:

$$G_2 + r = T_2 - 1$$

Therefore, we can rearrange the terms to calculate real taxes for year 2:

$$T_2 = G_2 + 1 + r$$

This equation says that the government must raise real taxes in year 2, T_2, above year 2's government purchases, G_2, to pay the principal and interest, $1 + r$, on the one unit of debt, B^g_1/P, issued in year 1. (Recall our assumption that G_2 does not change.)

Putting the results together, year 1's real taxes, T_1, fall by one unit and year 2's real taxes, T_2, rise by $1 + r$ units. How do these changes affect the total present value of real taxes paid by households? Recall the household's multi-year budget constraint:

$$C_1 + C_2/(1+r_1) + \cdots = (1+r_0) \bullet (B_0/P + B^g_0/P + K_0)$$
$$+ (w/P)_1 \bullet L^s_1 + (w/P)_2 \bullet L^s_2/(1+r_1) + \cdots + (V_1 - T_1)$$
$$+ (V_2 - T_2)/(1+r_1) + (V_3 - T_3)/[(1+r_1) \bullet (1+r_2)] + \cdots \qquad (15.7)$$

According to this equation, we have to divide year 2's real taxes, T_2, by the discount factor, $1 + r$, to compute a present value. Therefore, the overall effect of the changes in T_1 and T_2 on the present value of real taxes is given by:

decrease in year 1's real taxes + present value of increase in year 2's taxes

$$= -1 + (1+r)/(1+r)$$
$$= -1 + 1$$
$$= 0$$

Hence, households experience no net change in the present value of real taxes when the government runs a budget deficit in year 1 and pays off the debt with the necessary budget surplus in year 2.

In our simple example, the government's budget deficit does not affect the present value of real taxes. Moreover, we are assuming that real transfers, V_t, are zero in each period. Therefore, the budget deficit does not affect the present value of real transfers net of real taxes on the right-hand side of equation (15.7). We conclude that the budget deficit has no income effects on households.

We can interpret the result as follows. Households receive one unit extra of real disposable income in year 1 because of the cut in year 1's real taxes, T_1, by one unit. However, households also have $1 + r$ units less of real disposable income in year 2 because of the rise in year 2's real taxes, T_2, by $1 + r$ units. If households use the extra unit of real disposable income in year 1 to buy an extra unit of bonds, they will have just enough additional funds (i.e., $1 + r$ units) to pay the extra real taxes in year 2. Thus, the tax cut in year 1 provides enough resources, but no more, for households to pay the higher taxes in year 2. That is why there is no income effect. Nothing is left over to raise consumption or reduce labour supply in any year.

We can view the results as saying that households view real taxes in year 1, T_1, as equivalent to a real budget deficit in year 1, $(B_1^g - B_0^g)/P$. If the government replaces a unit of real taxes with a unit of real budget deficit, households know that the present value of next year's real taxes will rise by one unit. Thus, the real budget deficit is the same as a real tax in terms of the overall present value of real taxes. This finding is the simplest version of the **Ricardian equivalence theorem** on the public debt. (The theorem is named after the famous British economist David Ricardo, who first expressed the idea in the early 1800s.)[5]

We can interpret the results in terms of saving. The real budget deficit of one unit in year 1 means that real government saving is minus one unit. Since households do not change consumption, they place the entire extra unit of year 1's real disposable income into bonds. Therefore, real household saving in year 1 rises by one unit. Thus, the extra real household saving exactly offsets the government's real dissaving. The sum of household and government real saving – real national saving – does not change. Thus, another way to express the result is that a budget deficit does not affect real national saving.

ANOTHER CASE OF RICARDIAN EQUIVALENCE

Our basic result was that a deficit-financed cut in year 1's real taxes by one unit led to an increase by one unit in the present value of future real taxes. In our simple example, all of the higher future taxes appeared in year 2. More generally, some of the increases in real taxes would show up in later years.

To get a more general result, we can drop the assumption that the government runs enough of a budget surplus in year 2 to pay off all of the bonds issued in year 1. Assume, as before, that the government issues one unit of real debt, B_1^g/P, at the end of year 1. Recall that the government's budget constraint for year 2 is:

$$G_2 + r \bullet (B_1^g/P) = T_2 + (B_2^g - B_1^g)/P \qquad (15.10)$$

Suppose now that, in year 2, the government does not pay off the one unit of debt, B_1^g/P, issued in year 1. Assume, instead, that the government carries the principal of this debt, one unit, over to year 3, so that:

$$B_2^g/P = B_1^g/P = 1$$

If we substitute $B_1^g/P = 1$ and $B_2^g/P = 1$ into equation (15.10), we get:

$$G_2 + r = T_2$$

Therefore, year 2's real taxes, T_2, cover the interest payment, r, but not the principal, 1, for the real debt, B_1^g/P, issued in year 1. In other words, the government balances its budget in year 2: real taxes equal real purchases plus real interest payments.

[5]For discussions, see David Ricardo (1846), James Buchanan (1958, pp. 43–46, 114–122) and Robert Barro (1989). Gerald O'Driscoll (1977) points out Ricardo's doubts about the empirical validity of his own theorem.

If the government again balances its budget in year 3, we find by the same reasoning that year 3's real taxes, T_3, cover the interest payment, r, on the one unit of real debt. Similarly, if the government balances its budget every year, real taxes, T_t, cover year t's interest payment, r. The time profile for the changes in real taxes is:

- year 1: T_1 falls by 1
- year 2: T_2 rises by r
- year 3: T_3 rises by r

and so on. Hence, T_t increases by r units in each year after the first.

Think about the sequence of higher real taxes by r units each year. What quantity of real bonds would households need at the end of year 1 to pay these extra taxes? If households hold one more unit of real bonds, the real interest income in year 2 would be r, and this income could pay year 2's additional taxes. Then, if the principal of the bond – one unit – were held over to year 3, the real interest income of r could pay year 3's added taxes. Continuing this way, we find that the real interest income each year would allow households to meet their extra real taxes every year.

What, then, is the present value of the increase in real taxes by r units starting in year 2? This present value must be the same as the one extra unit of real bonds in year 1 needed to pay the additional real taxes in each subsequent year. But, obviously, the present value of one unit of real bonds in year 1 is one unit. Therefore, the present value of the additional future real taxes is one.[6]

Given the results about the present value of the higher future real taxes, the overall change in the present value of real taxes comes from combining two terms:

- -1: real tax cut in year 1
- $+1$: present value of real tax increases in future years.

Since the sum of the two terms is zero, we conclude, as in our first example, that a deficit-financed cut in year 1's real taxes, T_1, leads to no change in the overall present value of real taxes. Therefore, we find again that the deficit-financed tax cut in year 1 has no income effects on households.

RICARDIAN EQUIVALENCE MORE GENERALLY

We now have two examples in which a deficit-financed tax cut does not affect the present value of real taxes paid by households. To get this answer, we made a number of unrealistic assumptions. However, the result still holds if we relax most of these assumptions.

We can allow the initial real public debt, B_0^g/P, to be greater than zero. Notice that B_0^g/P enters as a part of households' sources of funds on the right-hand side of the multiyear budget constraint:

$$
\begin{aligned}
C_1 + C_2/(1+r_1) + \cdots = {} & (1+r_0) \bullet (B_0/P + B_0^g/P + K_0) + (w/P)_1 \bullet L_1^s \\
& + (w/P)_2 \bullet L_2^s/(1+r_1) + \cdots + (V_1 - T_1) \\
& + (V_2 - T_2)/(1+r_1) + (V_3 - T_3)/[(1+r_1)\bullet(1+r_2)] + \cdots
\end{aligned}
\tag{15.7}
$$

---

[6]We can verify this answer by summing the present values: $\dfrac{r}{1+r} + \dfrac{r}{(1+r)^2} + \dfrac{r}{(1+r)^3} + \cdots = \left(\dfrac{r}{1+r}\right) \bullet \left[1 + \left(\dfrac{r}{1+r}\right) + \left(\dfrac{r}{1+r}\right)^2 + \cdots\right]$

The infinite sum inside the brackets has the form of the geometric series $1 + x + x^2 + \cdots$, which equals $1/(1-x)$ if x is less than one in magnitude. In our case, $x = 1/(1+r)$. Therefore, we have

$$
\frac{r}{1+r} + \frac{r}{(1+r)^2} + \frac{r}{(1+r)^3} + \cdots = \left(\frac{r}{1+r}\right) \bullet \left(\frac{1}{1 - \left(\frac{1}{1+r}\right)}\right)
$$

$$
= \left(\frac{r}{1+r}\right) \bullet \left(\frac{1+r}{1+r-1}\right)
$$

$$
= \left(\frac{r}{1+r}\right) \bullet \left(\frac{1+r}{r}\right)
$$

$$
= 1
$$

However, if the time path of government purchases, G_t, is given (and if real transfers, V_t, are zero), we can show that a higher B_0^g / P requires the government to collect a correspondingly higher present value of real taxes, T_t, to finance the debt. This higher present value of real taxes exactly offsets the higher B_0^g / P on the right-hand side of equation (15.7). Thus, we still have no income effects on households.

If we allow real transfers, V_t, to be greater than zero, we find that a deficit-financed tax cut does not affect the present value of real transfers net of real taxes, $V_t - T_t$, on the right-hand side of equation (15.7). Hence, there are, again, no income effects on households.

We can allow for variations in the money stock, M_t, and the price level, P_t. In this case, the new feature is that the revenue from money creation – often called the inflation tax – should be viewed as another form of tax. That is, real taxes, T_t, have to be broadened to include the inflation tax. With this extension, we still find that a deficit-financed tax cut does not affect the present value of real taxes paid by households.

We can allow for tax cuts and budget deficits in future years, not just for year 1. These deficits will require higher real taxes in years further into the future. In each case, the higher present value of real taxes exactly offsets the present value of the tax cut. Therefore, we still get no effect on the present value of real taxes paid by households. This conclusion holds for any time pattern of budget deficits and tax cuts.

What if the government has a deficit-financed tax cut and finances the extra public debt forever by issuing new debt? In this case, it seems that future real taxes would never increase. However, this form of financing requires an explosive path for the public debt – it amounts to a form of chain letter or pyramid scheme in which the real debt rises at a rate that is ultimately unsustainable. Our assumption is that the government cannot carry out these types of chain letters.

In all of these cases, we find that the income effects are nil. The reason we keep getting this result is that we have held fixed the time path of real government purchases, G_t. These purchases have to be paid for at some point with real taxes, T_t. By varying its budget deficits, the government can change the timing of taxes. However, the government cannot escape levying the taxes at some point; this conclusion is an example of the economic adage that there is no such thing as a free lunch. If the government wants to change the present value of real taxes, it has to change the present value of its purchases, G_t. That is why the assumption of a fixed path of G_t is the really important assumption.

Economic effects of a budget deficit

What happens in the equilibrium business-cycle model when the government cuts year 1's real taxes, T_1, and runs a budget deficit? Economists often refer to this type of change as a stimulative **fiscal policy**. We know, if the path of government purchases, G_t, does not change, that the budget deficit has no income effects on households' choices of consumption and labour supply. Today's real tax cut is matched by a higher present value of future real taxes. There may, however, be substitution effects from the tax changes. These effects, which we explored in Chapter 14, depend on the forms of the taxes that are cut today and raised in the future. We begin by assuming that taxes are lump-sum, as in Chapter 13. Although this case is unrealistic, it does correspond to the one usually examined in macroeconomic textbooks. We will consider more realistic types of taxes in later sections.

LUMP-SUM TAXES

Suppose that the cut in year 1's real taxes, T_1, and the increases in future real taxes, T_t, all involve lump-sum taxes. The important feature of these taxes is that they have no substitution effects on consumption and labour supply. Recall that the budget deficit also has no income effects on consumption and labour supply. We conclude that, for a given real interest rate, r, and real wage rate, w/P, a deficit-financed tax cut would not affect consumption, C, and labour supply, L^s. (For convenience, we now omit the time subscripts on variables.)

A deficit-financed tax cut does not affect the marginal products of labour and capital, MPL and MPK. Therefore, the deficit does not shift the demand curve for labour (shown in Figure 14.4) or the demand curve for capital services (shown in Figure 14.5). Since the supply curve for labour does not shift, we find that the market-clearing real wage rate, $(w/P)^*$, and quantity of labour, L^*, are unchanged (Figure 14.4). Since the supply curve for capital services does not shift, we find that the market-clearing real rental price, $(R/P)^*$, and quantity of capital services, $(\kappa K)^*$, are unchanged (Figure 14.5). The fixity of R/P implies that the real interest rate, r, does not change.

Since the quantities of labour, L, and capital services, κK, do not change, we know from the production function, $Y = A \cdot F(\kappa K, L)$, that real GDP, Y, must be the same. The real GDP goes, as usual, for consumption, gross investment, and government purchases:

$$Y = C + I + G$$

We have just found that Y stayed the same. Recall that one of our assumptions is that government purchases, G, do not change. We also know that C is unchanged, because no income or substitution effects motivate households to change C. Therefore, we must have that gross investment, I, stays the same. This result tells us that today's budget deficit will not affect future capital stocks.

We can look at the results in terms of saving. Since the budget deficit has no income or substitution effects, households do not change consumption, C. However, a cut in year 1's real taxes by one unit raises households' real disposable income by one unit. Since C is the same, households must raise year 1's real saving by one unit. Therefore, the households willingly absorb the one unit of extra bonds issued by the government to cover its budget deficit. Or, as we put it before, the increase by one unit in real household saving fully offsets the reduction by one unit in real government saving. This offset means that real national saving in year 1 does not change.

We have found in our equilibrium business-cycle model that a deficit-financed tax cut does not stimulate the economy. In particular, real GDP, Y, gross investment, I, and the real interest rate, r, do not change. Since these results are controversial and important, we shall want to see how modifications of the model change the conclusions. We begin by assuming more realistic forms of taxes.

LABOUR-INCOME TAXES

Suppose that, instead of lump-sum taxes, the government levies taxes on labour income. As in Chapter 14, let τ_w be the marginal tax rate on labour income. Consider again a reduction in year 1's real taxes, T_1, financed by a budget deficit. We assume that the fall in T_1 is accompanied by a decline in the marginal income tax rate, $(\tau_w)_1$.

Since the path of government purchases, G_t, does not change, year 1's real deficit will require real taxes, T_t, to rise in future years. To keep things simple, while still bringing out the main results, assume that year 2's real taxes, T_2, rise by enough to pay off the extra real debt issued in year 1. Thus, real taxes do not change beyond year 2. We assume that the rise in T_2 goes along with an increase in year 2's marginal income tax rate, $(\tau_w)_2$.

The changes in marginal income tax rates, $(\tau_w)_1$ and $(\tau_w)_2$, affect the labour market in years 1 and 2. Figure 15.2 shows the effects for year 1. (The construction is the same as in Figure 14.4, except that we now consider a decrease, rather than an increase, in τ_w.) Figure 15.2 shows that the cut in $(\tau_w)_1$ raises labour supply in year 1. This increase

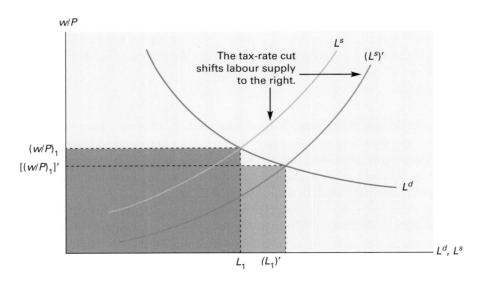

Figure 15.2 Effect of a decrease in year 1's labour-income tax rate on the labour market

The downward-sloping labour demand curve, L^d, comes from Figure 14.4. The upward-sloping labour supply curve, L^s, shown in light blue, also comes from Figure 14.4. A decrease in year 1's marginal tax rate on labour income, $(\tau_w)_1$, shifts the labour supply curve to the right to the dark blue one, $(L^s)'$. Consequently, year 1's market-clearing, before-tax real wage rate falls from $(w/P)_1$ to $[(w/P)_1]'$ on the vertical axis. The market-clearing quantity of labour rises from L_1 to $(L_1)'$ on the horizontal axis.

in labour supply leads, when the labour market clears, to a higher quantity of labour, $(L_1)'$. The higher labour input leads to a rise in year 1's real GDP, Y_1.[7]

The effects for year 2, shown in Figure 15.3, are the reverse. The increase in $(\tau_w)_2$ lowers labour supply in year 2. This decrease in labour supply leads, when the labour market clears, to a lower quantity of labour, $(L_2)'$. The reduced labour input leads to a decrease in year 2's real GDP, Y_2.

Our main finding is that a budget deficit allows the government to change the timing of labour-income tax rates and thereby alter the timing of labour input and production. Specifically, a budget deficit that finances a cut in year 1's tax rate on labour income motivates a rearrangement of the time pattern of work and production – towards the present (year 1) and away from the future (year 2).

Figure 15.3 Effect of an increase in year 2's labour-income tax rate on the labour market

The downward-sloping labour demand curve, L^d, comes from Figure 14.4. The upward-sloping labour supply curve, L^s, shown in light blue, also comes from Figure 14.4. An increase in year 2's marginal tax rate on labour income, $(\tau_w)_2$, shifts the labour supply curve to the left to the dark blue one, $(L^s)'$. Consequently, the market-clearing, before-tax real wage rate rises from $(w/P)_2$ to $[(w/P)_2]'$ on the vertical axis. The market-clearing quantity of labour falls from L_2 to $(L_2)'$ on the horizontal axis.

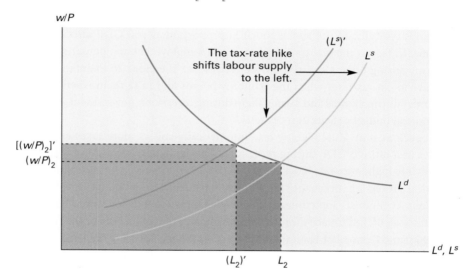

ASSET-INCOME TAXES

The effects of a budget deficit depend on the types of taxes that change. To illustrate, consider another form of tax studied in Chapter 14 – a tax on asset income at the rate τ_r. Assume now that year 1's budget deficit finances a cut in taxes on asset income, thereby resulting in a decrease in year 1's asset-income tax rate, $(\tau_r)_1$. Future taxes must, again, increase. We assume that only the tax rate, $(\tau_r)_2$, on year 2's asset income rises.

The results in Chapter 14 tell us that a cut in year 1's tax rate on asset income, $(\tau_r)_1$, raises year 1's after-tax real interest rate, $[1 - (\tau_r)_1] \cdot r_1$. In response, households save more and consume less. The increase in saving leads to a rise in year 1's gross investment, I_1. Therefore, for given real GDP, Y_1, year 1's consumption, C_1, must fall. In year 2, the tax rate on asset income, $(\tau_r)_2$, rises. The effects are in the opposite direction from year 1: households save less and consume more. Hence, year 2's gross investment, I_2, falls and year 2's consumption, C_2, rises. We see, accordingly, that the main effects are a rearrangement of the timing of investment and consumption. Investment moves towards year 1 and away from year 2, whereas consumption moves in the opposite direction.

[7] An additional effect is that the increase in L_1 tends to raise year 1's MPK. This change leads to an increase in year 1's capital utilization rate, κ_1, and, hence, to a rise in capital services, $(\kappa K)_1$. The increase in $(\kappa K)_1$ contributes to the rise in real GDP, Y_1.

In our previous example, we found that changes in the timing of labour-income tax rates caused changes in the timing of labour input, L, and real GDP, Y. In the present example, changes in the timing of asset-income tax rates cause changes in the timing of consumption, C, and investment, I. The general point is that, by running budget deficits or surpluses, the government can change the timing of various tax rates, thereby inducing changes in the timing of various aspects of economic activity: L, Y, C and I. In the next section, we consider whether it is a good idea for the government to induce these variations in the timing of economic activity.

THE TIMING OF TAXES AND TAX-RATE SMOOTHING

We have found that budget deficits and surpluses allow the government to change the timing of tax rates. However, it would not be a good idea for the government randomly to make tax rates high in some years and low in others. These fluctuations in tax rates cause unnecessary economic distortions, because they give households the wrong signals in determining how to choose the time pattern of labour, production, consumption and investment. Fortunately, governments usually do not behave in this erratic manner; rather, the public debt has typically been managed to maintain a pattern of reasonably stable tax rates over time. This behaviour is called **tax-rate smoothing**. This phrase signifies that the government maintains stability in tax rates even when economic disturbances occur.

One example of tax-rate smoothing concerns the response of income tax rates to economic fluctuations. Real government expenditures typically do not rise as much in proportion as real GDP does during booms, or fall as much during recessions. In fact, some real transfers, such as unemployment compensation and family assistance, tend to fall in real terms during booms and rise during recessions. Therefore, to maintain a balanced budget, the government would have to cut tax rates when the economy booms and raise them when the economy contracts. Instead of cutting tax rates during booms and raising them during recessions, governments typically run real budget surpluses in booms and real budget deficits in recessions.

Many tax systems, such as individual income tax, automatically collect more taxes as a ratio to GDP during booms and fewer taxes as a ratio to GDP during recessions. This tendency operates for a given tax law because a boom pushes taxpayers into higher tax-rate brackets, and because deductions do not rise along with GDP. The opposite forces operate during a recession. Because of the automatic tendency to run budget surpluses during booms and deficits during recessions, economists sometimes estimate what the budget deficit would have been if the economy had been operating at a level of 'full capacity' or 'full employment'. For discussions of the full-employment deficit, see E. Cary Brown (1956) and Council of Economic Advisers, *Economic Report of the President* (1962, pp. 78–82).

As another example, during wartime, government purchases rise substantially above normal. To maintain a balanced budget, tax rates would have to be abnormally high during wars. To avoid these unusually high wartime tax rates, governments tend to run real budget deficits during wars. In this way, the necessary increases in tax rates are spread roughly evenly over time. Tax rates rise somewhat during wartime but also increase afterwards to finance the public debt built up during the war. This wartime deficit financing explains much of the long-term evolution of the UK public debt, as shown in Figure 15.1.

STRATEGIC BUDGET DEFICITS

Decreasing the size of a government requires a reduction in both fiscal spending and taxes. However, cutting taxes is often an easier fiscal policy to implement. In this case, cutting taxes while holding government spending constant would lead to an increase in budget deficits. Some economists have argued that these deficits, and the consequent build-up of public debt, could create political pressure to curtail the growth of fiscal spending. Therefore, in the longer run, a tax reduction may be successful in forcing the ratio of total government expenditure to GDP to be smaller than it otherwise would have been.

This view of budget deficits gives rise to a new theory called **strategic budget deficits**.[8] The word 'strategic' is used because the models involve political strategies analogous to those analyzed in game theory. To get the basic

[8]This theory was developed by Torsten Persson and Lars Svensson (1989) and by Alberto Alesina and Guido Tabellini (1990).

idea, suppose that an administration is currently in power and favours a small government. Assume that this administration believes that it will be followed eventually by an administration that favours a large government. How can the current administration influence future government officials of a different political persuasion to choose relatively low levels of real purchases and transfers? One answer is to run a budget deficit that will leave behind a high ratio of public debt to GDP. The financing of this large public debt makes it politically difficult for the future government to select high levels of purchases and transfers.

Economics in Practice
'Unpleasant monetarist arithmetic'

Thomas Sargent and Neil Wallace (1981) analyzed effects from changes in the timing of the inflation tax; that is, the government's revenue from printing money. Their analysis applies especially to countries such as Argentina and Brazil, which have often relied heavily on the printing press for government revenue.

Suppose that the government cuts the current money growth rate in an attempt to reduce inflation. (See the discussion of money growth and inflation in Chapter 12.) Assume, however, that the government does not change its current or prospective real purchases and transfers. Assume also that the government does not change its current or prospective real taxes from the income tax or other forms of taxation. In this case, the decrease in current real revenue from printing money must correspond to an increase in the real public debt; that is, to a real budget deficit. As usual, the increased real public debt implies that the government's present value of future real revenue has to rise. However, if real taxes are fixed, the future real revenue has to come from future money creation. In other words, the government is changing the timing of the inflation tax, so that less is collected now and more later. The rise in future real revenue from money creation means that future money growth rates have to rise; that is, they have to be even higher than they were initially.

Because future money growth rates increase, today's reduction in money growth will be unsuccessful in the long run at reducing the inflation rate. The inflation rate will rise in the long run, along with the money growth rate. Moreover, if people anticipate the higher future inflation rate, the cut in the current money growth rate may not even reduce the inflation rate in the short run. The expectation of rising inflation rates tends to lower today's real quantity of money demanded, leading to a rise in the inflation rate in the short run. Sargent and Wallace use this analysis to argue that a programme to curb inflation by reducing money growth will be unsuccessful on its own. The programme has to be part of a fiscal plan that cuts current or prospective real government expenditure, or increases current or prospective real taxes.

THE STANDARD VIEW OF A BUDGET DEFICIT

Our equilibrium business-cycle model led to Ricardian equivalence, which implies that a deficit-finance tax cut does not affect real GDP and other macroeconomic variables. Many economists disagree with this proposition and predict, instead, that budget deficits raise real interest rates and reduce investment. Are there reasonable modifications of the equilibrium business-cycle model that generate these more standard predictions? We explore the necessary modifications in this section but do not settle the question of which theory of budget deficits is correct. In the end, the reader will have to weigh the theories and empirical evidence to decide which approach is most persuasive.

To bring out the main issues, we can simplify by returning to the assumption that taxes are lump-sum. The key point in the equilibrium business-cycle model was that a deficit-financed tax cut had no income effects on households' choices. Since the income effect was nil, a deficit-financed cut in year 1's real taxes, T_1, did not change consumption, C_1. Consequently, households saved all of the increase in year 1's real disposable income. Since real GDP, Y_1, did not change (because the inputs of labour and capital services stayed the same), and since government purchases, G_1, were unchanged, gross investment, I_1, did not change.

The starting point for the standard analysis is that a deficit-financed tax cut makes households feel wealthier; hence, there is a positive income effect. We look first at how these income effects modify our conclusions about budget deficits. Then, we consider arguments that economists have offered for why deficit-financed tax cuts make households feel wealthier.

Since a deficit-financed tax cut makes households feel wealthier, consumption, C_1, increases in the standard approach. Suppose, to keep things simple, that the quantity of labour supplied is fixed; that is, we ignore any income effects on labour supply. In this case, year 1's inputs of labour and capital services stay the same, and real GDP, Y_1, still does not change. Since C_1 increases, gross investment, I_1, has to decline for given government purchases, G_1. Thus, *a major new conclusion is that a budget deficit reduces investment.*

Another way to look at the results is that households respond to the increase in year 1's real disposable income partly with more consumption and partly with more saving. Most importantly, household saving no longer rises by the full amount of the tax cut. Thus, national saving falls and this decrease corresponds to the reduction in gross investment, I_1.

The longer-run effects depend on whether the government pays off the extra real public debt in year 2 or, instead, allows the debt to remain permanently higher. For the first case, we assumed in one of our earlier scenarios that year 2's real taxes, T_2, rose by enough to pay off the extra public debt. In this case, the effects in year 2 reverse those in year 1; in particular, investment is high in year 2. After year 2, the level of real public debt equals its original value, and there are no long-term effects on the capital stock.

As an example of the second case, we assumed in another of our scenarios that real taxes in each year, T_t, rose only by enough to pay the added interest expense each year. In this case, the stock of real public debt is permanently higher, and the capital stock, K, is permanently lower than it otherwise would have been. Therefore, future levels of capital services, κK, and, hence, real GDP, Y, will be lower than they would have been. Thus, additional real public debt contracts the economy in the long run.[9] These long-term negative effects on capital stock and real GDP are sometimes described as a **burden of the public debt**.[10]

In the standard approach, the smaller long-run stock of capital, K, implies a higher MPK (for a given labour input, L). This higher MPK leads to a higher real rental price, R/P, which implies a higher real interest rate, r. Therefore, a larger public debt leads, in the long run, to a higher r.

To reach the standard conclusions about the effects of budget deficits, we had to assume that a tax cut made households feel wealthier. We will now explore two of the more persuasive arguments for this assumption. The first one concerns the finiteness of life, and the second involves imperfections of credit markets.

Finite lifetimes

Suppose, again, that the government runs a budget deficit and cuts year 1's real taxes, T_1, by one unit. We know that the present value of the added future real taxes is one unit, the same as the initial tax cut. Suppose, however, that some of the future taxes needed to finance the public debt show up in the distant future – after the death of the typical person alive in year 1. In that case, the present value of the future taxes paid during the lifetimes of people living in year 1 falls short of one unit. Hence, these people experience a reduction in the overall present value of their real taxes.

Why does a budget deficit make people feel wealthier when they have finite lifetimes? The decrease in the present value of real taxes for current generations coincides with an increase in the present value of real taxes for members of future generations. Individuals will be born with a liability for a portion of taxes to pay the interest and principal on the higher stock of real public debt. However, these people will not share in the benefits from the earlier tax cut. Present taxpayers would not feel wealthier if they counted fully the present value of the prospective taxes on descendants.

[9]We can also allow for a negative income effect on labour supply. That is, households work less if the tax cut makes them feel wealthier.
[10]For discussions, see the papers in the volume edited by James Ferguson (1964). Note especially the paper by Franco Modigliani, 'Long-Run Implications of Alternative Fiscal Policies and the Burden of the National Debt'.

Budget deficits effectively enable members of current generations to die in a state of insolvency, where they leave debts – that is, public debts – for their descendants. Therefore, budget deficits make people feel wealthier if they view this governmental shifting of incomes across generations as desirable. However, most people already have opportunities for intergenerational transfers, which they have chosen to exercise to a desired extent. For example, parents make contributions to their children in the forms of educational investments, other expenses in the home and bequests. In the other direction – and especially before the growth of social security programmes – children provide support for their aged parents. To the extent that private transfers of this sort are operative, the government's budget deficit does not offer the typical person a new opportunity to extract funds from their descendants. Therefore, the predicted response to a rise in public debt would be to shift private transfers by the amount necessary to restore the balance of incomes across generations that was previously deemed optimal. In this case, even though people do not live for ever, a budget deficit would not make the current generation of households feel wealthier.[11] Therefore, we return to the case where budget deficits have no income effects on households.

As a concrete example, assume that a married couple plans to leave a bequest with a present value of £50 000 to their children. Then, suppose that the government runs a budget deficit, which cuts the present value of the couple's taxes by £1000 but raises the present value of their children's taxes by £1000. Our prediction is that the parents use the tax cut to raise the present value of their intergenerational transfers to the children to £51 000. The extra £1000 provides the children with just enough resources to pay their higher taxes. Parents and children then end up with the same amounts of consumption that they enjoyed before the government ran its budget deficit.

One concern is that these kinds of calculations assume that each person possesses considerable information and computational ability. More realistically, we should acknowledge that budget deficits make it harder for households to figure out exactly the future taxes that they or their descendants will bear. However, it is not obvious that this uncertainty would cause households systematically to underestimate the consequences of budget deficits for future taxes. In fact, the typical response to greater income uncertainty – caused, in this case, by uncertainty about future taxes – is to raise saving. This *precautionary saving* guards against a future that might be worse than anticipated. This behaviour implies that private saving may increase by more than one unit when the budget deficit increases by one unit. That is, national saving might increase in response to a budget deficit – the opposite of the standard view.

Imperfect credit markets

Thus far, we have assumed that the real interest rate, r, on private bonds equalled the rate on government bonds. Since households could issue private bonds, as well as hold them, our model assumes that households can borrow at the same real interest rate, r, as the government. In practice, credit markets are not this perfect. Many households that would like to borrow have to pay substantially higher real interest rates than the government. The borrowing rate is especially high if people borrow without collateral (such as a house or car).

When credit markets are imperfect, some households will calculate present values of future real taxes by using a real interest rate above the government's rate. We found before that a deficit-financed cut in year 1's real taxes by one unit led to an increase in the present value of future real taxes by one unit. However, we got this result when we calculated present values using the government's real interest rate, r. For households that face a higher real interest rate, the present value of the future real taxes will fall short of one unit.

To illustrate, suppose again that the government cuts year 1's real taxes by one unit and runs a budget deficit of one unit. Assume, as in one of our previous cases, that the government raises real taxes in year 2 by enough to pay the principal and interest on the one unit of new public debt. If the government's real interest rate is 2%, real taxes in year 2 rise by 1.02 units. To calculate the present value of these taxes, households would discount the 1.02 not by

[11]For a discussion of the interplay between public debt and private intergenerational transfers, see Robert Barro (1974). A different view is that parents use bequests to control their children's behaviour, rather than purely for altruistic reasons. For a discussion of this 'strategic bequest theory', see B. Douglas Bernheim, Andrei Shleifer and Lawrence Summers (1985).

the government's interest rate but by the real interest rate paid by households. If households use a real interest rate of, say, 5%, the result is:

$$present\ value\ of\ increase\ in\ year\ 2's\ real\ taxes = 1.02\,/\,1.05$$
$$\approx 0.97$$

Thus, the overall change in the present value of real taxes paid by households is:

$$change\ in\ present\ value\ of\ real\ taxes$$
$$= tax\ cut\ in\ year\ 1 + present\ value\ if\ increase\ in\ year\ 2's\ real\ taxes$$
$$= -1 + 0.97$$
$$= -0.03$$

Hence, the tax cut by one unit in year 1 decreases the overall present value of real taxes by 0.03 units. The effect would be larger if the government delayed its repayment of public debt beyond year 2.

Suppose now that some households (or businesses) have good access to credit and therefore use a real interest rate equal to the government's rate to calculate present values of future real taxes. For these households, a deficit-financed tax cut still leaves unchanged the overall present value of real taxes. What happens if the economy consists partly of households that face the same real interest rate as the government and partly of households that face higher real interest rates? In this case, a deficit-financed tax cut leaves unchanged the present value of real taxes for the first group and reduces the present value for the second group. Thus, in the aggregate, the tax cut makes households feel wealthier.

Why does the imperfection of credit markets make households feel wealthier in the aggregate when the government runs a budget deficit? By running a deficit, the government effectively loans money to households – the loan is one unit if real taxes fall in year 1 by one unit. Then the government effectively collects on the loan in future years when it raises real taxes. The real interest rate charged on these loans is implicitly the rate paid by the government on its bonds. Households view this loan as a good deal if the government's real interest rate is less than the rate at which households can borrow directly. That is why the overall real present value of taxes falls for households that use a high real interest rate to calculate present values.

The implicit assumption is that the government's use of the tax system is an efficient way to lend money to some households. That is, the government is better than private institutions, such as banks, at lending funds (by cutting taxes) and then collecting on these loans in the future (by raising future taxes). If the government is really superior at this lending process, the economy will function more efficiently if the government provides more credit; that is, in our case, if the government runs a larger budget deficit. By operating more efficiently, we mean that the available resources will be better channelled towards higher-priority uses. These uses might be for year 1's consumption or investment by households that previously lacked good access to credit.

In the end, the imperfection of credit markets can provide a reason why budget deficits affect the economy. However, the results do not resemble those from the conventional analysis, in which a larger public debt leads, in the long run, to lower levels of the capital stock and real GDP. With imperfect credit markets, budget deficits matter if they improve the allocation of credit; that is, if they alleviate some of the imperfections in private credit markets.

By the Numbers
Empirical evidence on the macroeconomic effects of budget deficits

An important prediction from the conventional analysis is that real budget deficits raise consumption and reduce national saving and investment. Over time, the reduction in investment leads to a lower stock of capital. This smaller capital stock implies a higher marginal MPK, which leads to a higher real interest rate, r.

Many economists believe that budget deficits reduce national saving and investment, and raise real interest rates. Nevertheless, this belief is not well supported by empirical evidence. For example, Charles Plosser (1982, 1987) and Paul Evans (1987a, 1987b) carried out statistical analyses of the effects of budget deficits on interest rates in a number of developed countries. Their main finding was that budget deficits had no significant effects on real or nominal interest rates.

Despite many empirical studies, it has proved difficult to reach definitive conclusions about the effects of budget deficits on consumption, national saving and investment. One difficulty concerns the direction of causation. As discussed before, budget deficits often arise as responses to economic fluctuations and temporary government purchases, such as in wartime. Since consumption, national saving and investment tend to vary as part of economic fluctuations and during wartime, it is hard to isolate the effects of budget deficits on these variables.

An empirical study by Chris Carroll and Lawrence Summers (1987) avoids some of these problems by comparing saving rates in Canada and the United States. The private saving rates were similar in the two countries until the early 1970s but then diverged; for 1983–85 (the final years in their study), the Canadian rate was higher by six percentage points. After holding fixed the influences of macroeconomic variables and tax systems, Carroll and Summers concluded that budget deficits did not affect national saving. That is, the higher private saving rates in Canada were just offsets to higher budget deficits. This finding is consistent with Ricardian equivalence.

The Israeli experience from 1983 to 1987 comes close to providing a natural experiment for studying the interplay between budget deficits and saving. In 1983, the national saving rate of 13% corresponded to a private saving rate of 17% and a public saving rate of –4%. (This measure of public saving includes public investment.) In 1984, a dramatic rise in the budget deficit reduced the public saving rate to –11%. The interesting observation is that the private saving rate rose to 26%, so that the national saving rate changed little, actually rising from 13% to 15%. Then a stabilization programme in 1985 eliminated the budget deficit, so that the public saving rate rose to 0% in 1985–86. The private saving rate declined dramatically at the same time, to 19% in 1985 and 14% in 1986. Therefore, the national saving rate remained relatively stable, going from 15% in 1984 to 18% in 1985 and 14% in 1986. Thus, the changes in private saving roughly offset the fluctuations in public saving and led to near stability in national saving. This experience therefore accords with Ricardian equivalence.

In other words, budget deficits matter, but in a desirable way. Therefore, we cannot use this reasoning to argue that budget deficits and public debt are burdens on the economy.

Social security

Retirement benefits paid through social security programmes are substantial in most other developed countries. Some economists, such as Martin Feldstein (1974), argue that these public pension programmes reduce saving and investment. We can use our equilibrium business-cycle model to examine this idea.

The argument for an effect on saving applies when social security is not a **fully funded system**. In a funded set-up, workers' payments accumulate in a trust fund, which later provides for retirement benefits. The alternative is a **pay-as-you-go system**, in which benefits to elderly persons are financed by taxes on the currently young. In this set-up, people who are at or near retirement age when the programme begins or expands receive benefits without paying a comparable present value of taxes. Correspondingly, members of later generations (including most readers of this book) pay taxes that exceed their expected benefits in present-value terms. In most countries, the social security systems operate mainly on a pay-as-you-go basis.[12]

Consider the economic effects of social security in a pay-as-you-go system. We focus here on income effects and neglect the types of substitution effects from taxes and transfers that we discussed in Chapter 14. The usual argument goes as follows. When a social security system starts or expands, elderly persons experience an increase in the

[12]Privatized arrangements, such as the main pension system in Chile, are fully funded but do not involve a government trust fund. For a discussion, see Jose Pinera (1996). The World Bank (1994) provides an overview of social security systems throughout the world.

present value of their social security benefits net of taxes. The increase in the present value of real transfers net of real taxes implies a positive income effect on the consumption of this group.

Young persons face higher taxes, offset by the prospect of higher retirement benefits. Thus, the present value of real transfers net of real taxes may fall for this group. However, the decline in this present value is not as large in magnitude as the increase for the currently old. Why? Because the currently young will be able to finance their future retirement benefits by levying taxes on members of yet unborn generations. Thus, the fall in consumption by the currently young tends to be smaller in size than the increase for the currently old. Hence, we predict an increase in current aggregate consumption. Or, to put it another way, total private saving declines. Since government saving does not change, national saving falls. The decline in national saving leads, in the short run, to a decrease in investment and, in the long run, to a reduced stock of capital.

This analysis of the economic effects of social security parallels our previous discussion of the conventional analysis of a budget deficit. In both cases, the increase in aggregate consumption arises only if people neglect the adverse effects on descendants. Specifically, an increase in the scale of a pay-as-you-go social security programme means that the typical person's descendants will be born with a tax liability that exceeds their prospective retirement benefits in present-value terms. If persons currently alive took full account of these effects on descendants, the income effects from a social security programme would be nil.

As in the case of a deficit-financed tax cut, more social security enables older persons to extract funds from their descendants. However, also as before, people value this change only if they give no transfers to their children and receive nothing from their children. Otherwise, people would respond to more social security by shifting private intergenerational transfers, rather than by consuming more. In many developed countries, the growth of social security has diminished the tendency of children to support their aged parents.

On an empirical level, there has been a great debate since the 1970s about the connection of social security to saving and investment. Martin Feldstein (1974) reported a dramatic negative effect of social security on capital accumulation. However, subsequent investigators argued that this conclusion was unwarranted.[13] The evidence for a broad cross-section of countries does not yield convincing evidence that social security depresses saving and investment.

Open-market operations

The inclusion of public debt in the equilibrium business-cycle model allows us to analyze **open-market operations**. An open-market purchase occurs when the central bank, such as the Bank of England, buys bonds – typically government bonds – with newly created money. (In this context, money refers to high-powered money, which is the sum of currency in circulation and reserves held by depository institutions at the central bank.) An open-market sale occurs when the central bank sells bonds for money. These open-market operations are the main way that central banks control the quantity of money. We want to know whether this realistic way of changing the quantity of money leads to results that differ from those of the unrealistic 'helicopter drops' of money that we studied in Chapters 11 and 12.

Consider an open-market purchase, whereby the quantity of money, M, increases by £1 and the stock of government bonds, B^g, decreases by £1. Assume that no subsequent changes in the quantity of money occur; that is, we are considering a one-time increase in M.

Table 15.2 shows that an open-market purchase of government bonds amounts to a combination of two policies that we have already studied. Suppose, first, that the government prints an extra pound of money, M, and uses the money to cut lump-sum taxes by £1 or raise lump-sum transfers by £1. For example, the government might have a helicopter drop of £1 of money – the unrealistic story considered in Chapters 11 and 12. This change is labelled as policy 1 in the table. Suppose, next, that the government raises lump-sum taxes by £1 or cuts lump-sum transfers by £1 and uses the proceeds to pay off £1 of government bonds, B^g. That is, the government raises taxes net of transfers and, thereby, runs a budget surplus. These changes are called policy 2 in the table. If we combine the two policies, we

---

[13]For a summary of the debate, see Louis Esposito (1978) and Dean Leimer and Selig Lesnoy (1982).

find that the quantity of money, M, rises by £1, taxes and transfers are unchanged, and the quantity of government bonds, B^g, falls by £1. Thus, we end up with an open-market purchase of government bonds, policy 3 in the table.

Table 15.2 Open-market purchases of government bonds

Government policy	Change in money, **M**	Change in government bonds, **B**^{g}	Change in taxes, **T**
1. Print more money and reduce taxes.	+£1	0	−£1
2. Raise taxes and reduce public debt.	0	−£1	+£1
3. Open-market purchase of government bonds.	+£1	−£1	0

Note: Policy 3 – an open-market purchase of government bonds – amounts to a combination of policies 1 and 2, which we have already studied.

We know from Chapter 11 that policy 1 – a one-time increase in the quantity of money, M, used to cut lump-sum taxes or raise lump-sum transfers – raises the price level, P, in the same proportion as the increase in M. We also know that there are no effects on real variables, including real GDP, Y, and the real interest rate, r. We know from our analysis in this chapter that policy 2 – the budget surplus created by an increase in taxes net of transfers – does not affect the same group of real variables. The budget surplus also does not affect the price level, P, because the nominal quantity of money, M, does not change. Therefore, the overall effect from policy 3 – the open-market purchase of government bonds – is that P rises in the same proportion as M, and the group of real variables does not change. That is, an open-market purchase has the same effects as the unrealistic helicopter drop of money considered in Chapters 11 and 12. We conclude that this unrealistic story gave us a reasonable and simple way to assess the linkages between money and the price level.

Summing Up

In this chapter, we allowed the government to borrow; that is, to run a budget deficit by issuing bonds. The government's budget constraint includes two new items: interest payments on the public debt and the proceeds from new debt issue.

In our equilibrium business-cycle model, changes in budget deficits have no income effects. The reason is that, if the path of government purchases does not change, a deficit-financed tax cut creates future real taxes with the same present value as the current tax cut. If we assume lump-sum taxes, the absence of an income effect implies that variations in budget deficits have no effect on a group of real variables, including real GDP, consumption, investment and the real interest rate. This result is known as Ricardian equivalence – taxes and budget deficits have equivalent effects on the economy.

Budget deficits affect the timing of taxes, and this timing matters if taxes are not lump-sum. For example, by running a budget deficit, the government can reduce today's tax rate on labour income and raise future tax rates on labour income. This change influences the time paths of labour input and real GDP. In most circumstances, variations in tax rates over time create unnecessary distortions in the economy. Therefore, the government is well-advised to avoid these distortions by following a policy of tax-rate smoothing. This policy keeps tax rates, such as those on labour income, stable despite economic fluctuations and temporary variations in government purchases, such as in wartime. To smooth tax rates, the government runs budget deficits during recessions and wars.

One deviation from tax-rate smoothing, known as strategic budget deficits, describes a government's use of deficits or surpluses to influence choices of government expenditure by future political administrations. By leaving behind a larger stock of public debt, a government can make it more difficult for a future administration to choose high purchases and transfers.

The standard view of budget deficits assumes that a deficit-financed tax cut has a positive income effect on consumption. A budget deficit tends, accordingly, to raise consumption and lower investment. In the long run, a larger public debt leads to a lower capital stock and a higher real interest rate. The income effect from budget deficits is often explained by the finiteness of life and the imperfections of private credit markets.

We analyzed pay-as-you-go social security systems and open-market operations by the monetary authority. An expansion of social security is analogous to a deficit-financed tax cut. Open-market operations have effects similar to those from the unrealistic helicopter drops of money considered in Chapters 11 and 12.

Key Terms and Concepts

balanced budget	fiscal policy	pay-as-you-go system	Ricardian equivalence
budget deficit	fully funded system	public debt	theorem
budget surplus	national saving	public investment	strategic budget deficits
burden of the public debt	open-market operations		tax-rate smoothing

Questions and Problems

A Review questions

1 Briefly compare the conventional view of government debt and the Ricardian view. What are the main differences in the assumptions and the conclusions?

2 Under what circumstances is an open-market operation neutral?

3 Suppose that the government announces a reduction in next year's tax rate on labour income. What intertemporal-substitution effect will this announcement have on the current quantity of labour supplied?

B Problems for discussion

4 Social security and the capital stock

Suppose that the government introduces a new social security programme, which will make payments to covered persons when they retire.

a What long-run effects do you predict on the capital stock, K?

b How does your answer to question a depend on whether the social security programme is fully funded or pay-as-you-go? (In a funded scheme, workers pay into a trust fund, which is then used to pay benefits. A pay-as-you-go system taxes current workers to pay benefits for current retirees.)

5 The income effect from a budget deficit

Suppose that, in year 1, the government cuts current, lump-sum taxes and runs a budget deficit. Assume that the real public debt remains constant in future years. Also, no changes occur in government purchases of goods and services, G, or in real transfers, V. Analyze the income effect from the government's tax cut. How does this effect depend on the following:

a finite lifetimes?

b the existence of childless persons?

c uncertainty about who will pay future taxes?

d the possibility that the government will print more money in the future rather than levying future taxes?

e the imperfection of private credit markets?

Money and
business cycles

PART VI

16 Money and business cycles I: The price-misperceptions model

Thus far, our macroeconomic model has stressed real factors, such as shifts in technology, as sources of business fluctuations. The government can affect real variables by changing its purchases of goods and services and its tax rates, but there is little evidence that these fiscal actions have been major sources of economic fluctuations in the economy. Many economists believe that monetary shocks – created mainly by the monetary authority – have been a principal cause of these fluctuations in the economy. In this chapter, we begin our analysis of monetary effects by studying the *price-misperceptions model.*

Effects of money in the equilibrium business-cycle model

We should start by recalling our results on the interactions between nominal and real variables in the equilibrium business-cycle model. One result from Chapter 11 is that a one-time change in the nominal quantity of money, M – interpreted in our model as currency – is neutral. This change leads to responses in the same proportion of nominal variables, such as the price level, P, and the nominal wage rate, w. Real variables, including real GDP, Y, employment, L, and the real interest rate, r, do not change.

We found in Chapter 12 that persisting changes in the nominal quantity of money affect the inflation rate, π, and thereby the nominal interest rate, i. A change in i affects the real quantity of money demanded, $D(Y, i)$, thereby influencing the quantity of real money, M/P. These changes have real effects, because increases in π and i induce people to spend more time and other resources to economize on real money holdings, M/P. Higher inflation leads to more resources expended on transaction costs. If we broadened the model to include costs of changing prices, we would find that higher inflation raises these costs as well. However, transactions costs and costs of changing prices are not important enough in normal times to have significant effects on real GDP.

Although money is neutral, at least as an approximation, we were able to use the model in Chapter 11 to derive implications for the empirical association between real and nominal variables. In our equilibrium business-cycle model, technology shocks affect real GDP, Y, and the nominal interest rate, i, and thereby influence the real quantity of money demanded, $D(Y, i)$. Typically, this real quantity demanded will be high in booms and low in recessions (because the effect from Y dominates that from i). If the nominal quantity of money, M, does not respond to changes in the real quantity demanded, the price level, P, will move in the direction opposite to the change in $D(Y, i)$. Therefore, the model predicts that P would be countercyclical – low in booms and high in recessions. If the monetary authority wants to stabilize the price level, P, it should adjust the nominal quantity of money, M, to balance the changes in the real quantity demanded, $D(Y, i)$. In this case, M will be procyclical.

The price-misperceptions model

Empirical evidence suggests that money is not as neutral as predicted by our equilibrium business-cycle model. The **price-misperceptions model** provides a possible explanation for the non-neutrality of money.[1] In this model, households sometimes misinterpret changes in nominal prices and wage rates as changes in relative prices and real wage rates. Therefore, monetary shocks – which affect nominal prices and wage rates – end up affecting real variables, such as real GDP and employment.

A MODEL WITH NON-NEUTRAL EFFECTS OF MONEY

The model retains most of the features of our equilibrium business-cycle model. We still maintain the microeconomic foundations that underlie the supply and demand functions for labour and capital services. We continue to assume that prices – prices of goods, wage rates and rental prices – adjust rapidly to clear markets. However, the important difference from before is that households have *incomplete current information* about prices in the economy. For example, a worker may know his or her current nominal wage rate and the prices of goods purchased recently. But the worker has less accurate information about wage rates available on other jobs, prices of goods encountered in the distant past or not at all, and so on.

The price-misperceptions model usually focuses on the labour market. We analyzed this market in Figure 9.13 in Chapter 9; Figure 16.1 reproduces the main parts of this analysis. Recall that an increase in the real wage rate, w/P, lowers the quantity of labour demanded, L^d. This demand comes from producers (households that own and run businesses) who pay the nominal wage rate, w, to workers and receive the price level, P, on sales of goods.

An increase in the real wage rate, w/P, makes work more attractive to households. Therefore, Figure 16.1 shows that a rise in w/P raises the quantity of labour supplied, L^s. More precisely, we found in Chapter 9 that the slope of the labour supply curve depends on the balancing between a substitution effect and an income effect. The substitution effect from a higher w/P motivates less leisure time – hence, more work – and more consumption. The income effect from a higher w/P motivates more leisure time – hence, less work – and more consumption. Thus, if the substitution effect dominates the income effect, the labour supply curve has a positive slope, as shown in Figure 16.1.

Now, we will allow for incomplete current information about prices across the economy. Consider the effect of the real wage rate, w/P, on the quantity of labour demanded, L^d. The demanders of labour are the employers.

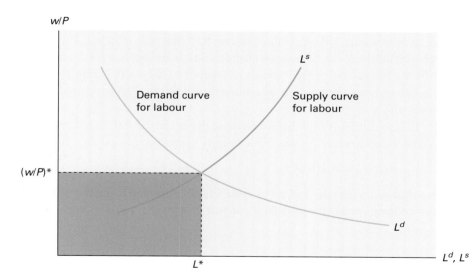

Figure 16.1 Clearing of the labour market

This figure reproduces our analysis of the labour market from Figure 9.13 in Chapter 9. A reduction in the real wage rate, w/P, raises the quantity of labour demanded, L^d. An increase in w/P raises the quantity of labour supplied, L^s. The market clears when the real wage rate is $(w/P)^*$ on the vertical axis and the quantity of labour is L^* on the horizontal axis.

[1] This model originated from Milton Friedman (1968c) and Edmund Phelps (1970). Later contributions were made by Robert Lucas; see his papers collected in Lucas (1981). For a survey of the main research through the 1970s, see Ben McCallum (1979).

We can reasonably assume that an employer has accurate current information about the nominal wage rate, w, paid to their employees. With respect to the price level, P, the price that matters is the one attached to the employer's own product. That is, the employer compares the nominal cost of labour, given by w, with the nominal amount, P, received on sales of the employer's good or service.[2] We can reasonably assume that the employer has accurate current information about prices of their own products. Therefore, the real wage rate that determines the quantity of labour demanded, L^d, is the actual value, w/P. Hence, we do not have to modify the labour-demand curve drawn in Figure 16.1.

Consider now the real wage rate that matters for labour supply, L^s. The suppliers of labour are the workers. For a worker, the relevant nominal wage rate, w, is the amount received from the employer. We can again reasonably assume that a worker has accurate current information about their own w. However, for the price level, P, the relevant variable is the price of a market basket of goods. These goods will be purchased from many locations at various times. Therefore, a worker will typically lack good current information about some of these prices. To bring in this effect, we denote by P^e the price that a worker expects to pay for a market basket of goods. The real wage rate that determines the quantity of labour supplied, L^s, is the ratio of w to this expected price; that is, w/P^e.

Consider again the effects from an increase in the nominal quantity of money, M. In Chapter 11, we found that the nominal wage rate, w, and the price level, P, rose in the same proportion as the increase in M. In particular, in Figure 16.1, an increase in M does not change the market-clearing real wage rate, $(w/P)^*$, and the market-clearing quantity of labour input, L^*. The constancy of $(w/P)^*$ and L^* accords with the result from Chapter 11 that a change in M is neutral; that is, it does not affect any real variables.

Consider, however, what happens when workers do not understand that an increase in the nominal wage rate, w, stems from a monetary expansion that inflates all nominal values, including the price level, P. Each worker may think, instead, that the rise in w constitutes an increase in his or her real wage rate, w/P. The **perceived real wage rate** is the ratio of w to the expected price level, P^e. This ratio, w/P^e, rises if the expected price level, P^e, increases proportionately by less than w. If w/P^e increases, the worker increases the quantity of labour supplied, L^s.

As an example, suppose that the nominal wage rate, w, is initially €10 per hour, and the price level is $P = 1$. Thus, the real wage rate, w/P, is initially 10 units of goods per hour worked. Assume that w doubles to €20 per hour. As a worker, how would you respond to this change? If P is still 1, w/P has gone up to 20 units of goods per hour worked, and it is attractive to work more hours. However, if P also doubles, so that $P = 2$, the real wage rate, w/P, is still 10 units of goods per hour worked. In this case, you have no reason to work more.

If the worker does not immediately observe the actual price level, P, the assessment of the higher nominal wage rate, w, depends on the change in the expected price level, P^e. If P^e starts at 1 and then rises to less than 2, the perceived real wage rate, w/P^e, goes up, and the worker will supply more labour. If P^e rises to 2 – that is, if the worker regards the higher w as just a sign of general inflation – w/P^e does not change, and labour supply stays the same.

To analyze the new effect graphically, we can use the revised version of Figure 16.1 shown in Figure 16.2. The labour-demand curve, L^d, is the same as before, because employers determine their quantity of labour demanded in accordance with the actual real wage rate, w/P.

The labour supply curves in Figure 16.2 are different from before, because the perceived real wage rate, w/P^e, determines the quantity of labour supplied. To understand the new labour supply curves, we can use the condition:

$$w/P^e = (w/P) \bullet (P/P^e) \qquad (16.1)$$

This equation implies that, for a given actual real wage rate, w/P, an increase in P/P^e raises the perceived real wage rate, w/P^e. In other words, if workers are underestimating the price level – so that $P^e < P$ – they must be overestimating their real wage rate; that is, $w/P^e > w/P$.

---

[2] The employer cares also about the prices of other inputs to production, including the nominal rental price, R, paid for capital services. In a more general model, another important input price would be for energy. We are assuming that the employer knows the values of all these input prices.

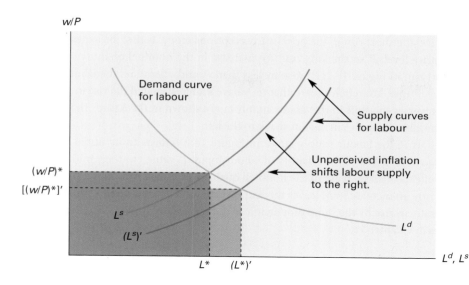

Figure 16.2 Effect of unperceived inflation on the labour market

A rise in P/P^e for suppliers of labour (employees) raises w/P^e for a given w/P. Therefore, the labour supply curve shifts to the right, from L^s to $(L^s)'$. We conclude that unperceived inflation raises labour input – from L^* to $(L^*)'$ – and lowers the real wage rate – from $(w/P)^*$ to $[(w/P)^*]'$.

To see how price misperceptions affect the labour market, assume that, initially, $P = P^e$ holds, so that $w/P^e = w/P$. The first labour supply curve, denoted by L^s in Figure 16.2, applies in this situation. As usual, along this curve, an increase in w/P raises the quantity of labour supplied, L^s.

Suppose, as in Chapter 11, that an increase in the nominal quantity of money, M, raises the price level, P. If the rise in P is only partly perceived by households, P^e increases proportionately by less than P. Consequently, P/P^e goes up, and equation (16.1) implies that w/P^e rises for a given w/P. Therefore, at any given w/P, the quantity of labour supplied is greater than before. We show this result in Figure 16.2 with the new labour supply curve, denoted by $(L^s)'$. This curve lies to the right of the original one, L^s. *Because of price misperceptions, the increase in P raises the quantity of labour supplied at a given w/P.*[3]

In the initial situation, where $P = P^e$, the labour market clears in Figure 16.2 at the real wage rate $(w/P)^*$ and the quantity of labour input L^*. With an unperceived rise in the price level, the market clears at the lower real wage rate, $[(w/P)^*]'$, and the higher labour input, $(L^*)'$. Thus, an increase in the nominal quantity of money, M, that creates an unperceived rise in the price level affects the real economy and is, therefore, non-neutral. Specifically, an increase in M raises the quantity of labour input, L.

The rise in labour input, L, will lead to an expansion of production. That is, real GDP, Y, increases in accordance with the production function:

$$Y = A \bullet F(\kappa K, L) \tag{16.2}$$

where κK is the quantity of capital services (the product of the capital-utilization rate, κ, and the stock of capital, K). For given κK, the rise in L implies an increase in Y.

As usual, we assume that the quantity of capital, K, is fixed in the short run. However, in the price-misperceptions model, the increase in money, M, tends to raise the capital-utilization rate, κ. The rise in labour input, L, tends to increase the marginal product of capital services, MPK. A higher MPK causes an increase in the demand for capital services. As in Chapter 10, this increase in demand raises the real rental price, R/P, and the quantity of capital services, κK (by raising κ). This expansion of κK reinforces the increase of real GDP, Y, in equation (16.2).

---

[3]An increase in the nominal quantity of money, M, might also raise the nominal wage rate, w, compared to the nominal wage rate, w^e, that workers expect to receive in future years. This effect arises if workers think that the change in w is temporary. An increase in w/w^e increases current labour supply, L^s, through an intertemporal-substitution effect. That is, workers work a great deal when w is perceived to be temporarily high and work relatively little when w is perceived to be unusually low. This intertemporal-substitution effect reinforces the result that an increase in M leads to a higher quantity of labour supplied.

MONEY IS NEUTRAL IN THE LONG RUN

The difference between the long run and the short run in the price-misperceptions model is that the expected price level, P^e, adjusts towards the actual price level, P, in the long run. An increase in the nominal quantity of money, M, raised labour input, L, in the short run in Figure 16.2; P^e rose by less than P, and, therefore, the labour supply curve shifted to the right. However, over time, households learn that they have underestimated the rise in P, and P^e increases accordingly. The rise in P^e reverses the shift in the labour supply curve shown in the figure. That is, w/P^e now decreases for a given w/P, and the labour supply curve shifts back to the left.

Eventually, when P^e rises as much as P, the labour supply curve in Figure 16.2 returns to its initial position, denoted by L^s. Therefore, the real wage rate, w/P, and the quantity of labour input, L, return to their initial values, $(w/P)^*$ and L^*. We conclude that the effects of an increase in the nominal quantity of money, M, on these real variables are only temporary. In the long run, an increase in M leaves the real variables unchanged. In this situation, the price level, P, and the nominal wage rate, w, rise by the same proportion as the increase in M. We conclude that, in the long run, money is neutral, just as in Chapter 11.

ONLY UNPERCEIVED INFLATION AFFECTS REAL VARIABLES

One important conclusion from the price-misperceptions model is that only unperceived changes in the price level, P, affect labour input, L, and real GDP, Y. The non-neutral effects that we found in the short run depended on the increase in the ratio of actual to expected prices, P/P^e. This change made workers believe that the real wage rate, perceived to be w/P^e, had risen and led, accordingly, to the shift to the right in the labour supply curve shown in Figure 16.2.

Suppose, instead, that an increase in the nominal quantity of money, M, raises expected prices, P^e, in the short run by the same amount as actual prices, P. In this case, the monetary change will be neutral, just as we found for the long run. The reason is that, when $P^e = P$, workers understand that the increase in their nominal wage rate, w, is due to a general increase in the nominal quantity of money, M, and the price level, P, and not to a rise in their real wage rate, w/P.

Consider, as an example, the long-run inflation analyzed in Chapter 12. In this situation, the price level, P, rises over time. However, the anticipated part of this inflation – the part considered in Chapter 12 – represents movements in P^e along with P. Therefore, in the price-misperceptions model, this anticipated inflation will not affect labour input, L, and real GDP, Y.

We get an analogous result for systematic monetary policy. Suppose that the monetary authority attempts to moderate economic fluctuations by printing a great deal of money in response to recessions. In the price-misperceptions model, this policy will have the intended real effects only if the actual price level, P, rises systematically above its expected level, P^e, when the economy is weak. This kind of policy is difficult to engineer; at times of recession, the monetary authority would have to fool people regularly into thinking that the price level, P, is lower than it actually is. That is, the expectation, P^e, would have to lag systematically behind the change in P. This systematic deception is inconsistent with the notion of rational expectations introduced in Chapter 12.[4] If people form price-level expectations, P^e, rationally, these expectations will take into account easily recognizable patterns, such as a tendency for the nominal quantity of money, M, and the price level, P, to rise in response to recessions. This adjustment of expectations tends to eliminate the real effects of systematic monetary policy.[5] That is, we return to a situation in which changes in the nominal quantity of money, M, are neutral, even in the short run.

Aside from the difficulty in systematically fooling workers, there is the question of why the monetary authority would want to deceive workers in this manner. One possibility is that central bankers have unusual preferences;

[4]Abraham Lincoln's perspective may be relevant: 'You may fool all of the people some of the time; you can even fool some of the people all of the time; but you cannot fool all of the people all of the time' (quoted in Alexander McClure, 1901, p. 124). Unfortunately, there is controversy about whether Lincoln actually made this famous statement.
[5]This finding is called the **irrelevance result for systematic monetary policy**. For the initial derivation, see Thomas Sargent and Neil Wallace (1975). Ben McCallum (1979) has an interesting discussion.

that is, they seek outcomes that differ from those that would be voluntarily chosen by well-informed households. However, we do not have to rely on central bankers having odd preferences. Under some circumstances, the economy might actually perform better if everyone could be tricked into working and producing more. To get this result, we have to assume that labour input, L, and, hence, real GDP, Y, are typically too low from a social perspective. Distortions in the economy, such as those from income taxation and welfare programmes, can lead to this outcome. Under these conditions, the monetary authority might make everyone better off if it can fool all workers and producers into raising L and Y. Thus, the monetary authority may be motivated to raise P above P^e even if the authority has normal preferences. However, even given this basis for creating unperceived increases in the price level, there remains the issue of whether this deception is feasible as an ongoing policy.

In contrast to systematic policy, the monetary authority can surely create unperceived changes in the price level, P, by behaving erratically. By randomly printing a considerable amount of money, M, at some times and little money at other times, the monetary authority could generate volatility in the price level, P. In this circumstance, the ratio of actual to expected prices, P/P^e, would be likely to fluctuate a great deal. Sometimes P would be higher than P^e, and sometimes P would be lower than P^e. This volatility would cause fluctuations in labour input, L, and real GDP, Y. Therefore, an erratic monetary policy would have real effects and, hence, not be neutral. However, this kind of 'monetary policy' would not tend to improve the workings of the economy.

Robert Lucas (1973) argued that the extent of the response to a monetary shock – that is, a change in the nominal quantity of money, M – depends on whether a country's monetary policy has a history of stability or volatility. In an unstable monetary setting, such as in many Latin American countries, households tend to view observed movements in nominal wage rates and prices, w and P, as reflections of general inflation. Consequently, monetary expansions do not usually fool workers into thinking that their real wage rate, w/P, has increased. Hence, in a Latin American type environment, monetary shocks tend to have small effects on labour input, L, and real GDP, Y.

In contrast, in a stable monetary setting – such as the United States and many other advanced economies since the mid-1980s – households are more likely to think that observed movements in nominal wage rates and prices, w and P, represent variations in real wage rates and relative prices. Consequently, monetary shocks tend to have significant effects on labour input, L, and real GDP, Y. A summary statement of the **Lucas hypothesis on monetary shocks** is that *the real effect of a given size monetary shock is larger, the more stable the underlying monetary environment*.

The Lucas hypothesis receives empirical support from cross-country studies for the post-World War II period.[6] First, it turns out that monetary shocks (measured by unanticipated changes in monetary aggregates) have a positive relation to real GDP in many countries. Second, as the theory predicts, the strength of this relation diminishes as a country's money growth rate and inflation rate become less predictable. Countries that have reasonably stable money growth and inflation turn out to be the ones in which monetary shocks have a significantly positive relation to real GDP. For countries such as Argentina and Brazil, where money growth and inflation have fluctuated violently, there is virtually no connection between monetary shocks and real GDP.

PREDICTIONS FOR ECONOMIC FLUCTUATIONS

In our equilibrium business-cycle model, we imagined that economic fluctuations resulted from shocks to the technology level, A. Then, we worked out the predicted cyclical patterns for a number of macroeconomic variables. The first row of Table 16.1 summarizes these predictions for five variables: the nominal quantity of money, M; the price level, P; the quantity of labour input, L; the real wage rate, w/P; and the average product of labour, Y/L. Recall that M is procyclical because of endogenous changes in the nominal quantity of money, as worked out in Chapter 11. The price level, P, is countercyclical for given M, as also discussed in Chapter 11. The procyclical patterns for L, w/P, and Y/L come from Chapters 9 and 10. The predicted patterns for these five variables accord with empirical observations, summarized in line 3 of Table 16.1. However, in the data, M and Y/L are only weakly procyclical.

[6]See Robert Lucas (1973), Roger Kormendi and Phillip Meguire (1984) and Cliff Attfield and Nigel Duck (1983).

Table 16.1 Cyclical patterns of macroeconomic variables in two models

	Nominal quantity of money, *M*	Price level, *P*	Labour input, *L*	Real wage rate, *w/P*	Average product of labour, *Y/L*
1. Equilibrium business-cycle model	procyclical	countercyclical	procyclical	procyclical	procyclical
2. Price-misperceptions model	procyclical	procyclical	procyclical	countercyclical	countercyclical
3. Empirical observations	procyclical (weakly)	countercyclical	procyclical	procyclical	procyclical (weakly)

Note: The cells show the cyclical pattern of five macroeconomic variables in three settings. First, is the equilibrium business-cycle model with economic fluctuations driven by shocks to the technology level, *A* (described in Chapters 9–11). Second, is the price-misperceptions model from this chapter, with economic fluctuations driven by shocks to the nominal quantity of money, *M*. Third, is the empirical pattern presented in Chapters 9 and 11.

Now, we can use the price-misperceptions model to get alternative predictions of cyclical patterns for macroeconomic variables. In this analysis, we imagine that economic fluctuations result from monetary shocks; that is, exogenous variations in the nominal quantity of money, *M*.

In the price-misperceptions model, an increase in the nominal quantity of money, *M*, raises the price level, *P*, and the nominal wage rate, *w*. The increase in the ratio of *P* to the expected price level, P^e, shifts the labour supply curve to the right, as in Figure 16.2. This shift leads to a rise in labour input, *L*, and a decline in the real wage rate, *w/P*. The increase in *L* tends to raise the MPK. The increase in MPK increases the input of capital services, κK, by raising the capital-utilization rate, κ.

The production function is still given by:

$$Y = A \bullet F(\kappa K, L) \tag{16.2}$$

The technology level, *A*, has not changed. Therefore, the rises in *L* and κK imply an increase in real GDP, *Y*. For a given production function and given κK, the rise in *L* encounters diminishing marginal product of labour, MPL. The average product of labour, *Y/L*, also tends to decline as *L* rises. Hence, we predict that a fall in *Y/L* accompanies the rise in *Y*.[7]

The second row of Table 16.1 summarizes the predictions from the price-misperceptions model for the five macroeconomic variables. The procyclical patterns for the nominal quantity of money, *M*, and labour input, *L*, are the same as those from the equilibrium business-cycle model and also conform to the data. Differences from the equilibrium business-cycle model show up for the price level, *P*, the real wage rate, *w/P*, and the average product of labour, *Y/L*. The price-misperceptions model predicts, counterfactually, that *P* will be procyclical, whereas *w/P* and *Y/L* will be countercyclical. These discrepancies suggest that monetary shocks, working through the channels isolated in the price-misperceptions model, cannot be the major source of economic fluctuations.

We can do better with a richer model that allows for both kinds of shocks – one to the technology level, *A*, and another to the nominal quantity of money, *M*. In this setting, the price level, *P*, would be countercyclical; and the real wage rate, *w/P*, and the average product of labour, *Y/L*, would be procyclical if the variations in *A* are usually the dominant source of economic fluctuations. However, monetary shocks also occur. Most importantly, this composite model predicts non-neutrality of money.

From the data, we know that nominal money, *M*, is weakly procyclical. (The procyclical pattern is more pronounced for broad monetary aggregates, such as M1 and M2, than for narrow aggregates, such as currency and the monetary base.) The equilibrium business-cycle model and the price-misperceptions model provide alternative explanations of this pattern. The equilibrium business-cycle model says that *M* is procyclical because the

---

[7]The increase in κK offsets the decline in the MPL. However, the real wage rate, *w/P*, has to fall overall to raise the quantity of labour demanded. Therefore, the MPL – which equals *w/P* in equilibrium – has to decline overall. Typically, a lower average product of labour, *Y/L*, accompanies a fall in the MPL.

central bank wants to stabilize the price level, P. This objective makes M move *endogenously* in the same direction as the real quantity of money demanded, $D(Y, i)$, which tends to move in the same direction as real GDP, Y. The price-misperceptions model says that an exogenous, unanticipated increase in M raises P more than expected and, thereby, raises real GDP, Y.

Although the nominal quantity of money, M, is procyclical in both models, the directions of causation are opposite. In the equilibrium business-cycle model, the causation runs from real GDP, Y, to M. In other words, money is endogenous. In the price-misperceptions model, the causation runs from exogenous (and unanticipated) changes in M to Y. Thus, to sort out the two stories, we have to observe something more than a positive correlation between the cyclical parts of nominal money and real GDP. This pattern accords with both models and, therefore, does not distinguish between them.

EMPIRICAL EVIDENCE ON THE REAL EFFECTS OF MONETARY SHOCKS
Friedman and Schwartz's Monetary History

The classic study of the interplay between money and output is the work by Milton Friedman and Anna J. Schwartz. Friedman and Schwartz (1963) analyze US monetary policy from 1867 to 1960, whereas Friedman and Schwartz (1982) also analyze monetary policy in the United Kingdom from 1875 to 1975. Their research considered, first, the historical sources of changes in the nominal quantity of money and, second, the interactions of these changes with variations in economic activity. The main conclusions in Friedman and Schwartz (1963) were (p. 676). "Throughout the near-century examined in detail we have found that:

1. Changes in the behaviour of the money stock have been closely associated with changes in economic activity, money income and prices.
2. The interrelation between monetary and economic change has been highly stable.
3. Monetary changes have often had an independent origin; they have not been simply a reflection of changes in economic activity."

The first two points are essentially a statement that nominal monetary aggregates are procyclical. We have also found this property, although the relation is not as strong or stable as Friedman and Schwartz suggested. The most important point, however, is their third one – the statement that the procyclical pattern for monetary aggregates cannot be explained entirely by endogenous money. Friedman and Schwartz made their third point by isolating historical episodes in which changes in the nominal quantity of money, M, resulted from largely exogenous factors. Overall, Friedman and Schwartz make a convincing case that exogenous changes in M have sometimes exerted significant influences on real economic activity. These findings support the price-misperceptions model.

Unanticipated money growth

Barro (1981) attempted to isolate the effects of monetary shocks on real economic activity by constructing measures of **unanticipated money growth**. The first step was to estimate anticipated money growth, using a set of explanatory values to determine the money growth rate that could have been predicted from historical patterns (using M1 as the definition of money). The variables included a measure of government spending and an indicator of the business cycle (based on the unemployment rate). Then, unanticipated money growth is determined by taking the difference between the actual and anticipated values. Barro (1981) found that an increase in unanticipated money growth raised real GDP over periods of a year or more. In a related study, Ben Broadbent (1996) observed that the positive link between unanticipated money growth and real GDP worked through surprise movements in the price level, P. This channel is the one isolated in the price-misperceptions model.

The results for unanticipated money growth are analogous to our finding in Chapter 11 that the cyclical parts of nominal monetary aggregates are, at least, weakly procyclical. That is, unanticipated money growth is similar to the cyclical part of money growth. The problem is that a positive relation of unanticipated money growth or the cyclical part of money to real GDP does not convincingly isolate causation from nominal money, M, to real GDP, Y. Even if the changes in M precede the changes in Y – as some economists have found – we cannot be sure about the direction of causation. The monetary authority might be adjusting M in response to anticipated future changes in Y; that is, the movements in money may still be endogenous.

Romer and Romer on monetary policy

In ongoing research inspired by the historical analysis of Friedman and Schwartz (1963), Christina Romer and David Romer (2004) pioneered the so-called 'narrative method' in isolating exogenous monetary shocks. They measure these shocks by looking at changes during meetings of the Federal Reserve's **Federal Open Market Committee (FOMC)** in the target for the **Federal Funds rate**. This rate is the overnight nominal interest rate, i, which the Federal Reserve monitors closely. In the short run, an increase in the Federal Funds rate goes along with a monetary contraction. This contraction typically shows up as reduced growth rates of monetary aggregates, such as currency, the monetary base and M1. Romer and Romer estimated the relationship of changes in the Federal Reserve's target for the Federal Funds rate to the Federal Reserve's forecasts of inflation and real GDP. Then, they measured monetary shocks as the difference between the actual change in the funds rate target and the one predicted from their estimated relationship. They found that unanticipated increases in the Federal Funds rate tended to reduce real GDP, whereas unanticipated decreases tended to raise real GDP. A recent study by Cloyne and Hürtgen (2016) applied this narrative method to data from the Bank of England and found similar effects of monetary policy on the UK economy.

A shortcoming of the Romer–Romer nararative method is that it does not clearly isolate the exogenous parts of monetary policy. As with the constructs of unanticipated money growth in Barro (1981), the new measures – essentially, unanticipated movements in the interest rate – might pick up responses of monetary policy to past or anticipated future variations in real economic variables. Thus, the correlation of the constructed monetary policy shocks with real GDP may still reflect reverse effects of real economic activity on the monetary variables.

A brief overview

At this point, the empirical evidence suggests that positive monetary shocks tend to expand the real economy, whereas negative monetary shocks tend to contract the real economy. However, the evidence is not 100% conclusive, and we surely lack reliable estimates of the strength of this relationship.

Economics in Practice
Incomplete information about prices: is it significant?

A key assumption in the price-misperceptions model is that households do not observe immediately the economy-wide price level, P. If households always knew the current P – perhaps because they looked regularly at a useful index, such as the consumer price index (CPI) – they would not get confused about movements in real wage rates. In particular, the perceived price level, P^e, would stay close to the actual value, P. Therefore, the perceived real wage rate, w/P^e, would stay close to the actual value, w/P. But then the model predicts that monetary shocks would be close to neutral.

Households can, in fact, observe quickly an index of consumer prices – with a one-month lag for the CPI. Of course, most people do not bother to monitor this index on a regular basis. But, presumably, they ignore this information because, in stable economies, it is not very important to keep a close watch on the general price level.

One reason that available price indices may not be so helpful is that each household cares about a different market basket of goods, each of which differs from the basket used to construct the indices. Then, in order to keep well-informed about prices, households would have to take detailed samples from a variety of locations. Since this process is costly, households would sometimes make errors in their interpretations of the prices and wage rates that they see. However, this argument cannot explain why variations in the general price level would be important enough to generate major errors in labour supply decisions. After all, a relatively small investment – looking at published price indexes – would be sufficient to eliminate the mistakes caused by general inflations of nominal prices and wage rates.

The bottom line is that ignorance about the general price level may account for small and short-lived confusions about relative prices and real wage rates. However, it is unlikely that large and long-lasting confusions would arise. The costs of being misinformed – and, therefore, making incorrect decisions about labour supply – seem excessive relative to the costs of gathering the necessary information on the general price level.

This viewpoint suggests that monetary shocks in the context of the price-misperceptions model can account for only a small part of observed economic fluctuations. This conclusion reinforces our findings about the cyclical properties of some key macroeconomic variables; notably, the price level, P, and the real wage rate, w/P. If monetary shocks and price-perception errors were of major importance, we would predict that P would be procyclical and w/P would be countercyclical. However, as noted in Table 16.1, the data show that P is countercyclical and w/P is procyclical.

REAL SHOCKS

We now consider how price misperceptions affect our previous analysis of a shock to the technology level, A – the main disturbance assumed in the equilibrium business-cycle model. We know from Chapters 9–11 that an increase in A raises real GDP, Y, but lowers the price level, P, at least if the monetary authority holds constant the nominal quantity of money, M. Conversely, a decrease in A reduces Y and increases P.

In the equilibrium business-cycle model, we assumed that households had accurate current information about the price level, P. We now assume, as in the price-misperceptions model, that the expected price level, P^e, lags behind the actual price level, P. For example, in a boom, when P declines, P^e decreases by less than P. Hence, P/P^e falls; that is, workers overestimate P during a boom. This overestimate of P means that workers underestimate their real wage rate, w/P: the perceived real wage rate, w/P^e, falls below w/P. It follows that the quantity of labour supplied, L^s, decreases for a given w/P.

The effect of this price misperception on the L^s curve is analogous to that shown in Figure 16.2, except in the opposite direction. At any real wage rate, w/P, the quantity of labour supplied is now lower. We show this shift to L^s in Figure 16.3. The original curve is labelled $L^s(A)$, where A is the initial technology level. The new curve is labelled $L^s(A')$, where A' is the higher technology level. The increase in the technology level from A to A' reduces the price level, P, and, therefore, shifts the L^s curve to the left.

An increase in the technology level also affects the labour-demand curve, L^d, as we know from our analysis in Figure 9.13 in Chapter 9. The increase in the technology level from A to A' raises the MPL and thereby increases the quantity of labour demanded at any w/P. We show this shift to L^d in Figure 16.3 as the movement to the right from the light blue curve to the dark blue one. Keep in mind our assumption that employers know the real wage rate, w/P. Therefore, price misperceptions do not affect the L^d curves.

Figure 16.3 shows that the increase in the technology level, A, raises labour, L, and the real wage rate, w/P. These changes are in the same direction as those in Figure 9.13. The new effect in Figure 16.3 comes from the shift to the left of the labour supply curve, L^s. We see graphically that this shift means that L rises by less than it would have otherwise.[8] Therefore, price misperceptions weaken the effect of a change in the technology level, A, on L and, hence, on real GDP, Y.

These new effects from price misperceptions apply only in the short run, when the perceived price level, P^e, lags behind the actual price level, P. In Figure 16.3, as P^e adjusts downward towards the lower P, the labour supply curve

---

[8]Labour, L, still has to increase overall. If L declined, real GDP, Y, would fall. Then the price level, P, would increase, and the L^s curve would shift in the direction opposite to that assumed in Figure 16.3.

Figure 16.3 Response of the labour market to a technology shock: effects of price misperceptions

The technology level, A, rises from A to A'. The labour-demand curves come from Figure 9.13. At any real wage rate, w/P, the quantity of labour demanded is higher along $L^d(A')$, than along $L^d(A)$. The increase in A also reduces the price level, P. Because of price misperceptions, the quantity of labour supplied falls at any w/P. Therefore, $L^s(A')$, lies to the left of the initial curve, $L^s(A)$. The increase in L, from L^* to $(L^*)'$, is less than it would have been if the L^s curve had not shifted. Therefore, price misperceptions lessen the response of L to a technology shock.

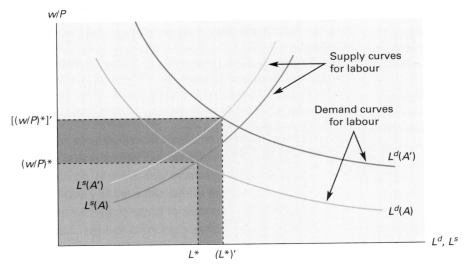

shifts to the right, back towards its initial position. Hence, the real wage rate, w/P, and the quantity of labour input, L, tend towards the values, $(w/P)^*$ and L^*, that applied in the original version of our equilibrium business-cycle model (Figure 9.13).

If we combine the findings about real shocks with the earlier ones for monetary shocks, we get the following summary of results for the price-misperceptions model:

- Because of price misperceptions, unanticipated increases in the nominal quantity of money, M, raise real GDP, Y and labour input, L, in the short run. Since money was neutral in the model without price misperceptions, we can also say that these misperceptions accentuate the real effects of monetary shocks.
- Price misperceptions lessen the short-run real effects of real shocks. A favourable shock to the technology level, A, still raises Y and L, but by less than before.

Rules versus discretion

We have found that unanticipated money shocks can affect the real economy in the short run. Given these results, it is not surprising that monetary authorities would be tempted to exercise their power to create money shocks as a way to influence real variables. However, economists have found that such temptations can lead to bad economic outcomes. The reasons for the bad results involve the distinction between rules and discretion. Under a **monetary rule**, the central bank commits itself to a designated mode of conducting policy. Under discretion, the authority leaves open the possibility for surprises; that is, for monetary shocks. In this section, we seek to understand why the economy might perform better in a committed or rule-like setting.

The ongoing debate over rules and discretion is an exciting research topic that involves the application of strategic analysis – a part of game theory – to government policy.[9] The initial inspiration came from the distinction between perceived versus misperceived price-level changes in the kind of model explored in this chapter. In this model, the

[9]The pioneering paper in this area – an important reason for their 2004 Nobel Prize in Economics – is by Finn Kydland and Edward Prescott (1977). Further developments are in Robert Barro and David Gordon (1983a, 1983b). Ken Rogoff (1989) has a useful survey of this literature.

real economy reacts to a change in the nominal quantity of money, M, only when the change is unanticipated – in particular, only when the money shock causes the price level, P, to deviate from its perceived level, P^e. Consequently, the monetary authority may be motivated to create price surprises as a way to affect real economic activity. However, under rational expectations, systematic surprises tend not to be attainable. Despite this difficulty, the temptation to act in a surprising manner remains, and this temptation can influence the equilibrium inflation rate, π. We will now work out a simple model of strategic interaction that determines π.

Suppose that the monetary authority can use its policy instruments – which could be open-market operations – to achieve a desired inflation rate, π. The authority seeks to raise real GDP, Y, and labour input, L, but can do so only by making π exceed the inflation rate that households expect, π^e. For given π^e, we assume that Y and L rise with π. The mechanism for this effect can be a link between misperceived price-level changes and labour supply, as in the model worked out before.

We assume that the monetary authority does not like inflation for its own sake. If π and π^e rise together, the economy experiences costs of inflation, perhaps due to transaction costs or costs of changing prices. Our assumption is that inflation and deflation are both costly; that is, costs of inflation are minimized when the price level is constant, so that $\pi = 0$. We also assume that, as π rises above zero, additional inflation becomes increasingly burdensome for the economy. More formally, the marginal cost of inflation rises with π.

For given inflationary expectations, π^e, the monetary authority faces a trade-off when considering whether to use its policy instruments to raise the inflation rate, π. An increase in π is beneficial because it raises the inflation surprise, $\pi - \pi^e$, and thereby expands real GDP, Y, and labour input, L. We assume that these increases in Y and L are attractive.[10] However, if π is already greater than zero, an increase in π is undesirable because it raises the costs of inflation.

The trade-off between the benefits and costs of inflation determines the inflation rate, denoted by $\hat{\pi}$, that the monetary authority selects. Typically, $\hat{\pi}$ will depend on the inflation rate, π^e, that households expect. As an example, if households expect zero inflation, $\pi^e = 0$, the authority might find it optimal to pick 5% inflation (i.e., $\hat{\pi} = 5$). If expected inflation rises (say, to $\pi^e = 5$) the authority might choose still higher inflation to keep ahead of expectations and, thereby, maintain a stimulus to real GDP and labour input. Thus, the policymaker might choose $\hat{\pi} = 8$. Typically, a higher π^e motivates a higher $\hat{\pi}$. However, as $\hat{\pi}$ rises, inflation may become increasingly burdensome for the economy. This consideration motivates the monetary authority not to react too strongly to a rise in π^e. Specifically, our assumption is that the response of $\hat{\pi}$ is always by less than the increase in π^e. For example, if π^e rises by 5 percentage points, from 0 to 5, $\hat{\pi}$ might increase by only 3 percentage points, from 5 to 8.

We show the graph of $\hat{\pi}$ versus π^e as the dark blue line in Figure 16.4. The important properties of this line are: first, $\hat{\pi}$ is greater than 0 when $\pi^e = 0$; second, the slope of the line is greater than zero; and, third, the slope is less than 1.0.

Consider how households form rational expectations of inflation in this model. A key assumption is that households understand the objective of the monetary authority. Each household recognizes that, if all households expect the inflation rate to be π^e along the horizontal axis, the authority will actually select the inflation rate $\hat{\pi}$ given on the vertical axis by the dark blue line in Figure 16.4. For example, if all households expect zero inflation, $\pi^e = 0$, the authority would set $\hat{\pi} = 5$. But, then, zero cannot be a rational expectation of inflation; no sensible household would expect zero inflation. Similarly, if all households expect 5% inflation, $\pi^e = 5$, the authority would set $\hat{\pi} = 8$. Thus, again, $\pi^e = 5$ is not a rational expectation. In this model, an expectation π^e will be rational only if the monetary authority is motivated to validate the belief; that is, to set $\hat{\pi} = \pi^e$. Thus, in Figure 16.4, the chosen $\hat{\pi}$ must lie along the light blue, 45-degree line, which shows outcomes for which $\hat{\pi} = \pi^e$.

The equilibrium inflation rate, π^*, is given from the intersection of the two lines in Figure 16.4. The value π^* satisfies two conditions. First, if $\pi^e = \pi^*$ on the horizontal axis, the monetary authority selects the inflation rate $\hat{\pi} = \pi^*$ on the vertical axis, as given by the dark blue line. That is, the authority is optimizing (by picking $\hat{\pi}$) for given inflationary expectations, π^e. Second, the expectation $\pi^e = \pi^*$ is rational because it gives the most accurate possible forecast of inflation.

---

[10] As discussed before, because of existing distortions in the economy, it may be socially desirable for the monetary authority to trick all households into working and producing more.

Figure 16.4 Inflation in a discretionary regime

The dark blue line shows the policymaker's optimal choice of inflation, $\hat{\pi}$, as a function of households' expected rate of inflation, π^e. The light blue, 45-degree line shows points where the chosen inflation rate, $\hat{\pi}$, equals the expected inflation rate, π^e. Under rational expectations, the pair $(\hat{\pi}, \pi^e)$ must lie on the light blue line. The value π^* is the equilibrium inflation rate in a discretionary regime. At π^*, the policymaker is optimizing for given expectations, and expectations are rational.

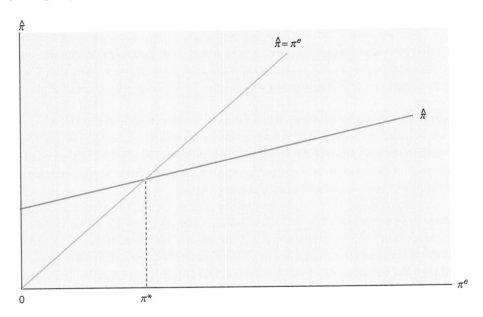

In this model, households have **perfect foresight** about inflation; that is, the forecast error is zero in equilibrium. In richer versions of this type of model, inflationary expectations would still be optimal forecasts of inflation, but the forecast error would generally be nonzero. For example, we would have nonzero forecast errors if the monetary authority sometimes makes unavoidable and unpredictable mistakes by randomly setting π different from $\hat{\pi}$.

The unappealing aspect of the equilibrium in Figure 16.4 is that it entails a high inflation rate, π^*, without any of the benefits that come from surprisingly high inflation. That is, in equilibrium, expected inflation, π^e, equals π^*. Recall that, in the underlying model, money growth and inflation stimulate real GDP, Y, and labour input, L, only when the inflation rate, π, exceeds its expectation, π^e. Thus, in the equilibrium displayed in Figure 16.4, Y and L receive no stimulus from surprisingly high inflation.

The outcomes would be more favourable if actual and expected inflation were lower than those that arise in equilibrium; for example, if $\pi = \pi^e = 0$. In this case, the inflation surprise, $\pi - \pi^e$, would again be zero, so that there would be no stimulus to real GDP, Y, and labour input, L. However, since π is low – specifically, zero – the economy would not suffer costs of inflation. Figure 16.4 makes clear, however, that $\pi = \pi^e = 0$ is not an equilibrium in the model. If the monetary authority managed to persuade households to expect zero inflation – so that $\pi^e = 0$ applied – the authority would actually opt for positive inflation. That is, if $\pi^e = 0$, π would be greater than zero along the dark blue line in the figure. Knowing this, households would not set $\pi^e = 0$ in the first place, because they know that this expectation is irrational.

The high-inflation equilibrium in Figure 16.4, where $\pi = \pi^e = \pi^* > 0$, is often referred to as the outcome under discretionary policy. This equilibrium prevails if the monetary authority cannot, or, at least, does not, make commitments about future monetary actions. In contrast, an authority that makes such commitments is viewed as operating under an explicit or implicit policy rule. One simple form of rule commits the monetary authority to adjust its instruments to approximate price stability; that is, to set $\pi = 0$ in each period. Another rule has the authority target a positive but low inflation rate. In the present setting, the commitment to zero inflation – if feasible – is the best option for the monetary authority.

Figure 16.4 illustrates the tension in a rule that specifies zero (or, more generally, low) inflation. When $\pi^e = 0$, the policymaker would like to renege on commitments by setting $\pi = \hat{\pi} > 0$ along the dark blue line. But then the outcomes would tend towards the discretionary equilibrium shown at the high inflation rate π^*. Thus, an important aspect of a rule is that the monetary authority be firmly committed to it. The authority has to ensure that it will not exploit an opportunity for surprisingly high inflation, *ex post*.

In some cases, a commitment to low inflation may not require a formal rule, which might even be embedded in a law. Instead, the authority may be able to build up a reputation for low inflation. Since a reputation for low inflation is valuable, a central banker may be able to convince households that they will not exploit short-run opportunities to create surprises by inflating at a rate higher than expected. These kinds of reputational equilibria are more likely to apply if the benefits from cheating (by creating surprisingly high inflation in the short run) are not too great, and if episodes of cheating generate a substantial loss of reputation.[11]

Over the last two decades, central banks in most advanced economies have become committed to low and stable inflation. In many countries, the commitments are reinforced by formal provisions stipulating that the central bank's objective is price stability. With increasing frequency, this objective is stated in terms of **inflation targeting**. In a regime of inflation targeting, the central bank commits to using its policy instruments, usually open-market operations, to attain a specified range of the inflation rate over a prescribed interval, such as a year. This commitment is reinforced by transparency about the central bank's objectives and procedures, including the regular publication of inflation reports. Table 16.2 lists 20 countries, beginning with New Zealand in 1989, that have adopted a formal regime of inflation targeting. In the Eurozone, the European Central Bank's primary objective is also to maintain price stability by aiming at an inflation rate of close to, but below, 2% over the medium term. In other countries, notably Japan and the United States, central banks have not adopted formal inflation targets but have also

Table 16.2 Countries with central banks that have adopted formal inflation targeting

Country	Date of adoption of inflation targeting
New Zealand	1989
Canada	1991
United Kingdom	1992
Australia	1993
Finland	1993 (dropped in 1999 on adoption of the euro)
Sweden	1993
Spain	1995 (dropped in 1999 on adoption of the euro)
Czech Republic	1997
Israel	1997
Brazil	1999
Chile	1999
Poland	1999
Colombia	2000
South Africa	2000
South Korea	2000
Thailand	2000
Hungary	2001
Iceland	2001
Mexico	2001
Norway	2001

Note: The list shows countries in which the central banks have formal procedures in place for targeting the inflation rate. This list comes from Frederic Mishkin and Klaus Schmidt-Hebbel (2001) and Alina Carare and Mark Stone (2003).

[11]For further discussion, see Robert Barro and David Gordon (1983b).

established reputations for maintaining low and stable inflation. However, a formal inflation-targeting regime may eventually prove irresistible even to these countries. In any event, the evolution of central-bank policies since the 1980s has been increasingly towards commitments to low and stable inflation.

Strategic interactions analogous to those for monetary policy arise in many areas in which policymakers perceive benefits from surprising the public. As examples, debtor countries may surprise foreign creditors by defaulting on international debts, governments may surprise owners of domestic capital by assessing high tax rates on capital that is already in place (a so-called **capital levy**), tax collectors may surprise taxpayers by announcing tax amnesties, and governments may renege on patents after inventions have been made. In all of these cases, surprises are tempting after the fact. However, if people's expectations take account of these temptations, the equilibria tend to have undesirable properties: little foreign borrowing, low investment, poor tax compliance and a small volume of inventions. To avoid these outcomes, governments are motivated to make commitments – sometimes involving laws and constitutional provisions – to resist temptations that arise after the fact. However, the credibility of these commitments is a major issue. Arguably, the degree of success of public institutions in resolving these commitment problems is a central feature that distinguishes prosperous countries from poor ones.

Summing Up

The empirical evidence suggests that variations in money are not neutral; monetary expansion seems to increase real GDP in the short run. In this chapter, we try to explain monetary non-neutrality by using the price-misperceptions model. In this model, an increase in the nominal quantity of money raises the price level and the nominal wage rate. However, in the short run, the price level perceived by households rises by less than the actual price level, and the perceived real wage rate increases. This perception raises labour supply, leading to a rise in the market-clearing quantity of labour and a fall in the market-clearing real wage rate. The increase in labour implies a rise in real GDP.

The price-misperceptions model with monetary shocks generates procyclical patterns for nominal money, the price level and employment. The model implies countercyclical patterns for the real wage rate and labour productivity. The predictions for the price level, the real wage rate and labour productivity conflict with empirical evidence. Thus, monetary shocks – at least within the price-misperceptions model – are probably not the major source of economic fluctuations. However, the inclusion of these shocks is a useful addition to the equilibrium business-cycle model, in which technology shocks are the underlying cause of economic fluctuations. In particular, the price-misperceptions model may explain why money is not neutral in the short run.

We discussed models of rules versus discretion in monetary policy. Under discretion, the policymaker makes no commitments about future policy. In this case, the incentive to create surprise inflation (as a way to expand the real economy) leads, in equilibrium, to high inflation. Moreover, this inflation is anticipated and, therefore, ends up not stimulating output and employment. Commitments to low and stable inflation, possibly sustained by central-bank reputation, generate better outcomes.

Key Terms and Concepts

capital levy	irrelevance result for	monetary shocks	price-misperceptions model
discretionary policy	systematic monetary	perceived real wage rate	unanticipated money
Federal Funds rate	policy	perfect foresight	growth
Federal Open Market	Lucas hypothesis on	policy rule	
Committee (FOMC)	monetary shocks	price stability	
inflation targeting	monetary rule		

Questions and Problems

A Review questions

1 What is a relative price? Is the real wage rate, w/P, an example of a relative price?

2 What do workers perceive about their real wage rate, w/P, when they see an increase in their nominal wage rate, w? Under what circumstances do workers make mistakes about their real wage rate?

3 Explain why it is reasonable to assume that individuals have imperfect information about prices throughout the economy. What are the costs of collecting and processing information about prices?

4 Can there be unanticipated changes in the nominal quantity of money, M, even when people have rational expectations? If so, does a policy-maker have the option of moderating economic fluctuations through surprise changes in M?

B Problems for discussion

5 The timing of money and output

Suppose that the data show that movements in nominal money are positively correlated with subsequent movements in real GDP. Does this finding demonstrate that money affects the real economy, rather than the reverse? If not, give some examples of endogenous money in which the movements of money precede those in real GDP.

6 Persisting effects on output

When expectations are rational, errors made in estimating the price level will not persist over time. How, then, can price-perception errors explain persistent excesses or shortfalls of real GDP from its trend?

7 The predictability of money growth

Suppose that the money growth rate becomes less predictable from year to year. What happens to the following:

   a the effect of a given-size money shock on real GDP, Y?

   b the effect of a given-size money shock on the price level, P?

8 Rules versus discretion

Assume that the monetary authority's preferred inflation rate is zero, but the authority also wants to reduce unemployment by making inflation surprisingly high.

   a Show how the equilibrium inflation rate can be high. Is the rate surprisingly high? Does the result depend on the authority's having the wrong objective or being incompetent?

   b Can the results improve if the policymaker has the power to bind themselves in advance to a specified inflation rate? If so, explain why this constraint (or rule) can improve matters.

   c Might the policymaker's reputation be a satisfactory alternative to a formal rule that dictates future policies?

   d Can you think of reasons, aside from reducing unemployment, why a policymaker might like surprisingly high inflation?

9 Irrelevance results for monetary policy

   a Under what circumstances does systematic monetary policy not matter for economic fluctuations?

   b Does the result in question a mean that the unpredictable parts of money growth do not affect real GDP?

   c Does the result in question a generalize to the idea that the systematic parts of all government policies are irrelevant for real GDP? Consider, as examples, the following:

      i a policy of cutting labour-income tax rates during recessions;

      ii a policy of raising government purchases of goods and services during recessions;

      iii a policy of enhancing the generosity of unemployment insurance programmes during recessions.

17 Money and business cycles II: Sticky prices and nominal wage rates

In Chapter 16, we developed a model where monetary shocks were non-neutral because of misperceptions about prices. In this chapter, we explore other models that economists have developed to explain the non-neutrality of money. In these models, the price level and nominal wage rate are sticky: they do not adjust instantaneously to clear all the markets. The lack of market clearing is a significant departure from our equilibrium business-cycle model. In the equilibrium business-cycle model – and also in the price-misperceptions model – the price level and nominal wage rate adjusted rapidly to balance quantities of goods supplied and demanded in each market. That is, until now, we assumed that all markets cleared. Now, we will relax this assumption.

As mentioned in Chapter 6, John Maynard Keynes (1936), in his *General Theory of Employment, Interest, and Money*, stressed the importance of stickiness in nominal prices and wages. His emphasis was on the stickiness of nominal wage rates. He thought it was unrealistic to assume that nominal wage rates adjusted rapidly to ensure continual balance between the quantities of labour supplied and demanded. Modern Keynesian economists usually focus instead on stickiness of nominal goods prices. As we shall see, the reason for the new focus is that it leads to a better fit with some features of economic fluctuations. We begin our analysis by introducing sticky nominal goods prices into a variant of our equilibrium business-cycle model.

The New Keynesian model

The usual explanation for **sticky prices** – nominal goods prices that do not react rapidly to changed circumstances – relies on two main ingredients. First, the typical producer actively sets the price of the good that he or she sells in the market. This price-setting behaviour differs from our previous analysis, where each perfectly competitive producer (a household or business) took the price as given by the market. Second, when choosing the price to set, each producer takes into account a cost of changing prices. This cost is sometimes called a **menu cost**, analogous to the expense that a restaurant incurs when it alters the prices listed on its menu.

Our previous setting of perfect competition applies most naturally to large-scale organized markets on which standardized goods are traded. Examples are stock exchanges (on which financial claims are traded) and commodity exchanges (on which claims to goods such as oil or corn are traded). In these organized markets, each trader takes as given the market prices of goods. That is, in most circumstances, each participant is small enough to neglect the impact of his or her actions on the market price.

The situation is different for markets with small numbers of sellers and buyers. For example, the markets for automobiles or computers have relatively few producers. Moreover, the goods traded on these markets are not fully standardized. Each kind of automobile or computer has different features, some of which are distinguished by brand names. These kinds of markets have substantial competition, but not the perfect competition associated with price-taking behaviour by all participants. Instead, each producer has some latitude in deciding what price to set. Economists call this environment **imperfect competition**.

In a perfectly competitive market, a producer who charges more than the market price would find that the quantity demanded would fall to zero. Conversely, a producer who asks less than the market price would find that the quantity demanded would soar towards infinity. In markets with imperfect competition, a decrease in a seller's price generates a finite increase in the quantity of goods demanded from that seller. Similarly, a rise in price leads to a finite reduction in the quantity demanded. Thus, each producer can make a meaningful choice of what price to charge. This perspective applies to many large companies, such as car manufacturers, but also holds for small businesses, such as corner shops. One reason that a small retailer, such as a grocery, has some latitude in setting its price is that its location is convenient for buyers who live nearby or are familiar with the shop. For this reason, a small increase in price above that charged by other shops would not, at least immediately, drive the quantity demanded to zero.

PRICE SETTING UNDER IMPERFECT COMPETITION

In this section, we examine how a producer in an environment of imperfect competition chooses the price of their goods. In the following section, we will learn how the producer takes menu costs into account when determining how to adjust prices to changed circumstances; for example, in response to a monetary shock.

To illustrate the main points, we will find it convenient to work with a formal model. Let $P(j)$ be the price charged for a good by firm j. As in our previous models, we can think of each business as owned and run by one of the households in the economy. The quantity of firm j's goods demanded, $Y^d(j)$, depends on how high $P(j)$ is compared to prices charged by other producers. For example, if firm k is a competitor – perhaps because it is the shop on the next corner – then a cut in k's price, $P(k)$, reduces $Y^d(j)$.

Generally, the quantity demanded of firm j's goods, $Y^d(j)$, will be more sensitive to prices charged on similar goods in nearby locations than to prices offered on very different products or in faraway locations. However, the model would become unmanageable if we tried to keep track of all of these prices. We can get the main results by assuming that the customers of firm j compare the price, $P(j)$, with the average of the prices charged by other firms. If we let this average price be P, then $Y(j)$ depends on the price ratio, $P(j)/P$. An increase in $P(j)/P$ lowers $Y^d(j)$, and a decrease in $P(j)/P$ raises $Y^d(j)$.

The quantity of goods demanded at firm j, $Y^d(j)$, depends also on the incomes of persons who are current or potential customers of the firm. For example, if the real income in the whole economy increases, the demand, $Y^d(j)$, will rise for each firm j.

Now, we move from the demand for firm j's goods to the production of these goods. The production function for firm j looks like the function we have used before:

$$Y(j) = F[\kappa(j) \bullet K(j), L(j)] \tag{17.1}$$

where $\kappa(j) \bullet K(j)$ and $L(j)$ are the quantities of capital services and labour used by firm j. To keep things simple, we ignore changes in the capital utilization rate, $\kappa(j)$, and we assume that the capital stock, $K(j)$, is fixed in the short run. We are also neglecting inputs of intermediate goods, which are materials and products produced by other firms. Extensions to allow for variable capital utilization and intermediate inputs are useful but do not change the basic conclusions.

Suppose that the nominal wage rate, w, is the same for labour used by all the firms in the economy. In other words, we are thinking of labour as a standardized service that is traded in the overall economy under conditions of perfect competition. More specifically, when we consider sticky nominal prices, we will ignore the possibility of sticky nominal wage rates; i.e., w will adjust to balance the total quantities of labour supplied and demanded in the economy. This assumption about the labour market can be questioned and was surely not the environment envisioned by Keynes (1936) in his *General Theory*. We will allow later for *sticky nominal wage rates*.

We begin with a set-up in which the nominal price charged by each firm, $P(j)$, is fully flexible. That is, it is convenient to construct our basic set-up while first ignoring any menu costs for changing prices. Given the nominal wage rate, w, and the average nominal price, P, charged by competitors, each firm sets $P(j)$ at the level that maximizes its profit.

To determine the profit-maximizing price, $P(j)$, we begin by considering the nominal cost of producing an additional unit of goods; that is, the **marginal cost of production**. To relate this concept to our discussion of labour demand in Chapter 7, recall that the marginal product of labour, MPL, is the ratio of additional output, ΔY, to additional labour input, ΔL. Therefore, for firm j:

$$MPL(j) = \Delta Y(j) / \Delta L(j) \tag{17.2}$$

If we rearrange this condition, we see that the added labour, $\Delta L(j)$, needed to raise output by $\Delta Y(j)$ units is:

$$\Delta L(j) = \Delta Y(j) / MPL(j) \tag{17.3}$$

The higher the $MPL(j)$, the lower the quantity of labour, $\Delta L(j)$, needed to raise output by the amount $\Delta Y(j)$. If we set $\Delta Y(j) = 1$, the labour needed to raise output by one unit is:

$$\Delta L(j) = 1 / MPL(j)$$

The nominal cost of each unit of labour is the nominal wage rate, w. Therefore, the added nominal cost of raising output by one unit is $w \cdot [1/MPL(j)]$. In other words, the nominal marginal cost of production for firm j is:

$$\textit{firm j's nominal marginal cost} = w / MPL(j)$$
$$= \textit{ratio of nominal wage rate to marginal product of labour} \tag{17.4}$$

Thus, for given $MPL(j)$, a higher w means a higher nominal marginal cost.

Under perfect competition, profit maximization dictates that each firm's nominal marginal cost, given from equation (17.4) by $w/MPL(j)$, equal its price, $P(j)$.[1] However, under imperfect competition, each firm can set $P(j)$ above its nominal marginal cost. The ratio of $P(j)$ to the nominal marginal cost is called the **mark-up ratio**:

$$\textit{firm j's mark-up ratio} = P(j) / (\textit{firm j's nominal marginal cost}$$
$$= P(j) / [w / MPL(j)] \tag{17.5}$$

where we used the formula for firm j's nominal marginal cost from equation (17.4). The mark-up ratio that a firm chooses depends on how sensitive a firm's product demand, $Y^d(j)$, is to $P(j)$. More market power – that is, less competition – tends to imply less sensitivity of demand to price and, therefore, motivates a higher mark-up ratio. If the sensitivity of demand becomes extremely high (because of greater competition), the mark-up ratio approaches 1.0. That is, we get close to the perfectly competitive outcome in which $P(j)$ equals nominal marginal cost. In our analysis, we assume that each firm's mark-up ratio is a given constant.

We can rearrange the formula for the mark-up ratio to get an expression for each firm's price:

$$P(j) = (\textit{firm j's mark-up ratio}) \cdot (\textit{firm j's nominal marginal cost}) \tag{17.6}$$

Therefore, for a given mark-up ratio, an increase in firm j's nominal marginal cost raises its price, $P(j)$, in the same proportion. For example, if nominal marginal cost doubles, $P(j)$ doubles. If we substitute the formula for nominal marginal cost from equation (17.4), we get:

$$P(j) = (\textit{mark-up ratio}) \cdot [w / MPL(j)] \tag{17.7}$$

Therefore, for a given mark-up ratio, an increase in the nominal wage rate, w, leads to a rise in the same proportion in the nominal price, $P(j)$. For example, a doubling of w causes all firms in the economy to double their nominal prices. Therefore, the average of these prices, P, also doubles.

In our model, we do not have to worry about the full array of individual prices, $P(j)$, that prevails in equilibrium. The important point is that, with imperfect competition, the profit-maximizing decisions of firms determine a

---

[1]If we rearrange the terms, the condition is $MPL(j) = w/P(j)$. Aside from the index j, this equation is the same as the condition for profit maximization worked out in Chapter 7 under perfect competition.

distribution of the $P(j)$. For example, if we think about corner shops, some of them will have relatively high $P(j)$, whereas others will have relatively low $P(j)$.

Each firm demands labour, and the total of these demands determines the economy-wide labour demand, L^d. As in our previous models, the equilibrium of the economy-wide labour market equates the aggregate quantity of labour demanded, L^d, to the aggregate quantity supplied, L^s. This condition determines the economy-wide real wage rate, w/P, as well as the total quantity of labour, L. Finally, if we know w/P and P, we can calculate the economy-wide nominal wage rate, w (by multiplying w/P by P).

SHORT-RUN RESPONSES TO A MONETARY SHOCK

Consider what happens when a monetary shock occurs. To be concrete, imagine that the nominal quantity of money, M, doubles. We found in Chapter 11 that this change in money was neutral. The price level, P, and the nominal wage rate, w, doubled. Real variables, including the quantity of real money balances, M/P, and the real wage rate, w/P, did not change.

With fully flexible prices and wages, money would still be neutral in the model that includes an array of imperfectly competitive firms. In this setting, each nominal price, $P(j)$, doubles when M doubles. Therefore, the average price, P, doubles, as in the model in Chapter 11. The economy-wide nominal wage rate, w, also doubles as before. These changes leave unchanged the real variables in the economy. The real variables now include not only the economy-wide real wage rate, w/P, but also the ratio of each firm's price to the average price, $P(j)/P$.

New results arise when we allow for stickiness in the nominal price, $P(j)$, set by each firm j. As mentioned before, these prices might change infrequently because of menu costs for changing prices. To illustrate the effects of price stickiness, we can consider the extreme case in which all of the $P(j)$ are rigid in the short run. The average price, P, would then also be fixed. If P is constant and the nominal quantity of money, M, doubles, each household would have twice as much real money, M/P, as before. However, nothing has changed to motivate households to hold more money in real terms. Each household would therefore try to spend its excess money, partly by buying the goods produced by the various firms.[2] Each firm j would then experience an increase in the quantity demanded of its goods, $Y(j)$.

How does a business react when it sees an increase in demand, $Y^d(j)$, while its price, $P(j)$, is fixed (by assumption)? We noted before that, under imperfect competition, the mark-up ratio is greater than 1.0. Since the price of goods sold, $P(j)$, is greater than nominal marginal cost, an expansion of production and sales, $Y(j)$, would raise firm j's profit. For example, if $Y(j)$, rose by one unit, the added nominal revenue would be $P(j)$, and the added nominal cost would be the nominal marginal cost, which is less than $P(j)$. Therefore, if $P(j)$ is fixed, a profit-maximizing firm would – over some range – meet an increase in demand by raising production, $Y(j)$.

To raise its production, $Y(j)$, firm j has to increase its quantity of labour input, $L(j)$. Therefore, the quantity of labour demanded, $L^d(j)$, rises by the amount:[3]

$$\Delta L^d(j) = \Delta Y(j) / MPL(j) \tag{17.3}$$

The important point is that, with a fixed price, $P(j)$, an increase in the nominal quantity of money, M, leads to an expansion of labour demand by each firm j.

How does an increase in the nominal quantity of money, M, affect the economy-wide labour market? Since each firm j increases its labour demand, $L^d(j)$, the aggregate quantity of labour demanded, L^d, rises at any given economy-wide real wage rate, w/P. We show this effect in Figure 17.1. The increase in the nominal quantity of money from its initial value, M, to the higher value, M', shifts labour demand to the right from the light blue curve to the dark blue curve.

---

[2]Households might also buy interest-bearing assets; that is, bonds. In the end, we would get the same results if we allowed for this additional channel of effects.

[3]The expansion of $L(j)$ reduces the marginal product of labour, $MPL(j)$, and therefore raises the nominal marginal cost of production, given by equation (17.4). At a fixed price $P(j)$, a profit-maximizing firm would be willing to meet an increase in demand up to the point at which the nominal marginal cost rose to equal $P(j)$.

Figure 17.1 Effect of a monetary expansion in the New Keynesian model

When the nominal quantity of money is M, the demand for labour, labelled $L^d(M)$, slopes downward versus the real wage rate, w/P, and is given by the light blue curve. When the nominal quantity of money rises to M' – but the price level, P, is held fixed – the demand for labour, labelled $L^d(M')$ along the dark blue curve, is larger at any given w/P. The supply of labour, L^s, slopes upward versus w/P. The increase in the nominal quantity of money from M to M' raises the real wage rate from $(w/P)^*$ to $[(w/P)^*]'$ on the vertical axis and increases labour input from L^* to $(L^*)'$ on the horizontal axis.

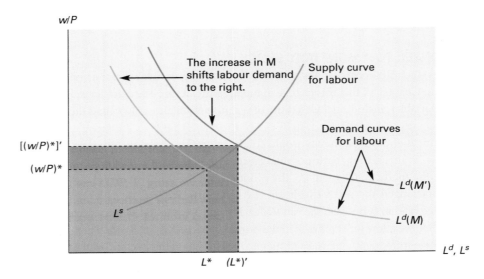

We assume, as in Figure 9.13 in Chapter 9, that an increase in the real wage rate, w/P, raises the quantity of labour supplied, L^s. Thus, L^s is given by the upward-sloping curve in Figure 17.1.

We see from Figure 17.1 that an increase in the nominal quantity of money from M to M' raises the market-clearing labour input from L^* to $(L^*)'$ on the horizontal axis. With the increase in labour input, each firm produces more goods in accordance with the production function:

$$Y(j) = F[\kappa(j) \bullet K(j), L(j)] \tag{17.1}$$

Thus, real gross domestic product (GDP), Y, increases.[4] Moreover, labour input, L, moves in a procyclical manner – it rises along with Y. In summary, we have shown that, in the New Keynesian model, a monetary expansion is non-neutral in the short run: an increase in the nominal quantity of money raises real GDP temporarily. This theoretical prediction is the same as in the IS-LM model presented in Chapter 6. Therefore, the New Keynesian model can be viewed as a modern version of the IS-LM model with the addition of microeconomic foundations that are emphasized in the equilibrium business-cycle model.[5]

NEW KEYNESIAN PREDICTIONS

Thus far, the predictions from the New Keynesian model are also similar to those from the price-misperceptions model considered in Chapter 16. That model also gave the result that a monetary expansion raised real GDP, Y, and labour input, L. However, one difference between the two models concerns the real wage rate, w/P. In the price-misperceptions model, an expansion of L had to be accompanied by a fall in w/P in order to induce employers to use more labour input. Thus, that model predicted – counterfactually – that w/P would be countercyclical. We now demonstrate that the New Keynesian model does not have this problem.

Figure 17.1 shows that a monetary expansion increases the market-clearing real wage rate from $(w/P)^*$ to $[(w/P)^*]'$ on the vertical axis. Therefore, the model generates a procyclical pattern for w/P. Thus, the New Keynesian

[4]We have not considered that the rise in real GDP, Y, increases the nominal quantity of money demanded, M^d. This change dampens the effect on Y from the expansion of the nominal quantity of money M.
[5]Romer (2011) provides a derivation of the IS and LM curves from the New Keynesian model.

model correctly predicts that w/P will be procyclical. The reason that the model gets this result is that employers are willing to employ more labour, even though w/P is higher. The key point is that, under imperfect competition, the mark-up ratio is greater than 1.0. The margin provided by this mark-up means that – at fixed prices of goods – firms can profitably use more labour to produce and sell more goods, even though the real cost of production has gone up (because w/P increased). The monetary expansion does cut into the mark-up ratios of firms. However, as long as the mark-up ratio remains above 1.0, firms are willing to expand labour input and production.

As in the equilibrium business-cycle model studied in Chapter 9, the prediction for procyclical labour input, L, in the New Keynesian model depends on the upward slope of the labour-supply curve, L^s, in Figure 17.1. That is, the analysis relies on the assumption that an increase in the real wage rate, w/P, motivates households to work more.

One respect in which the New Keynesian model works less well than the equilibrium business-cycle model concerns the average product of labour, Y/L. We found in Chapter 9 that Y/L was procyclical because of the direct effect of a change in the technology level, A, on the production function. This prediction for procyclical labour productivity accords with the empirical evidence discussed in Chapter 9.

In contrast, the New Keynesian model assumes that the technology level, A, is fixed. Therefore, we know from the production function that an increase in L tends to reduce the MPL and the average product of labour, Y/L. Hence, an expansion of L during an economic boom goes along with a reduction in the average product of labour, Y/L, whereas a decrease of L during a recession goes along with a rise in Y/L. Consequently, the New Keynesian model predicts, counterfactually, that Y/L would be countercyclical.

Keynesian economists have used the idea of **labour hoarding** to improve the model's predictions about labour productivity. Because of the costs of hiring and firing workers, employers are motivated to retain workers during temporary downturns. Therefore, businesses may 'hoard labour' in recessions as a cost-effective way of having labour available for the next upturn. Although labour input, L, still falls during a recession, it falls by less than it would if not for the hoarded labour. Moreover, during a recession, the 'excess' labour may not actually produce much output. The workers may be exerting less than full effort on the job, or they may be performing maintenance tasks that do not show up in measured output.[6] In either case, measured output per worker, Y/L, would be relatively low in a recession. Thus, we may be able to use labour hoarding to explain why the observed average product of labour, Y/L, is procyclical.[7]

PRICE ADJUSTMENT IN THE LONG RUN

Our analysis of the New Keynesian model applies in the short run, when we do not allow for adjustments in the prices, $P(j)$, set by each firm j. In the longer run, the prices adjust, and these adjustments tend to undo the real effects from a change in the nominal quantity of money, M.

To study the longer-run dynamics, go back to the formula for firm j's mark-up ratio:

$$\text{firm } j\text{'s mark-up ratio} = P(j)/(\text{firm } j\text{'s nominal marginal cost})$$
$$= P(j)/[w/MPL(j)] \tag{17.5}$$

We assumed, thus far, that $P(j)$ was fixed for each firm j. Therefore, the overall price level, P, was also fixed. We then got the result, in Figure 17.1, that an increase in the nominal quantity of money, M, raised the real wage rate, w/P, and the quantity of labour input, L. Since P is fixed, the increase in w/P must correspond to a rise in the nominal wage rate, w. We can see from equation (17.5) that, for fixed $P(j)$, the increase in w raises firm j's nominal marginal

---

[6]Jon Fay and James Medoff (1985) found from a survey of 168 manufacturing companies that the typical firm responded to a recession by assigning an additional 5% of its work hours to maintenance, overhaul of equipment, training and other activities that do not show up in measured output. This reallocation of labour can help to explain why measured output per worker, Y/L, tends to be low during a recession.
[7]A richer version of the new Keynesian model has a different way of explaining why the average product of labour, Y/L, is procyclical. The new feature is that goods produced by firms serve not only as final products, but also as intermediate inputs for other firms. A monetary expansion lowers mark-up ratios and, therefore, lowers the real cost of intermediate inputs. Consequently, firms use more of these intermediate inputs, and this increased use tends to raise the MPL and the average product of labour, Y/L. Therefore, Y/L can rise in a boom even though L increases.

cost and, thereby, lowers its mark-up ratio. Moreover, the increase in $L(j)$ reduces the marginal product of labour, $MPL(j)$. Equation (17.5) shows that the fall in $MPL(j)$ further raises firm j's nominal marginal cost and, therefore, further decreases the mark-up ratio.

Suppose, as an example, that firm j's preferred (profit-maximizing) mark-up ratio is 1.2; that is, the firm likes to set its price, $P(j)$, 20% above its nominal marginal cost, $w/MPL(j)$. With $P(j)$ fixed, the increase in the nominal wage rate, w, and the decrease in the marginal product of labour, $MPL(j)$, cut into the mark-up ratio and lower it to, say, 1.1. Since the mark-up ratio is still above 1.0, the firm meets the extra demand for its good at the fixed price, $P(j)$. However, the firm would still like to have a mark-up ratio of 1.2. Therefore, at least eventually, the firm would restore this ratio by raising its price, $P(j)$.

When each firm j raises its price, $P(j)$, the overall price level, P, increases. Therefore, for a given nominal quantity of money, M, real money balances, M/P, decrease. This change reverses the initial effect, whereby M rose for fixed P, and, therefore, M/P increased. In Figure 17.1, the shift to the right in the labour demand curve came from the effect of the higher M/P on the demand for each firm's good, $Y(j)$. As P rises and M/P declines, the demand for each firm's good, $Y(j)$, comes back down. Hence, the labour demand curve shifts to the left, back towards its initial position. In the long run, P rises in the same proportion as M, and the labour demand curve is back where it started. Thus, in the long run, we get back to our familiar conclusion that a change in the nominal quantity of money, M, is neutral: there are no effects on real variables, including the real wage rate, w/P, labour input, L, and real GDP, Y.

Our conclusion is that the real effect of a monetary shock in the New Keynesian model is a short-run result that applies only as long as prices fail to adjust to their equilibrium levels. In this respect, the results are analogous to those from the price-misperceptions model from Chapter 16. In that context, the real effect of a monetary shock applied only in the short run as long as households failed to perceive fully the economy-wide changes in prices. Thus, a key issue for the price-misperceptions model was whether the slow adjustment of price expectations was quantitatively significant. In the New Keynesian model, the parallel issue is whether the slow adjustment of prices is quantitatively significant.

Recently available data, discussed in the By the Numbers box 'Evidence on the stickiness of prices' give us a great deal of information about the frequency of price adjustment at the microeconomic level. These data do reveal stickiness of some prices; that is, prices for some types of products often do not change for several months. However, a tentative conclusion from empirical research with these new data is that price stickiness is insufficient to explain a major part of economic fluctuations. Thus, this evidence suggests that the New Keynesian model, although useful, might not explain a large part of economic fluctuations.

By the Numbers
Evidence on the stickiness of prices

A study by Luis Álvarez et al. (2006) quantified the stickiness in prices of goods and services contained in the consumer price index (CPI) and the producer price index (PPI) in the Eurozone. The flexibility of prices varies greatly, depending on the type of good or service. For prices contained in the CPI, prices change most frequently in energy and unprocessed food, and least frequently in services. For prices contained in the PPI, prices change most frequently in energy and food, and least frequently in capital goods. Overall, firms in the Eurozone change their prices about once a year on average. An earlier study by Mark Bils and Peter Klenow (2004) quantified the stickiness in prices of goods and services contained in the consumer price index (CPI) in the United States and found a much shorter median duration of prices of about 4–5 months.[8]

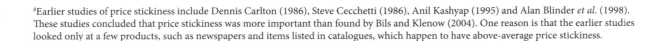

[8]Earlier studies of price stickiness include Dennis Carlton (1986), Steve Cecchetti (1986), Anil Kashyap (1995) and Alan Blinder et al. (1998). These studies concluded that price stickiness was more important than found by Bils and Klenow (2004). One reason is that the earlier studies looked only at a few products, such as newspapers and items listed in catalogues, which happen to have above-average price stickiness.

Mikhail Golosov and Robert Lucas (2006) used the Bils and Klenow findings to estimate how important the stickiness of prices is for US economic fluctuations. In the Golosov–Lucas model, one reason that firms want to change prices is individual shocks, which affect a specific firm's product demand or technology. For example, a rise in individual product demand motivates each firm to raise its relative price – $P(j)/P$ – in the model that we worked out before. The second reason to change prices is an economy-wide monetary disturbance. For example, an increase in the nominal quantity of money, M, motivates each firm to raise its nominal price, $P(j)$.

Both types of price change incur a menu cost. Because of these costs of changing prices, an individual firm does not always adjust its price, $P(j)$, in response to an individual shock or a monetary disturbance. Suppose that $[P(j)]^*$ represents a firm's 'ideal price', the price that would be chosen if menu costs were zero. Each firm will find it optimal to make a price change when $P(j)$ deviates substantially from $[P(j)]^*$. When a price change occurs, $P(j)$ will typically adjust by a substantial amount by an average of 7–8% upward or downward, as found by Emi Nakamura and Jon Steinsson (2006).

Golosov and Lucas construct a model that has an array of individual firms, each of which has the same menu cost for changing its price. (An extension to allow for differences in menu costs turns out not to affect the main results.) A higher menu cost motivates less frequent price changes. Golosov and Lucas assume that the menu cost takes on a value that generates a frequency of price change in the model that equals the average frequency found in the data by Bils and Klenow. Thus, in the Golosov–Lucas model of the economy, individual firms adjust their prices, on average, every 4–5 months.

One finding in the model is that, for this economy, individual shocks are responsible for most of the price changes. That is, most prices change in response to shifts in individual demand or technology, rather than economy-wide monetary shocks. The situation is different for an economy with high and variable inflation; Golosov and Lucas take Israel in the late 1970s and early 1980s as an example. In that high-inflation environment, most price changes occurred because of economy-wide monetary shocks.

In the Golosov–Lucas model, monetary shocks affect labour input and output, as in the New Keynesian model that we studied. However, it turns out that for an economy with low and stable inflation, observed monetary fluctuations account for only a small proportion of the observed fluctuations in real GDP. Golosov and Lucas conclude that, although money is non-neutral, monetary shocks play a minor role in economic fluctuations.

We can also use our analysis of price adjustment to see what the New Keynesian model predicts for the cyclical behaviour of the price level, P. When the nominal quantity of money, M, rose, P responded relatively little at first. Therefore, the expansion of real GDP, Y, was accompanied by little change in P. As P gradually increased, Y declined but remained above its initial level. Eventually, P rose in the same proportion as M, and, at that point, Y returned to its initial level. The upshot of this discussion is that Y is relatively high when P is relatively low.

We can also do the analysis in reverse, where a decrease in the nominal quantity of money, M, leads to a temporary decrease of real GDP, Y. In that case, we get that Y tends to be relatively low (e.g., just after the decrease in M) when P is relatively high.

Overall, the New Keynesian prediction is that the price level, P, tends to be relatively low during a boom – where real GDP, Y, is relatively high, and relatively high during a recession – where Y is relatively low. In other words, the model predicts that P is countercyclical. This prediction is the same as that in the equilibrium business-cycle model. As we saw in Chapter 11, the prediction for a countercyclical P accords with the data.

COMPARING PREDICTIONS FOR ECONOMIC FLUCTUATIONS

Table 17.1 extends Table 16.1 from Chapter 16 to include the cyclical predictions for five macroeconomic variables from the New Keynesian model. We can use Table 17.1 to compare these predictions with those from two alternative models – the equilibrium business-cycle model from Chapters 9–11 and the price-misperceptions model from Chapter 16 – and with the empirical patterns documented before.

Table 17.1 Cyclical patterns of macroeconomic variables in three models

	Nominal quantity of money, *M*	Price level, *P*	Labour input, *L*	Real wage rate, *w/P*	Average product of labour, *Y/L*
1. Equilibrium business-cycle model	procyclical	countercyclical	procyclical	procyclical	procyclical
2. Price-misperceptions model	procyclical	procyclical	procyclical	countercyclical	countercyclical
3. New Keynesian model	procyclical	countercyclical	procyclical	procyclical	countercyclical
4. Empirical observations	procyclical (weakly)	countercyclical	procyclical	procyclical	procyclical (weakly)

Note: This table extends Table 16.1 from Chapter 16. The cells show the cyclical patterns for five macroeconomic variables in four settings. First, is the equilibrium business-cycle model, with economic fluctuations driven by shocks to the technology level, *A* (described in Chapters 9–11). Second, is the price-misperceptions model from Chapter 16, with economic fluctuations driven by shocks to the nominal quantity of money, *M*. Third, is the New Keynesian model from this chapter, with economic fluctuations driven by shocks to *M*. Fourth, is the empirical pattern presented in Chapters 9 and 11.

Table 17.1 shows that, unlike the price-misperceptions model, the New Keynesian model correctly predicts a procyclical pattern for the real wage rate, *w/P*, and a countercyclical pattern for the price level, *P*. The one respect in which the New Keynesian model differs from the equilibrium business-cycle model and also deviates from the empirical pattern is for the average product of labour, *Y/L*. The New Keynesian model errs by predicting a counter-cyclical pattern for *Y/L*, although the idea of labour hoarding might fix this problem.

SHOCKS TO AGGREGATE DEMAND

Our discussion of the New Keynesian model focused on the economy's responses to an increase in the nominal quantity of money, *M*. A key part of the analysis was that each firm *j* experienced an increase in the demand for its goods, $Y^d(j)$, while its price, *P(j)*, was held fixed. The same results apply if $Y^d(j)$ rises for each firm *j* for reasons having nothing to do with money. The essential ingredient is an increase in the **aggregate demand** for goods.

One way for aggregate demand to rise is for households to shift exogenously away from current saving and towards current consumption, *C*. That is, households might become less thrifty for reasons not explained by the model.[9] The increase in consumer demand means that the typical firm *j* sees an increase in the demand for its goods, $Y^d(j)$. If the price level, *P*, is fixed in the short run, we can again use the analysis from Figure 17.1 to show that aggregate labour input, *L*, increases. Therefore, the increase in the aggregate demand for goods leads to an increase in real GDP, *Y*.

Another possibility is that the government could boost the aggregate demand for goods by increasing its real purchases, *G*. This expansion would again raise the demand, $Y^d(j)$, seen by the typical firm. As before, if the price level, *P*, is held fixed, labour input, *L*, and real GDP, *Y*, tend to rise.

The New Keynesian model has the property that an increase in the aggregate demand for goods may end up increasing real GDP, *Y*, by even more than the initial expansion of demand. That is, there may be a **multiplier** in the model – the rise in *Y* may be a multiple greater than 1.0 of the rise in demand.

The reasoning is that, at a fixed price level, *P*, the initial rise in the aggregate demand for goods leads to an equal-size increase in production, *Y*. This response applies if all firms have mark-up ratios significantly above 1.0 and are, therefore, willing to meet fully the extra demand at a fixed price. The expansion of *Y* leads to increases in real income, notably in real labour income, $(w/P) \cdot L$. This extra income motivates another increase in consumer demand, which adds to the demand for each firm's goods, $Y^d(j)$. The further increase in production, *Y*, in response to the additional demand generates the multiplier.

[9] The government might also stimulate consumer demand by cutting taxes. If households regard themselves as wealthier when taxes are cut – unlike the Ricardian case explored in Chapter 15 – current consumer demand would increase.

The Keynesian multiplier is an interesting theoretical result. However, economists have not verified empirically the existence of a multiplier. For example, we found in Chapter 13 that it was difficult to document an unambiguously positive effect from changes in government purchases, G, on real GDP, Y. The positive relation was clear only for the large temporary expansions of G during major wars. Moreover, even in these cases, the response of Y was less than the increase in G; that is, the multiplier was less than 1.

Money and nominal interest rates

In practice, central banks – such as the Bank of England – tend to express monetary policy as targets for short-term nominal interest rates, rather than monetary aggregates. In the United Kingdom, the Bank of England focuses on the official bank rate – the overnight nominal interest rate at which the Bank of England lends to commercial banks. The Bank of England's Monetary Policy Committee (MPC) meets 12 times per year. At each meeting, the MPC adopts a target for the official bank rate. Although monetary policy is not expressed in terms of monetary aggregates, adjustments of nominal interest rates nevertheless translate into changes in these aggregates.

In practice, a central bank uses open-market operations to achieve the desired target for its interest rate. Recall from Chapter 15 that open-market operations are exchanges between the monetary base (currency in circulation plus reserves held by depository institutions) and interest-bearing assets. These securities correspond to the bonds in our model. In an expansionary operation, the central bank creates a new monetary base to buy bonds. In a contractionary operation, the central bank sells bonds from its portfolio and uses the proceeds to reduce the monetary base.

The central idea is that, in the short run with sticky prices, open-market operations affect nominal interest rates – the official bank rate in the United Kingdom and the nominal interest rate, i, in our model. We can think of the relation between money and nominal interest rates from our familiar equilibrium condition in Chapter 11, whereby the nominal quantity of money, M, equals the nominal quantity demanded, $P \bullet D(Y, i)$:

$$M = P \bullet D(Y, i) \tag{17.8}$$

In our model, we have thought of M as nominal currency. Now, we should broaden the concept of M to the monetary base, which is the monetary aggregate affected directly by open-market operations. Through these operations, a central bank can control the quantity of monetary base on a day-by-day basis.

The equilibrium condition in equation (17.8) specifies a relationship between the nominal monetary base, M, and the determinants of the nominal quantity of money demanded: the price level, P; real GDP, Y; and the nominal interest rate, i. In the New Keynesian model, P is fixed in the short run. Thus, in the short run, if M increases, equilibrium requires some combination of higher Y or lower i to raise the nominal quantity of money demanded by the same amount as the increase in M. For a given Y, equation (17.8) says that a higher M has to match up with a lower i.

In our previous analysis, we thought of an expansionary monetary shock as an increase in the nominal quantity of money, M. Now, we can think of an expansionary monetary action as a decrease in the nominal interest rate, i.

If equation (17.8) were a fixed relationship, central banks could operate equivalently by changing the nominal quantity of money, M, or the nominal interest rate, i. However, in practice, the real quantity of money demanded, $D(Y, i)$, tends to fluctuate a great deal.[10] These fluctuations make it nearly impossible for central banks to designate in advance the precise time path for the monetary base or some other monetary aggregate needed to achieve a desired path for i. Such a designation would require knowledge about future quantities of real money demanded, $D(Y, i)$. Because this knowledge is unattainable, central banks tend not to conduct monetary policy by specifying

---

[10]As an example, we noted in Chapter 11 that the real quantity of money demanded has a great deal of seasonal variation. Central banks accommodate this seasonality by introducing an appropriate amount of seasonal variation in M. This seasonality in the monetary base avoids having seasonality in the nominal interest rate, i.

the path of a nominal monetary aggregate. More specifically, central banks have rejected proposals, originally put forward by Milton Friedman (1960, pp. 90–93), to have a **constant-growth-rate rule** for a designated monetary aggregate; Friedman's preferred candidates were M1 or M2. Such rules for money growth require i (or P or Y) to respond to each variation in the real quantity of money demanded.

Because of the shortcomings in rules based on monetary aggregates, central banks tend to frame their policies in terms of targeted adjustments in nominal interest rates, i. By targeting i, a central bank is led automatically to carry out the volume of open-market operations needed to obtain the required changes in the monetary base, M. For example, if the central bank wants to lower i, it raises M (through open-market operations) until the desired nominal interest rate prevails in the bond market. From equation (17.8), we know that the necessary increase in M equals the rise in real money demanded, $D(Y, i)$, caused by the fall in i (for given P and Y). However, an important point is that the central bank does not have to know the exact specification for $D(Y, i)$. It just keeps raising M until it sees the nominal interest rate that it wants.

As another example, suppose that the central bank does not want the nominal interest rate, i, to change, but that the real quantity of money demanded, $D(Y, i)$, increases. If the central bank kept M constant, i would have to rise to bring $D(Y, i)$ back down. Instead, the central bank raises M to balance the increase in $D(Y, i)$. (This adjustment is sometimes described as an *accommodation* of money demand.) Moreover, as in our previous example, the central bank does not have to know exactly how $D(Y, i)$ has changed. The central bank just keeps raising M (through open-market operations) until the nominal interest rate that prevails in the financial markets is the one that it wants – in this case, an unchanged i.

As we discussed in Chapter 16 and detailed in Table 16.2, since 1990, central banks in many countries, such as Hungary, Iceland, Israel, Norway, Poland, South Africa, Sweden and the United Kingdom, have adopted formal inflation-targeting procedures. In these regimes, nominal interest rates react to changes in the inflation rate; higher inflation induces higher nominal interest rates, and lower inflation induces lower nominal interest rates.

At this point, economists are confident that the response of monetary policy to inflation has been beneficial. That is, the success in curbing inflation derives from the policy of raising nominal interest rates sharply when the inflation rate rises and cutting rates sharply when the inflation rate falls. This policy can be expressed alternatively as having contractionary open-market operations when the inflation rate increases and expansionary open-market operations when the inflation rate decreases.

The benefits from adjusting nominal interest rates in response to other economic variables are less clear. That is, we do not know whether the economy has performed better or worse because a central bank has adjusted nominal interest rates in response to strength or weakness in the real economy, gauged particularly by the labour market.

The Keynesian model: Sticky nominal wage rates

As mentioned at the beginning of this chapter, the model in Keynes's (1936) *General Theory* relies on **sticky nominal wage rates**; that is, a failure of nominal wage rates to react rapidly to changed circumstances. To focus on the consequences of sticky nominal wage rates, we now simplify by assuming that prices of goods are perfectly flexible. Therefore, we can return to the model from previous chapters in which the suppliers and demanders of goods are perfect competitors. In this setting, the single nominal price, P, applies to all goods.

Keynes just assumed that the nominal wage rate, w, was sticky; that is, he assumed that w did not adjust rapidly to clear the labour market. Moreover, Keynes focused on a case in which w was higher than its market-clearing level. This assumption will imply (when we consider how the price level, P, is determined) that the real wage rate, w/P, will be above its market-clearing value.

In the Keynesian model, the labour market looks as shown in Figure 17.2. In this graph, the labour demand and supply curves are the same as those in our equilibrium business-cycle model (see Figure 9.13 in Chapter 9). Note that an increase in the real wage rate, w/P, lowers the quantity of labour demanded, L^d, but raises the quantity supplied, L^s. The only difference from before is that the nominal wage rate, w, is assumed not to adjust to generate the real wage rate, $(w/P)^*$, that balances the quantities of labour demanded and supplied. Instead, the prevailing real wage rate, $(w/P)'$, is greater than $(w/P)^*$.

At the real wage rate $(w/P)'$ shown on the vertical axis in Figure 17.2, the quantity of labour supplied is greater than the quantity demanded. Since the quantities supplied and demanded are unequal, we have to reconsider how the quantity of labour, L, is determined.

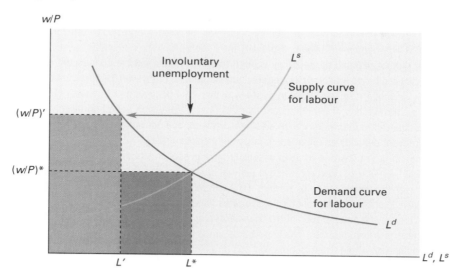

Figure 17.2 The labour market in the Keynesian model with sticky nominal wage rates

In the Keynesian model, the nominal wage rate, w', is fixed above its market-clearing value, w^*. Consequently, the real wage rate, $(w/P)'$, will be greater than the market-clearing value, $(w/P)^*$, on the vertical axis. At $(w/P)'$, the quantity of labour supplied, along the L^s curve, exceeds the quantity demanded, along the L curve. On the horizontal axis, the quantity of labour, L', equals the quantity demanded and is less than the market-clearing value, L^*.

Economics in Practice
Keynes and Friedman

John Maynard Keynes was a famous British economist who taught at Cambridge University. Important publications from 1919 to 1923 concerned German reparations payments and hyperinflation following World War I. His monumental work, *The General Theory of Employment, Interest, and Money*, appeared in 1936. This book worked out a new framework to provide remedies for economies caught up in the global depression of the 1930s. His model did not explain the origins of the Great Depression but did argue that market economies had a general tendency to experience persistently low aggregate output and persistently high unemployment rates. He argued that these poor aggregate outcomes could be improved by active fiscal policy – specifically, increases in government expenditure and cuts in taxes in response to a recession.

Although he discussed monetary policy, Keynes in the *General Theory* de-emphasized monetary shocks as a source of business fluctuations, and he downplayed monetary policy as an anti-recession device. In contrast, particularly since the 1980s, New Keynesian economists have embraced activist monetary policy as a centrepiece of countercyclical policy.

Whatever the merits of Keynes's model in the *General Theory*, there is no doubt about the extent of its intellectual influence. The *General Theory* essentially established macroeconomics as a distinct field of economics. Moreover, the term *Keynesian economics* is one of the most widely used phrases in the economics literature. The term refers to models in which government intervention at the macroeconomic level can help to improve the functioning of poorly performing market economies. Keynesian models typically assume, at least implicitly, that private markets can be trusted for microeconomic decisions; for example, how much to work and consume and which goods to buy and produce. The market failures in these models relate to aggregates, such as real GDP and overall employment. Correspondingly, the suggested government interventions are not microeconomic ones – such as controls on individual prices or detailed regulations of firms and households – but, rather, macroeconomic policies.

Milton Friedman, some of whose research we discussed in this and earlier chapters, was the only economist to rival Keynes for policy influence in the twentieth century. Friedman's main work appeared while he was at the University of Chicago; he is known as one of the pillars of the Chicago School of Economics. In contrast to Keynes, Friedman put the primary blame for the Great Depression from 1929 to 1933 on government failure, especially the Federal Reserve's monetary policy. The Fed did not respond aggressively enough to bank failures and the consequent sharp declines in broad monetary aggregates and the general price level. Documentation for this viewpoint is in the *Monetary History*, written by Friedman and Schwartz (1963). This interpretation of events meant that the Great Depression posed no dilemma for Friedman's broad preference for small government, and he found in the Fed's failures to prevent deflation an argument in favour of monetary rules.

Even today, there is no full consensus among economists on the sources of the Great Depression. However, there is general agreement that the monetary collapse – an aspect de-emphasized by Keynes – is a central part of the story. Many economists believe that the fall in monetary aggregates was particularly important because the accompanying deterioration of the financial sector led to collapses of credit and sharp increases in bankruptcies. The importance of the credit channel in explaining the size and duration of the Great Depression was stressed by the former chair of the Federal Reserve, Ben Bernanke, in his early research (Bernanke, 1983).

We use the principle that L equals the smaller of the quantities demanded and supplied – in this case, the quantity demanded, L^d. Hence, $L = L'$ on the horizontal axis. Labour input cannot be higher than this amount, because some demander of labour would then be forced to employ more labour than the quantity desired at the given real wage rate, $(w/P)'$. In other words, we assume that the labour market respects the rule of **voluntary exchange**. No market participant can be forced to hire more labour than the amount desired – or to work more than the amount desired – at the prevailing real wage rate.

Notice in Figure 17.2 that the quantity of labour supplied, L^s, at the given real wage rate, $(w/P)'$, is greater than the quantity demanded, L^d, which equals the quantity of labour, L'. The usual assumption about markets is that the nominal wage rate, w, would decline in this situation. That is, the eager suppliers of labour would compete for jobs by bidding down w. However, this response is ruled out by assumption in the Keynesian model, at least in the short run. The excess of the quantity of labour supplied (at the given real wage rate, $[w/P]'$) over L' is called **involuntary unemployment**. This amount is shown by the arrows in Figure 17.2. Involuntary unemployment is the difference between the quantity of labour that households would like at $(w/P)'$ (i.e., the quantity supplied, L^s) and the quantity that they actually get, L'.

Suppose, now, that a monetary expansion raises the price level, P. If the nominal wage rate, w, does not change, the rise in P lowers the real wage rate, w/P. We assume in Figure 17.3 that the increase in P reduces the real wage rate on the vertical axis from $(w/P)'$ to $(w/P)''$. This fall in w/P raises the quantity of labour demanded, L^d, and, thereby, increases labour input on the horizontal axis from L' to L''. Hence, in the model with sticky nominal wage rates, a monetary expansion raises labour input, L. The increase in L leads through the production function to an expansion of real GDP, Y.

As long as the nominal wage rate, w, is fixed, monetary expansions reduce the real wage rate, w/P, and raise labour input, L, through the mechanism shown in Figure 17.3. This process can continue until w/P falls to its market-clearing value, $(w/P)^*$, on the vertical axis. At that point, L reaches its market-clearing level, L^*, on the horizontal axis.[11]

---

[11]Further monetary expansion, with w still held fixed, would lower w/P below $(w/P)^*$. In this situation, the quantity of labour demanded, L^d, becomes larger than the quantity supplied, L^s. According to the principle of voluntary exchange, labour input, L, would then equal the quantity supplied, L^s. In this circumstance, reductions in w/P brought about by further monetary expansions would lower the quantity of labour supplied, L^s, and, thereby, reduce L. Thus, in the Keynesian model, too much monetary expansion would have adverse consequences.

Figure 17.3 Effect of monetary expansion in the Keynesian model with sticky nominal wage rates

In the Keynesian model, the nominal wage rate, w, is fixed above its market-clearing value, w^*. Therefore, on the vertical axis, the real wage rate, $(w/P)'$, is greater than the market-clearing value, $(w/P)^*$. On the horizontal axis, labour input, L', equals the quantity of labour demanded at $(w/P)'$. A monetary expansion raises the price level and, thereby, lowers the real wage rate to $(w/P)''$ on the vertical axis. On the horizontal axis, labour input rises to L', the quantity of labour demanded at $(w/P)''$. A sufficient monetary expansion would raise L up to the market-clearing value, L^*.

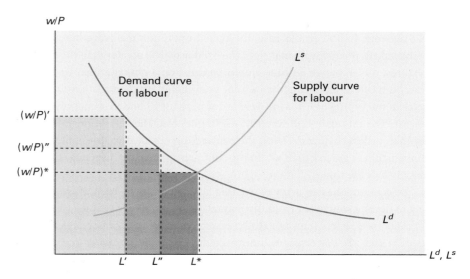

We see from Figure 17.3 that a monetary expansion raises labour input, L, and, thereby, real GDP, Y, by lowering the real wage rate, w/P. The Keynesian model is similar to the New Keynesian model in predicting that nominal money, M, and labour, L, would be procyclical. However, unlike the New Keynesian model, the Keynesian model predicts that w/P would be countercyclical – low when L and Y are high, and high when L and Y are low. We have stressed that w/P typically moves in a procyclical manner. Therefore, the Keynesian model has difficulty explaining the observed cyclical behaviour of w/P. In this respect, the model has the same flaw as the price-misperceptions model from Chapter 16.

Keynes himself recognized that his model had problems with respect to its predictions about the cyclical behaviour of the real wage rate, w/P. However, he did not come up with convincing solutions for this problem. One of the main motivations for the New Keynesian model – developed earlier in this chapter – is that it eliminates the counterfactual predictions for w/P. That is, as shown in Table 17.1, w/P is procyclical in the New Keynesian model. On the other hand, the New Keynesian model relies on sticky nominal prices, and many economists believe – like Keynes – that sticky nominal wage rates are more important in practice.

Long-term contracts and sticky nominal wage rates

For many workers, nominal wage rates are set for one or more years by the terms of agreements made with employers. These agreements are sometimes formal contracts between firms and labour unions. More commonly, firms and workers have implicit contracts that specify in advance the nominal wage rate over some period, often a fiscal or calendar year. The existence of these agreements has been offered as a defence for the Keynesian assumption that the nominal wage rate, w, is sticky. The contracting approach has also been used to explain why some nominal prices are sticky, for example, the prices of intermediate goods sold to businesses by regular suppliers.

There are many good reasons why trading partners would specify in advance the wage rates or prices on which services and goods will be exchanged. This presetting of wage rates or prices can prevent one party from demanding 'unreasonable' terms, *ex post*. That is, a wage or price agreement can alleviate what economists call the 'hold-up problem'. In the absence of a contract, an employer might, for example, lower the nominal wage rate after an employee has incurred substantial costs in moving to a job. Similarly, a supplier might raise the price for materials at a time when delays in a construction project are prohibitively expensive. Presetting the wage rate or price can avoid some of these problems.

Suppose that an employer and an employee agree on a fixed nominal wage rate, w, for the next year.[12] A natural choice is to set w equal to the best estimate of the average market-clearing nominal wage rate, w^*, that will prevail over the year. Although the chosen w may be a rational expectation of w^*, unanticipated events lead to mistakes. For example, if the inflation rate, π, is surprisingly high, the average price level, P, during the year will be higher than anticipated. If nothing else changes in the economy, the market-clearing nominal wage rate, w^*, would rise along with P to maintain the market-clearing real wage rate, $(w/P)^*$. In this case, the agreed-upon nominal wage rate, w, will fall short of the average w^* for the year. Conversely, if π is surprisingly low, the fixed w will be greater than the average w^* for the year.

When the contract expires, the employer and the employee agree on a new nominal wage rate, w, for the next year. This new w takes account of events during the current year, including the inflation rate, π. Thus, if expectations are rational, mistakes in the setting of w for this year – due perhaps to underestimation of inflation – tend not to be repeated the next year. The rationality of expectations implies also that deviations of w from w^* would not be systematically greater than or less than zero. Thus, the contracting perspective does not support the Keynesian emphasis on situations in which w is greater than w^*. In the contracting scenario, w greater than w^* and w less than w^* would each apply roughly half the time.

At any point in time, the economy has an array of existing labour contracts, each of which specifies a nominal wage rate, w, that is likely to deviate somewhat from the market-clearing value, w^*. Some of these agreements have w greater than w^*, and others have w less than w^*. However, aggregate shocks can create differences between the economy-wide averages of w and w^*. For example, unexpectedly low inflation tends to make w greater than w^* throughout the economy. Some macroeconomists have used this result to explain why a monetary contraction reduces employment and output. That is, the contracting approach has been used to fill a gap in the Keynesian model – explaining why the nominal wage rate, w, is sticky in the face of a monetary contraction.[13]

Unfortunately, this application of the contracting approach encounters logical problems. The Keynesian results emerge when the nominal wage rate, w, is fixed at too high a level *and* when the principle of voluntary exchange determines the quantity of labour, L. Suppose, for example, that w and, hence, w/P are too high, so that the quantity of labour supplied, L^s, is greater than the quantity demanded, L^d. In this case, voluntary exchange dictates that L equal the quantity demanded. This approach makes sense for an impersonal market. However, the idea is typically not applicable to a long-term contract, which is supposed to be the rationale for sticky nominal wage rates.

In an enduring relationship, in which explicit or implicit contracts arise, the trading parties do not have to change prices or wage rates at every instant to get the 'right' behaviour of quantities. Workers can, for example, agree in advance that they will work harder when there is more work to do – that is, when the demand for a firm's product is high – and work less hard when there is little work. Unlike in an impersonal auction market, these efficient adjustments in work and production can occur even if wage rates do not change from day to day.[14] The important point is that, in the context of labour contracts, stickiness of nominal wage rates does not necessarily cause errors in the determination of labour input and production.

To take a concrete example, suppose that inflation is sometimes lower than expected and sometimes higher. Rational firms and workers know that inflation – if not accompanied by real changes in the economy – does not alter the efficient levels of labour input and production. Therefore, it makes sense to agree on a contract that insulates the choices of labour input and production from the inflation rate. Over many years, when the effects of unanticipated

---

[12]The contracting approach motivates the presetting of a real wage rate, w/P, rather than a nominal wage rate, w. Yet, most labour agreements in advanced economies are not explicitly 'indexed'; that is, they do not contain automatic adjustments of nominal wage rates for changes in the price level, P. Apparently, firms and workers find it convenient to specify agreements in terms of the standard nominal unit of account – such as the euro – even though the future price level is uncertain. There is evidence, however, that higher and more variable inflation tends to generate shorter contracts and more frequent use of formal indexation of nominal wage rates.

[13]The original applications of the contracting approach to macroeconomics were by Donald Gordon (1974), Costas Azariadis (1975) and Martin Baily (1974). Applications to monetary shocks were made by Jo Anna Gray (1976), Stanley Fischer (1977) and John Taylor (1980).

[14]However, for large short-term increases in labour input, contracts often prescribe overtime premiums or other types of bonuses.

By the Numbers
Empirical evidence on the contracting approach

A number of empirical studies provide evidence about the macroeconomic implications of the contracting approach. Shaghil Ahmed (1987) used a data set for 19 industries in Canada over the period 1961–74. He used these data because an earlier study by David Card (1980) calculated the extent of **indexation**– automatic adjustment of nominal wage rates for changes in the price level – in each industry's labour contracts. Indexation ranged from zero to nearly 100%. According to theories in which labour contracts are the basis for the Keynesian model, industries with little indexation should show substantial responses of real wage rates and, hence, of employment and output, to nominal shocks. Industries with a great deal of indexation would be affected little by nominal disturbances.

Ahmed found that monetary shocks had positive effects on hours worked in most of the 19 industries. The important point for present purposes, however, is that the extent of an industry's response to these shocks bore no relation to the amount of indexation in the industry. Those with considerable indexation were as likely as those with little indexation to respond to monetary shocks. This finding is damaging to theories that use long-term contracts as the basis for the Keynesian sticky-wage model.

A study by Giovanni Olivei and Silvana Tenreyro (2007) suggests that the contracting approach may be important for understanding the real effects of monetary policy. They first observed that a preponderance of firms set wage rates towards the end of each calendar year, with the changes taking effect in January of the next year. In the contracting approach, this timing means that monetary disturbances that occur towards the end of the calendar year would be undone within a few months by the changes of wage rates in the next annual adjustment. In contrast, monetary disturbances early in the calendar year would take up to 12 months to be undone by the next adjustment.

Using this conceptual framework, Olivei and Tenreyro investigate whether the response of real GDP to monetary shocks looks different depending on the quarter of the year in which the shock occurs. They measure the shocks by unusual movements in the Federal Funds rate – the overnight nominal interest rate in the Federal Funds market, which comprises financial institutions, such as commercial banks. The unusual movements are those that cannot be explained by prior variations in real GDP, the GDP deflator and commodity prices. The main finding, for the period 1966 to 2002, was that the response of real GDP to a Funds-rate shock is substantial when the shock takes place in the first or second quarter of the year. A decline in the interest rate by one-quarter of a percentage point is estimated to raise real GDP by 0.2% over the following two years. However, the response is smaller if the shock to the Funds rate occurs in the third or fourth quarter of the year. In that case, a decrease in the Funds rate by one-quarter of a percentage point is estimated to raise real GDP by less than 0.1% over the following two years. Olivei and Tenreyro suggest that the difference in response arises because nominal wage rates tend to be sticky during the calendar year but flexible from the end of one calendar year to the beginning of the next.

inflation on real wage rates tend to average out, both parties to the contract would benefit from this provision. However, in an economic climate where inflation is high and unpredictable, firms and workers prefer either to index nominal wage rates to the price level, or to renegotiate contracts more frequently.

An important lesson from the contracting approach is that stickiness of the nominal wage rate, w, need not lead to the unemployment and underproduction that appears in the Keynesian model. Within a long-term agreement, it is unnecessary for w to move all the time in order for the economy to approximate the market-clearing quantity of labour, L^*. Thus, instead of supporting the Keynesian perspective, the contracting analysis demonstrates that observed stickiness of nominal wage rates may not matter very much for the workings of the macroeconomy. This reasoning applies also to the sticky prices in the New Keynesian model if we try to explain this price stickiness not from literal menu costs but, instead, from contractual agreements – for example, between producers and their suppliers.

Summing Up

In Chapter 16, we began our study of the non-neutrality of money by focusing on price misperceptions. In this chapter, we have considered another source of monetary non-neutrality: the stickiness of nominal prices and wage rates. This stickiness reflects costs of changing prices and wages.

The New Keynesian model features stickiness in prices of goods. In a setting of imperfect competition, individual firms set prices as mark-ups over nominal marginal costs of production. If prices are fixed in the short run, firms meet expansions of demand – over some range – by raising production and labour input. Therefore, a monetary expansion increases the economy-wide quantity of labour demanded. The boost to labour demand raises the real wage rate and, if the labour-supply curve slopes upward, the quantity of labour input. This expansion of labour allows for an increase in real GDP. The model thereby predicts that nominal money, labour and the real wage rate will be procyclical. The prediction for procyclical real wage rates – which is consistent with the data – distinguishes this model from the price-misperceptions model. However, the New Keynesian model has the counterfactual prediction that the average product of labour will be countercyclical. The idea of labour hoarding has been offered to eliminate this error.

An older-style Keynesian model relied on sticky nominal wage rates. If the nominal wage rate is typically too high, the quantity of labour supplied tends to exceed the quantity demanded. Employment equals the quantity demanded, and the shortfall from the quantity supplied equals the amount of involuntary unemployment. In this setting, a monetary expansion lowers the real wage rate, thereby raising the quantity of labour demanded and, hence, the level of employment. However, this model predicts, counterfactually, that the real wage rate will be countercyclical.

Key Terms and Concepts

aggregate demand	indexation	mark-up ratio	sticky prices
constant-growth-rate rule	involuntary unemployment	menu cost	voluntary exchange
imperfect competition	labour hoarding	multiplier	
	marginal cost of production	sticky nominal wage rates	

Questions and Problems

A   Review questions

1   Explain how an increase in the nominal quantity of money, M, reduces the nominal interest rate, i, in the New Keynesian model. Why does this effect not arise in the market-clearing model?

2   What is involuntary unemployment?

B   Problems for discussion

3   Sticky-wage models

How does the model with sticky nominal wage rates differ from the New Keynesian model? What are the relative strengths of the two kinds of models? Why do you think that Keynes emphasized sticky nominal wages, rather than sticky prices?

4   Perceived wealth in the New Keynesian model

Suppose a study finds that we are all wealthier than we thought. If we all believe in the finding of this study, what does the New Keynesian model predict for changes in real GDP, Y, and labour, L? Do we actually end up being 'wealthier'? Contrast these predictions with those from the equilibrium business-cycle model.

5   The paradox of thrift

Suppose that households become thriftier in the sense that they decide to raise current saving and reduce current consumer demand.

a   In the New Keynesian model, what happens to real GDP, Y, and labour, L?

b   What happens to the amount of saving? If it decreases, there is said to be a *paradox of thrift*.

c   Can there be a paradox of thrift in the equilibrium business-cycle model?

6   The New Keynesian model
   a   What are the main differences between the
       New Keynesian model and the equilibrium
       business-cycle model?
   b   Does a change in the nominal quantity
       of money, M, have real effects in the New
       Keynesian model? Is imperfect competition
       among producers sufficient to generate
       non-neutrality of money in this model?
   c   How does the New Keynesian model explain
       sticky prices?
   d   What does the New Keynesian model predict
       for the cyclical behaviour of the real wage rate
       and the average product of labour? Are the
       results consistent with the data?
   e   Are money-supply shocks the only kind
       of shocks that have real effects in the New
       Keynesian model? What other shocks have
       real effects in this model?
   f   What are the relative strengths of the New
       Keynesian and equilibrium business-cycle
       models?

7   The Keynesian multiplier
       Explain why there can be a multiplier in the
   New Keynesian model. How is the size of the
   multiplier affected by the following:
   a   adjustments of the price level, P?
   b   the extent to which mark-up ratios exceed
       1.0?
   c   reactions of the nominal quantity of money
       demanded, M^d, to real GDP, Y?
       Can there be a multiplier in the equilibrium
       business-cycle model?

International macroeconomics

PART VII

18 World markets in goods and credit

Thus far, we have carried out our analysis for a single, closed economy. Therefore, we have neglected the interactions among countries on international markets. Many macroeconomists, especially those in the United States, focus on a closed-economy framework. One justification is that the US economy is the largest economy in the world and represents a large share of the world economy, which really is a closed economy (if we neglect trade with Mars). Another rationale for the neglect of world markets, applicable particularly to the 1950s and 1960s, was that various restrictions inhibited the flows of goods and credit from one country to another. In particular, for the United States, the share of gross domestic product (GDP) that entered into international trade was not large.

With the opening up of international markets – often termed globalization – over the last 50 years, the practice of ignoring the rest of the world became increasingly unsatisfactory, even for the US economy. The ratio of US imports to GDP rose from 4.2% in 1960 to 16.5% in 2013, while the ratio of exports to GDP increased from 5% to 13.5%. The years from the mid-1980s through 2013 also featured large US borrowing from foreigners.

To study international trade, we have to extend our model to the world economy, which comprises many countries. We carry out the analysis from the perspective of a *home country*. To simplify, we think of the rest of the world as a single entity, which we call the *foreign country*. (The existence of many foreign countries will not affect our main results.) Residents of the home country buy goods and services from foreigners (imports) and sell goods and services to foreigners (exports). Residents of the home country also borrow from and lend to foreigners.

Sometimes, we assume that the home country has a negligible effect on the equilibrium in the rest of the world. This assumption is satisfactory if the home country is a minor part of the world economy. The European Union and the United States are an intermediate case between a small open economy and the world economy, which is a closed economy. That is, an economy such as the European Union and the United States is large enough to have a noticeable effect on the equilibrium of world markets.

We begin with a number of unrealistic assumptions, which we can later relax. Assume, first, that the goods produced in each country are physically identical. In addition, suppose that transport costs and barriers to trade across national borders are small enough to neglect. Finally, pretend that, instead of using their own money, all countries use a common currency, such as the euro or the US dollar. The idea of a common currency is that the households and businesses in each country use a single type of money and measure all prices in terms of this money. To be specific, we assume that the residents of each country hold money as euros and quote prices in units of euros.

Given these assumptions, goods in all countries must sell at the same euro price, P. If prices differed, households would want to buy all goods at the lowest price and sell all goods at the highest price. Thus, in an equilibrium where goods are bought and sold in all locations, all prices must be the same. This result is the simplest version of the law of one price. The idea of this law is that markets work to ensure that the same good sells at the same price for all buyers and sellers in all locations. We also simplify by ignoring inflation, so that the price level, P, is constant over time.

Suppose that the nominal interest rate for year t in the home country is i_t. Since we neglect inflation, the real interest rate, r_t, equals i_t. Suppose that the nominal interest rate in the rest of the world is i_t. Since we also neglect inflation in the rest of the world, the foreign real rate, r_t, equals i_t. In our previous analysis, we neglected differences among borrowers in creditworthiness. Now, we will go further, to neglect differences in creditworthiness between households in the home country and households in the foreign country. Furthermore, we assume that no transaction costs exist for carrying out financial exchanges across international borders. Given these assumptions, world credit markets would have to function effectively as a single market with a single nominal interest rate. That is, we have:

$$i_t = i_t^f$$

home nominal interest rate = foreign nominal interest rate

and

$$r_t = r_t^f$$

home real interest rate = foreign real interest rate

The nominal and real interest rates are the same for lenders and borrowers in the home and foreign country.

The balance of international payments

As before, the total output of goods and services in the home country is the real GDP, Y_t. When the country was closed to the rest of the world, Y_t had to equal the total real domestic expenditure on goods and services, which is the sum of consumption, C_t, gross investment, I_t, and real government purchases, G_t:

Closed economy:
$$Y_t = C_t + I_t + G_t$$

real GDP = real domestic expenditure (18.1)

Imagine that the home economy is closed initially and, therefore, satisfies equation (18.1). If the home country opens up to the rest of the world, its real GDP, Y_t, may differ from its real domestic expenditure, $C_t + I_t + G_t$. An excess of Y_t over $C_t + I_t + G_t$ adds to the home country's claims on the rest of the world, whereas a shortfall of Y_t from $C_t + I_t + G_t$ adds to the home country's debts to the rest of the world.

Let B_t^f be the net nominal holdings of foreign assets by the home country at the end of year t. These assets or debts could be held by the home country's households or government. We think of these assets as bonds, but they could also be ownership rights in capital. The addition to the home country's ownership of capital located in the rest of the world is called **foreign direct investment**.

In the national accounts, B_t^f is called the **net international investment position** of the home country. Note that B_t^f is a stock variable, analogous to the stock of government bonds, B_t^g. An excess of year t's real GDP, Y_t, over year t's real domestic expenditure, $C_t + I_t + G_t$, adds to the real net international investment position from the end of the previous year, B_{t-1}^f/P, whereas a shortfall subtracts from B_{t-1}^f/P.

The home country earns asset income on its net international investment position. Since all assets pay the same real interest rate, the net real asset income received in year t is:[1]

---

[1] In the national accounts, this term is part of the real **net factor income from abroad**. That is, $r_{t-1} \cdot B_{t-1}^f/P$ corresponds to real rental income less depreciation on the home country's net capital owned abroad. The net factor income from abroad also includes labour income – wage income of home residents working abroad less wage income of foreign residents working in the home country. In the model, we are assuming that all home residents work in the home country, and all foreign residents work abroad. For the United States, the net labour income from abroad is small compared with GDP. For countries that export many workers to other places, such as El Salvador, Mexico and Turkey, the net labour income from abroad is substantial in relation to GDP. Countries such as Germany and the Persian Gulf states, which import many 'guest workers' from other countries, have a sizeable negative net labour income from abroad.

$$net\ real\ asset\ income\ from\ abroad = r_{t-1} \bullet B^f_{t-1}/P \tag{18.2}$$

where r_{t-1} is the worldwide real interest rate on assets held at the end of year $t - 1$. The total real income of domestic residents in year t is the sum of real GDP, Y_t, and the net real asset income from abroad, $r_{t-1} \bullet B^f_{t-1}$. This total is called the **real gross national product (real GNP)**:

$$real\ GNP = Y_t + r_{t-1} \bullet B^f_{t-1}/P$$
$$real\ GNP = real\ GDP + net\ real\ asset\ income\ from\ abroad \tag{18.3}$$

The real GNP, $Y_t + r_{t-1} \bullet B^f_{t-1}$, determines the total sources of funds for the home country in year t. The uses of funds consist of real domestic expenditure on goods and services, $C_t + I_t + G_t$, and the change in the real value of the net international investment position, $(B^f_t - B^f_{t-1})/P$. This last term is called **net foreign investment**, because it represents the net acquisition of claims by the home country on the rest of the world. Thus, the budget constraint for an open economy is:[2]

> **Key equation (budget constraint for an open economy):**
>
> $$C_t + I_t + G_t + (B^f_t - B^f_{t-1})/P = Y_t + r_{t-1} \bullet B^f_{t-1}/P$$
>
> *real domestic expenditure + net foreign investment = real GNP on goods and services* (18.4)

For later purposes, we shall find it useful to express the budget constraint for an open economy in some alternative forms. If we move the real domestic expenditure on goods and services, $C_t + I_t + G_t$, from the left-hand side of equation (18.4) to the right-hand side, we get a result called the **balance of international payments**:

> **Key equation (balance of international payments):**
>
> $$(B^f_t - B^f_{t-1})/P = Y_t + r_{t-1} \bullet B^f_{t-1}/P - (C_t + I_t + G_t)$$
>
> *net foreign investment = real GNP − real domestic expenditure*
>
> *net foreign investment = real current-account balance* (18.5)

The right-hand side of equation (18.5) is the difference between real GNP and real domestic expenditure, and is called the real **current-account balance**. If the current-account balance is greater than zero, the home country is said to have a **current-account surplus**. If the balance is less than zero, the home country has a **current-account deficit**. If the balance equals zero, the home country has a **balance on current account**.

Equation (18.5) tells us that the real current-account balance equals net foreign investment. Therefore, if the current account is in surplus, net foreign investment is greater than zero, and the home country's net international investment position rises over time. Conversely, if the current account is in deficit, net foreign investment is less than zero, and the net international investment position falls over time. Note that the current-account balance and net foreign investment are flows. These flows determine how a stock variable – the net international investment position – changes over time.

We will find it useful to relate the balance of international payments to exports and imports. Exports are the goods and services produced in the home country that are sold to the rest of the world, and imports are the goods and services produced by the rest of the world that are bought by the home country. The difference between exports and imports, or net exports, is called the **trade balance**.[3] The trade balance equals the goods and services produced domestically,

---

[2]We have neglected transfers, such as foreign aid, from one country to another. If the home country makes net transfers to the rest of the world, the real amount of these transfers is a use of funds that adds to real domestic expenditure, $C_t + I_t + G_t$, on the left-hand side of equation (18.4).
[3]Some definitions of the trade balance consider only trade in goods. However, in practice, the distinction between goods and services is not so useful economically. For example, exports of services in the forms of transport, computer programming, and financial consulting are not economically so different from exports of steel or wheat.

which is the real GDP, Y_t, less the total of real domestic expenditure on goods and services, $C_t + I_t + G_t$. If Y_t is greater than $C_t + I_t + G_t$, the excess of the goods and services produced at home but not purchased at home must be going as net exports to the rest of the world. Similarly, if Y_t is less than $C_t + I_t + G_t$, the excess of the goods and services purchased at home but not produced at home must be coming as net imports from the rest of the world, so that net exports are less than zero. We therefore have that the trade balance, which equals exports minus imports, is given by:

$$trade\ balance = Y_t - (C_t + I_t + G_t)$$

$$trade\ balance = real\ GDP - real\ domestic\ expenditure \tag{18.6}$$

The trade balance is positive – or in surplus – if exports exceed imports, and negative – or in deficit – if imports exceed exports.

We can rearrange the terms in equation (18.5) to get another way to express the current-account balance:

Key equation (current-account balance and trade balance):

$$(B_t^f - B_{t-1}^f)/P = Y_t - (C_t + I_t + G_t) + r_{t-1} \cdot (B_{t-1}^f/P)$$

$$real\ current\text{-}account\ balance = trade\ balance + net\ real\ asset\ income\ from\ abroad \tag{18.7}$$

Thus, the real current-account balance differs from the trade balance by the net real asset income from abroad.

Suppose that the home country experiences a current-account surplus for a long time and, therefore, builds up a positive net international investment position with respect to the rest of the world, B_{t-1}^f/P. The net real asset income from abroad, $r_{t-1} \cdot (B_{t-1}^f/P)$, is then greater than zero, and equation (18.7) says that the current-account balance is greater than the trade balance. In other words, the home country can have a zero current-account balance even if its exports fall short of its imports, so that the trade balance is in deficit. The country pays for its excess imports with its net real asset income from abroad.

History of the UK current-account balance

Figure 18.1 shows the ratio of the nominal UK current-account balance to nominal GDP from 1772 to 2014. The main long-term pattern was a current-account surplus for most years before World War I, with a deficit emerging during World Wars I and II. The deficit was particularly large during World War II. The current account was roughly

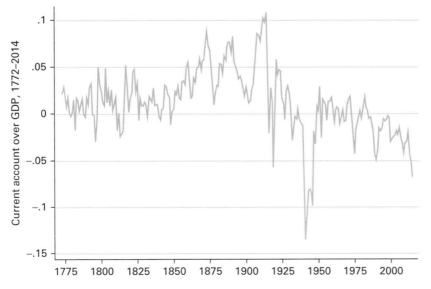

Figure 18.1 Ratio of UK current-account balance to GDP, 1772–2014

The graph shows the ratio of the nominal current-account balance to nominal GDP. The data on the current-account balance are from Three Centuries of Macroeconomic Data from the Bank of England (2015).

balanced from the end of the war to around 1985, when a persistent deficit emerged. The deficit over GDP from 1985 to 2014 has averaged 2.4%.

The upper part of Figure 18.2 shows the ratios of nominal exports and imports of goods and services to nominal GDP. These ratios illustrate the changing significance of international trade for the UK economy. The ratios averaged over 15% after the start of the Napoleonic Wars to the middle of the nineteenth century; over 30% for 1850–1914; and only 20 to 26% in the interwar period, 1921–40. After World War II, the ratios of exports and imports to GDP expanded to their previous ratios, remaining relatively stable thereafter.

The lower part of Figure 18.2 shows the ratio of the trade balance – nominal exports less nominal imports – to GDP. The variations in this ratio account for the main movements in the ratio of the current-account balance to GDP, shown in Figure 18.1. In particular, the large trade deficits account for the large current-account deficits emerging during World War II and those emerging since the late 1990s.

As discussed before, the current-account balance determines the change over time in the net international investment position. Figure 18.3 shows estimated values of this position, expressed as a ratio to GDP, from 1966 to 2014 for the United States and the United Kingdom. The available data start only in 1966 for the UK (1976 for the USA) because changes in the international investment position involve not only the current-account balance, shown in Figure 18.1, but also variations in the prices of assets and liabilities held in these two countries and in foreign countries. A substantial part of these price changes involve fluctuations in exchange rates, which we will discuss in Chapter 19.

The time patterns of the two countries are very similar. The ratio of the US net international investment position to GDP was 4.5% in 1976 increasing to peak at 10.6% in 1980 and decreasing thereafter to reach a staggering –40.7% in 2014. In the UK, the ratio of net international investment position to GDP was 3.2% in 1966, peaking at 21.1% in 1986 and declining thereafter. Although the year-to-year fluctuations depended on changes in prices of assets and liabilities, the main long-term influence was the current-account deficit (Figure 18.1). The net international investment position became negative in the 1990s and reached a staggering –24.1% of GDP in 2014.

Figure 18.2 Ratios of UK exports and imports to GDP, 1816–2014

The upper graphs show the ratios of nominal exports (dark blue) and imports (light blue) of goods and services to nominal GDP. The black graph shows the ratio of the trade balance (nominal exports less nominal imports) to nominal GDP. The data are from the Bank of England's Three Centuries of Macroeconomic Data (www.bankofengland.co.uk).

Figure 18.3 Ratio of US and UK net international investment position to GDP

These data are from the Office for National Statistics and the Bureau of Labor Statistics for the UK and USA, respectively. Changes in the net UK international investment position reflect the current-account balance (Figure 18.1) and also changes in dollar or pound prices of assets and liabilities held in the United States or United Kingdom and in foreign countries.

In our model, the net real asset income from abroad is the product of the real interest rate, r, and the net international investment position. Therefore, for given r, the net real asset income is high when the net international investment position is high, and vice versa.

Figure 18.4 shows UK net asset income from abroad, expressed as a ratio to GDP. (The variable used, the net factor income from abroad, includes a small amount of net labour income.) The ratio peaked around 2005, corresponding to a correction in the ratio for the net international investment position in Figure 18.3. The ratio for net asset income in Figure 18.4 fell from 1955 to 1980, reaching –1%. A puzzle emerges from 1999 to 2005, because net asset income varied between 0% and 2.5% of GDP, despite the large negative net international investment position during the same period. In particular, the net asset income remained positive in every year. The puzzle is also present in the 1980s: despite the positive net international investment position, around 20% of GDP in 1986, the ratio of net factor income remained between 0 and –1% of GDP. Mechanically, one reason for the outcome in the 2000s is that the rate of return on UK holdings of foreign assets has been higher than that on foreign holdings of UK assets. This was no longer the case more recently, as the net factor income turned negative in 2013. This was mainly due to huge negative returns on foreign direct investment abroad.

A similar pattern emerged for the USA starting in 1987. One reason for the low rate of return on foreign holdings of US assets is that a large and growing part of these holdings was in low-yielding US Treasury bonds. Most of these securities were held by foreign central banks, notably in Asia. In contrast, US holdings of foreign assets were concentrated more on stocks and direct investments in foreign companies, and these assets yielded higher returns. This set-up seems to be a good deal for the United States. The question is, why are foreigners willing to hold so much of their assets in low-yielding US securities – and will they continue to do so forever?

Figure 18.5 shows the last part of the UK current-account balance, the ratio to GDP of net UK transfers to foreigners. These transfers, omitted in equation (18.7), enter negatively into the UK current-account balance. The net UK transfers abroad were less than zero in almost all years since 1955, averaging –0.6% of GDP. The positive spike in the late 1940s – more than 1% of GDP – represents the large giving to World War II allies.

Figure 18.4   Ratio of UK net factor income from abroad to GDP, 1946–2014

Net factor income payments are income paid by foreigners to domestic capital and labour, less income paid by domestic residents to foreign capital and labour. The graph shows the ratio of the net factor income from abroad to nominal GDP. The data are from the Office for National Statistics (http://www.ons.co.uk).

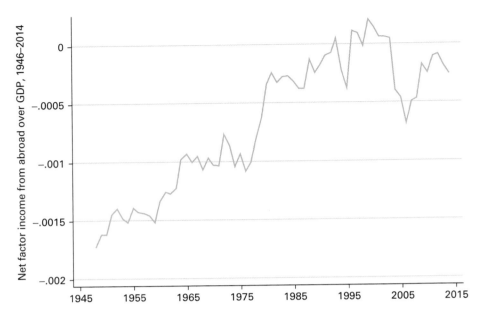

Figure 18.5   Ratio of net UK transfers abroad to GDP, 1946–2014

The graph shows the ratio of net nominal transfers abroad to nominal GDP. The positive spike in the late 1940s represents the large transfers to UK World War II allies. The data are from the Office for National Statistics (http://www.ons.co.uk).

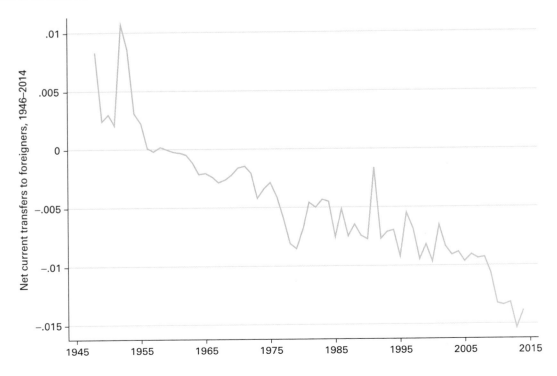

Determinants of the current-account balance

A primary purpose of our extension to a world economy is to understand changes in the current-account balance. We begin this analysis by extending our equilibrium business-cycle model to an open economy. To simplify, we neglect the extension from Chapter 10 to allow for a variable capital utilization rate, κ. In this case, we represent the input of capital services, κK, by the capital stock, K. Therefore, the production function is:

$$Y_t = A \bullet F(K, L_t) \tag{18.8}$$

As usual, we treat K as fixed in the short run.

To get a baseline for comparison, suppose, first, that the home economy is closed to the rest of the world. Since the economy is closed, we can use our previous analysis of the equilibrium business-cycle model to determine real GDP, Y_t, consumption, C_t, and gross domestic investment, I_t. Real GDP, Y_t, has to equal the total real expenditure on goods and services, as in equation (18.1):

$$Y_t = C_t + I_t + G_t \tag{18.1}$$

Since the market for capital services clears, the real rental price, $(R/P)_t$, equals the marginal product of capital, MPK (evaluated at the given capital stock, K). The real rate of return on capital equals $(R/P)_t$ minus the depreciation rate, δ. Since the real interest rate on bonds, r_t, has to equal the real rate of return on capital, we have:

$$r_t = MPK - \delta$$

real rate of return on bonds = real rate of return from owning capital $\tag{18.9}$

What happens if this closed economy gets access to the world credit market? We assumed earlier that the world credit market operates effectively as a single market. Consequently, the real interest rate in the home country has to be brought into equality with the real interest rate in the rest of the world.

Suppose, to begin, that the real interest rate in the rest of the world, r^f, is constant and happens to equal the real interest, r_t, determined in equation (18.9). That is, the home country would, if closed to the rest of the world, have the real interest rate $r_t = r^f$. In this case, the opening up to the world credit market would not change the real interest rate available to the home country's households. Therefore, decisions about consumption, saving, labour supply, and so on would not change. Consequently, the home country would end up with the same real GDP, Y_t, consumption, C_t, gross domestic investment, I_t, and so on. Therefore, the condition $Y_t = C_t + I_t + G_t$ would continue to hold in equation (18.1). We see, accordingly, that the trade balance would be zero:

$$trade\ balance = Y_t - (C_t + I_t + G_t)$$

$$trade\ balance = 0 \tag{18.6}$$

Recall that we add the net real asset income from abroad to the trade balance to get the real current-account balance:

$$(B_t^f - B_{t-1}^f)/P = Y_t - (C_t + I_t + G_t) + r_{t-1} \bullet (B_{t-1}^f/P)$$

real current-account balance = trade balance + net real asset income from abroad $\tag{18.7}$

Since the home country had initially been closed, it must have started with a zero net international investment position, $B_{t-1}^f = 0$. Therefore, the net real asset income from abroad is zero. Since the trade balance is also zero, we have that the current-account balance is zero. Therefore, although the home country has the opportunity to borrow and lend on the world credit market, this option is not exercised in equilibrium. However, this conclusion depends on our assumption that r_t, the real interest rate that the home country would have if it were closed, equals r^f.

To see how the world credit market can be important, start from the situation we have just described. Then assume that the technology level, A, in the home country rises, while the technology level in the rest of the world does not change. The increase in A raises the home MPK, evaluated at the given capital stock, K. Therefore, if the home country were a closed economy, the real interest rate, r_t, would rise, as indicated by equation (18.9).[4] If the home economy is a negligible part of the world economy, the foreign real interest rate, r^f, would not change.[5] Hence, the real interest rate, r_t, that the home country would have if it were closed is now greater than r^f.

What happens if the home country's real interest rate, r_t, rises above the foreign rate, r^f? Since we assumed that households and governments view all asset claims as equivalent, foreigners would want to do all of their lending in the home country, whereas domestic residents would want to do all of their borrowing abroad. Clearly, this response would not be an equilibrium. To see how markets come into equilibrium, we have to add something to our model.

Equation (18.9) says that the home country's real interest rate, r_t, must equal the rate of return on capital in the home country, MPK − δ. The rise in the home country's technology level, A, raises the MPK and, therefore, tends to raise r_t above the foreign rate, r^f (since $r_t = r^f$ applied initially). Since this divergence cannot apply in equilibrium, something has to give. Specifically, if r does not change (because the home country is small) and $r_t = r^f$ still holds, the rate of return on capital at home, MPK − δ, has to come back down to its initial value. The problem is that, if we treat the stock of capital at home, K, as fixed in the short run – that is, if we neglect the contribution of the current flow of net domestic investment to the stock of capital – there is no way for a rise in A not to increase the MPK.

One way that economists resolve this problem is to bring in **adjustment costs for investment**. The flow of net domestic investment (equal to gross investment, I_t, less depreciation, δK_{t-1}) leads over time to increases in the stock of capital, K_t, which appears as new plant and equipment. Businesses incur costs – called adjustment costs – for expanding the plant and equipment used in production. These costs effectively subtract from the rate of return on investment. Therefore, a large enough flow of gross investment, I_t, brings the rate of return on investment in the home country down to equal the given foreign real interest rate, r^f. Through this mechanism, an increase in the home country's technology level, A, motivates the home country to borrow a finite amount from foreigners to finance a high, but finite, flow of gross investment, I_t. To study the main effects on the current-account balance, we do not have to go through the details of this analysis. The main point is that an increase in the home MPK leads to a high, but finite, flow of gross domestic investment, I_t.

To see the effects of an increase in the technology level, A, on the current-account balance, go back to the definition:

$$(B_t^f - B_{t-1}^f)/P = Y_t - (C_t + I_t + G_t) + r_{t-1} \cdot (B_{t-1}^f/P)$$

real current-account balance = trade balance + net real asset income from abroad   (18.7)

On the right-hand side, the net real asset income, $r_{t-1} \cdot (B_{t-1}^f/P)$, is given – for example, at zero if the home country starts with a zero net international investment position, B_{t-1}^f/P. Real government purchases, G_t, are also given. The higher A raises the MPK and thereby increases gross domestic investment, I_t. This change reduces the current-account balance; that is, it moves it towards deficit. The question is, what happens to the difference between real GDP and consumption, $Y_t - C_t$?

We know that the increase in the technology level, A, raises real GDP, Y_t. This change reflects partly the direct impact of A on the production function and partly an effect from increased labour input, L_t. We know from Chapter 8 that the response of C_t depends on the strength of the income effect. If the change in A is permanent, C_t will rise by roughly as much as Y_t, so that $Y_t - C_t$ does not change.[6] In this case, we see from equation (18.7) that the current-account balance falls overall because of the increase in I_t.

We can gain insight into this result by considering real national saving. The total real income of the home country is real GNP, $Y_t + r_{t-1} \cdot (B_{t-1}^f/P)$, less depreciation of capital, δK_{t-1}. That is, real income equals real net national product

---

[4]The full increase in r_t includes a positive effect from higher labour input, L_t, on the MPK. If we allowed for an increase in the capital utilization rate, κ_t, as in Chapter 10, we would get a further boost to r_t.

[5]If the home country is the European Union, its economy would be large enough to have a noticeable impact on worldwide real interest rates. We could modify our analysis accordingly, but the same basic ideas still apply.

[6]The home real interest rate is fixed at the foreign value, r^f. Therefore, we do not get an intertemporal-substitution effect from a change in the real interest rate.

(real NNP). Real national saving equals real NNP less real expenditure on consumption and government purchases, $C_t + G_t$:

$$real\ national\ saving = Y_t + r_{t-1} \cdot (B^f_{t-1}/P) - \delta K_{t-1} - (C_t + G_t)$$

$$real\ national\ saving = real\ NNP - real\ expenditure\ on\ consumption\ and\ government\ purchases \qquad (18.10)$$

We can rearrange the right-hand side of equation (18.7) to get that the real current-account balance is:

$$(B^f_t - B^f_{t-1})/P = Y_t + r_{t-1} \cdot (B^f_{t-1}/P) - (C_t + G_t) - I_t$$

Then, if we add and subtract depreciation, δK_{t-1}, we get yet another way to express the current-account balance:

Key equation (current-account balance, saving and investment):

$$(B^f_t - B^f_{t-1})/P = Y_t + r_{t-1} \cdot (B^f_{t-1}/P) - \delta K_{t-1} - (C_t + G_t) - (I_t - \delta K_{t-1})$$

$$real\ current\text{-}account\ balance = real\ national\ saving - net\ domestic\ investment\ balance \qquad (18.11)$$

Note from equation (18.10) that the shaded term in equation (18.11) equals real national saving. Thus, we have shown that the real current-account balance is the difference between real national saving and net domestic investment.

In the case of a permanent increase in the technology level, A, we found that real GDP, Y, and consumption, C, rose by the same amount. Therefore, real national saving does not change in equation (18.10). Equation (18.11) shows, accordingly, that the rise in net domestic investment, $I_t - \delta K_{t-1}$, leads to a decline in the real current-account balance.

To summarize, we have the following results concerning the opening up of the home country to the world credit market:

- Suppose that the real interest rate, r, that would prevail in the home country if it were closed is greater than the rate in the rest of the world, r^f. In this case, the opening up of the home country to the world credit market results in a current-account deficit. The home country borrows from the rest of the world to pay for higher net domestic investment, $I_t - \delta K_{t-1}$.
- If the real interest rate, r, that would prevail in the home country if it were closed is less than the rate in the rest of the world, r^f, the results are the opposite. The home country has a current-account surplus – it lends to the rest of the world and has lower net domestic investment, $I_t - \delta K_{t-1}$.
- The final possibility – the first one we considered – is that the real interest rate, r, that would prevail in the home country if it were closed happens to equal the rate in the rest of the world, r^f. In this case, the current account is balanced, and the opening to the rest of the world does not affect $I_t - \delta K_{t-1}$.

These results may be surprising because the general view in popular commentary is that current-account deficits are a symptom of bad economic conditions. A better way to look at the current-account balance is to recall from equation (18.11) that it equals the difference between real national saving and net domestic investment. Thus, for given national saving, higher net domestic investment – often viewed as a good thing – goes along with a lower current-account balance, perhaps a current-account deficit. On the other hand, for given net domestic investment, greater national saving – also often viewed as a good thing – goes along with a higher current-account balance, possibly a current-account surplus. More generally, we cannot say that current-account deficits are necessarily a bad sign, or that current-account surpluses are necessarily a good sign. As we show in the following sections, we need more information about what is happening in the economy to make these kinds of judgements.

ECONOMIC FLUCTUATIONS

In this section, we use our open-economy version of the equilibrium business-cycle model to predict how the current-account balance varies with economic fluctuations. We assume that the home country is open to world credit markets and is small enough to have a negligible effect on the real interest rate, r^f, in the rest of the world. We treat r^f as constant, and we assume that the home country's economic fluctuations come from shocks to the technology level, A. Based on our analysis of the equilibrium business-cycle model in Chapters 9 and 10, we assume that the shocks to A are persistent over time but less than fully permanent.

Recall that the real current-account balance is given by:

$$(B_t^f - B_{t-1}^f)/P = Y_t + r_{t-1} \bullet (B_{t-1}^f/P) - \delta K_{t-1} - (C_t + G_t) - (I_t - \delta K_{t-1})$$

real current-account balance = real national saving − net domestic investment   (18.11)

We know that an increase in A raises net domestic investment, $I_t - \delta K_{t-1}$. We also have that consumption, C_t, rises, but by less than the increase in real GDP, Y_t (because the increase in A is less than fully permanent). Therefore, real national saving increases. The overall change in the real current-account balance in equation (18.11) depends on whether $I_t - \delta K_{t-1}$ rises by more or less than real national saving. In general, the overall effect on the real current-account balance is ambiguous. However, in usual empirical implementations of equilibrium business-cycle models, net domestic investment, $I_t - \delta K_{t-1}$, is highly sensitive to the rate of return on capital, $MPK - \delta$. In this case, the increase in net domestic investment dominates the rise in real national saving, and the real current-account balance falls. Thus, *the equilibrium business-cycle model predicts that the real current-account balance will be countercyclical – low in booms and high in recessions.*

To check out this prediction, Figure 18.6 uses UK data to compare the cyclical behaviour of the ratio of the current-account balance to GDP with the cyclical behaviour of real GDP. The ratio of the current-account balance to GDP is weakly countercyclical; from 1955 to 2014, the correlation with the cyclical part of real GDP was −0.32. Thus, as predicted, the current account tends to move towards deficit during a boom and towards surplus during a recession.[7]

As an example, consider the boom of the late 1980s. While real GDP rose above trend from 1987 to 1990 (the dark blue graph in Figure 18.6), the current-account deficit widened (the light blue graph). From the standpoint of equation (18.11), we have that the boom in net domestic investment, $I_t - \delta K_{t-1}$, dominated the rise in real national saving.

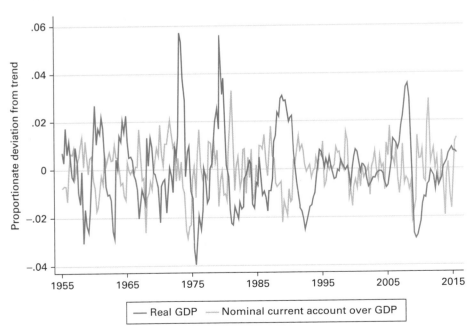

Figure 18.6 Cyclical behaviour of UK real GDP and the current-account balance

The dark blue graph is the deviation of real GDP from its trend. This deviation is measured in proportionate terms. The light blue graph is the deviation from trend of the ratio of the nominal current-account balance to nominal GDP. The data on GDP and the current-account balance are quarterly and seasonally adjusted. The ratio of the current-account balance to GDP is weakly countercyclical; it tends to fluctuate in the direction opposite to real GDP.

[7]The cyclical behaviour of the current-account balance reflects mainly the cyclical behaviour of the trade balance, which equals net exports of goods and services. Thus, the model also predicts that net exports are countercyclical.

Thus, much of the investment boom of the late 1980s was paid for by borrowing from the rest of the world, as reflected in the increasing current-account deficit. This result is an example of a current-account deficit reflecting good times: in this case, surging investment at home.

HARVEST FAILURES, GOVERNMENT PURCHASES, DEVELOPING COUNTRIES

In the context of economic fluctuations, we predicted that the real current-account balance would typically move towards deficit during a boom and towards surplus during a recession. However, we should not conclude that the current-account balance always moves towards deficit in good times and towards surplus in bad times.

To illustrate, consider a harvest failure, which results in a drop in the home country's real GDP, Y_t. If the harvest failure is expected to be temporary – applying, for example, only to this year's crops – the income effect is weak, and the response of consumption, C_t, is small. Therefore, $Y_t - C_t$ falls sharply – the home country's real national saving decreases almost one to one with the decline in Y_t. Moreover, although the harvest failure means less real GDP this year, there may be little impact on the MPK. In this case, there would be little response of net domestic investment, $I_t - \delta K_{t-1}$. Thus, the prediction from equation (18.11) is that a harvest failure leads to a current-account deficit. The home country borrows from abroad to maintain roughly stable consumption, C_t, and net domestic investment, $I_t - \delta K_{t-1}$. In this case, a current-account deficit is a symptom of bad economic times.

We can also use equation (18.11) to assess the effects on the current-account balance from changes in real government purchases, G_t. We know from Chapters 13 and 14 that a permanent increase in the home country's G_t tends to reduce its consumption, C_t, roughly one to one. Therefore, real national saving does not change, and we predict no effect on the current-account balance.

In contrast, a temporary increase in the home country's government purchases, G_t, such as in wartime, reduces consumption, C_t, much less than one to one. Therefore, real national saving falls, and we see from equation (18.11) that the real current-account balance moves towards deficit. In other words, if the home country has temporarily high G_t, perhaps because it is engaged in a war, it tends to finance much of these purchases by borrowing from foreigners. Again, a current-account deficit is a symptom of bad times.

The predictions about wartime government purchases are valid only if we can hold fixed the real interest rate in the rest of the world, r. If all countries are involved simultaneously in a world war and, therefore, all have temporarily high G_t, it is not possible for all combatants to borrow from non-combatants (which do not exist). Instead, the prediction is the one we reached for a closed economy in Chapter 13. For given real GDP, Y_t, real domestic expenditures – partly C_t and partly I_t – decline to make room for the temporarily high G_t. The fall in net investment means that, over time, the stock of capital, K_t, in each country is smaller than it otherwise would have been. Therefore, the MPK is higher in each country, and the real interest rate on the world credit market, r^f, rises over time.

Finally, we can get a prediction for how the current-account balance lines up with a country's long-term growth potential. Suppose that the home country is a developing country with a low capital stock, K_{t-1}, and a high MPK. This situation would apply if the developing country has good access to modern technology, has reasonably well-functioning legal and other institutions, and also has ample supplies of productive labour due to strong education and health. The high MPK means that the home country's net domestic investment, $I_t - \delta K_{t-1}$, would be high. The country would borrow heavily on the world credit market at the real interest rate r (if the country could be counted on to repay!) to finance high domestic investment and, thereby, high economic growth. In contrast, suppose that the home country is a developing country with weak opportunities for domestic investment, perhaps because it has poorly functioning government institutions, or because it lacks adequate education and health. In this case, we predict that the home country would have low net domestic investment, $I_t - \delta K_{t-1}$, and a current-account surplus. Thus, in these cases, a current-account deficit tends to be a sign of a favourable growth environment, whereas a current-account surplus is a sign of an unfavourable environment.

EXAMPLES OF INTERNATIONAL BORROWING AND LENDING

We can test our predictions about the current-account balance by considering empirical examples from a variety of countries. With respect to harvest failures, one study that supports our analysis involves wheat harvests in Australia from 1931 to 1985 (see John Scoggins, 1990). Poor harvests reduced real GDP in Australia but had little impact on the rest of the world and also had little effect on net domestic investment in Australia. Therefore, as predicted, poor harvests led to increases in Australia's current-account deficit. The harvest failures motivated Australians to borrow from foreigners to maintain levels of consumption.

A similar analysis applies to the massive harvest failure in Poland in 1978–81. In response to the temporary drop in real GDP, Poland's foreign debt in 1981 reached \$25 billion (US dollars), roughly half of the country's GDP.[8] Thus, as in Australia, a harvest failure motivated Poles to borrow from foreigners to maintain consumption.

For temporary government purchases, we can consider the linkage between war and the UK current-account balance from Figure 18.1. From 1914 to 1918 during involvement in World War I (but when the USA was not yet engaged in war), the UK borrowed large sums from the USA to finance temporarily high government purchases. The UK current-account deficit reached 6% of GDP in 1918. Note that, when this conflict became a world war in 1917, there were few non-combatant countries from which the UK, the USA and other countries could borrow. Similarly, the UK again ran a large current-account deficit starting in 1939, when war raged in Europe. The UK current-account deficit in 1940 was 14% of GDP.

For permanent changes in government purchases, we can consider the relation in the Eurozone between the cyclical part of government purchases (Figure 13.7) and the cyclical part of the ratio of the current-account balance to GDP in the United Kingdom (Figure 18.6). From 1955 to 2014, a period that excludes major wars, the correlation between the cyclical part of government purchases and the cyclical part of the ratio of the current-account balance to GDP was small in magnitude. This result accords with our model, because most of the changes in government purchases during this period were probably viewed as permanent.

Mexico's discovery of oil in the early 1970s allows us to apply our model to other events that affect international borrowing. By 1974, Mexico's oil prospects were great, but a significant amount of production had yet to material-ize. Prospective returns on investment were high in oil and related industries. Consumption – by households and government – rose because of the increase in prospective real income. Since real GDP was not yet high, Mexico's real national saving declined. Thus, overall, Mexico borrowed from foreigners to pay for high gross domestic investment and consumption. Consequently, Mexico's foreign debt increased from \$3.5 billion, or 9% of GDP, in 1971 to \$61 billion, or 26% of GDP, in 1981.

We also predicted that a developing country with a high MPK would run a large current-account deficit to finance high investment and rapid economic growth. As an example, from 1971 to 1980, Brazil's real per capita GDP rose by 5% per year. During this period, Brazil's foreign debt expanded from \$6 billion, or 11% of GDP, to \$55 billion, or 22% of GDP. For an earlier example of a promising developing country that borrowed heavily from abroad, consider the United States. In 1890, the US foreign debt reached \$2.9 billion, or 21% of GNP.

THE CURRENT-ACCOUNT DEFICIT AND THE BUDGET DEFICIT

In Chapter 15, we studied how budget deficits affect the economy. Think about a cut in year t's real taxes, T_t, corre-sponding to an increase in the real public debt, $(B_t^g - B_{t-1}^g)/P$. We assume that taxes are lump-sum, although we could also consider distorting taxes, as we did in Chapter 14. Most importantly, we assume that the time path of govern-ment purchases, G_t, does not change.

In the Ricardian approach, discussed in Chapter 15, a deficit-financed cut in year t's real taxes, T_t, did not affect the present value of real taxes paid by households. Therefore, households did not change consumption, C_t. Since the cut in T_t raised real disposable income and C_t did not change, real private saving in year t went up by the full amount of the tax cut. Hence, the increase in real private saving completely offset the reduction in real public saving, and real national saving did not change.

[8]The data on foreign debt for Poland (and for Mexico and Brazil, mentioned later) are from Morgan Guaranty Trust, *World Financial Markets*, February 1983; and Organization of American States, *Statistical Bulletin of the OAS*, January–June 1982.

If we allow for an open economy, the important issue is still whether a budget deficit affects real national saving. The real current-account balance is again given by:

$$(B_t^f - B_{t-1}^f)/P = Y_t + r_{t-1} \cdot (B_{t-1}^f/P) - \delta K_{t-1} - (C_t + G_t) - (I_t - \delta K_{t-1})$$

real current-account balance = real national saving − net domestic investment   (18.11)

In the Ricardian case, a budget deficit does not change real national saving. Therefore, equation (18.11) implies that the real current-account balance would not change. The reason is that the home country's households save the full amount of a tax cut and, therefore, willingly absorb all of the additional government bonds issued by the home government. Consequently, the home country does not borrow from the rest of the world to finance its budget deficit, and the real current-account balance does not change. Thus, *in the Ricardian case, a budget deficit does not create a current-account deficit.*

The conclusions are different if households do not save the full amount of the tax cut; that is, if a budget deficit reduces real national saving. For example, we mentioned in Chapter 15 that finite-lived households might feel wealthier when the government cuts taxes and runs a budget deficit. In this case, consumption, C_t, rises and real national saving declines. Equation (18.11) shows that the real current-account balance moves towards deficit. That is, the home country borrows from foreigners to pay for the rise in consumption. Hence, in this case, a budget deficit leads to a current-account deficit.

When budget and current-account deficits occur at the same time, an economy is said to be suffering from **twin deficits**. Economists applied this label to the US economy in the mid-1980s, when budget deficits were large and the ratio of the current-account deficit to GDP gradually widened. However, the current-account deficit disappeared at the beginning of the 1990s, despite the continued presence of budget deficits. Moreover, the current-account deficit rose again late in the 1990s, even though the budget shifted towards surplus. Later still, in 2002–06, twin deficits reappeared. Thus, the empirical observation is that twin deficits sometimes occur, but the pairing of current-account deficits with budget deficits is not a regular feature of the US economy or, it turns out, of other economies.

Even if budget deficits do not cause current-account deficits, twin deficits can arise as responses to other events. Consider, for example, a temporary expansion of government purchases, G_t, as in wartime. We found before that a temporary rise in G_t tends to move the real current-account balance towards deficit. We also know from Chapter 15 that a temporary increase in G_t motivates the government to run a budget deficit to avoid a large temporary increase in taxes. Therefore, the current-account deficit and budget deficit rise together in this case. However, we would not say that the budget deficit caused the current-account deficit. Rather, the two deficits moved in the same direction in response to a common shock – the temporary increase in government purchases because of the war.

Economics in Practice

Why was the US current-account deficit so large in 2000–2014?

We see from Figure 18.3 that the US negative international investment position has become very large relative to GDP since 2000. The persistent current-account deficits since 2000 in the USA have averaged 4%, which is unusual compared to the US history since 1820 (as are the large current-account deficits since 1999 in the UK data in Figure 18.1). An important question is: why did the current-account deficit become so large? We cannot be sure of the answer, but we can offer suggestions. For further discussion of this important puzzle, see Maurice Obstfeld and Kenneth Rogoff (2004).

We can start with 1991, when the United States ran a small current-account surplus. The ratio of the US current-account deficit to GDP rose during the 1990s, especially in the latter half, with the ratio reaching 4% in 2000. A key underlying factor was the strength of the economy, notably the rise in the ratio of gross domestic investment to GDP by four percentage points (from 13.4% in 1991 to a peak of 17.7% in 2000). Much of the investment boom reflected the growth of high-tech sectors, notably telecommunications and the Internet. Since the increase in investment exceeded the normal boom-time increase of real national saving, much of the added investment had to be financed by borrowing from foreigners. Hence, the rise in investment explains a good deal of the current-account deficit of 4% of GDP in 2000.

The economy went into a recession in 2001–02, partly because of the end of the technology boom in mid-2000 and partly because of the terrorist attacks of 11 September 2001. The ratio of gross investment to GDP declined to 15% in 2002, and this change would, by itself, have reduced the ratio of the current-account deficit to GDP. However, the US federal government substantially expanded its purchases, partly for defence and other aspects of national security and partly for other programmes. This increase in government purchases helps to explain why the current-account ratio stayed relatively steady in 2001–02 and then increased to 5% in 2003–07, correcting slightly to around 2% thereafter.

Some economists argue that the persisting budget deficits in 2003–06 made a major contribution to the current-account deficit. This argument is not compelling, because the ratios of the real budget deficit to real GDP were smaller in 2003–06 than they were in the mid-1980s and early 1990s. In those earlier periods, the ratio of the current-account deficit to GDP was much smaller than in 2003–06. Thus, budget deficits cannot be the main story.

The return to a strong economy, with the ratio of gross investment to GDP rising from 15% in 2003 to 17% in 2006, contributed to the current-account deficit, and some special factors mattered as well. One factor was the sharp rise in oil prices, which financial markets viewed as partly temporary. Another unusual force, mentioned near the beginning of this chapter, is that the rate of return on US holdings of foreign assets was much higher than the rate of return on foreign holdings of US assets. Therefore, although the estimated net international investment position of the United States became substantially negative (Figure 18.3), the net flow of payments to the United States remained positive, averaging almost 1% of GDP from 2000 to 2014. Throughout 2014, the United States effectively did not have to pay for its indebtedness to the rest of the world. This foreign generosity may have prevented the normal adjustment of the US economy towards a balanced current account.

The terms of trade

We have assumed, thus far, that only one type of good exists in the world. When we allow for heterogeneous goods, our analysis of the current-account balance will still be satisfactory if the market baskets of goods produced and purchased in the home country are similar to those produced and purchased in the rest of the world. However, one reason this condition may not hold is that countries – particularly small ones – tend to specialize in the goods they produce. For example, Chile produces a great deal of copper, Brazil a great deal of coffee, and Saudi Arabia a great deal of oil. Given these patterns of specialization, countries are affected substantially when the prices of their principal products change compared to prices of other goods. A particularly important price for the world economy is the oil price. All countries use oil, but the production of crude oil is concentrated in relatively few places. A rise in the price of oil, relative to other prices, is good for the small number of oil producers but bad for other countries.

To study these kinds of relative price changes in a simple way, pretend that the home country produces a single good that sells everywhere at the price P. The rest of the world produces another good that sells everywhere at the price P^f. When the home country exports goods, it receives $£P$ for each unit of goods exported. When the home country imports goods, it pays $£P^f$ for each unit of goods imported.

Consider the ratio P/P^f. This ratio is called the **terms of trade**. The units for the terms of trade are:

$$(£ \text{ per home good})/(£ \text{ per foreign good}) = \text{foreign good per home good}$$

Thus, the terms of trade give the number of units of foreign goods that can be imported for each unit of home goods exported. If the terms of trade, P/P^f, rise, or improve, the home country is better off because it gets more foreign goods in exchange for each unit of home goods. If P/P^f falls, or worsens, the home country is worse off because it gets fewer foreign goods in exchange for each unit of home goods.

In our equilibrium business-cycle model, economic fluctuations result from shocks to the technology level, A. For a single country, changes in the terms of trade have effects that are similar to changes in A. An improvement in the terms of trade resembles an increase in A, whereas a worsening of the terms of trade resembles a decrease in A. To see how this works, we have to incorporate the terms of trade into our equation for the current-account balance.

THE TERMS OF TRADE AND THE CURRENT-ACCOUNT BALANCE

Equation (18.7) gave the home country's real current-account balance when all goods sold at the single £ price P. If we multiply both sides of the equation by P, we get that the current-account balance in nominal terms is:

$$B_t^f - B_{t-1}^f = PY_t + r_{t-1} \cdot B_{t-1}^f - P \cdot (C_t + I_t + G_t)$$

nominal current-account balance = nominal GNP − nominal domestic expenditure

We have to modify this equation to bring in different prices for home and foreign goods. In the simplest setting, which brings out the main results, the home country exports all of its production, so that none of the real GDP goes directly to the home country's consumption, domestic investment and government purchases. Instead, the home country imports foreign goods to provide for consumption, domestic investment and government purchases.

Given these assumptions, the nominal income from the real GDP, Y_t, is still PY_t, where P is the euro price of home goods. The nominal expenditure on consumption, domestic investment and government purchases is $P^f \cdot (C_t + I_t + G_t)$, where P^f is the euro price of foreign goods. Therefore, the nominal current-account balance becomes:

$$B_t^f - B_{t-1}^f = PY_t + r_{t-1} \cdot B_{t-1}^f - P^f \cdot (C_t + I_t + G_t)$$

nominal current-account balance = nominal GNP − nominal domestic expenditure $\qquad$ (18.12)

If we divide both sides of equation (18.12) by P^f, we get that the current-account balance in real terms is:

$$(B_t^f - B_{t-1}^f)/P^f = (P/P^f) \cdot Y_t + r_{t-1} \cdot (B_{t-1}^f/P^f) - (C_t + I_t + G_t)$$

real current-account balance = real GNP − real domestic expenditure $\qquad$ (18.13)

Each term in equation (18.13) is a real value in the sense of being measured in units of foreign goods. The important new feature, shown by the shaded term on the right-hand side, is that Y_t, the real GDP in units of home goods, is multiplied by the terms of trade, P/P^f. If P/P^f rises and Y_t does not change, the home country has more real income in units of foreign goods. That is, the purchasing power of real GDP in terms of the foreign goods it can buy rises when the terms of trade improve. As before, we can express the real current-account balance in terms of real national saving and net domestic investment. If we rearrange the terms in equation (18.13), we get:

$$(B_t^f - B_{t-1}^f)/P^f = (P/P^f) \cdot Y_t + r_{t-1} \cdot (B_{t-1}^f/P^f) - \delta K_{t-1} - (C_t + G_t) - (I_t - \delta K_{t-1})$$

real current-account balance = real national saving − net domestic investment $\qquad$ (18.14)

How does an improvement in the terms of trade, P/P^f, affect the home country? The production function is still given by:

$$Y_t = A \cdot F(K, L_t)$$ $\qquad$ (18.8)

We assume that the capital stock, K, and the technology level, A, are fixed. To bring out the main results, we also assume now that the quantity of labour, L_t, equals a fixed amount L. In this case, real GDP, Y_t, will not change in equation (18.8). Recall, however, that Y_t is measured in units of home goods.

Equation (18.13) shows that an increase in the terms of trade, P/P^f, raises real GNP, measured in units of foreign goods, for a given real GDP, Y_t. Households respond to the higher real GNP by increasing consumption, C_t. The response of C_t is larger the more long-lasting the rise in P/P^f. As long as the change is less than fully permanent, C_t tends to rise by less than real GNP. Therefore, real national saving increases in equation (18.14). Thus, on this count, the real current-account balance moves towards surplus.

THE TERMS OF TRADE AND INVESTMENT

We have to consider whether an increase in the terms of trade, P/P^f, affects net domestic investment, $I_t - \delta K_{t-1}$. To study this effect, we must recalculate the real rate of return on capital in the home country. As before, an increase in the home country's capital stock, K, by one unit raises real GDP, Y, by MPK units. However, the price of K is now P^f, the foreign price level, because we assumed that the home country's domestic investment comes from imports of foreign goods. The price of Y is still the home price level, P, because home country output sells at P. Thus, buying one unit of capital at the price P^f yields a gross return of $P \cdot$ MPK. The gross real rate of return on capital is the ratio of $P \cdot$ MPK to P^f; that is, $(P/P^f) \cdot$ MPK. The net real rate of return subtracts the depreciation rate, δ:

$$net\ real\ rate\ of\ return\ on\ capital = (P/P^f) \cdot MPK - \delta \qquad (18.15)$$

The difference from before is that the MPK is multiplied by the terms of trade, P/P^f.

For a given MPK, equation (18.15) shows that an increase in the terms of trade, P/P^f, raises the net real rate of return on capital in the home country. Think, for example, of Chile as the home country, and consider the effect of an increase in P/P^f due to a rise in the world price of copper. The Chileans would see an increase in the net real rate of return on capital in the copper business and would therefore be motivated to invest more in this business.

The effect of higher terms of trade, P/P^f, on net domestic investment, $I_t - \delta K_{t-1}$, is analogous to the effect we considered before from an increase in the technology level, A. When A increased, the rise in the MPK raised the net real rate of return on capital. We noted that the response of $I_t - \delta K_{t-1}$ would be large, typically greater than the increase in real national saving. The same conclusion applies when the terms of trade, P/P^f, rise. In equation (18.14), we predict that $I_t - \delta K_{t-1}$ will rise by more than real national saving. Therefore, the real current-account balance moves overall towards deficit.

The conclusion is different if the rise in the terms of trade, P/P^f, is expected to be short-lived. In this case, the income effect is weak, the response of consumption, C_t, is small and real national saving rises strongly. Moreover, with adjustment costs for investment, net investment, $I_t - \delta K_{t-1}$, responds little to a temporary increase in the net real rate of return on capital. This is because businesses will find it unprofitable to pay large adjustment costs to expand their capital stock when the favourable return due to the high terms of trade is expected to be temporary. For example, Chile would not invest much in copper-mining facilities if a rise in the relative price of copper were expected to be short-lived. Therefore, in equation (18.14), $I_t - \delta K_{t-1}$ will rise by less than real national saving (which rose strongly), and the real current-account balance moves overall towards surplus.

To sum up, we predict that an increase in the terms of trade, P/P^f, that is expected to be permanent moves the current-account balance towards deficit. The reason is that the expansion of net domestic investment, $I_t - \delta K_{t-1}$, tends to be greater than the rise of real national saving. In contrast, we predict that an increase in P/P^f that is expected to be temporary moves the current-account balance towards surplus. In this case, the increase of $I_t - \delta K_{t-1}$ tends to be smaller than the rise of real national saving.

EMPIRICAL EVIDENCE FROM OIL PRODUCERS

An interesting way to assess our predictions about the terms of trade is to look at the effects from changing oil prices on the current-account balances of major oil-exporting countries. In this discussion, *think of the oil exporters as the home country and think of all other countries as the rest of the world.* The first column of Table 18.1 shows the world

Table 18.1 Oil prices and current-account balances of oil-exporting countries

Year	(1) Crude oil price (US dollars)	(2) Crude oil price (2000 dollars)	(3) Current-account balance (billions of 2000 dollars)	(4) Imports (billions of 2000 dollars)
1972	2.44	8.08	10	46
1974	11.50	33.14	193	92
1976	11.55	28.73	95	159
1978	12.78	27.90	−4	207
1980	35.71	66.01	189	231
1982	31.54	50.30	−21	199
1984	28.55	42.17	−15	185
1986	14.17	19.87	−41	129
1988	14.77	19.51	−26	137
1990	22.98	28.16	17	147
1992	19.04	22.04	−28	177
1994	15.95	17.66	−10	146
1996	20.37	21.69	20	165
1998	13.07	13.54	−20	169
2000	28.23	28.23	81	179
2002	24.95	23.94	32	185
2004	37.76	34.61	91	260
2005	53.35	47.57	172	300

Note: Sources are International Monetary Fund, *International Financial Statistics*, and Economist Intelligence Unit, *Country Data*. The crude oil price is an average world price per barrel in US dollars. Values expressed in 2000 dollars are divided by the US GDP deflator, based on 2000 = 1.0. The current-account balance is the total for major oil-exporting countries, expressed in 2000 dollars. (From 1996 on, these numbers exclude Iraq.) Imports are totals for major oil-exporting countries, expressed in 2000 dollars.

average US dollar price per barrel of crude oil from 1972 to 2005.[9] The second column shows this price in real terms, calculated by dividing the US dollar price of oil by the US GDP deflator (set to 1.0 in 2000). These values approximate the terms of trade for oil exporters.

Large increases in oil prices occurred with the rise of the Organization of Petroleum Exporting Countries (OPEC) in 1973–74 and 1979–80. Later increases appeared in 1990 (in the run-up to the Gulf War), 2000 and 2004–06. Table 18.1, column 3, shows that rises in oil prices typically led to current-account surpluses for the oil-exporting countries; for example, in 1974, 1980, 1990, 2000 and 2004–05. This pattern applies in our model to increases in the terms of trade that are perceived to be partly temporary. We also see, from column 4 of the table, that imports of oil-exporting countries responded strongly when oil prices remained at increased levels, such as from 1974 to 1978. Therefore, the current-account surplus tended to vanish; for example, in 1978, 1982 and 1992. This pattern corresponds in our model to increases in the terms of trade that are perceived to be long-lasting.

We can also use Table 18.1 to assess the responses to lower oil prices, such as in 1986, 1992–94 and 1998. In the short run, these changes tended to induce current-account deficits (column 3). However, when oil prices remained low for an extended period, the downward adjustment of imports (column 4), such as from 1980 to 1986, tended to eliminate the current-account deficits.

[9]Organization of the Petroleum Exporting Countries' (OPEC) oil is quoted exclusively in US dollars.

The volume of international trade

The trade balance is given by:

$$trade\ balance = Y_t - (C_t + I_t + G_t)$$
$$trade\ balance = exports - imports$$
$$trade\ balance = net\ exports \qquad\qquad (18.6)$$

Our model deals with the trade balance or net exports as part of the analysis of the current-account balance – see equation (18.7). When we studied the impact of the home country's technology level, A, and other variables on the current-account balance, the effects worked through changes in net exports. However, the model has nothing to say about the volume of international trade; that is, the absolute levels of exports and imports.

As an example, in 2014, US exports of goods and services totalled $2.3 trillion, and US imports of goods and services totalled $2.9 trillion. What difference would it make if exports and imports were each higher by $1 trillion, so that exports totalled $3.3 trillion and imports totalled $3.9 trillion? In the model, this change would have no effect. Since exports and imports are higher by the same amount, net exports and the current-account balance do not change. In the model, it does not matter if the United States exports an additional $1 trillion of goods and services and then buys back these (identical) goods and services as additional imports.

This feature of the model is a shortcoming, because the absolute levels of exports and imports are important in reality. Unfortunately, we cannot study these influences in a model that assumes that all goods are the same. The one-good assumption was a useful simplification for many macroeconomic issues, including the determination of the current-account balance. However, to explore the effects from changes in the terms of trade, we already had to make the model more realistic by assuming that the home country and the rest of the world produced different types of goods. To assess the benefits from greater international trade – a larger volume of exports *and* imports – we have to go further in allowing for heterogeneous goods and services.

In a realistic setting, many forms of goods and services exist. From the standpoint of efficient production, there are benefits from concentrating the production of some of these goods and services in particular locations. Some of the benefits from concentration arise because countries and localities differ in their relative quantities of factors of production, including skilled labour, unskilled labour, machinery, land, and so on. Countries with abundant skilled labour should specialize in the production of goods that use a great deal of this kind of labour; examples are sophisticated electronic equipment and computer software. Countries with more unskilled labour should specialize in the production of goods that use a great deal of these inputs; examples are agricultural products and textiles. Countries with a great deal of fertile land should also specialize in agriculture. These patterns of specialization require international trade, as well as trade across regions within a country.

Governments often restrict international trade by implementing a **tariff** (a tax on imports) or a **quota** (a limitation on quantities of imports). If trade is restricted in these and other ways, the economic outcomes will be inefficient, just as if the world technology level, A, were lower. In other words, if nations do not take advantage of opportunities for specialization, the world's overall output will be diminished. Or, to look at it conversely, greater openness to international trade through elimination of trade barriers is similar to an increase in A. With freer international trade, the world as a whole is able to produce more of each type of good for given world inputs of skilled labour, unskilled labour, land, and so on.[10]

We can use this analysis to broaden our interpretation of effects from changes in the technology level, A. We can view an increase in A as an expansion of world trade due to a decrease in government-imposed barriers, such

[10]This argument for the benefits from free international trade comes from the classical theory developed by David Ricardo (1819), Eli Heckscher (1919), Bertil Ohlin (1933), and Paul Samuelson and Wolfgang Stolper (1941). A more recent theory, pioneered by Elhanan Helpman and Paul Krugman (1985), focuses on benefits from specialization due to increasing returns to scale in the production of some goods. The exploitation of these economies of scale requires a country's production of these goods to exceed its expenditure on these goods; that is, a large part of output is exported. This theory complements the classical theory in that, in both cases, an opening up to international trade has effects analogous to an increase in the technology level, A.

as tariffs and quotas. Conversely, we can view a decrease in A as a depression of world trade due to the erection of new trade barriers. Our analysis predicts that freer trade will promote a boom, whereas more restricted trade will promote a recession. Empirical research on the determinants of economic growth, discussed in Chapter 5, supports the hypothesis that greater openness to international trade tends to raise a country's rate of economic growth.

Summing Up

This chapter extends the equilibrium business-cycle model to allow for international trade in goods and services, and for international borrowing and lending. Thus, we now have an open-economy version of the equilibrium business-cycle model.

The current-account balance for the home country determines the change over time in its net foreign assets. The current account is in surplus if real GNP is greater than real domestic expenditure on consumption, gross investment and government purchases. Otherwise, the current account is in deficit. The GNP adds to GDP the net real income on foreign assets (the net factor income from abroad). We can express the current-account balance as the trade balance (exports less imports) plus the net real income on foreign assets. We can also express it as the difference between real national saving and net domestic investment.

In the equilibrium business-cycle model, a favourable technology shock typically raises net domestic investment by more than real national saving. Hence, the current-account balance moves towards deficit. Thus, the current-account balance is countercyclical. The predictions are different if a disturbance affects real national saving but not the marginal product of capital. For example, the current account moves towards deficit in response to a harvest failure, or a temporary increase in government purchases, as in wartime.

If a budget deficit reduces real national saving, the current account would move towards deficit. However, in the Ricardian case, where a budget deficit does not affect real national saving, the current-account balance does not change.

The terms of trade are the ratio of export prices to import prices. Changes in the terms of trade have effects analogous to those from technology shocks. A permanent improvement in the terms of trade tends to create a current-account deficit, because the increase in net domestic investment tends to be larger than the rise in real national saving. A temporary improvement in the terms of trade tends to generate a current-account surplus, because the rise in net domestic investment is less than the increase in real national saving.

Elimination of trade barriers, such as tariffs and quotas, expands the volume of international trade. The economic effects are similar to those from increases in the technology level. Thus, we predict that freer trade creates a boom, whereas restrictions on trade generate a recession.

Key Terms and Concepts

adjustment costs for investment	current-account deficit	net factor income from abroad	real gross national product (real GNP)
balance of international payments	current-account surplus	net foreign investment	tariff
balance on current account	foreign direct investment	net international investment position	terms of trade
current-account balance	globalization	quota	trade balance
	law of one price		twin deficits

Questions and Problems

A　Review questions

1　If a country runs a budget deficit, must it also run a current-account deficit? How does the linkage between the two deficits depend on the relation between budget deficits and national saving?

2　Why is it infeasible for all countries to run a current-account deficit at the same time?

B　Problems for discussion

3　A change in the terms of trade

Suppose that the home country is Brazil, which produces a great deal of coffee for export. We considered in the text a change in the terms of trade that stemmed from a disturbance in the rest of the world. Suppose, instead, that a temporary shock at home – say, a failure of Brazil's coffee crop – raises the world's relative price of coffee. In this case, how does the disturbance affect Brazil's current-account balance?

4　A technology shock for a single country

Consider a temporary rise in the technology level, A, in the home country.

a　What happens to the home country's labour, L, capital utilization rate, κ, and real GDP, Y?

b　What happens to the home country's consumption, C, and current-account balance?

5　Taxes and the current-account balance

Discuss the effects on a country's current-account balance of the following changes in tax rates. (You should refer to the analysis of tax rates in Chapter 14.):

a　A permanent increase in the tax rate on labour income, τ_w;

b　A temporary increase in the tax rate on labour income, τ_w;

c　A permanent increase in the tax rate on asset income, τ_r;

d　A temporary increase in the tax rate on consumption, τ_c.

19 Exchange rates

In Chapter 18, we discussed international markets for goods and credit but said nothing about *exchange rates*. We could not discuss exchange rates because we assumed that all countries used a common currency, such as the US dollar, the pound or the euro, and that all prices were quoted in units of this currency. To analyze exchange rates, we have to introduce different types of currency – dollars, euros, pounds, yen, and so forth – and allow for prices to be quoted in these different currency units. This chapter makes the necessary extensions to consider these matters.

Different currencies and exchange rates

We will assume now that each country issues and uses its own currency, instead of using a common currency. To keep things simple, pretend that there are only two countries. Think of the home country as the United States and the foreign country as the United Kingdom. The US nominal quantity of money, M, is measured in dollars. The UK nominal quantity of money, M^f, is in pounds.

We now introduce a new market, called the **exchange market**, on which participants trade the currency of one country for that of another. In our model, traders exchange US dollars for UK pounds. Thus, households and governments can use the exchange market to convert dollars into pounds or pounds into dollars. We define the **exchange rate** or, more precisely, the **nominal exchange rate** to be the number of pounds received for each dollar. We use the word 'nominal' to distinguish from the *real exchange rate*, a concept introduced later. As an example of a nominal exchange rate, on 17 February 2016, 1 US dollar bought 0.69 UK pounds, or £0.69. Therefore, each pound bought 1/0.69 = 1.45 US dollars, or $1.45. The box below shows nominal exchange rates between the US dollar and other major currencies on 17 February 2016, as reported in *The Wall Street Journal*.

Let ε (the Greek letter epsilon) denote the nominal exchange rate between pounds and dollars. Thus, on 12 February 2016, we had $\varepsilon = 0.69$ pounds per dollar. Notice that a *higher* ε means that US currency is *more* valuable, because each dollar gets more pounds.[1] From the standpoint of the United Kingdom, the nominal exchange rate was $1/\varepsilon = 1.45$ dollars per pound. Thus, a higher ε means that UK currency is *less* valuable in terms of dollars, because each pound gets fewer dollars.

Figures 19.1 and 19.2 show the nominal exchange rates from 1950 to 2011 between the US dollar and the currencies of seven major countries – the United Kingdom, Canada, China, Japan, France, Germany and Italy.[2]

As an example, in 1950, 1.00 US dollar bought 0.36 UK pounds. Figure 19.1 shows that this nominal exchange rate did not change until 1968, when it rose to 0.42, 17% above the 1950 rate. That is, the US dollar became 17%

---

[1] We have to be careful, because some economists define the exchange rate in the opposite way; in this case, as dollars per pound, rather than pounds per dollar.
[2] Here, we discuss the value of a currency with respect to the US dollar simply because it is the most traded currency in the foreign exchange market.

Figure 19.1 Nominal exchange rates for Canada, China, Japan and the UK

The graphs show the value of each nominal exchange rate with the US dollar relative to the value that prevailed in 1950. In 1950, the nominal exchange rates were United Kingdom: 0.357 pounds per US dollar; Canada: 1.09 Canadian dollars per US dollar; China: 2.46 Chinese renminbi per US dollar (in 1952); Japan: 361.1 yen per US dollar. Data are from Penn World Table, 8.1 from Feenstra, Inklaar and Timmer (2015).

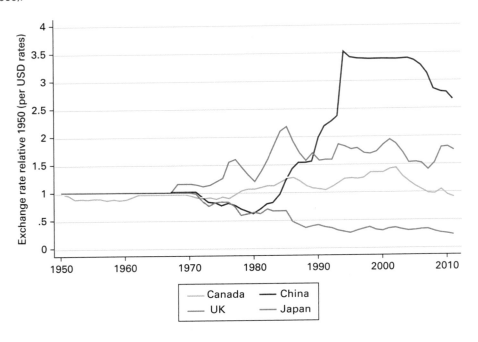

Figure 19.2 Nominal exchange rates for France, Germany and Italy

The graphs show the nominal exchange rate with the US dollar in euro-equivalent currency units. This is found by dividing the nominal exchange rate by the conversion rates from national currency to euro. The conversion rates with the euro were fixed at the start of 1999 at 6.56 French francs, 1.96 German marks and 1936.3 Italian lire. In 1950, the nominal exchange rates were France: 3.5 francs per US dollar; Germany: 4.2 marks per US dollar; Italy: 625 lire per US dollar. In 1999–2001, the separate currencies disappeared and were replaced by the euro. Data are from Penn World Table 8.1 from Feenstra, Inklaar and Timmer (2015).

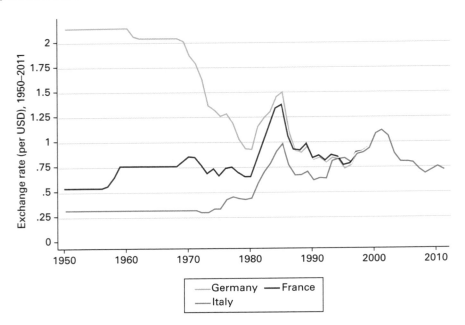

more valuable in terms of UK pounds. The highest rate in terms of UK pounds was in 1985, when the nominal exchange rate reached 0.77, 120% above the rate in 1950. In 2011, the US dollar had fallen to 0.62 UK pounds. This rate was 20% lower than in 1985 but still 75% higher than in 1950.

Similarly, Figure 19.1 shows US dollar nominal exchange rates with the Canadian dollar, the Japanese yen and the Chinese yuan. Notice that, since 1971, the rate between the US dollar and the yen fell substantially; that is, the dollar became less valuable in terms of yen. In 1950, 1 US dollar bought 361 yen, but in 2011, 1 US dollar bought only 80 yen. Therefore, the US dollar lost 78% of its value in terms of yen.

Figure 19.2 shows US dollar nominal exchange rates with the French franc, German mark and Italian lira. Separate rates applied from 1950 to 1998, after which the three currencies were replaced by a common currency, the euro.[3] Therefore, the US dollar nominal exchange rates with the currency of each of these countries have moved together since 1999.

By the Numbers
Exchange rates around the world

The financial press report two kinds of nominal exchange rates between a foreign currency and the US dollar. The first type, called a *spot exchange rate*, gives the current rate in units of foreign currency per US dollar. The second type, called a *forward exchange rate*, gives the rate applicable to a designated future date, again in units of foreign currency per US dollar. The forward rate applies to a contract for exchanging two currencies in the future, often one, three or six months ahead. By entering into a forward contract, market participants assure themselves of the rate at which they will be able to exchange currencies in the future.

Table 19.1 shows nominal exchange rates between major currencies and the US dollar on 17 February 2016, as reported in *The Wall Street Journal*. Although the *Journal* reported forward exchange rates for only a few major currencies, forward contracts on other currencies were available from fxstreet.com on 18 February 2016. Notice that the forward exchange rates for the British pound, euro and Swiss franc were declining with the future date. This pattern indicates that the financial markets expected the US dollar spot exchange rates for these currencies to fall over time. That is, the market expected the US dollar to depreciate relative to the British pound, euro and Swiss franc. However, the forward exchange rates for the Canadian dollar and Japanese yen were nearly flat, indicating that the markets expected little change over time in the US dollar spot exchange rate for the Canadian dollar and Japanese yen.

Table 19.1 Nominal exchange rates (foreign currency per US dollar) reported for 17 February 2016 in *The Wall Street Journal*

Country (currency)	Exchange rate	Country (currency)	Exchange rate
Argentina (peso)	14.922	New Zealand (dollar)	1.507
Australia (dollar)	1.392	Norway (krone)	8.543
Bahrain (dinar)	0.377	Poland (zloty)	3.953
Brazil (real)	3.985	Russia (ruble)	75.110
Canada (dollar)	1.367	Pakistan (rupee)	104.750
1 month forward	1.367	Peru (new sol)	3.504
3 months forward	1.365	Philippines (peso)	47.577
6 months forward	1.360	Saudi Arabia (riyal)	3.751
Chile (peso)	700.700	Singapore (dollar)	1.403
China (renminbi)	6.524	South Africa (rand)	15.471
Colombia (peso)	3359.320	South Korea (won)	1224.740
Denmark (krone)	6.708	Sweden (krona)	8.516

(continued)

[3] The conversion rates with the euro were set in 1999 at 6.56 francs, 1.96 marks and 1936 lire. The three currencies retained separate physical presences until 2001, after which only euro notes circulated.

Country (currency)	Exchange rate	Country (currency)	Exchange rate
Ecuador (US dollar)	1.000	Switzerland (franc)	0.992
Egypt (pound)	7.830	1 month forward	0.980
Eurozone (euro)	0.899	3 months forward	0.950
1 month forward	0.893	6 months forward	0.901
3 months forward	0.876	Thailand (baht)	35.610
6 months forward	0.851	Turkey (new lira)	2.956
India (rupee)	68.329	United Kingdom	0.700
Indonesia (rupiah)	13431.000	1 month forward	0.698
Japan (yen)	114.100	3 months forward	0.680
1 month forward	114.025	6 months forward	0.647
3 months forward	113.791	Uruguay (peso)	31.900
6 months forward	113.407	Venezuela (bolivar)	6.305
Mexico (peso)	18.363		

Purchasing-power parity

Sometimes countries allow their nominal exchange rates to move freely in response to market forces. These systems are called **flexible exchange rates**. In other circumstances, countries try to maintain a constant nominal exchange rate with respect to another currency, often the US dollar. These systems are called **fixed exchange rates**. We will begin with basic theoretical propositions about international finance that hold whether nominal exchange rates are flexible or fixed. The first of these propositions connects the nominal exchange rate between two currencies to the price levels prevailing in the two countries. In our model, we consider the nominal exchange rate between US dollars and UK pounds and the price levels in the United States and the United Kingdom.

THE PPP CONDITION AND THE REAL EXCHANGE RATE

The US price level, P, is measured in dollars per unit of goods. We denote the UK price level (or foreign price level) by P^f, measured in pounds per unit of goods. To start, assume that the goods produced and used in both countries are physically identical. We also ignore any transportation or other transaction costs for buying and selling goods in the two countries. Then, the central idea is that buying and selling goods has to look equally attractive in both countries for the households of both countries.

To see how this works, consider a household that has $1 of US currency. (The household could reside in either country.) The household can buy goods in the United States at the price P per unit of good. Therefore, with $1, the household gets $1/P$ units of goods. Suppose, instead, that the household uses the exchange market to get ε pounds for the $1. Then, with ε pounds, the household can buy $\varepsilon \cdot (1/P^f)$ units of goods in the United Kingdom. If this amount, $\varepsilon \cdot (1/P^f)$, is greater than $1/P$, the household would buy all goods in the United Kingdom. Conversely, if $\varepsilon \cdot (1/P^f)$ were less than $1/P$, the household would buy all goods in the United States. For the household to be indifferent about where to buy goods, the two amounts have to be equal:

$$1/P = \varepsilon \cdot (1/P^f)$$

quantity of goods that can be bought in US = quantity of goods that can be bought in UK   (19.1)

If equation (19.1) does not hold, households from both countries would want to buy all goods in one place: the cheaper country. We are interested in situations in which goods are bought and sold in both countries; that is, the United States and the United Kingdom are both economically active! Therefore, given our assumptions – that all goods are physically identical and transportation costs are negligible – equation (19.1) must hold.

We can rearrange the terms in equation (19.1) to get:

Key equation (purchasing-power parity):

$$\varepsilon = P^f/P$$

nominal exchange rate = ratio of foreign price to home price (19.2)

The equation between the nominal exchange rate and the ratio of prices of goods is called **purchasing-power parity (PPP)**. This condition means that the purchasing power in terms of goods for dollars (or pounds) is the same regardless of whether households buy goods in the United States or the United Kingdom.

For a concrete example, suppose that you have $100 and want to spend all of it on pizza. If each US pizza costs $10, you get 10 pizzas. Your alternative is to exchange the $100 for £70 if the exchange rate, ε, is 0.70 pounds per dollar. The number of pizzas you get in the United Kingdom depends on the UK price. If the price is £7 per pizza, you get 10 pizzas, just as in the United States. If the UK price is more than £7, you get fewer pizzas in the United Kingdom, and if the price is less than £7, you get more pizzas in the United Kingdom. To be indifferent about where to buy your pizzas (if it costs nothing to travel to the UK, and all pizzas are of the same quality), the exchange rate, 0.70 pounds per dollar, has to equal the ratio of the UK pizza price to the US pizza price. In our example, the ratio, 0.70, equals the £7 per pizza in the United Kingdom divided by the $10 per pizza in the United States. This 'pizza-parity' condition is the same as the more general PPP condition in equation (19.2).

The PPP condition in equation (19.2) applies when the price levels, P^f and P, refer to the same goods in the two countries. In practice, we would like to interpret P^f and P as price indices for market baskets of goods produced or consumed in the two countries. For example, we might use gross domestic product (GDP) deflators or consumer price indexes to measure P^f and P.

When we think of price levels as broad indexes, the PPP condition need not hold. One reason is that countries specialize in the production of different goods. Changes in the relative prices of these goods – that is, shifts in the terms of trade considered in Chapter 18 – will cause the PPP condition to fail. Another reason for failure of the PPP condition is that countries produce and consume **non-tradable goods** – such as personal services and real estate that do not enter into international trade. Because non-tradable goods cannot move from one country to another, the purchasing power of a currency in terms of non-tradable goods may depend on where one buys them.

To think about deviations from the PPP condition, it is useful to consider another concept of the exchange rate, called the *real exchange rate*. Whereas the nominal exchange rate, ε, specifies the number of UK pounds that a household gets for each US dollar, the real exchange rate specifies the number of UK *goods* that a household gets for each unit of US *goods*. When the PPP condition in equation (19.2) holds, the real exchange rate is 1.0. However, when PPP does not hold, the real exchange rate can differ from 1.0 and can also vary over time. At any point in time, the level of the real exchange rate will be a useful indicator of the extent of deviation from the PPP condition.

Formally, the real exchange rate is the ratio of the left-hand side of equation (19.2) to the right-hand side:

$$real\ exchange\ rate = \frac{\varepsilon/P^f}{1/P}$$ (19.3)

On the right-hand side, the denominator, $1/P$, is the number of goods that $1 buys in the United States. The numerator, ε/P^f, is the number of goods that $1 buys in the United Kingdom (after converting dollars for pounds on the exchange market). Therefore, the **real exchange rate** is the ratio of goods that can be bought in the United Kingdom, the foreign country, (say, with $1) to goods that can be bought in the United States, the base country, (also with $1).

To go back to our pizza example, if P is $10 per pizza, the denominator on the right-hand side of equation (19.3) is 0.1; that is, you get one-tenth of a pizza with your $1 in the United States. If ε is 0.70 and P^f is £7, the numerator is also 0.1; that is, you get one-tenth of a pizza with your $1 in the United Kingdom (after going through the exchange market). In this case, the real exchange rate for pizza is 1.0.

If we hold fixed the nominal exchange rate, ε, an increase in the ratio of UK to US prices, P^f/P, means that the United Kingdom has become relatively more expensive for buying goods (pizza, or goods in general). Therefore, the real exchange rate declines in equation (19.3), signifying that fewer goods can be bought in the United Kingdom compared to goods that can be bought in the United States. If we hold fixed P^f/P, an increase in the nominal exchange rate, ε, means that the United Kingdom has become relatively cheaper for buying goods. Therefore, the real exchange rate increases.

Table 19.2 shows real exchange rates in 2014 for selected countries, all compared to the United States. The definition of the real exchange rate is the one given in equation (19.3), where the price levels, P^f and P, refer to market baskets of goods contained in the GDPs. A value near 1.0 means that the basket of goods in a foreign country costs about the same number of dollars as the basket in the United States (the base country).[4] Higher values mean that goods are more expensive in the United States (the base country) than in the other country. Lower values mean that goods are more expensive in the other country than in the United States (the base country).

We see from Table 19.2 that most of the rich countries have real exchange rates not too far from 1.0. In 2014, the most expensive countries were Switzerland at 0.70, Australia at 0.74, Denmark at 0.75 and Sweden at 0.77. Rich economies that were less expensive than the United States were Singapore at 1.47, Hong Kong at 1.37, Japan at

Table 19.2 Real exchange rates for selected countries in 2014

Country	Real exchange rate	Country	Real exchange rate
Singapore	1.471	Russia	1.805
Hong Kong	1.372	Poland	1.761
Switzerland	0.695	Chile	1.520
United States	1.000	Turkey	1.883
Australia	0.741	Iran	3.175
Netherlands*	0.925	Mexico	1.678
Ireland*	0.909	South Africa	2.012
Sweden	0.769	Costa Rica	1.433
Denmark	0.750	Brazil	1.355
Belgium*	0.917	Thailand	2.632
Canada	0.897	Colombia	1.689
Germany*	0.971	China	1.742
United Kingdom	0.869	Ukraine	2.808
France*	0.921	Egypt	3.125
Japan	1.012	Indonesia	3.012
Italy*	1.007	Guatemala	2.028
Spain*	1.131	Vietnam	2.740
South Korea	1.193	India	3.610
Israel	0.906	Nigeria	1.845
Greece*	1.239	Pakistan	3.650
Czech Republic	1.600	Bangladesh	2.874
Hungary	1.786		

Note: Starting with the left column, countries are listed in descending order of real per capita GDP in 2011 (Penn World Table, 8.1 from Feenstra, Inklaar and Timmer [2015]). These real GDP numbers adjust for cross-country differences in the costs of the market basket of goods contained in the GDP. The real exchange rate, based on the prices of goods contained in the GDP, corresponds to the concept in equation (19.3). All real exchange rates use the United States as the base country. A value near 1.0 means that the market basket of goods costs about the same number of US dollars in the indicated country as in the United States. Higher values mean that the market basket of goods is less expensive than in the United States. Data are from World Development Indicators, World Bank.

*Value uses the domestic price levels and euro nominal exchange rates.

[4]Here, we no longer restrict the foreign country to being the United Kingdom but continue, for now, to consider the United States as the base country.

1.01, Italy at 1.01, Spain at 1.13 and South Korea at 1.19. Other rich countries had real exchange rates slightly less than, but close to, 1.0. Many middle-income and lower-income countries had real exchange rates well above 1.0. For example, India had 3.61, Thailand 2.63, South Africa 2.01 and Guatemala 2.03. The reason for these high real exchange rates is that poor countries tend to have relatively low prices for non-tradable goods, especially labour and real estate. This general pattern is called the **Balassa–Samuelson hypothesis**, named after the work of Bela Balassa (1964) and Paul Samuelson (1964).

The results in Table 19.2 show that the PPP condition in equation (19.2) does not hold exactly across countries and is way off for comparisons of high-income economies with middle- or lower-income economies. However, PPP works much better among advanced economies, such as the United States, Canada, much of Western Europe, Japan, and so on.

The consensus among economists is that, for rich countries, the PPP condition in equation (19.2) is not so accurate as a short-run proposition but is a good guide for long-run comparisons. (See the survey of empirical evidence by Alan Taylor and Mark Taylor, 2004.) That is, there is a long-run tendency for real exchange rates among the rich countries to approach values not too far from 1.0. This result means that we can use the configuration of real exchange rates at a point in time – such as the year 2014 in Table 19.2 – to forecast long-term changes in real exchange rates. Consider a country, such as Switzerland or Australia, whose goods were expensive relative to the United States in 2014; their real exchange rates were 0.70 and 0.74, respectively. The prediction is that these real exchange rates would increase in the long run to approach a value closer to 1.0. From the formula for the real exchange rate in equation (19.3), this prediction means that either the nominal exchange rate, ε, would rise or the ratio of foreign to home prices, P^f/P, would fall. That is, for a given ε, the inflation rate, π^f, in Switzerland or Australia should be lower than the inflation rate, π, in the United States.

We can be bolder and apply this reasoning to a comparison between the United States and China. In 2004, when China was still a relatively poor country, its real exchange rate (relative to the United States) was very high at 4.3. By 2014, China had reached the status of a middle-income country, and its real exchange rate (relative to the United States) had fallen to a value of 1.7, implying that goods in China had become more expensive (relative to the United States) than in the past. As discussed in Chapter 3, China has been growing rapidly for some time. If this rapid growth were sustained, China would be a rich country in 20–30 years. In that case, we would predict that the real exchange rate would continue to fall from 1.7 in 2014 to a value much closer to 1.0. The formula for the real exchange rate in equation (19.3) tells us that either the nominal exchange rate, ε, has to fall a great deal, or else the ratio of Chinese to US prices, P^f/P, has to rise a great deal. To be concrete, suppose that ε did not change and that the real exchange rate between China and the United States reached 1.0 in 20 years. In that case, P^f/P would have to rise by a factor of 1.7 over 20 years. For that to happen, the average inflation rate, π^f, in China would have to exceed the average US inflation rate, π, by about 2.7% per year.

THE RELATIVE PPP CONDITION

Now, we will consider changes, rather than levels, of the real exchange rate. The PPP condition says that the nominal exchange rate, ε, equals the price ratio, P^f/P:

$$\varepsilon = P^f/P \tag{19.2}$$

We mentioned that this condition is equivalent to saying that the real exchange rate, given by:

$$real\ exchange\ rate = \frac{\varepsilon}{P^f/P} \tag{19.3}$$

equals 1.0.

Equation (19.3) implies that the growth rate of the real exchange rate equals the growth rate of the nominal exchange rate, which we denote by $\Delta\varepsilon/\varepsilon$, less the growth rate of the ratio of foreign to home prices, P^f/P. The growth rate of P^f/P is the difference between the inflation rates of the two countries:

$$growth\ rate\ of\ P^f/P = \Delta P^f/P^f - \Delta P/P$$
$$growth\ rate\ of\ P^f/P = \pi^f - \pi$$

Therefore, we have:

$$\text{growth rate of real exchange rate} = \Delta\varepsilon / \varepsilon - (\pi^f - \pi) \qquad (19.4)$$

When the PPP condition in equation (19.2) holds, so that the real exchange rate equals 1.0, the growth rate of the real exchange rate equals zero. Therefore, the right-hand side of equation (19.4) must be zero. If we rearrange this condition, we get another key condition about international finance:

Key equation (purchasing-power parity, relative form):

$$\Delta\varepsilon / \varepsilon = \pi^f - \pi$$

$$\text{growth rate of nominal exchange rate} = \text{foreign inflation rate} - \text{home inflation rate} \qquad (19.5)$$

Equation (19.5) is called the **relative form of PPP**, whereas equation (19.2) is often called the **absolute form of PPP**. The relative form involves *growth rates* of nominal exchange rates and prices, whereas the absolute form involves *levels* of nominal exchange rates and prices. The relative form of PPP is more general than the absolute form. The absolute form requires the real exchange rate to equal 1.0. The relative form requires the real exchange rate to be constant, so that the growth rate of the real exchange rate in equation (19.4) equals zero. However, the level of the real exchange rate does not have to equal 1.0 for the relative form of PPP to hold.

Extensive research shows that the relative PPP condition does not fit the data well for advanced economies over short periods. That is, the real exchange rate can vary a great deal in the short run and is surely not constant (even at values different from 1.0). However, the relative PPP condition does pretty well for advanced economies in the long run.

Before exploring this issue, we first introduce another common measure of the real exchange rate: the **real effective exchange rate**, which uses a weighted average of price levels for trading partners as P^f in equation (19.3) and a weighted average of inflation rates for trading partners as π^f in equation (19.4). A value near 1.0 means that goods in the base country cost about the same as goods in its trading partners.[5] Higher (lower) values mean that goods are more (less) expensive in the base country than in its trading partners.

Table 19.3 shows the behaviour of inflation rates and nominal and real *effective* exchange rates from 1960 to 2015 for each of the G-7 economies (as the base country in each case) considered in Figures 19.1 and 19.2. There is a

Table 19.3 Inflation rates and nominal and real effective exchange rates for the United States and six other major economies, 1960–2015

Country	(1) Inflation rate, π_i	(2) Inflation-rate differential, $\pi^f - \pi_i$	(3) Growth rate of nominal effective exchange rate, $\Delta\varepsilon^i / \varepsilon^i$	(4) Growth rate of real effective exchange rate [(3) − (2)]
US	3.78	3.12	3.07	−0.05
Canada	3.79	0.93	0.40	−0.53
France	4.22	0.92	0.73	−0.19
Germany	2.23	2.77	2.95	0.18
Italy	5.92	−0.76	−0.76	0.00
Japan	3.10	2.66	3.77	1.11
UK	5.80	−0.22	−0.19	0.04

Note: All variables are in per cent per year. Periods are 1960–2015. The inflation rate, π_i, for country i is calculated from the CPI. The inflation-rate differential, $\pi^f - \pi_i$, is the difference between a measure of inflation of trading partners, π^f, and the inflation rate in the base economy, π_i. The growth rate of the exchange rate, $\Delta\varepsilon^i / \varepsilon^i$, is the growth rate of country i's nominal effective exchange rate. A negative number means that the currency i fell in value relative to the currencies of its trading partners. The growth rate of the real effective exchange rate is the growth rate of the nominal effective exchange rate (column 3) less the inflation-rate differential (column 2). A negative value means that goods produced in the base country became less expensive over time compared to goods produced in its trading partners. The data are from Real Effective Exchange Rates for 178 Countries: A New Database (bruegel.org) and the International Monetary Fund's *International Financial Statistics*.

[5] Here, we no longer restrict the base country to being the United States.

tendency for higher inflation-rate differentials from the average (column 2) to match up with higher growth rates of nominal effective exchange rates (column 3). However, the match-up was not close enough to make the growth rates of real effective exchange rates in column 4 equal zero. The real effective exchange rates grew by 0–1% per year for Germany, Italy and the United Kingdom. That is, these countries all became only marginally more expensive compared to their trading partners. Japan's real effective exchange rate grew by 1.11% per year. For Canada, France and the US, the real effective exchange rates fell by 0–1%.

Table 19.4 examines inflation rates and nominal and real effective exchange rates for a group of mostly middle-income countries that had high average inflation rates between 1960 and 1996. In this case, the relative PPP condition looks quite good, in the sense that the differential inflation rates compared with trading partners (column 1) match up well with the growth rates of nominal exchange rates (column 2). The changes in real exchange rates in column 3 are small in comparison with the growth rates of the nominal exchange rates.

Table 19.4 Inflation rates and nominal and real effective exchange rates for high-inflation countries

Country	(1) Inflation-rate differential, $\pi^f - \pi_i$	(2) Growth rate of nominal effective exchange rate, $\Delta\varepsilon^i/\varepsilon^i$	(3) Growth rate of real effective exchange rate [(2) – (1)]
Argentina	−68	−67	1
Brazil	−76	−74	1
Chile	−25	−29	−4
Colombia	−7	−8	−1
Iceland	−25	−26	−1
Indonesia	−25	−28	−3
Israel	−25	−26	−1
Peru	−49	−45	4
Uruguay	−20	−19	1

Note: Periods – defined to include times of high inflation – are 1960–96. The inflation rate for country i, π_i, is calculated from the consumer price index. The inflation-rate differential, $\pi^f - \pi_i$, is the difference between a measure of inflation of trading partners, π and the inflation rate in the base economy, π_i. The growth rate of the exchange rate, $\Delta\varepsilon/\varepsilon$, is the average growth rate of country i's nominal effective exchange rate with their trading partners. A negative number means that the base currency *fell* in value relative to *its trading partners*. The growth rate of the real effective exchange rate is the growth rate of the nominal effective exchange rate (column 3) less the inflation-rate differential (column 2). A negative value means that goods produced in the base country became less expensive over time compared to goods produced in its trading partners. The data are from Real Effective Exchange Rates for 178 Countries: A New Database (bruegel.org).

Interest-rate parity

Now, we will look at the connections between interest rates across countries. Assume that there is a different nominal interest rate in each country. We again think of the United States as the home country and the United Kingdom as the foreign country. The nominal interest rate in the United States, denoted by i, is expressed as dollars paid per year per dollar held as US bonds. The nominal rate i^f in the United Kingdom is expressed as pounds paid per year per pound held as UK bonds.

Consider a household that has one US dollar in year t and is choosing between holding a US bond or a UK bond. (The household could reside in either country.) Option 1, holding a US bond, is straightforward. The amount of dollars received in year $t + 1$ depends only on the US interest rate:

Option 1: Hold US bond

$$\text{dollars received in year } t+1 = 1+i \tag{19.6}$$

The second option is to use the exchange market to obtain UK pounds, buy a UK bond and use the exchange market a year later to convert back to dollars. In this scenario, it will be important that the nominal exchange rate between pounds and dollars might change over time. Therefore, we use the time subscript t to denote the nominal exchange rate, ε_t, for year t. In year t, the household can exchange its \$1.00 for ε_t pounds. By holding a UK bond with the nominal interest rate i^f, the household receives $\varepsilon_t \bullet (1 + i^f)$ of pounds in year $t + 1$. In year $t + 1$, each pound can be exchanged for dollars at the rate of $1/\varepsilon_{t+1}$ dollars per pound. Therefore, if the household converts its pounds back to dollars in year $t + 1$, it receives $\varepsilon_t \bullet (1 + i^f)/\varepsilon_{t+1}$ of dollars. Thus, the second option yields:

$$\textit{Option 2: Use exchange market and hold UK bond}$$

$$\textit{dollars received in year } t+1 = \varepsilon_t \bullet (1+i^f)/\varepsilon_{t+1} \qquad (19.7)$$

If there are no costs for using the exchange market and holding UK bonds, the two options must, in equilibrium, yield the same number of dollars in year $t + 1$. Otherwise, all households would hold bonds only in the country with the highest yield and borrow only in the country with the lowest yield. Therefore, equations (19.6) and (19.7) give the equilibrium condition as:

$$1 + i = \varepsilon_t \bullet (1+i^f)/\varepsilon_{t+1}$$

$$\textit{return on holding US bond} = \textit{return on using exchange market and holding UK bond} \qquad (19.8)$$

Before we interpret equation (19.8), we will find it helpful to simplify the result by using some algebra. Start by rearranging the terms to get:

$$1 + i^f = (1+i) \bullet (\varepsilon_{t+1}/\varepsilon_t)$$

The growth rate of the nominal exchange rate is:

$$\Delta \varepsilon_t/\varepsilon_t = (\varepsilon_{t+1} - \varepsilon_t)/\varepsilon_t$$

$$\Delta \varepsilon_t/\varepsilon_t = \varepsilon_{t+1}/\varepsilon_t - 1$$

We can therefore substitute $(1 + \Delta\varepsilon_t/\varepsilon_t)$ for $\varepsilon_{t+1}/\varepsilon_t$ in the equation above to get:

$$1 + i^f = (1+i) \bullet (1 + \Delta \varepsilon_t/\varepsilon_t)$$

If we multiply out the two terms on the right-hand side, we get:

$$1 + i^f = 1 + i + \Delta \varepsilon_t/\varepsilon_t + i \bullet \Delta \varepsilon_t/\varepsilon_t$$

The last term, $i \bullet \Delta\varepsilon_t/\varepsilon_t$, tends to be small – in fact, this term becomes negligible if we consider very short periods, rather than years. Therefore, we neglect this term. If we cancel out the 1s on each side of the equation and move i from the right-hand side to the left-hand side, we get the result we are looking for:

$$i^f - i = \Delta\varepsilon_t/\varepsilon_t$$

$$\textit{interest-rate differential} = \textit{growth rate of nominal exchange rate} \qquad (19.9)$$

To understand equation (19.9), imagine that the pound–dollar exchange rate, ε_t, is rising over time; that is, the dollar is becoming more valuable compared to the pound at the rate $\Delta\varepsilon/\varepsilon_t$. In order for US and UK bonds to yield the same return in dollars, the UK nominal interest rate, i^f, has to exceed the US nominal rate, i, by the growth rate of the nominal exchange rate, $\Delta\varepsilon/\varepsilon_t$. That is, the interest-rate differential has to compensate for the increase in the nominal exchange rate, which favours holding US bonds.

In practice, changes in nominal exchange rates are not known precisely in advance. Therefore, the growth rate $\Delta\varepsilon/\varepsilon_t$ in equation (19.9) must be replaced by the expected growth rate, $(\Delta\varepsilon_t/\varepsilon_t)^e$. When we make this change, we get an important result called **interest-rate parity:**

Key equation (interest-rate parity):

$$i^f - i = (\Delta \varepsilon_t/\varepsilon_t)^e$$

$$\textit{interest-rate differential} = \textit{expected growth rate of nominal exchange rate} \qquad (19.10)$$

The idea behind equation (19.10) is that for the two interest rates to offer the same deal – to have parity in the returns offered on bonds in the two countries – the difference in nominal interest rates, $i^f - i$, has to compensate for the expected growth rate of the nominal exchange rate, $(\Delta\varepsilon/\varepsilon_t)^e$.[6]

A number of real-world considerations prevent interest-rate parity from holding exactly. These considerations include uncertainties about asset returns and exchange-rate movements, the tax treatment of interest income in different countries, and government restrictions on currency exchanges and asset flows across international borders. For the main developed countries, departures from interest-rate parity are sometimes substantial in the short run but tend to be small in the long run.

We can use the results on interest-rate parity to compare real interest rates across countries. To make this comparison, we need our earlier result for purchasing-power parity in relative form:

$$\Delta\varepsilon/\varepsilon = \pi^f - \pi \tag{19.4}$$

We can revise this condition to express the terms as expected rates of change:

$$(\Delta\varepsilon_t/\varepsilon_t)^e = (\pi^f)^e - \pi^e \tag{19.11}$$

If we substitute this result for $(\Delta\varepsilon/\varepsilon_t)^e$ into the interest-rate parity condition from equation (19.10), we get:

$$i^f - i = (\pi^f)^e - \pi^e \tag{19.12}$$

interest-rate differential = difference in expected inflation rates

We can rearrange the terms to get an important result about real interest rates:

> Key equation (equality of expected real interest rates across countries):
>
> $$i^f - (\pi^f)^e = i - \pi^e$$
>
> *foreign expected real interest rate = home expected real interest rate* $\qquad$ (19.13)

Thus, the combination of the interest-rate parity condition – equation (19.10) – with the PPP condition in relative form – equation (19.11) – implies that expected real interest rates are the same in the foreign country (the United Kingdom) and the home country (the United States).

For advanced countries, expected real interest rates on government securities are not equal in practice, but the differences are usually not too large.[7] One reason for the discrepancies is that, as discussed before, the PPP condition in relative form – equation (19.11) – does not always hold; that is, real exchange rates are not always expected to be constant. We mentioned that, for advanced countries, real exchange rates tended to adjust over time towards values close to 1.0. Consider, for example, Switzerland and Australia, which were expensive compared to the United States in 2014 – the real exchange rates in Table 19.2 were 0.70 and 0.74, respectively. Our prediction was that these real exchange rates would increase towards 1.0 in the long run.

Recall that the formula for the real exchange rate is:

$$\text{real exchange rate} = \frac{\varepsilon}{P^f/P} \tag{19.3}$$

Our prediction of a rising real exchange rate for Switzerland and the US means that the expected growth rate of the nominal exchange rate, $(\Delta\varepsilon/\varepsilon_t)^e$, must be higher than the expected growth of P^f/P, which equals the difference

---

[6]Although the growth rate of the nominal exchange rate is unknown in advance, bondholders can ensure themselves of the future exchange rate by using a forward exchange contract, as described in the By the Numbers box 'Exchange rates around the world'. In that case, $(\Delta s_t/s_t)^e$ on the right-hand side of equation (19.10) is replaced by the forward premium on the exchange market, given by (forward – spot exchange rate)/(spot exchange rate). The equality between the interest-rate differential on the left-hand side of equation (19.10) and this forward premium is called *covered interest-rate parity*.

[7]For discussions, see Robert Barro and Xavier Sala-i-Martin (1990), Robert Cumby and Maurice Obstfeld (1984) and Frederic Mishkin (1984).

between the expected inflation rates, $(\pi^f)^e - \pi^e$. Therefore, instead of the equality in equation (19.11), we have the inequality:

$$(\Delta \varepsilon_t / \varepsilon_t)^e > (\pi^f)^e - \pi^e \tag{19.14}$$

If we substitute this inequality into the interest-rate parity condition in equation (19.10), we get:

$$i^f - i > (\pi^f)^e - \pi^e$$

Rearranging terms, we have:

$$i^f - (\pi^f)^e > i - \pi$$

foreign expected real interest rate > home expected real interest rate (19.15)

Therefore, our prediction for a country, such as Switzerland or Australia, with low real exchange rates in 2014, that is initially more expensive than the United States, is that the expected real interest rates in such a country will be higher than in the United States. One way to think about this result is that we predict that relatively more expensive countries will become cheaper over time. To make this adjustment, the countries must have relatively low inflation rates, which correspond to relatively high real interest rates.

Fixed exchange rates

Until the early 1970s and except during major wars, economically advanced countries typically maintained fixed nominal exchange rates among their currencies. Figures 19.1 and 19.2 show that, from 1950 to the early 1970s, the nominal exchange rates between six major currencies and the US dollar moved infrequently and by small amounts compared to what came later. For the six countries considered, the main exceptions to fixed nominal exchange rates in this period were the fluctuations in the Canadian dollar rate until the early 1960s and some realignments in the nominal exchange rates for the French franc, German mark and UK pound.

In Chapter 18, we assumed an extreme form of fixed nominal exchange rates – an environment where all countries used a common currency. Since there was only one money, the fixity of nominal exchange rates had to hold. Within a country, this arrangement is so common that it is usually taken for granted; for example, Massachusetts and California use the same US dollar and, therefore, maintain a fixed nominal exchange rate. However, until recently, the typical set-up for countries was that each one had its own currency. An important exception since 1999–2001 is the euro, now used by 19 European countries and likely to expand to cover additional countries in Europe. In earlier times, the main examples of common currencies were small countries that used another country's currency, or shared a single currency. For example, Panama and Ecuador use the US dollar; 12 countries in Africa use the CFA franc, which has been linked, aside from one devaluation, to the French franc (since 1999, the euro); and seven islands in the Caribbean use the Caribbean dollar, which is linked to the US dollar.

The fixed-exchange-rate regime that applied to most advanced countries from World War II until the early 1970s was called the **Bretton Woods System**.[8] Under this system, the participating countries established narrow bands within which they pegged the nominal exchange rate, ε, between their currency and the US dollar. Each country's central bank stood ready to buy or sell its currency at the rate of ε units per US dollar. For example, the German central bank (Bundesbank) provided dollars for marks when households (or, more likely, financial institutions) wanted to reduce their holdings of marks, and the reverse when households wished to increase their holdings of marks. To manage these exchanges, each central bank maintained a stock of assets as *international reserves*; for example, US currency or gold, or, more likely, interest-bearing assets such as US Treasury bills that could be readily converted into US currency. Then, the United States stood ready to exchange US dollars for gold (on the request of foreign official institutions) at a fixed price, which happened to be $35 per ounce. Thus, by maintaining a fixed nominal exchange rate with the US dollar, each country indirectly pegged its currency to gold.

Another historical example of a system of fixed exchange rates is the classical **gold standard**. In this set-up each central bank directly pegged its currency to gold at a fixed rate of exchange. The United Kingdom was effectively on the gold standard from the early eighteenth century until World War I, except for a period of suspension from

---

[8]The system was named in honour of the meeting site, Bretton Woods, New Hampshire, where the regime was set up.

1797 to 1821 because of the Napoleonic Wars. After departing from the gold standard during World War I, the United Kingdom returned to this system in 1926 but departed again during the Great Depression in 1931. The United States was on the gold standard from 1879 until the trough of the Great Depression in 1933, when the dollar price of gold was raised from $20.67 to $35 per ounce. Earlier periods involved a greater role for silver in the United States. From an international perspective, the high point of the gold standard was from 1890 to 1914.

Under a gold standard (or other commodity standard), each central bank pegs the value of its currency in terms of gold (or other commodities). An ounce of gold might, for example, be set at $20 in New York and £4 in London (roughly, the values prevailing in 1914). In this environment, the nominal exchange rate between UK pounds and US dollars had to be close to 0.2 pounds per dollar. Otherwise (subject to the costs of shipping gold), it would be profitable to buy gold in one country and sell it in the other. As with the Bretton Woods System, the classical gold standard would – if adhered to by the participants – maintain fixed nominal exchange rates among the various currencies.

It is possible for countries to maintain fixed nominal exchange rates in a regime that has no role for gold or other commodities. For example, from 1979 to 1992, several Western European countries kept the nominal exchange rates among their currencies fixed within fairly narrow bands. This arrangement, called the European Monetary System (EMS), effectively evolved into the euro, which became the common currency of 12 Western European countries over a transition period from 1999 to 2001. Although most countries in Western Europe use the euro, some important exceptions are the United Kingdom, Sweden, Denmark and Switzerland.

PURCHASING-POWER PARITY UNDER FIXED EXCHANGE RATES

To see the workings of a system with fixed nominal exchange rates, consider again the setting where the United States is the home country. We can still think of the United Kingdom as the foreign country, but we have to consider the pre-1971 environment in which the pound–dollar exchange rate was fixed in most years.

Suppose that the absolute PPP condition holds, so that the nominal exchange rate, ε, equals the ratio of the UK price level, P^f, to the US price level, P:

$$\varepsilon = P^f/P \tag{19.2}$$

Rearranging the terms, we get that the UK price level is given by:

$$P^f = \varepsilon P \tag{19.16}$$

Therefore, if the nominal exchange rate, ε, is fixed, P^f must move in lockstep with P. This condition means that the UK inflation rate, π^f, equals the US inflation rate, π:

Under fixed exchange rates :

$$\pi^f = \pi \tag{19.17}$$

The equality between the two inflation rates would not hold if we introduced deviations from the PPP conditions. However, we know that the PPP conditions work fairly well in the long run. Therefore, *if a country fixes its nominal exchange rate with the US dollar, the country must, in the long run, experience roughly the same inflation rate as the United States.*

The interest-rate parity condition is:

$$i^f - i = (\Delta \varepsilon_t / \varepsilon_t)^e \tag{19.10}$$

With a fixed nominal exchange rate, the expected growth rate of the nominal exchange rate, $(\Delta \varepsilon / \varepsilon_t)^e$, equals zero. Therefore, equation (19.10) implies that the UK nominal interest rate, i^f, equals the US rate:

Under fixed exchange rates :

$$i^f = i \tag{19.18}$$

The equality between nominal interest rates would not hold if we introduced deviations from the interest-rate parity condition. However, we know that this condition works fairly well, at least for advanced economies. Therefore, if a country – particularly an advanced economy – fixes its nominal exchange rate with the US dollar, the country must have roughly the same nominal interest rate as the United States.

THE NOMINAL QUANTITY OF MONEY UNDER FIXED EXCHANGE RATES

We will now study the determinants of the nominal quantity of money under fixed exchange rates. In working out these results, we think of the foreign country as economically small in relation to the United States. In particular, we assume that economic changes in the foreign country have negligible effects on US economic variables. Thus, our conclusions will fit better if the foreign country is economically smaller than the United Kingdom.

For a closed economy in Chapter 11, we stressed the relationship between a country's nominal quantity of money, M, and its price level, P. As before, we think of money as currency in circulation or, more broadly, as high-powered money, which includes deposits held by financial institutions at the central bank. The question is, how does our present analysis of fixed exchange rates relate to our discussion from Chapter 11? Somehow, we determined the UK price level, P^f, in equation (19.16) without saying anything about the UK nominal quantity of money, M^f.

As in Chapter 11, UK households demand a quantity of real money, M^f/P^f, that depends on UK real GDP, Y^f, and the nominal interest rate, i^f. We also have, from equation (19.18), that the UK nominal interest rate, i^f, equals the US rate, i. Therefore, the condition that M^f equal the nominal quantity demanded is:

$$M^f = P^f \cdot D(Y^f, i) \tag{19.19}$$

As in Chapter 11, the function $D(\bullet)$ determines the real demand for money in the United Kingdom. This real demand rises with real GDP, Y^f, and falls with the nominal interest rate, i.

If the absolute PPP condition holds, the UK price level is given by:

$$P^f = \varepsilon P \tag{19.16}$$

If we substitute for P^f from equation (19.16) into equation (19.19), we get:

$$M^f = \varepsilon P \cdot D(Y^f, i) \tag{19.20}$$

The nominal exchange rate, ε, is a fixed number. We are assuming that the US price level, P, and nominal interest rate, i, are determined independently of conditions in the United Kingdom. Therefore, for a given UK real GDP, Y^f, equation (19.20) prescribes the nominal quantity of money, M^f, that must be circulating within the UK. Hence, M^f cannot be freely chosen by the Bank of England, the UK central bank.

To understand these results, assume that the UK price level, P^f, accorded initially with the absolute PPP condition in equation (19.16). Assume further that the UK nominal quantity of money, M^f, equalled the amount given in equation (19.20) and, therefore, equalled the nominal quantity demanded.

Suppose that the Bank of England increases the nominal quantity of money, M^f, by an open-market purchase of UK government bonds, a form of open-market operation considered in Chapter 15. Table 19.5 shows a simplified balance sheet for the Bank. For the open-market operation that we are considering, the quantity of Bank assets in the form of UK bonds rises on the left-hand side of the balance sheet. Correspondingly, Bank liabilities in the form of UK currency, M^f, in circulation increase on the right-hand side of the balance sheet.

Our analysis of a closed economy in Chapter 11 suggests that the increase in M^f would raise the UK price level, P^f. However, if P^f rose, it would exceed the PPP level dictated by equation (19.16). Hence, for a given nominal exchange rate, ε, goods bought in the United Kingdom would become more expensive compared to goods bought in the United States. In response, households from both countries move away from buying goods in the United Kingdom and towards buying them in the United States. To facilitate this changed pattern of expenditure, households – or, more realistically, financial institutions – take their excess UK money to the Bank of England to exchange for US money. Note that, if the Bank is fixing the nominal exchange rate, it stands ready to exchange dollars for pounds at the rate of $1/\varepsilon$ dollars per pound. But then the UK nominal quantity of money, M^f, falls back towards its initial level. In Table 19.5, M^f declines on the right-hand side of the balance sheet. On the left-hand side, the Bank of England

Table 19.5 Simplified balance sheet of central bank (Bank of England)

Assets	Liabilities
International reserves (US dollar currency and Treasury bills, other foreign currency, gold)	UK currency, M^f
UK bonds	

loses assets in the form of US dollar currency or, more likely, US Treasury bills. These assets, along with other foreign currencies and gold, are called **international reserves** because they can be used readily to make payments with financial institutions, including other central banks.

The ultimate effect, on the left-hand side of the balance sheet in Table 19.5, is that the Bank has more assets in the form of UK bonds (bought in the initial open-market operation) and less international reserves. On the right-hand side, the net nominal quantity of money, M^f, is unchanged. The initial increase is fully offset by the return of money to the Bank. Only then does the UK nominal quantity of money, M^f, equal the nominal quantity demanded, as prescribed by equation (19.20). This unchanged M^f is consistent with an unchanged UK price level, P^f. That is, P^f accords with the PPP condition given in equation (19.16).

To complete the story, we have to assess the Bank of England's reaction to its loss of international reserves. One possibility is that the Bank allows the nominal quantity of money, M^f, to decline back to the level consistent with equation (19.20). In that case, the Bank ends up holding more UK government bonds and less international reserves, but the nominal quantity of money, M^f, is unchanged overall. This automatic response of the nominal quantity of money is a key element of the gold standard and other systems of fixed exchange rates. The mechanism means that, as long as the central bank fixes the nominal exchange rate, ε, it lacks control over the nominal quantity of money, M^f.

As another possibility, when the automatic mechanism tends to reduce the nominal quantity of money, M^f, the Bank of England might resist this tendency by initiating another open-market purchase of UK bonds. This process is called **sterilization**, because the Bank is attempting to sterilize or insulate the outstanding nominal quantity of money, M^f, from the losses of international reserves. In the present case, the Bank wants to engineer a monetary expansion even though this expansion is inconsistent with the fixed nominal exchange rate. Eventually, a policy of sterilization leads to a drain on reserves sufficient for the Bank to become unwilling or unable to maintain the nominal exchange rate. In other words, with a shortage of reserves, the Bank of England may no longer be willing or able to provide US dollars at the fixed rate of $1/\varepsilon$ dollars per pound. Instead, there may be a **devaluation**, which is a reduction in the value of the pound compared to the dollar. In the present case, a UK devaluation is a decrease in the exchange rate below $1/\varepsilon$ dollars per pound – so that ε, the number of pounds obtained for each dollar, increases. The important point is that the tendency of central banks to sterilize the flows of international reserves threatens the viability of fixed exchange rates.[9]

We should mention another possible reaction of UK policy to the loss of international reserves. Recall that this drain resulted from the Bank of England's excessive monetary creation. This policy tended to raise the UK price level, P^f, above the absolute PPP value given in equation (19.16). To counter the drain of international reserves, the UK government might impose trade restrictions, which artificially raise the cost of US goods for UK households. The more general point is that the UK government might interfere with free international trade to prevent the absolute PPP condition from holding. Thus, there are two types of ill effects from excessive monetary expansion in a regime of fixed exchange rates. One is the loss of international reserves, an outcome that tends, eventually, to cause a devaluation. Second, to avoid either devaluation or monetary contraction, the government may interfere with free trade. The frequency of these interferences during the post-World War II period was a major argument used by opponents of fixed exchange rates (see Milton Friedman , 1968a, ch. 9).

DEVALUATION AND REVALUATION

We discussed a situation in which the United Kingdom loses international reserves and is thereby pressured to devalue its currency. In other circumstances, the UK gains international reserves and is pressured to raise the value of its currency. An appreciation of the UK currency – an increase in $1/\varepsilon$, the number of dollars that exchange for each pound – is called a **revaluation**.

---

[9]This discussion uses a framework called the **monetary approach to the balance of payments**. This approach was developed by Robert Mundell (1968, part 2; 1971, part 2). The early origins of this theory are found in the eighteenth-century writings of David Hume; see Eugene Rotwein (1970).

The pressures for devaluation and revaluation in systems of fixed nominal exchange rates are not symmetric. Devaluations typically result from losses of international reserves. The threat of running out of reserves provides direct pressure for devaluation; for example, the Bank of England may no longer have the ability to exchange dollars for pounds at the rate of $1/\varepsilon$ dollars per pound. In the reverse situation, the Bank of England accumulates international reserves. In this case, the pressure to revalue is less direct. Mostly, the Bank has to decide that holding large quantities of international reserves is undesirable. An example in 2006 was the vast amounts of US Treasury bonds amassed by central banks in Japan, China and other Asian countries. Revaluation is a way to counter this build-up of international reserves.

Figures 19.1 and 19.2 (see p. 357) provide examples of devaluations and revaluations during the mainly fixed-exchange-rate period before the early 1970s. France devalued the franc by a total of 40% in 1957–58, Germany revalued the mark by 5% in 1961 and 7% in 1969, and the United Kingdom devalued the pound by 14% in 1967. In addition, several revaluations occurred in 1971–72, just as the Bretton Woods System was passing into history: Japan revalued the yen by 16%, Germany revalued the mark by 13% and Switzerland revalued the franc by 13%.

World history shows many examples of fixed-exchange-rate systems that ended with substantial devaluations. However, aside from the cases already mentioned up to the early 1970s, it is hard to find fixed-rate regimes that ended with substantial revaluations. From 2004–11, China revalued its currency – the renminbi – by a total of almost 22%, when it ended its fixed-rate system with the US dollar. In recent times, fixed-exchange-rate systems that culminated in large devaluations included the United Kingdom (32% devaluation in 1992, following a period of fixed exchange rates with major European currencies under the European Monetary System), Mexico (97% in 1994–95), South Korea (91% in 1997–98), Malaysia (67% in 1997–98), Thailand (109% in 1997–98), Indonesia (495% in 1997–98), Russia (266% in 1998), Brazil (71% in 1999) and Argentina (280% in 2002).

We will now consider the effects from an exogenous devaluation. Suppose that the Bank of England normally maintains a fixed nominal exchange rate with the US dollar (as it did before 1971). Then, for no particular reason, the Bank decides to lower the number of dollars, $1/\varepsilon$, paid out for each pound. That is, it increases the number of pounds, ε, paid out for each dollar.

Consider again the real exchange rate:

$$real\ exchange\ rate = \frac{\varepsilon}{P^f/P} \qquad (19.3)$$

which gives the number of goods that can be bought (with one US dollar) in the United Kingdom compared to the number that can be bought in the United States. If the United Kingdom devalues its currency – raises the nominal exchange rate, ε – the real exchange rate increases for a given ratio of UK to US prices, P^f/P. Therefore, the demand for UK goods rises. This increase in demand tends to raise the UK price level, P^f. Ultimately, P^f would rise by enough to restore the real exchange rate to its equilibrium level, something close to 1.0. The main point is that the UK devaluation creates inflationary pressure in the United Kingdom.[10]

Notice the two-way direction of causation between devaluation and inflation. We found before that expansionary monetary policy – increases in M^f and P^f – created pressure for devaluation. In this sense, domestic inflation tends to cause devaluation. Now, we see that an exogenous devaluation tends to raise P^f. In this sense, devaluation is itself inflationary.

---

[10]As in our previous analysis of the Bank of England and its balance sheet in Table 19.4, we can show that the process of raising P entails an increase in the UK nominal quantity of money M^f. This analysis works for a one-time devaluation. Additional effects arise if households expect future devaluations. This expectation raises the UK expected rate of inflation, $(\pi^f)^e$, which increases the UK nominal interest rate, i^f, in equation (19.10).

Economics in Practice
The Asian financial crisis

As discussed in Chapter 3, many of the fastest growing countries in the world since the 1960s are in East Asia. However, many of these countries experienced a setback in 1997–98, during the Asian financial crisis. The crisis began in July 1997 with the floating of Thailand's currency, the baht, which had been fixed to the US dollar since the early 1980s. The crisis spread rapidly to the Philippine peso (fairly stable against the dollar since 1990), Malaysian ringgit (nearly fixed against the dollar since the mid-1980s), Indonesian rupiah (which had been devaluing gradually against the dollar since the late 1980s) and South Korean won (fairly stable against the dollar since the mid-1980s). From summer 1997 to the worst point in 1998 (between January and September, depending on the country), the currency devaluations were between 60% and 110% for Thailand, the Philippines, Malaysia and South Korea, and around 400% for Indonesia. Since the changes in price levels were small in comparison, these steep devaluations of nominal exchange rates also represented sharp devaluations of real exchange rates. Other East Asian economies experienced much milder devaluation (Singapore and Taiwan), or no devaluation (China and Hong Kong).

What caused the Asian financial crisis? At the time, many observers thought that these star growth performers in Asia were being unfairly punished by irrational world currency markets. However, subsequent analyses found problems in government policies and incentive structures, especially in domestic financial systems. The set-ups encouraged excessive borrowing on world markets, especially by banks and finance companies, to invest in construction and other projects. Although many investments were highly speculative, the limited risks borne by key decision makers – financiers and entrepreneurs – led to excessive borrowing and investing. In addition, many loans were influenced by government pressure and were directed to politically favoured companies, which were often unprofitable.

Increased knowledge about the investment and lending structure in some East Asian countries led to the marking down of asset values on stock, bond and real estate markets. These adjustments and cutbacks in investments contributed to the financial crisis and led to widespread bankruptcies, especially of banks and construction companies. The financial distress led to broad contractions of real economic activity; for example, Thailand's fall of real GDP in 1998 was its first decrease since the 1950s.

By 1999, the East Asian countries that suffered from the financial crisis had rebounded to positive economic growth, though at rates below pre-crisis levels. Some domestic financial regulations and government policies had been improved to promote lending based on sound commercial principles, rather than weak individual incentives or government pressure. Thus, despite the pain of the Asian financial crisis, some useful long-term lessons were learned.

Flexible exchange rates

The international system of fixed nominal exchange rates anchored on the US dollar broke down in the early 1970s. One reason was the excessive creation of US dollars and the consequent rise in the US price level after the mid-1960s. This inflation made it increasingly difficult for the United States to maintain convertibility of the dollar into gold at the set rate of $35 per ounce. President Nixon decided, in 1971, to raise the dollar price of gold and to curb flows of gold from the United States to foreign central banks. These actions signalled the end of the Bretton Woods System, whereby currencies were linked to gold through the US dollar.

Since the early 1970s, most advanced countries have allowed their currencies to vary more or less freely to clear the markets for foreign exchange. We see from Figures 19.1 and 19.2 that the nominal exchange rates of six major currencies with the US dollar have fluctuated substantially since the early 1970s. Many middle- and lower-income countries, especially the high-inflation countries covered in Table 19.4, have also maintained flexible exchange rates. The table shows that the nominal exchange rates rose sharply over time for these high-inflation countries.

Groups of countries, such as the members of the European Monetary System from 1979 to 1992 and the euro countries since 1999, have maintained fixed exchange rates among their currencies. Argentina maintained a fixed exchange rate with the US dollar from 1991 to 2001, China maintained a fixed exchange rate with the US dollar from 1994 to 2005, and other Asian countries maintained fixed exchange rates with the US dollar over various periods. Nevertheless, the most important development since the early 1970s has been the increased reliance on flexible exchange rates. To study this system, we have to extend the model to consider the determination of exchange rates in a flexible-rate system.

We, again, think of the United Kingdom as the foreign country and the United States as the home country. The absolute PPP condition still gives a relation between the UK price level, P^f, and the US price level, P:

$$P^f = \varepsilon P \qquad\qquad (19.16)$$

The difference from the fixed-exchange-rate set-up is that the nominal exchange rate, ε, is not a fixed number. Because of adjustments of ε in a flexible-rate regime, P^f need not move in lockstep with P even if the absolute PPP condition always holds.

The Bank of England can now use its policy tools to achieve a desired path of the price level, P^f. As in our analysis of a closed economy in Chapters 11 and 12, this process involves adjustments of the UK nominal quantity of money, M^f, and the UK nominal interest rate, i^f. Given the path of P^f, the United Kingdom can allow the nominal exchange rate, ε, to adjust (or float) freely to satisfy the absolute PPP condition in equation (19.16). Thus, the important point is that the United Kingdom can choose a monetary policy that is independent of that chosen by the United States.

Fixed and flexible exchange rates: A comparison

Every country has a choice about whether to have a flexible exchange rate or a fixed exchange rate, tied, for example, to the US dollar (or the euro or a basket of currencies). Each system has pluses and minuses, and we cannot say that one system is superior at all times for all countries. However, we can list the pluses and minuses in the two set-ups.

- An extreme form of fixed nominal exchange rate is a common currency. This arrangement applies within countries; for example, California and Massachusetts use the same money, the US dollar. This set-up is enormously convenient; it greatly facilitates trade in goods and assets across state borders. The same kind of convenience applies to the use of a common currency across national borders. Thus, the decision to adopt a common currency, the euro, by 12 Western European countries in 1999–2001 encouraged trade in goods and assets among these countries. Fixed nominal exchange rates between different currencies are less convenient for transactions than a common currency, but a fixed exchange rate is more convenient than a flexible exchange rate. One way to make this point is to observe that choices of fixed exchange rates are not about whether to have them at all but, rather, to decide over what range of economic activity, legal jurisdiction and physical territory they should apply. Should fixed nominal exchange rates apply only within each independent country and not across any international borders? From an economic standpoint, the identification of independent moneys with independent countries is unlikely to be optimal.
- One advantage of a flexible nominal exchange rate is that it introduces an additional way to satisfy the PPP condition, $P^f = \varepsilon P$, in equation (19.16). For a given US price level, P, fixity of the nominal exchange rate, ε, means that the foreign price level, P^f, has to adjust on its own to satisfy the PPP condition. This adjustment might be difficult if some prices adjust slowly, as in the new Keynesian model developed in Chapter 17. Then, in the transition to a new equilibrium value of P^f, the economy might suffer from reduced output and higher unemployment. Some of this difficult transition might be avoided by the rapid adjustment of the nominal exchange rate, ε, in a flexible-rate system. Economists believe that this sticky-price argument is more important for countries that are very different from one another, that trade little with one another, and that have little mobility of labour and capital between them. Thus, this argument suggests that fixed nominal exchange

rates – including common currencies – work better between economies that are basically similar, have a great deal of trade, and have considerable mobility of labour and capital between them.

• Related to the previous point, a fixed-exchange-rate system precludes an independent monetary policy, at least in the long run. To put it the opposite way, a flexible-rate system allows for an independent monetary policy at every point in time. This independence might be useful if the monetary authority uses its policy instruments wisely to improve the functioning of the economy. For example, with the kinds of sticky prices assumed in Chapter 17, monetary policy can be used to avoid periods of depressed output and high unemployment. Fixed nominal exchange rates preclude this kind of helpful monetary policy.

• The independence of monetary policy under flexible exchange rates is not always desirable. For example, in the price-misperceptions model developed in Chapter 16, output and employment respond to unexpected movements in the price level and monetary aggregates. Under these conditions, the monetary authority may want to surprise households with unexpected inflation, and this temptation tends to generate an equilibrium with high and variable inflation. An advantage of a fixed nominal exchange rate is that it commits the monetary authority not to pursue this kind of monetary policy. That is, if the central bank is committed to maintaining the nominal exchange rate, it cannot simultaneously create major surprise movements in the price level and monetary aggregates. From this standpoint, a fixed-rate system might produce better outcomes than a flexible-rate system. However, this conclusion is tempered by the realization that governments and central banks can renege on promises to maintain a fixed nominal exchange rate. As an example, Argentina adopted a strong form of fixed exchange rate with the US dollar in 1991. This commitment was part of a broader programme of economic reform, and the fixed exchange rate worked well through 1998 to improve the workings of the Argentine economy. However, after an economic crisis in 1999–2001, the Argentine government and central bank went back on their promise that 1 peso was worth 1 US dollar. A sharp devaluation made the nominal exchange rate about 3 pesos per dollar. The economy suffered dramatically in 2002 from the change in regime, essentially going through an economic depression.

Summing Up

In Chapter 18, all countries used a common currency. In this chapter, we allowed for different currencies and, therefore, for exchange rates between the currencies. The nominal exchange rate specifies the amount of foreign currency, such as UK pounds, that trades for each US dollar. In contrast, the real exchange rate specifies the number of UK (or foreign) *goods* that exchanges for each unit of US (or home) *goods*.

The condition for absolute PPP says that the nominal exchange rate – say, pounds per dollar – equals the ratio of the UK (or foreign) price level to the US (or home) price level. Equivalently, the real exchange rate equals 1.0. This condition does not hold exactly, because economies specialize in the production of different goods, and the costs of non-traded goods and services depend on where one buys them. For advanced economies, real exchange rates deviate from 1.0, but not by too much. For middle- and lower-income countries, real exchange rates are usually far above 1.0; that is, market baskets of goods and services are cheaper than in the United States.

The relative form of the PPP condition says that the growth rate of the nominal exchange rate equals the difference between the inflation rates of the UK (foreign) and US (home) countries. Equivalently, this condition says that the growth rate of the real exchange rate equals zero. This condition does not work so well in the short run for advanced economies but does much better in the long run. It also works well for middle-income countries with high inflation.

The interest-rate parity condition says that the difference between the UK (foreign) and US (home) nominal interest rates equals the expected growth rate of the nominal exchange rate. When combined with the relative form of the PPP condition, the interest-rate parity condition implies that expected real interest rates are the same in the two countries. The interest-rate parity condition explains a great deal about cross-country behaviour of interest rates, especially for rich countries. However, this condition need not hold exactly if we allow for differences across countries in tax systems, uncertainties about asset returns and exchange-rate movements, and government restrictions on currency exchanges and cross-border asset flows.

Fixed exchange rates applied to the advanced countries under the Bretton Woods System, which prevailed from the end of World War II until the early 1970s. Fixed rates also apply to common-currency systems, such as the euro regime adopted in 1999–2001 by 12 Western European countries. With a fixed nominal exchange rate, the UK (foreign) inflation rate has to be similar to that in the United States. Therefore, a country with a fixed nominal exchange rate cannot carry out an independent monetary policy. An attempt to have an independent monetary policy in a fixed-rate system can lead to losses of international reserves and, consequently, devaluation of the currency.

Under flexible exchange rates, a country can have an independent monetary policy. This policy can be managed to achieve a desired price level. The nominal exchange rate then adjusts to be consistent with this price level.

The choice between fixed and flexible exchange rates depends on a number of factors. Fixed exchange rates, especially a common currency, reduce the transaction costs for trades in goods and assets. Flexible exchange rates allow for an independent monetary policy, which can sometimes be managed wisely to avoid depressed output and high unemployment. Fixed exchange rates can usefully commit the central bank to low and stable inflation. However, by devaluing, governments and central banks can break the promise to maintain a fixed exchange rate.

Key Terms and Concepts

absolute form of PPP	exchange rate	monetary approach to the	real exchange rate
Balassa–Samuelson	fixed exchange rates	balance of payments	PPP
hypothesis	flexible exchange rates	nominal exchange rate	relative form of PPP
Bretton Woods System	gold standard	non-tradable goods	revaluation
devaluation	interest-rate parity	purchasing-power parity	sterilization
exchange market	international reserves	real effective exchange rate	

Questions and Problems

A Review questions

1 In a flexible-exchange-rate system, a country such as Brazil that has a persistently high inflation rate, π, will experience regular depreciation of its nominal exchange rate with the US dollar. Explain why this happens. Why might the Brazilian government like this system?

2 Explain the condition for interest-rate parity in equation (19.11). Explain how this condition leads to the equality for expected real interest rates across countries in equation (19.14).

3 We have mentioned as examples of fixed-exchange-rate systems the classical gold standard, the Bretton Woods System and a set-up with a common currency. Explain how each of these systems operates to maintain a fixed nominal exchange rate.

4 Explain the conditions for absolute and relative purchasing-power parity in equations (19.2) and (19.5).

5 Explain how the nominal exchange rate differs from the real exchange rate. Which rate is pegged in a system of fixed exchange rates?

6 Does the central bank have discretion over the quantity of domestic money in a fixed-exchange-rate system? Show how an attempt to carry out an independent monetary policy can lead to devaluation or revaluation. Why might the attempt lead to trade restrictions?

B Problems for discussion

7 Futures contracts on foreign exchange

If a person buys a one-month futures contract on the euro, they are agreeing to purchase euros next month at a dollar exchange rate set today. The buyer of this contract goes long on the euro and does well if the euro appreciates (more than the amount expected) over the month. Similarly, the seller of a futures contract agrees to sell euros next month at a dollar exchange rate set today.

The seller goes short on the euro and does well if the euro depreciates (more than expected) over the month.

Consider a euro bond with a maturity of one month. This bond sells for a specific number of euros today and will pay out a stated number of euros in one month. How can a person use the currency futures market to guarantee the dollar rate of return from buying the euro bond and holding it for one month?

8 Shipping gold under the gold standard

Suppose (using unrealistic numbers) that the price of gold is $5 per ounce in New York and £1 per ounce in London. Assume, initially, that gold can be shipped between New York and London at zero cost.

a Assume that the dollar-pound exchange rate is $6 per pound. If a person starts with $1000 in New York, what can the person do to make a profit? If the cost of shipping gold between New York and London is 1% of the amount shipped, how high does the exchange rate have to rise above $5 per pound to make this action profitable?

b Go through the same exercise when the exchange rate is $4 per pound, from the perspective of someone who starts with £200 in London.

c The results determine a range of exchange rates around $5 per pound for which it is unprofitable to ship gold in either direction between New York and London. The upper and lower limits of this range are called *gold points*. If the exchange rate goes beyond these points, it becomes profitable to ship an unlimited amount of gold. Can you show that the potential to ship gold guarantees that the exchange rate will remain within the gold points?

9 Flexible exchange rates and inflation rates

Equation (19.5) relates the growth rate of the exchange rate between the foreign and home currency to the difference in inflation rates for the two countries. Use the International Monetary Fund's International Financial Statistics to calculate growth rates of exchange rates and inflation rates for some countries. (Use countries other than those shown in Tables 19.2 and 19.3.) Do the results accord with equation (19.5)?

10 A shift in the demand for money

Consider an increase in the real demand for money, M^d/P, in China.

a Under a fixed exchange rate with the United States, what happens to China's price level, P, and nominal quantity of money, M?

b Under a flexible exchange rate, with a fixed M, what happens to China's price level, P, and exchange rate, ε?

11 President Nixon's departure from the gold standard in 1971

Under the Bretton Woods System, the United States pegged the price of gold at $35 per ounce.

a Why did trouble about the gold price arise in 1971?

b Was President Nixon right in eliminating the US commitment to buy and sell gold from foreign official institutions at a fixed price? What other alternatives were available? For example, what was the classical prescription of the gold standard? The French suggested a doubling in the price of gold. Would that change have helped?

Bibliography

Abraham, Katharine. 1987. 'Help-Wanted Advertising, Job Vacancies, and Unemployment', *Brookings Papers on Economic Activity* 1, 207–243.

Acemoglu, Daron, Gallego, Francisco A., and Robinson, James A. 2014. 'Institutions, Human Capital and Development', *Annual Reviews of Economics* 6 (January): 875–912.

Acemoglu, Daron, Johnson, Simon, and Robinson, James A. 2001. 'The Colonial Origins of Comparative Development: An Empirical Investigation', *American Economic Review* 91 (December): 1369–1401.

Acemoglu, Daron, Naidu, Suresh, Restrepo, Pascual, and Robinson, James A. 2015. 'Democracy Does Cause Growth', Working Paper, MIT Department of Economics.

Ahmed, Shaghil. 1987. 'Wage Stickiness and the Nonneutrality of Money: A Cross-Industry Analysis', *Journal of Monetary Economics* 20 (July): 25–50.

Alesina, Alberto, and Tabellini, Guido. 1990. 'A Positive Theory of Fiscal Deficits and Government Debt', *Review of Economic Studies* 57 (July): 403–414.

Alogoskoufis, George S. 1987a. 'Aggregate Employment and Intertemporal Substitution in the U.K.', *Economic Journal* 97 (June): 403–415.

Alogoskoufis, George S. 1987b. 'On Intertemporal Substitution and Aggregate Labor Supply', *Journal of Political Economy* 95 (October): 938–960.

Álvarez, Luis J., Dhyne, Emmanuel, Hoeberichts, Marco, Kwapil, Claudia, Bihan, Hervé Le, Lünnemann, Patrick, Martins, Fernando, Sabbatini, Roberto, Stahl, Harald, Vermeulen, Philip, and Vilmunen, Jouko. 2006. 'Sticky Prices in the Euro Area: A Summary of New Micro-evidence', *Journal of the European Economic Association* 4, (April–May): 575–584.

Ando, Albert, and Modigliani, Franco. 1963. 'The "Life-Cycle" Hypothesis of Saving: Aggregate Implications and Tests', *American Economic Review* 53 (March): 55–84.

Attfield, Cliff, and Duck, Nigel. 1983. 'The Influence of Unanticipated Money Growth on Real Output: Some Cross-Country Estimates', *Journal of Money, Credit, and Banking* 15 (November): 442–454.

Azariadas, Costas. 1975. 'Implicit Contracts and Underemployment Equilibria', *Journal of Political Economy* 83 (December): 1183–1202.

Baily, Martin N. 1974. 'Wages and Employment under Uncertain Demand', *Review of Economic Studies* 33 (January): 37–50.

Balassa, Bela. 1964. 'The Purchasing Power Parity Doctrine: A Reappraisal', *Journal of Political Economy*, 72 (December): 584–596.

Barro, Robert J. 1974. 'Are Government Bonds Net Wealth?' *Journal of Political Economy* 82 (November/December): 1095–1118.

Barro, Robert J. 1978. 'Comment from an Unreconstructed Ricardian', *Journal of Monetary Economics* 4 (August): 569–581.

Barro, Robert J. 1981. 'Unanticipated Money Growth and Economic Activity in the United States', in R. Barro (ed.) *Money, Expectations, and Business Cycles*, New York: Academic Press.

Barro, Robert J. 1987. 'Government Spending, Interest Rates, Prices and Budget Deficits in the United Kingdom, 1730–1918', *Journal of Monetary Economics* 20 (September): 221–247.

Barro, Robert J. 1989. 'The Ricardian Approach to Budget Deficits', *Journal of Economic Perspectives* 3 (Spring): 37–54.

Barro, Robert J., and Gordon, David B. 1983a. 'A Positive Theory of Monetary Policy in a Natural Rate Model', *Journal of Political Economy* 91 (August): 589–610.

Barro, Robert J., and Gordon, David B. 1983b. 'Rules, Discretion and Reputation in a Model of Monetary Policy', *Journal of Monetary Economics* 91 (August): 101–121.

Barro, Robert J., and Sahasakul, Chaipat. 1983. 'Measuring the Average Marginal Tax Rate from the Individual Income Tax', *Journal of Business* 56 (October): 419–452.

Barro, Robert J., and Sahasakul, Chaipat. 1986. 'Average Marginal Tax Rates from Social Security and the Individual Income Tax', *Journal of Business* 59 (October): 555–566.

Barro, Robert J., and Sala-i-Martin, Xavier. 1990. 'World Real Interest Rates', in *NBER Macroeconomics Annual 1990*. Cambridge, MA: MIT Press.

Barsky, Robert B., and Miron, Jeffrey A. 1989. 'The Seasonal Cycle and the Business Cycle', *Journal of Political Economy* 97 (June): 503–534.

Beaulieu, Joseph J., and Miron, Jeffrey A. 1992. 'A Cross-Country Comparison of Seasonal Cycles and Business Cycles', *Economic Journal* 102 (July): 772–788.

Bernanke, Ben S. 1983. 'Nonmonetary Effects of the Financial Crisis in the Propagation of the Great Depression', *American Economic Review* 73 (June): 257–276.

Bernheim, B. Douglas, Shleifer, Andrei, and Summers, Lawrence H. 1985. 'The Strategic Bequest Motive', *Journal of Political Economy* 93 (December): 1045–1076.

Bils, Mark. 1989. 'Testing for Contracting Effects on Employment', Working Paper no. 174, Rochester Center for Economic Research, January.

Bils, Mark, and Klenow, Peter. 2004. 'Some Evidence on the Importance of Sticky Prices', *Journal of Political Economy* 112 (October): 947–985.

Bird, Roger C., and Bodkin, Ronald G. 1965. 'The National Service Life Insurance Dividend of 1950 and Consumption: A Further Test of the "Strict" Permanent Income Hypothesis', *Journal of Political Economy* 73 (October): 499–515.

Blinder, Alan S., Canetti, Elie R. D., Lebow, David E., and Rudd, Jeremy B. 1998. *Asking About Prices: A New Approach to Understanding Price Stickiness*, New York: Russell Sage Foundation.

Bloom, Murray T. 1966. *The Man Who Stole Portugal*, New York: Charles Scribner's Sons.

Board of Governors of the Federal Reserve System. 2003. *The Use and Counterfeiting of United States Currency Abroad*, Part II, Washington, DC: U.S. Government Printing Office.

Bolt, Jutta, and van Zanden, Jan Luiten. 2014. 'The Maddison Project: Collaborative Research on Historical National Accounts', *Economic History Review* 67 (3): 627–651.

Bomberger, William A., and Makinen, Gail E. 1983. 'The Hungarian Hyperinflation and Stabilization of 1945–1946', *Journal of Political Economy* 91 (October): 801–824.

Boskin, Michael J., with Dulberger, Ellen R., Griliches, Zvi, Gordon, Robert J., and Jorgenson, Dale. 1996. *Toward a More Accurate Measure of the Cost of Living*, Advisory Commission to Study the Consumer Price Index, Washington, DC: U.S. Government Printing Office.

Bresciani-Turroni, Costantino. 1937. *The Economics of Inflation*, London: Allen & Unwin.

Broadbent, Ben. 1996. 'Monetary Policy Regimes and the Costs of Discretion', unpublished Ph.D. dissertation, Harvard University.

Brown, E. Cary. 1956. 'Fiscal Policy in the Thirties: A Reappraisal', *American Economic Review* 46 (December): 857–879.

Browning, Martin, and Collado, M. Dolores. 2001. 'The Response of Expenditures to Anticipated Income Changes: Panel Data Estimates', *American Economic Review* 91 (June): 681–692.

Buchanan, James M. 1958. *Public Principles of Public Debt*, Homewood, IL: Irwin.

Cagan, Phillip D. 1956. 'The Monetary Dynamics of Hyperinflation', in Milton Friedman (ed.) *Studies in the Quantity Theory of Money*, Chicago: University of Chicago Press.

Carare, Alina, and Stone, Mark R. 2003. 'Inflation Targeting Regimes', Working Paper, International Monetary Fund, January.

Card, David. 1980. 'Determinants of the Form of Long-Term Contracts', Working Paper no. 135, Princeton University, June.

Carlson, John A. 1977. 'A Study of Price Forecasts', *Annals of Economic and Social Measurement* 6 (Winter): 27–56.

Carlton, Dennis. 1986. 'The Rigidity of Prices', *American Economic Review* 76 (September): 637–658.

Carroll, Chris, and Summers, Lawrence H. 1987. 'Why Have Private Savings Rates in the United States and Canada Diverged?', *Journal of Monetary Economics* 20 (September): 249–279.

Caselli, Francesco, and Coleman, J Wilbur. 2001. 'Cross-Country Technology Diffusion: The Case of Computers', *American Economic Review* 91 (May): 328–335.

Caselli, Francesco, and Feyrer, James. 2007. 'The Marginal Product of Capital', *Quarterly Journal of Economics* 122 (2): 535–568.

Cass, David. 1965. 'Optimum Growth in an Aggregative Model of Capital Accumulation', *Review of Economic Studies* 32 (July): 233–240.

Cecchetti, Stephen G. 1986. 'The Frequency of Price Adjustment: A Study of the Newsstand Prices of Magazines', *Journal of Econometrics* 31 (April): 255–274.

Central Statistical Office. *Annual Abstract of Statistics*. London, various issues.

Clark, Truman A. 1986. 'Interest Rate Seasonals and the Federal Reserve', *Journal of Political Economy* 94 (February): 76–125.

Cloyne, James, and Hürtgen, Patrick. 2016. 'The Macroeconomic Effects of Monetary Policy: A New Measure for the United Kingdom', *American Economic Journal: Macroeconomics*, forthcoming.

Coe, David T., and Helpman, Elhanan. 1995. 'International R&D Spillovers', *European Economic Review* 39: 859–887.

Cole, Harold L., and Ohanian, Lee E. 2004. 'New Deal Policies and the Persistence of the Great Depression: A General Equilibrium Analysis', *Journal of Political Economy* 112 (August): 779–816.

Council of Economic Advisers. 1962. *Economic Report of the President*: 78–82.

Cumby, Robert, and Obstfeld, Maurice. 1984. 'International Interest Rate and Price Level Linkages Under Flexible Exchange Rates: A Review of Recent Evidence', in John F. O. Bilson and Richard C. Marston (eds) *Exchange Rate Theory and Practice*, Chicago: University of Chicago Press.

Darby, Michael R. 1976. 'Three-and-a-Half Million U.S. Employees Have Been Mislaid: Or an Explanation of Unemployment, 1934–1941', *Journal of Political Economy* 84 (February): 1–16.

Darby, Michael R., Haltiwanger, John C., Jr, and Plant, Mark W. 1985. 'Unemployment Rate Dynamics and Persistent Unemployment under Rational Expectations', *American Economic Review* 75 (September): 614–637.

Deane, Phyllis, and Cole, W. A. 1969. *British Economic Growth, 1688–1959*. 2nd edn, Cambridge: Cambridge University Press.

DeLong, J. Bradford. 1998. 'Estimating World GDP, One Million B.C. – Present', Working Paper, University of California, Berkeley, Department of Economics.

Dotsey, Michael. 1985. 'The Use of Electronic Funds Transfers to Capture the Effect of Cash Management Practices on the Demand for Demand Deposits', *Journal of Finance* 40 (December): 1493–1503.

Easterly, William M. 2001. *The Elusive Quest for Growth: Economists' Adventures and Misadventures in the Tropics*, Cambridge, MA: MIT Press.

Esposito, Louis. 1978. 'Effect of Social Security on Saving: Review of Studies Using U.S. Time Series Data', *Social Security Bulletin* 41 (May): 9–17.

Evans, Paul. 1987a. 'Interest Rates and Expected Future Budget Deficits in the United States', *Journal of Political Economy* 95 (February): 34–58.

Evans, Paul. 1987b. 'Do Budget Deficits Raise Nominal Interest Rates? Evidence from Six Industrial Countries', *Journal of Monetary Economics* 20 (September): 281–300.

Fair, Ray C. 1979. 'An Analysis of the Accuracy of Four Macroeconometric Models', *Journal of Political Economy* 87 (August): 701–718.

Fair, Ray C. 1987. 'International Evidence on the Demand for Money', *Review of Economics and Statistics* 69 (August): 473–480.

Fay, Jon A., and Medoff, James L. 1985. 'Labor and Output over the Business Cycle: Some Direct Evidence', *American Economic Review* 75 (September): 638–655.

Feenstra, Robert C., Inklaar, Robert, and Timmer, Marcel P. 2015. 'The Next Generation of the Penn World Table', *American Economic Review* 105 (October): 3150–3182.

Feinstein, C. H. 1972. *National Income, Expenditures, and Output of the United Kingdom, 1855–1965.* Cambridge: Cambridge University Press.

Feldstein, Martin S. 1974. 'Social Security, Induced Retirement, and Aggregate Capital Accumulation', *Journal of Political Economy* 82 (September/October): 905–928.

Ferguson, James M. (ed.). 1964. *Public Debt and Future Generations,* Chapel Hill: University of North Carolina Press.

Fischer, Stanley. 1977. 'Long-Term Contracts, Rational Expectations, and the Optimal Money Supply Rule', *Journal of Political Economy* 85 (February): 191–206.

Fisher, Irving. 1926. *The Purchasing Power of Money,* 2nd edn, New York: Macmillan.

Fleisher, Belton M., and Kniesner, Thomas J. 1984. *Labor Economics: Theory, Evidence, and Policy,* 3rd edn, Englewood Cliffs, NJ: Prentice-Hall.

Flood, Robert P., and Garber, Peter M. 1980. 'An Economic Theory of Monetary Reform', *Journal of Political Economy* 88 (February): 24–58.

Friedman, Milton. 1956. 'The Quantity of Money – A Restatement', in Milton Friedman (ed.) *Studies in the Quantity Theory of Money,* Chicago: University of Chicago Press.

Friedman, Milton. 1957. *A Theory of the Consumption Function,* Princeton, NJ: Princeton University Press.

Friedman, Milton. 1960. *A Program for Monetary Stability,* New York: Fordham University Press.

Friedman, Milton. 1968a. 'Free Exchange Rates', in *Dollars and Deficits,* Englewood Cliffs, NJ: Prentice-Hall.

Friedman, Milton. 1968b. 'Inflation: Causes and Consequences,' in *Dollars and Deficits.* Englewood Cliffs, NJ: Prentice-Hall.

Friedman, Milton. 1968c. 'The Role of Monetary Policy', *American Economic Review* 58 (March): 1–17.

Friedman, Milton. 1969. *The Optimum Quantity of Money and Other Essays,* Chicago: Aldine.

Friedman, Milton, and Schwartz, Anna J. 1963. *A Monetary History of the United States, 1867–1960,* Princeton, NJ: Princeton University Press.

Friedman, Milton, and Schwartz, Anna J. 1982. *Monetary Trends in the United States and the United Kingdom: Their Relation to Income, Prices, and Interest Rates, 1867–1975,* Chicago, IL: University of Chicago Press.

Fullerton, Don. 1982. 'On the Possibility of an Inverse Relationship Between Tax Rates and Government Revenues', *Journal of Public Economics* 19 (October): 3–22.

Galí, Jordi, López-Salido, J. David , and Vallés, Javier. 2007. 'Understanding the Effects of Government Spending on Consumption', *Journal of the European Economic Association,* 5 (March): 227–270.

Garber, Peter M. 1982. 'Transition from Inflation to Price Stability', *Carnegie-Rochester Conference Series on Public Policy* 16 (Spring): 11–42.

Goldfeld, Steven M. 1973. 'The Demand for Money Revisited', *Brookings Papers on Economic Activity,* no. 3, 577–638.

Goldfeld, Steven M. 1976. 'The Case of the Missing Money', *Brookings Papers on Economic Activity,* no. 3, 683–730.

Goldfeld, Steven M., and Sichel, Daniel E. 1990. 'The Demand for Money', in Benjamin M. Friedman and Frank H. Hahn (eds) *Handbook of Monetary Economics,* vol. 1, Amsterdam: North Holland.

Golosov, Mikhail, and Lucas, Robert E., Jr. 2006. 'Menu Costs and Phillips Curves', unpublished, MIT, March, National Bureau of Economic Research, December.

Gordon, Donald F. 1974. 'A Neo-Classical Theory of Keynesian Unemployment', *Economic Inquiry* 12 (December): 431–459.

Gort, Michael, and Klepper, Steven. 1982. 'Time Paths in the Diffusion of Product Innovations', *Economic Journal* 92 (September): 630–653.

Gray, Jo Anna. 1976. 'Wage Indexation: A Macroeconomic Approach', *Journal of Monetary Economics* 2 (April): 221–236.

Greenwood, Jeremy, Hercowitz, Zvi, and Huffman, Gregory. 1988. 'Investment, Capacity Utilization, and the Real Business Cycle', *American Economic Review* 78 (June): 402–417.

Griliches, Zvi. 1957. 'Hybrid Corn—An Exploration in the Economics of Technological Change.', *Econometrica* 25 (October): 501–522.

Griliches, Zvi. 1998. *R&D and Productivity: The Econometric Evidence,* Chicago: University of Chicago Press.

Hahm, Joon-Ho. 1998. 'Consumption Adjustments to Real Interest Rates: Intertemporal Substitution Revisited', *Journal of Economic Dynamics & Control* 22 (February): 293–320.

Hall, Robert E. 1979. 'A Theory of the Natural Unemployment Rate and the Duration of Unemployment', *Journal of Monetary Economics* 5 (April): 153–170.

Hall, Robert E. 1989. 'Consumption', in Robert J. Barro (ed.) *Modern Business Cycle Theory,* Cambridge, MA: Harvard University Press.

Hall, Robert E. 2005. 'Employment Efficiency and Sticky Wages: Evidence from Flows in Labor Market', Working Paper no. 11183, National Bureau of Economic Research, March.

Havránek, Tomáš. 2015. 'Measuring Intertemporal Substitution: The Importance of Method Choices and Selective Reporting', *Journal of the European Economic Association* 13 (December): 1180–1204.

Hawtrey, Ralph G. 1932. 'The Portuguese Bank Notes Case', *Economic Journal* 42 (September): 391–398.

Heckscher, Eli. 1919. 'The Effect of Foreign Trade on the Distribution of Income', *Ekonomisk Tidskrift.*

Helpman, Elhanan, and Krugman, Paul R. 1985. *Market Structure and Foreign Trade,* Cambridge, MA: MIT Press.

Hercowitz, Zvi. 1981. 'Money and the Dispersion of Relative Prices', *Journal of Political Economy* 89 (April): 328–356.

Heston, Alan, Summers, Robert, and Aten, Bettina. 2002. *Penn World Table Version 6.1.* Center for International Comparisons at the University of Pennsylvania (CICUP), October.

Hsieh, Chang-Tai. 2003. 'Do Consumers React to Anticipated Income Changes? Evidence from the Alaska Permanent Fund', *American Economic Review* 93 (March): 397–405.

Hubbard, R. Glenn. 2002. 'Tax Notes 30th Anniversary', unpublished Working Paper, Columbia University, December.

International Monetary Fund. *International Financial Statistics,* various issues.

Jappelli, Tullio, and Pistaferri, Luigi, 2010. 'The Consumption Response to Income Changes', *Annual Review of Economics* 2 (September): 479–506.

Jaumotte, Florence. 2000. 'Technological Catch-up and the Growth Process', unpublished Ph.D. dissertation, Harvard University, November.

Jones, Charles I. 1995. 'Time Series Tests of Endogenous Growth Models', *Quarterly Journal of Economics* 110 (May): 495–525.

Jones, Charles I. 2005. 'Growth and Ideas', in Philippe Aghion and Steven Durlauf (eds) *Handbook of Economic Growth,* Amsterdam: Elsevier.

Jovanovic, Boyan, and Lach, Saul, 1997. 'Product Innovation and the Business Cycle', *International Economic Review* 38 (February): 3–22.

Judson, Ruth. 2012. 'Crisis and Calm: Demand for U.S. Currency at Home and Abroad from the Fall of the Berlin Wall to 2011', Board of Governors of the Federal Reserve System International Finance Discussion Paper 1058.

Kashyap, Anil K. 1995. 'Sticky Prices: New Evidence from Retail Catalogs', *Quarterly Journal of Economics,* 110, 245–274.

Kendrick, John W. 1961. *Productivity Trends in the United States,* Princeton, NJ: Princeton University Press.

Kenny, Lawrence W. 1991. 'Cross-Country Estimates of the Demand for Money and Its Components', *Economic Inquiry* 29 (October), 696–705.

Keynes, John Maynard. 1923. *A Tract on Monetary Reform,* Macmillan: London.

Keynes, John Maynard. 1936. *The General Theory of Employment, Interest, and Money,* New York: Harcourt Brace.

Koopmans, Tjalling C. 1965. 'On the Concept of Optimal Growth', in *The Economic Approach to Development Planning,* Amsterdam: North Holland.

Kormendi, Roger C., and Meguire, Phillip G. 1984. 'Cross-Regime Evidence of Macroeconomic Rationality', *Journal of Political Economy* 92 (October): 875–908.

Kreinin, Mordechai E. 1961. 'Windfall Income and Consumption—Additional Evidence', *American Economic Review* 51 (June): 388–390.

Kuznets, Simon. 1948. 'Discussion of the New Department of Commerce Income Series', *Review of Economics and Statistics* 30 (August): 151–179.

Kydland, Finn E., and Prescott, Edward C. 1977. 'Rules Rather than Discretion: The Inconsistency of Optimal Plans', *Journal of Political Economy* 85 (June): 473–491.

Kydland, Finn E., and Prescott, Edward C. 1982. 'Time to Build and Aggregate Fluctuations', *Econometrica* 51 (November): 1345–1370.

Kydland, Finn E., and Prescott, Edward C. 1990. 'Business Cycles: Real Facts and a Monetary Myth.' *Federal Reserve Bank of Minneapolis, Quarterly Review* (Spring): 3–18.

Lahaye, Laura. 1985. 'Inflation and Currency Reform', *Journal of Political Economy* 93 (June): 537–560.

Landsberger, Michael. 1970. 'Restitution Receipts, Household Savings, and Consumption Behavior in Israel', unpublished Working Paper, Research Department, Bank of Israel.

Lane, Philip R. 2012. 'The European Sovereign Debt Crisis', *Journal of Economic Perspectives* 26 (Summer): 49–67.

Leimer, Dean, and Lesnoy, Selig. 1982. 'Social Security and Private Saving: New Time Series Evidence', *Journal of Political Economy* 90 (June): 606–629.

Lindsey, Lawrence B. 1987. 'Individual Taxpayer Response to Tax Cuts, 1982–1984', *Journal of Public Economics* 33 (July): 173–206.

Lucas, Robert E., Jr. 1973. 'Some International Evidence on Output-Inflation Trade-offs', *American Economic Review* 63 (June): 326–334.

Lucas, Robert E., Jr. 1977. 'Understanding Business Cycles', *Carnegie-Rochester Conference on Public Policy* 5: 7–29.

Lucas, Robert E., Jr. 1981. *Studies in Business-Cycle Theory,* Cambridge, MA: MIT Press.

Lucas, Robert E., Jr. 1988. 'On the Mechanics of Economic Development', *Journal of Monetary Economics* 22 (July): 3–42.

Maddison, Angus. 2003. *The World Economy: Historical Statistics*, Paris: OECD.

Malthus, Thomas R. 1798. *An Essay on the Principal of Population*, London: W. Pickering, 1986.

McCallum, Ben T. 1979. 'The Current State of the Policy Ineffectiveness Debate', *American Economic Review* 69 (proceedings, May): 240–245.

McClure, Alexander K. 1901. *Abe Lincoln's Yarns and Stories*, New York: W. W. Wilson.

Miron, Jeffrey A. 1986. 'Financial Panics, the Seasonality of the Nominal Interest Rate, and the Founding of the Fed', *American Economic Review* 76 (March): 125–140.

Mishkin, Frederic S. 1984. 'Are Real Interest Rates Equal Across Countries? An Empirical Investigation of International Parity Conditions', *Journal of Finance* 39 (December): 1345–1357.

Mishkin, Frederic S., and Schmidt-Hebbel, Klaus. 2001. 'One Decade of Inflation Targeting in the World: What Do We Know and What Do We Need to Know?', Working Paper no. 8397, National Bureau of Economic Research, July.

Mitchell, B. R., and Deane, Phyllis. 1962. *Abstract of British Historical Statistics,* Cambridge: Cambridge University Press.

Mitchell, B. R., and Jones, H. G. 1971. *Second Abstract of British Historical Statistics.* Cambridge: Cambridge University Press.

Modigliani, Franco, and Brumberg, Richard. 1954. 'Utility Analysis and the Consumption Function: An Interpretation of Cross-Section Data', in Kenneth Kurihara (ed.) *Post-Keynesian Economics,* New Brunswick, NJ: Rutgers University Press.

Morgan Guaranty Trust. 1983. *World Financial Markets,* New York, February.

Mulligan, Casey B. 1995. 'The Intertemporal Substitution of Work – What Does the Evidence Say?' Population Research Center Discussion Paper Series no. 95-11, July.

Mulligan, Casey B. 1998. 'Pecuniary and Nonpecuniary Incentives to Work in the United States during World War II', *Journal of Political Economy* 106 (October): 1033–1077.

Mulligan, Casey B. 2001. 'Capital, Interest, and Aggregate Intertemporal Substitution', unpublished Working Paper, University of Chicago.

Mulligan, Casey B., and Sala-i-Martin, Xavier. 2000. 'Extensive Margins and the Demand for Money at Low Interest Rates', *Journal of Political Economy* 108 (October): 961–991.

Mundell, Robert A. 1968. *International Economics,* New York: Macmillan.

Mundell, Robert A. 1971. *Monetary Theory,* Pacific Palisades, CA: Goodyear.

Musgrave, Richard. 1959. *Theory of Public Finance,* New York: McGraw-Hill.

Muth, John F. 1961. 'Rational Expectations and the Theory of Price Movements', *Econometrica* 29 (July): 315–335.

Nakamura, Emi and Steinsson, Jon. 2006. 'Five Facts about Prices: A Reevaluation of Menu Cost Models', unpublished, Harvard University, August.

North, Douglas, and Weingast, Barry. 1989. 'Constitutions and Commitment: The Evolution of Institutions Governing Public Choice in Seventeenth Century England', *Journal of Economic History* (December): 803–832.

Nuvolari, Alessandro, Verspagen, Bart, and von Tunzelmann, Nick. 2011. 'The Early Diffusion of the Steam Engine in Britain, 1700–1800: A Reappraisal', *Cliometrica* 5 (October): 291–321.

Obstfeld, Maurice, and Rogoff, Kenneth. 2004. 'The Unsustainable U.S. Current Account Position Revisited', unpublished Working Paper, Harvard University, October.

Ochs, Jack, and Rush, Mark. 1983. 'The Persistence of Interest Rate Effects on the Demand for Currency', *Journal of Money, Credit, and Banking* 15 (November): 499–505.

O'Driscoll, Gerald P., Jr. 1977. 'The Ricardian Nonequivalence Theorem', *Journal of Political Economy* 85 (February): 207–210.

Ohlin, Bertil. 1933. *Interregional and International Trade,* Cambridge MA: Harvard University Press.

Olivei, Giovanni, and Tenreyro, Silvana. 2007. 'The Timing of Monetary Policy Shocks', *American Economic Review* *American Economic Review* 97(3) (June): 636–663.

Organization of American States. *Statistical Bulletin of the OAS,* various issues.

Parker, Jonathan A. 1999. 'The Reaction of Household Consumption to Predictable Changes in Social Security Taxes', *American Economic Review* 89 (September): 959–973.

Persson, Torsten, and Svensson, Lars E. O. 1989. 'Why a Stubborn Conservative Would Run a Deficit: Policy with Time-Inconsistent Preferences', *Quarterly Journal of Economics* 104 (May): 325–345.

Phelps, Edmund S. 1970. 'The New Microeconomics in Employment and Inflation Theory', in Edmund S. Phelps (ed.) *Microeconomic Foundations of Employment and Inflation Theory,* New York: Norton.

Pinera, Jose. 1996. *Empowering Workers: The Privatization of Social Security in Chile,* Washington, DC: Cato Institute.

Pinkovskiy, Maxim and Sala-i-Martin, Xavier. 2009. 'Parametric Estimations of the World Distribution of Income', NBER Working Paper no. 15433.

Plosser, Charles I. 1982. 'Government Financing Decisions and Asset Returns', *Journal of Monetary Economics* 9 (May): 325–352.

Plosser, Charles I. 1987. 'Fiscal Policy and the Term Structure', *Journal of Monetary Economics* 20 (September): 343–367.

Porter, Richard D., and Judson, Ruth A. 2001. 'Overseas Dollar Holdings: What Do We Know?', *Wirtschaftspolitische Blatter* 48: 431–440.

Radford, R.A. 1945. 'The Economic Organisation of a P.O.W. Camp', *Economica* 12 (November): 189–201.

Ramaswami, Chitra. 1983. 'Equilibrium Unemployment and the Efficient Job-Finding Rate', *Journal of Labor Economics* 1 (April): 171–196.

Ricardo, David. 1819. *Principles of Political Economy and Taxation.* 2nd edn, London: John Murray.

Ricardo, David. 1846. 'Funding System', in J. Ramsey McCulloch (ed.) *The Works of David Ricardo,* London: John Murray.

Rogoff, Kenneth S. 1989. 'Reputation, Coordination, and Monetary Policy', in Robert J. Barro (ed.) *Modern Business Cycle Theory,* Cambridge, MA: Harvard University Press.

Romer, Christina D. 1986. 'Spurious Volatility in Historical Unemployment Data', *Journal of Political Economy* 94 (February): 1–37.

Romer, Christina D. 1988. 'World War I and the Postwar Depression: A Reinterpretation Based on Alternative Estimates of GNP', *Journal of Monetary Economics* 22 (July): 91–115.

Romer, Christina D. 1989. 'The Prewar Business Cycle Reconsidered: New Estimates of Gross National Product, 1869–1908', *Journal of Political Economy* 97 (February): 1–37.

Romer, Christina D., and Romer, David H. 2004. 'A New Measure of Monetary Shocks: Derivation and Implications', *American Economic Review* 94 (September): 1055–1084.

Romer, David. 2011. Advanced Macroeconomics. 4th edn, New York: McGraw-Hill Education.

Romer, Paul M. 1990. 'Endogenous Technological Change', *Journal of Political Economy* 98 (October): S71–S102.

Rotwein, Eugene, (ed.). 1970. *David Hume – Writings on Economics*, Madison: University of Wisconsin Press.

Runkle, David E. 1991. 'Liquidity Constraints and the Permanent Income Hypothesis: Evidence from Panel Data', *Journal of Monetary Economics* 27: 73–98.

Sala-i-Martin, Xavier. 2006. 'The World Distribution of Income: Falling Poverty and . . . Convergence, Period', *Quarterly Journal of Economics* 121 (May): 351–397.

Samuelson, Paul A. 1964. 'Theoretical Notes on Trade Problems', *Review of Economics and Statistics* 46 (May): 145–154.

Samuelson, Paul A., and Stolper, Wolfgang F. 1941. 'Protection and Real Wages', *Review of Economic Studies* 9 (November): 58–73.

Sargent, Thomas J. 1982. 'The Ends of Four Big Inflations,' in Robert E. Hall (ed.) *Inflation: Causes and Effects*, Chicago: University of Chicago Press.

Sargent, Thomas J., and Velde, Francois R. 1995. 'Macroeconomic Features of the French Revolution', *Journal of Political Economy* 103(3) (June): 474–518.

Sargent, Thomas J., and Wallace, Neil. 1975. 'Rational Expectations, the Optimal Monetary Instrument, and the Optimal Money Supply Rule', *Journal of Political Economy* 83 (April): 241–254.

Sargent, Thomas J., and Wallace, Neil. 1981. 'Some Unpleasant Monetarist Arithmetic', *Federal Reserve Bank of Minneapolis, Quarterly Review* (Fall): 1–17.

Scoggins, John F. 1990. 'Supply Shocks and Net Exports', unpublished Working Paper, University of Alabama at Birmingham.

Shimer, Robert. 2003. 'The Cyclical Behavior of Equilibrium Unemployment and Vacancies: Evidence and Theory', Working Paper no. 9536, National Bureau of Economic Research, February.

Solow, Robert M. 1956. 'A Contribution to the Theory of Economic Growth', *Quarterly Journal of Economics* 70 (February): 65–94.

Solow, Robert M. 1957. 'Technical Change and the Aggregate Production Function', *Review of Economics and Statistics* 39 (August): 312–320.

Sonderhefte zur Wirtschaft und Statistik. 1929. Berlin: R. Hobbing.

Souleles, Nicholas S. 1999. 'The Response of Household Consumption to Income Tax Refunds', *American Economic Review* 89 (September): 947–958.

Stuart, Charles E. 1981. 'Swedish Tax Rates, Labor Supply, and Tax Revenues', *Journal of Political Economy* 89 (October): 1020–1038.

Taylor, Alan M., and Taylor, Mark P. 2004. 'The Purchasing Power Parity Debate', *Journal of Economic Perspectives* 18 (Fall): 135–158.

Taylor, John B. 1980. 'Aggregate Dynamics and Staggered Contracts', *Journal of Political Economy* 88 (February): 1–23.

Thornton, Henry. 1802. *An Enquiry into the Nature and Effects of the Paper Credit of Great Britain*, London: J. Hatchard.

U.S. Department of Commerce. 1975. *Historical Statistics of the U.S., Colonial Times to 1970*, Washington, DC: U.S. Government Printing Office.

U.S. President. 1962. *Economic Report of the President*, Washington, DC: U.S. Government Printing Office.

Van Ravestein, A., and Vijlbrief, H. 1988. 'Welfare Cost of Higher Tax Rates: An Empirical Laffer Curve for the Netherlands', *De Economist* 136: 205–219.

Walre de Bordes, J. van. 1927. *The Austrian Crown*, London: King.

Warren, George F., and Pearson, Frank A. 1933. *Prices*, New York: Wiley.

World Bank. 1994. *Averting the Old Age Crisis*, Oxford: Oxford University Press.

World Bank. 2006. *World Development Indicators*, Washington, DC: IBRD, World Bank.

Glossary

absolute convergence The tendency of real per-capita GDP in poor economies to grow faster than in rich ones, so that poor economies catch up over time to rich ones. The term 'absolute' means that the convergence is not conditioned on other economic variables.

absolute form of PPP The version of purchasing-power parity that involves levels of exchange rates and prices.

acyclical Having no regular relation with the business cycle; that is, with detrended real GDP.

adjustment costs for investment Costs that have to be paid to change the quantity of capital (plant and equipment) used in production.

after-tax real interest rate The real interest rate calculated after netting out the real income tax paid on the interest earnings.

after-tax real wage rate The real wage rate calculated after netting out the real income tax paid on the wage income.

aggregate demand The total demand for goods and services in the forms of consumption, gross investment and government purchases.

aggregate supply The total supply of goods and services produced in an economy.

Ak model A growth model in which the production function is linear in capital; that is, $y = Ak$, where y is output per worker and k is capital per worker.

average product of capital The ratio of output (real GDP) to the capital stock.

average tax rate The ratio of taxes to a measure of income. See *marginal tax rate*.

balance of international payments The summary statement of a country's international trade in commodities, bonds and international reserves.

balance on current account A zero current-account balance.

balanced budget Equality between the government's purchases, transfers and interest payments, and the government's tax revenue.

Balassa–Samuelson hypothesis Theory that, in poor countries, the prices of non-traded goods and services are low compared to prices of traded goods. Therefore, a market basket of goods and services tends to be less expensive in poor countries than in rich ones.

barter Direct exchange of one good for another, without the use of money. See *medium of exchange*.

bond A contract that gives the holder (lender) a claim to a specified stream of payments from the issuer (borrower).

bond market Market on which bonds are traded.

boom A period in which real GDP is high and rising.

Bretton Woods System A system of international payments established after World War II in which each country pegged the exchange rate between its own currency and the US dollar. The United States exchanged dollars for gold at a fixed price ($35 per ounce), thus pegging the value of each country's currency to gold.

budget constraint An equation relating the sources of funds in a period, such as wage and asset income and initial assets, to the uses of funds in that period, such as consumption and end-of-period assets.

budget deficit Excess of the government's purchases, transfers and interest payments over the government's tax revenue.

budget line A graph of the combinations of consumptions over two periods that satisfy the household's two-period budget constraint.

budget surplus Excess of the government's tax revenue over the government's purchases, transfers and interest payments.

burden of the public debt The possible negative effect of the public debt on saving and investment and, hence, on the stock of capital available later.

business cycle Pattern of real GDP rising during a boom and falling during a recession.

capital levy Tax rate on capital when levied after investments have been made.

capital stock Stock of goods in the forms of plant and equipment, used as input to production.

capital-utilization rate Rate at which stock of capital is used in production.

chain-weighted real GDP A method for constructing real GDP in which the relative-price weights continually adjust for the changing composition of production.

checkable deposits Deposits issued by financial institutions against which account holders can write cheques.

classical economics A school of economic thought which focuses aggregate supply and stresses that economies function most efficiently with minimal government interference.

closed economy An economy isolated from the rest of the world.

Cobb-Douglas production function A particular functional form of the production function, developed by Charles Cobb and Paul Douglas and widely used to represent the technological relationship between the amounts of inputs, such as capital and labour, and the amount of output produced by those inputs.

commodity money Money that takes a physical form, such as gold and silver coins.

common currency A regime in which all countries use the same currency and quote prices in units of this currency.

conditional convergence The idea that real per-capita GDP in poor countries grows faster than in rich countries, for given values of government policies, propensities to save money and have children, and other variables.

constant-growth-rate rule A rule for monetary policy in which a specified monetary aggregate grows at a constant rate.

constant returns to scale The property of a production function that a proportionate increase in all inputs results in an equiproportionate increase in output.

consumer durables Consumable commodities purchased by households that last for a long time. Examples are cars, furniture and appliances.

consumer non-durables and services Consumable commodities purchased by households that last for a short time.

Consumer Price Index (CPI) A weighted average of prices of consumer goods, measured relative to a base year.

consumer semi-durables Consumable commodities purchased by households that last for longer than a year but with a lifetime of use that is significantly less than durable goods. Examples are clothes and footwear.

convergence The tendency of real per-capita GDP in a poor economy to grow faster than in a rich one. Therefore, the poor economy's real per-capita GDP tends to catch up over time to that in the rich economy.

copyright Property right over the use of a book, trademark or similar object.

countercyclical Moving in the direction opposite to the business cycle; that is, to detrended real GDP.

CPI Consumer Price Index.

currency Non-interest-bearing paper money issued by the government.

currency union A group of countries that use a common currency.

current-account balance The value of goods and services produced by domestic residents (including the net factor income from abroad) plus net transfers from abroad, less the expenditure by domestic residents on goods and services. If the current-account balance is positive (negative), the current account is in surplus (deficit).

current-account deficit A negative current-account balance.

current-account surplus A positive current-account balance.

cyclical part of real GDP The difference between real GDP and its trend.

deflation A sustained decrease in the general price level over time. See *inflation*.

demand curve A curve expressing the relation between the quantity demanded and the price of a good or service.

demand for money The amount of money that households desire to hold, expressed as a function of real GDP, the nominal interest rate, transaction costs and other variables.

depreciation The wearing out of capital goods over time.

devaluation An action by the central bank that raises the number of units of a country's currency that exchange for other currencies.

diffusion of technology Spread of technology from one country or region to another.

diminishing average product of capital Tendency for the average product of capital to fall as capital per worker rises.

diminishing marginal product of capital Tendency for the marginal product of capital to fall as capital per worker rises.

diminishing marginal product of labour Tendency for the marginal product of labour to fall as the quantity of labour rises, for given capital input.

discount factor The relative value of a unit of currency in different periods of time; for example, the relative value of a euro between one year and the next. The nominal discount factor is 1.0 plus the nominal interest rate.

discounted Use of the discount factor to express future income or expenditure in units comparable to current income or expenditure.

discouraged workers Workers who leave the labour force following a period of unemployment.

discretionary policy A set-up in which government policy is not restricted by prior commitments.

disequilibrium Absence of equilibrium in a market; lack of market clearing.

double taxation Taxation of something twice. For example, corporate profits are taxed at the corporate level and then taxed again at the household level when paid out as dividends.

duration of unemployment The length of time that a spell of unemployment is expected to last. The duration of unemployment is inversely related to the job-finding rate.

economic fluctuations Variations in real GDP during a business cycle.

economies of scale in cash management The property of the demand for money that the desired average real money-holding increases less than proportionately with a rise in real GDP.

employment The number of persons working at jobs in the market sector.

employment rate The ratio of employment to the labour force.

endogenous growth theory Long-run economic growth that is explained by the interactions within a model.

endogenous money The automatic response of the quantity of money to changes in the economy. Money is endogenous under the gold standard and in regimes in which the monetary authority targets nominal interest rates or the price level.

endogenous variables Variables determined by the model.

equilibrium Condition that determines quantities and prices in a market. *Quantity supplied equals quantity demanded* is an example of an equilibrium condition.

equilibrium business-cycle model (EBC model) A model of economic fluctuations that uses equilibrium conditions to determine how shocks affect real GDP and other macroeconomic variables. In our model, supply and demand functions accord with microeconomic foundations. Given these functions, the key equilibrium conditions are that markets have to clear.

exchange market Market in which the currency of one country is traded for that of another country.

exchange rate The number of units of a country's currency that trades for one unit of another currency, such as the US dollar. See *nominal exchange rate*.

exogenous technological progress Improvements of technology that are not explained within the model.

exogenous variables Variables that are not explained within the model.

expectations of inflation Forecast of the inflation rate.

expected real interest rate The real interest rate that is expected to be earned (or paid) after adjusting the nominal interest rate by the expectation of inflation.

exports Goods and services produced by the residents of the home country that are sold to foreigners.

Federal Funds rate The interest rate on loans made in the Federal Funds market, which is the market for very short-term borrowing and lending between financial institutions, such as commercial banks, in the United States.

Federal Open Market Committee (FOMC) A committee of the Federal Reserve that has responsibility for open-market operations.

fiat money Money, such as paper currency, that has value due to government fiat, rather than intrinsic value, such as gold.

finite horizon Finite planning period used by households in determining consumption, saving and labour supply. See *infinite horizon*.

fiscal policy The choice of government spending, taxes and borrowing to influence the level of aggregate economic activity.

fixed exchange rates Systems in which countries peg the exchange rate between their currency and other currencies, such as the US dollar. Examples of fixed exchange-rate regimes are the gold standard, the Bretton Woods System and a currency union.

flat-rate tax A kind of income tax in which the amount of tax is a constant proportion of taxable income. See *graduated-rate tax*.

flexible exchange rates Systems of international payments, prevalent since the early 1970s, in which countries allow the exchange rates for their currencies to fluctuate so as to clear the exchange market.

flow variable A variable, such as real GDP or consumption, expressed per unit of time, such as a year.

foreign direct investment Purchases of capital goods by home-country residents in foreign countries.

fully funded system (for social security) A system in which each individual's payments accumulate in a trust fund and retirement benefits are paid out of the accumulated funds. See *social security; pay-as-you-go system*.

GDP Gross domestic product.

GDP in constant prices Gross domestic product expressed in terms of dollars from a base year. See real GDP.

GDP in current prices Gross domestic product expressed in current prices. See nominal GDP.

general equilibrium Clearing of all markets at the same time.

general price level The price per unit of goods and services. The average price of all goods and services.

globalization The increased tendency for production and other economic activities to be carried out on a worldwide basis.

GNI Gross national income.

GNP Gross national product.

gold standard A system of international payments under which countries agree to buy or sell gold for a fixed amount of their currencies. The high point of this system was from 1890 to 1914.

goods market A market in which goods and services are exchanged for money.

government's budget constraint The equation showing the balance between the government's sources and uses of funds.

graduated-rate tax A kind of income tax in which the marginal tax rate rises with taxable income. See *flat-rate tax*.

Great Depression The worldwide decline in aggregate economic activity in the United States and many other countries from 1929 to 1933.

Great Recession The decline in aggregate economic activity across the world in the late 2000s.

gross domestic income (GDI) The total income received by all sectors of an economy, including wages, profits and taxes net of subsidies.

gross domestic investment Total expenditure on capital goods, including business spending on plant and equipment, the net change in business inventories, and residential construction. This total contains no adjustment for depreciation.

gross domestic product (GDP) The market value of an economy's domestically produced goods and services over a specified period of time, such as a year.

gross investment Purchases of capital goods with no adjustment for the depreciation of the existing capital goods.

gross national income (GNI) The total income claimed by the residents of a country over a specified period of time; GNI equals gross domestic income plus the net factor income from abroad.

gross national product (GNP) The total market value of the goods and services produced by the residents of a country over a specified period of time; GNP equals gross domestic product plus the net factor income from abroad.

gross value added (GVA) The total value of goods and services produced in an economy over a specified period of time, such as a year.

gross world product (GWP) The combined gross national product of all the countries in the world.

growth accounting A formula that relates growth of real GDP to the growth of inputs, capital and labour, and to technological change.

help-wanted advertising Media advertising for job openings; used as a proxy for job vacancies.

high-powered money The total amount of Federal Reserve notes (currency) and non-interest-bearing deposits (reserves) held at the Fed by depository institutions; the monetary base.

household budget constraint in nominal terms The equation showing the balance between a household's sources and uses of funds. In this case, the equation is in nominal terms.

household budget constraint in real terms The equation showing the balance between a household's sources and uses of funds. In this case, the equation is in real terms.

household consumption expenditure Purchases of goods and services by households for use in consumption.

human capital Skills and training that are embodied in workers and add to productivity.

hyperinflation A sustained period with an extraordinarily high inflation rate, such as in Germany after World War I.

imperfect competition A competitive environment in which each business has some pricing power. See *perfect competition*.

implicit GDP deflator The price index that relates the gross domestic product, measured in nominal terms, to real GDP.

imports Goods and services produced in foreign countries that are purchased by the residents of the home country.

imputed rental income Rental income on capital, such as owner-occupied housing, that is not explicitly paid and received.

income effects The effects of higher income on choices such as consumption and labour supply.

indexation A system of contracts, such as for labour, in which payments are revised upwards or downwards automatically for increases or decreases in the general price level, so as to keep the real value of payments independent of inflation.

indexed bonds Bonds on which the nominal payments of interest and principal are automatically adjusted for inflation to ensure a contracted real interest rate.

inequality Differences in levels of real income across persons in an economy or across economies.

infinite horizon Planning period of indefinite (infinite) length used by households in determining consumption, saving and labour supply. See *finite horizon*.

infinite-horizon budget constraint Budget constraint for a household over an infinite horizon.

inflation rate The percentage change in a price index between two periods of time, such as from one year to the next.

inflation targeting A regime for monetary policy in which the central bank adjusts nominal interest rates to achieve a target inflation rate.

infrastructure capital Capital, often publicly owned, in the form of transport, communications, energy and water provision, and so on.

intellectual property rights Ownership rights in discoveries and ideas.

interest rate The ratio of the interest payment to the amount borrowed; the return to lending or the cost of borrowing.

interest-bearing assets Assets, such as bonds, that pay interest.

interest-rate parity Equalization of interest rates across countries, adjusting for prospective changes in exchange rates.

international reserves Assets, such as US dollars and gold, that are commonly used for international transactions and as stores of value by central banks and other financial institutions.

intertemporal-substitution effect The effect on current consumption (leisure) when the cost of future consumption (leisure) changes relative to that of current consumption (leisure).

inventories Stores of commodities held by businesses either for sale or for use in production.

investment-saving curve An equilibrium condition of the goods market.

investor sentiment The overall attitude of investors toward investment.

involuntary unemployment The inability of workers to obtain employment at the prevailing market wage; a feature of Keynesian models.

irrelevance result for systematic monetary policy The theoretical finding that a systematic policy of changing the quantity of money in response to the state of the economy is predictable and therefore powerless to affect real variables.

IS-LM model A macroeconomic model based on the insights of John Maynard Keynes on the relationship between interest rates and output level in the goods and money markets.

job-finding rate The rate at which workers move from unemployment or outside the labour force to employment.

job-separation rate The rate at which workers move from employment to unemployment or outside the labour force.

Keynesian economics A school of economic thought which focuses on aggregate demand and stresses that government policies can be used to counter recessions.

labour force The total number of employed workers plus the number of unemployed.

labour hoarding The tendency of firms to retain their workers during a recession. Labour hoarding may explain the tendency for measured labour productivity to fall during recessions and rise during booms.

labour market The market on which workers sell, and producers buy, labour services.

labour-force participation rate The fraction of the population (sometimes the non-institutional population) that participates in the labour market.

Laffer curve A graph showing that tax revenues initially rise as the marginal income tax rate rises, but eventually reach a maximum and subsequently decline with further increases in the marginal tax rate.

law of one price The condition that identical goods in different places must sell at the same price when the price is expressed in a common currency.

legal tender A characteristic of money, whereby its use as a medium of exchange is reinforced by government statute.

life-cycle models The theory of the choices of consumption and leisure that are made when the planning horizon equals an individual's expected remaining lifetime. The theory predicts that an individual will build up savings during working years and exhaust them during retirement years.

liquidity-money curve An equilibrium condition of the money market.

liquidity trap A situation in which monetary policy is ineffective because increases in money supply fail to decrease interest rates.

Lucas hypothesis on monetary shocks The hypothesis that the effect of a given-size money shock on real GDP is larger, the less volatile money growth is historically.

lump-sum tax A tax paid by an individual to the government in which the amount paid does not depend on any characteristic of the individual, such as income or wealth.

lump-sum transfer A transfer payment from the government to an individual in which the amount paid does not depend on any characteristic of the recipient, such as income or wealth.

M1 The monetary aggregate that comprises currency held by the public, checkable deposits and travellers' cheques. M1 comprises the assets that serve regularly as media of exchange.

M2 M1 plus household holdings of savings deposits, small-time deposits and retail money-market mutual funds.

marginal cost of production The added nominal cost to a producer from raising output by one unit.

marginal product of capital (MPK) The increase in output from an increase in capital services by one unit, while holding fixed the technology and the quantity of labour.

marginal product of labour (MPL) The increase in output from an increase in labour by one unit, while holding fixed the technology and the quantity of capital services.

marginal propensity to consume The proportion of additional income spent on consumption.

marginal tax rate The fraction of an additional unit of income that must be paid as tax. In a graduated-rate system, this tax rate rises with the level of income. See *average tax rate*.

market-clearing approach The viewpoint that prices, such as the wage rate, rental price and general price level, are determined to clear markets.

market-clearing conditions Conditions that quantity supplied equal quantity demanded in a market.

mark-up ratio In imperfect competition, the ratio of the price charged to the marginal cost of production.

maturity The date at which a bond expires and its principal is repaid.

medium of exchange A commodity or other item used as a means of payment; money.

menu cost Cost that must be paid to adjust a nominal price or wage. New Keynesian models rely on these costs to rationalize the sluggish adjustment of prices.

microeconomic foundations The microeconomic analysis of individual choices that underlies the macroeconomic model of the economy.

monetary aggregate Total nominal quantity of a concept of money, such as the monetary base, M1, or M2.

monetary approach to the balance of payments Analyses of the balance of international payments and exchange rates that stress the nominal quantity of money and the demand for money in each country.

monetary base Another name for high-powered money.

monetary rule A regular procedure for altering the nominal quantity of money in response to developments in the macro economy.

monetary shocks Unanticipated changes in the nominal quantity of money.

money The usual means of payment or medium of exchange in an economy. Money also serves as a store of value. Money may take the form of paper currency, commodities or deposits at financial institutions.

money growth rate The proportionate change per year in the nominal quantity of money.

MPK The marginal product of capital.

MPL The marginal product of labour.

multiplier The change in aggregate output per unit of increase in real aggregate demand. In Keynesian models, the multiplier can be greater than 1.0.

multiyear budget constraint The budget constraint for a household over more than one year.

national income The income earned from aggregate production. National income equals gross domestic product less depreciation, which equals net domestic product.

national-income accounting The summary statement of gross domestic product and its components during a year.

national saving Total saving carried out by the residents of a country; the sum of private and public saving.

natural unemployment rate The average unemployment rate that prevails in an economy in the long run. The unemployment rate tends to adjust over time toward the natural unemployment rate.

NDP Net domestic product.

neoclassical growth model A model of economic growth that extended the Solow growth model to allow for household choices of saving rates.

net domestic investment Gross private domestic investment less depreciation.

net domestic product (NDP) Gross domestic product less depreciation.

net exports The difference between the value of exports and the value of imports.

net factor income from abroad Net income earned by the residents of a country from claims on foreign assets and from labour supplied to foreign countries.

net foreign investment The change in a country's net holdings of foreign assets.

net international investment position The stock of foreign claims held by home residents (including the home government) net of the stock of home claims held by foreign residents (including foreign governments).

net investment The change in the capital stock; gross investment less depreciation.

net national income (NNI) Gross national income less depreciation.

neutrality of money The theoretical finding that once-and-for-all changes in the nominal quantity of money affect nominal variables, such as the general price level, but do not affect real variables, such as real GDP.

new Keynesian model Models that attempt to explain the role of sticky prices and aggregate demand in the Keynesian framework. These models incorporate imperfect competition and allow for menu costs of changing prices.

NNI Net national income.

nominal Measured in current prices; valued at current prices; unadjusted for changes in the general price level.

nominal exchange rate The exchange rate between one currency and another. See *real exchange rate.*

nominal GDP Gross domestic product expressed in current prices.

nominal interest rate The amount paid as interest per euro borrowed for each period; the rate at which nominal assets held as bonds grow over time.

nominal rental price The nominal amount paid per year for each unit of capital used in production.

nominal saving The current euro value of real saving, calculated by multiplying real saving by a price index.

nominal wage rate The nominal amount paid per year for each unit of labour used in production.

non-rival good A good used by one household that does not reduce the quantity available for other households. An idea is an example of a non-rival good.

non-tradable goods Goods and services, such as labour services and real estate, that do not enter readily into international trade.

open economy An economy that conducts trade with the rest of the world.

open-market operations The purchase or sale of government securities by the central bank in exchange for high-powered money.

patent Property right over the use of an invention.

pay-as-you-go system (for social security) A system in which benefits to retired persons are financed by taxes on the current working generation.

perceived real wage rate The real wage rate as perceived by workers. In the price-misperceptions model, the perceived

real wage rate is the ratio of the nominal wage rate to the expected price level.

perfect competition Market setting in which each participant is sufficiently small to neglect any influence on the market price. A perfect competitor assumes that they can buy or sell any quantity desired at the market price.

perfect foresight A situation in which expectations of inflation or of other variables are accurate, so that there are no forecast errors.

permanent income Long-run average real income. The hypothetical amount of real income that, when received constantly throughout a household's planning horizon, has the same real present value as the actual flow of income.

planning horizon The number of years that enter into the household's plan for choosing consumption, saving and labour supply.

policy rule A rule or commitment for government actions with regard to money or other variables.

population growth Increase over time in population.

poverty An estimated level of real income required to pay for basic necessities of life.

PPI Producer price index.

PPP Purchasing-power parity

present value The value of future euro expenses or receipts, expressed in terms of current euro equivalents.

price level Euro price of a market basket of goods and services.

price stability Rough constancy over time in the price level.

price taker A participant in a market who regards the market price as given. See *perfect competition.*

price-level targeting A rule for monetary policy that dictates maintenance of price stability.

price-misperceptions model A model of economic fluctuations in which some participants incorrectly perceive the general price level. Money is not neutral in this model.

principal of bond The euro amount borrowed, to be repaid at maturity.

procyclical Moving in the same direction as the business cycle; that is, with detrended real GDP.

producer price index (PPI) A weighted average of prices of raw materials and semi-finished goods, measured relative to base-year prices.

production function The relationship between the quantity of output and the quantities of inputs to production, such as labour and capital.

productivity Output measured relative to quantities of inputs, such as labour.

productivity slowdown A reduction in the rate of growth of output per worker, thought to have occurred in OECD countries after the early 1970s.

profit The difference between revenue and costs for a firm.

propensity to consume The response of real consumer expenditure to a rise in real income.

propensity to save The response of real saving to a rise in real income.

public debt The euro stock of interest-bearing government bonds.

public investment Investment by government in plant and equipment or in public infrastructure.

purchasing-power parity (PPP) The condition that the exchange rate between the foreign and home currencies equals the ratio of prices of foreign goods to prices of home goods.

quantity theory of money The theory that changes in the nominal quantity of money account for the bulk of long-run movements in the general price level. This theory usually assumes that money is neutral in the long run.

quota A limitation on the quantity of goods that can be imported or exported.

Ramsey model A form of the neoclassical growth model due to the economist Frank Ramsey.

rate of economic growth Proportionate change per year in real GDP.

rational expectations The viewpoint that individuals make forecasts or estimates of unknown variables, such as the general price level, in the best possible manner, utilizing all information currently available.

real business-cycle (RBC) model A theory of economic fluctuations that relies on real disturbances rather than monetary shocks. The RBC model is a type of equilibrium business-cycle model.

real demand for money A function that determines the quantity of real money demanded.

real disposable income Income measured after taxes and in real terms.

real effective exchange rate A weighted average of real exchange rates of a country with respect to its trading partners.

real exchange rate The exchange rate between the foreign and home currencies divided by the ratio of the foreign price level to the home price level.

real gross domestic product The real value of the nominal gross domestic product.

real gross national product The real value of the gross national product.

real gross world product The real value of the gross world product.

real interest rate The nominal interest rate on a bond less the inflation rate. The rate at which the real value of assets held as bonds grows over time.

real money demand The ratio of the nominal amount of money demanded to the price level.

real money supply The ratio of the nominal amount of money supplied to the price level.

real rental price The real value of the nominal rental price.

real saving The change in the real value of assets held by households or by the economy as a whole. The real value of nominal saving.

real terms Measured in units of goods; valued at base-year prices; values adjusted for inflation by deflating by a price index.

real wage rate The real value of the nominal wage rate.

recession A period of decline in real GDP. A shortfall of real GDP from trend.

relative form of PPP The version of purchasing-power parity that involves changes in exchange rates and in the ratio of foreign to home prices.

rental market A market in which capital services are bought and sold at the rental price.

rental price The price charged per year for using a unit of capital.

research and development (R&D) Expenditure dedicated to discovery of new goods and improved methods of production.

reservation real wage The real wage rate that is just high enough to induce someone to accept a job.

retail price index (RPI) A price index that measures the change in the cost of a representative sample of retail goods and services.

revaluation An increase in the value of a country's currency in terms of another currency, such as the US dollar.

revenue from printing money Revenue that the government obtains by printing paper currency.

Ricardian equivalence theorem The theoretical finding that, for given government purchases, an increase in current taxes has the same effect on the economy as an equal increase in the government budget deficit.

risk premium The higher rate of return required on risky assets, such as corporate stock, compared to safe assets.

rival good A good that, if used by one person, cannot be used by another person.

saving The change in a household's assets over a year. The difference between total income and consumption.

seasonally adjusted data Adjustment of economic variables, such as real GDP, for normal seasonal variations.

shocks Exogenous disturbances that affect the macro economy. A shift to the technology level is an example of a shock.

social security Transfer payments made by the government to households to cover old-age pensions, survivors' benefits and disability insurance.

Solow growth model A model of economic growth. Key elements are a production function with capital and labour inputs, the saving rate, the population growth rate and the rate of technological progress.

Solow residual See *total factor productivity growth*.

sources of funds In a budget constraint for households or government, the sources of funds are initial assets and various types of income.

standard deviation A measure of the variability of a variable. The standard deviation is the square root of the variance. The variance is the average squared deviation from the mean.

standard of living Level of consumption that can be sustained, given a household's long-run income.

steady state A long-run situation in which variables such as capital per worker and real GDP per worker are not changing.

steady-state growth A long-run situation in which variables such as capital per worker and real GDP per worker are growing at a constant rate.

sterilization An action by the central bank that prevents increases (decreases) in the amount of international reserves from increasing (decreasing) the nominal quantity of money in the country.

sticky nominal wage rates Sluggish adjustment of the nominal wage rate to changed conditions in the labour market. A characteristic of the Keynesian model.

sticky prices Sluggish adjustment of goods prices to changed conditions in the goods market. A characteristic of the new Keynesian model.

stock market A market on which households trade shares of ownership in firms. The owners of stock receive the dividends paid out by firms.

stock variable A variable, such as capital or money, expressed in units of goods or units of a currency. Stock variables do not have a dimension per unit of time. See *flow variable.*

stores of value Forms of holding assets, such as bonds, money and ownership of capital.

strategic budget deficits Manipulation of budget deficits to influence choices made by future government regimes.

subsistence level Standard of living regarded as the minimal requirement for sustaining life.

supply curve A curve expressing the relation between the quantity supplied and the price of a good or service.

tariff Tax levied on international trade, usually on imports.

tax-rate smoothing Fiscal policy aimed at maintaining stable tax rates over time.

technological progress Inventions and improved knowledge about methods of production that generate continuing upward shifts of the production function.

technology level The level of the production function. A higher technology level means that real GDP is higher for given inputs of capital and labour.

term structure of real interest rates The relation of real interest rates to the maturity of bonds.

terms of trade The price of a country's produced tradable goods expressed relative to the price of the world's produced tradable goods.

TFP growth Total factor productivity growth.

three-equation Keynesian model A modern version of the Keynesian model featuring the IS curve, the Phillips curve and a monetary policy rule.

total factor productivity growth (TFP growth) The growth rate of unobserved technology that is calculated by taking the difference between the growth rate of output and a weighted average of the growth rates of observed inputs, such as labour and capital.

total hours worked Total worker-hours per year; the product of employment and average hours worked per year for each worker.

trade balance The difference between the value of exports of goods and services and the value of imports of goods and services.

transaction costs Costs incurred in the process of making sales or purchases, such as brokerage fees or the value of the time required.

transfer payment Transfers of funds from government to individuals, such as welfare payments.

transition path In a growth model, such as the Solow model, the path from the initial position to the steady-state position.

trend real GDP The smooth part of the time series on real GDP. We view this trend as reflecting long-run economic growth, rather than economic fluctuations.

twin deficits Simultaneous appearance of budget and current-account deficits.

two-year budget constraint The budget constraint for a household over two years.

unanticipated money growth The difference between actual money growth and anticipated money growth.

unemployment The number of persons in the labour force (and, therefore, classified as seeking work) without a job.

unemployment insurance The government programme of providing temporary benefits to workers who have lost their jobs and are currently unemployed.

unemployment rate The ratio of unemployment to the labour force.

unexpected inflation The difference between the actual inflation rate and the expected inflation rate; the forecast error made in predicting inflation.

user costs Additional costs incurred while using capital goods; for example, the costs of electric power, security services, and so on.

uses of funds In a budget constraint for households or government, the uses of funds are expenditures on goods and services and final values of assets.

utility The level of happiness of a household, measured in units called utils. Utility increases with increases in either consumption or leisure. See *utility function.*

utility function The relationship between the amount of utility obtained and the amounts of consumption and labour chosen by the household.

vacancies The difference between the number of job openings at firms and the level of employment.

vacancy rate The ratio of vacancies to the total number of jobs that firms want occupied.

value added The increase in value of a product at various stages of production.

voluntary exchange Voluntary sales and purchases made at going prices.

wage rate The euro amount paid and received on the labour market for each hour of labour services.

Index